BURLESQUE
A Final Tribute:
LEGENDS RECIPES & MINSKY'S FILES

BY JANE BRIGGEMAN

BURLESQUE A Final Tribute: Legends Recipes & Minsky's Files
By Jane Briggeman
Copyright © 2021 Briggeman
No part of this book may be reproduced in any form or by any means, electronic, mechanical, digital, photocopying, or recording, except for inclusion of a review, without permission in writing from the publisher or Author.
No copyright is claimed for the photos within this book. They are used for the purposes of publicity only.

Published in the USA by:
BearManor Media
1317 Edgewater Dr #110
Orlando, FL 32804
www.bearmanormedia.com

Paperback ISBN 978-1-62933-771-5
Case ISBN 978-1-62933-772-2
BearManor Media, Orlando, Florida
Printed in the United States of America
Book design by Robbie Adkins, www.adkinsconsult.com

Dedication

This book is dedicated to **ALL** members of "The Golden Days of Burlesque Historical Society," as well as those who performed for the Minsky's into the late 1970s. I have enjoyed the time I've been allowed to spend around the burlesque legends, and feel blessed to have met many wonderful people throughout this great adventure; they will never be forgotten. I miss so many, too many to name, performers that we have lost over the years; and I appreciate everyone who has contributed and helped preserve this history. A very special thank you goes to the late Pat Elliott Minsky Shapiro for her help and devotion in our combined efforts to preserve Harold Minsky's Files. Pat died in late 2004, just a short time after sending me his material. For continued emotional support and friendship over the years I want to thank: Dee Milo, Beverly Roberts, Taffey O'Neil, K.C. Layne, Vicki O'Day, Nocturne, Lee Angel, and Dusty Sage. I also want to remember a few women who are no longer with us: Zorita, who died in 2001; Stacy Farrell, 2005; Mimi Reed, 2006; "Aunt" Pat Flannery, 2011; Daphne Lake, 2015; and Joni Taylor, who died in 2017. Lastly to Sunny Dare, who pushed me to move home to the Midwest in late 2006; sadly, she died in 2008.

Acknowledgements

BURLESQUE A Final Tribute: Legends Recipes & Minsky's Files, as with all of my books, was a group effort. If it were not for the continuous help and support from members of "The Golden Days of Burlesque Historical Society," and their families, there would be no stories to tell, no photos to share, and none of this history would be preserved. As I was wrapping up this book I also received some help from a few people who worked for Harold or Pat Minsky in the 1970s; Brigid Itnyre, Jeanette Telders, Nancy Schuneman, and Berri Lee. Dusty Sage, Maureen Girard, Janelle Smith, C.F. Miller, and others, also helped with photos. I stand and applaud all of you. Thank You!

It has always been important to me to remember old-time performers and entertainment history. Therefore, if mentioned in Minsky's Files, you may find "notes" throughout this book about some additional performers, club owners, places, or people.

I also want to thank my Publisher Ben Ohmart and the team of creative personnel at BearManor Media; including Robbie Adkins and Stone Wallace. Without their patience, understanding, and expertise, my books would not exist.

After retiring, I returned to Iowa in search of a home of my own. On the morning of July 5, 2018, an explosion and fire destroyed the house where I was staying in Fertile, Iowa. I managed to save my laptop with the manuscript for this book; but three large irreplaceable boxes of burlesque material and photos, including the actual Minsky Files, were lost. For me, the biggest loss was my fourteen year old cat "Otis." Luckily, most of the BHS Collection and many of my personal items were in storage. Sadly, I have had to search out photos for this book.

For additional burlesque history please check out my other books published by BearManor Media; *BURLESQUE: A Living History*, *BURLESQUE: Legendary Stars of the Stage (2nd Edition)*, and *BURLESQUE: A Collection of Comedy Blackouts*. Also, please check out another book published by BearManor Media, written by Dusty Sage; *Burlesque in a Nutshell – Girls, Gimmicks & Gags*.

Table of Contents

Introduction vii

A Final Tribute 1

Sintana 16

Burlesque Legends Recipes and other Tid-Bits 29

Minsky's Files 131

Introduction

Most of my books revolve around those people I have gotten to know through "The Golden Days of Burlesque Historical Society." The BHS, as it was commonly called, has fluctuated in size; but over the years we worked together to find and reconnect people who worked in legendary burlesque, by or before 1965. Even though the numbers have dwindled, the few who survive, continue to stay connected and work together to preserve the history. The majority of the people written about in my books are legendary performers. The material in this particular book has mostly been supplied by legendary dancers; there are very few men left today who worked in old-time burlesque. The dancers were called ecdysiasts, exotic or striptease dancers, or specialty dancers; specialty dancers rarely removed their clothing. All dancers were trained to perform a variety of well rehearsed routines, usually wearing expensive costumes and sometimes using props like balls, balloons, or snakes. They also worked with other performers – such as comics, straight men, and talking women; as well as live musicians and sometimes variety acts. They were considered to be true entertainers. Some who worked in burlesque also performed in vaudeville, movies, clubs – nightclubs or supper clubs, television, or live theatre.

In 2004, before dying, Patricia Elliott Minsky Shapiro sent me package after package of materials that came from the files of Harold Minsky, her late husband. The files were primarily from the 1960s through the very early 1980s, but there was also some earlier material. After Harold died in 1977, Pat carried on the Minsky tradition and produced a few shows herself. Some of the same material Pat sent to me was also given to the University of Nevada, Las Vegas – both copies and originals. Needless to say I found the material interesting and it fits into my style of books. My style meaning, I think it's important to remember people and to do so in a positive manner. Most of the people written about in the Minsky section, the largest in the book, are a part of the history revolving around the world of Minsky's Burlesque. With so many articles, letters, and reviews, it's meant to take you back in time to relive the burlesque experience through Harold Minsky's eyes.

This book also contains a small tribute to "Exotic World." It includes a selection of photos I took at the museum during the few short months I spent at the ranch in 1994. I wanted to do something to remember Dixie Evans – she made the museum special; however, if it weren't for Jennie Lee, there wouldn't have been an "Exotic World." Doing a search you will find that "Exotic World" in Helendale, California, no longer exists. The property is listed for land value only – the trees Jennie Lee planted, and Dixie Evans spent every morning watering, are dead or dying. All that remains is 40 acres of sand, some remnants of buildings, the wells, and a lot of memories from years gone by.

The section on Sintana was a request from her family and friends who wanted the woman and teacher they knew and loved to be remembered.

Lastly, the recipe section in this book primarily comes from the burlesque legends themselves. When I say "legend," I mean LEGEND – so few remain. These true legends spent the last few years sending me their favorite recipes. One humorous response I received is as follows:

"Hi Jane, Do I cook? If it weren't for Smucker's Peanut Butter and Uneeda Biscuits I would have succumbed to starvation years ago. NO, I don't cook, but I like to use the cooking terminology when I'm out in public. For instance: I like to RENDER things ---- perhaps RENDER them helpless. I like to CARMELIZE things, preferably onions, scallions, leeks, etc. I love to use a DRIZZLE of extra virgin olive oil (the extra virgin part is hard to come by in today's world) and then put whatever remains into a REDUCTION sauce until it disappears.

If you want directions to any of these processes let me know and I'll fax you post-haste. Do you have any other foolish questions? Paul DeSavino Jr."

I received recipes from many legends, but I thought Paul's words were worth sharing as well. I realize this is a massive book; and I worked as quickly as possible to complete it in the hopes that some of those who contributed would still be alive to see it in print.

For additional stories regarding old-time burlesque please refer to my other books: *BURLESQUE: Legendary Stars of the Stage - 2nd Edition*, and *BURLESQUE: A Living History*. I am proud to say both books won IPPY's – major independent publishing awards. To read more old-time Blackouts, look for: *BURLESQUE: A Collection of Comedy Blackouts*. All are published by BearManor Media and available through them and Amazon.Com.

P.S. A TRUE burlesque legend did not work on a pole!

A Final Tribute

Jennie Lee, "The Bazoom Girl," passed away on March 24, 1990; Dixie Evans, "The Marilyn Monroe of Burlesque," passed away on August 3, 2013. Both women had strong, passionate ties to "Exotic World," which was often simply called "the ranch." Jennie Lee created "Exotic World" out in the Mojave Desert on "an old goat farm" in Helendale, California; it was her baby. Following Jennie's death, Dixie Evans eventually became the worker-bee and public face to the museum.

Jennie Lee, "The Bouncing Bombshell." This may be one of her first 8 X 10 photos.
Courtesy: Pat Flannery

Front of the first Exotic World Flyer.
Courtesy: C.F. Miller

Jennie Lee always loved animals, evident in this 1949 photo. Courtesy: Pat Flannery

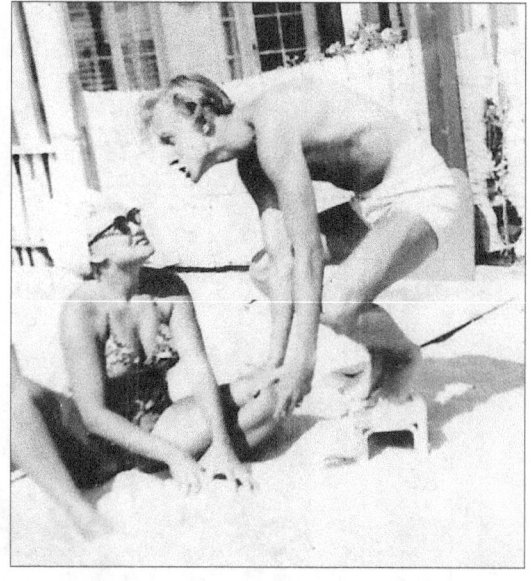

Jennie and husband, Danny Wanick, just being themselves. Courtesy: Pat Flannery

Jennie Lee all dressed up for a night on the town. Courtesy: Pat Flannery

Jennie Lee posing in front of the Wanick homestead beloved palm tree. Courtesy: Pat Flannery

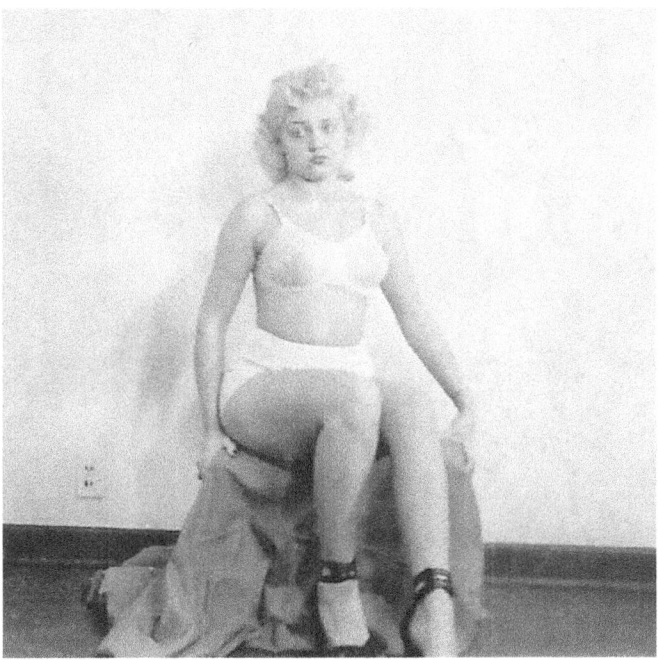

A young Jennie Lee looking quite dejected. Courtesy: Pat Flannery

I never met Jennie, but I connected with Dixie in mid-1992, and moved to Helendale in August of 1994 to try and help in any way I could. I spent nearly six months at the ranch, and quickly learned that the museum's main goal was to run a yearly competition showcasing young dancers. For me, however, my main interest in burlesque has always been about preserving the history; so I got out of the way.

I have my memories of Dixie and the ranch, and no one can take them away from me. I remember my nephew Charlie's expression after Dixie performed her Marilyn Monroe impression for him, and the stern lecture she gave me about driving with the car window down while resting my arm in the open window frame. "You could lose your arm," she said, and would then go into graphic detail. I also remember Dixie pulling a very large dead scorpion out of the swimming pool one day and taking it out onto the acreage, away from the house, and burying it. I helped with museum tours, a variety of projects, and the mail; I even wrote the first newsletter mailed to patrons of the museum while I was at the ranch. Dixie and I both watered trees on a daily basis; and I met my first, very large black widow spider while living in the guest cottage. There were many nights when I would sweep baby scorpions into a dustpan and take them out into the desert, only to have them creep back under the door the following night. I also met Dusty Sage, Liz Mauk, and Barbara Burrows, local women who pitched in to help whenever possible. But, in my opinion, if it were not for Dixie Evans, "Exotic World" would have died with Jennie Lee. Mostly people came to the museum to meet Dixie and hear her stories; SHE was the draw.

1952 photo of Dixie Evans from Wolf Bait magazine. Courtesy: Burlesque Historical Society

May 4, 1957 photo from the cover of This Week in Miami Beach. *At the time Dixie Evans was starring at Place Pigalle. Courtesy: Burlesque Historical Society*

Autographed front cover of the Exotic World flyer picturing Dixie Evans. Courtesy: C.F. Miller

During my brief stay at the ranch I also connected with Tanayo, Stacy Farrell, Novita, Doreen "Dodie" Gray, Dee Milo, and several other burlesque legends. They missed Jennie a great deal; as well as staying in touch with colleagues from burlesque who attended the various events and reunions Jennie organized over the years. It was Tanayo who first asked for my help in finding old friends, which began a letter writing campaign in 1995. Many people who worked in legendary burlesque were found due to those letters. Doreen Gray sent me Pat Flannery's address, just days before "Dodie" died in 1999. Pat and I used to talk every Saturday morning; and thanks to her daughter Bekki, Pat attended our 2009 gathering in Wisconsin. (Dan Barry and *The New York Times* did a fabulous piece on that gathering.)

Jennie Lee, "The Bazoom Girl." Courtesy: Pat Flannery

Dancers performing onstage in a burlesque show at the theatre in Los Angeles. Courtesy: Pat Flannery

Tanayo at an Exotic World event. Courtesy: Burlesque Historical Society

Stacy Farrell performing at one of the very first Miss Exotic World competitions. Courtesy: Burlesque Historical Society

Rosie Mitchell, stage name "Novita," in 2008. Courtesy: Novita

Doreen Gray, 1949. Courtesy: Pat Flannery

The remains of a large poster from Cabaret Bremen, where Jennie Lee and Dee Milo performed on the same bill in Mexico. Courtesy: Dee Milo

Dee Milo performing at Exotic World in the early 2000s, in a gown created by Carmela, "The Sophia Loren of Burlesque." The gown is only a small piece of the collection belonging to "The Golden Days of Burlesque Historical Society." Courtesy: Burlesque Historical Society

Doreen "Dodie" Gray and Pat Flannery performing together in a burlesque comedy scene. Courtesy: Pat Flannery

The goal was always to find and reconnect people who had worked in legendary burlesque; and to save what history we could in the process – which I believe has been a success. If I had not connected with Dixie, even briefly, a long time ago, there would have been no group called "The Golden Days of Burlesque Historical Society;" and even fewer books written regarding legendary burlesque.

So, Rest in Peace, Jennie Lee and Dixie Evans - I think of you both, often. The photos taken at the ranch in 1994 are in honor of all the hard work Dixie did at "Exotic World." But if it were not for Jennie, having the initiative to create a burlesque museum as well as keep friends and performers connected, how much history from the last decades of legendary burlesque would still exist?

Autographed program cover of the 6th Annual Exotic Dancers League convention held in 1963. Courtesy: C.F. Miller

Jennie Lee as Diamond Lil, 1956. Courtesy: Pat Flannery

Jennie Lee at Exotic World; photo taken in November 1989. Courtesy: Rob Powell

Mid 1990s, Dixie Evans at Exotic World Ranch. Courtesy: Authors Collection

Program from the 2005, 15th Anniversary, Miss Exotic World Extravaganza. Courtesy: C.F. Miller

Many years from now, after the sands at 29053 Wild Road in Helendale, California, have been built upon again; it wouldn't surprise me if the new owners didn't awake to the sounds of music and revelry. I believe the memories of "Exotic World" will live on and on…

*Exotic World Front Gate. All of the photos in this section are from 1994.
All Courtesy: Authors Collection*

Exotic World driveway, approaching the house and museum.

Exotic World courtyard.

Exotic World pool and stage area.

Jennie Lee collected all she could for her museum and to preserve legendary burlesque. Bambi Sr. can tell you a funny story about that.

Display case at Exotic World; one of many.

More display case items.

There were costumes…

...And even more costumes.

...Everywhere.

There were photos...

Sintana

In the summer of 2015 I received not one, but several letters, asking if I would do something to remember Candace Huntsman Lehrman White. Candy was an exotic dancer known on the burlesque stages during her early years as "Candy Cane," and later as "Sintana." Frequently billed as "The Fabulous Flame" or "The Queen of the Exotics," she died in 2010. Typically, but not always, people remembered in my books are those I have come in contact with. It's easier to write about people as you get to know them through their letters, phone calls, or at gatherings. So this was not an easy section for me to write, and I requested and received help from her family and friends. As my research continued I truly thought it was important to write something about this woman; after all, what is remembered, lives.

"Sintana" officially retired from burlesque in 1975, but while still performing, became involved with the Ravenwood Church and Seminary of Wicca. She was interviewed by Marilyn S. Futterman for the book, *Dancing Naked in the Material World*, published in 1992, and stated the following:

"I was an emancipated minor. I went to a nunnery and left at sixteen. I literally married the first man I met. He knew Harold Minsky, so I went to work in Vegas in a chorus line at the Dunes. I had no training, no background, and I was extremely naïve. I couldn't keep time. I only lasted a week or so. I was not chorus material. The choreographer suggested the burlesque circuit. I went to Baltimore to star in burlesque as a feature. I criedlike crazy and had a little mental breakdown. Then I was okay.

Minsky Follies advertisement for the show at the Silver Slipper starring Sintana. Courtesy: Sybil Carswell and Carl Simone

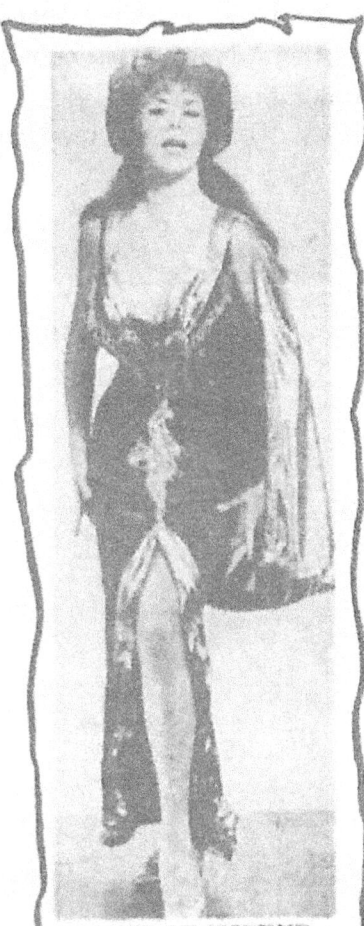

DEBUTS AT SLIPPER— Sensuous Sin-Tana, internationally famous as "The Fabulous Flame," is making her Las Vegas debut at the Silver Slipper as one of the stars of "Life Begins at Minsky's." The popular burlesque show also stars comedians Irv Benson and Jack Mann and the magnificent Minsky Mannequins.

Newspaper clipping marking Sintana's debut in the Harold Minsky show at the Silver Slipper in Las Vegas. Courtesy: Sybil Carswell and Carl Simone

Newspaper ad promoting Sintana's appearance at the 2 O'Clock Club in Baltimore. Courtesy: Sybil Carswell and Carl Simone

I came into burlesque during a transition period when pornography was being introduced into the movies, which was really the death of burlesque. It went from an eight piece orchestra down to three broads and a tape recorder. I watched the transition from Bunny Yeager in swimsuits playing volleyball to hard-core pornography. I was naïve and a very inhibited person. Extremely inhibited. But with the combination of lights, audience, and music, I was like a different person. It hits you before and after you come offstage. I was scared to death of men, and the stage was a buffer between me and them. I never considered what I did "sexy," though I portrayed an animalistic sexuality that was not a basic part of my nature. In a relationship I would never be that uninhibited. Never.

I think I was always a little bit ashamed about what I did. I was never an advocate of total nudity."

Early photo of Candace; was this when she was performing as Candy Cane? Courtesy: Sybil Carswell and Carl Simone

Another early photo of a young dancer named Candy Cane. Courtesy: Sybil Carswell and Carl Simone

Born in Kansas in 1937, Candy, as she was called as a child, was the granddaughter of a deeply religious dairy farmer. The farm was always her "happy place," even though she did not get along well with her step-father. As a teenager she spent a year at a Roman Catholic nunnery but left at the age of 16, and returned to public school. She found few people lived up to her family's religious standards.

Immediately after graduating from high school, at age 17, Candy married James (Jimmy) Montello. Having limited experience, the young couple found work in circus and carnival shows. Candy worked as a dancer. Known as "Monty Mitchell," in the carnivals, Jimmy worked on the crew until his death many years later. The marriage did not last, leaving Candy with an infant daughter to raise. Desperate to support her child she turned to exotic dancing. In the early days, she performed as "Candy Cane." She later changed her stage name to "Sintana," and performed in burlesque theatres and clubs all across the country including: Nevada, Maryland, Kentucky, Florida, New York, Ohio, and Georgia. She may have also returned to work in the circus during the summer months; many performers did during that time period.

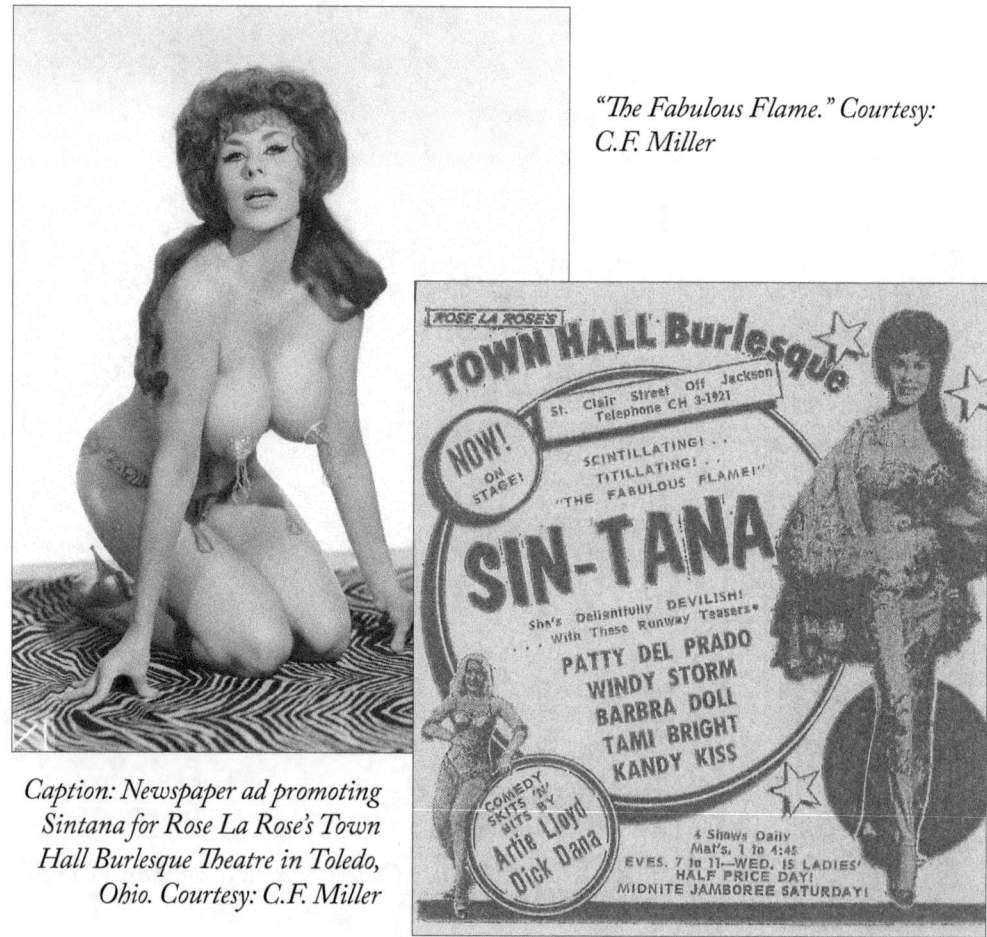

"The Fabulous Flame." Courtesy: C.F. Miller

Caption: Newspaper ad promoting Sintana for Rose La Rose's Town Hall Burlesque Theatre in Toledo, Ohio. Courtesy: C.F. Miller

"Sintana's" daughter Sybil wrote, "I so remember as a child being in the theatre backstage with all the people who would soon be onstage to perform. The comedians, the poker games, the girls. I would stand just offstage and they would throw me their clothes or costumes. I would hang them up in their dressing rooms. The tips were great! I thought I had a real important job. They were very loving, kind, real people. I would watch them onstage, intensely. Especially Mom, I was so proud of her."

Sintana headshot. Courtesy: C.F. Miller

By now, Candy was living in New York City with her then husband Mark Lehrman; in the Fall of 1972 the couple headed to Buffalo to help her daughter who was pregnant. In December Candy became a grandmother to a baby boy. Candy and Mark returned to New York City after the birth of the baby, but shortly thereafter headed to Florida. According to various documents Candy soon returned to New York City and was running a burlesque club until she left the city for good in late 1974.

During the years 1973 and 1974, "Sintana" managed a burlesque club called "Sintana's Burlesk" at 63rd Street and Lexington Avenue in New York City. As the years went by, she had become more and more disturbed by what she saw as the "blending of burlesque and the pornography industry, and the abuse of young dancers." I have tried to find more information about this particular club, even what currently stands at that address, but information is scarce. So, I contacted the New York Historical Society Reference Library, and they did a search for me. The information I found on the internet just did not sound right, so I emailed and asked the following question:

"For a couple years in the early 1970s Candy was supposed to have owned "Sintana's Burlesk" - a theatre or perhaps a club - at 63rd Street and Lexington Ave in New York City. Can you tell me anything about it - and is a building still there that may have been used for such a purpose?" They provided me with the following information in an email, along with several attachments. The email reads:

Ad for Sintana's Burlesk. Courtesy: Burlesque Historical Society

"Thanks for your email and interesting question. We do have Manhattan telephone books for the late 1960s but did not find "Sintana" or her given name Candace Lehrman listed. I did, however, find "Sintana's" 1973 advertisement for dancers in the open newspaper database.

The newspaper ad, from the *New York Amsterdam News*, caters to the African-American and Harlem communities.

This information places her burlesque club at 714 Lexington Avenue, which is near 63rd Street but a bit further south at 57th and 58th Streets; then, across from Alexander's Department Store. We don't have a 1973 phone book to see if the club was listed, but we do find advertisements in *The New York Times*.

The building can be researched because its tenants caused some controversy. Also the Department of Buildings provides certificates of occupancy that give a glimpse of the building's use at certain moments of time. The one attached, from 1974, is amusing in that it calls the second floor a "physical culture and health establishment," but it seems to be referring to the massage parlor and suggests that "Sintana" had left that location by November 1974.

Finally, of not much interest except maybe to you, I found an ad for a 1974 Mercedes for sale by putting "Sintana's" phone number, 752-6394, into a newspaper search. I hope this helps."

The email was signed "With best regards, Mariam Touba, Reference Librarian."

To begin with, the short article about Alexander's Inc., ran in *The New York Times* on October 30, 1969. A branch of their store, called "Experiment One," is reported to have leased a 2000 square foot store at 714 Lexington Avenue which was scheduled to open across from Alexander's main store at 58th Street and Lexington. The footage does not match up between this short article and the Certificate of Occupancy information which follows. Was the paperwork inaccurate or the article?

From the *New York Amsterdam News*, May 28, 1973 Classified Ads section there was a small advertisement that reads:

"GO-GO DANCERS; Professionals or beginners. Will train at no fee. Learn while you earn big $$$. Interview after 11:30am with photo. Work East Side: 714 Lexington, Phone Sintana 752-6394 or West Side: 210 W. 49th St. Phone Carl 245-9382."

The New York Times ran advertising for "Sintana's Burlesk" on April 11, 1973, and again on July 5, 1973. The advertising mentions; all live shows, all nude revue, group rates, and shows changed weekly. There were continuous shows seven days a week, starting at 11am, and running through 3am. The address listed was 714 Lexington Avenue, between 57th and 58th Streets. The phone number listed was 752-6394.

The Department of Buildings, Certificate of Occupancy has two dates on the paperwork that I was provided by the New York Historical Society; October 31, 1974, and November 26, 1974. Most of the form is illegible but it does list 714 Lexington Avenue as the street address. It also explains the tenants "permissible use and occupancy." The cellar, on the ground floor was used for storage. The first floor, listed as a Retail Store, was 120 square feet and could accommodate up to 50 people. The additional three floors could all accommodate up to 20 people. The second floor was 60 square feet, and the third floor was 110 square feet. They are both listed as Physical Culture and Health Establishments. The fourth floor, was listed as an Art Studio and 95 square feet.

I also received a copy of an article from *The New York Times* dated May 14, 1975. The article was titled "East Siders' Group Unites to Oust a Peep Show and Pornography Parlor." At first I thought the worst, but from my calculations "Sintana's Burlesk" had closed around November 1974. The adult bookstore,

"Lexington Front Page," moved into the same location as the club in December of 1974. It turns out Alexander's held the lease on the ground floor of 714 Lexington Avenue since perhaps 1969 and had sublet it out over the years. An attorney stated in the article that while sitting vacant Alexander's lost potential revenues of $75,000, so they were not concerned as to what business the latest tenant would be conducting.

The advertisement for the car was posted in *The New York Times*, December 19, 1975. It was for a 1974 Mercedes 280 Sedan; white with a blue interior, with an electric sunroof, air-conditioning, all power AM/FM stereo, power antenna, and in immaculate condition. 7,200 was also listed but did not state if that was miles or the asking price.

Sybil filled in some blanks on the car. She says, "That was not my mother's car. However, she may have been selling it for someone, or someone may have given it to her to sell as a gift or to pay off a debt."

Stage Door Exotics Revue sign from the club. Courtesy: Sybil Carswell and Carl Simone

After closing the club Candy headed to Buffalo, New York, where she may have performed at the popular club, "The Stage Door." However, feeling disillusioned, Candy danced less and less as "Sintana." After taking some time off from her burlesque career her daughter remembers her mother working in a bakery, and then working in product promotion, where Candy met a Wiccan Priest who sparked her interest in the Old Religion.

Club table card; check out the artwork. Courtesy: Sybil Carswell and Carl Simone

When a friend in Atlanta became ill, Candy travelled to Georgia to help with his care and started Ravenwood in a dilapidated, two-story Victorian house on Moreland Avenue. She became known in the area among Wiccans simply as "The Lady," a term of endearment and respect for a woman, and teacher, of considerable knowledge and commitment to the craft. Besides serving as a center for Wicca, Ravenwood became known as a refuge for abused girls and battered women. At the time, Candy stated, "They'd call or come by in the middle of the night, seeking safety, needing help and sanctuary."

In 1975, Candy, aka "Lady Sintana," founded the Ravenwood Church, the state's first Pagan congregation; in 1977, she hung a sign in front of her home offering education about the Old Religion to the public. By 1982, the High Priestess had successfully challenged the Internal Revenue Service, and Ravenwood became one of the first Pagan congregations in the country to be granted tax-exempt status as a church. Across the country, she was considered the person who shattered legal barriers and opened minds to the practice of the Old Religion. Even those of us who have never met "The Lady," have benefited from the religious rights and liberties she fought so hard to attain.

One with nature, Lady Sintana. Courtesy: Sybil Carswell and Carl Simone

"Her mission in life was to bring respect and legality to the Pagan religion," said her late husband David John White, aka "Lord Merlin," the Elder High Priest of Ravenwood. "She not only won legal battles, but she won over hearts as well. Her main idea was not to convert people, but to have some venue where people could learn the truth."

It was 1978 when White met the former burlesque dancer; four years later, the couple married and embarked on a shared mission to educate people about the Old Religion. Wicca is a pre-Christian, nature-centered matriarchal religion from Western Europe that dates back more than 800 years to the Celts. It is the wisdom of knowing and working within the balance of nature, positive and negative; as well as being aware and having respect for all life and feelings.

Lady Sintana. Courtesy: Sybil Carswell and Carl Simone

In the mid-1980s, "Lady Sintana" moved Ravenwood to a neighborhood on the south side of Decatur. There the Wiccan center continued to survive court challenges and zoning battles, as well as provide a safe, but public space, for students continuing on their path of self-discovery, harmony, balance, and spiritual practice.

In 1996, Candy left Georgia and moved west, first to California and then to Washington state, to care for her terminally ill mother. After her mother passed, she returned to a small community in western North Carolina and lived with her daughter. Candace White maintained close ties with Ravenwood, working tirelessly to educate the public about her nature-centered religion, and to this day she remains a revered figure in her coven. When asked about her departure, she reaffirmed that she was still interested in keeping the old traditions alive, but also explained that she believed Ravenwood had come to the point where it had "to grow beyond myself."

Candace Huntsman Lehrman White died from complications of lung cancer on September 17, 2010, but she lives on in the hearts and minds of all who knew her, as well as those who knew of her. Ravenwood has moved several times over the years, and is now located in a private home.

(Notes: I cannot tell you how many non-smoking legendary burlesque performers, who worked in clubs in the 1960s through the 1980s, have died from lung cancer.

David John White, aka "Lord Merlin," was born in Banbury, Oxfordshire, England on July 12, 1935, and died in Ball Ground, Georgia on September 23, 2011. It is reported that a small wildlife sanctuary in north Georgia, was named in his honor.)

The Ravenwood Church sign. Courtesy: Lady Maia of Ravenwood

Burlesque Legends Recipes and other Tid-Bits

I only wish old chums Electra, Carmela – The Sophia Loren of Burlesque, and Peggy Lloyd were still alive when I decided to include a section such as this in a burlesque book. They would have been the first to send recipes. Electra participated in many chili cook-offs; she had a wall in her Reno home covered with jars of spices. Carmela liked to cook and filled my freezer when I lived in Las Vegas; she also introduced me to her favorite Las Vegas buffets – she loved eating chicken feet. Peggy gave me her mother's old cookbook; she grew the herbs used in her recipes in her own backyard and often joked that when there was a water shortage in Las Vegas, she would go out and pee on her plants. These women loved to cook. For more biographical information, or photos, on those who contributed to this section, check out; *BURLESQUE: A Living History,* and, *BURLESQUE: Legendary Stars of the Stage 2nd Edition.* So let the recipes and tid-bits begin.

The one and only, the ORIGINAL, Electra. Courtesy: Dusty Sage

Carmela, "The Sophia Loren of Burlesque." Courtesy: C.F. Miller

Peggy Lloyd in the Fall of 2000. Courtesy: Authors Collection

Lilli Marlene

Some of the routines for which Lilli Marlene was famous included "Lili Marlene Underneath the Lamplight," which required the assistance of a male partner dressed as a World War II sailor. She also performed to the music, "The Rites of Spring," with fire, thunder, and smoke coming from a specialized machine; and she shared the stage with thousands of bubbles from a bubble machine in yet another fan favorite routine. In 1973, Lilli Marlene performed in her final burlesque show in Chicago, after her agent passed away. Lilli, who loves to cook, and her husband, maintain a very active lifestyle and are surrounded by loving family, friends, and their Dachshunds.

How appropriate is this photo of Lilli Marlene? I like it a whole lot. Courtesy: Lilli Marlene

Apricot-Sage Cookies

Lilli says, "These are my favorite cookies by far and I often bake them twice a week for afternoon tea! Savory herbs and sweet cookies don't normally go hand in hand, but the flavor that occurs when tart apricot meets soft sage is exceptionally delicious."

1¾ Cups all purpose flour
2 Tablespoons snipped fresh sage or 2 teaspoons dried sage
1/3 Cup sugar
¼ Cup yellow cornmeal
3 Tablespoons milk
½ Cup butter; apricot preserves or jelly

1. Preheat oven to 375 degrees. In bowl stir together flour, sugar, and cornmeal. Using pastry blender, cut in butter until mixture resembles fine crumbs. Stir in sage. Add milk. Stir with fork to combine; form into ball. Knead until smooth; divide in half.
2. On a lightly floured surface, roll half the dough out at a time to ¼ inch thickness. Use a 2 inch round cookie cutter to cut out dough.
3. Place cut outs 1 inch apart on ungreased cookie sheet and bake about 10 minutes or until the edges are firm and very lightly browned. Transfer to wire rack and cool.
4. Spread the bottoms of half the cookies with apricot preserves. Top with remaining cookies. You can freeze unfilled cookies up to 3 months. Thaw cookies and fill with apricot jelly.

Lilli Marlene. Courtesy: Lilli Marlene

*Lilli Marlene dressed in a Roaring 20s costume for a Christmas party in 2019.
Courtesy: Lilli Marlene*

Brandied Shrimp and Grits with Leek Sauce

1 LB colossal shrimp (fresh or frozen)
¼ Cup honey
3 Tablespoons Dijon mustard
3 Tablespoons olive oil
¼ teaspoon red pepper or pepper flakes

Mix honey, mustard, olive oil, and pepper together; marinate shrimp in the mixture. Set aside.

For the sauce:
1 Leek (cleaned and chopped)
2 Cloves garlic (chopped)
1 teaspoon fresh ginger (chopped fine)
1 Tablespoon flour
Olive oil
¼ Cup brandy
¼ Cup half-and-half
½ Cup chicken broth

Heat the olive oil in a frying pan; then sauté' the leeks for 2 minutes. Add garlic and ginger; stir until fragrant. Turn down heat; dust garlic and ginger with flour and stir until light yellow. Add brandy and chicken broth while stirring gently for 1 minute. Add half-and-half and the marinated shrimp with the remaining marinade. Sauté' shrimp and sauce together for 2 minutes or until shrimp turns pink. Remove from heat. Do not overcook shrimp. Serve over stone ground grits.

Not your Mothers French Toast

4 One inch thick French bread slices
3 Eggs
½ Cup half-and-half
2 Tablespoons brandy
1 Tablespoon vanilla
A pinch of nutmeg
2 Tablespoons sugar and cinnamon mix
1 Banana (cut into one inch pieces)
2 Cups of Wheaties
Mixed berries

Beat eggs, half-and-half, vanilla, brandy, and nutmeg together in a shallow dish. Cut a round hole out of the middle of the bread slices and stick a piece of banana into it. Repeat with all the bread. Soak bread in egg mixture until well saturated. Spread the Wheaties on a plate and turn bread slices into the Wheaties until covered on all sides. Fry in butter for 2 minutes on each side and sprinkle with sugar cinnamon mix. Serve with mixed berries and dust with powdered sugar.

Rahmschnitzel

4 Slices of pork loin cut ¼ inch thick
½ Cup flour blended with pepper and salt on a dinner plate for breading
1 Cup Panko or bread crumbs on another dinner plate
2 Eggs, whipped with 1 Tablespoon water in a bowl
4 Tablespoons olive oil
1 Cup onion (chopped)
4 Cloves of garlic (minced)

2 Tablespoons paprika
½ Cup dry red wine
2 Tablespoons Dijon mustard
½ Cup heavy whipping cream
1 Cup chicken stock

Cut and pound the pork slices thin, then press the slices into the flour mixture on both sides, dip into the egg wash and coat evenly with the Panko crumbs. Set aside.

In a heavy frying pan over medium heat, brown meat with olive oil about 4 minutes on each side. Remove from pan and keep warm in oven.

To the same pan add; onions, garlic, paprika, mustard, and cook until tender, about 4 minutes.

Turn down the heat and sprinkle 2 Tablespoons of flour into pan, stir a few times, and then add the wine. Mix and cook a few seconds just to evaporate the alcohol, then add the stock; bring to a simmer whisking until smooth. Turn down the heat and wait 30 seconds before adding heavy cream. Stir to mix for 1 minute and remove from heat. Place one schnitzel on each plate, pour some sauce over it; sprinkle with chives and serve with potatoes, noodles, or rice, and a green salad.

Salad with Papaya Dressing

1 Firm ripe papaya (10 to 12 oz) halved lengthwise
1 Tablespoon finely grated peeled, fresh ginger
1 Tablespoon minced onion
1 Tablespoon chopped fresh tarragon
1 teaspoon minced garlic
1 teaspoon dry mustard
2 Tablespoons fresh lemon juice
½ teaspoon salt
1/8 teaspoon black pepper
½ Cup olive oil
Lettuce leaves

Scrape seeds from papaya and save 4 Tablespoons of seeds. Discard remaining seeds, and then peel papaya halves and slice. Press ginger through garlic press into a small bowl to extract juice, about 1 teaspoon, discarding the pulp. Whisk in papaya seeds, onion, tarragon, garlic, mustard, lemon juice, salt and pepper, and add oil in a steady stream; whisking until emulsified.

Divide lettuce and papaya slices among four plates and drizzle with dressing.

Barbara Kemp

Barbara Kemp was a member of the Hudson Theatre chorus line in Union City, New Jersey. During her brief career, other women she performed with, in that chorus line, included: Athena, Ellye O'Connell, Hope Diamond, Joan Torino, Laura Lee, Lorraine Terbuggen, and Maria Bradley.

Some of the Hudson Theatre girls, from left to right: Athena, deceased; Maria Bradley; Joan Torino, deceased; Hope Diamond; and Ellye O'Connell, deceased. Courtesy: Maria Bradley

Hope Diamond. Courtesy: C.F. Miller

Spaghetti with Ricotta

1 LB thin spaghetti
8 Tablespoons melted butter
15 Oz Ricotta cheese
Grated cheese
Salt and Pepper to taste

Cook pasta per directions on box. Place in a warm serving dish; stir in melted butter and Ricotta, toss to blend. Top with grated cheese, and salt and pepper. (Serves 6)

Stuffed Hot Dogs

Barbara wrote, "I loved them when I was a kid." Six hot dogs cut part way through. Fry 6 pieces of bacon almost done. Stuff the hot dogs with favorite cheese, wrap bacon around it, and hold in place with tooth picks. Bake until cheese is melted and bacon is crisp; about 15 minutes at 350 degrees uncovered or place under broiler for about 10 minutes, checking often.

Ham with Cherry Apple Sauce

3 LB ham (can be canned)
3/4 Cup apple juice divided
2 Tablespoons cornstarch
1 Cup chopped apples
1/2 Cup cherry jelly

Bake ham according to package instructions. Combine 1/4 cup apple juice with cornstarch in a small bowl, beat until smooth and set aside. Place apples, jelly, and remaining apple juice in a large saucepan and heat over medium heat for about 5 minutes. Add cornstarch mixture and cook about 1 minute longer until thickened. Slice ham and serve with sauce. (About 8 servings)

Danish Pastry

Stir together 2 3/4 cups flour and 1 teaspoon salt. Cut in 1 cup Crisco. In measuring cup beat 1 egg yolk and enough water to make 2/3 cup. Mix well and stir into flour mixture. On a floured board, roll out half the dough to a 17 X 12 rectangle. Fit onto the bottom and up the sides a little of a 15 1/2 X 10 1/2 pan. Sprinkle with crushed cornflakes - about 1 1/2 cups. Top with 2 cans apple pie filling or about 12 apple slices, 1 cup sugar, and 1 teaspoon cinnamon. Roll out the remaining dough to 15 1/2 X 10 1/2 and cover the apples. Cut slits in the top and bake 50 minutes at 350 degrees. You can brush with beaten egg white, if you want, before baking. While still warm, brush with a mixture of 1 cup powdered sugar and 3 - 4 teaspoons of milk. When cool, cut into bars or squares.

Baked Bean Casserole

Fry 1/2 pounds or more of bacon until crisp. Cool and crumble. Fry 2 cups of red onion, until soft, in the bacon drippings along with 3 or 4 sliced Italian sweet sausage - optional. Drain: 1 can lima beans, 1 can kidney beans, 1 can butter beans, and 1 can of hot chili beans. You can use any bean combo you like. The beans, when finished, will have a lot of juice but that is okay. Use a slotted spoon to remove if you do not like that much juice. Add 1 - 2 cans of Boston Baked Beans (I use Bush's, do NOT drain), 1/2 cup apple cider vinegar, and 1/2 cup brown sugar. I usually end up adding a little more sugar before I put it in the oven. Stir together well in an oven safe dish and bake for 90 minutes at 350 degrees. I have also cooked it in a crock pot on high for 4 hours and just put it under the broiler for 15 minutes before serving. Add more sugar or vinegar to taste when cooked.

Kim Summers

Kim Summers performed in production shows, burlesque theatres, and supper clubs all across the United States for over twenty-five years. She danced occasionally in shows at many of the major hotels in Las Vegas, including, *Minsky's Follies* at the New Frontier, and *Thoroughly Modern Minsky* at the Thunderbird. Kim also worked with such performers as Sally Rand, comedienne Billie Bird, and comic Sid Fields, who was featured as the landlord on *The Abbott and Costello Show* on television. In 1984, Kim retired, but continued to work as a dance studio operator, choreographer, and taught dance for many years. Kim Summers died on June 20, 2019.

Kim wrote, "My Mother used to make this all the time. It's a favorite of mine."

Pork Chops and Oven Baked Beans

6 Pork chops (bone-in)
1 Large can baked beans
1 Tablespoon brown sugar
1/2 Cup Ketchup

1 teaspoon Worcestershire sauce
1 Onion (diced)
2 Garlic cloves (minced)

Brown pork chops with onion and garlic. Mix all the other ingredients in a bowl. After the pork is browned, spoon mixture over chops and bake in the oven for 20 minutes at 350 degrees.

The Summer Affair; Kim Summers and her dance partner. Courtesy: C.F. Miller

Lite Shrimp Scampi

1 Onion – medium (thinly sliced and halved)
2 or 3 Garlic cloves (pressed or crushed)
1/2 Tablespoon Italian Seasoning
1 Tablespoon Worcestershire sauce
1 Cup white wine
2 Tablespoons white wine
1 Pack "Butter Buds" - mixed according to box directions
1 Cup mushrooms (fresh and sliced)
1 LB large shrimp (peeled and deveined)

Sauté together in two Tablespoons of white wine the onion and garlic, until they are translucent. Next, add the Italian Seasoning, Worcestershire sauce, and the rest of the wine. Cover and simmer for 15 minutes. Finally add the now liquid "Butter Buds," mushrooms, and shrimp. Cover and simmer for about 5 more minutes or until the shrimp are pink and curled, stirring occasionally. Serve over rice. (Serves 4)

Marg Connell

Performing as "The Irish Mist," Marg worked clubs and theatres across the Eastern Seaboard, west into Ohio and Minnesota, and into Canada. Paul Jordan and John Sullivan were her primary agents in Boston. I have not heard from Marg in a few years so I believe she has died; I truly enjoyed our chats.

Marg wrote, "This is a recipe from a busy nurse who I worked with at St. Mary's Hospital in Lewiston, Maine in 2002. This is how she gave it to me, and it's very good."

'Mom's Delight'

Hamburger - cooked and drained
Elbow macaroni – cooked
Cream of mushroom soup

Mix all together. Simmer - add quantity of ingredients to your liking. This makes up quickly, any quantity, and is REALLY good.

Honey Cold Remedy

Mix equal parts:
Honey (Maine Honey was mentioned)
Fresh lemon juice
Whiskey

"Heat the mixture to hot, but never boiling. It works wonders!" (Electra also always swore to the wonders of honey.)

Dee Milo

From 1949 to 1964, Dee Milo, billed as the "Venus of Dance," performed in burlesque theatres, clubs, and USO Shows across the United States, Japan, and Mexico. For the more than forty-five years since, Dee has been involved in the healing arts community; including the practice of energy healing and creating the CDR Balancer.

Electra. Courtesy: Dusty Sage

Dee Milo, reconnecting with her burlesque past, in 1995 photo shoot. Courtesy: Dee Milo and Earl Hansen

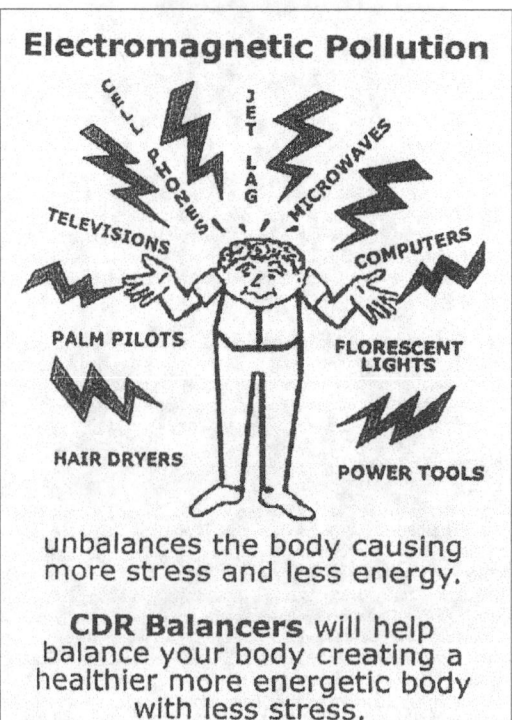

Design taken from old CDR Balancer paperwork. Courtesy: Dee Milo

Dee Milo on a vacation to Hawaii almost 20 years ago. Back then she went everywhere with her camera. Courtesy: Dee Milo

When asked if she had any recipes to share, her response was quite simply, "I have no recipes except for a can opener." I lived on the same property as Dee for six years; I don't think she uses a can opener very often. The property, at that time, was covered with a variety of fruit trees. We also grew our own vegetables; we dried or froze the things we didn't eat fresh. To this day I especially miss having access to all those fresh fruits – frozen grapes, yum. My advice is, if you have room to plant, grow as much of your own food as possible.

Pat Flannery

Pat Flannery grew up surrounded by music; her mother had been a performer in vaudeville and nightclubs. Pat loved to dance, and began her professional dancing career in chorus lines at the age of sixteen. After World War II, she went to Los Angeles and found work in the movie industry. There was plenty of work to be had at MGM and Paramount; she performed as an extra in many of the big-name musicals, including "Meet Me in St. Louis." In the early 1950s, Pat began dancing in nightclubs and burlesque, performing as a satirical dancer, singer, and talking woman primarily on the West Coast and in Alaska. Her favorite burlesque comics included "Beetle Puss" Lewis and Joe DeRita. Pat Flannery retired from burlesque in 1960; she died in 2011. It's because of the close friend-

ship between "Aunt" Pat and Jennie Lee that the BHS has so many Jennie Lee photos; both women also loved animals.

The following recipe is from Pat Flannery's daughter, Bekki Vallin:

"This just came to me, and it's something for the book. Fresh sautéed mushrooms in butter on toast and fresh ripe sautéed tomatoes in olive oil with melted sharp cheddar cheese on toast. You cut nice sized slices of tomatoes and cook them on one side, then after you flip them put the cheese onto melt. Simple but delish and mom (Pat Flannery) loved it and so do I." – Bekki Vallin

Pat Flannery. Courtesy: Bekki Vallin

K.C. Layne

It was in the mid-1960s, just as the last theatres were closing and the best acts were performing in supper clubs, that K.C. began dancing. In those early days she was known as "Joani Layne," later on she began using the initials K.C. Upon retiring from burlesque, she worked in films, and later became an accountant. K.C. Layne now paints, and you will find her work hanging in art galleries.

"This recipe I picked up from Mademoiselle Gee Gee when I first started in the mid-1960s. She always carried a hot plate, and cooked in her hotel room. Her room always smelled so good."

Brown ground beef (or ground round) Potatoes - diced
Onions – diced   1 Can of drained whole kernel corn
Season with: crushed red peppers, salt, pepper, parsley, etc. Cook until potatoes are done.

Early photo of K.C., while performing as Joani Layne. Courtesy: K.C. Layne

Barbecue Ribs

2 Slabs baby back ribs
2 Jalapeño peppers
5 - 10 Cloves garlic and/or garlic powder
1 Tablespoon cayenne pepper
2 Tablespoons chili pepper
2 Tablespoons paprika
1 – 2 Tablespoons of salt
Any Barbeque sauce, I use KC Masterpiece.

Cut the ribs apart so they are individual, and put into a large stockpot, preferably stainless steel, and cover with cold water. Put on high heat; when they come to a boil add the seasoning and vegetables.

Then cover with a heavy plate only, right in the boiling water face down. Do not put a lid on. Boil for at least 1 1/2 hours to 2 hours, until they seem to almost fall off the bone. With a slotted spoon, remove the ribs to a baking dish or dishes, and then brush the barbeque sauce over the ribs, and put into a 350 degree oven for 20 to 30 minutes. Walla, best eating ribs around!

K.C. Layne, 4'10" Stick of Dyno-Mite. Courtesy: K.C. Layne

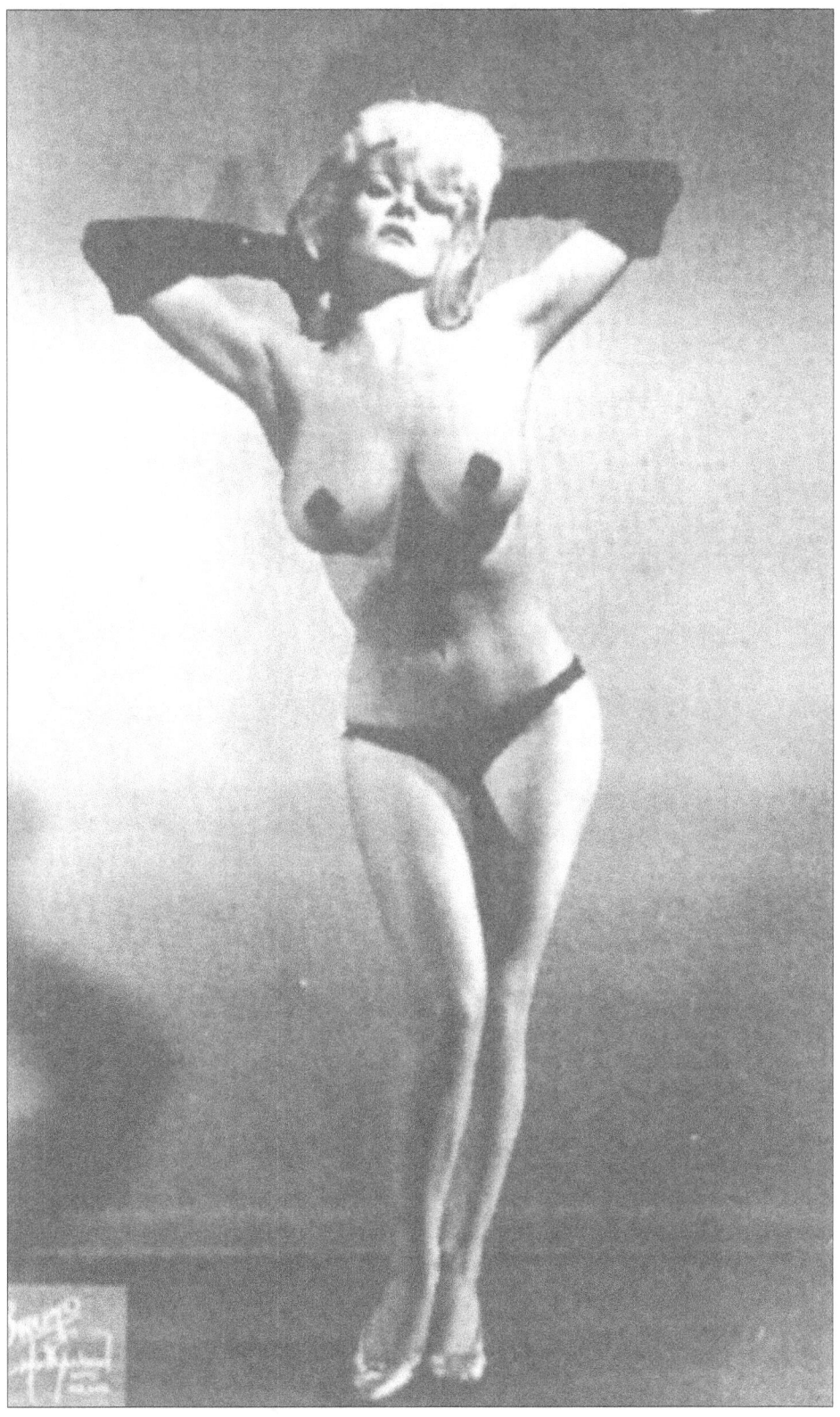
A voluptuous K.C. Layne. Courtesy: K.C. Layne

K.C. Layne, 4'10" Stick of Dyno-Mite. Courtesy: K.C. Layne

Mademoiselle Gee Gee. Courtesy: K.C. Layne

Banana Bread – from my mom, Zetta Wymore

Ingredients:
1¼ Cups sugar
½ Cup butter – softened
2 Eggs
1½ Cups ripe bananas – mashed (3 to 4 medium)
1/3 Cup unsweetened apple juice
½ Cup buttermilk
1 teaspoon vanilla
2½ Cups flour
1 teaspoon baking soda
1 teaspoon salt
1 Cup nuts – chopped (if desired)

Grease the bottom only of a 9X5X3 loaf pan, or 4 or 5 small individual loaf pans. Preheat oven to 350 degrees.

Mix sugar and butter together in a large bowl. Stir in eggs until everything is blended together well. Add bananas, buttermilk, apple sauce, and vanilla. Beat until smooth. Stir in remaining ingredients, except nuts, just until moistened. Stir in nuts. Pour into pan, or pans.

Bake about 60 to 75 minutes, or until inserted toothpick in center of bread comes out clean. Cool 5 minutes, loosen sides of loaf; then remove from pan. Cool completely before slicing.

Lemon Bars – from my Aunt Verna Mae Smith

Ingredients:

CRUST
1 Cup butter
½ Cup sugar
2 Cups flour

FILLING
5 Tablespoons flour
1 teaspoon baking powder
2 Cups sugar
4 Eggs slightly beaten
¼ teaspoon grated lemon rind
½ Cup lemon juice

Crust: Cream butter and sugar together; add flour. Spread in ungreased jelly roll pan. Bake at 350 degrees for 15 minutes, or until crust starts to brown around edges. Remove from oven.

Lemon Filling: Stir together 5 Tablespoons of flour, baking powder, sugar, and add to slightly beaten eggs. Beat until blended. Add lemon rind and juice. Beat well; filling will be thin.

Pour lemon filling over hot crust. Bake until golden brown, about 18-20 minutes. Sprinkle with powdered sugar, and cut into squares.

Apple Butterscotch Cookies

¼ Cup butter
1 Cup brown sugar
½ Cup half-and-half
1 Egg
½ teaspoon baking soda
1 teaspoon salt

½ teaspoon nutmeg
2 Cups flour
1 Cup Cameo or Rome Beauty apples
– pared and chopped
½ Cup butterscotch chips
1 Cup pecans – chopped

Preheat oven to 350 degrees. Cream together butter and sugar; beat in half-and-half, egg, soda, salt, nutmeg, and flour. Add apples, chips, and nuts. Drop by teaspoonfuls onto greased cookie sheet. Bake for 12-15 minutes. Be careful not to over bake. To make the glaze, combine 2 cups of powdered sugar, 1 teaspoon cinnamon, and 3 to 5 Tablespoons of apple juice. Drizzle over cooled cookies.

Microwave Fudge

3 Cups sugar
1 Cup butter (2 sticks)
2/3 Cup evaporated milk
1 Package semi-sweetened chocolate chips (OR if you want peanut butter fudge, use 1 package of peanut butter chips and 1/3 cup peanut butter)
1 Jar Kraft marshmallow crème
1 teaspoon vanilla
1 Cup walnuts or pecans

Put butter in large microwavable bowl. Cook on high for 1 to 1½ minutes. Remove and add sugar and milk. Stir well. Microwave on high for 5 minutes; stirring after 2½ minutes. Finish cooking on high.

Remove and stir well, scraping sides. Put back in and microwave for another 5½ minutes; stirring after 3 minutes. Finish cooking on high.

Remove and add chocolate chips, then stir. Add marshmallow crème, stir; then add vanilla, stir, and lastly add nuts. Pour into lightly greased 9X13 baking pan. Cool and cut into squares. Enjoy!

Butterscotch Haystacks

1 Package (11 oz) Nestle Toll House butterscotch flavored morsels
½ Cup creamy peanut butter
1 or 2 Cans Chow Mein noodles (8.5 to 10 oz)
3½ Cups of miniature marshmallows (7 oz)

Microwave morsels in large, microwavable bowl on medium high for 1 minute; stir. Microwave an additional 10-20 second intervals, stirring until smooth. Stir in peanut butter until well blended. Add Chow Mein noodles and marshmallows; toss until all ingredients are coated. Drop by rounded Tablespoon onto waxed paper-lined trays. Chill or let set; store in sealed container. (Makes about 6 dozen)

Scalloped Corn

1 Can cream style corn
2 Cans whole kernel corn
2½ Cups crushed crackers
1 Package shredded Velveeta cheese
8 Oz evaporated milk
1 Cup crackers finely crushed
1/3 Cup melted butter
Salt and Pepper to taste

Combine 1 can of cream style corn and 1 can of whole kernel corn in medium casserole dish. Cover with crushed crackers and cheese. Pour evaporated milk over ingredients in dish. Layer the last can of whole kernel corn on top, and add salt and pepper. Mix finely crushed crackers with melted butter, and sprinkle over dish as topping. Bake at 350 degrees for 30 minutes.

Prize-Winning Meatloaf

1½ LBs ground turkey
1 Can diced tomatoes, with juice
¾ Cup Quaker Oats – quick or old-fashioned, uncooked
1 Egg or 2 egg whites – lightly beaten
¼ Cup onion (chopped)
½ teaspoon salt – optional
¼ teaspoon black pepper
Garlic, crushed red pepper, basil, parsley – all to taste

Preheat oven to 350 degrees. In large bowl, combine all of the ingredients, mixing lightly but thoroughly. Press into a 8X4 inch loaf pan. Bake 60 minutes to medium doneness – until not pink in the center and juices show no pink color. Let stand 5 minutes; drain off any juices before slicing.

Customize recipe by using lean ground beef, and adding canned (drained) or frozen (thawed) corn. You can also add chopped green or red pepper, and sliced mushrooms. Also, you can sprinkle the top of the baked meatloaf with 1 cup of shredded cheese. Return loaf to oven for 3 minutes to melt the cheese.

Vicki O'Day

Vicki O'Day, also known as "Astarte, Goddess of Fertility," danced in burlesque clubs mostly on the West Coast from 1964 to 1979; she also performed in Alaska and Canada. In 1965, while in Denver, Vicki appeared in the movie *A Day in the Life of a Stripper* with Tempest Storm. She has been a chef, activist, ombudsman, dog-sitter, housewife, mother, grandmother, and a friend to many since she retired from the burlesque stage.

Vicki's Salsa

1 Pint (1 Cup) fresh strawberries
1 Cup tomatoes – no seeds
1 Small red onion
1 or 2 Jalapeños
2 Garlic cloves
1 Lime – juiced
1 Tablespoon olive oil

Mix together well and chill for minimum of two hours.

Vicki also suggested, instead of sugar, to add black pepper to fresh strawberries. She says it may not sound good, but it is really very tasty.

A rather serious pose of Vicki O'Day. Courtesy: Vicki O'Day

Coconut and Rum Pancakes

2 Eggs
5 Tablespoons melted butter
¾ Cup milk
¼ Cup cream of coconut (sweetened)
2 Tablespoons rum

1¼ Cups flour
1 Tablespoon sugar
4 teaspoons baking powder
Salt (to taste)

Pour egg mixture into dry ingredients just until moist. Scoop the batter onto a lightly oiled frying pan over a medium-high heat, using approximately 1/4 cup for each pancake.

A very young Vicki O'Day. Courtesy: Vicki O'Day

Rum French Toast

4 Eggs
1 Cup (½ milk – ½ heavy cream)
3 Tablespoons rum (dark is best)
2 Tablespoons sugar
¼ teaspoon nutmeg
1 Pinch salt

Use with thick sliced (good) bread; 4 Tablespoons of butter, vegetable oil, and garnish with fruit.

Tempest Storm, 1992. Courtesy: C.F. Miller

Cilantro - Buttermilk Dressing

1 Cup mayonnaise
1 Cup sour cream
1 Cup buttermilk
1 Cup chopped cilantro leaves
2 Tablespoons Parmesan or Romano cheese

1 teaspoon dry mustard
½ teaspoon celery seeds
½ teaspoon coriander seeds
¼ teaspoon pepper

Blend together, makes 3 cups; store in the refrigerator.

Herb Dressing

2/3 Cup salad oil (a good olive oil)
2/3 Cup cilantro (chopped)
1/3 Cup fresh lemon juice
2 Tablespoons tarragon vinegar (champagne or white wine)

1 teaspoon salt (to taste)
½ teaspoon dried tarragon
½ teaspoon chervil
¼ teaspoon oregano

Blend together; great with avocado, red onions, and/or on a spinach salad.

Onion Soup

¼ Cup butter
2½ Cups onions – thinly sliced
3 Tablespoons brown sugar
1 teaspoon pepper

3 Tablespoons flour
8 Cups beef broth
1 Cup dry red wine
¼ Cup A-1 Steak Sauce

In soup kettle add onions, brown sugar, and pepper. Cook over <u>low</u> heat until onions are lightly browned. (About 1 hour.)

Sprinkle onions with flour; stir to blend. Stir in broth; add wine or additional broth, steak sauce, and salt. Bring to boil; reduce heat, cover, and simmer for 45 minutes.

Homemade Croutons

3 Cups cubed French bread
2 Tablespoons olive oil
2 Tablespoons melted butter

¼ teaspoon oregano, basil, salt and pepper

Bake croutons at 350 degrees for 15 minutes or until browned. Serve in soups or on salads.

Helpful Hints

Vicki writes, "Many things found in hardware stores can also be helpful in kitchens. Examples are: Instead of pie weights use a ball chain. It can be picked up with a fork or a pair of tongs. When making pie dough, add vodka to the water. It makes it easier to roll and evaporates when baking. The next time you stay at a hotel, or go to a Dollar Store, bring home a shower cap. They can be used for bowl covers. Knee high nylons make good strainers. Rubbing alcohol, often used for cleaning, can be added to towels and dishrags. It helps reduce odors. And lastly, fabric stores sell cheese cloth by the yard."

Daphne Lake

Born and raised in Buffalo, New York, Daphne began her show business career in 1963 by working in a carnival sideshow. Daphne soon became the snake charmer in the show, briefly, and then she took a job as a "Bally Girl" in a girl's show. While the carnival wintered in Gibsonton, Florida, Daphne spotted a newspaper ad for a theatre in St. Petersburg that was looking for dancers. She made the trip, applied for the job, and got hired at $75 a week. Using the name "Jezebelle," she performed in three shows a day, seven days a week. By 1970, she was a featured performer,

Daphne Lake, "Miss Elegance;" a good chum and a wise woman. Courtesy: Daphne Lake

billed as "Daphne Lake." She created routines that revolved around the use of fire, marshmallows, or feathers.

Daphne wrote, "Owners were demanding favors, and there were more and more porn shows in the clubs. They placed more importance on how many bottles of champagne we conned the customers into buying than how glamorous our wardrobe was, or that we could even do a dance with fire. I couldn't work that way, so I just gave up. Theatres were almost all gone, and the ones that remained were doing really hard-core porn revues. I did my last show on a Saturday, and then I went to work in an office the very next Monday. I worked with a lot of the older girls in the theatres. Many had started dancing at the age of fourteen, and they knew little else. I realized I wasn't going to be able to support myself in burlesque, so as I got older, I kept up on my education."

Billed as "Miss Elegance," Daphne Lake never worked the West Coast, but she did perform in theatres and clubs on the East Coast, in the Midwest, in the southern United States, and also in Canada. In 1973, she retired from dancing. Daphne Lake died on March 17, 2015.

K.C. Layne and Daphne Lake at the 2006 BHS gathering at the Stardust Hotel and Casino in Las Vegas. Courtesy: Authors Collection

Hearty Lamb Vegetable Soup

6 Cups water
1/2 - 1 Cup of barley – washed
1 Small onion or 1/4 large onion - in chunks
1 - 2 Ribs of celery - in chunks
2 Tablespoons chopped dry parsley or 4-5 whole sprigs fresh parsley (Daphne preferred fresh)
1/2 teaspoon dried thyme - optional
1-2 Cloves of fresh garlic

1 Large or 4 small cubes of bouillon (Daphne used vegetable bouillon)
Bones, meat bits, and degreased juices from a leg of lamb
1 Large can of stewed tomatoes - chunky
1 Can of Veg-All mixed vegetables (Daphne preferred large veggies)
Salt to taste - optional
Splash of wine - optional
Hot pepper sauce (to taste)

Before making the soup, pour the juices from the cooked lamb into a bowl and cover with Saran Wrap. Once the juices are cold, the fat will solidify on top. Remove and discard that fat. Juices should be like jelly. Bones and juices can be stored in a good quality freezer bag for up to one year, in the freezer.

To make the soup: pour canned tomatoes, chunks of onion, celery, garlic, parsley, bouillon, and thyme into blender. Blend together until the mixture is like a chunky salsa.

Pour mixture into soup kettle or pressure cooker. Add lamb bones. Add some water into the blender jar. Whip it around to get the rest of the mixture from the jar. Add that water to the soup kettle; then add plain water until the soup kettle is about 3/4 full. Add washed barley. Boil until barley is cooked and soup bone releases marrow. (About 12 minutes boiling in a pressure cooker or about 60 minutes in a regular soup kettle.)

After barley is cooked, add drained canned vegetables, salt and wine (if desired), and then add hot sauce drop-by-drop (less IS more). (WARNING: If using pressure cooker, wait until the pressure is FULLY released BEFORE opening.) Allow soup to sit a few moments so that the vegetables can heat and soup can cool to eating temperature. It's really good with hot, crusty bread!

Spreckels Pound Cake

1 Cap (bottle cap) almond flavoring
2 1/3 Cups Spreckels granulated sugar
½ teaspoon salt
½ teaspoon nutmeg or mace
1 teaspoon grated lemon rind
2 Cups (1 LB) butter, softened
1½ teaspoons of vanilla or brandy extract
4 Cups sifted cake flour
10 Eggs

Blend sugar, salt, nutmeg, and lemon rind in a large mixing bowl. Cream together sugar mixture and butter until light and fluffy. Add extract and vanilla flavoring. Blend flour into creamed mixture gradually; continue blending until thoroughly mixed. Beat eggs into mixture, one at a time; beating well after each addition.

When smooth, turn batter into greased and floured 10 inch tube pan. Bake in slow oven at 325 degrees for 80 minutes or until cake tester comes out clean and cake is golden brown. Turn cake out on cooling rack; cool thoroughly. Let stand in airtight container at least 24 hours before serving. Yield: one 10 inch cake, or 24 servings. The recipe can be divided in half to make a smaller cake.

Daphne notes: Use cake flour; regular flour makes the cake too heavy. She preferred loaf pans, but used round pans as well.

Baklava

½ LB sweet butter, melted
¾ to 1 LB Filo (Phyllo) pastry leaves
1 or 2 LBs blanched almonds, chopped
1 LB shelled walnuts
2/3 Cup sugar
4 teaspoons ground cinnamon
2 teaspoons allspice
3 Dozen whole cloves

Ingredients for Syrup:
2 Cups honey
2 Cups water
2 Cups sugar
2 Cinnamon sticks OR 2 teaspoons ground cinnamon
1 teaspoon grated orange peel
1 teaspoon vanilla extract

Combine all the ingredients for the syrup in a sauce pan; bring to a boil, simmer for 10 minutes, strain, and allow to cool.

Coarsely grind or chop the walnuts and almonds, and mix thoroughly with the cinnamon, allspice, and sugar.

Brush a 9X13X2 inch pan with butter; lay a sheet of Filo in the bottom, brush with butter, cover with another sheet of Filo, brush with butter, and repeat process until you have used about a dozen sheets. Then spread one thin layer of the nut mixture on top of the Filo; cover with a sheet of Filo, brush with butter, cover with another layer of nuts, and repeat the process until all the nuts are used. Then cover with the remaining Filo sheets, brushing each sheet with butter. With a very sharp knife, cut the top Filo sheets into triangles; cutting diagonally across the pan. Insert a clove in the center of each triangle, and bake at 350 degrees for 90 minutes. When the Baklava is evenly browned, remove from oven, and pour the cooked syrup evenly over it, so that it penetrates the layers and covers the Baklava. Allow to cool several hours before serving.

Daphne notes: If more than ½ LB of butter is used, it gets too greasy. More cinnamon and allspice is being used to add flavor; less can be used if preferred. Strain the syrup before using it. More, or less, walnuts or almonds can be used in the recipe; chopping them coarse or fine is up to the cook. Do not eat the cloves!

Daphne wrote, "The only place that I worked, in Buffalo, was "The Stage Door." They only hosted me twice. Then the business went to crap and I had to stay on the road to keep working. Whenever I was offered a long-term contract, I stayed. I looked into going back on the road a couple of times, but all that was left was the mob-run clubs in the Midwest and Boston. I declined; it was too dangerous. If they liked you, they might want to keep you. If they didn't like you, they might hurt you. As it was, one of them tried to frame me on a weapons charge in Youngstown. I was onstage at the time, wearing a G-string, high heels, pasties, and a smile. When the cops asked me if the gun was mine, (they found it in my open bag in the kitchen/dressing room,) I looked at the officer and asked him, 'And just <u>where</u> would I be able to hide such a <u>huge</u> gun?' (It must have been at least a 45 caliber, although I didn't know much about guns at the time.) They arrested the manager of the club and let me leave town. I never went back to Youngstown after that!"

Jennifer Fox

Jennifer writes, "As far as recipes, I do not cook. I wish I did. I would love to contribute but do not want to poison anyone. In one of your letters you mentioned Tony Midnite said I should write a book. First, I must say how beautiful his gowns were. When you went for your fitting you did not know what he had in mind. But you really felt special going onstage in a Midnite gown. I remember one time going to pick up a gown at his studio, where I saw a gold sequin gown and lime green coat. I remember thinking I wish I had ordered those colors. To my surprise it was what he had designed for me. And all the under pieces, bra, panty, attached panel, G-string; all sequined and finished so beautifully. In my first professional photo shoot with Maurice Seymour I wore a fuchsia and silver gown and coat. He must have taken 100 photos. I think part of it was because Tony's gowns photographed so well."

Jennifer Fox.
Courtesy:
Jennifer Fox

Jennifer Fox. Courtesy: Jennifer Fox

Susan Mills

Here is comic Steve Mills favorite supper:

Mashed Potatoes and Chicken
Mashed potatoes
Boiled chicken - shredded in small pieces
Shredded cheddar cheese
Butter

I combine the chicken with the mashed potatoes and butter and some milk. I put a generous layer of cheddar cheese on top, and put in the oven in a small casserole dish for about 20 minutes at 350 degrees.

Susan writes, "Steve could eat this, and never have a problem with digestion. Of course, it was made with a lot of LOVE!"

Steve Mills was a popular and well known vaudeville and burlesque comic; Susan, his wife, also performed in burlesque. Later in life he appeared as the lead comic in the Ann Corio show, *This Was Burlesque*, which began as an Off-Broadway show in 1962. He continued on with the show when it landed on Broadway in 1965, and also performed with the touring company. Many legends were involved with that show including Paul Morokoff (choreographer) and Rex Huntington (costumes).

When Steve died in 1988, his obituary in the *Orlando Sentinel* read as follows:
"Steve Mills, 92, Performed as Comic in Vaudeville Shows; March 12, 1988. Warwick, R.I. – Steve Mills, 92, one of the last of the great vaudeville comedians who worked with the Shubert organization in the 1930s and 1940s, died Wednesday. After serving as an Army bugler in 1918, Mills joined the vaudeville and burlesque circuits. In 1924, he performed in Billy Gilbert's *Whiz Bang Babies*, and was lead comedian for Billy Minsky at the National Winter Garden Theatre in New York. After signing with the Shubert organization in the early 1930s, Mills appeared in *Three Little Girls, No, No Nanette,* and *Prince of Pilsen*. After burlesque ended in New York in 1937, Mills played New England nightclubs until 1944, when he rejoined Shubert to perform in the operettas *Wildflower* and *The Firefly*. He also played in *A Lady Says Yes* in New York with Carole Landis, before returning to New England clubs. In the 1960s and early 1970s, Mills appeared on TV talk shows and performed with Mildred Natwick and Hans Conried on Broadway in *70 Girls, 70* in New York in 1971, the *Best of Burlesque* show in Las Vegas, Nevada, and the Minsky Show in Miami. He last appeared on stage in 1977."

When I mentioned to Susan I was including some information about Steve, including his obituary, she wrote, "Sounds good, but when printing Steve's obit,

Susan and Steve Mills. Courtesy: Susan Mills

be careful for the details. All the obits written were not accurate. He was born on October 9, 1895 and died on March 9, 1988. He died in my arms, in his house in Warwick, Rhode Island. You might add that he drank a half bottle of champagne every night, and still loved his barbershop quartets; amongst other things."

Since we are on the topic of burlesque comics, I thought I would also include some tid-bits from straight man Lee Stuart:

Lee and Elaine Stuart, a legendary burlesque husband and wife duo. Courtesy: Lee Stuart

"I worked with Freddie Frampton in Louisville at the National. Freddie was a very funny guy with a W.C. Fields accent. He also shared Fields' love of the bottle. Across the alley from the stage door was a side entrance to the tavern. After each show Freddie would drop in for a few drinks. This day between the afternoon show and the evening show the manager hired an alligator wrestler as a specialty act. The guy had two alligators that he tied to a wall at the bottom of the stairs. When Freddie made his way into the theatre for the night show with a fair load on, he saw these two alligators at the foot of the stairs. He paused mid-stairs, eyes wide, and white as a sheet; he turned and up the steps he went, back to the bar. 'Give me a shot Gus, you ain't gonna believe what I just saw in the basement!' It took the manager and another comic several minutes to explain the situation so Freddie would return to the theatre. We loved hearing Freddie explain, 'Hell man I've seen pink elephants, tigers, and lions, but never an alligator. I may quit drinking.' He didn't quit, nor slow down."

Lee also wrote, "I know you know of the Kane time. The Kemp time was on the East Coast and when we were laid off for the summer we could find several weeks on the Kemp time. It belonged to an agent in Charlotte, North Carolina. He booked one nighters up and down the East Coast from New England to Florida and used a lot of burlesque people. Each show carried a stripper for closing. Ruth Swank was the feature in the cast we were on. She later died in a car crash on icy roads south of Duluth. The dates were mostly in Army camps and small theatres. It didn't pay much, but it beat a lay off. The agent was T.D. Kemp; brother of Hal Kemp, the big band leader."

Another from Lee Stuart, "This old joke was still popular among performers backstage after many years. It had its beginning in the era of minstrel shows. It seemed this large show had fallen on hard times when one night Bozo the top comic passed away. The rest of the comics gathered around old Bozo and discussed how to give Bozo a proper burial. They had no money, so it was decided they would do it themselves. Early next morning they loaded old Bozo in a wheelbarrow they borrowed from a stagehand and pushed Bozo to the outskirts of town where they dug a hole. They placed the body in the hole and stood around for several minutes. Someone said it would be nice if someone gave a eulogy. They stood looking from one to the other in silence. Finally one spoke up and said, 'You guys wait here until I go back to town and get a STRAIGHT Man.' Most performers thought this was funny, but comics failed to see the humor. People not in the business would not get it at all."

Joni Taylor

I thought it was appropriate to follow words from a straight man with recipes from a talking woman.

In 1952, Joni Taylor began her career working in the chorus line at the in Pittsburgh. As her career progressed Joni went on the road, working in bits with comic Charlie Robinson and dancing as a co-feature. She performed as a pretty young dancer, or she blackened her teeth and played the hausfrau in comedy scenes; she was always adaptable. In 1964, Joni left burlesque, but filled-in whenever AGVA called for a last-minute replacement. She loved to dance; but was also very proud to have worked with many top-notch comics and straight men from the last decades of legendary burlesque.

I stayed with Joni for six months after I returned to the Midwest from Utah; she had a big heart, loved all animals – especially cats - and I assure you she was a GOOD cook! She died in September 2017.

A young Joni Taylor backstage at the Pittsburgh Casino Theatre. Courtesy: Joni Taylor

Originally opened as the Harris Theatre in 1911, it was renamed the Casino Theatre in 1936. The Pittsburgh, Pennsylvania theatre closed in 1966. Courtesy: Burlesque Historical Society

Joni Taylor, almost always had a smile on her face. Courtesy: Joni Taylor

Barbara Curtis, Al Anger, Joni Taylor, and Sam DiRando on Joni and Sam's wedding day in 1959. Courtesy: Joni Taylor

Joni Taylor. Courtesy: Joni Taylor

Joni Taylor and Sunny Dare at the 2006 BHS gathering at the Stardust Hotel and Casino in Las Vegas. Courtesy: Authors Collection

Broccoli and Pasta

¾ Cups virgin olive oil (in large pan or skillet) heat until hot

Add 8 large garlic cloves, cook until lightly browned

Add 1 small onion, and brown

1 Small green or red pepper, sauté until lightly cooked

Add 2 cups of chicken broth or bouillon – boxed or canned

Add 1 Tablespoon of oregano, 1 Tablespoon of parsley, 1 Tablespoon of crushed basil leaves, and 1½ Tablespoons of crushed red pepper seeds, (more or less); bring to simmer.

Add 1 head of fresh, cut broccoli, or 1 large bag of frozen

Add salt and pepper to taste. Cook on low heat for 15 to 20 minutes. Serve over Linguini al dente noodles, cooked 6 to 7 minutes. Sprinkle with grated cheese.

Buffalo Chicken Dip

1 Package (8 oz) cream cheese, softened

½ Cup blue cheese dressing

½ Cup Frank's Red Hot Sauce

½ Cup crumbled blue cheese or mozzarella

2 Cans (12.5 oz) canned white chunk chicken

Stir cream cheese into 9 inch pie or cake plate until smooth. Stir in remaining ingredients. Bake in preheated 350 degree oven for 20 to 25 minutes until hot and bubbly. Stir, and serve with a variety of crackers and fresh vegetables.

Delicious Cranberry Sauce

1 LB bag of fresh cranberries   1 Whole orange, including rind

Grind cranberries and orange together; add 2 cups of sugar and let stand for three hours.

Then mix 1 large box of strawberry Jell-O with 3½ cups of hot water. When Jell-O starts to jell add cranberry mixture, and add ½ cup celery, ¾ cup crushed pineapple, and ¾ cup of walnuts – chopped fine. Mix well and chill; make it the day ahead of when you want to serve it. Joni said, "It's absolutely delicious."

Apple Cake

2 Cups flour	3 Eggs
1 teaspoon cinnamon	1 Cup oil
1 teaspoon baking soda	6 Cups of apples – peeled, cored, and sliced
½ teaspoon salt	
1¾ Cups sugar	1 Cup of chopped nuts

Sift and measure flour. Sift again after adding cinnamon, baking soda, and salt. Add remaining ingredients; then mix and add apples, nuts, and mix again. Bake in greased and floured 9X13 cake pan for 60 minutes in preheated 350 degree oven. Dust with powdered sugar. Serve warm, or cold, with whipped topping. Mixture looks like a big glob when first put in the pan, but will settle while baking.

Stacy Farrell

Stacy Farrell began her career in burlesque in the chorus line at the Follies Theatre in Los Angeles when she was nineteen years old. At that time the chorus line consisted of about twenty girls. Stacy told me, "In the old days, in order to work in burlesque, you had to know how to dance. We did everything: tap, ballet, toe, and jazz. We had to parade around the stage with grace, always smiling at the audience. We also had to do scenes with the comics. This gave us all-around experience to go on and do many other things."

Stacy's career as a dancer spanned five decades, beginning in the 1930s and ending in 1974. Stacy and Jennie Lee were close chums; and occasionally, towards the end of her career, Stacy would perform in one of Jennie's clubs. But after a long illustrious career on some of the biggest and best burlesque stages, when

Press photo from 1973 of the demolished Follies Theatre in Los Angeles. Courtesy: Los Angeles Times

told she had to appear nude to dance in clubs, Stacy retired. Not interested in performing in the nude, she bought her own club in North Long Beach, California. Stacy Farrell passed away in November of 2005.

Stacy Farrell died long before the concept of this book was even thought of, but I wanted to include her because she was a great friend. She wasn't much of a cook, but she could mix a mean drink. I spent many weekends at her home. We often went out to eat; she really liked Chinese food, and we'd also shop for things to nibble on over the weekend. Though she has been gone for many years, I still have a key to her home. The following words are from Mary Woodard, a woman who used to work for Stacy.

"Stacy Farrell was always so alive and fun, even in the midst of personal sorrow. Everyone loved her and every year on her bar's anniversary, all her old burlesque buddies would come down and Stacy would close the bar to the public so that they could have a party. It was a blast! One year, I made a fabulous gold lame' gown to wear. I worked as a bartender a couple nights each week while attending college.

Stacy's bar had been called the "Wagon Wheel" when I was a little kid. It was only a mile or so from my home and I grew up watching the place transform from a square dance hall to Stacy Farrell's. She had these gigantic posters of herself framed on the outside walls in a fabulous sequined evening gown while holding a huge trophy for winning the "Most Beautiful Stripper" award. When her band, manager, and bartenders defected to a newly opened bar, I stayed and won Stacy's love and loyalty. She never forgot a friend.

Here's a funny. One day when I was pregnant with my second child (years after leaving Stacy's) I was at the bank at 10am. As I parked, this older blonde bombshell in short-shorts and high heels climbed out of a sports car…it was

Jennie Lee and Stacy Farrell having a grand time at Stacy's club. Courtesy: Burlesque Historical Society

Stacy. I looked so fat and drab that I just couldn't bring myself to get out of my car and talk to her! She was fabulous and always the life of every party.

I left California in 1980 and have never returned there to live. I kept in sporadic touch with Stacy until then, but my husband's job took us all over the world and I lost touch - my bad. Stacy impacted my life in many ways. She told me that she had hired me because I reminded her of herself. What a compliment! When I interviewed for the job, she asked, 'How are you going to work in those heels?' And I answered, 'I ALWAYS work in heels!' What a smart ass thing to say to the woman who would be my boss. But she laughed and hired me. Stacy had a great, all out laugh that I can still hear. And she never got really mad either. What a babe!

Thanks for the walk down "Memory Lane," Jane. Even at my age I still recall those two years with Stacy as a fun, fun time in my life. Your books must be a wonderful joy for you - to have been able to pass on a unique piece of history to others. Guess everyone has a Stacy story, huh?

And thanks for answering my email, even with such sad news. I'm sure you are right about Stacy perhaps willing herself to die. She should've been in an

Stacy Farrell standing in front of her club in North Long Beach, California. Courtesy: Burlesque Historical Society

actor's home or something, somewhere that she could've relived her life on a daily basis."

Stacy Farrell used to tell me tales of her bar in Long Beach; and just for the record, she gave me my first taste ever of a Martini. She also gave me a book Jennie Lee had once given her; Stacy was my "California Mama." When Stacy Farrell passed away in 2005 she had been a part of "The Golden Days of Burlesque Historical Society" since the group began in 1995. Sometime, around 1998, she was declared legally blind and had to give up driving. At that time, she was driving a bright yellow sports car, which she totally loved and hated to give up.

The following is an email train of tid-bits from three ladies of the BHS, who all sent recipes for this book; Sequin, Lily Ann Rose, and The Fascinating Jennifer.

Sequin wrote, "Hello Jane. I received my newsletter today, and have something to contribute to the book on Harold Minsky. I did my "Farewell to Burlesque" show at Minsky's Adams Theatre in Newark. I will have to get into my box of photos and look for one particular picture of him admiring a new gag award necklace on me. I have another shot throwing my garter out to the audience that was taken that night too. I may have the write-up from the press party we threw following the show, but I'm not sure. Is that the type of thing you are asking for?"

Lily Ann Rose wrote, "Ah, sweet memories… My days in the chorus at the Casino Burlesque Theatre are some of my sweetest. I loved the gals, the funny men, and the beautiful stars! Some of my fondest memories are of the times I was the talking woman for the hilarious team of Sharples and Naples. Keep the memories coming."

The Fascinating Jennifer responded to that email with, "Lily, that brought back a memory of when I was in the chorus and I was doing a bit with Freddy Lewis. I was standing on a box in a black bra and panties. The bit was going on…

Autographed photo of Sequin to Joni Taylor. Courtesy: Joni Taylor

Freddy had a cane in his hand and in a quick motion he flipped the cane between my legs and caught it on the other side. The audience laughed, but I didn't like it at all. I said in a quiet voice to Freddy, 'You do that one more time and I will walk right off the stage.' I have a deep voice and for some reason it carried throughout the theatre. Everything stopped for about three seconds and then continued. He later apologized. I don't know now why it bothered me, but at the time it did. However, I liked Freddy, he was a sweetheart!"

Tina Mack chipped in with, "Here's my idea of the perfect recipe. Give husband credit card. Call and order pizza. Send husband to get it. Done! Ha!"

The Fascinating Jennifer

In 1954, the Casino Burlesque Theatre in Boston hired Jennifer to dance in the chorus line. After learning stage presence, she was asked to do a solo striptease routine, which was of no interest to the young dancer. After watching Sequin's routine, which contained no bumps and grinds, Jennifer began creating her own costumes and routines, and she frequently filled-in onstage at the theatre when needed. In 1957, "The Fascinating Jennifer" toured on the Bryan and Engle circuit as a co-feature. By 1958, she was performing as a feature, and continued to work in burlesque theatres until her retirement in 1963. Jennifer died on October 18, 2015.

Autographed photo The Fascinating Jennifer gave to Joni Taylor. Courtesy: Joni Taylor

The Fascinating Jennifer. Courtesy: Burlesque Historical Society

Cousin Mike's Spaghetti Sauce

Ingredients:
- 4 Large cans of whole tomatoes
- 3 Small cans of tomato paste
- *1½ LBs ground beef and pork (half and half)
- 3 or 4 Cloves garlic – finely chopped
- ½ Cup olive oil (pure)
- 12 Sausages (6 hot, 6 sweet)
- 1 Tablespoon Italian Seasoning
- 1 Tablespoon oregano
- 1 Tablespoon parsley
- 1 Tablespoon honey
- 2 Bay leaves
- *2 Eggs
- *1/3 Cup grated cheese
- *1/2 Cup Italian bread crumbs
- *1 teaspoon minced garlic
- *1 teaspoon minced onion
- 1 Cup red cooking wine
- 1 Cup water

Optional Ingredients:
- 1 Thick slice of onion – cubed (makes sauce sweeter)
- Mushrooms

Sauce:

Pour oil into pan with sausages and garlic; simmer until sausages are slightly browned. In a large mixing bowl, combine tomatoes and paste by hand; pour into pan. Bring to a boil, stirring frequently. Sprinkle oregano and Italian Seasoning over sauce; then add the honey and bay leaves.

Meatballs:

Mix all * ingredients thoroughly and place into sauce, stirring carefully.

    At this point, add mushrooms

    Pour wine and water into sauce

    Simmer for at least 6 hours

Italian Stuffing for Turkey

Ingredients:
- Small box of Progresso Italian flavored bread crumbs
- 1 Can black olives – pitted and cut in half
- ½ LB Provolone cheese – cut in small pieces
- ½ LB Genoa salami – cut in small pieces
- 4 Hard boiled eggs – cut in small pieces

Add all the ingredients into a bowl. Next add enough water so that the stuffing is moist, but not too wet. It's better to leave it a bit dry when stuffing a turkey or chicken because the juices from the bird will make it moist. It can also be made in a baking dish and in that case you would add more water.

(Notes: Directions were not included for baking as a separate dish, so I am including something that might work. Use your best judgment. Preheat oven at 350 degrees; lightly grease a 9X13 inch baking dish, and bake for 30-40 minutes or until the top is brown and crisp.)

Italian Sauce

Ingredients:
- 4 Cans of crushed tomatoes
- 1 Can of tomato paste
- 6 Hot or sweet sausages
- 4 Cloves of garlic – chopped
- ½ to ¾ Cup of fresh parsley – chopped
- 6 Whole basil leaves – remove after sauce is finished
- 2 Tablespoons of sweet basil
- ¼ Cup of Italian Seasoning
- 1 teaspoon red crushed peppers
- 6 Tablespoons olive oil
- 1½ Cans of water

In a large sauce pan add the olive oil, garlic, and 2 cans of tomatoes. Next add all seasonings, and the other 2 cans of tomatoes. Stir well and add 1 can of water. Put tomato paste in ½ can of water and mix until smooth, then add to sauce. Add sausages. Bring to a boil and then lower flame and simmer for 6 hours.

Italian Meatballs

Ingredients:
1 Egg
¼ Cup of Italian seasoned bread crumbs
¼ Cup of Italian grated cheese
4 Cloves of garlic – minced
¼ Cup of fresh parsley
4 Tablespoons of the Italian Sauce
2 LBs of Hamburger

Place hamburger in a large bowl and add all the ingredients. Mix well and make meatballs; drop them in the Italian Sauce. This recipe of sauce and meatballs has been in my family for generations and is now being passed on to the younger members of my family.

"The Fascinating Jennifer" wrote, "One night I went onstage to do my number and when it came time to take off my dress the zipper got stuck in the material. I struggled with it for awhile while dancing around; I even went to the wings and had someone try from there while I faced the audience. They couldn't get it unstuck and I went on dancing around, laughing, struggling, and I never did get it unstuck. I think I heard a few boos as the number ended."

Lily Ann Rose

At the age of fourteen, Lily Ann Rose followed her mother and three aunts into the world of burlesque, in Boston. In the late 1940s she learned to twirl tassels and worked with some of the best comics and straight men of the day. To learn more, I would suggest reading her book, *Banned in Boston: Memoirs of a Stripper*, by Lillian Kiernan Brown. In the meantime I hope you enjoy some of the recipes she shared for this book.

Salmon Lovers Spread

1 Can red salmon
1 Red onion, diced
¼ Cup green olives, pimento stuffed, sliced
1 Tablespoon olive oil
Juice of 1 lemon
Dash of horseradish
Dash of Dijon mustard
Dash of mayonnaise

Cream all ingredients together until the spread consistency is smooth and creamy. Garnish with parsley and green onion.

Lily Ann Rose. Courtesy: Lillian Brown

Broiled Grapefruit

2 Grapefruits 4 Maraschino cherries
4 Tablespoons of sugar

Slice grapefruits in half, remove seeds and separate from skin for easy removal. Sprinkle with sugar. Place cherries in center of each half. Place under hot broiler until lightly browned on top. Serve immediately.

Ceviche

2 Cups raw fish, shrimp, clams
½ Cup lime juice
1 Cup tomato juice or V-8
1 Small onion, chopped
1 Tomato, chopped
1 Green pepper, or chili, chopped
½ Cup cilantro, chopped
Tabasco to taste

Cover raw fish completely with lime juice and set in refrigerator overnight or until fish is "cooked" in the juice. Add remaining ingredients. Serve in cocktail glasses.

Pizza Crust

2 Packages active dry yeast or 2 cakes compressed yeast
½ Cup water
1 Tablespoon salt
2 Cups lukewarm water
7 Cups sifted all-purpose flour

Soften yeast in ½ cup warm water. Combine salt and 2 cups of lukewarm water; beat in 2 cups of the flour. Blend in softened yeast; then stir in 4 cups of the flour, or enough to make a "soft dough." Turn out on a lightly floured surface. Cover; let rest for 10 minutes. Then knead until smooth and elastic, 5 – 8 minutes. Work in the remaining cup of flour. Divide dough into 2 portions. Place on floured surface and roll out to the desired size. Leave crust approximately ¼ inch thick. Place onto lightly greased pizza pans. (Makes 2 large pizzas)

Pizza Toppings

1 Can (28 oz) Italian style tomatoes
2 Cans (6 oz) tomato paste
1 Tablespoon crushed oregano
1 Tablespoon whole basil
1 Can (8 oz) mushrooms
1 Green pepper, sliced or chopped
1 Onion, sliced or chopped
Crushed garlic
2 Sticks pepperoni, thinly sliced
Sauté sausage and / or hamburger as desired
2 Packages mozzarella cheese, finely shredded

Drain tomatoes and crush finely. Add tomato paste, basil and oregano; mix well. Put ½ of mixture on each crust. Sprinkle with shredded cheese, mushrooms, peppers, onions, hamburger, sausage, and pepperoni. Preheat oven to 450 degrees. Brush edges of crust with olive oil before placing in oven. Bake until crust browns. Makes 2 combination pizzas; other toppings optional.

Hush Puppies

½ Cup onion, diced
1 Cup self-rising flour
1 Cup cornmeal
½ Can beer

Mix together the dry ingredients. Add onions and beer until thick biscuit consistency. Drop by spoonfuls into hot oil, 375 degrees, until brown. Test inside for doneness. Serve immediately with fried catfish.

Spiders

These sounded like fun; the recipe comes from a friend of Lily Ann's, Patricia Huml.

1 Package (12 oz) butterscotch or chocolate morsels
1 Can (5 oz) Chow Mein noodles
1 Cup skinless peanuts

Melt morsels over very low heat. Mix all the ingredients together well, and then spoon onto waxed paper. (Makes about 5 dozen)

Old Fashioned Chocolate Pound Cake

2 Sticks butter (1/2 LB)
½ Cup Crisco (8 level Tablespoons)
3 Cups sugar
5 Eggs
3 Cups cake flour
½ teaspoon baking powder
4 Level teaspoons cocoa
1 Cup milk
1 teaspoon vanilla

Cream together the butter, sugar, and Crisco. Add eggs one at a time. Sift together all the dry ingredients. Add alternately with milk to the creamed mixture, and then add the vanilla. Bake in a 9X10 inch pan at 325 degrees for 80 minutes.

Variance: Fold in 1 cup of mashed bananas, ¼ cup of crushed nut meats, and 1 teaspoon of freshly ground nutmeg. Bake at 325 degrees for 90 minutes.

Italian Bread Crumbs

2 Cups grated bread crumbs
3 Large garlic cloves, crushed and diced
½ Cup parsley, chopped
½ teaspoon sugar
½ Cup grated Romano cheese
Salt and pepper to taste

Mix all ingredients together until well mixed. These will store well in a jar in the refrigerator until ready to use.

Italian Wedding Soup

1 LB ground beef	1 Egg
1 LB chicken parts or chicken stock	2 Cups Cece beans (Chick Peas/Garbanzo)
3 Carrots	½ Cup Tubettini or Orzo pasta
3 Onions	1 Bunch escarole (washed 3 times and cut up)
Parsley	
Italian bread crumbs	
2 Cups tomatoes	

Place vegetables in large pot and cover with soup stock. Cook until tender. Add bread crumbs and egg to meat and mix into meatball consistency. Form into tiny meatballs and drop into soup. 10 minutes before serving, add pasta.

Chicken Stock

2 LBs chicken parts will do, skin on	1 Carrot whole, washed not peeled
1 Bunch of celery tops	Salt and pepper to taste
1 Onion whole, do not peel, just wash off loose skin	

Wash and place all ingredients in a 12 quart stock pot. Cover with 8 quarts of water. Bring to a boil and simmer for 4 hours. Remove chicken, skin, and bones – reserving the meat. Strain the broth and store in the refrigerator until cold. Skim the fat, removing it before using the stock in a recipe; but store with the fat on as it protects your broth.

The broth is ready to use in recipes that require chicken stock. With the chicken meat you can make pot pies, chicken and dumplings, or just plain good old chicken soup.

Katherine's Favorite BBQ Sauce

(Katherine is Lily's daughter)	¼ Cup celery seed or fresh celery
1 Can tomato paste	¼ Cup Karo or dark cane syrup
¼ Cup vinegar	¼ Cup Ketchup
¼ Cup sugar (white or brown)	3 Cups of V-8 or tomato juice
¼ Cup onion, chopped	

This is for oven bake BBQ – not for open flame BBQ. Mix ingredients in a saucepan and bring to a boil. Pour over chicken, beef, or pork; oven bake slowly at 325 degrees.

Fruit Wine

This also comes from a friend of Lily's, Willis Butcher.

3½ Gallons of water
5 LBs sugar (real cane sugar not beet)
1½ Gallons of fruit (grapes, berries, etc.)

Press out fruit into crock. Add water and 2 pounds of sugar. Cover; stir once a week. In 10 days, add the additional 3 pounds of sugar. It's ready to bottle in about 3 weeks. Strain and bottle; makes 5 gallons.

Sequin

Sequin began her career in show business at the age of seventeen, in the midst of World War II, when she was hired as a nightclub singer in Oakland, California. After touring with Buddy Johnson and later Jack "Madman" Mitchell, Sequin, with the aid of her friend and artist Ted Littleton, created a striptease act and began her burlesque career at "Strip City" in Los Angeles. Lili St. Cyr was her role model. Touring as "Sequin, Beauty to the 4th Dimension," she worked theatres and clubs throughout the United States. Dick Richards, the dancer turned agent, was instrumental in booking Sequin on to the Ohio Burlesque Circuit until she appeared at Minsky's in 1957. There, she met future husband Tony Tamburello. Tony, musical director for Tony Bennett, created a nightclub routine with special material which he and Sequin performed until they married a year later and Sequin retired. Sequin died on December 16, 2016.

Lili St. Cyr. Courtesy: C.F. Miller

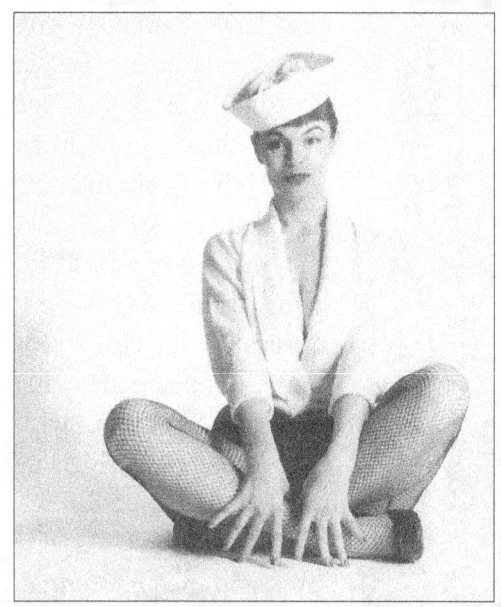

A variety of photos of Sequin. For a number of years the BHS used to search for performers that others in the group were looking to reconnect with. It took nine years to find Sequin. Courtesy: Mary Jane Tamburello-Ellis

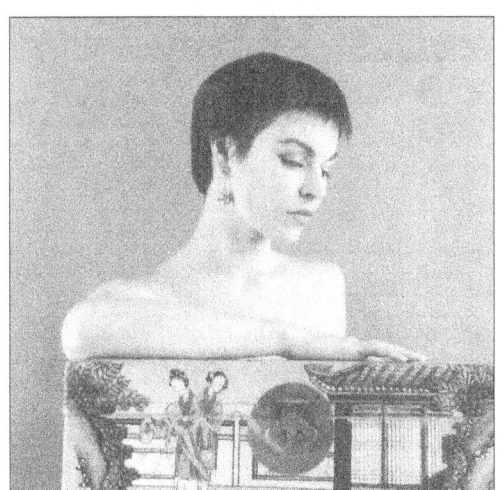

Stromboli

Set out the deep fryer and heat oil to 365 degrees.

In large bowl:

    2 Cups sifted flour   ¼ teaspoon salt

Make a well in center; add 3 eggs, one at a time. Mixing slightly after each is added. Add ½ teaspoon of vanilla.

Mix well to make a soft dough. Turn dough onto lightly floured surface, and knead. Divide into halves. Lightly roll each half ¼ inch thick to form a rectangle. Cut into strips ¼ inch wide. Roll, with palm of hand, into strips similar to the thickness of a pencil. Cut into pieces ¼ to ½ inch long.

Fry only as many pieces as will float in a single layer until lightly browned; turn to brown evenly. Drain, over fryer, before removing to absorbent paper towel until all pieces are done.

Cook in a skillet, over low heat for about 5 minutes:

    1 Cup of honey   1 Tablespoon sugar

Remove from heat and add pieces of fried dough. Stir constantly until all are coated. Remove with slotted spoon to plate. Chill slightly and arrange in a cone shaped mound. Sprinkle with sprinkles or multi-colored candies. Adding cinnamon to the honey and sugar mixture is another option. Manja!

Chicken Salad - my grandson Dae Ellis's recipe

2 Cups cooked chicken breast - cut into bite size cubes
½ Cup red onion - diced
1 Medium Granny Smith apple – peeled and diced
½ Cup raisins
½ Cup walnuts – chopped
4 Tablespoons honey or brown sugar
½ Cup mayonnaise or Miracle Whip (more if you want)
½ teaspoon curry powder

Mix together well and chill.

Italian Tuna Surprise

Ingredients:
1 LB spaghetti
1 LG can solid white tuna – gently broken into chunks
1 LG can Campbell's tomato soup
1 Onion – chopped
1 Cup curly parsley – chopped
Olive oil

Serves 4 - 6

Put a pot of water on to boil and cook spaghetti al dente. Sauté parsley and onion in olive oil; when the onion is soft add the tuna. Next add the tomato soup and heat until bubbly. Turn off the heat, drain pasta, and add soup mixture. Gently combine into pasta, and serve with grated parmesan cheese.

Adjust amounts to suit your families taste – more soup, a little garlic, more tuna, onion, etc. Oil packed tuna is too strong for our taste, so we use the white solid tuna.

Spinach Salad – my daughter Mary Jane Tamburello-Ellis's recipe

1 or 2 Packages of baby spinach (fresh)
½ LB bacon – fried crisp and crushed
½ Red onion – chopped
½ Cup apple cider vinegar
¼ Cup sugar

Optional: Mandarin orange slices, sliced strawberries, blueberries, pine nuts, crumbled blue cheese, or chopped walnuts.

Wash and "spin dry" the spinach thoroughly and put in a large bowl. Tear spinach leaves into bite size pieces, and add onion and any optional ingredients you want to use. Mix lightly.

Fry bacon until crispy and let "drain" on paper towel. Pour off all but 2-3 Tablespoons of the fat. Add vinegar and sugar, and bring to a boil. Cook until the sugar dissolves. This makes your vinaigrette.

When ready to serve, pour the hot vinaigrette lightly over the spinach mixture and add the crispy bacon bits. Toss lightly. If needed, salt and pepper to taste.

Sequin wrote, "The following is a favorite recipe my step-mom would make when I was a kid. I made it on the road when I performed as well; I always carried a 'kitchen in a box.' It contained: pots, herbs, silverware, cups, plates, a can opener, an electric frying pan, an electric coffee pot, casserole dishes, and a hot plate."

Ingredients:
1 LB ground beef
1 Onion – chopped
1 Package of egg noodles
1 Package of shredded cheddar cheese
1 Can of tomato sauce
1 Can of creamed corn
Salt, pepper, and Grandma's Spanish Seasoning

Cook egg noodles. Fry ground beef; then add corn and tomato sauce when beef is cooked. Season the beef mixture with Grandma's Spanish Seasoning. Drain noodles when cooked and put in second frying pan, pouring the beef mixture over it. Cover entirely with shredded cheese and cook slowly with the lid on, until cheese has melted. If I had an oven, I'd put all the ingredients into a casserole dish and bake 20-30 minutes until the cheese bubbles. Serve with a salad and French bread.

Sandra Ellis

In 1936, Sandra Ellis, a native New Yorker, auditioned for *Minsky's Burlesque* after seeing an ad in a local New York newspaper. She was hired immediately and danced at Billy Minsky's Republic Theatre on 42nd Street and Broadway, at the Continental Theatre, and at the beautiful Oriental Theatre at 52nd Street and Broadway. Sandra Ellis remained with the Minsky organization until the City of New York closed down all the burlesque theatres.

Sandra didn't send any recipes, just shared how she cooks fresh fish and a tidbit. Sandra Ellis, who also contributed to the Eddie Lynch section in this book, passed away in her sleep on November 9, 2019; she was 102 years young.

Sandra wrote, "Place fresh fish, skin down, in a thin baking pan. Put a pad of non-salted butter on top, along with a dash of paprika. Bake or broil – I prefer broiled – for about 10-15 minutes at around 350 degrees. I also prefer fish with no bones, like Cod. Fruits and veggies are more to my liking. That's my cooking. I am not now, or never was a cook – had no time for it. I am not a meat eater – but once in awhile when the stores have fresh fish, like Pollock or Flounder, I'll get two pounds and freeze some.

Have I told you that when Alan Alda was a little boy, maybe two or three years of age, I was his father's (Robert) dance partner at the *Minsky's Follies* in New York City? In Alan's book, *Don't Stuff the Dog*, he mentions how we, the performers, would play with him between sets."

Burlesque Artists Association Membership card for Sandra Ellis. Courtesy: Sandra Ellis

(Notes: Mimi Reed also told me a similar story about playing with Alan Alda when he was a child backstage at the theatres. If Mimi were alive I know she would have contributed to this book. She, and her partner Thareen Auroraa, loved to cook. They treated me to a home cooked meal in Studio City, California on my 45th birthday, many years ago. It was then that Mimi gave me the bellows used to blow up the balloons she danced with when performing as a specialty dancer.)

Mimi Reed and Thareen Auroraa in the 1960s. Courtesy: Mimi Reed

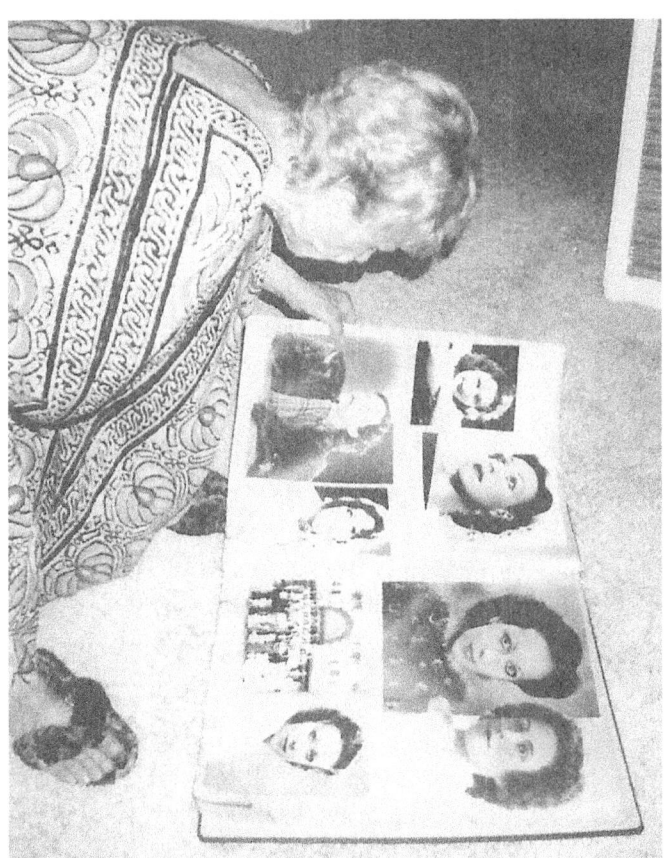

Mimi Reed showing me her scrapbook at a visit to her home in 2000. Courtesy: Authors Collection

My landlady in California, Eleanor Oliver, helped at two BHS reunions in Las Vegas, and shared the following recipe. (Ellie and dancer Sheila Rae were close friends for many years.)

Ellie's Tacos

Hormel Chili and Beans – (meat optional)
Corn Tortillas
Lettuce – chopped
Cheddar cheese – (sharp) shredded
Onions – diced
Tomatoes – diced
Taco sauce – or hot sauce

Heat the beans; add browned hamburger if you want, and warm the tortillas. Then make yourself a Taco – they are good.

Patty O'Farrell

Patty O'Farrell. Courtesy: Patty O'Farrell

Patty O'Farrell worked in burlesque theatres across the Midwest, including Louisville, Cincinnati, Chicago, and Kansas City, Kansas. In her early years, she preferred performing in theatres where she got to meet many of the comics and work in the comedy scenes. As time passed, she favored working in various clubs across the country. In 1964, Patty was booked into a club called the Roadhouse in West Sacramento and decided to call California home. In between shows at the Roadhouse, she performed at a variety of clubs across the country including the Driftwood in Sacramento, but always returned to the Roadhouse. Known for twirling tassels, Patty retired from burlesque in 1975. Patty O'Farrell died on December 12, 2018.

Avocado Boats

4 Avocadoes (halved length wise)
4 Fresh tomatoes (peeled)
2 Medium onions (diced)
2 Tablespoons oil
1 Clove of garlic
½ teaspoon thyme
8 Fresh mushrooms (chopped)
1 Can taco dip (Granny Goose 10.5 oz)
2 Cups grated cheese
1 Package tortilla chips (Granny Goose)
12 Black olives
Salt and Pepper

Scoop out the insides of the avocadoes, and save shell halves. Dice avocadoes into small pieces. Put into a large bowl and set aside. Next, sauté together in oil the diced onion, garlic, mushrooms, and seasonings; then add fresh tomatoes and blend ingredients together. Pour over diced avocadoes and mix well. Spoon the mixture into empty shell halves. Spoon 2 or 3 Tablespoons of taco dip over top, or whatever is desired. Heap cheese abundantly on top and place olive slices down the middle. Bake in hot oven for 10 to 15 minutes or broil until cheese melts. Place tortilla chips on ends to form a boat. Serve on a platter with remaining chips. (Serves 8)

Wayne's Corn Boats

1 Small can of corn
1 Can of tomato sauce (8 oz)
1½ LBs hamburger
2 Tablespoons onion (minced)
1 Egg
1 Cup instant mashed potatoes
¼ Cup water
¼ Cup Ketchup
½ Capful Kitchen Bouquet
¼ teaspoon Italian Seasoning
¼ teaspoon onion salt
Few drops of Worcestershire sauce
4 Slices American cheese
Salt and Pepper to taste
4 12X12 inch strips of aluminum foil

Mix corn and ½ can of the tomato sauce together. Heat in a sauce pan and add salt. Mix hamburger, egg, potatoes, and seasonings together. Form into 4 equal balls. Divide each ball, making one a little larger than the other. Take the larger part and form a boat by making a well in the center. Scoop corn mixture into boat, then place a slice of cheese folded in half on top of corn mixture. Place the rest of the hamburger on top to seal together. Wrap aluminum foil around ball. Bake in 400 degree oven for 45 minutes.

Patty's, then 10-year old son, Wayne, created the Corn Boat recipe. These two recipes were published in *The Sacramento Union* in November 1977.

La Savona

La Savona originally came to the United States from Czechoslovakia, which is now the Czech Republic. She was an attraction in many European cities where dancing was recognized as a sensuous, ancient art form. Her burlesque career began in New York City where she worked as a special attraction on the same bill with Blaze Starr. When Blaze left, La Savona became the star of the show. She toured in theatres and clubs throughout the United States, Canada, and Europe. She is perhaps best known for her "Scheherazade Oriental" number. La Savona died on December 6, 2017.

La Savona. Courtesy: C.F. Miller

Blaze Starr. Courtesy: C.F. Miller

Plum Dumplings – from cousin Jana Kopecka

Ingredients:
2 Eggs
2 Cups sifted flour
2 Cups boiled potatoes – riced
1 Cup fine bread crumbs
12-15 Plums, washed
¼ Cup cinnamon sugar
Butter and salt (light)

Cream 2 Tablespoons of butter, then beat in the eggs and salt. Gradually beat in the flour and riced potatoes. The dough should be stiff enough to knead thoroughly. On a floured board roll out the dough to ¼ inch thickness; then cut into 3 inch squares. Lay one plum on each square, sprinkle with a little cinnamon sugar and fold edges over the plum. Shape with hands into a ball. The wall of dough should be very thin. Drop the dumplings into boiling salted water; cover and simmer for about 15 minutes. Brown bread crumbs in 1-1/3 cup of hot butter. Roll the dumplings in buttered bread crumbs, and sprinkle with cinnamon sugar. Recipe makes about 5 servings. (These can also be made with other fruits like strawberries. Note to self: pit the plums.)

Stuffed Peppers (Texas Hash)

This recipe, (originally from Elva Brown, sister-in-law of La Savona) will feed five or six people. For two or three servings, cut the recipe in half – or be prepared to deal with yummy leftovers.

10X10 Casserole dish

11" Skillet at least 2½" deep – bigger would be better for the full recipe.

Ingredients:
- 9 or 10 Large peppers (mango or sweet)
- 2 LBs ground beef
- 1½ Cups yellow onion – finely chopped
- 1 Cup peppers – finely chopped
- 1 Cup uncooked rice (Minute Rice)
- 2 Cans (15 oz) tomato puree
- ¾ Cup water (approximately)
- 1 Tablespoon Worcestershire sauce
- 1¾ teaspoon salt
- Dash of Black Pepper
- 2 Tablespoons of Crisco

Prepare peppers by cutting out the stems, and then chopping off the tops and removing the seeds. Chop the tops up fine and use as part of the 1 cup of chopped pepper. Usually it will take only one additional pepper to make the proper amount, leaving 8 or 9 to stuff.

Add the two Tablespoons of Crisco to skillet, heat and stir in onions and pepper. Cook until the onions are tender and slightly yellow. Add the ground beef and cook until browned.

Drain off the excess fat. Add the puree, sauce, salt, and water; then stir in the rice. Simmer and stir for 2 to 3 minutes. The amount of water needed depends on how much juice you get from the meat and vegetables. You need enough to soften the rice, yet not making the stuffing soupy. Normally, 1 cup of rice would require 1 cup of water.

Grease the casserole dish and place the peppers in an upright position. Fill the peppers with the ground beef mixture. Put any excess mix around the peppers.

Cover the dish and place in a preheated 350 degree oven for about 40 minutes, or until the peppers are soft.

Cooking time can be cut in half by par boiling the peppers for 5 minutes before stuffing. If the stuffing appears to get a bit dry you can add a bit more water; if too "soupy" take the lid off the last few minutes. This can also be served as a hash without the stuffed peppers. In this case you can add an extra half-cup or so of chopped pepper. Some chopped tomatoes can be added if desired.

Ann Pett

Ann Pett. Courtesy: Burlesque Historical Society

When Ann was a young woman she left the Midwest and joined the Mardell Dancers as an actress/chorus girl in a mini-musical performing in forty theatres throughout the south. Upon reaching New York, by day she worked for Fortune Pope, who owned radio station WHOM; at night, she rehearsed dance routines for gangster Mickey Cohen. The shows she danced in were performed in a chain of burlesque theatres throughout the East Coast. They included beautiful girls, costumes, a live orchestra, and famous comics. In the late 1950s after touring the circuit, Ann returned to New York City for additional training in voice, dance, and acting. She soon found herself performing in a road show that toured the United States which featured her as, "Ann Pett, The Cosmopolitan Girl." Ann also worked for Harold Minsky, choreographer and theatrical agent Dick Richards, Sol Richman Productions, and she had a long run in Ann Corio's show, *This Was Burlesque*. I believe Ann Pett died in New York City from Covid-19 in early 2020.

Ann sent a magazine recipe for Salade Nicoise but I decided not to include it – almost all of the ingredients were French. However, I am including the following about her dear friend Penny Powers, who also worked for Harold Minsky. Ann wrote, "A prize winning Maryland Guernsey cow first put Penny Powers into the limelight at age 13. She then went on to Philadelphia to appear on a Paul Whiteman television show, where she received her 1st dance award. The limelight kept shining on Penny when she appeared on the Merv Griffin *One in a Million* television show."

Honey Standish

Honey Standish was born in Kansas and raised in Texas; she was a proud eleventh descendent of Captain Myles Standish, who escorted the Pilgrims to America in 1620. In 1944, Honey started her career as a performer in circuses and carnivals. She quickly turned to working on the burlesque stage as a chorus line dancer, where she solely performed from 1945 to 1949 at the Rialto Theatre in Chicago. She wrote, "I was the one who led the chorus line on and offstage." But her real love was art. Since 1954, she resided in the Detroit area; in 1959, she created the La Belle Miel Art School, a private school for children and adults. Honey demonstrated and taught students in all media including painting, charcoal, ceramics, and free-form sculpture. Honey, won many awards in a variety of Michigan art shows; shows were also held every summer in Honey's own backyard garden. In addition to her numerous one-woman shows, Honey was invited to hang her artwork at a number of prestigious shows and galleries, including the Macomb Art Society, Michigan Art Education Association, National Art Education Association, Lakeside Palette Club, Women's Caucus for Art, Detroit Institute of Art, Toledo Art Museum, and the Chicago Art Institute. Honey died quite suddenly at home in 2014. (All the material I had for this section was destroyed in the 2018 fire.)

In 1989 Honey wrote, "I've cooked and would make up recipes whenever I got bored with everyday cooking and life, so when I made up a new dish I hoped it wouldn't kill us all. I cook like I paint. I put things together and make them work, or at least hope they will."

Honey's Peanut Butter – Team Flakes Cookies

December 1965

2 Cups of Team Flakes (discontinued; substitute)
¼ Cup butter – soft
1 Egg
1½ Cups of brown sugar
½ Cup of granulated sugar
1¼ Cups of flour
½ teaspoon baking powder
¾ teaspoon baking soda
½ teaspoon salt
¾ Cup peanut butter
¼ Cup buttermilk

Mix together the dry ingredients and peanut butter. Then add the buttermilk and the Team Flakes last. Blend together, then drop from spoon. Bake at 350 degrees for 10 minutes.

Tuna Casserole

July 1974

1 Can of tuna fish
1 Egg
Add to 2 cups of cooked rice
½ Cup chopped celery
1½ Cups chopped zucchini (small ones)
1 Onion cut up (minced)

Sauté celery, zucchini, and onion together in butter; then add these ingredients to the rice, tuna, and egg mix. Bake in deep dish at 325 degrees for one hour. Salt and pepper to taste; serves 4.

Swedish Meatballs

1964

1 LB ground round
½ Cup dry bread crumbs
1 Egg
2/3 Cup of sweet milk (fresh milk)
2 Tablespoons chopped onion
1 teaspoon salt
1/8 teaspoon pepper
1/8 teaspoon nutmeg
Roll into ½" diameter Balls
Brown in fat or oil

Add ¼ cup hot water; simmer 20 minutes in the gravy made by meatballs. Add a beef bouillon cube to hot water, and add to the pan of meatballs if you want to make more gravy.

Creole Soup

December 1966

2 Cups brown stock
½ Can of chopped tomatoes
2 Tablespoons flour
2 Tablespoons butter
1 Tablespoon horseradish
1 Chopped onion – small

1/8 Chopped green pepper (more if you like)
¼ teaspoon salt and pepper
Pinch of cayenne
1 Cup of macaroni (Cook and drain)

Sauté peppers and onions in butter for 4 minutes; add stock, salt, pepper, cayenne, and strain. Add cooked macaroni, tomatoes, and horseradish.

Spanish Rice

1962

1 or 2 Cups of rice
1 Onion – minced

1 Green pepper – minced
¼ Cup celery – diced fine

Cook in butter or oil for 15 minutes.
Add:

2 Cups of tomatoes
2 teaspoons of salt
1/8 teaspoon of pepper (more to taste)
Pinch of oregano or teaspoon of soy sauce

2 Dashes of hot sauce (Tablespoon)
2 teaspoons of Worcestershire sauce
½ teaspoon of marjoram
½ teaspoon of thyme

Combine in pot and cook for 30 minutes until simmering. Then add rice and continue to cook until it becomes as thick as you like.

All in One Meatballs

February 1965

1 LB ground round
1 Egg – beaten
¼ teaspoon thyme
1 Medium onion – minced
2 Stalks celery – chopped

3 Tablespoons Ralston Wheat
1 Jigger of red wine
Salt and Pepper to taste
1 teaspoon seasoning salt
¼ Cup flour

Mix together and roll the meatballs in flour; cook in hot oil until browned. Add a can of cream of vegetable or cream of mushroom soup, and ¼ cup of water. Chop and add 2 small (boiled) potatoes. Cook for 20 minutes.

Hidden Treasures Cookies

½ Cup butter
½ Cup sugar
½ Cup brown sugar
1 teaspoon vanilla
1 Egg
1 Cup flour
1 teaspoon baking powder
1 teaspoon salt
1 Cup small gumdrops (not black)
½ Cup flaked coconut
1 Cup Instant Ralston

Beat butter, sugars, vanilla, and egg until smooth; then add flour, baking powder, and salt. Blend and mix in gumdrops, coconut, and cereal. Drop on cookie sheet with teaspoon. Bake at 375 degrees for 12 minutes. (Makes 6 dozen)

Peanut Blossoms

Sift Together:
1¾ Cups flour
1 teaspoon baking soda
½ teaspoon salt
Cream Together:

½ Cup shortening
½ Cup peanut butter
½ Cup sugar
½ Cup firmly packed brown sugar

CREAM WELL
Add:
1 Unbeaten egg
2 Tablespoons milk
1 teaspoon vanilla

Blend, shape, and roll in sugar. Bake for 8 minutes in 375 degree oven. Take out and add Red Hots, chocolate chips, or gumdrops. Put back in oven and bake for another 2 to 5 minutes. Recipe makes 3 dozen cookies.

Honey's Stuffed Cabbage

June 1965

7 Large cabbage leaves
1 LB hamburger
1 Cup cooked rice
2 Tablespoons chopped pepper – red or green
¼ Cup chopped onions
½ Cup catsup
1 teaspoon thyme leaves
1 teaspoon dried parsley or ¼ cup fresh
½ teaspoon salt and pepper – to taste
½ teaspoon of seasoning salt

4 Tablespoons of flour – mix in with rice, onions, peppers, and other ingredients. If the flour is mixed in while the rice is hot, the ingredients will blend better. Let stand.

Wilt cabbage leaves. Roll ingredients into leaves and put in greased baking pan. Cook for 45 minutes at 350 degrees.

Honey's Catsup
September 1956

½ Gallon of tomato juice
3 Onions – chopped
1½ Green pepper – chopped
1 Tablespoon sea salt
¼ Cup vinegar
2 Tablespoons hot sauce
2 Tablespoons Worcestershire sauce
2 Tablespoons of Heinz 57 Sauce
1 teaspoon celery seed
1 Tablespoon onion juice
1 Tablespoon cayenne pepper
1 teaspoon chili powder
1 teaspoon allspice
1 Tablespoon cloves
1 Tablespoon garlic salt or 4 cloves – chopped
¼ Cup brown sugar
½ Cup sugar
2 Tablespoons black pepper corns

Combine in 6 quart pan or cooker. Add the tomato juice. Cook for 1 hour, then strain. Put back in pan and cook 20 minutes more. Then put in jars and seal. You can use the strained onions, peppers, and spices with meat, as a sauce.

Chili
1956

4 LBs ground beef
6 Onions
6 Tomatoes
1 Can tomatoes
2 Tablespoons Worcestershire sauce
2 Tablespoons Heinz 57 Sauce
5 Tablespoons chili powder
1½ Tablespoons cayenne pepper
2 Tablespoons brown sugar
¼ Cup sugar
¾ Cup vinegar
1 Tablespoon celery seed
2 Tablespoons salt
2 Tablespoons pepper
5 Cups of water

Brown the meat, and add the onions, spices, and brown sugar. After the meat is browned, put in a large pot, and add the water. When mixture is hot, add the tomatoes. Put in the oven and bake for 90 minutes, or longer. The longer it cooks, the better the flavor. (Today we can use a crock pot.)

Honey's Oat Bran Pancakes
July 1989

For one or two people
½ Cup oat bran
¼ Cup flour
1 Egg
1 Tablespoon baking powder
¼ Cup milk
1 Tablespoon brown sugar
½ teaspoon salt
1 Tablespoon virgin olive oil or corn oil

Beat up well to a medium thin batter. Batter will make six 5" pancakes, or more if smaller.

Salsa Chicken and Rice

September 2001

1½ Cups cooked rice

Place the chicken on top of the rice (you can also use duck breast) in a lidded casserole dish. Add salt, pepper, ½ teaspoon garlic or 2 chopped cloves, rosemary, and basil on top of the chicken or duck. Pour salsa, one bottle or homemade, over everything. Put in a 350 degree heated oven and cook for 90 minutes. Take the lid off, and add cheddar cheese on top of salsa, (optional), and cook for another 30 minutes.

Homemade Salsa

2 Mangoes cut/cubed
½ Papaya – medium, cut/cubed
1 Red onion cut/cubed
1 Green pepper cut/cubed

Salt, pepper, garlic, chopped basil, and 1 lemon – juiced. Mix together and refrigerate overnight.

Honey's Salsa

6 Meaty tomatoes – chopped fine
2 Yellow peppers – chopped fine
2 Large red peppers – chopped fine
2 Medium onions – chopped fine
Then in a large bowl add:
1 Tablespoon sugar
2 Tablespoons honey
3 Tablespoons mustard seeds (Dijon)
½ Cup blended onion juice
½ Cup white vinegar
¼ Cup pickle juice – dill

Mix everything together well and let sit overnight to blend. Put in jars or bags; will keep two weeks – but it also freezes well. Eat with meat like burgers, brats, or hot dogs.

Macaroni Salad

Let macaroni sit in a bowl of hot water for an hour, or until soft. Then add:

1 Onion – chopped
1 Green pepper – chopped
1 Orange pepper – chopped
1 Tablespoon yellow mustard seed (Dijon)
½ Cup ranch dressing
1 teaspoon sugar
¼ Tablespoon dill pickle juice
Salt and pepper to taste

Mix everything together well and chill. Serve with tomatoes.

Eggplant and Apple Bread

October 1968

½ Eggplant or 1½ cups cubed
1 Apple cubed
1 Bouillon cube
¼ Cup butter
Salt and pepper to taste
Dash of sweet basil (optional)

1 Long loaf of Italian or French bread – hollowed out. Set aside the bread that has been removed from the loaf.

Add bouillon cube to ¼ cup water. Cook until cube has been absorbed into the water. Then pour over the bread from the inside of the loaf, and add the eggplant and apple mix. Mix together well, and place in the hollowed out bread shell. Wrap in tin foil and bake at 350 degrees for 35 minutes. (Experiment and add some cheddar cheese to the top of the mixture in the bread shell.)

Fried Chicken Golden Surprise

1968

1 Chicken – cut in pieces; flour, salt, and pepper each piece. Fry until at least half cooked – will bake for an hour in the next step of this recipe.

1 Clove garlic – or 1 teaspoon garlic salt
½ Cup alphabet macaroni
1 Can Golden Mushroom Soup

Mix together garlic, macaroni, and soup. Place chicken in baking dish, and pour the soup mixture over the chicken. Bake at 325 degrees for one hour. This dish goes well with green beans and pumpkin pie. (Serves 4)

BBQ Sauce

¼ Cup chopped onions
¼ Cup lemon juice
1 Tablespoon butter
½ Cup water
2 Tablespoons vinegar
1 Cup chili sauce
2 Tablespoons brown sugar
½ teaspoon salt
¼ teaspoon paprika
1 Tablespoon Worcestershire sauce

Simmer about 20 minutes.

Corn Bread

1 Yellow cake mix
3 Eggs
½ Cup buttermilk
1½ Cups yellow cornmeal
1 teaspoon baking soda

Preheat oven to 375 degrees. Mix all ingredients together well. If the batter is too thick, add another ¼ cup of buttermilk. Pour into a 9X2 inch pan. Bake until brown on top. Cut into squares and serve with butter and honey.

Celery Seed Dressing

Blend together:

2/3 Cup sugar	1/8 teaspoon onion juice
1½ Tablespoons celery seed	¼ Cup vinegar
1 teaspoon dry mustard	Beat together:
1 teaspoon salt	1 Cup salad oil

Gradually beat everything together until all the ingredients thicken up. Chill before serving. Strain out celery seeds after it sets for 24 hours.

Butterscotch Brownies

Cream in a bowl:

¼ Cup butter   1 Cup brown sugar

Next, beat together:

1 Egg	½ teaspoon salt
1 teaspoon vanilla	1 teaspoon baking soda
¾ Cup sifted flour	

Optional: chopped nuts and butterscotch morsels.

Preheat oven to 350 degrees. Mix all the ingredients together well, and put in a greased 9 inch pan. Bake for 30 minutes; then let sit to cool.

Hollandaise Sauce

2 Egg yolks	1 Tablespoon lemon juice
½ Cup melted butter	Pinch of cayenne
½ teaspoon salt	

Beat eggs until thick. Add salt and cayenne pepper. Next, slowly add 3 Tablespoons of butter, beating constantly. Then add the rest of the butter and lemon juice. Serve with hot asparagus, broccoli, fish, etc.

Thin White Sauce

1 Tablespoon butter	1 Cup milk
1 Tablespoon flour	Salt and pepper to taste

Melt butter and blend in flour until smooth. Add milk until boiling point is reached. For thicker sauce add more flour. Cook 3 minutes and serve with vegetables.

Drop Cookies

2 Cups firmly packed brown sugar
2/3 Cup soft butter
2 Eggs
2/3 Cup buttermilk or sweet milk
1 teaspoon vinegar
1 teaspoon vanilla
½ teaspoon cinnamon

1 Cup chopped nuts or flavored morsels – optional
3 Cups flour
1 teaspoon baking powder
½ teaspoon baking soda
1 teaspoon salt

Preheat oven to 350 degrees. Sift together flour, baking powder, baking soda, and salt; set aside. Cream sugar and butter together; then add beaten eggs, buttermilk, vanilla, and cinnamon into the bowl. Add nuts or morsels if desired, and mix everything together. If too dry, add a bit more milk. Drop by teaspoon onto greased cookie sheet, and bake for 8-12 minutes. (Makes 6-10 dozen)

Oatmeal Cookies

1 Egg
½ Cup butter
1 Cup brown sugar
1 Cup flour

½ teaspoon baking soda
1 teaspoon baking powder
1/8 teaspoon salt
2 Cups rolled oats

Preheat oven to 375 degrees. Beat egg and fold in the rest of the ingredients. Drop teaspoon size cookie dough drops onto greased cookie sheet. Bake 8-10 minutes.

Ham Glaze

1 LB dark brown sugar
¼ Cup vinegar

1 teaspoon dry mustard
¼ teaspoon ground cloves

Blend ingredients together. 20 minutes before ham has finished cooking, remove from oven. Score ham and pour mixture over the meat. Bake for an additional 20 minutes at 400 degrees. Glaze will cover a 12-15 LB ham.

Apple Sauce

October 1956

3 Dozen apples - chopped

Cook until they easily mash up, and then run them through a colander. You can also use a potato masher.

1 Cup of sugar
3 Tablespoons of cinnamon

½ teaspoon allspice
2 teaspoons salt

Mix everything together well. (Makes 8½ pints)

Sausage Patties

½ LB of ground sausage
1/3 Cup rolled oats
¼ Cup evaporated milk
1 teaspoon dried mustard

Mix ingredients together. Fry until brown on both sides, and thoroughly cooked.

Honey Angel Cake

1 Cup flour
1 Cup sugar
1½ - 2 Egg whites
½ teaspoon salt
1½ teaspoons cream of tartar
½ Cup honey
2 Drops almond extract
1 teaspoon vanilla

Warm an ungreased angel food cake pan. Sift flour and sugar four times. Beat egg whites and salt until foamy. Add cream of tartar and beat until stiff. Gradually add honey, vanilla, and almond extract. Fold in the flour, and slowly pour into cake pan. Bake 30 minutes in a 400 degree oven.

Oatmeal Banana Cookies

1 Cup whole wheat (pastry) flour
1 Cup wheat germ
½ Cup sugar
1 teaspoon salt (½ teaspoon if you prefer less salt)
½ teaspoon nutmeg
¾ teaspoon cinnamon
¼ Cup butter

Cream butter and add the flour, wheat germ, and spices.

Then add:
1 Egg
1 Cup mashed bananas
1¾ Cups oats
½ Cup nut meats – chopped fine (optional)

Blend all ingredients together well, and drop teaspoon full onto baking sheet tray. Bake for 10-15 minutes at 375 degrees, or until they are light brown. As soon as you pull them from the oven, place a ½ pecan on each cookie.

Batter Recipe for Fried Chicken

June 1956

1 Cup milk or buttermilk
1 Egg
1 Cup flour
¼ Cup cornmeal
2 teaspoons of Lea Perrins Worcestershire sauce
1 teaspoon paprika
Salt and Pepper

Place all of the ingredients in a mixing bowl and beat well until thoroughly mixed. Batter chicken and place in hot frying pan. Cook on low heat for 60 minutes or longer if frying over two pounds of chicken.

Fried Rice

2 Tablespoons butter	3 Chicken bouillon cubes dissolved in
¾ Cup uncooked white rice	2½ cups boiling water
2 Large mushrooms chopped fine	Finely chopped green pepper, carrots, and onion to taste

Heat butter in large frying pan. Add rice, mushrooms, and onions. Cook until golden brown. Stir in bouillon; cover, and cook until tender. (30 minutes) Add carrots and green peppers. Mix well and cook for a few more minutes. Serve immediately – serves 8.

Golden Cake

Heat oven to 325 degrees.
Place in sifter –

3 Cups flour	4 teaspoons baking powder
1 teaspoon salt	

Sift together
Beat 12 egg yolks together until lemon yellow in color
Slowly beat in:

2 Cups sugar	2 Tablespoons lemon juice
1 Cup boiling water	

Slowly sift in flour.
Bake in an ungreased 10 inch tube pan 50 to 60 minutes.

Cocoa Cake

Heat oven to 375 degrees
Cream well:

½ Cup of shortening	1 Cup sugar

Add:

1 Beaten egg	2 teaspoons vanilla

Mix well
Place in a sifter –

2 Cups sifted flour	1 Tablespoon baking powder
½ Cup cocoa	

Alternately combine flour and the other ingredients with 1¼ cups of milk. Bake in two greased layer cake pans for 20 to 25 minutes.

Fudge Cake

Heat oven to 375 degrees
Cream well:
1½ Cups sugar   ½ Cup shortening
Add:
2 Beaten eggs
Place in a sifter –
2¼ Cups sifted flour   1 teaspoon baking soda
1 teaspoon baking powder   ½ Cup cocoa

Alternately combine flour with 1 Cup milk (sour), 1/3 cup water, and 1 teaspoon vanilla. Bake in two 9 inch greased layer cake pans 25 to 30 minutes.

Miss White Fury

Miss White Fury was a fan favorite, who performed under the name "Miss White Fury and her Twin 44's," but also danced as "Patti Kelly." Her parents, performers Rusty and Dusty Farnham, worked in vaudeville and early radio. From 1953 to 1983 Fury performed on burlesque circuits across the country as a feature attraction. Resplendent with platinum white hair, gorgeous white costumes, and twirling large white tassels, she was in demand and an extremely popular performer.

Patti always considered the comics and straight men the real stars of the burlesque shows. She wrote, "I consider myself a lucky person to have been involved in the days of burlesque, when shows were real shows. The theatres had first and second acts, openings, closings, finales, and costumes. I made many friends I will never forget. Everyone was important, including the fabulous casts, the house people, the stage managers, theatre owners, and the orchestra players. Georgia Sothern was a wonderful, exciting feature to watch. Some of the gals in "The Golden Days of Burlesque Historical Society" were great talking women. They knew every scene and every comic. Gals like Grace Reed, Eileen Hubert, and Barbara Curtis. I never tired of watching the scenes and blackouts by such comic favorites as Irving Benson, Bert Carr, Maxie Furman, Harry Conley, and Ray Kolb.

I had such a wonderful life on the road. Mostly good and fun things happened. A great deal of time was spent creating a new act with new costumes and props. Dancers such as Taffey O'Neil were so beautiful. Every time I hear "Sophisticated Swing," I think of her. Sally Marr ("Boots Malloy"), and her son, Lenny Bruce, were a blast. All of these people and many more, made up some of the greatest shows on earth!"

Miss White Fury and her Twin 44's. Courtesy: Burlesque Historical Society

After retiring from burlesque, "Fury" became an instructor, and opened her own ballroom dance studio; over the years she also owned restaurants, a tavern, retail shops, and a talent agency. Being happy, healthy, and close with her family and friends is what mattered most to her. After my mom died in 1996 Patti invited me for a visit. I spent two weeks in Oregon and had a great time. Sadly, Miss White Fury was last known to be living in a healthcare facility in South Carolina; I suspect she has since died.

A young Miss White Fury. Courtesy: C.F. Miller

She once asked, "Why can't burlesque theatres be revived, instead of people thinking that topless, bottomless, table-dancing, pole-dancing, and lap-dancing is burlesque?"

Ham and Cheese Loaf

1 Round loaf of French bread
2 Cups shredded cheddar cheese
6 Oz softened cream cheese
1½ Cups sour cream
1 Cup diced, cooked ham (5 ounces)
½ Cup chopped green onion
1 Can diced green chilies (3 oz)
1 teaspoon Worcestershire sauce
2 Tablespoons oil
1 teaspoon butter, melted

Mix all ingredients. Hollow out loaf of bread. Cut the bread that you removed from the loaf into squares for dipping. Pour the mixture into the bread shell; then wrap in foil and bake at 350 degrees for 60 minutes.

Old Fashion Lemon Sauce

Double this!
½ Cup butter
1 Cup sugar
¼ Cup water
1 Egg, well beaten
3 Tablespoons lemon juice
Grated rind (zest) of 1 lemon
2 Tablespoons lemon juice
1 teaspoon vanilla

In a saucepan, combine butter, sugar, and water. Then add well beaten egg, 3 Tablespoons lemon juice, and lemon zest. Cook over medium heat, stirring constantly until it comes to a nice rolling boil. Remove from heat and stir in the 2 Tablespoons of lemon juice and vanilla. Serve hot over bread pudding. (Yields 1½ cups)

Old Fashion Bread Pudding

3 Cups bread crumbs
2 Cups milk, scalded, add ¼ cup butter
½ Cup sugar
2 Eggs, slightly beaten
¼ teaspoon salt
1 teaspoon cinnamon or nutmeg, or both
½ Cup seedless raisins (optional)

Heat oven to 350 degrees. Spray 1½ quart (9X13) baking dish with Pam. Place bread crumbs in dish. Add together scalding milk, (let cool slightly,) beaten eggs, sugar, spices, and salt. Mix together well, and then pour over bread crumbs. Bake 40 to 45 minutes until inserted knife comes out clean. ("Fury" recommends doubling the recipe.)

Peanut Butter Crisps

1 Cup shortening
1 Cup sugar
1 Cup brown sugar
1 Cup chunky peanut butter
2 Eggs, beaten
1 teaspoon vanilla
3 Cups flour
2 teaspoons baking soda
½ teaspoon salt

Cream together the shortening, sugars, and peanut butter. Add eggs and vanilla; then add dry ingredients and mix together well. Form into 1 inch balls. Place on oiled cookie sheet 2 inches apart. Press with back of floured or sugared fork to flatten, making crisscrosses. Bake at 375 degrees for 8 minutes or until set. (Makes five dozen)

Fresh Apple Cake

2 Cups sugar
2 teaspoons vanilla
Juice of ½ lemon
3 Cups flour
3 Cups peeled and chopped apples

1¼ Cups cooking oil
2 Well beaten eggs
1 teaspoon salt
1¼ teaspoons baking soda
1½ Cups chopped pecans

Combine sugar, oil, vanilla, eggs, lemon juice, and salt in mixing bowl. Beat well. Mix flour and soda. Add to first mixture and beat together well. Add apples and pecans. Again, mix together well. Bake in tube pan at 325 degrees for 90 minutes.

Chilies Relleno Reno

2 Cans Ortega chilies (whole or fresh)
Pepper Jack cheese, diced
¾ Cup evaporated milk
2 Tablespoons flour

4 Eggs
Grated cheddar cheese
Chili peppers

Slice Pepper Jack cheese and put 1 slice into each chili. Mix flour, eggs, and milk together. Pour over chilies, and then sprinkle with cheddar cheese. Bake at 350 degrees for 35 to 40 minutes until set. Serve with tortillas, salsa, and black olives.

Broccoli Casserole

1 Package frozen broccoli (10 oz) – chopped (or fresh)
½ Cup onion – chopped
¾ Cup celery – chopped

1 Can cream of mushroom soup
1 Cup uncooked rice (Minute Rice)
3 Tablespoons butter
1 Jar of Cheez Whiz (8 oz)

Cook broccoli and set aside. Cook rice and set aside. In a large pot, sauté butter, onions, and celery. Over a low heat, add cream of mushroom soup and Cheez Whiz. Heat only until cheese melts. Add rice and broccoli; mix everything together. Place in an ungreased baking dish. Bake at 350 degrees for 60 minutes. It's yummy, and can be a main dish. (I wonder if real cheese could be substituted for the processed cheese?)

Italian Chicken Breasts

4 to 6 Large chicken breasts (skinless)
2 Large packages spaghetti sauce mix
1 Large package onion soup mix
1 Cup white wine
Ripe olives, sliced
Mushrooms, sliced
Parmesan cheese

Line large baking dish with foil so that the chicken can be placed flat with the foil folded over the top to seal. Combine the spaghetti sauce mix and the onion soup mix in a paper bag. Shake and mix well. Drop the chicken breasts into the bag and shake to coat well. Place chicken in dish, and then pour the wine over the chicken. Top with mushrooms. Seal foil well. Bake at 350 degrees for 60 minutes. Then, open foil to brown for an additional fifteen minutes. Top with olives. Serve with the sauce from the pan and Parmesan cheese. It's great with a green salad!

Brunch Potatoes

4 Small to medium potatoes, diced into ½ inch cubes
1 Small yellow onion, chopped
1 Cup diced, cooked ham – ½ inch pieces
¼ Cup roasted red pepper, chopped (optional)
Spray oil
Salt and pepper to taste

Spray a light coating of oil on a non-stick stir fry pan or skillet. Toss in potatoes and heat over medium high flame. Cover and cook for 15 minutes, stirring every 3 to 5 minutes until potatoes are "just" done. Remove lid and add onion and ham. Cover for another 5 to 7 minutes or until onion is translucent, and everything is browning nicely. Add red pepper (if desired) and a few dashes of salt and pepper. Remove from heat and serve. (Makes 4 servings)

Patti's Salsa to Nick with Love

4 Medium tomatoes, chopped
½ Cup finely chopped onion
½ Cup finely chopped celery
½ Cup finely chopped green bell pepper
¼ Cup olive oil
1 Tablespoon finely chopped jalapeno pepper
2 Tablespoons finely chopped green chili pepper
2 Tablespoons red wine vinegar
1 teaspoon mustard seed
1 teaspoon salt
Dash of pepper

Combine all ingredients and mix together well. Cover and refrigerate for several hours or overnight. (Makes about 3 cups)

Toffee

1 LB butter
2 Cups sugar
6 Tablespoons water
6 Tablespoons light Karo

2 Cups chocolate chips
2 Cups chopped nuts (pecans, almonds, and / or peanuts)

Melt butter, and then add the rest of the ingredients. Cook over low heat until caramel color. Stir constantly. Pour onto buttered foil lined pan. Spread with chocolate chips. Press nuts into chips when cool, and then break into pieces.

Madam Lazonga Killer Kahlua

4 Cups water
5 Cups sugar
Mix together in a large saucepan and bring to a boil.

Then add:
½ Cup instant coffee (not decaf)
5 Cups water

Mix everything together well and bring to a boil. Take off the heat and let cool for 60 minutes. Then mix in one fifth of pure grain alcohol and 2 ounces of vanilla. It is now ready to drink, or bottle up.

Christmas Champagne

1 Package strawberry Kool-Aid
1 Can (8 oz) orange juice, mixed with 1½ cans of water
1 Can (8 oz) lemonade juice, mixed with 1½ cans of water
1 Can (4 oz) pineapple grapefruit juice
1 Bottle (28 oz) ginger ale

Prepare Kool-Aid according to package. Combine all juices and chill for 4 hours. Add ginger ale right before serving.

Frankie Ray Perilli

Frankie Ray began his career as a nightclub comic. For several years, he co-starred with pal Shecky Greene at the Wits End Club in New Orleans. When Greene signed a contract to work on *The Colgate Comedy Hour* television show, Frankie also came to Hollywood to work as a writer for the program. In addition to creating material for Greene, he also wrote for Dean Martin and Don Rickles. His other projects included writing movie scripts, producing, and working as an emcee in burlesque. He was very proud to have written the European cult film, *The Doberman Gang*, with business partner Lou Garfinkle. Frankie and Lenny Bruce were also close friends, and it's only because of Frankie I got to meet

Lenny's mom Sally Marr, also known as "Boots Malloy." Frankie Ray Perilli died on March 8, 2018.

I think you'll enjoy the following story Frankie sent with his recipe. It has a simple title, and the words are his.

Lenny Bruce

Lenny loved my mother Mary's pasta and through the years he'd come over to my parents' house on Sundays. Around the late 1940s, we came from Chicago to live in a house on a street called Riverdale near Boyle Heights in Los Angeles. Our table was never fancy but the food was always good. Lenny got to like my mother's Penne Arrabbiata. It was a little ways from Hollywood and Lenny hated restaurants… the hassling with waitresses, a limited menu, etc. He liked a good cafeteria once in awhile. He was like this before he became famous and even more so later. It got to be where he would say, "Let's go see your mother and father, and eat." My father, Marco, liked Lenny a lot. Later I moved the family to a street in West Hollywood on Poinsettia Drive. Lenny and I drifted apart, but once in awhile he'd call. I hadn't heard from Lenny for about a year at one point. My father would say, "Ma, where's dat guy?" I kept tabs on him though through his wonderful mother, Sally Marr.

Then on the morning of August 6th, 1966, I got this call, "Frank, it's me, Lenny." Good thing he announced himself. He sounded hoarse and sick, and said, "I've been thinking about Mary's Arrabbiata sauce. You think she would make some penne for me?" I said, "Sure, you come over tonight." He yelled, "No schumuck! I want it now!" I said, "I'll see you in an hour." Lenny said, "Love ya!" and hung up. My poor mother never cooked pasta that early in the day. I said, "Ma, just leave it in the pot." I drove up the hill with the pot of penne alongside me. Lenny is waiting in the driveway. He runs to the car and pulls the pot out of my hand, tosses the lid off and puts his head in the pot like a horse would do to a bag of oats. When he was through, he handed me the pot. It was spotless. He ate at least a half pound of penne, but wouldn't touch the bread. Then he said, "I gotta go back to work. I'll call you tonight. I didn't forget about our plans to make movies." Then he gave me a hug and said, "I really love you, Frank."

I'm standing in the driveway, holding the pot, as I watch him walk into the house. He turned, and I started to laugh. He had red gravy all around his mouth. It made me think back to my childhood on the West Side of Chicago. The whole neighborhood ate pasta on Sundays. After we ate, we'd run out onto the streets to play, and we all had gravy around our mouths. Lenny yelled, "What are you laughing about?" I waived for him, "Go and type, I'll tell you later." He smiled while he rolled his stomach, an indication that the pasta had hit the spot. After I had gotten into my car, he yelled, "Wait!" He ran toward me, stopped and pulled some half dead roses from his garden. He handed them to me and said, "Give these

Frankie Ray Perilli. Courtesy: Frankie Ray Perilli

to Mary. Tell her, keep these roses alive. Love you." He turned and ran back to the house. When I got home, my mother looked into the pot. She says, "Ooh, what a nice boy Lenny is. He washed the pot." I said, "Wash it, again, Ma." I didn't want to tell her he licked the pot clean. I then took a nap.

When I got up, I drank some wine and took a bath. It was hot that day. Later I got a call from a very close pal, Joey Di Amore. He told me Lenny had been found dead in his bathroom. I said, "Maybe he choked on Mary's penne, he ate it so fast." Joey said, "No, Lenny overdosed." I got in my car and ran back up the hill again, and was tempted to look in the bathroom where Lenny was lying on the floor. I said, "Screw it." I wanted to remember the last time I saw him; happy and content with that look of the gravy around his mouth.

This is my mother Mary's recipe. She said she learned it from a Neapolitan neighbor back in Chicago. Mary was Calabrese, but in one tenement building you would find Italians from Rome, Bari, Naples, Sicily, and even Northern Italy. So the women would borrow recipes from each other.

*Frankie Ray Perilli.
Courtesy: Frankie Ray Perilli*

*A more dapper Frankie Ray Perilli.
Courtesy: Frankie Ray Perilli*

(Frankie also noted that Al Capone used to put garlic on his bullets so that his victims would suffer.)

Penne Arrabbiata

¼ Cup extra virgin olive oil
2-3 teaspoons of red chili pepper flakes
1 Can imported Italian tomatoes (28 oz)
3 Garlic cloves, peeled
Salt
1 LB imported penne
Handful chopped Italian parsley

Heat the extra virgin olive oil in a skillet over moderate heat. Add the chili pepper flakes. As soon as the flakes begin to add some color to the oil, lift out the tomatoes from the can and crush them with your fingers as you add them to the skillet. An alternative is to set a food mill over the skillet and puree the tomatoes directly the skillet. Stir the pureed tomatoes, mixing well with the oil and chili pepper flakes. Squeeze the garlic cloves through a press directly

Lenny Bruce, 1960s. Courtesy: Frankie Ray Perilli

into the sauce. Add salt to taste. Cook the sauce over moderately high heat until the tomatoes begin to break down and the sauce thickens, approximately 15 minutes. Meanwhile, cook the penne in abundant boiling salted water until al dente. Quickly drain and place in a serving bowl along with the tomato sauce. Add chopped parsley and mix the pasta well with the sauce.

Sally Marr attending the Lenny Bruce Posthumous 68th Birthday Benefit for the "Comic Book Legal Defense Fund" in October 1993. Courtesy: Frankie Ray Perilli

It was such a treat for me to meet Sally Marr in 1995, and sadly, even be invited to her funeral in 1997. Frankie also sent the following story to include in this book. He wrote:

"It was my idea, to have Sam Kinison dedicate a Star on Hollywood Boulevard for Lenny (Bruce). I wrote to Sam, thinking he would help, because he was the only one I could think of that would have made Lenny laugh. I never got an answer. When I discussed it with Sally she said, "Listen, schumuck, Sam doesn't read letters! You bring that script to Ciro's Pomodoro Restaurant. I'll tell Sam to meet us there after his show, and then you can pitch your idea to him." Sally was about 88 years old at the time, and if she could take those late hours, I could too; so I agreed to go.

But let me digress. Let's go back to a strip joint called "The Near and Far." The club was owned by Mickey Cohen, and Sally and I were the emcees. Sally would work until the first intermission, then so as not to lose the crowd, I would go on with no band. Of course once the girls weren't on that stage, a lot of people did leave. Girls would often sit with the customers and order drinks. In most towns, it was called "B-Drinking," and the girls would get a cut on every drink, but that was illegal in Los Angeles, and West Hollywood, where "The Near and Far" was located. The girls were not forced to drink, but if they felt like it they would help out the club. Now when Sally sat at a table out front, she would talk about me while I was struggling with my act onstage. She would say, "Look how good this kid is! He is a real trooper. You wouldn't guess they're going to repossess his car tomorrow!" Now the guy sitting with Sally, wanting to impress the other girls at the table, would usually answer, "How much does he owe?" Sally would say, "Two lousy payments." The man would say, "How much is the payment," to which she replied, "$125." The man wrote out a check for $375, and said, "Say, here's three payments worth." Then Sally would say, "Let him do an impression especially for you. Who is your favorite movie star?" After responding, Sally would holler up saying, "Frank, this guy is a fan. Do Lewis Stone." I learned to do a lot of different impressions very quickly."

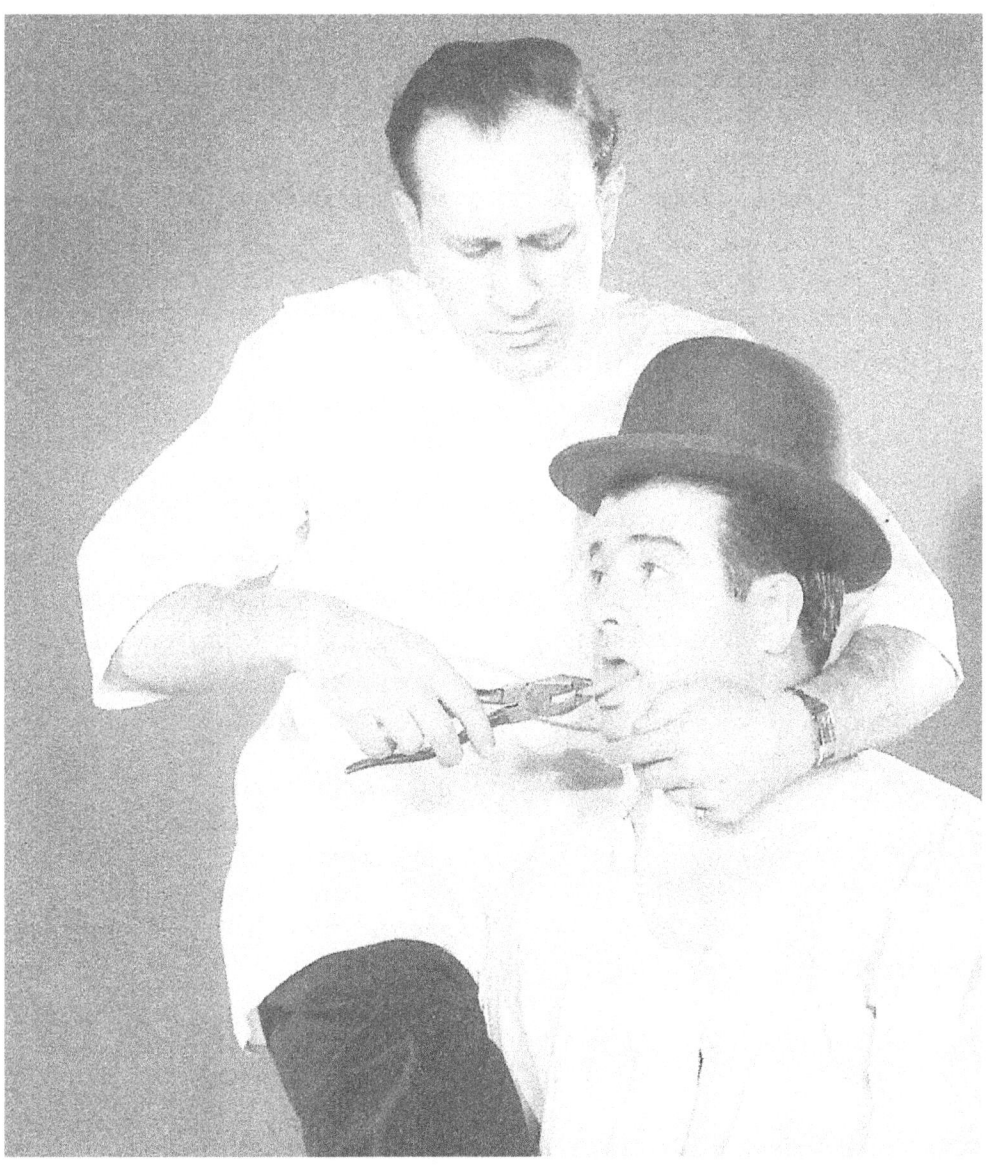

Bud Abbott and Lou Costello. Courtesy: CBS Photo Archives

(Notes: Lenny Bruce has yet to get a Star on the Hollywood Walk of Fame, even though he opened doors for today's comics.)

Frankie also contributed the following tid-bits:

"I think the funniest Abbott and Costello gag wasn't in any of their movies, but in a Mel Brooks film. A parade of English soldiers march in; then a slew of Abbott's march in as a voice comes from the crowd shouting, out of left field, sounding like Lou Costello, "A-B-B-O-T-T!"

Here's how you can make a great strawberry milk shake a la Costello; a milk shake is a cool beverage made of milk and flavoring that is mixed, beaten, or shaken until frothy. It is usually named after the predominant flavor used, in this case strawberries. Ice cream is frequently used in making milk shakes, both for flavor and richness. In most cases, the ice cream is so well mixed with the rest of the ingredients, that a spoon is not required to consume the beverage.

In soda fountain parlors, a milk shake that contains dissolved ice cream is known as a "frosted," while one that has un-dissolved ice cream, in the manner of an ice cream soda, is called a "float." Malted milk powder is sometimes used in making milk shakes, giving the beverage a definite richness. Such drinks are known as "malted milk," "malteds," or "malts," rather than milk shakes. Again, the name of the chief flavoring prefixed to the title, strawberries.

Using a blender, add all ingredients and remember that the ideal milk shake is a compromise between froth and liquid, and that it must be cool, if not actually cold. The ingredients should be chilled before use and the person making the shake should work quickly, to keep the ingredients from getting too warm in the process. Milk shakes are served immediately after being made, before the froth has had a chance to subside. They may be served with or without straws, depending on individual taste, but a spoon should be required only in the case of an ice cream float."

Val Valentine

Val writes, "I have no recipes for you; I never was big in the kitchen." She can say that, yet Val Valentine made dinner for me and a couple gal pals for my birthday in 2007. Seems to me we went home with a full belly and some good memories!

Val Valentine. Courtesy: C.F. Miller

Miss Orchid Mei

Miss Orchid Mei is a present-day neo-burlesque dancer. I asked Mei if she would like to contribute a recipe for the book. She has always been very supportive of the BHS and her story was included in *BURLESQUE: A Living History*. She says her grandmother's peanut butter cookies are amazing.

Miss Orchid Mei. Courtesy: Miss Orchid Mei

Miss Orchid Mei. Courtesy: Miss Orchid Mei

Grandma's Peanut Butter Cookies

¾ Cup butter
½ Cup peanut butter
¾ Cup brown sugar
3 Eggs
¼ Cup milk
1 Cup chopped nuts (optional)

1 teaspoon vanilla
1½ Cups flour
1 teaspoon baking soda
1¼ teaspoons salt
1 Cup regular quick cooking oatmeal

Cream together the butter, peanut butter, and sugar until light and fluffy. Add eggs one at a time; beating after each. Blend in the milk and vanilla. Then combine the flour, baking soda, and salt; stir until thoroughly blended. Stir in the dry ingredients, the oatmeal and nuts. Add 1 cup of chocolate chips for extra goodness. Drop by teaspoons onto a greased cookie sheet. Bake at 350 degrees for 10-12 minutes. It yields about 4½ dozen cookies depending on size.

Taffey O'Neil

From 1953 to 1972, Taffey O'Neil performed as a headliner on burlesque stages throughout the United States. After her first year of dancing, Taffey actually preferred working supper clubs to theatres and nightclubs. When asked why, she said, "It was always couples who came to supper clubs to see the shows together. Supper clubs presented more of a family atmosphere, and the shows presented a variety of entertainment."

Preferring to dance on the West Coast to be near her family, Taffey did spend 1963 on the road. However, she only appeared on the East Coast and Midwest burlesque circuits four times during her career. When asked about her billing, she stated, "I never used anything but my name." Lili St. Cyr's name was mentioned when asked if there were any dancers she admired, but Taffey went on to say that she "never idolized any one particular dancer."

The late Irving Benson once said about Taffey, "What a lovely lady! She is one of my all-time favorite people I have ever met in show business. A real lady! No matter how many years pass, I'd know her anywhere. She will always have that same sweet face."

Taffey O'Neil. Courtesy: Al Baker Jr.

Taffey O'Neil has been a part of "The Golden Days of Burlesque Historical Society" since the group was formed in 1995. She and her late husband Howard attended nearly every gathering, and I consider them "family."

Advertisement for the triumphant return of Taffey O'Neil at the Tiffany Club in Los Angeles. Courtesy: Taffey O'Neil

Best Damn Carrot Cake

2 Cups sifted flour	1 1/2 teaspoons baking soda
1 teaspoon salt	2 Cups sugar
2 teaspoons cinnamon	

Combine all dry ingredients; sift into mixing bowl.

1 1/2 Cups of canola or vegetable oil	8 Oz can of crushed Dole pineapple
4 Eggs	1 1/2 Grated carrots
2 teaspoons of vanilla	1 Cup chopped walnuts

Add eggs into dry mixture one at a time and mix with whisk; combine all the other ingredients and mix with wooden spoon.

Pour mixture into greased and floured 9X13 baking pan. Preheat oven to 350 and bake 45 to 50 min.

Frosting

8 Oz of cream cheese	1/2 teaspoon vanilla extract
1/2 Cup of softened butter	3/4 of a 1 LB box of powdered sugar

Use electric hand mixer to mix ingredients. Wait for cake to cool to room temperature before applying frosting. After the cake is frosted top with chopped walnuts; chill in refrigerator.

The following I wanted to include because they are <u>good</u>:

Apple Crisp from Sandi Neumeier

Ingredients:

10 Medium apples - 3 Red Delicious, 3 Yellow Delicious, 2 Macintosh, 2 Granny Smiths, or just a variety of different apples. (Gala, Brae Burn are good choices for firmer, less juicy apples; and Cortland's in place of Macintosh are okay too.) Do not use too many Macintosh, they are too juicy.

1/2 Cup white sugar
1 teaspoon cornstarch
1/8 teaspoon nutmeg

2 teaspoons cinnamon (use a coarser brand)

Core and slice apples, just not too small; blend mixture together and coat the apples. Pour into a lightly buttered 9X13 cake pan.

Topping:

1 Cup of Old Fashion rolled oats
1 Cup of brown sugar (packed tightly)
1/2 Cup of flour

1/2 teaspoon cinnamon
1/2 Cup butter (melted)

Sprinkle evenly on top. Bake at 350 degrees for 35 to 45 minutes or until golden brown. If apple crisp is too juicy after baking, drain to one corner and scoop out excess juice. Sometimes apples are too juicy for baking.

Sandi Neumeier is a former co-worker, who made this for me to be served at the BHS Reunion held in Wisconsin in 2009. It is delicious and everyone who attended the gathering enjoyed it a lot. Sandi says it's best served warm with ice cream, but it's yummy no matter how it's served!

Kringla from Karen Erickson

Ingredients:

1½ Cups white sugar   1/2 Cup shortening

Mix these together and then add 1 egg slightly beaten

Sift together:

1 teaspoon baking soda
3½ Cups flour
1 teaspoon baking powder

1/2 teaspoon salt
1 Cup buttermilk (or cream)

Add the buttermilk alternately with the flour mixture. Add 1 teaspoon vanilla and 1/2 teaspoon cardamom and mix in. Cover with Saran Wrap and keep in refrigerator overnight. Roll in pencil shape and form into knot. Bake at 400 degrees for 10 to 12 min. They should be just slightly browned at edges.

From left to right; Marg Connell, Nocturne, La Savona, Anne Pett, Orchid Mei, and Bambi Brooks at the 2009 BHS gathering in Baraboo, Wisconsin. Four of these women contributed to this section; Nocturne is the daughter of "Laughing" Lou La Mar.
Courtesy: Authors Collection.

This is another fan-favorite from the Midwest and something many of us grew up eating. Karen graduated from high school with my brother, and tolerated me as a kid. I was always bugging her at the community swimming pool where she worked as a lifeguard.

Grandma Long's Banana Nut Bread from Debbie Long Hatz

Ingredients:
1 Cup white sugar
¼ Cup butter
2 Beaten eggs
3 Tablespoons sour milk*
2 Cups flour
½ teaspoon salt
1 teaspoon baking soda
1 teaspoon baking powder
3 Medium bananas
½ Cup nuts (optional)

Mix ingredients in order given in a large bowl. Begin by mixing sugar, butter, eggs, and milk together. (Debbie notes, to create sour milk, add a little vinegar to the milk you have, or just use the milk you have on hand – it does not alter the recipe.) Then sift in flour, salt, baking soda and powder. Stir until mixed thoroughly. Mash bananas and stir into dough. You can also add 1 cup of another fruit, such as: blueberries, diced peaches, pineapple; or chocolate chips. (What about butterscotch or peanut butter chips?) Pour into greased and floured pans – fill half + full. This recipe equals 3 – 4 small loaves, or 1 – 2 large loaves. Bake about 1 hour in 350 degree oven.

Who can't resist homemade banana bread? This recipe comes from another classmate of my brother's, and it is so good.

The final recipe is mine!

Chili – As simple as it gets

Brown 1 pound of Hamburger; throw it in a crock pot. Sauté' an onion – or leave it raw; add it to the crock pot. Add 1 can of black beans, 1 can of Bush's Grilling Beans, 1 can of Hunt's diced tomatoes, and 1 can of Hunt's tomato sauce – don't drain any of them. Don't forget the McCormick's Chili Seasoning mix. Add two or three heaping Tablespoons of brown sugar, and extra garlic – if you like. Turn on the crock pot and walk away. That's it in a crock pot, but it tastes so good, especially on a cold winter day!

A Peek into Harold Minsky's Files

In June of 2000 "The Golden Days of Burlesque Historical Society" held a gathering at the "Gold Coast Hotel and Casino" in Las Vegas, Nevada. Several of these gatherings have been held over the years in California, Las Vegas, and even Baraboo, Wisconsin – home of the "Circus World Museum." But at this particular get-together Barbara Curtis and Lorraine Lee Richards, two of the best talking women in the business, introduced me to Pat Elliott Minsky, aka Trish Shapiro.

Postcard of the Gold Coast Hotel and Casino in Las Vegas, Nevada. Courtesy: Authors Collection

After studying dance in New York City, Pat Elliott performed in theatres, clubs, and Las Vegas production shows from 1963 to 1967. In the summer of 1967 Pat married burlesque producer Harold Minsky. After their marriage, Pat worked behind the scenes learning the business end of producing the Minsky Shows. Sadly, Harold died on Christmas day 1977; yet in 1978 Pat went on to co-produce at least two shows under the Minsky banner. She went back to school, enrolling at UNLV, and remained actively involved with charities, as well as producing her own photography and glass art, which were presented in shows and galleries.

Beginning in August of 2004 Pat sent the Burlesque Historical Society multiple packages containing Harold Minsky's Files; each contained individually named folders. Pat Elliott Minsky Shapiro died from cancer in November, but before her passing she sent me a final email telling me to use the materials the best way I knew how – to me that meant a book.

I received two complete sets of materials from Pat; the first contained a variety of documents, and the second contained photos and correspondence from those seeking employment within the Minsky shows - mostly from the 1960s into the 1980s. Did the materials contain information regarding every show Harold produced? No, there were holes. However, everything included in this section was copied and quoted (with or without quote marks at times), along with – references, dates, writers, resources, and notes whenever possible. This was all written before a house explosion and fire destroyed everything Pat sent me, on July 5, 2018; all photos set aside for this book were lost as well. However, another set of Minsky documents can be found at UNLV; are they identical to what I received? I have no idea.

For those who don't know the early Minsky history, there were four Minsky brothers: Abe, Billy, Herbert K., and Morton. Their father, Louis, unable to rent out the National Winter Gardens Theatre after acquiring it, turned it over to Billy and Abe to do with it what they wanted. They tried several things before becoming successful with stock burlesque; their principals were surrounded with a large chorus, often as many as thirty girls, and they maintained a runway. The Minsky theatres featured many of the best dancers in the business: Carrie Finnell, Hattie Beall, Margie Pennetti, Mildred Cozierre, and Mae Dix. Customers came in droves, and Minsky's set the pace for all stock burlesque theatres to follow. In late 1924, Billy and his financial partner, Joseph Weinstock, opened the 125th Street Apollo Theatre. Soon, a second theatre they opened, the Republic, brought in customers day and night, filling the theatres to their capacity. Not only was burlesque considered respectable, but big business; and this time, on Broadway. By 1928, Minsky shows were very lavish productions with as many as eighteen principals, ten of whom were women. Alternating their principals between theatres, Minsky's could guarantee long engagements. This was something stock burlesque performers considered very important. Mae Dix and Minnie Fitzgerald had long engagements, and Steve Mills and Bobby Wilson were favorite long-term comics in the Minsky theatres; and the art of strip teasing became a popular form of entertainment.

In 1935, three years after Billy Minsky died, thirty-five of the thirty-eight vaudeville troops in operation on the East Coast had at least one striptease or exotic dancer on its card. Not only did this art form remain a part of burlesque shows, but also began catching on in nightclubs, Broadway shows, and cabarets.

Billy, Morton, and Herbert K. Minsky sitting for the camera. Courtesy: Bettmann Archives

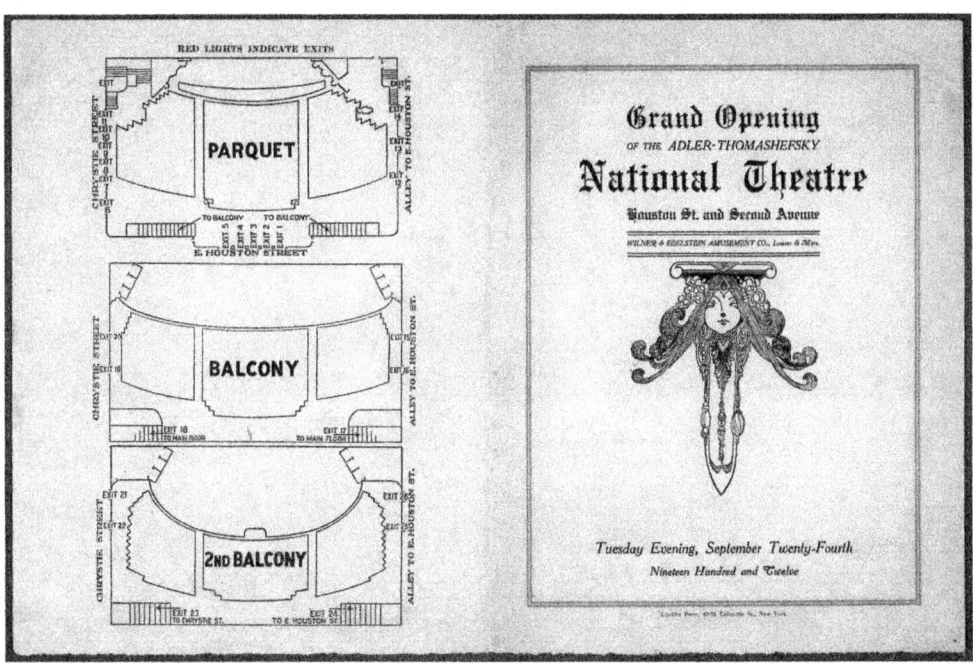

Front and back covers from the 1912 National Theatre Grand Opening Program. Courtesy: C.F. Miller

Burlesque shows also included comics and straight men, skits, house singers, a specialty dancer, a variety act or two, and chorus lines; despite popular belief, these shows weren't solely comprised of the art of strip teasing. In 1937, when the burlesque theatres started closing down in New York City, about one thousand performers were put out of work, as well as an equal number of stagehands and musicians. So, you no longer could see a burlesque show in New York City, but shows could still be seen across much of the country. Burlesque was a very popular form of entertainment, and is a part of our history and culture; it was often called the "Poor Man's Ziegfeld Follies."

Minsky's Burlesque, by Morton Minsky and Milt Machlin, is one the best books found for the in-depth story regarding the Minsky's. (Morton was Harold's uncle.) The book is referenced because one of the first clippings I start with, (from the "A" Files), was a Letter to the Editor written by Morton Minsky and printed in *The New York Times* on December 26, 1981. But let's begin with Harold Minsky's obituary...

The Apollo Theatre. Courtesy: Burlesque Historical Society

Marquee of Billy Minsky's Republic Burlesque Theatre.
Courtesy: New York Daily News Archive

"A" is For...

From the AP Press:

"December 26, 1977; Minsky, 62, dies of cancer LAS VEGAS (AP) Funeral services were scheduled today for Harold Minsky, 62, a member of the family that introduced burlesque to the American public. Minsky, who died of cancer at his home Sunday, opened his follies on the Las Vegas Strip in 1957. The production's success during a six-year run at the Dunes Hotel encouraged other hotels to open similar lavish shows, contributing to Las Vegas' development as a major entertainment center. "His lifelong ambition was to keep the true flavor of burlesque alive," said Jerry Lucas, a Minsky associate for 15 years and general manager of the production company. "Burlesque isn't strip joints. Minsky's was always in good taste." Minsky began his show business career in 1934, at the age of 19, when he took over as manager as one of his family's New York burlesque theatres. Until Mayor Fiorello La Guardia shut them down in 1941, the Minsky family operated as many as nine theatres in New York. Lucas said Minsky's will continue operating burlesque revues under the same name, which was trademarked several years ago. "The only way this was possible was because the name Minsky was synonymous with burlesque," Lucas said." (Harold Minsky; March 14, 1915 – December 25, 1977)

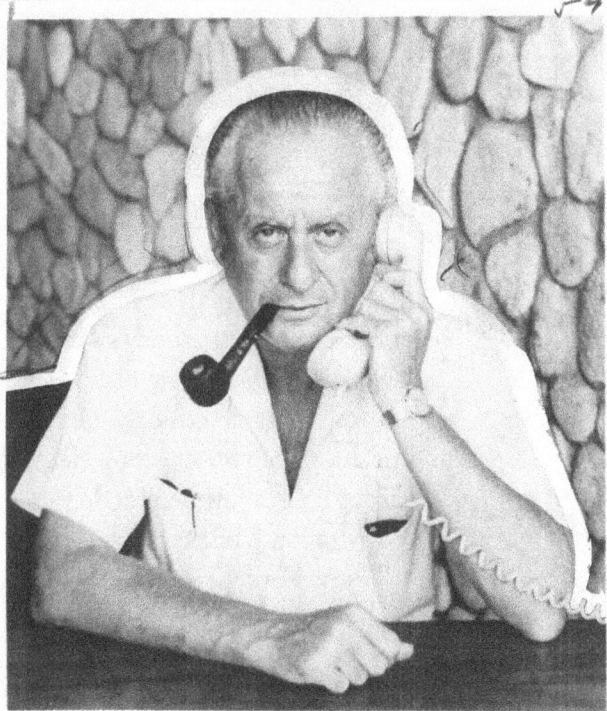

January 30, 1977 Press Photo of Harold Minsky marked up to be cropped for publication. Courtesy: Authors Collection

The next item comes from *The New York Times*, and reads:

"The Day La Guardia Killed Burlesque"

Letter to the Editor:

Your December 12th news feature on the centennial of Mayor Fiorello H. La Guardia's birth interested me. I wish, though, that you had given more space to the Mayor's behavior, which was oddly anti-democratic at times. Let me cite my experience as the sole survivor of the four Minsky Brothers of burlesque fame.

My three brothers (Abe, Billy, and Herbert) and I were operating six theatres in Metropolitan New York, plus others throughout the country, when on April 30, 1937, we were put out of business for corrupting the morals of the city.

La Guardia accomplished this by denying the renewal of burlesque theatre licenses. We were then featuring Phil Silvers, Abbott and Costello, Red Buttons, Joey Faye, Jack Albertson, Gypsy Rose Lee, and others of great talent in our burlesque extravaganzas; in competition with Ziegfeld, White, Rose, and the Shubert's. We were known as the "Poor Man's Ziegfeld."

Brooks Atkinson, Robert Garland, A. J. Liebling, and other outstanding critics of the theatre sang the praises of the Minsky shows at every opportunity. They had genuine fun at the Minsky's and expressed it in a variety of literary forms.

While you are lauding La Guardia's virtues, I think you should remember his lack of foresight in closing the Minsky Theatres. He used autocratic power to affect the closing. The burlesque industry lacked funds to fight for its constitutional rights.

The word "burlesque" and the name "Minsky" were banned. Liberals of that day felt that the censorship groups were too powerful to oppose. It was a complete surrender! La Guardia had eliminated an original source in the development of today's theatre. My opinion is that he did this not because of any ethical standards but to gain votes for re-election through a sensational tactic.

Morton Minsky
New York, December 15, 1981

Mayor Fiorello La Guardia. Courtesy: New York Daily News Archive

A bunch of bananas; Joey Faye, Phil Silvers, Jack Albertson, and Herbie Faye. Phil Silvers, among others, often played comic for straight man Jess Mack – whose mentioned on later in this book. Courtesy: Burlesque Historical Society

Gypsy Rose Lee. Courtesy: C.F. Miller

"A" also stands for the Aladdin Hotel and Casino in Las Vegas, Nevada. The initial Aladdin Hotel was the first major casino to open on the Las Vegas Strip in the 1960s, eight years after the area's boom period ended in 1958 with the debut of the Stardust Hotel. The original site of the Aladdin had been undeveloped desert property until 1962, when Edwin S. Lowe, a toy manufacturer and investor from New York, bought the land. He built the Tallyho, a small hotel without a casino. Lowe's venture suffered from the lack of gambling and closed shortly after it opened. The Kings Crown Inns of America, Inc., purchased the property in November 1963 and renamed it the Kings Crown Tallyho Inn; it too ran into financial difficulties and was unable to obtain a gaming license, closing sometime in 1965. The hotel remained closed until Milton Prell, the previous owner of the Sahara Hotel, acquired the property in January 1966. Prell envisioned a hotel and large casino with a theme based on the ancient Persian folk tale of a boy named Aladdin whose oil lamp

Large early postcard of the Aladdin Hotel and Casino – showing two views; and it only cost 5 cents to mail. Courtesy: Authors Collection

contained a genie granting wishes. After extensive renovations, Prell's Aladdin debuted on April 1, 1966, with a gourmet restaurant and Nevada's largest casino.

In May 1967, the Aladdin gained worldwide publicity when Elvis Presley married Priscilla Beaulieu at the hotel. However, Prell suffered a stroke later that year, and in 1969 sold the resort to the Parvin-Dohrmann Corporation, owner of the Fremont Hotel in downtown Las Vegas. In 1972, the Aladdin was sold again, this time to Sam Diamond, Peter J. Webbe, Sorkis J. Webbe, and Richard L. Daly, along with a group of investors based in Detroit and St. Louis. The new owners pumped millions into improvements, including a 7,500-seat performing arts theatre which replaced the golf course. But the new owners rapidly got into trouble. First they spent big on renovations and were not seeing much of a return on their investment; secondly they were tied to the mob. By the late 1970s, Nevada's Gaming Control Board learned of allegations of hidden ownership in the Aladdin by organized crime. An investigation led to the hotel's closure and sale. The Aladdin then went through a series of new owners, including Ed Torres and Wayne Newton; most were unsuccessful. On November 25, 1997 the Aladdin closed; and on April 27, 1998 the hotel was imploded with only the Aladdin Theatre for the Performing Arts left standing. The implosion paved the way for a new, reconstructed version of the Aladdin that eventually went through even more renovations and became the Planet Hollywood Resort and Casino in April of 2007.

After 33 years, the legendary Aladdin Hotel and Casino was imploded on April 27, 1998. Courtesy: Authors Collection

There were two separate folders that revolve solely around shows Harold Minsky produced at the Aladdin Hotel between 1968 and 1972. It almost appears, by reading the contracts and paperwork, that these shows were popular enough to run forever. The cast members for those shows and what they got paid to perform was as follows:

Minsky's Burlesque in 1968: Show opened Friday, December 20, 1968 and ran sixteen weeks with continuous two week options. The cast members mentioned included: Barbara Curtis, talking woman, $350 per week; Dick Richards, comedian, $400 per week; Patricia Gomez, dancer, $400 per week; Looney Lewis, comic, $400 per week; and Suzette Summers, strip, $400 per week.

Written, as typed, those performing at the Aladdin in Minsky's Burlesque in 1969 included: The Agostinos, (Frank and Denise) Adagio Act, $940.38; Herbie Barris, comedian, $339.50; Looney Lewis, comic, $475; Dick Richards, comic, $350; Sandy O'Hara, strip, $374; Bert Gehan, straight man, $339.50; Suzette Summers, strip, $350; Tracy Carol, dancer, $350; Elna Fisher, dancer, scale; Cathy Oakes, chorus, scale; Julie Freeman, chorus, scale; Jimmy Mathews, comedian, $339.50; Pat Burns, straight man, $339.50; Michel Stany, male dancer, lead dancer, scale; Karyn Kay, chorus, scale; Sharon Holmes, chorus, scale; Wendy Farrington, chorus, scale; Robin Faria, chorus, scale; Betty Francisco, chorus, scale; Orie Sasaki, lead dancer, nude, scale; Joan Symes, chorus, scale; Joni Carson, strip, $850; Miss Loni, foot juggler, $650; Dyanne Thorne, straight woman, scale ($470.19 for 16 shows); Alisa Gregory, chorus, scale; Rick Hamilton, male dancer, lead dancer, scale; Jodie Lamb, nude, lead dancer, scale; and Jean Douglas, chorus, scale.

(Notes: BHS Members, Jimmy Mathews died in October 2004; Dyanne Thorne died January 28, 2020.)

The list for 1970 was short and included: Diane Lewis, strip, $450; Jack Mann, straight man, scale; Irving Benson, comedy star, $700; and Carrie St. Clair, strip, $400. I assume many performers from the 1969 cast stayed on with this show.

The list from 1971, for the most part, did not share wages and included: Ratanya, strip, $400; Paul Gilbert, comedian; Pat Allen, showgirl, scale; Diane Marlo, exotic, strip, scale; Don Crawford, lead male dancer, scale; Beverly Whiting, dancer, scale; Debra Duke, showgirl, scale; Joe La Vigna, principal singer, scale; Jim Rogers, lead dancer, scale; Linda Stuart, showgirl, scale; Yvonne Kraemer, dancer, scale; Anne Gubbins, dancer, scale; Sharon Holmes, dancer, scale; Ann Marie Aaron, dancer, scale; Virginia Jones, lead dancer, scale; Maria Clair, showgirl, scale; Sally Gray, principal singer, scale; Toni Shain, principal singer, scale; Marge Allen, showgirl, scale; Betty Francisco, lead dancer, scale, and Nathalie Saam,

Tommy "Moe" Raft and Berri Lee appearing in Minsky's Burlesque '72 at the Aladdin Hotel in Las Vegas. Courtesy: Berri Lee

showgirl, scale. It was also noted that Sam Diamond was the President of the Aladdin, and Moe Lewis was the Entertainment Director; and 12/8 was written in pencil by Paul Gilbert's name.

Lastly we have the list for 1972, which included: Diane Lewis, strip, $450; Suzette Summers, strip, $370; Marilyn Wild, showgirl, scale; Carme Pitrello, straight man, scale; Ricki Dunn, pickpocket, $500; Tommy "Moe" Raft, comic, $1,000; Berri Lee, comedy magician, $450; and Joe DeRita and Frank Scannell, comedy team, $1,250.

(Notes: Samuel B. Diamond was born on August 3, 1909, in Canada, and died on April 15, 1997 in Las Vegas. Diamond came to Las Vegas in 1945 and began his gaming career at the Last Frontier the next year. When mobster Ben "Bugsy" Siegel opened his opulent Flamingo in 1947, Diamond accepted the floor man job and eventually wound up owning an interest in the resort. During his lifetime he would also become part owner of the Pioneer Club, Club Bingo, the Aladdin, and the Silver Slipper.

In 1976, Diamond became General Manager of the Fremont Hotel, then under the control of Alan Glick and his Argent Corporation. Diamond began running the Fremont eight months after selling much of his Aladdin stock and stepping down as its President and General Manager. Diamond was promoted to Executive Consultant for Argent in June 1976. However, he apparently was not with Argent when the hammer came down in the late 1970s. State gaming officials eventually ousted Glick and Argent amid allegations the company, which at the time also owned the Stardust and Hacienda hotels, ran a casino skimming operation for Midwest mob families. In mid-1977, according to news clippings, Diamond was attempting to gain Nevada Gaming Commission approval to operate a poker room at the Aladdin.

Sam Diamond was a legendary, old-school casino boss who believed in the popular old-style Las Vegas philosophy of giving the customer the best for their money. He is buried in the Woodlawn Cemetery in Las Vegas.

The November 9, 1974 issue of *Billboard* magazine noted that services had been held in Las Vegas for Moe Lewis, age 65, Entertainment Director for the Fremont, Aladdin, and Stardust hotels. He died of cancer. Lewis, before moving to Las Vegas in 1960, operated the Embers Restaurant in New York in the 1950s, along with the nightclub, Basin Street East. He was born Morris "Moe" Levy on August 12, 1909 in Yonkers, New York, and died October 26, 1974 in Las Vegas, Nevada. Lewis may have been associated with Howard Hughes, as well as other hotels such as the Sands and the Landmark.

Betty Francisco, 62, of Las Vegas, died on July 13, 2003. She was a professional dancer, choreographer, director, and producer, who was well known in the Las Vegas entertainment industry. Born Betty Milton on March 22, 1941, she began her show business career after battling polio. Betty became a principal dancer in many Las Vegas productions including *Minsky's Burlesque, Viva Les Girls* and *Bare Touch of Vegas*. (I met her at the Minsky Reunion in 2000 in Las Vegas.)

Paul Gilbert, 1961.
Courtesy: Fairfax Media

Paul Gilbert, was born Ed MacMahon on December 27, 1918 in New York, New York (Manhattan), and died on February 13, 1976 in Hollywood, California.

Born into a vaudevillian family, the young man trained with South American aerialists and traveled with the circus until a dramatic 65-foot fall ended his highflying career, according to a 1954 article in *Time* magazine. After the fall Gilbert continued to work in the entertainment field: acting, singing, dancing, and performing comedy. He also served in the United States military as a fighter pilot.

Paul Gilbert's talents were frequently on display during the next few decades, performing in television, films, and for Harold Minsky. Gilbert and his fourth wife, actress Barbara Crane, adopted Jonathan and Melissa Gilbert, who became part of the cast of the hit television series, *Little House on the Prairie*, (1974-1983). Actress and producer Sara Gilbert, daughter of Paul's wife Barbara and her second husband, Harold Abeles, took the Gilbert surname in 1984.

Carme Daniel Pitrello, Jr., was born in Lockport, New York on December 28, 1933, and passed away on December 4, 2016, at the Plant Hospital in Clearwater, Florida.

Carme Pitrello. Courtesy: We the Italians

Before enlisting in the Army at the age of 18, Carme played semi-pro football with the Lockport Essos. He also began entertaining in and around Lockport and Buffalo: singing, performing comedy routines, and impersonations. His early years as an Army Ranger included combat in Korea in the 1950s; he was one of only three in his unit to survive. Upon returning to the States, he was reassigned to Desert Rock, Nevada during the testing period of 13 atomic bombs. He spent time in Las Vegas on the weekends, where he made a number of friends. In 1969 Carme moved his family to Las Vegas, where he expanded his gift for performing.

With over ten thousand performances during his 40 years on the Las Vegas Strip, his talents created opportunities to work with many famous entertainers. He performed at the: Frontier, Dunes, Aladdin, Sahara, Thunderbird, Sands, Hacienda, Riviera, Desert Inn, and the Union Plaza, where he set attendance records in the long-running production show, *Natalie Needs a Nightie*. He did the entire show in drag and according to those "in the know," was one of the ugliest women you could possibly imagine. As the years passed, he left Las Vegas and began entertaining passengers on cruise ships; as well as entertaining in theatres, clubs, and community centers across the state of Florida. Carme was inducted into the Las Vegas Hall of Fame in 2012.

Ricki Dunn was born Fred Revello in Newark, New Jersey, on April 2, 1929. He died on January 29, 1999, and is buried at the Lakeside Cemetery in Colon, Michigan. He was a successful entertainer best known for his pickpocket act.

Dunn ran away from home as a teenager to join the circus, developing his skills in the "Ten-in-One" shows. He was an assistant to Card Mondor, an Australian magician and stage performer. By the early 1950s, Ricki had teamed with Channing Pollock and Robert Orben, and later developed his pickpocket act while perfecting his "Chick Cups" and "Cards Across" routines.

Dunn, known as "America's Funniest Pickpocket," worked at all the major nightclubs, hotels, casinos, and on cruise ships around the world. His act, billed as "Ricki Dunn is a Thief," worked in cities like Miami, Chicago, New York,

Ricki Dunn. Courtesy: Pat Elliott Minsky/ Burlesque Historical Society

and Las Vegas. During his 20 minutes onstage he would steal everything from wallets, neckties, glasses, and belts, and have his audience roaring with laughter. His signature closing routine was "The Drinking Trick."

In 2006, Ricki Dunn's book, *The Professional Stage Pickpocket*, was published posthumously. The book relates various experiences of his career that spanned over 50 years; as well as his routines and how to steal almost every kind of item you can imagine. If one is lucky enough to find this book it also contains a DVD of a Ricki Dunn live performance at "The Magic Castle" in Los Angeles.

Berri Lee, born in Australia, came to America at a young age. After high school he moved to Los Angeles where he began to study acting, worked in films, and professional little theatre. Seeing the young man perform, Lucille Ball took him under her wing at Desilu Studios and taught him more about comedy. He also joined Actors Studio West as well as the Jerry Lewis Workshop. Taking on part-time jobs to support himself, Berri got a job in Hollywood at "The Magic Castle," not as a magician but as a parking valet. With the constant exposure from the various entertainers, Berri explored his opportunities for performing as a comedy magician.

MINSKY'S MADMEN — Berri Lee, billed as the "Mad Magician," and Tommy Moe Raft, generally considered the maddest of the burlesque "Top Bananas," share a moment of high glee in the current Minsky's Burlesque '72 in the Bagdad Theater of the Aladdin. Suzette Summers is the featured "exotic" in this gay girly-girly romp.

One night Cary Grant saw him perform, and offered to help in any way he could. Grant introduced Lee to Ed Sullivan, and shortly thereafter Berri

Photo from the September 1, 1972 Las Vegas Review-Journal *promoting "Minsky's Madmen" Berri Lee and Tommy "Moe" Raft appearing in* Minsky's Burlesque '72 *at the Aladdin. Courtesy: Berri Lee*

Cover of the 1969 Vegas Visitor *magazine with Cary Grant and Berri Lee on the cover.*
Courtesy: Berri Lee

appeared on one of Sullivan's final shows. The next stop was Las Vegas where Lee became one of the busiest men in town. He worked for over twenty years as the starring comedy magic act in many of the major hotel showrooms. Over the years he also performed in Reno, Lake Tahoe, Laughlin, on several television shows, major cruise lines, and at celebrity golf tournaments. But as Las Vegas evolved, so did the type of entertainment people came to see. Berri Lee now calls Florida home, where he continues to appear in venues throughout the state.

The Ed Sullivan Theater marquee. Berri Lee appeared on one of Sullivan's final shows.
Courtesy: Berri Lee

Ed Sullivan and Berri Lee. The Ed Sullivan Show *was a television variety show that ran from 1948 to 1971 on CBS.*
Courtesy: Berri Lee

Reno Hilton Hotel Marquee. Courtesy: Berri Lee

Berri Lee. Courtesy: Berri Lee

Joseph La Vigna was born in Philadelphia on June 17, 1944, and died in Las Vegas on July 3, 2014. According to his obituary Joe's passions were singing and cooking. He performed in musical theatre and traveled all over the United States in his early years before coming to Las Vegas in the early 1970s, where he worked at the Aladdin Hotel for Harold Minsky. It is noted that Joe was a fabulous chef and opened "The Gourmet Factory," a successful gourmet kitchen store which featured cooking classes. Always the chef, he then created "Affairs Catering." His parties apparently were legendary, and he catered parties throughout the Las Vegas valley until his passing. Joe La Vigna, "The Executive Singing Chef," is buried at the Memory Gardens Cemetery in Las Vegas, Nevada.

Irving Benson, probably the last surviving comic from vaudeville and legendary burlesque, died on May 19, 1916; he was 102 years young.

A young Irving Benson. Courtesy: Burlesque Historical Society

He was born Irving Wishnefsky on January 31, 1914, in Brooklyn, New York. His parents were Jewish immigrants from Poland. He often appeared in local talent shows before he turned 10 years of age, and by the time he entered show business he had changed his name to Benson.

Benson won an amateur contest as a dancer in the 1920s, and, by the mid-1930s, he was touring the country telling jokes. He got his start in vaudeville, but as vaudeville died he turned to burlesque. Over time, he climbed to the top of the bill as the featured "first comic," or, "top banana." During World War II, he entertained the troops with the USO.

Jack Mann and George "Beetlepuss" Lewis. Courtesy: Burlesque Historical Society

For 30 years, starting in 1946, he was part of a comedy duo with straight man Jack Mann, appearing all over the country, including New York's Palace Theatre. As theatres began to close, Irving moved to Las Vegas.

He always delivered his punch lines with a hangdog expression, and a matter-of-fact voice with the perfect timing honed by thousands of performances. He also came of comic age at the same time as other vaudeville and burlesque comedians, including Red Skelton, Jackie Gleason, and Phil Silvers.

A very young Red Skelton. In 1929, when he was sixteen, he joined the Mutual Wheel. He was the youngest featured burlesque actor in the business at that time. Courtesy: Metro-Goldwyn-Mayer

In the 1960s, Benson became known to television viewers through his appearances with Milton Berle, another comedian from the vaudeville tradition. Pretending to be an audience member named Sidney Spritzer, Benson interrupted Berle's monologue with a blizzard of insults. For years, Benson — as Spritzer — was featured in Milton Berle's performances around the country. (Check out YouTube.) In the early

2000s, when Berle was in his 90s, he and Benson got together again for a tour in Florida.

Irving made his first appearance on *The Tonight Show* in 1962 and became a favorite of Johnny Carson, who often acted as Benson's straight man. In addition to his nightclub routines, he occasionally acted in touring theatrical productions and in television shows, including a 1979 appearance on *Happy Days*.

Johnny Carson and Irving Benson appearing together on The Tonight Show *in 1977. Courtesy: Irving Benson*

He never forgot his lines, never lost his timing, and never forgot where the world of vaudeville had taken him. In 2010, actors and filmmakers John C. Brown and Bart Williams released a documentary about Irving Benson, *The Last First Comic*. It is available on Amazon.

Irving's wife of 79 years, the former Lillian Waldowsky, died in March of 2016.

Irving Benson was a member of "The Golden Days of Burlesque Historical Society" for nearly twenty years. Irving was a good chum and a wonderful resource; he would always answer all my questions, no matter how stupid they may have seemed to him.)

The next item in this folder was the AGVA and Associated Booking Corporation Agreement between the Aladdin Hotel and Patava, Inc., dated October 25, 1968. It included the Standard Form of Artists Engagement Contract, along with the seven page Agreement drawn up by the lawyers. The Standard Form, stapled to the Agreement, stated the show was to commence on December 20, 1968; it was to consist of a cast of 25, and run for sixteen (16) consecutive weeks. The shows were to run seven (7) days a week; two shows per night, and three (3) shows on Friday and Saturday. The contract included the option to run the show for two additional, and consecutive sixteen (16) week periods. The Aladdin Hotel was to pay Patava, Inc., $13,000 per week. The Form was signed by: Edward Torres, General Manager for the Aladdin Hotel, Harold Minsky for Patava, Inc., and Art Engler for the Associated Booking Corporation.

Additional information from the Agreement included: the twenty-five employees would consist of a chorus and principals, a stage manager, one wardrobe mistress, and Harold Minsky, as the Director; and the show would last seventy-five minutes. The show would conclude by the end of April 10, 1969, unless the option for an extension was exercised by the hotel in writing by the end of the eighth week. The Aladdin would furnish and pay of the orchestra, consisting of seven members; they would also furnish and pay for stagehands and an assistant wardrobe mistress, if needed. The Agreement was signed by Torres and Minsky.

Suzette Summers marquee at the Esquire Theatre, in Toledo, Ohio in July of 1968. Courtesy: University of Toledo Digital Repository

Also in this folder were AGVA contracts for comic Dick Richards and dancer Suzette Summers. Both performers were signed through the Jess Mack Agency, located at 1501 Broadway in New York City, for a period of eight weeks; and both performers were to receive $350 per week. They were to begin work on April 11, 1969, and to perform in thirteen shows per week at the Aladdin Hotel. Richards signed his contract on April 3, and Summers signed hers on April 8.

The next item was an Agreement dated July 18, 1969, and signed by Harold Minsky and Edward Torres, the General Manager of the Aladdin Hotel. It was a typical contract which was to commence in the main showroom at the Aladdin for a period of fifty-one (51) weeks beginning on December 19, 1969 and ending on December 11, 1970. The following was spelled out:

Minsky was to provide the following personnel: seven dancers, ten showgirls, two comics, one straight man, one straight woman, one singer, three specialty dancers, one stripper, a stage manager, and a wardrobe mistress. He was also obligated to produce a maximum of sixteen shows per week; but the hotel would have the right to schedule the times for the shows each week, and whether it was one, two, or three shows per day. Each show had to run at least seventy-five minutes. Minsky was to be paid $16,000 per week, which included the increase under the terms of the AGVA contract commencing January 1, 1970. The hotel was to provide a seven piece orchestra for show rehearsals, and the show; also the stage lighting, stagehands, and an assistant wardrobe mistress, if needed.

What was different in this contract was it stipulated the names of the strips. Lili St. Cyr and Tempest Storm were both to perform for eighteen weeks; the other names mentioned were Joni Carson and Babette Bardot. The Aladdin also had the option to extend the original Agreement for two additional weeks, but must exercise that right in writing by the end of the forty-third week. Minsky would receive the same payment as the other fifty-one weeks.

Autographed photo of Tempest Storm. Courtesy: C.F. Miller

Autographed photo of Lili St. Cyr performing as "Shanghai Lil" at The Forbidden City in Honolulu. Courtesy: C.F. Miller

There was also a letter from the Associated Booking Corporation, dated July 18, 1969. It was signed by Minsky and Art Engler, and spelled out the usual ten percent payment Agreement between Minsky and the agency.

Something else of interest were two pages breaking down the entire cost of the show for the Aladdin Hotel, and it was dated December 19, 1969. It is typed as it was written. The first page lists the following: Audition – Advertising and Publicity, $366.36; Travel Expense, $76.69; Wardrobe – Labor and Golda, $2,556

Babette Bardot marquee at the Circus Circus Hotel and Casino in Las Vegas, 1969. Courtesy: Burlesque Historical Society

and $6,025.92; Wardrobe – Finished and Unfinished, $7,188.47; Wigs, $1,039; Music, $3,167.72; Scenery and Props, $11,877.75; Lighting, $1,529.19; Professional Fees, $9,700; Rehearsal Payroll (Gross), $7,250; Additional Tax – Corporation pays, $258; Miscellaneous Expense (petty cash), $1,000. It comes out to $52,035.10 according to the total listed on the bottom of the first page.

The second page lists weekly expenses and monthly expense. The weekly expenses listed are: AGVA, $98; Associated Booking Corporation, $1,600; S. Elkman, $125; Bank of Las Vegas, $200; Weekly Payroll, $10,600; Scenery, $75; Advertising and Publicity, $100; Petty Cash Expenses, $50; Payroll Tax, $1,000, and Insurance and Personal Tax, $25. This all adds up to a total of $13,873.

The monthly expenses were as follows: Telephone, $400; Electric, $50; Gas, $50; First Western Savings, $292.50; Dardy, $400; Tal Lease, $302.10; Humble, $75; Hotel and Maintenance, $750; Shoe Repair, $100; Dry Cleaning, $40; Wig Maintenance, $40; Scenery Repair, $150; Props – Repair and Replacement, $100; Dressing Room Maintenance, $80; Miscellaneous Tax, $100; Answering Service, $28; Legal and Accountant Fees, $400; Wardrobe – Replacement Stockings, $160; Water, $20; Office Expense (printing, etc.), $30; and Miscellaneous, $200. This all adds up to a grand total of $3,757.60.

The Aladdin Hotel and Casino marquee advertising the Minsky show in 1969. Courtesy: Pat Elliott Minsky/Burlesque Historical Society

The last two items for 1969 ran in publications, the first in the *Las Vegas Sun* and the second in *Variety*. Let's start with Ralph Pearl's column "Vegas Daze and Nights." The following ran on December 26, 1969. In-part the column reads:

"Let's face it, Kiddies, you just haven't lived until you've watched a top banana in all burlesque, Looney Lewis, playing Rhett Butler in an outrageously funny fashion in the brand-new edition of *Minsky Burlesque '70* at the Aladdin. Harold Minsky's latest girlie clambake, incidentally, has to be the most rollicking, sexiest frolic ever put together by the nation's number one girlie show provocateur. It stars the torrid, flame-haired and bosomy Tempest Storm, one of the more outstanding ecdysiasts in the saloon business, also a bevy of curvy Minsky femmes and guy dancers, stripper Suzette Summers, Jimmy Mathews, Dyanne Thorne, saucy Sharon Richards, and a belting femme named Jeannie Thomas. If you've been wondering whatever happened to big league burlesque, look no farther. It's at the Aladdin."

The following review, written by Will, appeared in the "Nitery Review" column, in the December 30, 1969 issue of *Variety*. It reads:

"Las Vegas, December 29 – In for a year with only top line changes planned, this edition by Harold Minsky goes well over his previous production on just about all counts. First of all, he has been budgeted upward, and that boon aids materially in the booking of top acts, along with the settings, costumes, et al. Last year's run was a very good draw for the Aladdin, with the incoming revue looming just as good, if not better.

In Tempest Storm, the marquee pull is evident. She looks fit, blazingly adorned with highlighted day glow crimson hair. Super endowments are hers almost beyond the nth degree and she knows how to use every inch of her flesh for enticement. The prevalent instant nudity zip does not affect her ambulation in the least. Miss Storm attends to the ritual of the tease, gradually divesting while legging to broad rhythms until the final runway strut. With only the briefest of public appliqué showing at the finish, she bows to modest applause. The fate of today's stripper is just this – rapt attention throughout the act, yet the hesitant smattering of hands in punitive consideration of their talent.

Jimmy Mathews. Courtesy: Pat Elliott Minsky/ Burlesque Historical Society

Looney Lewis earned his position of top banana for this edition. All of last year, he was whacked about in the hoary burlesque "Fight Scene," by a succession of boxers; Freddie Little, Ferd Hernandez, among the punchers. He heads two blackouts this outing. A "Gone With the Wind" spoof, with shapely talking gal, Dyanne Thorne, and interruptions from the house by straight man Pat Burns. It needs trimming, but has some rib tickling moments. The "Crazy House" romp is ludicrous with crossovers by Jimmy Mathews, Jerry Lucas, Pat Burns, Miss Thorne, Hernandez, and Suzette Summers pulling variable shades of ho-hoing.

Teri Starr and Dyanne Thorne at the 1999 BHS gathering held at the Imperial Palace in Las Vegas. Courtesy: Authors Collection

Mathews reveals his ability to grab laughs through some rubbery mugging and general schtick in "The Gun Ain't Loaded" blackout. Miss Thorne works well in this scene and blonde cutie, Sharon Richards, from the line also projects amusingly.

Suzette Summers is another holdover. Her peeling, a standout before, continues to take in the orbs. Savage moves while dropping leopard-skin coverings keep the jungle motif in fast action. She has the sumptuous body with good looking face, a combination that is most advantageous to her Strip trips. She also has developed into a very capable talking woman among the various sketches.

Miss Loni has a fast-paced interlude of risley kinetics dance, scissoring her legs with skill as she foot-flips large balls, plastic lighted barbells, outsize playing cards, and Lucite boxes. She makes a score immediately, continuing without letup until flesh flaring of all objects lighted and whirling in surrounding darkness.

Warbler Jeannie Thomas reveals sensitivity and excellent tonal quality. The brunette looker illustrates production lyrics with considerable style, moving smoothly among the choreos. These dance rounds, patterned by Jerry Norman, are his best Minsky designs to date. The girl gambolers are fleet, and the provocative nude mannequins keep the stage alive with their pulsing movements; a potent combination. Ornamenting the three numbers are nudists Orie Sasaki, Betty Stowell, and Jodie Lamb. All discharge vibratory oscillations, attended by two muscular, dynamic males, Michel Stany and Rick Hamilton.

Plaudits go to Josephine Spinedi for costuming, executed by Eastwood; the spectra settings by Winn Strickland, built by Nevada Scenic Studios, Inc.; lighting by Bob Kiernan, and charts by Irv Gordon, transmitted ably by Hank Shank's Septet.

Lili St. Cyr replaces Tempest Storm on February 20. Will."

(Notes: Josephine Spinedi was educated at the Arts Educational School of London in classical ballet with a minor in art. She began her professional dancing career at age 16 in Italy, where she also assisted some of Italy's top costumers and fashion designers. When her dance troupe came to Las Vegas, Spinedi also continued designing wardrobe for producer Matt Gregory's scaled-down hip shows *The Feminine Touch, Mod, Mod World*, and *Pony Express*, as well as shows for Harold Minsky.

Just some of Josephine Spinedi's designs can be viewed at: http://digital.library.unlv.edu/collections/showgirls/josephine-spinedi)

On January 17, 1970, the *Las Vegas Sun* ran the following brief comment in the Ralph Pearl column. It reads:

"We ran into an old pal from the El Rancho Vegas days, Lili St. Cyr, still stunning and still the number one Ecdysiast in show business today. She was at the Flamingo with her boss Harold Minsky and his charming Pat, to catch the Zsa Zsa Gabor show. Lili will headline the *Minsky Burlesque '70* at the Aladdin February 20th."

In the folder there was also a cast list for *Minsky's Burlesque '70*, which included what some performers were paid. Most were paid AGVA scale; line captains, swing girls, and those who performed in scenes were paid an extra $50 per week. Looney Lewis was paid $600 per week. Jimmy Mathews, Jerry Lucas, Pat Burns, Suzette Summers, Dyanne Thorne, Jeannie Thomas, and Betty Francisco (line captain) were a part of the cast along with fifteen others. There were two "swing girls," and Sharon Richards performed in the scenes. It also lists two dancers, per show, who had specific days off per week, Monday through Sunday.

There was also a RIDER for the July 18, 1969 contract between the Aladdin Hotel and Minsky that was dated May 6, 1970. It reads as follows:

"It is agreed that for the weeks ending May 7, 1970 and May 14, 1970, the contract price is amended to $15,500.00 per week.

It is agreed that for the weeks ending May 21, 1970 and May 28, 1970, the contract price is amended to $13,850.00 per week.

It is agreed that starting with the week ending June 4, 1970 and continuing for the remaining weeks of this contract, the contract price is amended to $13,200.00 per week.

It is further agreed that the personnel depicted in Paragraph One in said contract is amended as follows:

For a two week period only, starting May 1 and concluding May 14, 1970 on the basis of fourteen shows per week, seven days per week, personnel will consist of: 1 comic, 10 principals, 14 chorus (dancers and showgirls), 1 wardrobe mistress, 1 stage manager, and 5 extras (2 girls working in scenes, 2 swing girls, 1 captain).

For a two week period only, starting May 15 and concluding May 28, 1970 on the basis of thirteen shows per week, six days per week, personnel will consist of: 1 comic, 10 principals, 12 chorus (dancers and showgirls), 1 wardrobe mistress, 1 stage manager, and 3 extras (2 girls working in scenes, 1 captain).

Starting with the week of May 29, 1970 and for the remaining weeks of this contract, on the basis of thirteen shows per week, six days per week, personnel will consist of: 1 comic, 8 principals, 12 chorus (dancers and showgirls), 1 wardrobe mistress, 1 stage manager, and 5 extras (4 girls working in scenes, 1 captain).

It is agreed that the running time of the show will be a minimum of sixty-five minutes.

All other terms and conditions set forth in the master contract and RIDERS therein remain the same."

Harold Minsky and just some of the ladies from one of his shows. Courtesy: Janelle Smith Collection

Also in this folder was an AGVA Standard Form of Artists Engagement Contract dated August 13, 1971. It was between the Prell Hotels, doing business as the Aladdin Hotel, and Harold Minsky, also known as Patava, Inc. It was for fifty-one consecutive weeks; thirteen shows per week, six nights a week, starting on or about December 20, 1971. The specific starting date was to be determined by, or around, October 1, 1971. The Aladdin was to pay Patava, Inc., $16,500.00 per week. The Agreement was signed by Moe Lewis, Entertainment Director for the Aladdin, Harold Minsky, and Art Engler for Associated Booking Corporation. There was a "Date Rider" attached to the contract stating the show was to commence on December 24, 1971. The document was dated October 5, 1971, and signed by Moe Lewis and Art Engler.

Specific information in the Agreement states:

Minsky was to produce a show in the main showroom on the premises at the Aladdin Hotel, and he would provide sufficient personnel to include the following: a chorus of (14) dancers and showgirls, eleven (11) principals, a stage manager, and a wardrobe mistress. The hotel would have the right to approve all performers that would appear in the production, as well as have the right to select the number of shows Minsky would produce. Although, Minsky was not to produce more than thirteen (13) shows during any six (6) days of each week. However, if the hotel asked for additional shows to exceed the thirteen (13) shows, six (6) days per week, or additional shows on day seven (7), the hotel would be required to pay the minimum basic wage, including overtime scale, together with all additional union benefits as well as federal and state taxes. The hotel would also have the right to determine whether there should be one, two, or three shows on any one day; those shows would run a minimum of seventy-five minutes per show.

Minsky was to produce, stage, and direct, at his sole expense, as well as furnish all the ingredients for the show, including: personnel, costumes, choreography, and musical arrangements. The hotel would provide the publicity and advertising. If Minsky was unable to do his job, and a substitution needed to be made, it had to be done so with the consent of the hotel.

It was also agreed upon that on or before 12:00pm on the sixth day of each week during the term of this agreement, the hotel would pay Minsky $16,500.00 dollars. Minsky would pay all taxes, AGVA dues, and welfare benefits. The hotel would also furnish and pay for an orchestra for all the shows, conforming with all regulations, and consisting of a minimum of seven (7) playing musicians. They would also provide said orchestra for show rehearsals of approximately five (5) hours for each two (2) days prior to any opening of any new shows, or change of, or addition of new principals. The hotel would also supply stage lighting as Minsky required, stagehands, and an assistant wardrobe mistress, if needed.

The following comments were included in this Agreement: "This writing contains the entire understanding and agreement between the parties, replacing all prior understandings with respect to the subject matter hereof."

As well as: "If any conflict should exist between any provision hereof, and any such law or collective bargaining agreement, this Agreement then shall be modified, but only to the extent necessary to remove such conflict, and so modified shall continue in full force and effect."

Like a few other contracts I have seen, it also included the comment that reads: "In the event this Agreement shall be suspended by reason of a strike or lockout, and during the term of such strike or lockout, the Producer shall be obligated to pay its employees the minimum basic scale, the consideration to be paid by Operator to Producer during the term of such strike or lockout shall equal the minimum basic scale for the Producer's employees and no more."

For good measure the verbiage "Act of God" was also thrown into that paragraph. It was signed and dated on August 23, 1971 by Harold Minsky and Moe Lewis.

In November 1971, a RIDER was attached to the above Agreement extending Minsky's Burlesque to continue to perform at the Aladdin for an additional twenty-three (23) consecutive weeks from December 24, 1971 through and including June 1, 1972. The hotel was to notify Minsky in writing by April 1, 1972 if the show was to continue beyond June. The RIDER was signed by Sam Diamond, Moe Lewis, and Harold Minsky.

Postcard from Minsky's Burlesque '72 *presented nightly in the Bagdad Theatre as a tribute to the "most beautiful girls in the world" at the Aladdin Hotel. Courtesy: C.F. Miller*

There was one additional RIDER in this folder dated June 15, 1972. It was signed by Sam Diamond and Art Engler. It reads:

"RIDER to contract dated August 13, 1971, between Prell Hotels, Inc., dba Aladdin Hotel, Las Vegas, Nevada, and the Producer, Patava, Inc.

It is hereby mutually agreed that starting on June 30, 1972 the cast of the show *Minsky's Burlesque '72* shall be reduced as follows: Two (2) showgirls, One (1) straight man.

It is agreed that with this reduction of cast personnel starting with the week ending July 6, 1972 and continuing through the week ending December 2, 1972, the contractual price will be reduced to $15,850.00 per week.

It is finally agreed that if at any time during the run of this engagement that circumstances facilitate adding to the cast complement, such scales involved shall be paid by the Operator, Aladdin Hotel, Inc."

The next item in the Aladdin folder was a standard AGVA contract dated December 8, 1971. It was to engage the services of Paul Gilbert, comedian, to perform at the Aladdin for a period of eight (8) consecutive weeks beginning on December 24, 1971. Gilbert was to work thirteen (13) shows a week, six (6) days weekly; two (2) shows per night on week nights, and three (3) shows on Saturday. It did not list his wages, but it lists his agent as: William Loeb Management, 233 South Beverly Drive, Beverly Hills, California. It also listed Gilbert's home address as: 11477 Dona Pegita Drive, Studio City, California. The contract was signed by Paul Gilbert and Harold Minsky.

The following short article appeared in the *Las Vegas Sun* newspaper on December 24, 1971. Titled "Minsky's Burlesque '72; Aladdin Has Girls, Girls, Girls," no author was mentioned. It reads as follows:

"Beautiful girls, music, comedy and the excitement that makes Las Vegas the entertainment capital of the world have been combined in *Minsky's Burlesque '72*, opening Christmas Eve at the Aladdin Hotel.

Minsky productions have featured the most beautiful girls in abundance, and producer Harold Minsky has prepared an extravagant revue for the Bagdad Theatre where every night will be fun night.

The outstanding revue, staged by Jerry Norman, will be presented twice nightly with reservations a must, especially during the holiday season. A special show is scheduled for 1:30am on Saturdays.

Minsky's Burlesque '72 will feature striptease artists and burlesque sketches galore with Rudi Eagan and his orchestra providing the musical backing.

Elegant, colorful costumes, designed by Josephine Spinedi, will partially drape the gorgeous selection of beauties in the production. Musical arrangements are by Ken Tiffany.

The highlight of the musical revue is expected to be an illusion whereby four separate stripteases are performed by eight girls. "This has to be seen to be believed," according to Minsky."

The following "Nitery Review" appeared in *Variety* on both January 7, 1972, and on January 12, 1972. It was written by Will, and reads as follows:

"Aladdin, Las Vegas, Harold Minsky's "Burlesque '72," with Paul Gilbert; 2 drink minimum.

Berri Lee and chorus dancers performing in Minsky's Burlesque '72 at the Aladdin Hotel. Courtesy: Berri Lee

Harold Minsky has another orb-teasing package in his newly mounted *Minsky's Burlesque '72*, which sports comic Paul Gilbert, a couple of strippers and a collection of anatomical delights that move to the choreographic direction of Jerry Norman. It will do very good biz for new owners of this spa as they set course on the choppy competitive seas of the Vegas Strip. Show is set for indefinite run.

Gilbert has had much experience with comedy as standup gagster, thesping legit, and cracking the old burlesque barrel from time to time. He certainly knows and shows his ability to flip and toss verbal cuties to various femme cuties and male stooge, Jerry Lucas, in standard "Crossovers" mania immediately following opening line production, and in "Fireman" scene later on. Sarasue Gleiss is the baby-voiced talking woman in this sketch and shares gab with Ann Marie Aaron in Gilbert's doctor howlarity, proven on many a nitery stage.

The days of the tried and true strip routine could be numbered, with gimmicks taking the place of the old artful peek-a-boo struts. Ratanya has what she calls a "Maori Specialty," which is the whirling of white balls on long ropes as she moves about, and mini-lighted bulbs at strategic points for finish. Real attention grabbers, however, occur during Diane Marlo's "Tre Exotique" romp, with marshmallow pasties upon each breast, temptingly thrust before ring-siding males to bite off. The walkabout is nothing unusual. Ditto her bare facts.

Immediately following Ratanya is "The Showgirl Strip," where eight very well-proportioned lassies go through a razzle-dazzle take-off and put-on routine.

The production numbers are standouts, Norman having outdone himself with this opus. Especially notable is the "Space Number of Webs," elastic and otherwise, with Don Crawford featured in contortions among the web patterns. Debra Duke is a fine form feature in the dazzling opener. Lead girl dancers Virginia Jones and Betty Francisco are matched in fleet work with Crawford and Jim Rogers. The Minsky Singers, Joe La Vigna, Toni Shain, and Sally Gray blend well in the lyrical illustrations for production rounds.

The Josephine Spinedi costumes are quite spectrumatic throughout, whirling in front of the bright settings by Wynn Strickland. The charts by Ken Tiffany are performed with brio by Rudi Eagan's Septet."

There was one line regarding Minsky in Ralph Pearl's column "Vegas Daze and Nights," in the *Las Vegas Sun* on April 1, 1972. It simply reads: "Attention Harold Minsky, Aladdin Hotel; Please confirm or deny, but what about the buzz I'm getting from a reliable source in Carson City that you're interested in taking over Kings Castle Hotel in Lake Tahoe?"

(Notes: April 1, 1972 was also the night Tommy "Moe" Raft opened in *Minsky's Burlesque '72* at the Aladdin Hotel.)

The final item regarding the hotel was a Xerox of a letter on Aladdin Hotel and Casino stationery. The mailing address was: P.O. Box 14217, Las Vegas, Nevada 89114. The telephone number was: (702) 736-0111; and it was dated May 3, 1972. It was addressed to, and reads:

Mr. Al Sachs
Vice President
Recrion Corporation
Stardust Hotel
Las Vegas, Nevada
Dear Mr. Sachs:
Pursuant to my telephone conversation with Mr. Moe Lewis, please be advised that the Aladdin Hotel Corporation has agreed to retain *Minsky's Burlesque '72* intact through December 2, 1972, as per the Contract dated August 13, 1971.

Kindly execute the enclosed copy and return to me at once. Thanking you for past favors, I remain
Respectfully yours,
Aladdin Hotel Corporation
Sam Diamond
President

On the bottom of the letter were the initials "AS."

Other paperwork in this folder had a lot to do with AGVA – the American Guild of Variety Artists. AGVA is an entertainment union representing performers in variety entertainment, including: burlesque, circuses, showrooms and cabarets, comedy showcases, dance revues, magic shows, theme park shows, and arena and auditorium extravaganzas. (There was some overlap between the jurisdictions of AGVA and Actors' Equity.) AGVA was the successor to the American Federation of Actors organized by Sophie Tucker, among others, and affiliated with the American Federation of Labor. In 1939 the AFL dissolved AFA due to financial irregularities, and issued a new charter to AGVA.

In 1966-67, the Las Vegas AGVA wage scales, rehearsal conditions, and payment break downs included the following:

Minimum salaries for the chorus ranged from $167.85 to $271.13, depending on if the dancers worked six days or seven; and 13 to 21 shows. For a principal, pay ranged from $250.00 to $403.84. Six hours of rehearsal per week was included as part of their salary. Overtime rehearsal rate was $3.00 per hour. Saturday and Sunday rehearsal rate was $4.50 per hour.

A young, elegant, Sophie Tucker. Courtesy: Dusty Sage

The paperwork went on to state the following:

"If an Artist is brought to place of employment prior to date of the engagement for rehearsal purposes, and rehearsal necessitates living away from home, then that Artist shall be paid one half of the minimum basic agreement scale until the start of the engagement.

In no event shall rehearsal periods extend beyond three weeks. Any extension of the three week period shall be paid on a full contractual basis.

If a Chorus Artist is required to step out of line to lead a production number, or work in bits, the Artist shall be paid no less than an additional Twenty-Five percent of his or her contractual salary."

In March of 1969, wages were listed as follows:

"Chorus Artists: Basic minimum of $228.00 for up to 13 shows in six days; $17.54 per show for all shows over 13 in the six day period; and $35.08 per show for all shows on day seven.

Principals: Basic minimum of $336.76 for up to 13 shows in six days; $25.90 per show for all shows over 13 in the six day period; and $51.80 per show for all shows on day seven.

Rehearsal Pay: For the first three weeks of rehearsal prior to the start of a new show; $125.00 per week, Monday through Friday, maximum seven hours per day, thirty-five hours per week.

Overtime rehearsal rate, Monday through Friday, $5.00 per hour; Saturday and Sunday rehearsal rate, $7.50 per hour.

Supplemental Pay: The extra weekly compensation for "stepping out of the line," "swinging," and for "captain," will be $50.00 per week; and the compensation for "Understudy of Principals" will be $25.00 per week until performing as the Principal, at which time compensation will be that of the Principal. Performers now receiving supplemental pay for the above will not have the dollar amount reduced during their current engagement."

Wage scales for AGVA performers working in Minsky's shows in 1970 and 1971 were the following:

"Chorus Artists 1970: $237.12 for 6 days, up to 13 shows; for 6 days, over 13 shows – per show, $18.24; and day seven – per show, $36.48. In 1971: $246.60 for 6 days, up to 13 shows; for 6 days, over 13 shows – per show, $18.97; and day seven – per show, $37.94.

Principal Artists 1970: $353.17 for 6 days, up to 13 shows; for 6 days, over 13 shows – per show, $27.17; and day seven – per show, $54.34. In 1971: $367.30 for 6 days, up to 13 shows; for 6 days, over 13 shows – per show, $28.25; and day seven – per show, $56.50."

This was also the first time Singers and Lounge Performers in Musical Groups appeared on Minsky's AGVA, Las Vegas Branch, minimum wage scale paperwork. It reads as follows:

"Singers: 1/1/69 thru 12/31/71 – Artists whose principle activity is singing and who are featured as production singers individually and/or collectively shall be regarded as Principal Artists.

Lounge Performers in Musical Groups: Artists performing with musical groups in lounges as band or orchestra singers, and go-go girls, working under the direction of a musician as head of the group or band. Work week not more than 6 days of 6 consecutive hours with rest periods similar to the musicians in the group.

1/1/6 – 12/31/69 ---- $266.00
1/1/70 – 12/31/70 ---- 4 percent Increase
1/1/71 – 12/31/71 ---- 4 percent Increase

Rehearsal Pay: 1/1/69 – 12/31/71 -- For the first three weeks of rehearsal prior to the start of a new show; $125.00 per week, Monday thru Saturday, maximum seven hours per day, forty-two hours per week. Overtime rehearsal rate, Monday thru Saturday, is $3.00 per hour; Sunday rehearsal rate, $4.50 per hour. Vacation and sick leave benefits start 1/1/70."

"B" is For...

"B" is for a Minsky File called "Burlesque Comics/Straight Men," which also contained information on some talking women. The material included: biographies, reviews, press releases, some letters, and sadly, a lot of photographs.

Let's start with a couple of newspaper articles on Barbara Curtis, one of the best talking women in burlesque. The first article was from *The Standard-Times* in New Bedford, Massachusetts on August 29, 1967. In-part it reads:

"Wild Wiggles, Giggles Catapult Cape Show by Brad Hathaway, staff writer – HYANNIS – It was like old home week at the Old Howard in Boston here last night as the buxom lassies of *Minsky's Burlesque Follies* did their best to bump, grind and wiggle across a fun-filled stage at the Cape Cod Melody Tent.

Phil Silvers. Courtesy: Burlesque Historical Society

The girls are strictly for the looking, and the ribald acts spiced in between will leave you hurting with laughter. Just leave the prudes and kids at home.

Harold Minsky has been producing burlesque since 1936. Among the stars who got their start in the Minsky shows are Phil Silvers, Lili St. Cyr, Gypsy Rose Lee, and Georgia Sothern.

There's a local touch to the Melody Tent production as Barbara Curtis teams with several terrific comics in the cast of five rollicking and risqué scenes.

Miss Curtis, daughter of Mr. and Mrs. George F. Pierce of 14

Barbara Curtis. Courtesy: Janelle Smith Collection

*Milt Douglas.
Courtesy: Burlesque Historical Society*

Quelle Lane, Marion, has been with Minsky's eight months, and in show business most of her life.

She's perfect and gets superb support from Dick Bernie and Danny Jacobs in the 'He-Haw Club" scene and in 'School Days." Then she teams with Jack Rosen and Danny Jacobs in the hilarious "Lifesaver," and with Milt Douglas in "The Honeymooners."

You'll get your bellyful of laughs with this crew, without a doubt."

The article goes on to mention the other performers in the show including: Monique Monet, Lisa Duran, Yolanda Moreno, singer Frankie Vale, and the Minsky girls and dancers. The final paragraph reads:

"For looking and laughing, *Minsky's Burlesque Follies* can't be beat. The show will play at 8:30pm nightly through September 3, with the exception of Friday. On that day there will be a late show at 10:30pm, with the regular performance getting under way at 7pm."

The second article was from the *Boston Herald Traveler* on September 6, 1967. It came from the Samuel Hirsch column "Hirsch on Theatre," and was titled "Lunch with Burlesquers All Dressed to Kill." It reads as follows:

"A press luncheon at the Playboy Club for stars of *Minsky's Burlesque Follies*

Monique Monet was the featured performer in Life Begins at Minsky's which opened in the Marine Room of the Edgewater Beach Hotel on September 20, 1967. Credit: Authors Collection

Autographed photo of Lisa Duran. Courtesy: Janelle Smith Collection

now playing at Frank Connelley's Carousel Theatre in Framingham seems at first glance – to be an over-statement.

However, in the interests of education, and since we had heard how Harvard boys had studied for years at the Old Howard, we joined our colleagues in a visit with Dick Bernie, a baggy-pants comic, Barbara Curtis,

Front of Yolanda Moreno flyer. Courtesy: C.F. Miller

"a talking woman," and Corinne Anderson and Arian Michelle, both Minsky dancers.

They were dressed in the height of fashion and talked about their work as a serious theatrical form. Actually, these were not the strippers, but actors and dancers. Several of the Minsky Girls were supposed to be there to talk about their ancient art, but they were late.

"Maybe they couldn't find their costumes," quipped Bernie, a dead-pan, sandpaper voiced comic in a checked sport jacket. "Or else their tassels were tangled."

A shapely waitress in a scant bunny costume pranced by with a menu. The conversation stopped while the orders were taken and the burlesque people inspected her with some amusement.

"Nudity is a business," said Barbara Curtis, a statuesque blonde in a smart red suit. "We don't stop to think about it. I was married to a burlesque comic, Al Anger, and before he died he used to say he enjoyed seeing the girls all dressed up after the show. He said they had more character with clothes on. He knew their names then."

When the bunny left, her fluffy bunny's tail wagging behind her, a question was asked about the topless waitress fad. "Ridiculous," snorted Barbara. "There's no illusion when you see a woman walking that way with a tray of food. On the stage, there's an illusion; stage lights and music and some grace to it. Besides, they're infringing on our territory."

Bernie, who's been in the business close to 30 years, and has worked vaudeville, Broadway shows, motion pictures, and television, (you've seen him with Jackie Gleason's *The Honeymooners*), was a top banana with Ann Corio. He says burlesque is coming back because of the new interest women have in the shows. There are three burlesque companies touring this summer and Harold Minsky's show has been playing Las Vegas for the last 17 years – after burlesque was closed for good in New York in April 1942.

Dick Bernie and Steve Mills clowning around backstage. Courtesy: Susan Mills

Jackie Gleason. Courtesy: C.F. Miller

Burlesque – which had its start in America in 1865 when it was known as "burleycue" and "leg shows," is synonymous with the name Minsky. Harold's father, Abe, and his uncles, formed a dynasty that at one point filled 15 New York theatres.

Out of this bawdy atmosphere came some of the great American stage, screen, and radio comedians. Among those were: Al Jolson, W.C. Fields, Fannie Brice, Sophie Tucker, Jack Pearl, Bert Lahr, Leon Errol, Phil Silvers, Bobby Clark, Willie Howard, and Weber and Fields. The training was tough, a trial by fire, because rowdy audiences in those days heckled the comic, threw vegetables

1928 Press Photo of Fannie Brice waving from a passenger train in a Chicago railroad station. Courtesy: Chicago Sun-Times/ Chicago History Museum Archives

Popular piece of sheet music from 1922 picturing Al Jolson on the cover. Courtesy: Authors Collection

Photo of Sophie Tucker from 1917 sheet music "Sweet Cookie Mine."
Courtesy: Authors Collection

Bobby Clark and Fannie Brice performing together in a Vaudeville routine at the Rialto Theatre.
Courtesy: Dusty Sage

across the footlights, and yelled, "Get the hook." Fistfights in the front aisle broke up the comic monologues, and sometimes police raids carried them off to jail.

In 1920, the striptease transformed burlesque into a disrobing arena. The favorite shout became, "Take 'em off!" and bumps and grinds and G-strings competed with the sure-fire comic bits. Prohibition, the growth of Broadway revues, and an invention called "the movies" finally killed burlesque.

Now it's coming back again and the trouble is it's hard to find comedians who know the gags. "They don't know how to mug anymore," said Bernie, a man with what is called "a rubber face" and an inexhaustible bag of one-line quips.

He has a line in one of the skits when he mentions a local town, the one they're playing. He changes it to suit the place. Here, he starts to say, "Framing…" and pauses. "I can't say the rest of it, it's against my religion!"

He said that with tent shows there are no more stage-door Johnnies. "No stage doors – only grass. So, now they're grasshoppers. Mosquitoes are a bigger problem than mashers."

And the girls insist there are no more strip teasers in the business; only exotic dancers, ecdysiasts, tassel twirlers, Go-Go girls, and Bunnies.

And now it's *Minsky's Burlesque Follies*. It's educational again, and high camp."

"B" was also for a Biography – Irving Benson's. There was no date, nor was it accredited to any writer.

"From the time that he could walk or talk it was destined that Irving Benson would become the number one vaudeville comic in the United States. At age eleven he won his first amateur contest as a dancer. Acting came next and he kept busy at this until age twenty-one when he went into burlesque and became the youngest featured comic in this field. Periodically over a period of several years he did nightclubs and vaudeville, but always returned to his first love, the burlesque stage.

During World War II he toured with a USO Show, George Gershwin's *Girl Crazy*, playing one of the leads.

After this it was on to summer stock where he played starring comedy roles, in such plays as, *You Can't Take it With You, Boy Meets Girl*, and *Guys and Dolls*.

In 1962, while appearing in New York, Irving was seen by Johnny Carson and since then has been a frequent guest on *The Tonight Show*. During appearances on the show, Johnny Carson plays straight man for Irving, which is one of the highest compliments that can be paid to a comedian by a fellow comedian.

In 1964 Irving appeared at the Thunderbird Hotel in Las Vegas for producer Monte Proser as a co-star in *High Button Shoes* and *Anything Goes*.

Milton Berle and Bill Dana selected Irving out of over 200 comics to play Berle's "Man in the Theatre Box" (Sidney Spritzer) on *The Milton Berle Show*. Besides appearing as a regular with Milton Berle on his show, Benson has done over 20 *Hollywood Palace* shows with Berle as host, as well as with other stars.

He has worked for Harold Minsky for the past 17 years as Minsky's star and "top banana" and has appeared in the Minsky shows in Chicago, New York, and in Las Vegas at the Dunes, New Frontier, Silver Slipper, and the Thunderbird Hotels.

Irving, the elf-like comedian, has proved to the entire entertainment industry that the old adage

Irving Benson appearing on The Hollywood Palace show in 1969. Courtesy: Irving Benson

Backstage after a Minsky show at the Dunes Hotel in Las Vegas. From left to right: Dick Dana, Irving Benson, Eddie Lynch – stage manager at the Dunes and a part of the Minsky organization for twenty years – Joe DeRita, and Tommy "Moe" Raft. Courtesy: Pat Elliott Minsky/ Burlesque Historical Society

"big talent can come in a little package," is true.

Since Irving has had such great success on *The Tonight Show* starring Johnny Carson, *The Milton Berle Show*, and the *Hollywood Palace*; he has recently completed a pilot for Screen Gems, as well as Dodge, Biz, AT&T, and Cain's Coffee television commercials. He is now looking in the direction of motion pictures and television. Because Irving is a completely untapped source of talent in these areas it is a sure bet that both the television and motion picture screens will be filled in the near future with one of the greatest natural comedians of our time."

(Notes: There is more about Irving throughout this book. Monte Proser is worth looking up; he had an interesting career.)

The following article was added to the "B" Files shortly after Harold died. It was part of an obituary for comic Herbie Barris, from the *Las Vegas Sun* newspaper, dated December 31, 1977. It reads in-part as follows:

"Las Vegas Comedian Dies At 68; Las Vegas comedian Herbie Barris, 68, who appeared in revues produced by Barry Ashton and the late Harold Minsky, died Wednesday in a local hospital.

A burlesque comic, Barris appeared with Milton Berle, Charles Vespia, and the late Tommy "Moe" Raft during his career. He appeared in Las Vegas many times, frequently at the Silver Slipper. His last appearance was two years ago at the Hollywood Palladium in a show produced by Minsky.

A Las Vegas resident eight years, he was born September 19, 1909 in New York."

Herbie Barris.
Courtesy: Burlesque Historical Society

The following was a press release and titled, "Burlesque Comics DeRita and Scannell Tabbed for Minsky 'Top Banana' Billing." It reads:

"Old-timers and burlesque fans are looking forward to Harold Minsky's teaming of Joe DeRita and Frank Scannell at the Aladdin starting Friday, February 18, when the comedy duo are billed as the top bananas in *Minsky's Burlesque '72*.

Theirs is a limited six-week engagement, ending on March 29, after which the Bagdad Theatre star will be the winsome Mr. Tommy "Moe" Raft.

DeRita is world famous as one of the "Three Stooges." He joined Moe Howard and Larry Fine in 1958 after years of vaudeville and burlesque touring, and untold dozens of radio shows and movies. He was starring in a Minsky show in Las Vegas 14 years ago when movie director Henry King saw him and signed him to appear in Gregory Peck's *The Bravados*. Not long after that, he became 'Curley' in the "Three Stooges."

His straight man, Frank Scannell, has been in show business for over 50 years and that includes everything from burlesque and vaudeville, to 'legit' and musical comedy. During the past 25 years, Frank has appeared in more than 200 motion pictures and TV shows. His way with a comedy line earned him feature 'laugh-parts' opposite Phil Silvers, Red Skelton, Lucille Ball, Joe 'Curley' DeRita, and the "Three Stooges." One of Frank's notable moments in the film industry came in the hit movie, *Airport*.

The pair are presented twice nightly; 10pm and 12:30am, with three shows on Saturday at 9pm, 11:30pm, and 1:30am. The Rudi Eagan Orchestra backs the show. Reservations are suggested by Maitre d' Allan Chapin."

The photo caption that went with the press release reads:

"Aladdin Hotel: 'Curley' of the 3 Stooges and straight man Frank Scannell, Minsky Headliners at Aladdin.

Joe 'Curley' DeRita and his funnyman partner, Frank Scannell, are co-starring attractions in *Minsky's Burlesque '72* at the Aladdin. Joe joined Moe Howard and Larry Fine in 1958 to become one of the celebrated "Three Stooges." He has been featured in Harold Minsky's burlesque romps since 1950. Frank Scannell, a 50-year veteran of the theatre has over 200 television and motion picture performances to his credit. He has been 'straight man' for the likes of Phil Silvers, Red Skelton, and Lucille Ball. His most recent film credit was in *Airport*.

DeRita and Scannell are to be viewed twice nightly in the Bagdad Theatre at 10pm and 12:30am, and three times on Saturday; 9pm, 11:30pm, and 1:30am. Rudi Eagan's Orchestra backs the show."

Another press release found in the folder simply reads, "For Immediate Release, Please." It was written by Lee Fisher, of the Aladdin Hotel, in Las Vegas, Nevada.

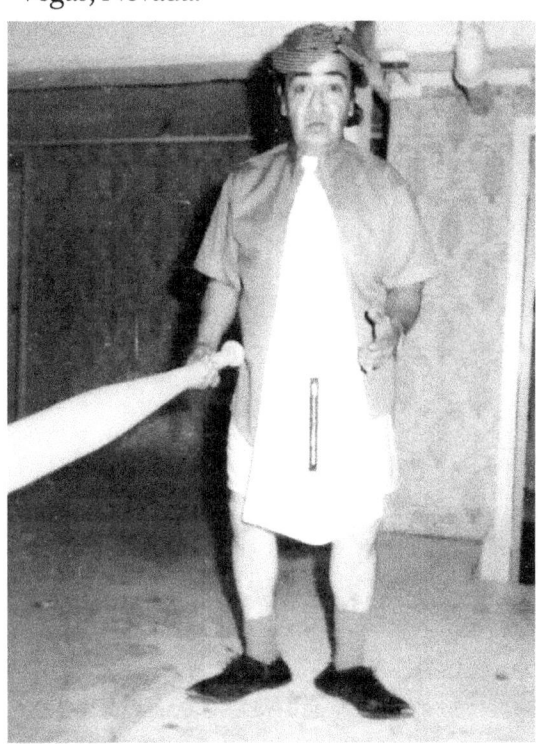

Tommy "Moe" Raft. Courtesy: Berri Lee

Tommy "Moe" Raft Labeled Burlesque's "Top Banana."

"This is a story about a "Top Banana." His name is Anthony Ray Bonefilio from Los Angeles, California. He is better known in the show biz world of burlesque as Tommy "Moe" Raft.

It has taken Tommy almost half a century to earn his reputation as the undisputed "Top Banana" or Number One Comedian in burlesque. After all, there were such old-time "greats" as Jackie Gleason, Lou Costello, Red Buttons, and Phil Silvers who earned their top-star status in the footloose land of bump-and-grind… Or lesser known comedian's comedians like Rags Ragland, Herbie and Joey Faye, Billy "Bumps" Mack, Joey Yule (Mickey Rooney's pappy), Harry Clexx, Jack LaMont, Irving Benson, or Al Ferris.

Tommy, star of the current *Minsky's Burlesque '72* at the Aladdin Hotel, slipping into his baggy pants backstage, reflects on his long career which started when

Rags Ragland. Courtesy: Janelle Smith Collection

he left Hollenbeck Junior High School in Los Angeles during the 1929 stock market crash. "Would you believe it?," he says, "I won a ukulele contest in Los Angeles at the Olympic Auditorium. This got me four weeks with Fanchon and Marco at Loews State at fantastic money, $250 per week. Imagine a kid, 16, earning that kinda loot in the Depression."

After that, he made his maiden bus trip. "I musta ridden nine million miles on buses," he chirps. The first one carried *The Hotsie Green Revue* to Denver. It was supposed to be a big national tour. The entire troupe was stranded. But Tommy was lucky. The manager of the Denver Rivoli caught his act, as they say, and brought him into his tab show, *The Rendezvous Revue*. Tommy started "doing bits." His salary slowly escalated from $75 per week to $100. A year later, it was $125. He stayed there almost five years, emerged a finely-honed burleycue comic making $175 and learned all the "shticks" he could from the masters of his art, including the generous clown-and-comic, Bozo St. Claire, who took a great delight in watching Tommy evolve as a promising comedian.

San Francisco got its first look at the 5 feet, four inch funnyman in 1936 when he opened at the Capital Theatre in Paul West's *Bravo!* The top banana in the burlesque revue was Al Ferris. By the time Tommy checked out of the show two years later he was earning $225 a week.

Few persons around, during the soup-kitchen days of 1938, would describe that period as "a very good year." Tommy says, "I lucked out; got me a good spot at the Gaiety Theatre in Minneapolis. Jack LaMont was the top banana then. I stayed six months and got two-six-bits ($275)."

In 1939, he made his Brooklyn debut at the Star Theatre. Irving Benson was the top banana. Tommy stayed three years. He practiced his pratfalls and double-takes; rehearsed endlessly on the "half-skull," the slow-burn, double-takes-in reverse, and all the bits of comedy mugging that were required to flesh-out the repertoire of a burlesque top banana.

And so it came to pass 30 years ago that Tommy "Moe" Raft moved into the big time as a top banana. Harold Minsky hired him for the Gaiety Theatre in New York. "Ya gotta understand that this was the same thing as an ordinary act playing the Palace," Tommy explains. "Here I was on the same boards where guys like Silvers and Ragland and Buttons and Faye had made big names for themselves."

The Gaiety was his home "until gangrene set in," which in Tommy's lingo means he stayed for more than three years. When he tried to enlist in the army for World War II, Tommy says he got one of the biggest laughs of his career. Only thing wrong, he comments, is that it came from the enlisting Sergeant. "Here I was 115 pounds of muscle and they turned me down for size. How do you like that?"

So Tommy toured; and how he toured. He says there is no city in this nation he hasn't been in. Some of the towns were so small he says, "They only had a street on one side." Whatever that means.

In 1945 he found himself working for Minsky again, this time in New Orleans at the Opera House. "Eddie Lynch was the stage manager," Tommy remembers. Two years later he was playing the Brown Derby Club in Chicago on Washington Street. "Ted Smith, the emcee got sick. That's when I found out I could be a master of ceremonies, too." Tommy and his line of chorines cured Chicago's blues for almost four years. When Tommy finally kissed-off Chicago, it was with regret. After all, "Chicago's gotta couple great tracks." To Tommy "Moe" Raft, there is only one major weakness, one major sport and one divinely important mission in life; to pick nine straight winners on a nine-race card. To him, the form divine is the Racing Form. He will tell you with an evil glitter in his eye of the day at Hialeah, "When I picked six in a row; Pow!"

Tommy was asked about the biggest 'yuck' he ever got on stage. It was the time he was playing the Garrick Theatre in St. Louis. He was playing a guitar in the act and

The Garrick Theatre in St. Louis, Missouri.
Courtesy: Burlesque Historical Society

moved closer to the lip of the stage to establish the true artist's search for rapport with his audience. There was an organ at the lip of the stage. But Tommy didn't notice that there was a two-foot gap between the stage and the pit organ. He disappeared behind the organ and dropped ten-feet into the pit. A cloud of dust billowed into the theatre. One could hear guitar strings snapping and popping all over the place. The din when he landed could be heard across the street. The drummer went down with him. The place was in an uproar. When Tommy climbed back up on the lip of the stage, torn, bedraggled, and grimy, the whole audience went absolutely ape with laughter. The manager happened to be in the wings during the fiasco. "Why not keep it in the act, Tommy?" he howled from the wings. With Tommy's fully-loaded, burlesque-burnished repertoire of choice stage "shticks," and terminology, the entire crowd was treated to a non-scheduled performance. In it, he mastered the essence of contempt. "The manager liked to die," Tommy giggled.

Baggy-pants and all, Tommy is in for another long run in the girl-filled Minsky extravaganza at the Aladdin; which thus becomes a living laboratory for anyone interested in the fine American art of burlesque – especially if the party happens to yearn to be a "Top Banana" one day."

Straight man and agent Jess Mack. Courtesy: Burlesque Historical Society

On August 2, 1971, Jess Mack, a theatrical agent who once worked as a straight man, wrote the following letter to Harold Minsky:

Dear Harold,

Both – Dick Richards, and Earl Van and his wife, are in Canada at present --- (different places.) Am trying to get in touch with both of them, and as soon as I do, will talk to them about Lake Geneva and get back to you. Enclosed find photos of Earl Van and his wife. He worked for you at the Slipper several years ago.

I am also enclosing photos of Monkey Kirkland and Ralph Clifford. Also Billy King – who does Tramp Comedy and has a couple

Earl Van.
Courtesy: Burlesque Historical Society

Monkey Kirkland, at age 25.
Courtesy: Lady Midnight

of good scenes, namely; the "Balloon Scene" and Abbott and Costello's "Who's on First" Baseball Scene. I had him with the Ann Corio show last year.

I have also been in contact with Steve Mills, who recently closed with the Broadway show *70 Girls 70*, he wants $400 a week, plus. I am trying to get him to accept $300. He also has a wife. So does Richards and Van… and I feel almost certain that they will ask for the food for their wives! If we get Van and his wife, then it will be okay because she will be the talking woman, and I will make certain that she agrees to work with the other comic.

Have you decided on a feature for Lake Geneva?

I spoke with Roland Muse on Saturday and we discussed Zianne in Miami Beach. She has an offer to go to the Place Pigalle Club in Miami. Do you have intentions of holding her over in Miami? If so, then I think we'd better issue her a

Billy King performing onstage. Courtesy: Pat Elliott Minsky/Burlesque Historical Society

In 1958, straight man Lee Clifford and talking woman Barbara Curtis backstage at the Roxy Theatre in Cleveland, Ohio. Courtesy: Barbara Curtis and Joni Taylor

contract before she accepts the Pigalle offer. Will leave that up to you…

I will keep you posted as soon as anything materializes here. Best of wishes,

Sincerely;

Jess Mack

P.S. Just want to check out the Straight Man again --- Ralph Clifford is working here in New York with Kirkland – and Lee Clifford is in Atlantic City until September 5. He too is a good man, and worked for you at the Slipper also. Will let you decide which CLIFFORD you want! Jess

Ralph Clifford wrote to Minsky on February 23, 1972:

Dear Mr. Minsky,

I have read that Tommy "Moe" Raft will follow Joe DeRita. Quite likely, he will do scenes requiring the strong support of a seasoned (yet not necessarily septuagenarian) straight man. I respectfully submit my qualifications for your consideration.

During my hiatus I have seen all the burlesque shows in town and yours is un-despicably the leader. Understandably, I prefer to be part of the Minsky Revue which represents the highest standards of burlesque.

With best wishes for your continued success, and looking forward to once again being a member of your organization.

Sincerely,

Ralph Clifford

I also found a resume for Looney Lewis in this folder. He had scratched off some information, and added new items by pen. This is what I learned: Loney, with a deleted "o" from his first name, lived at the Bryant Hotel at 54th Street and Broadway, in New York City, Room #305. He was 70 years of age, weighed 140 pounds, and stood 5'6" tall. The age and weight were scratched through – he had typed this resume up when he was 65 and weighed 155 pounds. His eyes were listed as blue-gray, and his hair as bald – wigs. He stated he performed as "Characters – heavy drama; High and Low comedy, and Whimsy – dialects."

He wrote: "This year marks my fiftieth anniversary in show biz. Prior to Broadway was the Top Banana in Burlesque."

Straight man Ralph Clifford and comic Jimmy Mathews. Courtesy: Pat Elliott Minsky/Burlesque Historical Society

Handwritten notes on Broadway included: "*Dreyfus in Rehearsal,* and *Unexpected Guests.*" Also: "*Foxy,* Stand-by for Bert Lahr; *Gypsy,* Hotel Owner – Burlesque Boss; *Two's Company,* opposite Bette Davis, Stand-by for David Burns; *Two on the Aisle,* Characters and Stand-by for Bert Lahr; *Jacobowsky and the Colonel,* Replaced J. Edward Bromberg, featured role; and *One Touch of Venus,* Detective, opposite Mary Martin."

Notes on Broadway tours included: "All of the above except *One Touch of Venus,* and *Two's Company. Do-Re-Mi,* Gangster, opposite Phil Silvers; *A Funny Thing Happened on the Way to the Forum,* National Company opposite Dick Shawn, also at the Riviera Hotel in Las Vegas, the David Burns role; *Diary of Anne Frank,* Kermit Bloomgarden Production, played the Dentist and understudy for Francis Lederer, lead; and *Ziegfeld Follies,* Pre-Broadway with Kaye Ballard."

Notes on Stock included: "Starred and featured in heavy dramatic roles, plus high and low hoke comedy and whimsy. In such shows as: *Fair Lady, Of Thee I Sing, Student Prince, Merry Widow, Brigadoon, Carousel, Annie Get Your Gun,*

I Remember Mama, Anything Goes, Naughty Marietta, Forum, and several heavy original drama try-outs, etc."

Notes on Television included: "Ed Sullivan, Fred Allen, Dean Martin, Lucille Ball, Ann Margret Special, etc."

Lastly, handwritten notes by Looney Lewis on "Last Four Seasons" included: "Starred for Harold Minsky for over one year in Las Vegas, and toured top Nightclubs across country. I have also performed in Grand Opera, Circus, and Vaudeville. And I recently starred with Mamie Van Doren and Denice Darcel in tent shows (theatre) in the round; Double Talk Expert."

There was also a note from Irving Siders in the folder, no date, with a newspaper clipping stapled to it, which reads:

Dear Harold,

The press was just excellent in Latham, Nevada. They grossed around $48,000 for the week which wasn't too bad. This may help to break the ice for a theatre tour next season which I have started working on.

Irv

In a 1978 handwritten letter, which accompanied this photo, Looney Lewis explained to Pat Elliott Minsky, "Am sending the only photo of myself onstage. The rest I lost in a fire." (The woman was not identified and I understand losing priceless material in a fire.) Courtesy: Pat Elliott Minsky/ Burlesque Historical Society

The newspaper clipping reads in-part:

"*Minsky's Burlesque Follies* is a fast-paced, slick production which reminds one more of a Las Vegas Revue than the musty offerings at the Old Howard in Boston.

The accent is still on comedy in the Colonie Coliseum presentation with Looney Lewis and his troupe of second bananas getting all the laughs still in the hoary old sketches of past years.

Looney shares the spotlight with Mamie Van Doren, an attractive former movie sex symbol whose singing voice is slight but warm in its handling of some of the latest up-tempo songs. Miss Van Doren makes two appearances, with her first being the most successful since she concentrates on singing, although she has an ingratiating manner with an audience." It continues on with:

"Tommy Finnan's direction of the production accents speed, and the show moves rapidly with dancing interspersed with comedy and a magic act that is quick and effective.

Mary Rooney not only performed under her real name, but also danced under the names "Chris Snow" and "Crystal La-Vegas." Courtesy: C.F. Miller

Fortunately, the comedy is highlighted and Lewis is a throwback to all the baggy-pants comedians of burlesque. His timing is excellent and he makes effective use of expressions and gestures. Lewis and his cohorts have a wild time with a first-act fight scene and later in the well-known "Crazy House" routine. His companions, Patricia Hall, Tommy Spencer, and Aldo Venturi, match Lewis in his pace and timing.

No burlesque show would be complete without an ecdysiast and Mary Rooney fits the bill perfectly. An agile dancer, Miss Rooney has the physical requirements for an effective performer of the burlesque art. Surprisingly, her act is the only moment of nudity in an otherwise tame production. Martin Kelly"

A similar, but much longer column was found online, regarding the same show, from a Schenectady, New York newspaper in 1971.

(Notes: Irving Siders, a producer who exported the sights and sounds of Broadway to theatres across the nation, died on October 13, 1999, at Mount Sinai Medical Center in Manhattan, following a massive heart attack he suffered four days earlier. He was 81, and never regained consciousness after the attack.

The son of a mechanic and shopkeeper, Siders grew up in Boston, and was educated at the Boston Latin High School before hitting the road at the age of 16. He "ran off to be a band boy," for pianist Fats Waller. Being on the road, was a city-a-day profession, which introduced Irving to the world of jazz, clubs, and show people. During World War II Irving worked on the docks, but after the war he soon returned to the music business, reaching a high level at Verve Records. He became a talent manager and booking agent, setting up tours for jazz performers like Ella Fitzgerald and the Count Basie Band.

In the mid-1970s Irving turned his attention to theatre, and worked as a co-producer on the Broadway production of *The Poison Tree*, which opened and closed in a single week in January 1976. He quickly returned to working the turf he knew best, "the road." Over the next twenty years he organized national tours of dozens of Broadway productions, from serious drama to musicals. It was his knowledge of Waller's music that helped him become a driving force behind the creation of the rollicking musical *Ain't Misbehavin'*. His credits also include the national tour of Michael Bennett's *Dreamgirls*. In 1987 he brought a tour of the show back to New York, staging a revival at the Ambassador Theatre. It was nominated for a Tony for best revival. He hoped a staging would make it to London, he told *Playbill On-Line* just two weeks before his death.

Apart from Broadway, Irving Siders work in the entertainment field included booking the talent at the Playboy Clubs and serving as personal manager for singers Vaughn Monroe and Bobby Rydell. He also worked with many of the major stars and star makers of the American theatre, including Harold Minsky. "He got along with both the Shubert's and the Nederlander's. There aren't too many people who can say that," composer Mitch Leigh said, of two of the nation's largest theatre owners.)

In March of 1977, Looney Lewis wrote the following letter to Jerry Lucas, which was also in this folder:

Hello Jerry,

Hope this note finds you and "yours" well. When last we met in that ill fated Hollywood caper, I, knowing that you always leveled with me, asked you why I was (as I thought) on Minsky's "shit" list. You assured me that the only thing wrong was my salary demands. There for the following may be of interest to you and Pat Minsky.

Enclosed is from my latest Broadway disaster. (Cost me six months of waiting.) Closed in one week and prior to that was another disaster for David Merrick, big show with Ruth Gordon, Sam Levene, and Avery Schreiber. Garson Kanin directed it; six months work which ran two weeks.

So – I got me a real good talking woman; looks real good, around 28 or 30 years of age, and a promising straight man. <u>And</u> because money was tight, I rewrote the "fight scene" where the referee is also the fighter. Thus saving the salary of a fighter! He, the straight man, also is a top singer that can really hold his own with the best. He can do a singing specialty or sing the girl numbers. Thus you have three people that can do your entire show <u>without</u> salary for fighter <u>plus</u> a great singer <u>and</u> they can be bought for a <u>reasonable figure</u>. My salary will be reasonable too.

Best regards to the Minsky family and yours as ever,
Looney Lewis

After reading his letter I dug back into the box of materials and found the March 1977 *Playbill* for *Unexpected Guests*. Among those in the cast with Lewis, were: Jerry Stiller, Zohra Lampert, and Robert Earl Jones, father of James Earl Jones. Lewis played Mr. Mullin; Annie Ives played the part of his wife. Some of what *Playbill* wrote about Lewis included:

"Loney Lewis (Mr. Mullin) is currently celebrating his fiftieth anniversary in show business. He began his career doing dramatic roles with the Washington Square Players which later became the Theatre Guild, but soon abandoned his dramatic career to enter burlesque as a comedian. After years of burlesque and vaudeville, he is still amusing audiences in nightclubs throughout the country. In addition to his acting career, Mr. Lewis is a professional portrait artist."

There was also a clipping from the *New York Post* dated March 4, 1977, which reads:

"The comedy, *Unexpected Guests*, by Wichita playwright Jordon Crittendon, closes Sunday, a $200,000 loss to producer-director Chuck Grodin and friends. Looney Lewis, onetime burlesque favorite, effectively played a father role. He was listed in the program as 'Loney Lewis.' "When I left burlesque for the stage, they took an 'o' out of my name and put it at the end of my salary," Lewis explained."

Unexpected Guests opened on March 2, 1977, and officially closed on March 6, after only six performances. *Dreyfus in Rehearsal,* with Ruth Gordon, also had a very short run, from October 17 through October 26, 1974.

Looney Lewis was not the only comic from burlesque who performed in *A Funny Thing Happened on the Way to the Forum*. Dick Richards was also involved in a production of that show. The following article, also part of the "B" File, was sent to Pat with the following note:

1/13/81

Dear Pat – We leave Toronto around February 1st and go home. If you have any opening for us – it would be nice to work a "Minsky" show again. Please keep us in mind.

Sincerely,
Lorraine and Dick Richards

"Fun With Dick and Lorraine," by Jack McIver; *Toronto Star:*

"After 41 years making 'em laugh on the burlesque circuit Dick Richards is still finding A Funny Thing Happened…

Dick Richards. Courtesy: Lorraine Lee

Lorraine Lee. Courtesy: Lorraine Lee

"It was a tough day, the day I was born. I couldn't walk, I couldn't talk, I had no hair on my head, and my parents wouldn't let me down. The worst thing was, I was unemployed."

Things got better for Richard Gluck, though. He learned to walk and talk, sing and dance, play the piano, and act, and he changed his name to Dick Richards. "It's such a catchy name, 900 other guys latched on to it." Finally, in 1939, he headed out on the burlesque circuit.

Heading out on the burlesque circuit at that time might sound professionally risky, if not suicidal – burlesque, after all, had turned the corner and was doing a slow spin into a brick wall – but Dick Richards persevered, and if he didn't become another George Burns, or Bert Lahr, he at least found reasonably steady employment.

His itinerary since those early days reads like a Greyhound Bus schedule: Baltimore, Toledo, Norfolk, Dayton, New York, Pittsburgh, St. Louis, and Kansas City. You expect to find Topeka and Cucamonga listed in it.

Sing and dance, play a little piano, pick up a USO show here, a cruise there, do a little stand-up comedy, steal a few jokes, borrow a few, write a few; "Anything, as long as it got a laugh," and work the rooms while the naked showgirls were changing whatever it is naked showgirls change.

Richards went wherever he could get work, warmer climates preferred, and somehow he spent a lifetime in a profession that's supposed to have drawn its last breath 20 years ago.

That background has brought Dick Richards to Toronto again. In the 1940s or '50s, he's not sure of the exact decade, he played the old Casino Theatre on Queen Street West, but now he's back, and, for the first time, he's working in the 'legitimate theatre.' Until the end of the month, the tiny, 5-foot-nothing, crew-cut comedian will continue to steal the show as "Senex, the Citizen of Rome," with the more-than-willing, if-not-particularly-able, libido, in *A Funny Thing Happened on the Way to the Forum*, at the St. Lawrence Centre.

The star, Gina Mallet, wrote that he stole the show as he scampered geriatrically about the stage, looking like a small boy caught with his hand stuck in the candy jar.

Richards, wearing a mini-toga, his bone-white legs bracketed by big old Bermuda shorts and sweat socks, is hilarious as the hen-pecked, lecherous Senex, but in real life, his bone-white legs bracketed by sneakers and too-short trousers, the 60-year-old Borscht Belt veteran is much happier talking about his skills as a cook and his other hobbies, jewelry-making and antique collecting, than he is discussing his career.

This star doesn't greet visitors in a Four Seasons suite, but in a rented apartment on Charles Street East, just down the road from the Waldorf Astoria. He's happier here – the apartment has a kitchen, and as he says, "I'm not at the mercy of waiters and restaurants; I don't even believe in restaurants."

Every few minutes, Richards gets up and prowls about the apartment, wandering into the kitchen, pulling back the drapes to gaze out the window, checking for lint on the rug; he's obviously uncomfortable in an interview situation, and keeps asking, "Isn't that enough?"

His third wife, Lorraine, a pleasant red-head, is with him on this trip. They've been married for 23 years. "If the fourth one's as good as this one, I'll be a happy man," he says.

He got the Toronto job 'by accident,' when one of those naked showgirls from his past mentioned his name to Marvin Gordon, choreographer for *A Funny Thing*....

He's enjoying the run, but thinks he got more laughs from his burlesque revues than he's getting with ...*Forum*.

Richards allows that he was born in New York to 'intellectual' parents, (his father taught engineering at Cornell,) that he attended the Julliard School of Music on a scholarship, (piano is still a hobby,) and that he dropped out of New York University to work a cruise to South America as a musician.

He ended up working the Borscht Belt, in the Catskill Mountains, but gave up the piano for the stage when he learned performers were making $25 a week, compared with his $12. "Then," he says, "I went to work in a burlesque show, and stayed in burlesque a long time. When burlesque shows fell apart, in the early 1960s, my wife and I took a job in the West Indies."

Things suddenly got better. Burlesque, in the past decade, has enjoyed a revival as a nostalgia item, and Richards has found himself in demand as a performer in revues from Miami to Las Vegas, from the Playboy Club in Chicago to the Roosevelt Hotel in New Orleans. "Still," he says, "If I don't have any work, I can be home a long time."

He and Lorraine maintain an apartment on Staten Island, (they have no children,) but he thinks they'll move out of New York for good soon.

1962 Press Photo of Red Buttons. Courtesy: Authors Collection

If you want Dick Richards to wax nostalgically about those good old days of burlesque, about working with Red Buttons, about how he never met George Burns, or about how Johnny Carson once saw him work the Playboy Club in Chicago, you'd better drop by his apartment and hold him down; he's in no mood for talking today. There he goes again, back to the window.

In fact, if Dick Richards never quite made it to the big time, if he never challenged Bert Lahr, Jack Albertson, or Jimmy Durante, as a king of burlesque, it may be because he's really just a shy little guy. And – an unusual characteristic for a show-biz veteran – a nice little guy."

Lastly, "B" was also for: burlesque blackouts, bits, skits, scenes, routines, or whatever you want to call them. The following is original material by comic Monkey Kirkland, who occasionally worked for Harold Minsky.

Monkey Kirkland. Courtesy: Pat Elliott Minsky/Burlesque Historical Society

Baseball Honeymoon

Cast of five:
Comic
Straight
Character – Man
2 women

PROPS: DRESSED BED, OIL CAN, SETTEE, CHAIR, TWO VASES, TWO SIDE TABLES, BASEBALL BAT, COUNTER, REGISTER BOOK, PENCIL, TWO BASEBALLS, BASEBALL CHEST PROTECTOR, BASEBALL FACE-MASK.

(Monroe "Monkey" Kirkland: March, 18, 1949)

(SET OPENS IN ONE; PULLS AWAY TO SPLIT SET – IN FULL) (BEDROOM AND LIVING ROOM)

(OPENS IN ONE WITH CLERK BEHIND SMALL COUNTER DISCOVERED ON)

Clerk: Well, this certainly has been a busy day for me, and my business! What a business I'm doing! Every room in this hotel has been taken except for the one next door to me. (NAME), the famous baseball player is staying here, and to think how fortunate I was to get him to spend his honeymoon here, at my hotel.

Comic: (ENTERS) Hey, jerk! You got a room?

Clerk: Have you a reservation?

Comic: What the hell? Do I look like an Indian?

Clerk: Here, put it in the book.

Comic: Oh no! I'm wise to you! I put it in the book and you (BUS) slam it shut!

Clerk: No-no-no! Your cognomen! Let me see your cognomen.

Comic: What, here? (STARTS BEHIND DESK TO SHOW CLERK)

Clerk: What's your name? Here, write your name in the book; right here.

Comic: (TAKES PEN AND WRITES) I. P. Brown.

Clerk: You don't say! (OR: You look healthy!) Maid! Maid! Show this man to his room. (MAID ENTERS WHEN CALLED)

Maid: Walk this way sir... (COMIC DOES COMEDY WALK IMITATING MAID. BOTH EXIT: BLACK OUT – PULL AWAY TO SPLIT SET) (MAID FOLLOWED BY COMIC ENTERS THE BEDROOM) ...now this is your room, sir. In the event that you want anything, just call me, and I'll come. Don't forget, if you need anything, just call me. (GRINDS, BUMPS, AND EXITS)

Comic: Can I depend on that? (BASEBALL PLAYER AND WIFE ENTER OTHER SIDE)

BBP: Well, here we are.

Wife: You know darling, I certainly felt as if everyone in that lobby was staring at me when we walked out of the dining room downstairs!

BBP: (TAKES OFF COAT, THEN TAKES TWO BASEBALLS OUT OF HIS TROUSER POCKETS) Look darling; see what I have for you?

Wife: Oh, just look at those two beautiful balls you have! (COMIC DOES SHOE BUS)

BBP: Look what I can do with them. I can bounce them on the floor. (BBP BOUNCES ONE BALL HARD ON THE FLOOR. COMIC DOES

BUS) ...and look honey! See how high I can throw this one... (THROWS BALL TOWARD CEILING)

Wife: Oh, my! It almost reached the ceiling. Gosh but you're wonderful!

Comic: Hell! You're telling me!

BBP: You know, dear, you might think that when a man reaches the heights that I have, that he would have things easy; but such is not the case. You have no idea as to how many women ask me to autograph my balls for them.

Comic: I never had that kind of luck.

Wife: You know, dearest, in the rooming house where I used to live, there was an awfully nice young fellow living there; but he only had one ball.

Comic: That's one for Ripley!

Wife: (PICKS UP CHEST PROTECTOR) What's this?

BBP: Oh that? I wear that when I play with the ball. That's a chest protector. Now you see, dear, when a ball hits me in the chest, it won't hurt me!

Comic: (JUMPS ON BED – DOES PILLOW BUS) Damn, Sam! It can't be done!

Wife: (PICKS UP FACE MASK) And what's this?

BBP: That's a mask. When the pitcher goes into the box, I put this on so that the balls don't hit me in the face.

Comic: Going into the box? He should have a gas-mask.

Wife: (HAS BACK TO BBP) Just think of that.

BBP: Honey, look at my bat.

Wife: (TURNS AROUND TO SEE BAT) Isn't it big and shiny! Is it an old one?

BBP: No.

Comic: Don't believe him lady, he's had it since he was born.

Wife: Let's play with your bat and ball. I'll sit over here, and you stand over there, and I'll throw your ball to you and you can give it a good sock. (COMIC DOES BUS)

Comic: It's a damned good trick if he can do it!

BBP: You know, dear, that when I get out on the field, I throw my bat over my shoulder, and you should hear how the women in the grandstand get up and cheer me!

Comic: With a bat like that, they <u>should</u> cheer you!

BBP: Look, baby, how strong and hard it is. (BOUNCES BAT ON FLOOR)

Comic: (BREAKS HAT – YELLS) Maid! Maid! Maid!

Maid: (ENTERS) What's the matter?

Comic: (PUTS PILLOW CENTER OF BED, GRABS OIL CAN, OILS SPRINGS – GENERAL BUS) Hey, maid. How about you and I playing a game of ball?

Maid: I can't.
Comic: Why not?
Maid: Wet grounds!
BLACKOUT

Doctor – Plumber

Cast of four:
Comic
Straight
2 Women
PROPS: DESK, TELEPHONE, PAPERS, STETHOSCOPE, CHAIRS, DOCTOR'S WHITE COAT, PLUMBER'S TOOL KIT, HALL TREE.
(Monroe "Monkey" Kirkland; February 27, 1949)

(DOCTOR'S OFFICE – IN TWO)
(PULL AWAY TO INTERIOR DOCTOR'S OFFICE. DOCTOR'S WIFE IS TALKING ON THE PHONE)
Wife: Hello, Operator? I want...(LOCAL 12340). Hello, is this the Pioneer Plumbing Company? This is Dr. Maloney's wife speaking. Would you send a man over immediately? The pipes in the bathroom are leaking. (HANGS UP AND EXITS) (DR. ENTERS WITH GIRL FROM LEFT)
Doc: Right this way, Miss. I'm sorry to inform you, but you have a very bad case.
Girl: You say it's very bad?
Doc: Yes, a very bad case of Leakage of the Heart.
Girl: Leakage of the Heart, eh?
Doc: Yes, and it's quite critical, too.
Girl: Is there anything you can do for me?
Doc: I'm afraid that it's beyond my ability as a doctor, to do very much for you. You have such a severe case.
Girl: Oh, dear.
Doc: However, there's an eminent physician from Paris who arrived in this country only a few days ago. Now he may be able to help you. In fact he may be able to cure you completely.
Girl: Where can I meet him?
Doc: Well, it's just a coincidence, but he's due here in my office at any moment, you see we have an appointment for a consultation.
Girl: Fine. Then I'll meet him here.
Doc: Yes, that will be quite alright. His name is Plumber.
Girl: Plumber?

Doc: Yes, Dr. Plumber. I've never seen him myself, but they say he's an exceptionally brilliant man. However, he is also quite eccentric.
Girl: Eccentric?
Doc: Yes. They say he likes to disguise himself as a tramp or a bum, and pretend that he is someone else.
Girl: That is being eccentric.
Doc: Now, should you meet the Doctor, please remember to do everything that he says.
Girl: Everything?
Doc: Everything. Don't forget that he's a genius, and besides, he may be able to cure you!
Girl: In that case, I'll do everything that he tells me to do.
Doc: Now, if you'll step this way to the waiting room, I'll call you when the Doctor arrives. (BOTH EXIT LEFT IN ONE) (COMIC RINGS BELL OFFSTAGE – ENTERS LEFT IN TWO)
Comic: You ring the bell and no one answers. What did they do? Draft the maid? I was sent here by the Pioneer Plumbing Company, and I hope that I'm in the right house...I hope...I hope... (DOCTOR ENTERS LEFT X'S COMIC) Hello Maloney.
Doc: Yes? And who are you?
Comic: Plumber.
Doc: Plumber! Well-well-well! How do you do Doctor?
Comic: (BEWILDERED) Doctor? What do you mean, Doctor?
Doc: Why, your disguise is perfect!
Comic: What do you mean? This is my Pershing Square suit.
Doc: Oh, I've heard all about your eccentricities.
Comic: Oh? You mean the wife and I? Well, we've split.
Doc: Just a moment, I'll tell the patient that you're here. Oh Miss...the Doctor has arrived. (GIRL ENTER LEFT X'S COMIC)
Comic: Hello, Babe!
Girl: Is this the great Dr. Plumber?
Doc: Yes, won't you be seated.
Comic: Now just a minute! I came here to fix a leak.
Doc: Yes, and you're just in time!
Comic: Well, where's the leak?
Doc: (POINTS AT GIRL) Right there.
Comic: And such a pretty girl, too.
Doc: Doctor, do you think you can stop it?
Comic: Well, I may not be able to stop it, but I'll plug it up a bit.
Doc: If you don't mind, Doctor, I'd like to talk to you.

Comic: (HUMORING; X'S) What do you want to talk about.
Doc: Have you got your stethoscope with you?
Comic: Have I got what?
Doc: I said have you got it with you?
Comic: I've always got it with me.
Doc: Always?
Comic: Yes.
Doc: Did you bring it from the old country?
Comic: Oh, yes, I dragged it right along.
Doc: I presume that you've had it quite awhile?
Comic: Oh, yes! I've had it all my life. You see it was a present from my father, (PAUSE) and I think the old man was Scotch.
Doc: Well, if you've had it all your life it must be getting old.
Comic: Oh, it's crawling up in age a bit.
Doc: Not too old?
Comic: Oh, hell no! Don't listen to rumors.
Doc: I thought that while you're working on the young lady, you'd like to use mine.
Comic: No, thanks, junior; I'd rather stick to my own, (PAUSE) I'm more familiar with it.
Doc: But you see, I have a new one!
Comic: A new one?
Doc: Oh, yes. My old one got burnt. (COMIC SKULLS)
Comic: What do you mean?
Doc: My office caught on fire.
Comic: How do you do, Dr. Maloney!
Doc: So I traded it in on a new one.
Comic: You can't trade them in!
Doc: Oh yes you can! The new ones are bigger and better.
Comic: I think I'll do a little trading in!
Doc: I'm sure you'll like the new ones. (HANDS COMIC STETHOSCOPE)
Comic: They are much better than the old ones. (BUS WITH STETHOSCOPE)
Doc: Well, I'll leave you two alone. If you need me, I'll be in the Ante-room.
Comic: Tell Auntie I'll be in later. (DR. EXITS) So, you're the little lady who's sick.
Girl: Yes.
Comic: Nothing serious I hope.
Girl: I think it is.

Comic: Well, I'll have to examine you. Come here. (BOTH DOWN FRONT) (COMIC PUTS STETHOSCOPE ROUND HER NECK) Two beers! (LISTENS ON GIRLS CHEST) Say, Ah. I believe you have too many clothes on.

Girl: You mean you want me to take off my dress? (REMOVES DRESS) (COMIC LOOKS AROUND, MUGS, CHASES GIRL AROUND TABLE. FINALLY AFTER BUS TAKES GIRLS HAND, BOTH TAKE DOWN FRONT, COMIC LOOKS AT GIRLS BREASTS)

Comic: I think you have a very bad case of mumps. You still have too many clothes on. You retire to the Ante-room, and take off some more clothes. I'll be in later.

Girl: I'll be waiting, Doctor! (BUMPS, EXITS) (DOCTOR'S WIFE ENTERS RIGHT)

Wife: Plumber?

Comic: Yes?

Wife: I've got a leak in the bath-tub.

Comic: Well, go ahead! It's your bath-tub!

BLACKOUT

OTHER OPTIONAL TAG-LINES:
Well, go ahead. I won't look.
OR
One place is as good as another.
OR
I've got to see that!
OR
It's your house. Do as you wish.

Pork Chops

Cast of four:
Doctor
Husband
Comic
Wife
SET IN FULL.
PROPS: COUCH, CHAIR, BASKET WITH WEENIES.
(Monkey Kirkland; June 14, 1951)

Doctor: I think the best thing for your wife is a complete change. Send her away for a rest. Her imagination is just overwrought. Here take this prescription and give her these tablets until you can find a nice quiet place for her to rest. (EXIT DOCTOR)

Husband: Thank you Doctor. Now honey, don't you worry. Everything is going to be alright. I'm just going down to the drug store for a moment, but I'll be right back. So you just lie there and rest. (HUSBAND EXITS)

Wife: (LAUGHS) He thinks I'm crazy. Ha! He's the one that's nuts. They can't kid me; I know that I'm Tallulah Bankhead.

Comic: I'm the butcher boy, lady. I've brought your meat.

Wife: Why, if it isn't the Count—

Comic: The Count? (LOOKS AROUND) Oh, the Count. Yes Ma'am, 27 cents please for the meat and I'll...

Wife: Why Count, how nice to see you. How long have you been in this country? Oh, I remember so well those nights on the Riviera when you played the piano for me. Please Count, play something for me now. Get the piano and move it over here. Look out, don't walk into the fireplace—-Now the stool-- (BUSINESS WITH PIANO) Stop!! Stop, do you hear me. It's my husband! He'll kill you if he finds you here. We've got to do something! Quick! Hide! Yes, under the piano--- Hello darling, I didn't expect you back so soon. Dear, you remember the Count? Count, this is my husband. What are you doing? Take your hand out of your pocket. I can explain everything. The Count was just going to play the piano for me. The piano was here and he moved it over there. Look out! (TO COMIC) He's got a gun. Don't you dare shoot! I'm warning you! I'll kill you first! There, take that. (GUN SHOT OFFSTAGE) Oh my God! What have I done? I've killed him! Oh please forgive me! I didn't mean to do it. Oh----- Listen! Do you hear those sirens? They've come to take me away. Don't let them take me away! Hello Officer, I can explain everything. You see, the Count here was playing--------------- They've got me in a cell--- (SCREAMS) Look—- a million rats! I hate rats! (GRABS COMIC) This is all your fault! If it hadn't been for you, this would have never happened. Oh, they've got me in the Court Room. What's that, your Honor? Guilty? What? The electric chair? But, your Honor, I don't want to die! Let me explain. The Count was going to play the piano. What's that? I've got to die? Very well, but before I go... Moe, sing me a song. (OFFSTAGE) Look down, look down, that lonesome road, before you travel on... Ah, that makes the going easier. Why, I could die laughing. (EXITS LAUGHING HYSTERICALLY)

BLACKOUT

Ghost

Cast of three:
Comic
Straight
Bit-Man (as Ghost)
SET: OPENS IN ONE; TO FULL INTERIOR OF HAUNTED HOUSE.
PROPS: SMALL TABLE, TWO CHAIRS, SMALL PAIL, TWO DOZEN METAL SLUGS, ONE BANANA EACH SHOW, SHEET FOR GHOST, CANDLE, AND MAP.
(Monroe "Monkey" Kirkland; April 12, 1949)

(OPENS IN ONE IN STREET-SCENE; COMIC AND STRAIGHT ON FROM LEFT)
Straight: Come on! You're always dragging behind like an old cow's tail.
Comic: I'm no hind end of an animal! Where are we?
Straight: We're going into the old haunted house.
Comic: Haunted house? Spooks? The hell with you!
Straight: A spook won't hurt you!
Comic: No, but he'll make me hurt myself.
Straight: You've never met a spook. You've never seen a ghost. You've never been intimate with a ghost.
Comic: Hell, yes! Three or four times.
Straight: You've been intimate with a ghost?
Comic: Oh! I thought you said a goat!
Straight: While we are in the haunted house, let's search for the pot of gold that's hidden there.
Comic: A pot of gold?
Straight: Yes.
Comic: If we find it we'll be rich.
Straight: Certainly. Come on, let's go. (THEY EXIT RIGHT, AD-LIBBING. PULL AWAY TO TWO. STRAIGHT TAKES CENTER, COMIC RIGHT. BUS LOOKING AROUND; STRAIGHT LIGHTS THE CANDLE. OVER THE MIKE: Whooooooooooo!)
Comic: That's all! (STARTS TO GO. STRAIGHT GRABS HIM AND THROWS HIM RIGHT)
Straight: What's the matter with you?
Comic: Did you hear that?
Straight: Yes, that was only an echo.
Comic: A who-co?

Straight: An echo! You see, everybody has an echo. An echo is a reverberation of the sound vibration of your voice. When you speak your voice goes out into space and rebounds. In other words you speak and it comes back and hits you. Watch this... Hello. (OVER MIKE: Hello) See? Now listen. How are you? (OVER MIKE: How are you?) See? Now watch. (CLAPS HANDS THREE TIMES. SAME BUS OVER MICROPHONE) Now you try it.

Comic: Hello. (OVER MIKE: Hello) How are you? (OVER MIKE: Alright. How are you?) (COMIC STARTS TO GO; STRAIGHT GRABS HIM) That wasn't me!

Straight: Certainly that was you!

Comic: Are you sure?

Straight: Certainly. Try it again.

Comic: How are you? (OVER MIKE: Shawkreft Du Shwinyock) Oh no! (STARTS TO GO; STRAIGHT STOPS HIM)

Straight: What's the matter with you?

Comic: I didn't say that!

Straight: Of course you did!

Comic: If I did, I wasn't looking!

Straight: Now use your hands... that should be easy for you. (COMIC SKULLS THIS BUS CLAPPING HANDS ANSWERED FROM OVER MICROPHONE) To hell with that! (STARTS TO GO; STRAIGHT GRABS HIM)

Comic: I didn't do that!

Straight: You certainly did. You can't fool an echo.

Comic: Can't fool an echo, eh? (CLAPS ONCE; OVER MIKE, ONCE. CLAPS TWICE; MIKE TWICE. CLAPS THREE TIMES; MIKE THREE TIMES. CLAPS TWICE; MIKE TWICE. GOES TO CLAP ONCE, MUFFS; CLAP OVER MICROPHONE. COMIC STICKS THUMB TO NOSE; LAUGHS) I fooled the echo!

Straight: Come on! Sit down. (STRAIGHT TAKES CHAIR BEHIND TABLE. COMIC TO HIS LEFT) There's a long story attached to this haunted house. Thirteen years ago an old miser lived here. Of course you know what a miser is?

Comic: Sure, a guy that eats mice!

Straight: No, No! A miser is a man who hoards his gold.

Comic: I know a lady that's got a million in gold.

Straight: Who?

Comic: Mae West.

Straight: How did she manage to save a million dollars?

Comic: She hoarded. (WHORED IT)

Straight: Never mind! Well, as I was saying, the old miser lived here and every night he used to sit at this table and count his gold piece by piece. (SLUGS POUR INTO PAIL ONE AT A TIME; THREE OR FOUR SLUGS. STRAIGHT PAYS NO ATTENTION TO SOUND)

Comic: Listen!

Straight: What's wrong?

Comic: Someone is counting slugs!

Straight: As I was saying, the old miser was counting his gold, piece by piece. (THREE SLUGS DROP INDIVIDUALLY AND THEN ALL DROP)

Comic: He hit the jack-pot!

Straight: Then one night as the miser was counting his gold, he heard a knock at the door. (KNOCK OFFSTAGE)

Comic: (GETS UP) Come in… (TO STRAIGHT) Hey! Someone's at the door!

Straight: This happened thirteen years ago!

Comic: That must have been the echo!

Straight: (VERY EXCITED) Now picture the miser counting his gold. He knows that someone is trying to get in, and he's right. It's two assassins of the night! Again the knock comes on the door, and into the room comes the murderers. One of the murderers has a dirk in his hand, that long! (BUS WITH HANDS)

Comic: How long?

Straight: That long. (BUS WITH HANDS)

Comic: (PUSHES STRAIGHTS HAND) Put it back, I saw it the first time.

Straight: The murderer plunged the knife into the miser's heart. (HITS COMIC OVER HEART WITH LEFT HAND)

Comic: (JUMPS UP HOLLERING) I'm stabbed! Take them off me!!

Straight: The miser fell to the floor dead! Drowned in a pool of his own blood!

Comic: Goodnight little children! I hope you sleep well! (OR BUS OF GROAN OVER MIKE, WITH COMIC MUGGING THE ACTION UNTIL A SATISFIED SIGH ENDS PIECE OF BUS)

Straight: But…

Comic: I knew there was going to be a butt!

Straight: They say that every night at the stroke of twelve midnight, the miser's ghost walks in this very room…

Comic: (SCARED BUS) What time is it now?

Straight: Five minutes to twelve.

Comic: Five minutes to twelve?

Straight: Yes, five minutes to twelve. (COMIC STARTS TO GO. STRAIGHT GRABS HIM AND SAYS) Where are you going?

Comic: I'm going home.

Straight: What for?

Comic: I forgot something.

Straight: What did you forget?

Comic: I forgot to stay there!

Straight: What do you want to go home for now? If you go home now you'll have to walk. Wait five minutes and I'll send you home in a wagon.

Comic: That's what I'm afraid of.

Straight: Remember! We came here in search of a pot of gold. Now if we find the pot, and it isn't filled…

Comic: Don't worry… I'll fill it!

Straight: (TAKES MAP OUT OF POCKET AND PUTS IT ON THE TABLE) Now let's look at the map. It will tell the location of the gold. (STRAIGHT KEEPS LOOKING AT MAP AND IGNORES COMIC; MEANWHILE, KEEPING UP LINE OF CHATTER ABOUT MAP. A GHOST COMES THROUGH CENTER AND SLAPS COMIC'S FACE, RIGHT SIDE, AND EXITS FAST. COMIC PUSHES STRAIGHT)

Comic: What the hell's the matter with you?

Straight: Huh?

Comic: Don't be a wise guy! I'm scared enough as it is without you slapping my face!

Straight: I didn't slap your face!

Comic: Well, don't do it again! (STRAIGHT GOES ON READING DIRECTIONS; GHOST ENTERS AND SLAPS STRAIGHT'S FACE ON LEFT SIDE AND EXITS. STRAIGHT PUSHES COMIC)

Straight: What the hell's the idea? Don't hit me in the face! I don't like it!

Comic: You got hit?

Straight: Yes I got hit and don't do it again!

Comic: Well, I'll be seeing you! (STARTS OFF AND STRAIGHT STOPS HIM) I'm hungry. I haven't had a bite to eat all day. (STRAIGHT TAKES BANANA FROM POCKET)

Straight: Here's a banana, eat it. (BUS COMIC PEELING BANANA; IE: ONE SKIN, TWO SKIN, ETC) (COMIC STARTS TO EAT BANANA AND STRAIGHT STOPS HIM BY CALLING HIS ATTENTION TO MAP. GHOST ENTERS TAKES SMALL PIECE OF BANANA, AND EXITS. COMIC GOES TO TAKE BITE, DISCOVERS BANANA PARTIALLY GONE. MUGS IT – LOOKS AT STRAIGHT)

Comic: The banana is for me?

Straight: Sure, I gave it to you.

Comic: Well, let me eat it!

Straight: Who the hell's stopping you?

Comic: If you want a piece of banana, ask for it!

Straight: I don't like banana.

Comic: Well, leave it alone then! (COMIC PEELS BANANA AGAIN. GOES TO EAT IT, STRAIGHT STOPS HIM AS BEFORE. GHOST ENTERS; TAKES ANOTHER PIECE, EXITS. COMIC SKULLS STRAIGHT, FEELS MOUTH, THEN PEELS BANANA DOWN TO LAST PIECE. STRAIGHT CALLS ATTENTION TO MAP AGAIN; GHOST ENTERS, TAKES LAST PIECE OF BANANA AND EXITS. COMIC LOOKS AT BANANA. SCREAMS, THROWS SKIN ON TABLE. BOTH JUMP UP AT SAME TIME)

Straight: What's the matter?

Comic: The banana!

Straight: What's the matter with it?

Comic: It's gone!

Straight: Sure it's gone! You ate it!

Comic: Well if I did eat it, it's the most tasteless banana I ever ate!

Straight: I'm wasting my time in here with you. You stay here and search for the pot of gold in this room, and I'll look in the next room. (STARTS TO GO; COMIC GRABS HIM)

Comic: You're not going to leave me here alone!

Straight: If you need me, just holler and I'll hop right back in.

Comic: Hop, hell! You fly in! (STRAIGHT STARTS TO GO; TAKES THREE STEPS. COMIC YELLS; STRAIGHT TURNS AND FACES COMIC)

Straight: What do you want?

Comic: Where the hell have you been?

Straight: I was just walking back!

Comic: Don't walk back! Fly back! (STRAIGHT EXITS OFF LEFT; AND COMIC WALKS DOWN CENTER. GHOST ENTERS AND GETS RIGHT BEHIND COMIC. COMIC WALKS UPPER LEFT; GHOST FOLLOWS CLOSE BEHIND. REPEATS SAME BUS TO RIGHT. GHOST REMAINS UNSEEN BY COMIC. COMIC TAKES ONE STEP BACK, BUMPS INTO GHOST. MUGS) Is that you (NAME)? Talk to me! This is no time to play jokes! (BUS FEELING BEHIND AND TOUCHING SHEET – STARTS, BUT LEGS WON'T MOVE. BUS TRYING TO MOVE LEGS. BUS TRYING TO MOVE HEAD. FINALLY MOVES HEAD SEEING GHOST. COMIC LOOKS STRAIGHT AHEAD; GHOST DOES QUICK EXIT. COMIC BUS OF TRYING TO CALL STRAIGHT; FINALLY REGAINS VOICE AND YELLS. STRAIGHT RUNS IN)

Straight: What is it? What's wrong?
Comic: He was here! He was here!
Straight: Who was here?
Comic: The miser's ghost!
Straight: You're crazy! Nobody's here but you and I!
Comic: I tell you he was here. A big giant, nine feet tall! His face all white and no eyes! (WHILE HE IS TRYING TO EXPLAIN TO STRAIGHT, GHOST ENTERS AND TAKES POSITION IN BACK OF STRAIGHT TO HIS RIGHT. BUS OF COMIC TRYING TO TALK)
Straight: What's the matter with you? (COMIC FINALLY TURNS STRAIGHT'S HEAD TO FACE GHOST. STRAIGHT SCREAMS; GHOST EXITS) Why don't you do something?
Comic: (BUS OF PULLING BACK OF PANTS) I did! (OR – I think I did!)
BLACKOUT

"C" is For...

There were two folders in the "C" File. One was titled "Chateau de Ville," and the other "Condado Beach, Puerto Rico." There was also a single article on Cindy Raft; it had no date. It was written by Esther Lynn, and titled "Former Strip Dancer is now a Talent Agent by Day – Wine Goddess by Night."

"Cindy Raft has show business in her blood... figuratively! Her mother, Tera, was a dancer and AGVA booking agent; her father, Tommy "Moe" Raft, was, perhaps, one of the most respected of the burlesque comics around. Proclaimed by many as "the funniest man in show business" and admired by Milton Berle, Danny Thomas, and the late Lenny Bruce, the sad-faced comedian spent more than 25 years performing in revues produced by Barry Ashton and the great Harold Minsky. When she was old enough, Cindy joined her father onstage, working her way up to lead dancer and line captain. She appeared with the

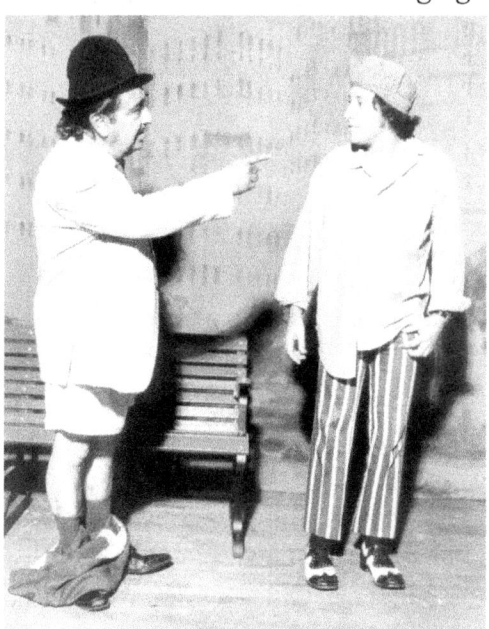

Tommy "Moe" Raft and Berri Lee appearing together in Minsky's Burlesque '72 at the Aladdin Hotel. Courtesy: Berri Lee

Top Banana in *Minsky's Burlesque* at the Aladdin and Fremont in Las Vegas, as well as around the Chicago theatre circuit. Tommy "Moe" Raft died in 1974.

In the 1980s, Cindy decided to expand her show business horizons. While still performing, she began serving as a talent coordinator for television and convention projects, doing choreography for and producing small revues, as well as booking specialty acts into Rocky Sennes, Frederic Apcar, and Dick Francisco productions. As her behind-the-scenes responsibilities increased, Cindy danced less and less, finally giving up performing to devote all of her time and energies to her growing agency.

These days, no, make that nights, thanks to the help of her competent assistant Sandy Dagel, in addition to her agency work, Cindy is back in "Show Business" – sort of. As one of the six Caesars Palace Wine Goddesses, Cindy contributes to the experience of the Bacchanal Room diners – giving them the Royal Treatment by pampering the gentlemen with shoulder massages and feeding them grapes and gifting the women guests with Caesars perfume – just like in the days of the Roman Empire. Cindy says, to be a "Goddess" is one of the most enjoyable jobs she has ever had – probably the reason she is still at it after seven years.

During the past year, the "Cindy Raft Entertainment Agency" has handled a number of the very big projects including events for Polaroid, Paramount Pictures, and the National Association of Television Producing Executives, who were honoring Emmy Award winner Kelsey Grammar. In addition, Cindy has booked entertainers Rich Little, (who has flown in on a Lear Jet for the party), and the dynamite combination of Foster Brooks and Las Vegas' own Babe Pier, (watch for an up-coming DIRT ALERT story on comic/impressionist Babe), who regularly perform together in Northern and Southern Nevada, Laughlin, and throughout the Florida condos circuit. Day or night, Goddess Cindy Raft is a busy lady who loves what she is doing and finds all of her jobs challenging and rewarding."

(Notes: Cindy Raft still actively runs the "Cindy Raft Entertainment Agency." She married Babe Pier on August 1, 1987; Pier passed away from cancer on July 31, 2012.)

The Chateau de Ville folder included an advertisement placed in *Variety*, dated March 5, 1975. It reads: "Minsky's Goes Legit in 1975. Always a Blockbuster in Clubs and Hotels, now bigger than ever in Dinner Theatres." The ad provided locations for all Chateau de Ville Dinner Theatres in Rhode Island, Massachusetts, and Connecticut; as well as the dates the show would be playing. It also listed additional dinner theatre productions including the shows in Grand Rapids, Michigan; Dallas, Texas; and in Valparaiso, Indiana. It went on to list performances at Playboy Clubs in St. Louis, Missouri; Chicago, Illinois; and the

Shoreham Americana Hotel in Washington D.C. The show was to be a full two hour long production, and the ad gave special thanks to Irving Siders.

Also in this folder were two copies of a RIDER dated February 4, 1975. One was an actual contract, including dates and locations; the other was a draft with notes written in pencil. It had a line at the bottom for an artist's signature, along with a line that had the actual signature of Jerry Lucas, the General Manager of the show. The RIDER appears to have been solely for the Chateau de Ville Dinner Theatre shows. In-part it reads:

This contract is for twenty-two (22) out of twenty-three (23) weeks with the following work dates:

Warwick, Rhode Island ---- 2/8/75 thru 3/23/75
Randolph, Massachusetts ---- 4/1/75 thru 4/27/75
Framingham, Massachusetts ---- 4/29/75 thru 6/1/75
Saugus, Massachusetts ---- 6/3/75 thru 6/29/75
East Windsor, Connecticut ---- 7/1/75 thru 7/27/75

Beneath that, written in pencil:

Extended – 4 weeks ---- 8/5/75 – 8/31/75 – 4 weeks

The RIDER continues on with:

The work week is six (6) days per week – eight (8) shows per week with no more than two shows per day.

Beneath that, in pencil was: 7,750.00 week

As one continues through this folder you discover the RIDER was definitely a draft because there were two different Agreements included. It appears the first, between Minsky and the owner of the Chateau de Ville Dinner Theatre chain, Gerald Roberts, was for a trial run involving two cities: Saugus, Massachusetts and Hartford, Connecticut. The second was for the run of five different cities. There was also a program included from one city; and between the trial dinner theatre runs, there were cast changes. So let's start with the first Agreement and the first cast; but first an introduction to Gerald Roberts.

(Notes: Gerald Roberts, produced theatrical productions and concerts in and around Boston, and later Los Angeles, was 80 years old when he died from complications of a brain tumor at his home in Brookline, Massachusetts on March 12, 2010.

Over the years, he worked with a range of performers including the Beatles. The group was setting out on what was to be their last tour of America, when a New York-based agent called Roberts, in 1966, and asked whether he wanted to produce their Boston appearance. Roberts eagerly said yes. He thought it would be ideal to hold it at Suffolk Downs, a thoroughbred race track in East Boston, and got in touch with Bill Veeck, a former baseball team owner who managed the track at the time. Negotiations ensued, and Veeck agreed to offer the venue to Roberts for $1,000, as long as Roberts paid his operations staff, and the requisite payroll taxes and insurance. The Beatles August concert was announced in an advertisement that ran in *The Boston Globe*.

The next day, Roberts's secretary got an angry call from Veeck. Roberts recalled in notes he had typed up, intending them to be part of his memoir someday, that he returned his call and after a barrage of choice expletives, Veeck screamed, "You never told me it was the Beatles." I was prepared for the onslaught and replied, "Bill, you never asked." After a brief pause, he roared in laughter and responded, "You ... you just conned a con man."

Of the Beatles, Gerald Roberts wrote, "I found them to be true gentlemen, an opposite of most rock groups and a pleasure to be with. The band was transported to the venue in a hearse, and then brought in through the stable entrance on the Revere side to avoid the throngs of fans."

Roberts grew up in Roxbury, and earned his bachelor's degree in accounting from Northeastern University in the late 1940s. After graduating he was soon working as an accountant for several Boston Celtics basketball players. In 1964, he helped client, Frank Connelley, secure a loan to buy a bankrupt theatre-in-the-round circus tent, the Carousel Theatre in Framingham, Massachusetts. The two became co-owners, initially putting on plays for children. He also booked acts for big bands and theatrical productions, producing shows for jazz greats like Dizzy Gillespie, Sarah Vaughan, and B. B. King. He often played chauffeur, picking up the stars in his Mercedes, and enjoyed telling stories about each and every one of them.

Roberts became completely involved with theatre in the early 1970s, teaming up with the Chateau de Ville Dinner Theatre chain to put on shows. The chain included five theatres in southern New England. After moving to Los Angeles, he and a business partner took over the Mayfair Theatre in Santa Monica. The theatre had opened in 1911, and was reopened in the mid-1980s as the New Mayfair Theatre. After an earthquake caused heavy damage to the theatre in 1994, Roberts moved back to Massachusetts, settling in Brookline. After retiring he took a memoir-writing class at the Brookline Senior Center, with plans of writing his memoirs – which sadly never happened. Gerald Roberts is buried in the Sharon Memorial Park in Massachusetts.)

What follows are the bodies of the "Agreements." The first copy was from 1975, parts of which were changed and initialed by Gerald Roberts. It was not signed by Harold Minsky, but it was signed by Roberts and Chuck Eddy, Vice President of the Associated Booking Corporation. The second, a "Memorandum of Agreement," was from May 18, 1976, and signed by both Harold Minsky and Gerald Roberts.

I

"This Agreement made and entered into this 20th day of January, 1975 between Chateau de Ville Dinner Theatres, Inc., hereinafter referred to as the Operator and Shokow, Ltd., a Nevada Corporation, hereinafter referred to as Producer.

Operator hereby engages the Producer to secure, provide and supply a package "Musical Revue" known as "Minsky's Burlesque" in the capacity of an Independent Contractor, for presentation in the Chateau de Ville Dinner Theatres in Saugus, Massachusetts and Hartford, Connecticut for a period of eight (8) (consecutive was crossed out and initialed) weeks commencing Tuesday, June 3, 1975 through (Sunday, July 27, 1975 was crossed out and initialed.) Exact itinerary of the two locations are to be agreed upon.

Each performance to last approximately two (2) hours, plus an intermission and shall be presented six (6) nights weekly, Tuesday through Sunday, and eight (8) shows weekly, not to exceed two (2) shows in any one night.

II

Producer agrees to furnish, and supply, at his sole expense, a cast of no less than fifteen (15) persons.

Producer further agrees to supply all costumes, shoes, hose and accessories, scenery, backdrops, props, musical arrangements and special material, and any and all things necessary for the presentation of the show.

III

Operator hereby agrees, at his sole expense, to furnish and supply the premises above (including all necessary items for rehearsals) and a follow spotlight and operator for all rehearsals and performances.

Operator shall furnish and pay for the orchestra for necessary rehearsal time and all performances for this engagement and the orchestra shall consist of five (5) musicians, with the exact instrumentation to be advised.

IV

For and in consideration of the package "Musical Revue" as above described to be supplied and furnished by the Producer, the Operator hereby agrees to pay the Producer the sum of Seven Thousand Seven Hundred Fifty Dollars ($7,750.00) weekly as follows: (The next four lines were crossed off and initialed by Gerald Roberts. It was all regarding payments being made to the Associated Booking Corporation, something Roberts was not willing to do; the following comment was added.) Weekly payments shall be made each Saturday to Shokow, Ltd. by (cashiers was crossed off and initialed) check or cash.

V

Operator shall provide and pay for transportation from Framingham, Massachusetts to Saugus, Massachusetts or Hartford, Connecticut, and also provide transportation from Saugus, Massachusetts or Hartford, Connecticut to the Boston Airport for all members of the cast, including luggage, props, instruments, etc. In addition, Operator shall provide transportation from the lodging site of the cast to the theatres and return for each performance.

VI

Producer warrants that he is providing at his expense, all insurance required by law, such as Workman's Compensation Insurance, etc., relative to his employees. Operator warrants that he will carry the necessary third party liability insurance to hold the Producer harmless from third party claims in connection with the presentation of said "Musical Revue."

VII

Producer's capacity herein is that of an Independent Contractor exclusively and in no manner, shape or form, shall be construed or interpreted as that of being a partnership, joint venture or otherwise.

It is further agreed that the Producer, as employer, is solely responsible for the payments of all salaries of all performers, including the required with-holding and unemployment taxes, and Workmen's Compensation Insurance relative to any and all employees of the Producer.

VIII

Operator agrees to use the registered Trademark I insignia, i.e. ® in all advertising including, but not limited to, table cards, lobby displays, billboards, newspapers, etc.

Producer agrees that it will use the Trademarks, "Minsky's," "Minsky's Follies," "Minsky's Burlesque," and "Minsky's Burlesque Follies," in the metropolitan area of the location of the engagement, during the term of this engagement and any renewal thereof, exclusively for shows produced by Producer for Operator. Producer reserves the right to inspect any pictures and written material for publicity and advertising to insure that said Trademarks are being properly used.

Operator and Producer acknowledge that no rights to said Trademarks have been or are transferred to the Operator by this Agreement.

Any billings by the Operator of, "Minsky's," "Minsky's Follies," "Minsky's Burlesque," or "Minsky's Burlesque Follies," shall be headline billing.

In all advertising, signs or billings, wherein the names "Minsky's," "Minsky's Follies," "Minsky's Burlesque," or "Minsky's Burlesque Follies," are used, the words "Minsky" or "Minsky's" shall be in larger type than any of the other words used in any advertising or billings. HAROLD MINSKY shall, whenever possible, be identified as the Producer in all advertising and billing.

The words "Minsky" or "Minsky's" as it may be associated with "Follies," "Burlesque," or similar words, shall not be used by Producer in any other capacity in the metropolitan area of the location of the engagement during the term of this Agreement.

In WITNESS WHEREOF, the parties hereto have set their hands the day and year first written above."

The following was actually on Chateau de Ville Productions, Inc. stationery. It listed Gerald Roberts as the Producer, and the address as: 161 Highland Avenue, Needham Heights, Massachusetts 02194. The telephone number was (617) 449-4150. It reads as follows:

Memorandum of Agreement

This Agreement made and entered into this 13th of May 1976 between Chateau de Ville Productions, Inc., hereinafter referred to as the Producer, and Shokow Ltd., a Nevada Corporation, hereinafter referred to as Show.

I

Producer hereby engages Show to secure, provide, and supply a Package Musical Revue, "Minsky's Burlesque," in the capacity of an Independent Contractor for and to the Producer, for presentation in the Chateau de Ville Dinner Theatre at: Framingham, Massachusetts, from July 10, 1976 to August 8, 1976; Randolph, Massachusetts, from August 10, 1976 to August 22, 1976; Saugus, Massachusetts, from August 24, 1976 to September 5, 1976; Windsor, Connecticut, from September 10, 1976 to October 3, 1976; and Warwick, Rhode Island, from October 5, 1976 to October 31, 1976. (Windsor is optional – to be notified by Producer by July 14, 1976. Warwick is also optional – to be notified by Producer by August 1, 1976.) There will be a minimum of six (6) performances and a maximum of nine (9) performances per week at the option of the Producer. The performance shall last approximately two hours, plus an intermission. There will be no performances on Mondays.

II

Show agrees to furnish and supply, at his sole expense, the items listed in the attached RIDER. Show further agrees to supply all costumes, shoes, hose and accessories, props, musical arrangements, with instrumentation for an agreed-upon orchestra, special material, and any and all things necessary for the presentation of a quality production at a level consistent with Producer's standards.

III

Producer hereby agrees, at his sole expense, to furnish and supply the above-mentioned premises and the items listed in the attached RIDER.

IV

For and in consideration of the Package Musical Revue as above described to be supplied and furnished by the Show, the Producer hereby agrees to pay the Show the sum of $8,250.00 per week (six days) payable on Sunday of each week after the last performance. Show will be paid $2,750.00 for July 10 and 11; and $4,125.00 for September 10, 11, and 12.

V

Show warrants that it is providing at its own expense all insurance required by law, such as Workmen's Compensation Insurance, etc., relative to its employees. Producer warrants that he will carry the necessary third party liability insurance to hold Show harmless from third party claims in this production.

VI

Show's capacity herein is that of Independent Contractor exclusively, and in no manner, shape or form shall be construed or interpreted as that of being a partnership, joint venture or otherwise.

VII

It is further agreed that Show, as employer, is solely responsible for the payments of all salaries of all performers, including the required withholding and payroll taxes relative to all employees of Show.

In Witness Thereof, the parties hereto have set their hands the day and year first written above.

Harold Minsky, President of Shokow Ltd.
Gerald Roberts, President of Chateau de Ville Productions.
May 18, 1976

The last item in the folder was a list of cast members.
Comics – Dick Richards and Lou Ascol (Equal Billing)
Straight Man and Woman – Eddie Innes and Ilona Adams
Exotic Dancers – Janet Boyd (Robin)
Specialty Acts – Berri Lee
Singer – Joseph La Vigna
Lead Dancers – Donald Crawford and Rhonda LaMont
Dancers – Barbara Sheehan and Christina Sheehan
Showgirls – Robin Duran, Barbara Hunt, Dona Reynolds, and
    Robin Zito

(Notes: Janice "Robin" Zito was born on February 22, 1952, and died from injuries sustained while trying to rescue a dog on May 29, 2009. She loved animals, and is buried at the Ogden City Cemetery in Ogden, Utah.)

The Condado Beach, Puerto Rico folder was dated 1973, but contained items starting from 1969. The first item was actually an Option Agreement entered into on March 14, 1969 between the Executive House, Inc., Condado Beach Hotel, San Juan, Puerto Rico, and (Minsky) Patava, Inc. The two parties were exercising an option on their original contract dated November 7, 1968. In-part the option reads:

"Commencing Tuesday, April 8, 1969, the Minsky's Follies Revue shall continue for eight (8) consecutive weeks through and including Sunday, June 1, 1969.

Operator has an additional six (6) consecutive options of four (4) weeks each:

First option must be exercised on or before May 5, 1969.

Second option must be exercised on or before June 2, 1969.

Third option must be exercised on or before June 30, 1969.

Fourth option must be exercised on or before July 28, 1969.

Fifth option must be exercised on or before August 25, 1969.

Sixth option must be exercised on or before September 22, 1969.

It is agreed and understood that the contract price per week commencing April 8, 1969 shall be reduced by One Thousand Dollars ($1000.00) weekly to a total of Eight Thousand One Hundred Thirty Dollars ($8130.00) per week. It is further agreed and understood that Seven Hundred Fifty Dollars ($750.00) per week shall be deducted from the contract price and sent to Associated Booking Corporation, 401 N. Michigan Avenue, Chicago, Illinois; the balance shall be payable to Patava, Inc., or its representative each week."

Image from postcard of street level view of the Condado Beach Hotel in San Juan, Puerto Rico. Courtesy: Authors Collection

It went on to say that the Executive House had the privilege of requesting a new show upon six (6) weeks' notice. If a new show was requested the contract price would be $9130.00 per week for the first eight weeks, and $8130.00 per week there-after. $850.00 per week, for the first eight weeks would be deducted and sent to the Associated Booking Corporation; $750.00 per week if the show was held over beyond eight weeks.

The Executive House would also have the privilege of requesting replacement Acts or Performers; however, if they made such a request they would be responsible for the roundtrip air coach transportation for any new performers from their point of origin, but not to exceed any distance greater than Las Vegas, Nevada to San Juan, Puerto Rico. It was also agreed that if Harold Minsky decided to change any of the performers in the show, then he would be responsible for their roundtrip transportation. The only exception in regards to this Agreement was the replacement of the girl singer which was to be made as of April 8, 1969; Minsky paid for those transportation costs.

The above conditions were the modification of the original contract dated November 7, 1968; the original contract was not in the folder.

The contract was signed by: Carl Devoe, President of Executive House, Inc., Harold Minsky, and Chuck Eddy, Manager of the Chicago Office of Associated Booking Corporation.

The next item was a letter to Chuck Eddy from Marcel Wortman, Vice President and General Manager of the Condado Beach Hotel. It was dated May 27, 1969 and reads:

Dear Mr. Eddy:

After duly signed by both parties, Condado Beach Hotel and Patava, Inc., this letter will serve as an Agreement to the following:

1) Our letter dated April 22, 1969 giving termination to Minsky's Follies as of June 1, 1969, should be disregarded and in consequences we are hereby giving full force to the Agreement signed on March 14, 1969.

2) We are exercising the following three options of four weeks each:

From Tuesday, June 3, 1969 to Sunday, June 29, 1969.

From Tuesday, July 1, 1969 to Sunday, July 27, 1969.

From Tuesday, July 29, 1969 to Sunday, August 24, 1969.

And an additional option of one week:

From August 26, 1969 to Sunday, August 31, 1969.

3) If the situation described in the third paragraph of your letter dated May 19, 1969, may arise, we shall share the cost of the Air Fare on a 50 percent basis.

Kindest personal regards.

It was signed by Harold Minsky and Marcel Wortman.

The last Agreement in this folder was entered into between the Executive House and Condado Beach Hotel, in San Juan, Puerto Rico and Harold Minsky on September 30, 1970.

Thanks to those who worked for Harold Minsky in the 1970s, this photo can be identified as the cast who performed in Puerto Rico. Courtesy: Janelle Smith Collection

The show was to be presented in the Fiesta Room in the Condado Beach Hotel for a period of sixteen (16) consecutive weeks beginning Tuesday, December 22, 1970, and running through and including Sunday, April 11, 1971. Each performance was to last approximately one hour and presented six nights per week, with Monday off, and a maximum of twelve (12) shows weekly. The off night each week could be changed with a two week notice; however, there was to be no more than twelve (12) nights of performances, consisting of two (2) performances each night, in any two (2) week period.

The Executive House had the option to cancel this engagement at the end of the first eight (8) weeks, or any time thereafter by giving four (4) weeks advance notice in writing of such cancellation. In the event of such a cancellation, they would pay Minsky $1000.00 per week for any unplayed weeks of the original sixteen week period. However, the penalty payment for unplayed weeks would not exceed $6000.00.

Minsky agreed to supply a cast of no less than fifteen (15) performers. He would also supply all costumes, shoes, hose and accessories, scenery, backdrops, props, musical arrangements, and special material necessary for the presentation of the show. Executive House agreed to provide two "prop boys" for backstage, and a follow spotlight and operator for all rehearsals and performances. They would also furnish and pay for two (2) – five (5) hour rehearsals with the orchestra, as well as all performances. The orchestra would consist of no less than eight (8) musicians.

Minsky was to receive $7500.00 per week, plus fifteen (15) roundtrip air coach tickets from Las Vegas to San Juan. If Minsky elected to provide a larger cast than fifteen, the Hotel would provide one way transportation for any additional cast members. If any of the extra members in the cast left the show early, Minsky was to pay for their return transportation. If, however, the extra cast members remained in the show through the completion of the contract, Executive House would pay for their return transportation. If any additional cast member flew into Puerto Rico from a city of origin closer than Las Vegas, their roundtrip air fare would be paid for by the Executive House, no matter what. The performers were all expected to stay at the Condado Beach Hotel throughout the run of the show. The contract also stipulated that $750.00 per week would be paid to the Associated Booking Corporation in Chicago; and both parties were responsible for their share of insurances, taxes, and complying with all union or guild regulations.

The contract was signed by Carl Devoe, President of the Executive House, and Chuck Eddy for the Associated Booking Corporation.

(Notes: Carl Devoe was a former partner of the law firm of Goldberg, Devoe, Shadur, and Mikva. He grew up on the West Side of Chicago, and worked his way through Kent Law School by teaching tap dancing. In 1945, he co-founded the firm with Arthur J. Goldberg, who went on to become Secretary of Labor under President John F. Kennedy, an Associate United States Supreme Court Justice, and an Ambassador to the United Nations. Devoe and Goldberg met while serving together in the Office of Strategic Services during World War II. In the early 1960s Devoe became the founding president of the Executive House hotel chain, which included the Chicago Executive House on East Wacker Drive. In 1981, the Chicago law firm was called one of the 13 great small law firms in the country. Carl Devoe died on March 24, 1997 in the Alden Lincoln Park Rehabilitation Health Care Center; Arthur J. Goldberg died in 1990.)

This folder also included some individual pages, with photos, that were ripped from the *San Juan Diary;* "San Juan's Oldest English Language Magazine Founded May 28, 1959." Tony Beacon published and edited the weekly tourism and gossip magazine. In 1975 Beacon relocated to Miami where he worked in local publicity, and attempted to set up a similar publication for the Miami area. Each individual page reads as follows:

"Delightful Dianne O'Connor, is the featured singer with the sensational *Minsky's Burlesque Follies of '69* at Fiesta Room – The Condado Beach Hotel's Fiesta Room is Girlville with the sensational *Minsky's Burlesque Follies of '69* setting up fun headquarters in the elegant supper club. One of the delightful attractions in Harold Minsky's big laugh-filled show is lovely Dianne O'Connor, featured vocalist, and a feast for the eyes along with a covey of lovely dolls who made Minsky Burlesque an American Institution. Beautifully costumed and sharply produced, *Minsky's Burlesque Follies of '69* is truly the show that made Las Vegas blush (but happily). – January 17, 1969."

"Gorgeous Linda Gable starts conflagration every night in Minsky's red hot *Minsky's Burlesque Follies '69* at Fiesta Room – Blessed with a mass of flaming red hair, a gorgeous body and a scintillating personality, lithe Linda Gable, a superb stripper, sets the Condado Beach Hotel's Fiesta Room on fire every night in the red hot *Minsky's Burlesque Follies '69*, a blockbuster show that is terrific at the box office. When Linda struts her stuff, you know burlesque will always enliven the entertainment scene. *Minsky's Burlesque Follies '69* features great comedy skits, blackouts, excellent music, and an acre of beautiful showgirls and fast-stepping dancers. – January 31, 1969."

"Here's what the well-(un)dressed showgirls wear in the sensational *Minsky's Burlesque Follies '69* at Condado Beach Hotel's Fiesta Room – The beautiful showgirls in the sensational *Minsky's Burlesque Follies '69* are now drawing capacity crowds to the Condado Beach Hotel's Fiesta Room where some of the most breath-taking costumes ever seen in a show in Puerto Rico. This statuesque lovely displays what the well-(un) dressed girls are featuring in the fun-filled revue. The dazzling dancing girls are equally beautiful in the lightning-fast Follies, complete with a gorgeous stripper and knockabout comedians. – February 7, 1969."

"Tantalizing Tulsa Denning torrid dancer in the spicy *Minsky's Burlesque Follies '69* at the Fiesta Room – Deliciously named Tulsa Denning is the delectable lead dancer who keeps ringsiders sitting at attention as she whirls through her torrid routines in the spicy *Minsky's Burlesque Follies '69* at the Condado Beach Hotel's Fiesta Room twice every night. Tulsa paces a flower garden of smooth dancing dolls and statuesque showgirls in the racy revue that is the best traditional burlesque fun. *Minsky's Burlesque Follies '69* has been a box office bonanza at the Fiesta Room for the past three months. – March 28, 1969."

"Sensational Suzette Summers featured Exotic Dancer in Minsky's Burlesque Follies Revue is back at the Condado Beach Hotel, and there to lend her striptease artistry to this purely-American entertainment idiom is the exotic Suzette Summers. A protégé of Harold Minsky, sexy Suzette closed recently at the Aladdin Hotel in Las Vegas in order to join her mentor's *Minsky's Burlesque Follies '70* in San Juan. Comic Looney Lewis provides the slap-stick, baggy-pants tomfoolery as he fends off the straight lines served up by Barbara Curtis and Patrick J. Burns. The vocal talents of singer Candy Graham, the skillful dancing of Dick Colacino and Ann Gubbins, boxer Ferd Fernandez, and a bevy of eight beautiful showgirls and dancers round out the fun-filled *Minsky's Burlesque Follies '70* at the Condado Beach Hotel's Fiesta Room. – June 26, 1970."

Barbara Curtis. Courtesy: Janelle Smith Collection

The folder also included one complete *San Juan Diary* magazine from January 24, 1969. This publication had a full-length article in the "Diary Nightclub Review" column about the Minsky show. No author was mentioned, but I suspect it was written by Tony Beacon. It reads:

"Titillating, tantalizing *Minsky's Burlesque Follies '69* is a blockbuster of broad fun and gorgeous girls (twice a night) at Condado Beach Hotel; a blistering Fiesta Room show complete with stripper and belly laughs. I have been a longtime aficionado of burlesque, but nothing I have ever ogled anywhere in the U.S. could equal *Minsky's Burlesque Follies '69* now blistering the stage at the Condado Beach Hotel's festive Fiesta Room, where cheering crowds are splitting their sides howling at this blockbuster show, a gags-and-girlie masterpiece by the genial King of Burlesque – Harold Minsky. Sensational is the only word to describe this tobasco-flavored revue, complete with stripper, belly laughs, and a platoon of gorgeous long-stemmed dancers and showgirls who light up the Fiesta Room stage like a fireworks display! Broad comedy is the hallmark of burlesque and Minsky has been quite astute in maintaining this tradition in his rang-dang-do show at the

Fiesta Room. The staging, costuming and music glitter with high professional polish, but a boatload of ad libs and waggery keeps the show on a delightfully informal plane – and the capacity audience eats it up. Now hear this: *Minsky's Burlesque Follies '69* is being presented twice nightly (at 10pm and 12:30am) to accommodate the vast audiences attracted by the magic of the famous Minsky name. That's the tipoff on a great show. The standard burlesque pattern is followed and herein lies the secret of the many years of success of the Minsky shows. Today, there are certain producers who disdain the word burlesque, but those who have adopted this style of presentation usually have hit shows. Minsky's is not merely a show it is an institution! After the zippy overture is played by the Pepito Torres Orchestra in Broadway style, *Minsky's Burlesque Follies '69* erupts in an explosion of beautifully constructed charmers who are living dreams in eye-popping costumes of gold glitter, filmy ostrich feathers – and little else! I'll tell you right now that these dolls are as gorgeous as any dancers and showgirls ever to appear in a San Juan nightclub; and the dancers can really dance, too! While pretty (and stacked) blonde Dianne O'Connor sings "I Believe in You," the girls are joined by fantastic male dancing star Michel Stany, (what a physique for the ladies in the room to ogle), and stunning lead dancer Tulsa Denning in a wild strip act in which Stany starts taking off his tie, his belt, and shirt, and intersperses his own stripping by removing the feathers adorning Tulsa, (love that name), and pretty soon she is revealed in such brief attire that it can all be placed in a pillbox! When Tulsa starts dancing with that luscious body the room temperature soars. This is an adult show, boys and girls. Laura Del Mar, Carol Smith, and Kathie Ruth are the delectable dancing dolls and they can really swing. Those whistle-bait-figured showgirls return in slightly concealing but most revealing costumes to undulate sexily while Dianne O'Connor sings, "I've Got to Travel On," in jump tempo. These dancers and showgirls are not merely exquisite decorations in the revue, they are talented performers, adding flash and dash to the spicy action. By this time, the crowd is in a highly receptive mood and when comedian Dick Bernie, ably abetted by straight man Bert Gehan, takes the spotlight, you know this is pure, unadulterated burlesque! Dick shatters your laugh nerves with his broad and risqué bits about being in jail for 30 days, statutory rape, wives, his wife posing for a house painter, a letter from his wife, and his job as a private eye. Bernie and Gehan are joined by blondelicious straight woman Bobbye Mack, (and how she can be called a straight woman with all those curves is beyond me). Bobbye wants Bernie and Gehan to find her lost twin sister, Sophia Plunk. Taking notes, Bernie garbles it into "lost sin twister." Bobbye offers a big reward and the scene climaxes in a rib-smashing blackout. Great! The ravishing dancing girls melt the stage in vary-colored, peek-a-boo harem costumes as Dianne (in blue see-through pantaloons) sings about "Fabulous Places." Michel Stany dances lithely in gold and white. As Dianne swings on "Hajji Baba," the fire-and-ice showgirls (all collectors' items) literally make male eyes bulge as they parade in sensational costumes that scream sexiness. To remove the suspense for the "Bashful Bachelor Brigade," the girls are Sandra Carter, Marian Marlo, Lori Field, Lynn Brooks, Bo Kapp, and a mysterious girl from Czechoslovakia whose first name is Eva, but who refuses to give her last name. These charmers range from tall to short, and from blonde to brunette to redhead – and all are terrific. Michel Stany and Tulsa Denning, plus dancers Laura Del Mar, Carol Smith, and Kathie Ruth, send the club up in flames with their torrid twerking. So far, the show is a smash hit, but when beautiful, flame-haired Linda Gable undulates onstage to perform her celebrated strip it's time to bar the doors (to keep Linda from getting away)! Clad in a white gown with white fur stole Linda is a dream and when she peels off the stole and the gown and wiggles into a gauzy negligee, she adds more red cells to the pounding blood of every guy in the room. In pink light Linda is a vision of visions to behold as she dances to "Don't Go Away Mad." Wowie! I am still laughing at the tremendously funny "School Days" skit, featuring Dick Bernie, Bobbye Mack, Bert Gehan, Tulsa Denning, and Laura Del Mar. With shapely Bobbye as the teacher and the others as students, this routine is a masterpiece of double meanings on innocent words. The answer to how now brown cow will not be repeated here. Bernie can't win because every time he makes a crack, Bobbye smashes him on the noggin with a rolled newspaper – typical burlesque howls. Gehan's spelling of Mississippi will fracture you, and Dick's spelling of cat is wild. The poetry session is a rowdy exercise in verification that must be seen. In the "English Lesson," the words ascot and Messrs. Damon and Pythias are given titillating definitions. The blackout with a kiss involving Bernie, Gehan, and Bobbye, makes everyone literally fall in the aisles with laughter. Michel Stany and the four dancing dolls scorch the stage in a cleverly conceived routine, and then Stany and Tulsa Denning start a conflagration of their own with their fiery and sensual dancing. Dianne O'Connor sings "After Tears Comes Laughter," while the showgirls light up the stage again in gold glitter wraps, then Dianne segues into "The Beat Goes On," and the smooth sexy showgirls remove the wraps to stand revealed in pert pantaloons and little else – for the most delicious costuming I've ogled in a long, long time to sock over a red hot finale. This is a fast, wacky and funderful show that makes an hour seem more like minutes. I have a notion a lot of guys from every hotel in town are going to reserve tables for both the 10pm and 12:30am show, with countless repeaters. Special credit goes to superb choreographer Jerry Norman, who has a terrific dancing unit; he even has the showgirls executing their routines with the skill of dancers. While praise must also go to hard-working stage manager Jerry Lucas, who manages to bring some degree of order to the frenzy backstage. This

Bobbye Mack. Courtesy: Pat Elliott Minsky/Burlesque Historical Society

show has everything – and then some. A special Beacon Bouquet to Condado Beach General Manager Marcel Wortman for engaging the sensational *Minsky's Burlesque Follies '69* for a long run at the Fiesta Room. This is a glittering, girl-studded show that proves conclusively that there's nothing better than a dame! See this show as often as Maitre D' Ernesto Velez can get you a reservation! A nightlife must!"

(Notes: The above article was written as a single paragraph. I left MOST of the punctuation alone, but some of the run-on sentences were too much for me. What really floored me were the words in bold type, which made absolutely no sense. Every few words something appeared in bold type, words like: platoon, broad, hallmark, tipoff, hit institution, ladies, brief, pillbox, not, jail, twin, poetry, hour, minutes, and order. Those are just a few of them; plus the author of the review created his own words – watch for them.)

The other item in this folder was a dinner menu and wine list from the *Minsky's Burlesque Follies '69*. You would have enjoyed seeing the prices; sadly, it was destroyed in the fire!

"D" is For...

"D" starts us out with "The Dunes Hotel, 1957 – 1961." This File contained a few newspaper articles and the actual Agreement dated May 10, 1959, between M & R Investment Company, Inc., and Harold Minsky.

Postcard of the Dunes – you can't miss the Sheik. Courtesy: Authors Collection

Anyone researching the Dunes Hotel and Casino will find a few different versions; but all are very similar. For a little background on the Dunes, I have pieced together the following:

In the early 1950s, the Tax Commission in Las Vegas, the casino industry's governing body, was flooded with proposals for new hotels. In August 1953, the commission deferred acting on four gambling licenses, representing more than $15 million in new investment, pending on receiving more information about the projects' finances. The original names of the four potential properties may be unfamiliar to history buffs, and only three ultimately opened their doors. The Casa Blanca Hotel, planned for the Strip (Highway 91) and Race Track Road, would be owned by brothers David, Meyer, and Louis Gensburg (who owned the land), and a combination of businessmen, including two of the Marx Brothers, Harpo (Arthur) and Gummo (Milton). The Araby, slated for land across the highway from the Flamingo, was fronted by Rhode Island restaurateur Joseph Sullivan (many people thought he was a front man for Raymond Patriarca of the New England crime family); Al Gottesman, a Floridian who formerly owned a chain of theatres, and Bob Rice, a costume jewelry dealer. Lastly, the Sunrise, a project slated for north of the Last Frontier, was headed by Los Angeles hotelier Frank Fishman.

Portion of the 1932 sheet music cover from the film Horse Feathers *starring the Marx Brothers. The song, "Everyone says I Love You." Courtesy: Authors Collection*

None of these hotels opened under their original names. The Casa Blanca Hotel morphed into the Riviera, and Race Track Road became Riviera Boulevard. The Araby kept its Middle Eastern theme but opened as the Dunes. The Sunrise became the Royal Nevada, and did open, but not with its original owner. Lastly, the Desert Spa, the fourth potential property, became an obscure piece of Las Vegas trivia.

Of the seven resorts that were scheduled to open in 1955, none ended the year with their original owners or management. Two did not open, although the Stardust ultimately did; two others almost closed before the year was out, and the remaining three — Riviera, Dunes, and the New Frontier — became viable casinos but only after significant changes.

The Dunes debuted on May 23, 1955. Its opening show didn't quite match the star power at the New Frontier or Riviera, but its stage was wider than any in town, with enough room for forty chorus girls, and its dinner theatre was the first in Las Vegas to add balcony seating. Al Gottesman, who was in charge of entertainment, opted for a revue titled *New York — Paris —Paradise*, which starred dancer Vera-Ellen. With only 194 rooms, the Dunes was smaller than the other properties on the Strip, and its chief owners had no experience with gambling, although they had hired a staff with extensive hotel and restaurant experience. The Dunes boasted that it had the country's largest swimming pool, and the 30-foot fiberglass sultan, (designed by YESCO,) that welcomed new arrivals, gave the resort an identity. However, that was not enough to bring in the visitors. The casino struggled immediately, and the public firing of headliner Wally Cox, after a disappointing July debut, brought the hotel the wrong kind of attention.

Photo of the Genie while it was still on the hotel.
Courtesy: Burlesque Historical Society

Several other Las Vegas properties, at this time, were struggling as well. The Dunes owners, eager to cut their losses, leased their new casino to the operators of the Sands, led by Jake Freeman. An attorney for Gottesman, Sullivan, Rice, and the other major Dunes investors cited a "persistent losing streak" at the casino as the reason for its financial difficulties, but in fact players were too scarce. Having less than 200 rooms severely handicapped the resort to provide much income for the casino, even if the house had been unlucky.

The Sands hoped to turn around the Dunes fortunes by replicating its own success, based in no small part on quality entertainment. Frank Sinatra, riding on a camel, kicked off the "new" Dunes three-day Arabian Nights themed opening celebration in early September. Sands entertainment director, Jack Entratter, took over booking duties for the Dunes as well, but aside from opening night with Sinatra, he kept the big named entertainment for the Sands. In November, for instance, Billy Gray and Georgia Gibbs headlined the Dunes, while Nat King Cole was the top attraction at the Sands. Under Sands management, the Dunes didn't improve; the following year, Sands executives declined to renew their lease, and for a time the $5 million resort operated without its casino.

Press Photo from September 12, 1955 of Frank Sinatra surrounded by harem girls as he presided over the festivities at the reopening of the Dunes Hotel. He arrived on a camel. Courtesy: Authors Collection

April 1956 Press Photo of Teamster Boss Dave Beck giving his blessing to heir apparent Jimmy (Jimmie) Hoffa. Courtesy: Authors Collection

In 1956, the Dunes was sold to James "Jake" Gottlieb, whose Chicago freight company (Western Transportation) had received a business loan from the Teamsters Union Pension Fund controlled by labor boss James Riddle "Jimmy" Hoffa. Gottlieb, who allegedly had ties to organized crime figures in Chicago, sold a small interest in the hotel to a fellow Chicagoan, Major A. Riddle. Riddle, a nightclub and Indiana trucking company owner, may have also had ties to the "Chicago Outfit." The pension fund, which Hoffa used to help bankroll additional Las Vegas casinos, loaned Gottlieb and Riddle $4 million.

While Riddle was making up his mind as to whether or not he should actually take an interest in the hotel, he got a phone call from Bill Miller. Miller was an old pro at booking entertainment. While at the Sahara, he put that hotel on firm financial ground with his booking of lounge acts like Louis Prima and Keely Smith, as well as showroom headliners such as Marlene Dietrich. "He encouraged me about the possibility of bringing top acts to the hotel. So through his insistence, we formed M & R Investment Company with Miller as President and myself as Vice President. However, about a year later we began to disagree about the running of the hotel. So I bought him out," Major Riddle told George Stamos, in a 1979 interview.

1945 sheet music featuring Louis Prima. Courtesy: Authors Collection

Sheet music from the 1930 film The Blue Angel, starring Emil Jannings with Marlene Dietrich. Courtesy: Authors Collection

Accepting the deal, and the money, Riddle added rooms, and in early 1957 brought the *Minsky's Follies* to the resort; the first show to feature bare breasted showgirls in Nevada. The first of the *Minsky's Follies* series debuted on January 10, 1957, with *Minsky Goes to Paris*. The show reopened the Arabian Room and featured Lou Costello, of Abbott and Costello fame, as the star.

The uproar was immediate from the local Catholic priests and the "Legion of Decency," to the city and county officials who were fielding a multitude of angry phone calls, and to the halls of the State Legislature. "Bare breasted girls onstage in Las Vegas, we can't have that!" The newspaper editorials were filled with column after column denouncing the move away from wholesome entertainment. With straight faces they

1948 Press Photo of Bud Abbott and Lou Costello. Courtesy: Burlesque Historical Society

worried that it would bring the wrong element to Las Vegas. Miller and Riddle didn't care, the show was a big success. In the first week alone it set a record for turnout which stood until the 1990s; 16,000 people attended the Minsky show at the Dunes. The show ran for an unprecedented six weeks, and people were more than happy to stay around and gamble after seeing the show. Minsky's Follies, in various editions, played the Dunes for the next four and a half years. Pinky Lee, a vaudevillian comic and television host, was the star of the Minsky's Follies in the summer of 1958. Lee broke Lou Costello's six-week run record by being held over to standing room only crowds for eight weeks. In May 1959, Harold Minsky signed a two-year contract extension to continue to produce shows for the Dunes. The contract paid $100,000 a year.

The innovations that Riddle was implementing, though, cost money, and he needed more cash. Casinos typically found they could rely on only two sources when finances were limited: the Teamsters Union Pension Fund or the Bank of Las Vegas, operated by E. Parry Thomas, who represented a group of Utah bankers. Thomas reasoned that Las Vegas casino executives would respond in kind if treated like legitimate businessmen. He was right, but often faced critics

Front and back of the Pinky Lee postcard from the Dunes Hotel. This postcard was promoting the Minsky show which was performing at the Dunes. Courtesy: Authors Collection

1962 Press Photo of Elvis Presley and Major A. Riddle. Courtesy: Authors Collection

stating he was nothing more than a "mob banker." In 1962, Riddle went looking for investors. He decided to sell 50 percent of his stock to veteran gamblers Sid Wyman and Charles Rich, as well as Wendell Fletcher and George Duckworth. Duckworth had invested as well, at various times, in the Sands, the Riviera, and the Royal Nevada hotels.

In May 1964, the beloved "Sheik" was removed from the roof of the Dunes hotel and placed into storage. The hotel also underwent structural changes as the new "Diamond" tower began to rise. Gottlieb flew to Las Vegas frequently from Chicago, solely to chart the progress of the tower; he approved everything. He also worked with Riddle to upgrade the clientele of the hotel. Both men wanted to attract well-heeled gamblers and high-rollers. Major Riddle even worked out a contract with junket entrepreneur, and Las Vegas legend, Julius "Big Julie" Weintraub to bring East Coast gamblers to the Dunes.

Dunes postcard from Las Vegas with the Genie showing the back way, past the golf course. The Genie stood forty feet high. Courtesy: Authors Collection

The "Sheik" would be brought out of storage once the new interstate highway, I-15, was completed. He would be placed on the back of the golf course near the highway exit for Dunes Road amid hopes it would encourage motorists to use that exit for the Dunes Hotel.

In 1968, Riddle executed an exchange of stock with M & R Investment and Continental Connector Company located in Brooklyn, New York. As a result, Continental Connector Company became the parent corporation. Not long after that, Meshulam Riklis and Isidore Becker, owners of the American International Travel Service and the Riviera Hotel and Casino, purchased 30 percent of Continental Connector Company stock to gain control of the hotel. Riddle, however, blocked them by teaming with Irving J. Kahn, a prominent Dunes stockholder.

After Kahn's death in 1973, his attorney, Morris Shenker, arranged with Kahn's estate to buy his interest in the Continental Connector Company. The Teamsters Central States Pension Fund loaned Shenker the money he needed to gain control of the Dunes; thus, he became Chairman of the Board and Chief Controlling Officer. Shenker and Riddle continued to work together as the 1960s came to close. They had big plans for the Dunes as a new decade was dawning.

As the 1970s dawned, rumors ran rampant that Howard Hughes was interested in buying the Dunes property. Hughes had come to town in 1966 for a brief visit. The brief visit turned into a much longer stay and Hughes purchased the Desert Inn rather than move out of the penthouse. Since then, he had been buying various Strip properties including the Sands and the Frontier. With Hughes most recent purchase, the Castaways, he struggled in his negotiations with the Nevada Gaming Board for a gaming license. Hughes was informed that he was teetering on a monopoly and would not be approved. So he offered to remove gaming from the

1975 Press Photo of Morris Shenker.
Courtesy: Authors Collection

Castaways in exchange for purchasing the Dunes. The Nevada Gaming Board said no.

In 1976, Morris Shenker sued the Teamsters Union for $140 million. He claimed that they had backed out of a $40 million loan to expand the Dunes. The lawsuit was dismissed but the Justice Department became interested in the case as they were yet again investigating the Teamsters Union for its ties with organized crime.

In October 1977, the Securities Exchange Commission filed a civil suit against Shenker, the Pipefitters Welfare Education Fund, and the Pipefitters Local Union #562 Pension Fund. They charged the defendants had used $23.5 million in labor pension funds to help keep the Dunes on an even financial keel. Shenker's actions and associations had also garnered the attention of the Justice Department. The Dunes was already having a hard time shaking the rumors of being involved with organized crime, and it only made things even worse when eight members of the Colombo crime family stayed at the hotel in 1980.

Stuart and Clifford Perlman, founders of Caesars World, agreed to buy the Dunes in 1983 for $185 million, and even took over operation of the property for several months, but the sale ultimately fell through. In 1984, Morris Shenker filed for bankruptcy, and soon after, Major Riddle's company M & R Investment Company, also filed for bankruptcy, leading to the resort's sale. The sultan statue, by now on the golf course, caught fire in 1985, reportedly due to an electrical short. In 1987, Japanese investor Masao Nangaku purchased the Dunes but could not make it a financial success.

On November 17, 1992, the Dunes was sold for the last time to developer Steve Wynn's company, Mirage Resorts, Inc. The Dunes closed the doors forever on January 26, 1993 at midnight. Employees danced to a calypso band and enjoyed free prime rib at the Sultan's Table before watching the giant marquee go dark. Over 1,300 employees were out of work. Many had worked there for over ten years and some as long as twenty-five.

All gambling was halted at 5:15am on January 27, 1993. Chips were collected, as well as the coins from the slot and video poker machines. Gaming agents taped the coin slots shut and hung "out of order" stickers on the screens. The coins were delivered to the counting room and the chips and cash were delivered to the main cage. Arthur Andersen and Company arrived early Monday morning to perform the final audit.

A liquidation sale was conducted by National Content Liquidators to clear the property of its contents as a prelude to the building's demolition. Like many of the legendary properties of its era, it could no longer compete with the newer and more exciting mega-resorts that were being built.

On April 23, 1993, Ed Hassen of YESCO dismantled the flashing neon palms, which were sold at auction and shipped to the buyer in Taiwan.

On October 27, 1993, the Dunes was demolished in a grand ceremony that involved major fireworks displays and the use of several "cannon blasts" from the ship "HMS Britannia" at the Treasure Island Hotel and Casino. Over 200,000 people watched its demise. The Dunes sign itself was lit and read "No Vacancy" as if it were still open. Everything except the South Tower was destroyed.

Remains of the Dunes Hotel after it was imploded on October 27, 1993.
Courtesy: Authors Collection

The 15-year-old South Tower was demolished nine months later in July 1994, with no fanfare and minimal media attention. The demolition also held symbolic significance for the city. Longtime residents knew that the Dunes had been controlled by the mafia, having first been built with money from it, as well as maintained through various mob-controlled pension funds. For many, the demolition signaled the end of significant mafia control and influence in Las Vegas. It has been suggested that a number of mobsters who came to Las Vegas became model citizens, good businessmen, dedicated family men, and civic leaders. Is that true? Only they, their families, and community would know.

The Bellagio now stands in its place. The Dunes golf course is now occupied by parts of the Monte Carlo, New York-New York, CityCenter, the now-demolished Boardwalk Hotel and Casino, and the Cosmopolitan. During the construction of the Bellagio, workers found four bags of Dunes casino chips that had been buried at the site.

(Notes: "Major Riddle, casino tycoon, dies at age 73;" his obituary ran in the July 10, 1980 *Chicago Tribune*, and can be read online.

Major A. Riddle was born in Louisville on November 15, 1906, and died in Las Vegas on July 8, 1980. A relative of Major A. Riddle writes, "He did have some shady businesses such as the Plantation Clubs in both Indiana and Chicago.

Up front they seemed like dance clubs but in secret rooms they gambled, and drank alcohol during prohibition. When they got raided, he paid off the officials. He also did some money runs over between Chicago and the Indiana state line for Al Capone. He had a guy on each side of his Packard, standing on running boards with machine guns, as he carried a vast amount of money and would pay off the cops that stopped him. This is also how he made money, besides investing in oil. Then he was asked to go to Las Vegas and help the struggling Dunes Hotel out because he had a golden touch in helping struggling businesses. He did turn around the Dunes and created many jobs; he was a man with vision. He was also the pioneer of the buffet for locals and charged very little."

The *Billboard* magazine from July 4, 1942, mentions Major Riddle, and the Plantation Club he owned at that time as being in Moline, Illinois. I have yet to find any other mention of him owning other clubs. It should also be noted that Major A. Riddle and James Riddle Hoffa were distant cousins.

Riddle was also an honorary pallbearer at Bennie Bickers funeral. In Dallas, in the 1930s, Bickers was a lieutenant, bodyguard, and driver for Ben F. Whitaker. Whitaker had been a lieutenant under mob boss Warren Diamond, before he became the mob boss of Dallas. Whitaker's two main lieutenants were Bickers and Benny Binion; Binion moved to Las Vegas in 1947 and received a Nevada gaming license in 1951.

I am also enclosing a few notes on the other hotels and casinos Major A. Riddle owned:

Riddle built, and opened, the Silver Nugget Casino in North Las Vegas in late 1964.

In 1976, Riddle purchased and demolished the old Thunderbird Hotel, and built the Silver Bird Hotel and Casino on the property. The Silver Bird opened on January 1, 1977; by 1980, the resort had 400 hotel rooms. In 1981 the Silver Bird was purchased from the Riddle estate by Ed Torres for $500,000. Torres renamed the Silver Bird the El Rancho, after the El Rancho Vegas, which burned down in 1960.

The Silver City Casino opened in 1974; Gene Lucas was the general manager and Fred Crossley was the day shift boss. In 1979 it was purchased by Circus Circus Enterprises. Eddie Kover, a former Vaudevillian and film actor, came out of retirement and made the coffee shop at the Silver City Casino one of the most successful in Las Vegas.

Lastly, the Holiday International Hotel and Casino opened by Major Riddle Enterprises in 1977, and was closed in 1980 when Riddle died. It is now the Main Street Station.

Major A. Riddle's estate was involved in multiple legal situations after his death; additional information can be found on the internet.

Mayfair Theatre advertisement promoting the vaudeville team Miles and Kover. Courtesy: Dusty Sage

Press Photo of Morris Shenker and Jimmy Hoffa, year unknown. Courtesy: Gangland Wire

Morris A. Shenker was born in Russia in 1907, and died August 9, 1989 in Santa Monica, California. He was an attorney best known for representing labor leader Jimmy Hoffa, and as a former owner of the Dunes Hotel in Las Vegas. (Hoffa had links to organized crime and disappeared in 1975.)

Because of his ties to the Teamsters and other alleged mob connections, Shenker, who operated the Dunes Hotel and Casino in the 1970s, ran afoul of the Nevada Gaming Commission. Despite state and federal investigations, Shenker escaped indictment until February 1989 when a federal grand jury accused him of conspiring to conceal hundreds of thousands of dollars from the Internal Revenue Service and bankruptcy creditors. He denied any wrong doing.

Shenker, involved in bankruptcy proceedings from 1967 to 1973, filed for bankruptcy again in 1984 after a $34 million court verdict went against him for money he borrowed from the Culinary Workers Pension Fund for resorts in Southern California and other projects. He, and his estate, were involved in court battles over his finances for several years.

Morris A. Shenker died of pneumonia at age 82, owing the IRS an estimated $55 million. Fictionalized versions of Shenker appear in the 1961 film *Hoodlum Priest*, as "Louis Rosen," and in the film *Casino*.

There is also a lot of information on the internet about the Teamsters Union Pension Fund; Chicago based, the fund was once nicknamed "the mob's bank." They provided almost $250 million worth of low-interest loans to casino developers, many with ties to organized crime, which brought unprecedented growth to the Las Vegas Strip and the city's downtown area. In return, the crime groups reaped untold millions in secretly skimmed profits. In 1958, the Dunes Hotel received a loan for $4 million dollars. Additional loans from the fund flowed to a list of new hotel-casino projects on or near the Las Vegas Strip. Jimmy Hoffa also personally made arrangements for loans to Morris Shenker when he became involved with the Dunes Hotel.

By 1977, the United States government forced the Teamster Union Pension Fund to cede oversight of the fund to outside regulators. The union would lend no more money to Nevada casinos. Nevertheless, the fund proved that a significant amount of the expansion and success of the Las Vegas casino industry in the 1950s, 1960s, and 1970s resulted from major financing provided by a source closely associated with organized crime. In 1983, a federal grand jury in Kansas City indicted fifteen organized crime figures on charges related to skimming, and in 1984, eleven of them received long prison terms.

There is also information online regarding the Chicago Outfit; also known as the Outfit, the Chicago Mafia, the Chicago Mob, or the Organization. It's an Italian-American crime syndicate based in Chicago, Illinois, dating back to the 1910s. The Outfit reached the height of its power in the early 1960s, when it controlled casinos in Las Vegas and "skimmed" millions of dollars over the course of several decades. They used the Teamsters Union Pension Fund, with the aid of Meyer Lansky and Jimmy Hoffa, to also engage in massive money laundering through the Outfit's casinos.

It has been rumored that $2 million skimmed from the casinos was used to build the Old Neighborhood Italian-American Club. The club, considered to be the hangout of old-timers as they lived out their golden years, was founded by Angelo J. "The Hook" LaPietra, who died in 1999.)

Before moving on to the actual Agreement signed between Harold Minsky, Major Riddle, and Robert Rice, I want to mention a column I found written by Jane Ann Morrison for the *Las Vegas Review-Journal* on May 28, 2015. There was no title, but in-part it reads:

"After 48 years researching the mob, author and gaming consultant Bill Friedman knows the difference between "good hoods" and "bad gangsters," and his new book *30 Illegal Years To The Strip* examines the differences between the two.

One example of a "good hood" was the late Morris "Moe" Dalitz, who came from the illegal liquor world spawned by prohibition in the 1920s and transitioned into legal gambling in Las Vegas.

Another, Major A. Riddle, described dating Virginia Hill, when she was a sweet girl in the 1930s before she linked with Ben Siegel. Later, she became a foul-mouthed fun-time girl. Riddle told Friedman he wouldn't have dated her then.

Friedman said his goal was not to correct the record about organized crime, although he did that throughout, condemning false or speculative information. His goal was to show who these men actually are. According to Friedman, "They were the most fascinating men and I wanted to understand them; who and what they really were, the good, the bad and the ugly. All organized crime wants is to separate you from money, but gamblers want to separate you from money without pushing you around, without hurting you physically. That's what distinguished the good hoods from the bad gangsters."

Historic photo of flamingo sitting atop the original tower at the Hotel. Courtesy: Authors Collection

So where did the "hoods" hang out when they came to Las Vegas? Binion's, Dunes, Flamingo, and the Sands – according to my research, these were considered the best of the old mob hangouts.

What follows was the six page 1959 Agreement between Harold Minsky and the Dunes Hotel and Casino. It is typed as it was written; it was drawn up by the Las Vegas Law Offices of Goldwater, Singleton, Dickerson, and Miles.

AGREEMENT

"This Agreement, made this 15th day of May, 1959, by and between M & R Investment Company, Inc., hereafter referred to as "Company," and Harold Minsky, hereafter referred to as "Minsky."

WITNESSETH:

WHEREAS, the Company is the operator of the Dunes Hotel, in Las Vegas, Nevada, and is desirous of presenting at such hotel a musical revue or revues, under the supervision and direction of Minsky; and

WHEREAS, the Company is desirous of procuring the services of Minsky and the use of his name; and

WHEREAS, Minsky is desirous of producing musical revues for the Company at the Dunes Hotel, Las Vegas, Nevada;

NOW, THEREFORE, in consideration of the mutual promises and agreements hereinafter set forth, and for other good and valuable consideration, the receipt of which is hereby acknowledged, the parties here to mutually promise and agree as follows:

The term of this contract shall be for two years, beginning on the 26th day of June 1959, and terminating on the 26th day of June 1961.

During said two year term of this Agreement, Minsky shall be retained as producer and director of the musical revues presented at the Dunes Hotel, Las Vegas, Nevada, and shall be the exclusive producer and director of said revues and shows, regardless of whether or not the Company presents a principal performer not selected by Minsky, and whether or not the title of the show or revue bears the name "Minsky." It is further understood and agreed by and between the parties hereto that in the event the company hires, retains or presents a principal name performer to be presented in any revue or show produced by Minsky, the Company must consult with Minsky with regard to the presentation, part, performance, or use of said principal performer. In the event the Company does not desire to use the name of Minsky in any show produced and directed by Minsky, as heretofore described, it is understood and agreed that Minsky shall be and remain the producer and director of said show or revue, regardless of the billing given to any principally performer.

Minsky's fees as producer as heretofore described shall be at the rate of Twelve Hundred and Fifty ($1250.00) per week for each week of the term of this agreement. Minsky's fees shall be payable at the end of each weekly period and shall not be subject to any deductions whatsoever, except advances or bills owed to the Company.

Minsky shall devote full time and effort, as may be necessary for the organizing and rehearsing and production of the show at the Dunes Hotel, and in connection therewith shall spend whatever time is necessary at the Dunes Hotel for the proper supervision, direction and management of the show, it being understood that Minsky's fees shall be payable as herein provided irrespective of whether or not he is present at the Dunes Hotel. The Company shall also pay for any and all transportation charges for Minsky and his wife to anywhere in the United States of America, when such transportation is required for or connected with the production of said show. It is further understood and agreed that Minsky shall be, and he is hereby, granted the privilege of charging food and drink at the Dunes Hotel and shall not be required to reimburse the Company for said charges.

During any period of this Agreement for which Minsky's services are contracted hereunder, Minsky agrees not to engage in or otherwise aid in the presentation of any show in Clark County, Nevada, or permit the use of his name in any manner whatsoever in conjunction with any presentation in Clark County, Nevada. In the event that the Company does not exercise its option to extend the terms of this contract in the manner and at time herein provided, then this contract shall come to an end and none of the restrictions herein imposed upon Minsky shall thereafter be binding.

It is understood that any show produced by Minsky under the terms of this contract may bear an entitlement including the word "Minsky;" provided however, that the Company may present a show not bearing the entitlement including the word "Minsky," it being understood and agreed that Minsky shall be and remain the producer of any show not thereby entitled with the word "Minsky," as herein provided. In the event that the Company violates or breaches any of the terms of this agreement, Minsky shall have the option of directing the Company to forthwith cease and desist from the use of the name "Minsky" in conjunction with the show then being presented, and on receipt of such notice the Company shall comply therewith.

In the event the name of Minsky shall be used in the entitlement of any show produced by Minsky, then Minsky shall, in the organization and presentment of the show, have the sole right to select all of the principals and performers required by him, subject to the right of the Company to reject any principal or act selected by Minsky, provided notice of such rejection is given prior to the commencement of the show. Minsky is expressly authorized, upon approval by the Company, to execute all necessary contracts for employment of acts, principals and other performers, expressly provided, however, that, within the limit of the budget provided, Minsky shall have the sole and exclusive right to hire chorus girls, and the express authority to enter into contracts of employment with them, as an authorized agent of the Company. It is understood that the amount to be expended for talent in conjunction with the show to be presented under this Agreement shall be a minimum of $10,000.00 per week, and a minimum of $10,000.00 shall be expended for any show for the purchase or rental of costumes. It is understood that the use of the word "talent" in this Agreement is limited solely to performers and not to the persons engaged in the conjunction with the show.

Minsky shall have the sole right to select a choreographer and stage manager for the show, whose compensation shall be paid for by the Company.

After the commencement of the show, the Company shall have no right to change the manner, presentation or nature of the show, or any right or authority to interfere with the show, or make changes therein without the approval of Minsky.

It is understood that any and all costs, charges, disbursements, or otherwise, in conjunction with the organization and presentation of the show shall be solely the obligation of the Company.

It is understood that if Minsky desires to have Charles E. Hogan assist in the presentment of the show, all compensation due and payable to him shall be payable by Minsky, except that the Company shall furnish room and board for Charles E. Hogan for a period not exceeding one week, and transportation to and from Chicago.

This contract or any of the rights provided for herein are not assignable or transferable by the Company by direct act on its part, or by operation of law. In the event of the appointment of a Receiver, Trustee, or any Custodian of the Company, its business or assets, then and in such event, any and all rights to options of renewal exercisable as referred to in paragraph three hereof shall be extinguished.

All written notices required to be served or delivered under this Agreement shall, as to the Company, be personally served on any officer of the Company, or sent by registered mail to the Company at the Dunes Hotel, Las Vegas, Nevada; and as to Minsky, service may be effected personally on him, or by registered mail to his residence, as herein first stated.

The parties hereto acknowledge that Minsky contemplates the organization of a road show originating from Las Vegas, Nevada, and from the Dunes Hotel. In the event Minsky organizes and produces a show originating from the Dunes Hotel in Las Vegas, Nevada, the Company shall be entitled to receive from Minsky fifty percent (50%) of the net profits derived from the performance of said show, providing, however, that there shall be deducted from said profits an agent's commission, if any, and a booker's commission, in the sum of five percent (5%) which shall be payable to Charles E. Hogan, of 203 North Wabash, Chicago, Illinois; and provided, further, that Charles E. Hogan shall be the exclusive booker for said road show. This Agreement between the parties with regard to the organizing and producing of road shows, as set forth in this paragraph, shall be operative and effective only so long as the parties hereto are doing business under and within the terms of this entire Agreement between the parties, and shall not be effective or operative in the event that the other Agreements of the parties, as set forth herein, are for any reason no longer applicable. In the event that costumes or materials owned by the M & R Investment Company, Inc., are used during the operation described in this paragraph, M & R Investment Company, Inc., shall be entitled to and receive a reasonable compensation for the use of such costumes and properties.

The parties further acknowledge that the nature of the performances by the parties set forth in this Agreement requires mutual confidence and respect of the personalities who are parties to this Agreement, and, for that reason, the Company hereby grants to Minsky the right, privilege and option to terminate this Agreement and all the terms hereof in the event that a majority of the Directors of the Company, as of the date of this Agreement, are no longer in office or associated with the Company, or in the event that this Agreement and its terms are for any reason assigned to a person, firm, corporation, or co-partnership in which the present Directors of the Company are not interested, either as investors, partners or stockholders. This option shall be exclusive with Minsky, and it is understood and agreed that it is not extended or granted in any way to the Company.

It is agreed by and between the parties hereto that in the event the name "Minsky," or the show produced by Minsky, is used by way of a photographic article in writing or any other manner, as the result of which the M & R Investment Company, Inc., or any of its affiliates, receives compensation of any amount, the amount of compensation so received shall be divided twenty-five percent (25%) to Minsky, and seventy-five percent (75%) to M & R Investment Company, Inc., or any of its affiliates. It is further understood and agreed that the use of the name "Minsky" or any reproduction by way of photograph, or otherwise, of the show produced by Minsky shall not be done without the consent of Minsky, in writing first hand and obtained. This paragraph includes brochures, souvenir programs, television, or the use of any media for which M & R Investment Company, Inc., or any of its affiliates, receives compensation as set forth in this paragraph, it being understood and agreed that the media mentioned herein is by the way of description only and not by way of limitation.

This contract supersedes and makes null and void any and all written Agreements, if any, heretofore in existence between the parties.

IN WITNESS WHEREOF, the Company has caused these presents to be signed by its proper and authorized officers, and caused its corporate seal to be hereunto affixed, and Minsky has hereunto set his hand the day and year first above written."

The contract was signed by: Major A. Riddle, President of M & R Investment Company, Inc., Robert Rice, Secretary, and Harold Minsky.

On August 5, 1958, the *Los Angeles Herald-Express* ran the following article, "The Minsky Story," written by Don Bailer.

"Las Vegas 'Sextravaganza' Producer Tells Technique. On September 6, 1957, Las Vegas swank Dunes Hotel opened a new and – for Vegas – revolutionary type of entertainment, a nude girlie extravaganza staged by Harold Minsky, the New York burlesque legend. That night, about a half-century and 3000 miles from the birth of Minsky Burlesque at New York's National Winter Garden, the remnants of burlesque and of the old Ziegfeld-Shubert-George White-Billy Rose extravaganzas came to life again, and a new rage was on its way to sweeping success in brash, free-wheeling Las Vegas. Today, the first of two installments of "The Minsky Story."

Gone is the gleam in baldhead row – dimmed by the crew cuts of the Crosby boys.

Billy Rose, 1947. Courtesy: C.F. Miller

Stage-door Johnny has taken his chocolates and roses and wandered disconsolately away – his place taken by poolside Trujillo's proffering sports cars and wedlock.

This is the new visage – the Las Vegas visage – of the re-birth of the girlie show, the Nude Deal of the entertainment world.

And the man responsible for it is Harold Minsky, veteran of the lusty heyday of burlesque – now extinct – in New York City.

The name Minsky has been synonymous with burlesque for half a century, since 1908, when Abe Minsky launched the glorified vaudeville show with window dressing.

Today the name Minsky is emerging in a new, but not entirely new concept. It's the

Harold Minsky, with a showgirl and the costumer, in the late 1950s. Minsky was highly involved with all aspects of his shows. Courtesy: UNLV

same old Minsky drawing card, with Ziegfeldian lavish window-dressing for the windowed undressing – Broadeville, 1958!

"The main difference is money," Harold Minsky explains today in comparing his father's shows at the old National Winter Garden, the old Ziegfeld Follies, and his current girlie extravaganzas at the Dunes in Las Vegas.

"My father used to mount 52 shows a year for about $3500 a show, plus talent and behind-the-scenes salaries. In those days a Ziegfeld Follies used to cost about $30,000 to produce. The current Minsky Show at the Dunes cost me $133,000 for production costs alone; salaries and other such costs not included."

For example, consider those costuming ingredients for the current show: 300 pounds of rhinestones, two miles of nylon, two bushels of sequins, and 1,650,000 pieces of mirror glass.

It took 134 seamstresses, designers, and tailors a total of 7000 man-hours to complete the wardrobe. But the result was some of the most striking and expensive garments ever to uncover the feminine form. That is the extravaganza-nude formula Minsky has applied with such crackling success in Las Vegas.

As for that success, Harold Minsky recalls the sagacious words of his father, who said, "That in addition to taste, resourcefulness, creative ability, artistry, and the other basics, a showman must possess business acumen and have your hand on the public pulse."

Harold had all the basics, and when he arrived in Las Vegas and got his hand on the public pulse, it was a quick and successful move to the public purse.

Here's how Minsky reads the Vegas pulse, "Las Vegas is an around-the-clock New Year's Eve, where nobody goes to bed and money is spent as if it were rubies."

The Dunes owner, Major A. Riddle, has signed Minsky to another full-year contract and is breaking ground for a plush 19-story addition to his hotel. This is the new home of Minsky extravaganzas, dizzy Las Vegas, where a staggering sum is merely drinking money.

Men wise in the ways of show business – but not quite as alert historically as they might be – look today at the success of Harold Minsky's nudie spectaculars at Las Vegas and call him heir apparent to the crown once worn by the likes of Florenz Ziegfeld, the Shubert's, Billy Rose, and George White. The fact is, that showmanship crown may simply be coming home to roost on the family brow from which it was frankly filched by other showmen.

Ziegfeld always maintained his Follies formula came from the Paris Follies Bergere – but for 20 years he was a regular Friday night patron at Minsky's National Winter Garden, always in the same seat, 4th row center, on the aisle.

But the frankest confession of "artistic thievery" is a matter of record in the New York Supreme Court. Ziegfeld and his closest competitors, the Shubert Brothers, joined legal forces in a suit against one of their former dancers, George

Florenz Ziegfeld. Courtesy: Authors Collection

White. They charged that his annual "Scandals" show was plagiarism. White's reply was, "All of us go down to Minsky's on the East Side and steal both his ideas and whenever we can, his talent."

The roster of Minsky burlesque alumni, the talents which were suckled there and weaned into great personal stardom, includes such names as: Fannie Brice, Bert Lahr, Harry Richman, Sophie Tucker, Joe Penner, Jack Pearl, Clark and McCullough, Belle Baker, Pinky Lee, Red Buttons, Phil Silvers, Abbott and Costello, Gypsy Rose Lee, Robert Alda, and Rags Ragland.

Minsky currently has four girlie extravaganzas touring the country, a successful stock company at the Rialto

*George White.
Courtesy Burlesque Historical Society*

Fannie Brice pictured on the sheet music cover from 1928 film My Man.
Courtesy: Authors Collection

Early photo of Bert Lahr performing during his vaudeville days, 1914. Courtesy: Authors Collection

Cover of Joe Penner's Joy Book. Courtesy: Dusty Sage

Paul McCullough and Bobby Clark – Clark has the drawn on spectacles. Courtesy: Authors Collection

1936 photo of Bud Abbott and Lou Costello in front of a Minsky sign. Courtesy Dusty Sage

Gypsy Rose Lee. Courtesy: C.F. Miller

Theatre in Chicago, and at the Adams Theatre in Newark, but he makes no bones about Vegas being his flippant new frontier.

With the new contract he has signed, he made the decision to plunge all in, making Vegas the new jackpot of nudie spectacular showmanship – and the first two bars have already flipped into line.

Tomorrow – What is "A Minsky Girl?" – Her geography, her professional longevity, her history?"

"The Minsky Story – Part II" By Don Bailer

"Producer Tells How He Picks Showgirl Beauties—Harold Minsky, the name synonymous for half a century with New York burlesque, today is the big name in a new rage of girlie extravaganza entertainment in Las Vegas. Today, the last of two installments of "The Minsky Story," tells how these beautiful girls are picked for their jobs.

There are some interesting figures on Minsky showgirls, and not just ones like 38-23-35. For instance, forty percent of them marry rich men; and the average professional life of a Minsky showgirl is six years, from age 18 to 24. There are exceptions, but normally the maximum they can stretch it to is age 26. After that, they have had it.

But Harold Minsky is careful to stress that part about there being exceptions – his wife, for example, and anybody else's who might take offense at the suggestion that age 26 is over the hill.

Dardy Orlando and Harold Minsky. Courtesy: Janelle Smith Collection

His wife of 12 years, Dardy, is an ex-showgirl and an extremely beauteous one. They are the parents of two children, Ava, 5, and Danny, 10.

Dardy, and a sister Barbara, were once featured as a specialty team at the Earl Carroll Theatre in Hollywood, which is now the Moulin Rouge. Another sister, still quite famously active is, Lili St. Cyr.

Minsky speaks eloquently and authoritatively on the subject of showgirls in general and Minsky girls in particular.

What is the ideal Minsky girl? This is what he says:

Autographed photo of Lili St. Cyr at Ciro's in West Hollywood. Courtesy: C.F. Miller

"She's five feet, 10 inches tall in her heels. She has at least a 36-inch bust, but no larger than 38. Her waist is 22 or 23 inches, and her hips never more than 35.

Her legs must be like tapered rose stems and her ankles sufficiently narrow so that an ordinary man's hand can completely close around them. She should have small feet, but not so small they look like clubs.

Her complexion and skin must be youthful and unblemished. She can be a golden blonde, but not platinum, because platinum hair is something like gilding the lily. She can also be red-haired, but not hennaed; or a genuine brunette, but not ranging in the in-between hues which makes a girl appear drab.

Her eyes must be large, her lips full, and she must have a chin, so she doesn't resemble an egg.

Her neck should be long and swan-like, her shoulders narrow, but never drooping; and her back like a figure eight, vertically cut in half.

She should have a pleasant, modulated voice, good diction qualities, and high intelligence."

That is the ideal Minsky girl. Harold Minsky is also particularly proud of the educational caliber of his girls.

"Of the forty girls in the Dunes Hotel line," he points out, "all are high school graduates; six have college MAs; fourteen have their BAs; all told, twenty-two have been to college for at least two years, and seven presently are taking college correspondence courses.

This helps them to hold their husbands after the honeymoon tinsel palls, because they are able to talk intelligently to a man. Over the years fewer Minsky marriages have ended in divorce courts than those of any other profession.

And all Minsky showgirls and chorus girls don't set their sights only for millionaires. About forty percent of them do marry rich men, but statistics show that thirty-one percent marry struggling musicians, and eighteen percent marry successful actors. Four percent return to their home towns and marry childhood sweethearts, and seven percent marry moderately successful businessmen, writers, or show business executives."

Minsky has even carried his statistics beyond the point where the girls marry up and leave.

"More than sixty-five percent have children the first year of marriage," he says, "And eighty percent have children sometime during the first five years of marriage. Only two percent of the marriages among the girls in a show ends in separation and/or divorce."

If his recitation of all these facts, figures, specifications, and intelligence levels will help shatter that image of a chorine as a frowsy, gum-chewing, dim-witted dumb "goll from Joisey," Mr. Minsky will be satisfied."

There were two more articles in the "D" File. The following had a date, but no year; however, that can be figured out by its content. It was from the Las Vegas August 14th column, "Bill Slocum Everywhere," and it reads:

"Anybody who says Las Vegas will stand for absolutely anything just doesn't know this bulwark of American morality.

The town that thinks nothing of all night gambling, all night drinking, and several other interesting pastimes that usually occur in the wee hours, is suddenly offended.

It has been offended by the female bosom. That is the uncovered female bosom.

Comics who tell jokes that would make a stevedore shrink are toasts of the town. But a few little old American, English, and French girls have conservative old Las Vegas in a dither.

It seems that one Harold Minsky, a distinguished scion of America's first family of flesh peddlers, came to town with a revue last September that it is still here and doing a fantastic business at the Dunes.

Mr. Minsky's first line of attack was undraped ladies, and he undraped his ladies somewhat more above the waist than had ever before been attempted here among the grass roots of American morality and good taste.

The people filled the Dunes and lingered to have a go at craps, roulette, and 21. And they kept filling the place and they kept lingering and the props got richer.

Then the brand new Stardust imported the *Lido Revue* from Paris and did turn-away business on precisely the same theory that was doing so well at the Dunes.

Postcard of the El Rancho Hotel and Casino. Courtesy: Authors Collection

Autographed photo of Sally Rand. Courtesy: C.F. Miller

El Rancho Vegas, an olden-time, conservative type gambling hall, added six unhampered wenches to its show. The Silver Slipper, which has always been frankly a burlesque house, removed the only rule it ever had regarding its show. Miss Sally Rand, a promising new-comer to the business, is currently headlining the Silver Slipper extravaganza.

And the accumulated monotony of the new idea in Las Vegas show business came tumbling down around the heads of the happy casino owners who had found this newer and far cheaper way of filling their halls.

The natives got sore; the local gapers, ever-watchful against anything that will hurt Las Vegas, began to grumble. Casino owners who didn't have girlie epics became critical; and most frightening of all, the churches began complaining.

Las Vegas doesn't want any trouble with anybody,

particularly religious groups. It is far too vulnerable on too many counts that conflict with stand and religious practices, notably ridiculous marriage and divorce customs.

The "Battle of the Bosoms," as it is being called here, has split the tightly-knit casino owners as nothing ever did. They are afraid that perhaps this fight into mild nudity may be the mistake they have always feared. This town has always been fearful of "taking one step too many," and bringing upon it the wrath of the nation.

El Rancho Vegas has already draped its half-dozen wenches. But Major A. Riddle, president of the Dunes, says, "We don't plan to change." He does not think he is hurting anybody's morals and he knows his clients like it.

The Las Vegas politicians have kept a hands-off attitude – sure proof the owners haven't yet decided what to do about this threat to the good name of Las Vegas.

But you can be sure of this: the persuasive gentlemen who have sunk fortunes earned by their muscle into Las Vegas will very quickly persuade the recalcitrant owners to get in line and dress their fillies if any real danger to Las Vegas' future as a Golden Goose is suspected."

The final article was from the *Las Vegas Review-Journal*, dated March 18, 1961. It's the "Las Vegas Spotlight" column by Gene Tuttle. It was the fourth in a special Saturday series of thumb-nail sketches of the producers along the Strip. This column was all about, you guessed it… Harold Minsky

"Despite his father's plea to study law and become an attorney, Harold Minsky, brought up in the theatre since his birth in New York City, let the grease paint in his blood sway him away from law and into the theatre where he has made a great name for himself.

This June will mark Minsky's 28th year in show business and he is just as eager over each show as if it were his first. Right now he is busy planning for the new Zsa Zsa Gabor show.

"I love this life," said Harold, as he rested in his office at the Dunes Hotel, where he has been staging shows for the past three years. "I first started working in the box office, then I graduated to stagehand – then manager, and so on up the ladder."

Harold learned all about show business from his father, A.B. Minsky. Besides working in the theatre, he managed to take some courses at Columbia University to broaden his education.

His first produced show was at the Gaiety Theatre on 48th Street in New York. "It was a real burlesque show with nudes and all," grinned Harold who has become known as America's top producer of nude shows. "While I was at the Gaiety we turned out such stars as Phil Silvers, Red Buttons, Rags Ragland, and

Minsky's Gaiety Burlesque Theatre, street level view, on 42nd Street in New York City, 1937. Courtesy: Bettmann Archives

Pinky Lee." In his round in New York, Harold Minsky produced shows at the Eltinge Theatre, the Oriental, and at the Gotham Theatres.

"It was ten years ago that I first came to Las Vegas and staged the third show ever held in the Desert Inn, *Minsky's Follies*. Since then I came out here many times with shows and acts," explained Harold. "Finally, Major Riddle of the Dunes made me an offer and I decided to settle down here."

Minsky didn't confine his activities to New York and Las Vegas, but he has opened many clubs and theatres across the United States. When he opened a theatre in New Orleans, he had playing in the orchestra such new name personalities as Al "The King" Hirt and Louis Prima. Now Al Hirt is appearing, perhaps because of Harold, in the Dunes Hotel lounge.

Minsky staged many top shows at the Colonial Inn in Miami Beach, and he has put together shows and sent them out on tours all across the nation. Trujillo invited Minsky and his show to the islands and built a theatre for him to appear in. The show lasted five months and did record business.

Minsky Goes To Paris, was Harold's first Dunes presentation which clicked solid and sold him on being a Las Vegas resident. He brought to the Strip the Minsky touch of presenting nudes in colorful production numbers.

Looking toward the future, Minsky is now in negotiations with an English nightclub to bring in one of his famous *Minsky's Follies* for a fall run."

"E" is For...

Almost everything in these Files refers to Eddie Lynch. It included copies of: early programs, contracts, letters, numerous newspaper articles, clippings, and columns.

There is more about Sandra Ellis in the recipe section, but in a letter from March 4, 2016, Sandra wrote:

"Of course I knew Eddie Lynch quite well. He was our dance master (choreographer) for all the Minsky shows. He arranged all the routines for us line girls and showgirls – which I doubled on as I was tall, 5'9". Eddie was about 5'9" and medium build, with a round face, glasses, and he was a great non-temperamental person. He was very patient, and I liked him so much. Eddie was also very light on his feet. He did one bit with us girls dancing around Robert Alda to the tune of, if I remember, either "Stairway to the Stars," or "Stay in My Arms Cinderella." I often took care of Alan Alda backstage, when he was a small child. I go back in time thinking about all of this. When the Minsky's Theatres in New York closed down in 1939, I did dance in nightclubs, but it was not the same. The Minsky's were such wonderful people to work for. I married in early January of 1944, and that was the end of my career."

Sandra Ellis. Courtesy: Sandra Ellis

Let's continue on with the three Lynch contracts, which were from 1935, 1937, and 1939. They were not as long, or as "specific," as the other contracts I've included in this book. The following contract was between Eddie Lynch and Herbert K. Minsky, Harold's uncle.

"AGREEMENT MADE this 5th day of July, 1935, by and between Joan Amusements Corporation, hereinafter referred to as the "Owner," and Edward

Chorus line from unknown theatre; date unknown as well – but Ann Corio is believed to be fourth from the left. Courtesy: Dusty Sage

Robert Alda. Courtesy: Burlesque Historical Society

Lynch, hereinafter referred to as the "Producer."

WITNESSETH:

The owner hereby engages the producer to put on the show called *Life Begins at Minsky's*, stage all dance routines, select costumes, and supervise the lighting of said show, all subject, however, to the approval of the managing producer, Herbert K. Minsky.

It is understood and agreed that the said show, *Life Begins at Minsky's* shall open on July 17, 1935, at Hollywood, California, and the term of this Agreement shall commence on said July 17, 1935, and shall continue for the run of said play, to wit, *Life Begins at Minsky's*.

The said producer hereby agrees to attend personally, at Hollywood, California, at the opening, to wit, July 17, 1935, and to render his exclusive services and to perform the services required in Paragraph 1: and further agrees to hold himself in readiness and on call to give his personal services and best efforts to revamp, rehearse, and replace girls, or such services as may be needed in such production of the show, at his own time, except that the owner shall pay to the producer any and all expenses incurred by him and shall pay the transportation to any city wherein the producer shall be called, the royalties to be paid under this Agreement, however, shall continue.

The owner hereby agrees to pay to the producer the sum of Two Hundred ($200.00) Dollars on July 10, 1935, and a weekly sum of One Hundred ($100.00) Dollars commencing July 17, 1935 for each and every week that the said show, *Life Begins at Minsky's*, shall continue.

The owner agrees to pay to the producer, in addition thereto, to wit, the weekly royalties, the transportation of the producer to and from California, and to and from any other city or town where the producer may be required to attend when needed to make adjustments or re-polish any numbers which may be required in said show, *Life Begins at Minsky's*.

IN WITNESS WHEREOF, the parties hereby have subscribed this instrument the day and year first above written."

This contract was signed by Herbert K. Minsky, of Joan Amusement Corporation, and Edward Lynch.

Eddie Lynch backstage with some of the chorus line dancers. Courtesy: Maureen Girard

The next Agreement was between Eddie Lynch and the Morningside Hotel, in Hurleyville, New York.

"This AGREEMENT made and entered into on the 17th day of March 1937, by and between Charles Golembe, Proprietor – Authorized Representative of The Morningside Hotel, hereinafter known and designated by the term of the party of the first part; and Eddie Lynch of 2538 Crescent Avenue, N.Y.C., hereinafter known and designated by the term of the party of the second part. Now, therefore in consideration of the sum of one dollar to each in hand paid, and for other good and valuable considerations, it is agreed as follows:

WITNESSETH:

Party of the first part, hereby engages and employs the exclusive services of the party of the second part Eddie Lynch in the capacity of entertainer for the summer season commencing May 15, 1937 and terminating Labor Day, 1937. Party of the first part agrees to pay and party of the second part agrees to accept, the sum of One hundred and twenty-five dollars, ($125.00) weekly, for the above term to be paid weekly, the first weekly salary to become due and payable on May 22, 1937, and every week thereafter, during the period of employment herein. The party of the first part agrees to provide suitable bed, board, and lodging to the aforesaid Eddie Lynch free of all charges. Party of the first part will pay transportation one way.

For services rendered in arranging this contract the Resort Entertainment Bureau, Inc., 148 West 46th Street, is to receive 10 percent of the earnings of the party of the second part amounting to $12.50 weekly. The party of the second part hereby agrees that the party of the first part deduct the above mentioned amount and pay same in full to the Resort Entertainment Bureau, Inc., on or before August 15, 1937. It is also agreed that should the party of the first part re-engage the services of the party of the second part for the following seasons, said party of the second part must be engaged through the Resort Entertainment Bureau, Inc."

The final contract was between Eddie Lynch and the E. M. Loew Circuit, from 1939. It reads as follows:

"This AGREEMENT made the 20th day of October 1939 by and between Edward Lynch and E. M. Loew Circuit Inc.

NOW, THEREFORE, IT IS MUTUALLY AGREED AS FOLLOWS:

That the E. M. Loew Circuit Inc. agrees and does herewith employ Edward Lynch to produce shows at the Gaiety Theatre, Boston, Massachusetts for a period of six (6) consecutive weeks, to commence on the 25th day of October, 1939 and to terminate on the 29th day of November, 1939.

That the employer will pay to Edward Lynch the sum of $125.00 per week for each and every week that he shall be so employed in the production of shows at the Gaiety Theatre, and it is mutually understood that the services of Mr. Lynch are to be exclusively for the Gaiety Theatre.

It is understood and agreed that the employer shall have the right to extend the six (6) weeks period of hiring hereinabove mentioned for the balance of the theatrical season, which expires on or about May 15th, 1940 providing that the employer shall advise Edward Lynch in writing at least three (3) weeks prior to the expiration of the six (6) weeks hereinabove mentioned that this contract shall be extended to the expiration of the theatrical season as above mentioned.

IN WITNESS WHEREOF, the parties have hereunto set their hands and seals on the day of October, 1939."

It almost appears as if the signatures were signed by the same person. The names signed were: Edward Lynch, per Joseph Brooks; and E. M. Loew Circuit Inc.

(Notes: The following obituary was published in *The New York Times* on November 17, 1984.

"E. M. Loew, the president and chairman of the board of E. M. Loew's Theatres Inc., died yesterday, November 16, 1984, at Mount Auburn Hospital in Cambridge, Massachusetts, after a long illness. He was 86 years old and had homes in Milton, Massachusetts, and Palm Beach, Florida. Mr. Loew, a native of Austria, was a former owner of the Foxboro Raceway in Boston and the Latin Quarter Nightclubs in Manhattan and Miami."

The following testimony, given on April 8, 2003 by Brenda Loew, was in support of the designation of the Gaiety Theatre as a Boston Landmark to the Boston Landmarks Commission, Room 900, Boston City Hall, in Boston, Massachusetts. Sadly, the theatre was torn down in 2005.

"Good evening,

My name is Brenda Loew. I am the great niece of the late pioneering theatre chain magnate, nightclub, and race track owner E. M. Loew.

E. M. owned the Gaiety Theatre for nearly 50 years before he died in 1984. Throughout my life I knew the Gaiety only as the Publix Theatre -- until just recently, when I was contacted by the "Friends of the Gaiety."

Upon careful review of all the information presented to me, I am attending this hearing to request the Commission take action on the proposal, and designate the Gaiety Theatre a historic landmark. I assure you that E. M. Loew, who was so often honored for his philanthropic service to community, religious, and charitable organizations, would have wanted that.

A search of Boston area news archives tells the story: Here in Boston, as any American in history, E. M. epitomized the pioneering entrepreneurial spirit that built America during the twentieth century. E. M. came to America in search of the American Dream almost a century ago. He was a waiter at Jacob Wirth's restaurant. That legendary Boston institution and historic landmark is still located just around the corner from the Gaiety.

In the 1930s and early 1940s, Boston newspapers characterized E. M. as a Horatio Alger rags to riches story. By 1937, the papers reported that E. M. Loew was the largest single owner of movie theatres in New England.

E. M. Loew broke down social barriers. He was a Jew who moved into Milton. He bought the Peabody Estate on Brush Hill Road, and built the B'nai

Jacob Orthodox Shul on Blue Hills Parkway in honor of the memory of his youngest brother, Jack.

During World War II, E. M. brought over the rest of the Loew family from Vienna, saving them from Hitler's concentration camps. Family always came first with E. M.

E. M. was the flamboyant owner of Bay State Raceway in Foxboro, Boston's Latin Quarter Nightclub, the New York Latin Quarter, and the Miami Latin Quarter on Palm Island right next to Al Capone's house.

After the deal to buy the Red Sox from the Yawkey family fell though in the 1960s, E. M. sold land adjacent to the racetrack in Foxboro for a dollar to Billy Sullivan for the Patriot's first football stadium.

Yes, E. M. Loew was Boston's own success story, a man who electrified the city of Boston and other cities and towns throughout the East Coast with marquees bearing his name, including the Lynn Open Air Drive-in on the Lynnway, the first drive-in East of the Mississippi.

Members of the Landmarks Commission: You are stewards who will determine the options of what will follow; what the legacy of visionary builders of empires like E. M. Loew will be.

In North Adams, E. M. Loew's Mohawk Theatre has already been designated a historic landmark.

Designating the Gaiety a historic landmark will enrich the neighborhood and the city, and enhance the possibilities and the opportunities for future generations of Bostonians, tourists, students, arts patrons, cultural events, and businesses.

Invest in this resource. Pass along a chain of tradition as an inheritance and a legacy that will eventually be even more beneficial than when it was received.

I request the Commission designate the Gaiety Theatre a historic landmark. Thank you.")

On to the clippings, and there were many; sadly most did not have any dates. I did my best to put them in chronological order when possible, and I have included dates, if known.

The following clipping, with no date, was attached to a copy of a note from the General Press Department of the Messrs. Lee and J.J. Shubert and Shubert Theatrical Company; C.P. Greneker, General Representative. The telephone number listed was, 7200 LACKAWANNA; the office address was, 227 West 45th Street, New York City. The note was dated September 23, 1926, and even though the signature was hard to read, I believe it was signed by J.J. Shubert. It reads:

Mollie King appeared in the 1919 Shubert production Good Morning Judge. *Courtesy: Authors Collection*

"To Whom It May Concern: Mr. Edward Lynch was formerly employed in the Press Department of the Shubert Theatrical Company. He is an honest, reliable young man, and anyone employing him would make no mistake. Yours Very Truly,"

Portion of sheet music cover from 1916 picturing Al Jolson. The Song, "Down Where the Swanee River Flows." The show, Robinson Crusoe, Jr., *was performed at the Winter Garden Theatre. Courtesy: Authors Collection*

The attached newspaper clipping reads:

"Eddie Lynch, stage director of Boston and New York shows, has moved up in the theatrical world from selling newspapers on the Common, then on the trains to Gotham, singing songs in a Washington Street cabaret, at the age of 15, where blossomed his opportunity. Al Jolson came to town. He was told about Eddie. Eddie eagerly went back to New York with the famous comedian as a warbler in a Broadway show. He took to dancing and was so good at it that Jolson made him work overtime to teach the same steps to his chorus line. Between show weeks, Eddie in the last two years has made seven trips to Hollywood as a technical advisor to movie land's song and dance pictures."

The next clipping was short, but sweet:
"Signed by Minsky's: Edward F. Lynch, dance director for several of the more important Shubert productions during the past five years, has been signed to produce the divertissements which the Minsky's will present at their Oriental Theatre, on Broadway near 52nd Street. They will open September 3rd with the *Oriental French Follies.* The *American Legion Follies* will follow."

Included with the clipping was an advertisement that read: "Wanted Show Girls and Dancers; Experience unnecessary, 2 weeks training free for theatre reviews. 40 weeks work guaranteed. Apply all week, 1 to 5 P.M. to Mr. Lynch; Michael Studio, 743 8th Avenue, New York City."

The Oriental Theatre.
Courtesy: Burlesque Historical Society

There was an original program in the File from the Oriental Theatre on Broadway, near 51st Street. It provided the following information: Beginning Friday, September 10, 1937, Oriental French Follies Mgmt presents, *Follies Brassiere*, in 18 Scenes. The show was Staged and Directed by Edward Lynch, Wardrobe by Eva Collins, Scenery by Mischa Salmon, and Orchestra Direction by Michael Azzara. Cast members included: Barbara Doane, Elise, Jimmy DiPalma, Al Parker, Al Golden, Jr., Annette, Gladys Fox, Queenie King, Steve Mills, John Kane, Hank Henry, Sylvia Simms, Walker and Walker, Jeanne and Gloria, Miss Julie Bryan, and the "Frenchiest Girls on Broadway." Dave Rosen was the House Manager; John Kane the Stage Manager. The following comment was also in the program: "Shows continuous from 10am to Midnight; *American Legion Follies* was to begin the following Friday, and "The Toast of Broadway," Margie Hart, would be coming soon."

The following early clippings revolved around the Minsky Shows in New York, sadly there were no dates. There are several write-ups included here, separated only by quotation marks.

Margie Hart.
Courtesy: Janelle Smith Collection

"Race Course Lends Itself To Burlesque. Billy Minsky's Brooklyn Theatre today will present a new Minsky Traveling Road Show, *Win, Place and Show*. This is a typical burlesque offering, filled with racy humor, slapstick comedy, singing and dancing, plus a cast of featured performers whose talents have been lauded in previous appearances here.

With speed as his watchword, Edward Lynch, noted producer of Minsky's *A Perfect '36*, now current at Minsky's Music Hall, Miami Beach, Florida, and Minsky's Playhouse in Hollywood, has turned this opus into a colorful production."

Early photo of Billy Minsky's Republic Burlesque Theatre. Courtesy: New York Daily News Archive

Front cover of a Minsky's Burlesque Music Hall Program – Million Dollar Pier in Miami Beach, Florida. Courtesy: Dusty Sage

(Notes: There was a copy of the program from *A Perfect 1936* in the File, and I was especially tickled to read Howard Montgomery's name as a member of the cast. Stacy Farrell loved the guy, and always told me what a fine dancer he was. Howard came to some of our earliest gatherings in California; he was fun and a very fine gentleman.)

A section of the program from *A Perfect 1936* reads: "Entire Production Under personal Direction of Harold Kay Minsky, assisted by Edward Lynch." The cast included: Joan Carroll, Ginger Britton, specialty dancer Anita Jakobi, Murray Briscoe, Pat "Paradise" Paree, Madeline Winters, Howard Montgomery, Melba Brian, Max Furman, Alma Maiben, Stanley Simmonds, Mike Sachs, Floyd Hallicy, Alice Kennedy, Harriet Carr, Sunny Vale, George Broadhurst, and Sam Raynor. There were sixteen scenes in Act I, and eleven in Act II.

More clippings read:

"Ann Corio is the attractive feature of *Girls in Blue*, musical revue devised by Edward Lynch, which is playing Billy Minsky's Brooklyn Theatre this week. Others in the cast are: Gay La Bar, Evelyn Brooks, Louise Phelps, Chique Rione, Sammy Weston, Carmen, Johnny Barry, Frank Smith, and Joe DeRita."

Ann Corio. Courtesy: Burlesque Historical Society

A young Joe DeRita, later known as "Curly-Joe" in The Three Stooges. Courtesy: Dusty Sage

"*Footlight Flashes* at Minsky Theatre; Beginning next Sunday, March 29th, Billy Minsky's Brooklyn Theatre will present a new Minsky Traveling Road Show, *Footlight Flashes*.

This production was ably staged by that well-known producer, Eddie Lynch, with whom there is none to compare for his musi-gal revues. While such favorable comments have been heard concerning the lavish production, and the efficiency of its chorus, the company roll of honor has not been over-looked in presenting to the public that glamorous prize winning beauty, Maxine DeShon, our own Miss America, who possesses an infectious smile. Also in the cast is Rags Ragland, a comic genius whose screamingly funny eccentricities are always greatly enjoyed; as well as: Max Furman, Bert Grant, Marvin Lawler, Franklin Hopkins, Alma Maiben, Boots Burns, Pat Paree, Dolly Hendricks, Annette, and a host of others including thirty dancing Minskyettes."

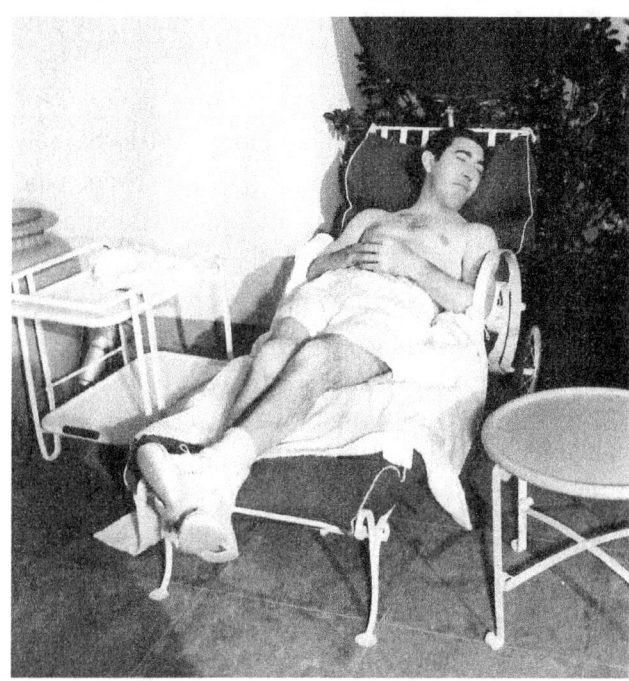

Rags Ragland. Courtesy: Janelle Smith Collection

"Billy Minsky's Presents *There Goes Rusty*, beginning next Sunday, February 16. Billy Minsky's Brooklyn Theatre, will present, *There Goes Rusty*, a stupendous musical production featuring the cream of beauty and talent. Never have such extraordinary scenic effects and devices graced a burlesque revue in the past. Edward Lynch, the producer, has created a vast number of visionary novelties, utilizing nearly every color on the spectrum, with the consequent result that *There Goes Rusty* is veritably the season's most amazing spectacle. Mr. Lynch has assembled a particularly distinguished roster of beauties, whose talents are widely known in the entertainment field."

"Novel Color Effects Used In Burlesque; Billy Minsky's Brooklyn Theatre today will present *There Goes Rusty*, a musical production featuring scenic effects unusual for burlesque. Edward Lynch, producer, has created a number of colorful novelties.

The dialogue fashioned by the Minsky's, is handled by ace comics. The ensemble has been given lilting tunes, capers, and a score of deft marches.

Cordons of funsters, singers, and dancers who will entertain you include such well known performers as: Edna "Hot-Cha" Dee, Marie Voe, June White,

Annette, Margie Hart, Bab, Bruce and Betty, Harry Clexx, Steve Mills, Al Pharr, Wen Miller, Tom Bundy, Shuffles LeVan, and a host of others."

"*Peaches in Paris* Comes to Minsky's beginning Sunday, January 12. Billy Minsky's Brooklyn Theatre will present *Peaches in Paris*, a brand new traveling road show featuring: Billie Bird, Alice Kennedy, Jean and Joan Carroll, Ginger Britton, Gertrude Foreman, Nellie Casson, Vic Plant, Chick Hunter, Johnny Kane, Joe Devlin, George Tuttle, Stanley Simmonds, Mike Sachs and Company, Jack Montague, Toots Miller, Peaches Joyce, and a host of others.

1946 street advertising for a show at Walker Evan's Burlesque Theatre in Chicago, starring Ginger Britton. Courtesy: Dusty Sage

The production was conceived and staged by Edward Lynch, who recently established a reputation for musical pictures on the West Coast. These productions are on a more elaborate scale than ever before and of the musi-gal variety, replete with vaudeville specialties, singing and dancing specialties, and a big beauty chorus."

(Notes: There were two programs in the File from Billy Minsky's Brooklyn Burlesque. One from September 29, 1935, *Silk Stocking Revue*, and the second, *Good Ship Lollypop*, which only provides November 3 as a date.

The cast for *Silk Stocking Revue* included: Elsa Lang, Murray Green, Rose Heatherly, Sam Gould, Johnny Cook, Murray Lewis, Suki Yama, Cynthia Michel, Gene Shuler, Buddy and Betty Abbott, the Dancing Madcaps, Charles Robinson, Ruth Coburn, Ann Valentine, Nora Ford, and Ginger Britton. The program also promoted the show for the following week of October 6, *Pretty Faces*, featuring: Margie Hart, Dagmar, Pat Paree, Lillian Murray, as well as mentioning the Ethiopian Princess Orelia as the added attraction.

The program for *Good Shop Lollypop* contained more pages and information than the *Silk Stocking Revue* program. The front page promoted the following weeks

Margie Hart. Courtesy: Janelle Smith Collection

Mike Sachs. Courtesy: Burlesque Historical Society

show starting November 10, *You're a Honey*, which would feature: Sunya "Smiles" Slane, Dagmar, Ginger Britton, Jean Lee, Alma Maiben, Edna Dee, Elsa Lang, plus the comedy trio of Maxie Furman, Clyde Bates, and Jack Hunt. The cast for *Good Shop Lollypop* included: Robert Alda, Scratch Wallace, Harry Reed, Babe Morgan, Al Darr, Charlie Schultz, Jack LaMont, Phyllis Vaughn, Collette, Mike Sachs, Alice Kennedy, the Dancing Madcaps, Paul Neff, Sylvia, Leipzig, and Ceil Von Dell.

There was also a column in this program entitled "Minsky Gossip." It reads:

"The Gay White Way has gone Minsky in a big way. In fact they have become Minsky conscious. Being aware of the fact that Minsky discovers talent and grooms them for bigger and better jobs on Broadway, these nightclub impresarios make their weekly pilgrimage to the Republic and Brooklyn Theatres in search of suitable material for their floor shows. And while we welcome them with open arms and take their cash we, however, feel a wee bit slighted. Not that we object to them signing up a number of our gorgeous charmers but the fact remains that as yet we haven't been invited to dine at their clubs. Grateful or not the Minsky's are slighted.

Much has been written about *Life Begins at Minsky's* – the nu-deal revuesque which created a sensation in Miami Beach last winter, played five months in Hollywood where the entire movie colony went gaga and is now at the Columbia Theatre in San Francisco. This lavish revue will grace the Brooklyn stage late next month with the entire cast and production intact. You never witnessed a show like this in your young lives and when you see it you will shout our names from the house-tops. It's now our turn to receive the Christmas gifts.

In *Strip Girl*, the Broadway comedy which opened last week, Mayo Methot plays the role of a specialty artist. The locale of the play is the stage of Minsky's Republic and unfolds bits of comedy scenes which are familiar to you. A ticket for *Strip Girl* will set you back $3.30, but at Minsky's Brooklyn where "burlesque reigns supreme," the prices are so low that you can buy four seats for our show for the price of a Broadway play. Minsky's is the poor man's Ziegfeld.

Every theatre has its midnight show with the movies throwing in a couple of extra midnights during the week (the canned actors haven't a chance to talk back) but our midnight show every Saturday night "tops" them all. It's the night of nights in Brooklyn and one you cannot afford to miss. It gives everyone a chance to greet his neighbor, pay or collect a debt (forgive us for mentioning it), and inquire about the mothers-in-law health. Aside from that there's the show that is worth the talk. A gay evening of laughs is a two and half hour peppy, rip-roaring show which ends at about three o'clock. Then for a dance or a cup of coffee, see the girl friend home, and you will be just in time for early mass.

Two amiable managers, Mr. John Kane and Mr. George Finch, are always on hand to greet you. Complaints or praises they receive graciously, and if you wish to inform them of an organization contemplating a theatre party they will thank you from the bottom of their hearts and include us in it."

What I also enjoyed about this particular program was the advertising. Some of the ads included:

"Irish Tea Room; 324 Livingston Street, Brooklyn, 'The Leaves Will Tell,' Free Readings, Lunches 25 – 35 cents." They were open evenings and Sunday.

"Vivian Beauty Salon; 560 Fulton Street, Brooklyn, in the Arcade, Personality Permanent $3.00 Complete." The phone number was STerling 3-9557.

"Chop Sticks Chinese – American Restaurant; 530 Fulton Street, Brooklyn, Luncheon – 35 cents – Dinner, Delicious Food – Good Service."

"Lotus Beauty Salon; 10 De Kalb Avenue, Brooklyn, opposite Dime Bank, Beauty Items 3 for 50 cents, Monday to Thursday, Permanent Waves $3.00 Complete, Bleaching and Dyeing." The phone number was CUmberland 6-0166.

"Barney's, For Value, Shoes for Men; 8 Fourth Avenue, Brooklyn, opposite Long Island Depot, Well Known Makes – Slater's, London, Ralston, Nunn-Bush, Florsheim, and Douglas, $1.97 - $2.97."

"Rosman's Restaurant; 392 Flatbush Avenue, Brooklyn, opposite the Theatre, Complete Lunch – 45 cents, Delicious Dinner – 55 cents."

"George's Restaurant; 366 Livingston Street, Brooklyn, near Flatbush Avenue, Special Blue Plate 35 cents – A La Carte, Spaghetti Any Style 35 cents – Beer – Wines."

"Paramount Parking Terminal; 85 De Kalb Avenue, Brooklyn, Park in Safety, Work Done While You Are in the Theatre – Lubricating, Fender Work, Washing, Auto Repairing."

"Vincent's Beauty Parlor; 35 Nevins Street, Brooklyn, 'Best Work at Cut Prices,' Four Beauty Items $1.00, Monday to Thursday, Expert Operators, Open 9am to 9pm." The phone number was CUmberland 6-7833.

"Fort Greene Cabaret; 110 De Kalb Avenue, Brooklyn, Dining – Dancing – Entertainment, No Cover Charge."

"Fay's; 635 Fulton Street, Brooklyn, Home Made Candies, All Candies Made on Premises, Simply Delicious."

"Joost and Morin; 72 De Kalb Avenue, Brooklyn, Plumbing – Heating, Oil Burners, Gas Appliances." The phone number was STerling 3-1613.

"Tri-Boro Beauty Salon; 583 Fulton Street, Brooklyn, around corner of Theatre, All Beauty Items 25 cents, Permanent Ringlets $1.50 up, Scalp Treatment."

"Brooklyn Roseland; Fulton and Flatbush Avenues, Brooklyn, 'Brooklyn's Foremost Ball Room,' with Charming Hostesses, Bar – Buffet Service – Beer.")

There were more clippings as well:

"Musical Play to Open; The Morningside Playhouse will offer an intimate musical comedy tomorrow, when Edward F. Lynch, producer and director, will offer *Mount High*, starring Sid Tomack and the Reis Brothers. Others in the cast of this musical are: Allen and Kent, Marion Joyce, Cecile Bronson, Robert Brinn, the De Meranvilles and others. The scenery was designed and executed by Ivan Lemkowitz."

Included in this folder were copies of programs from The Morningside Theatre; *Campus Days* from Saturday, July 18, 1936, and *Naughty Nauticals* from Saturday, July 25, 1936. Both shows were staged by Eddie Lynch; and the orchestra was under the direction of Simon "Sy" Sugar. Both shows included the following cast members: Sid Tomack, Edna Lee, Arnold Spector, Ann Quartin, Byrnes and Swanson, and Al and Sid - the Reis Brothers. Tootsie Stone, Jackie Mills, Bernice Wald, and Don Byrnes were also in the cast for *Campus Days*.

And this:

"Jovial Irishman Behind Scenes at Minsky's; Behind the scenes at the Plaza Theatre is a good-looking, jovial Irishman – Eddie Lynch. He's been Harold Minsky's right-hand man for years. 'Twas "Smiling Eddie" who whipped into shape the opening burlesque show at Minsky's Plaza on a few days notice.

Eddie, though still in his 30s, has more than 25 years of show business under his belt. He started as a teenage hoofer. First, it was Broadway musicals and vaudeville, then a long stretch in Hollywood. There, he was assistant to Busby Berkeley when the latter was top man at Warner's and directed the great musicals when Warner's turned to "talkies" in the late 1920s and early 1930s."

Unknown performer and Eddie Lynch looking over paperwork in his office. Courtesy: Maureen Girard

There were also several pages containing clippings and articles from 1938. Let's start with an article from January 21, 1938.

"Showboat Burlesque Will Make Fish Wild, New York, (U.P.) – A seagoing burlesque, which is expected to combine the best features of a ferryboat ride and a striptease show, last night was offered to patrons of art in the raw who have been denied their fun since a ban was declared on public undressing in New York.

Two enterprising ex-burlesque directors, David Rosen and Edward F. Lynch, have hired a boat and 35 young ladies, all guaranteed to be "100 percent experts" in the business of disrobing.

"The show will be held in the middle of the Hudson River," Lynch said. "It will be called a nautical review, but the only thing nautical about it will be the name and the locale. The feature of this show will be striptease work. Every member of the chorus, as well as the showgirls, will be a stripper. This is going to be a happy combination of the shoreline and the waste line."

The new "showboat burlesque" would attempt to evade the legal ban on striptease shows, issued last summer by License Commissioner Paul Moss, and ratified by the American Federation of Actors, by holding off the undressing until the boat shoves off.

The exact itinerary has not been planned, Lynch explained, but the general plot is for the show to remain "inoffensive" until it reaches the middle of the river. New Jersey is on the far side.

"After that," Lynch said, "it will be up to the customers. It will be every man for himself, and the show will make Mount Vesuvius seem like cold soup. The gals will keep taking off clothes until the customers yell, 'stop!'"

Lynch said in 25 years of show business he has never heard a customer yell, 'stop!'

Among the leading ladies will be two young ladies addicted to ripping off their underwear in the fashion made popular by Gypsy Rose Lee. Lynch said Miss Julie Bryan, Gypsy Rose's former understudy, would probably make the clientele forget they ever saw Miss Lee.

He said he would have 25 chorus girls and at least a dozen specialty girls in the cast, and when the new "Noah's Ark" swings into the stream and the girls begin to get down to nature, even the fish will stop swimming."

This article, along with some similar clippings, appeared in several East Coast area newspapers. Did this "Noah's Ark" burlesque show ever actually happen? I truly have no clue.

Julie Bryan shows how easily her costume is slipped off to a photographer in her dressing room backstage at the Oriental Burlesque Theatre in New York City. Courtesy: New York Daily News Archive

Sheet music from George White's Scandals of 1919. The song, "Up Above The Stars." Courtesy: Authors Collection

Another clipping from 1938 included the following from the "Voice of Broadway" column, written by Dorothy Kilgallen. "Miss Midnight's Notebook" reads:

"Fable from the Forties: Eddie Lynch, once a chorus boy known as "Apple Cheek Eddie," became the producer who brought the Minsky's to Broadway. He used to sneak into the Broadway hits at night, disguised as a candy butcher, and write down the blackout sketches, which would then turn up a couple of evenings later in the local burlesque shows.

One night George White caught him making notes on the blackouts during a performance of the "Scandals," and chased him down Broadway for blocks, screaming, "There goes that so and so who's been stealing our sketches."

This week Eddie Lynch, all dressed up in white tie and tails, took his girl to see the out-of-town premiere of a new musical. He even paid for his tickets! And as the show unfolded Eddie grew whiter and whiter.

You see, Eddie still produces burlesque shows for the entire country. And it startled him to see that every comedy scene in the new musical was identical with the ones in the burlesque divertissement he was opening there the next night."

And then there was this bit of information:

"Eddie Lynch, the Troc producer, has received an offer from the *American Weekly* to serialize his memoirs. If Eddie really lets go, they should be hotter than Fanny Hill."

Something similar reads:

"Eddie Lynch, the Troc producer who once was a Hollywood dance director with Busby Berkeley, is writing a book which will tell "all" about many of the ex-burlesquers who have climbed to movie fame."

The Troc Burlesque Theatre in Philadelphia, Pennsylvania. Courtesy: C.F. Miller

(Notes: I have not been able to find any record of Eddie Lynch writing such a book about his life, or about burlesque.)

There were several more clippings; I believe they were all from different newspapers:

"Eddie Lynch Produced *Hit Parade of Tunes*; A real hit is the *Hit Parade of Tunes*, a new show that just opened at the Globe Theatre. Eddie "Apple Cheek" Lynch produced it, and it's another good job to his credit."

"Eddie Lynch, the Balanchine of Burlesque, is serious about wanting to bring ballet to the masses. He's trying to hire ballerinas to replace the traditional gum-chewing burleycue chorines."

"Eddie Lynch, the Troc producer, has had a terrific offer to go to Frisco and stage a burlesque spectacle during the conference. After all, what could the delegates look at that's more American than burlesque?"

"Max Hoffman, son of the famous Gertrude, now in the cast of *Good Night, Ladies*, reminiscing with Eddie Lynch, the Troc's impresario, about the days when they were in *Sweet Adeline, Golden Dawn*, etc., and roommates of a guy named Archie Leach – later known as Cary Grant."

"A glamorous movie star narrowly missed getting slugged in a local nightclub when she sent a note to handsome Eddie Lynch, the dance director, and it was intercepted by his girl friend, an ex-wrestler."

"When Gypsy Rose Lee was in Cleveland recently, Eddie Lynch, producer at the Roxy Theatre there, thought she high-hatted her burlesque friends. So he took revenge. He billed a stripteaser in the following week's show as 'the young Gypsy Rose Lee.'"

"A special number produced by Eddie "Apple Cheek" Lynch that is the highlight in *Mermaids and Models*, is the cellophane number. The 18 lovely chorus girls are in a garden setting, standing on high steps. With all the lights turned on, and the girls dressed in cellophane, you see the effects of a softly beautiful cascading waterfall."

"Sherry Lea, who gave up a movie career to go into burlesque, because the "kids were more sincere there," was offered a deal by Eddie Lynch, top burlesque director, which guarantees her $1,000 a week in 3 years."

A paragraph in the "Man About Boston" column, written by George W. Clarke, reads:

"Almost everyone in the theatre was in Philadelphia for J. J. Shubert's opening of *A Lady of ?*, which seems to have left no question in the minds of those who reviewed it – it seems to be funny in all the spots where the star, Carole Landis, isn't… and, aside from that, is Lynch, ex of E. M. Loew and now of burlesque, reported at the Philadelphia Variety Club that two of the blackouts were current at his place."

(Notes: The show was re-titled *A Lady Says Yes* prior to opening at the Broadhurst Theatre in New York City on January 10, 1945. It would only run for 87 performances.)

And finally:

"Pawtucket's First Unit This Year; Patrons Want More – Pawtucket, R.I. – Indicative of improved conditions in Southern New England and the clamor for stage shows is business done by Eddie Lynch's *Too Hot For Paris* unit at E. M. Loew's Capitol Theatre, November 13 to 15.

Playing three shows daily, the attraction drew close to 10,000. This was first unit to play Pawtucket this season, and house manager Hy Rodman went after business with extra advertising in the Providence and Woonsocket dailies. Three thousand cards handed to patrons Tuesday and Wednesday, inviting comments on show and expressions as to whether more such attractions were desired, brought over 600 replies, with comments praising the attraction and saying, 'Give us more.'"

The following clipping was from the *Philadelphia Record* on September 24, 1944. It's short and reads:

"Carol Lord Headlines New Burlesque at Troc: Burlesque's pin-up girl, Carol Lord, headlines the new show at the Troc Theatre this week, beginning with a midnight performance, tonight.

Hirst Circuit ad for traveling burlesque shows. Courtesy: Dusty Sage

Autographed photo of George Lewis to Lois de Fee; don't know why he added "Benny Wop" into his signature. There was a comic who went by the name Benny "Wop" Moore; Lewis went by "Beetlepuss." Courtesy: Dusty Sage

Others on the bill are: Chickie O'Dell, dancer Evelyn Lang, comics Eddie Lloyd and Franklyn Hopkins, and I. B. Hamp and Gertrude "Gertie" Beck.

Vaudeville specialties include a novelty by Herbert Loe and song hits of the day by Tommy Lane.

The Trocettes present new dance routines by Eddie Lynch, and music is by Merrick Valinote and Harry Kahn's Swingsters."

(Notes: The following article, not in the Minsky Files but which may be of interest to burlesque fans, was in the *Billboard* magazine on September 5, 1942. The title of the article is "Comics Set for 26 Hirst Units; 23 Houses Start." It is a short article which provides many names and just some good information. It reads:

"PHILADELPHIA. August 29 – Izzy Hirst's office has practically completed castings of comics for 26 burlesque units to play the Hirst and Midwest wheels. Unit line-up includes: 1) Manny King and Billy Wallace; 2) Bob Ferguson and Max Coleman; 3) George Murray and Bert Carr; 4) George Lewis and I. B. Hamp; 5) Billy Ainsley and Eddie Innes; 6) Shorty McAllister and Stinky Fields and Bobby Faye; 7) Mike Sachs and Bobby Vail; 8) Billy Walsh and Billy Hagen; 9) Jack Diamond and Murray Leonard; 10) Harry Conley and Billy Foster.

11) Bozo Snyder, Joe Cowan and Bill Lloyd; 12) Hap Arnold, Russell

Billy "Cheese and Crackers" Hagen. Courtesy: C.F. Miller

Comic Tommy "Bozo" Snyder without stage makeup on. Courtesy: Lee Stuart

Comic Joey Cowan. Courtesy: Burlesque Historical Society

Trent and Harry Levine; 13) Billy "Boob" Reed and Meggs Lexing; 14) Marty Collins and Al Anger; 15) Benson and Ryan and Billy Fields; 16) Looney Lewis, Little Jack Little and Al Rio; 17) Billy "Bumps" Mack, comic to fill; 18) Harry Clexx and Benny Moore; 19) Hap Hyatt and Dusty Fletcher; 20) Paul West and Johnny D'Arco and Lew Fine; 21) Kenny Brenna and Frankie Belasco; 22) to fill; 23) Freddy Binder and Jack Rosen and Jimmy Coughlin; 25) Jack "Tiny" Fuller, comic to fill; 26) Frank X. Silk and "Slats" Taylor.

Because of limited transportation facilities and curb on freight cars, traveling units will be limited to seven to nine people. In addition to two or

Paul West and Meggs Lexing. Courtesy: Lee Stuart

three comics, traveling unit will comprise a single stripper, straight man, singer, and dancer. While the choruses will be house units, the girls will be rotated from time to time.

In addition, props and scenery are being held down to an absolute minimum. However, no shortages are expected along those lines, since every one of the 23 houses on the wheels is pretty well stocked with stage accessories. The houses will pick up their own vaudeville acts. Also, strippers to augment the regular strip with the unit will also be picked up by the houses themselves.

Routes call for the units to rotate eight weeks in the East and eight weeks in the West. Starting the season with 23 houses, two of which are single-day stands, wheels expect to add several more full-week stands."

Burlesque ticket for a show at the Gaiety Theatre in Boston. Note the spelling of the name Sacks. Over the years I have often seen names misspelled. Courtesy: Dusty Sage

While researching the spelling of the name of a comic, I came across the following article from the *Austin Daily Herald*, in Minnesota, from August 11, 1952. Mike Sachs and his wife Alice Kennedy sometimes worked for the Minsky's. It reads:

"Mike Sachs, Blind Burlesque Comedian, Dies. NEW YORK (UP) – Michael (Mike) Sachs, who continued as a burlesque comedian for seven and a half years after going totally blind, died of a stroke early today.

His wife, who has been his stage partner for 19 years, said he was "so very happy" last night at the thought that they were going to play the season's opening August 23 at the Old Howard, Boston burlesque house.

Sachs died in Boulevard Hospital near his Long Island City home. He was 62.

He lost the sight of his right eye at the age of five when a blank cartridge exploded while he was at play. He lost the sight of the other eye in 1945.

His wife, the former Alice Kennedy, said the veteran of a half century on the stage "never made a false step" while playing his comic burlesque roles in his years of blindness. He knew the stages well, and she gave him cues. They were married in June, 1951.")

The following clipping was from an unknown newspaper, dated Thursday, August 16, 1945.

"Desert Scene is One of Many at Globe. The chorus in *Bathing Beauties*, now at the Globe Theatre, again comes through with some spectacular routines under the direction of Eddie (Apple Cheek) Lynch. The outstanding number is a Russian dance in which half of the girls are dressed in black and the other half are in white. They stand in a line, one girl back of the other, so that only the lead girl is seen, while the arms of the other girls are visible. The various motions of all of their arms are quite effective.

Another scene is on the desert. Several Arab tents are around, and some camels lie, or rest, (or what-ever it is when a camel sits down) in the background. The girls are dressed in yellow harem costumes and dance, while Bob Ridley sings desert songs."

The following two clippings were from unknown Los Angeles newspapers; the year, also unknown. Separated by quotation marks, they read:

"Minsky Stager Now at Follies; Edward Lynch, former dance director for Minsky's, is now under contract to the Follies Theatre. He directed the new show, *Is She Good*, which gets under way tonight at the midnight offering."

"Follies Boasts Top Talent. The present performers at the new Follies Theatre are something about which the owners can boast. For the first time in burlesque history, the current show can point the acknowledged world leaders in four divisions of the art.

One may glimpse, first, the greatest laugh act of the stage today, 300 pound Carrie Finnell; second, the highest salaried dancer of burlesque, tiny Betty Rowland; third, the best known comic, Joe Yule; and fourth, the leading dance and scenic director of the past decade, Eddie Lynch.

In this week's show, *Not Tonight Daddy*, and for a couple of weeks to follow, this quartet of headliners will remain. In mid-September or soon thereafter, redheaded Betty will begin a screen leading role."

Carrie Finnell, an extremely popular performer in burlesque. Courtesy: Burlesque Historical Society

(Notes: The Files contained even more programs, including four from the Follies Theatre: *Frolics and Thrills*, from April 7, 1934; *Hot-Cha Babies*, from April 28, 1934; *Oriental Nights*, from May 5, 1934; and *Let's Make Whoopee*, from May 12, 1934. Dances and Ensembles were staged by Eddie Lynch; the shows were all produced by George Clark, and the sets were created by James Monroe Johnson. The cast members included: Alice Duval, Sally O'Day, Bobbie Young, Billie Bird, Sylvia Rogers, Billie Beaton, Louise Phelps, Jimmie Chubb, Jack Russell, Eddie Collins, Gene Darby, Leon DeVoe, and Al Ferris. And according to all of

Press Photo from 1949 of Joe Yule – Mickey Rooney's father. Courtesy: Authors Collection

the programs, "The background of 40 dazzling and youthful dancing beauties are by no means to be overlooked. In fact, we know they will be well looked over!")

The next four items came from "Clippings, Inc.," which was located at 15 Whitehall Street, New York City. The press clipping agency dated the selections February 16, 1947. Most were short, a couple of lines; but one was quite lengthy.

The first was from *The Hollywood Reporter*, and ran in the "Rambler Reporter" column. It reads:

"There is a movement among the Broadway producers to bar a fellow named Eddie Lynch, a burlesque producer, from opening nights. He comes to look at the scenery, he hopes to rent if the show folds."

Another reads: "Eddie Lynch has been engaged to stage and direct 14 chorines who will make up the group Gypsy Rose Lee will head over her Royal American Shows tour."

Included was a small ad that reads: "Wanted – at once, Chorus Girls; Experience Unnecessary. Apply 1pm to 3pm, 7pm to 3pm. Kentucky Hotel, with Rehearsal Clothes, Room D – Mr. Lynch."

The final clipping in this group was a full-length article from the New York Associated Press. It reads as follows:

"Burlesque Going Elegant; Girls Now 'Exotic Dancers' – New York, (AP) – Burlesque, for years the blowzy, brash, black sheep of show business, is going elegant. At least, Eddie Lynch says it is. Eddie, an old-timer who is a producer for the Eastern Burlesque Wheel, says; "The days of bums bringing in their lunch and taking their shoes off, is over."

He boasts, "We play to a general ladies and gentlemen audience. The strippers have graduated from a garter belt to silver for capes, platform shoes, hats and gloves – and they take 'em off to symphonic music."

His reference to strippers was a slip of the tongue. Those ladies now are referred to as "exotic dancers."

There's been a delicate shift of emphasis from flesh to comedy. In the salty slang of the trade, Lynch explains, "We're featuring comics. We book a first and second banana, you know, comics; a 'yes' man (straight man), two strippers and a featured strip, the dame who rides in the Pullman."

Boston is an important stop-over on the burlesque circuit. Four houses were running there at the start of the season and two are still flourishing. San Francisco and Los Angeles are the only other cities supporting two burlesque theatres. New York is the only big city where burlesque isn't acceptable. It has been banned there for several years.

Burlesque business has been off slightly since most of the servicemen were mustered out, according to *Billboard*. The magazine estimates that a minimum of

750 strippers are working now, plus 150 comics and 75 straight men. Twenty-six theatres belonging to the big wheels are lighted.

There are a number of independent houses, ranging from reputable spots that book from both wheels, down to spit-in-the-corner places showing double-feature grade Z pictures for a nickel and featuring one live act. The latter, sometimes termed "scratch houses," hire the floaters or "gypsies" of the profession. "Burlesque," Mr. Lynch claims, "is the only place where anybody can get a chance anymore."

Kids are broken in on what the performers call "Burma Road," a derisive tag for Rochester, Dayton, Toledo, and Youngstown. After eight weeks they're supposedly ready for the big league. Atlantic City is the Valhalla of the business. "A couple of weeks at the Globe," Mr. Lynch says, "and you can write your own ticket."

Insiders say the real "characters" are the musicians in the orchestra pit. Mr. Lynch tells a story about last year in Cleveland when he was sitting out front watching one of his units and smelled something burning. Pungent smoke was curling up from the pit. He peered over and saw the drummer working over an electric plate.

Mr. Lynch ran for the house manager, and asked, "Don't you smell fish burning?" The house manager nodded, "Sure, it's Friday," he said.

Eddie Lynch, seated on the left side of the photo with a woman on his lap, at a cast party. Courtesy: Maureen Girard

The following article, mentioning Lynch, ran in the Los Angeles *Daily News* on April 29, 1947. It was written by David Hanna for his column, "David Hanna on Broadway."

"NEW YORK, April 29 – (Exclusive) – Eddie Jaffe, a man who has been in show business for many years in capacities such as agent, publicity man and producer, has been lying awake nights brooding over the fact that in this era of nostalgic entertainment, the movies have overlooked burlesque.

Jaffe is particularly concerned by the fact that people are inclined to think of burlesque only as a "Girlie Show" with the emphasis on the striptease. The public has forgotten that burlesque once was accepted family entertainment which did just what its name implies. It burlesqued other shows, satirized public figures, and poked fun at anything that seemed topical and humorous.

Fannie Brice performing a fan dance with palm fronds. Courtesy: Bettmann Archives

Consequently burlesque was a medium which cradled some of America's finest comedians. To mention a few who grew up on the wheel, there are Phil Silvers, Rags Ragland, Bud Abbott, Lou Costello, and the late W.C. Fields and Will Rogers; and of course, Fannie Brice.

These are the performers who graduated from the burley bits into Broadway revues, the screen and radio. Jaffe points out that there are others no less talented but not so lucky. A great many still are working in burlesque. These Jaffe hopes to assemble sometime this summer to make a picture. It won't be anything fancy – just a thin story line to tie the thing together with all the action centered on the filming of the great burlesque routines for which the comedians are known.

To help him in the project (which will be shot at a New Jersey studio,) Jaffe has engaged Eddie "Apple Cheek" Lynch whose nom de theatre is "the poor man's Ziegfeld." His nickname "Apple Cheek" goes back to the time when he used to be an errand boy for theatrical press agents. Newspapermen of the day remember him fondly as the lad who used to throw his employers' releases into the nearest sewer so that he could go to the ball game.

Lynch grew out of such habits as he gained stature in the amusement world. He became a burlesque director and a rough estimate of his work through the years would indicate that he has staged some 5000 shows. He has shuttled all over the country and wearily explains his success as the result of a long memory and respect for a short budget.

Among the comedians who have been lined up for this celluloid tribute to burlesque are "Stinky and Shorty" – a team that is almost as old as the business itself. Stinky, who is celebrating his 50th year as a burly funnyman, came to America in 1905 with Charlie Chaplin to work for Oscar Hammerstein in an act called, "A Night in an English Music Hall."

His partner, Shorty, used to work with Stan Laurel in England, and for many years he was a member of the legendary Keystone Kops. One of the few original 'Keystoners' still alive, he certainly is the only one still active in show business today.

1944 program from the Empire Burlesque Theatre in Newark, New Jersey. The show featured "Stinky" Fields and "Shorty" McAllister. Courtesy: Burlesque Historical Society

Another old-timer whose slap-stick will be immortalized in the Jaffe picture is Billy "Cheese and Crackers" Hagen. He has been in burlesque for 45 years all because he was knocked out in a fight. A member of America's first Olympic team in 1908, Hagen boxed as a professional and amateur, simultaneously. He used his real name for the former, and billed himself as Hayden when he went up against the non-pros.

Fighting against Aurelia Herrera, the hard-hitting Mexican lightweight, Billy took the drubbing of his lifetime in the very first round. That finished his days in the ring, so with his wife he conceived a burlesque boxing bit and went on the stage. He's still doing the same routine – and the laughs are just

as plentiful as they were at the turn of the century.

Hagen is the comic who won national publicity for his craft when during the war he was obliged to put his important prop, a putty nose, in a safe at the Empire Theatre in Newark every night. Putty, it seems, was impossible to get.

The next day, before the first performance, he would send a most dignified messenger into the manager's office, always with the same request, "Mr. Hagen would like to take his nose out of your safe."

Hear "Tapestries of Life" by David Hanna, and featuring Theodore Von Eltz, tonight, KNX, 9:30."

Billy "Cheese and Crackers" Hagen. Courtesy: Burlesque Historical Society

Comic Billy "Cheese and Crackers" Hagen, straight man Floyd Hallicy, and May Joyce performing in "The Baseball Player's Honeymoon" scene. Courtesy: Burlesque Historical Society

Just as I found the previous column interesting, I consider the following to be a gem as well. It was an article written by Paul Wilder for the *Tampa Morning Tribune*. It's titled "In Our Town, How the Lovely Showgirls Train for a Season of Travel with the Midway," and dated, April 22, 1949. It reads:

"The piano tinkles… workmen nail up blue velvet backdrops… a dozen tall girls in blue jeans, play suits and just plain dresses prance back and forth… a harried man pounds the beat with his foot and shouts, "One, two, three, four, turn; one, two, three, four, back…"

It's the dreary rehearsal for Gypsy Rose Lee's girl show going out with the midway in a few weeks.

Scenery men, unmindful of the flashing legs and moving shoulders, pound unhurriedly. Other workers carry lumber in and out, as an electrician works on spotlights and portable wiring.

Over and over, over and over, the producer, Eddie Lynch, of New York, calls the girls back to repeat their steps.

The showgirls, all over five feet eight, and two standing six feet tall, were recruited in New York. They are paid anywhere from $50 to $75 a week, and according to experience. Part of the money is withheld from their weekly checks until the end of the season. Thus, if a girl collects $60 a week during the tour, and stays with the show, she'll collect the rest in "bonus" of about $350.

Their costumes, provided by the show, already have run to $22,000, including Gypsy Rose Lee's own grand finale costume made of more than a million rhinestones, weighing over 70 pounds. The dress cost more than $2200, not including a $160 petticoat which Miss Lee decided not to wear anyway because she can't get it on and off fast enough in changes.

Even the stockings, costing $15 a pair, are provided by the show. When the unit goes on tour there will be a $10 prize for the showgirl who makes her nylons wear the longest. There will also be fines by the stage manager for girls, who sit down in their costumes, rumpling or damaging the material, and who may mistreat the wardrobe. Money from the fines will be put into a kitty to pay for a party at the end of the 26-week season.

Producer Eddie Lynch, who worked with Earl Carroll and Arthur Hammerstein as producer, and who has just come from producing Milton Berle's show for television, is an old hand at dealing with showgirls. In 17 years of show business he figures he's hired and trained more than 1000 girls.

There are three rules in picking showgirls, he says: "(1) Never pick them with their clothes on. Girls who appear gorgeous in 'New Look' dresses may turn out to be bowlegged or knock-kneed, so they spell OX when standing together. (2) Beware of falsies, a big problem in show business. The wardrobe matron's job is discovering bogus attractions. (3) Beware of paint and powder. Get the girls who are youthful and wholesome in appearance without paint."

"Hair is also one of the producer's problems," Lynch says. "On Monday there may be two blondes in the show, and eight brunettes. On Tuesday there may be eight blondes and two brunettes. On Wednesday the remaining two brunettes will be redheads, so they will be the outstanding girls. Present fad among the showgirls over the country is honey blonde, but they may change overnight, according to the style set by some movie star. The girls in this show have blossomed out with upswept hairdos because Gypsy has her hair upswept.

The show now has 12 regular girls and two spares, who will be available for work in the line in case of emergency. They aren't required to do much dancing, just walk prettily around the stage to music and sing some numbers like, "We're the Darlings of the Show; We'll Bring out the Wolf in You." They also provide a scenic background for the show's star, Miss Lee. The showgirls will perform the bally calls out front, to draw in the customers, as well as parading inside the show. It's a snap for the first 10 weeks," Lynch say, "but after that it becomes a grind, and you really have to work."

Then he goes back to, "One, two, three, four, turn; just a little more class, dear. One, two…" as he continues to count."

Photo from 1949, Gypsy Rose Lee standing between Carl J. Sedlmayr Sr. and Carl J. Sedlmayr Jr. of the Royal American Shows. The men presented the show, Gypsy Rose Lee and her Royal American Beauties; *it was produced by Eddie Lynch. Courtesy: C.F. Miller*

(Notes: The folder contained a copy of a flyer that goes hand-in-hand with the preceding article. It was from the Royal American Shows and reads: "Carl J. Sedlmayr presents Gypsy Rose Lee and her Royal American Beauties in a Gay Glittering Revue." The show was produced by Edward Lynch; it starred Gypsy Rose Lee, and featured, among others: The Four Reasons, a musical combo; Bill Frazer; The Beaucaires, a novelty dance troupe; Boyd Bennett; and Brandy Bryant. In small print, in parenthesis, at the very bottom of the flyer it reads: "Miss Lee's Finale Gown weighs ninety-seven pounds. It is made of one million, one hundred thousand, three hundred and twenty-seven rhinestones, sewn on by hand!" The credits state that Miss Lee's Specialty Costume was executed by Anna Delta Winslow.)

The final Lynch clipping I'm including, comments once again about the book Eddie was supposedly writing; but there was no date, author, or anything else listed as to what newspaper the article appeared in. It reads:

"Lynch Gives 'Burlesk' Needed Novel Punch. Edward Francis Lynch, production manager for Harry Brock at the Empire Theatre, in the current attraction, *Red Rhythm*, is presenting his fifth musical review. He joined Brock this season through a chance meeting on the golf links last summer, and together they decided that burlesque, one of the passé branches of the entertainment world, needed modern ideas and many radical changes.

The oldsters shook their heads when Brock, a New York hotel owner, decided to put burlesque on a new basis two years ago. Now they nod their heads with pleasure at whatever he does. An ideal assistant is Lynch. He, too, believes that laughter and beauty are a good combination for entertainment.

Lynch is a New Jersey chap, hailing from Jersey City. Gus Edwards wanted an apple-cheeked boy for his famous juvenile act which from time to time featured such stars as Eddie Cantor, Georgie Price, George Jessel, and Walter Winchell; and roly-poly Lynch got the job. He did a 'Little Lord Fauntleroy' until he outgrew his suit. It was cheaper to get a new actor than a new suit, so Lynch found himself working for C.P. Greneker, a Shubert press representative, when the road tour ended.

Lynch has a knack of adapting himself to any job and soon found writing, providing he could give his imagination full rein, an ideal career. Greneker let him go whole hog on publicity for Shubert productions, and in the eight years Lynch was a glorifier for these shows he used up more adjectives than any 10 theatrical prevaricators on Broadway. He still holds that record, as his worn-out dictionary will prove.

But putting others in the spotlight became tiring to young and ambitious Lynch. He took to staging such Broadway successes as *Rose Marie, Golden Dawn,*

Good Boy, and *Sweet Adeline*, for the road. This process is very interesting, according to Lynch. It requires merging ten or twelve scenes into two or three, and reducing a cast of 50 actors down to 15 or 20 with a skeletonized chorus for a background. The idea is to retain the play with its highlights without any of its expenditures.

From these glorified tabloids to burlesque was an easy step. This type of entertainment specializes in timely topics, obviously satirized, and risqué jokes, smartly dramatized. To offset these blackouts, Lynch indulges in his fantastic ideas for ballets and chorus routines. He has done more to improving the choruses in burlesque than anyone else in recent years. Lynch declares that burlesque represents the best features of musical revue – the blackout - coupled with the headliners of vaudeville. More than any other type of entertainment it is helping to bring back the "flesh" shows to the cinema-ridden public.

The Empire has already broken its last year's records for the same period. The reason for this, Lynch puts forward, is that the shows at the Empire Theatre are first and foremost laugh shows.

Lynch has made burlesque his career and is now writing a book on this all-absorbing subject in collaboration with Manuel Seff and Marian Spitzer.

In *Red Hot*, the next attraction at the Empire Theatre, starting this Sunday, Lynch has incorporated some of his most daring ideas, and he is anxious to see how the public will react to them."

(Notes: Looking under Marian Spitzer's name I did not find anything about burlesque; however, I did buy a copy of her book *The Palace*. When looking under the name of Manuel Seff, I also found nothing connecting him to Eddie Lynch.)

The most recent item from the "E" File, in regards to Eddie Lynch, was a letter from Lynch to Pat Minsky Shapiro, dated June 14, 1981. The letter, written on Caesars Palace stationery, was notarized; it was an appraisal and reads:

Dear Pat,

As you well know, I have been associated with the Minsky family in the field of stage productions for over forty-five years now. During this time, I have worked in the various fields of show business including choreographer, producer, and stage manager for the Minsky family in particular. I have assisted your late husband, Harold, in the buying of scenery and costumes for his numerous stage productions and since last working for Harold in 1966, I have been stage manager for Caesars Palace where I am presently involved in the current costs of live stage productions. For these reasons, I consider myself to be well qualified in doing this appraisal for you.

First of all, I would like to say that I arrived at the total amount of $26,190.00 based on the following: the condition of the costumes, the quality and durability of the materials used, as well as the fair market value, and the cost of reproducing the costumes at the current costs of materials.

I found the condition of the costumes to be mostly good to very good condition. The materials which the costumes, trim on the costumes, and headpieces are made of include quality materials such as: silk, lamé, chiffon, sequins, mirrors, beads, boa, rhinestones, pearls, feathers and applied materials. Real hair, as opposed to synthetic, was used in the making of the headpieces and wigs.

I have taken into consideration also, the fact that such materials as sequins, rhinestones, and beads have increased in value as they are durable materials. Their durability means that they can be reused as the costs to replace them have increased considerably.

I feel that to replace these costumes at today's market would be more than double that amount.
Sincerely,
Eddie Lynch

"E" is also for the Edgewater Beach Hotel. Just a brief history of the hotel follows.

The Edgewater Beach Hotel was a resort hotel complex in the far-north neighborhood community of Edgewater in Chicago, Illinois. It was designed by Benjamin H. Marshall and Charles E. Fox. The original section was built

Aerial photo of the Edgewater Beach Hotel. Courtesy: Uptown Chicago History

in 1916 for owners John Tobin Connery and James Patrick Connery, and was located between Sheridan Road and Lake Michigan at Berwyn Avenue. An adjacent south tower building was added in 1924. The hotel closed in 1967, and was entirely demolished by 1971.

The developers also built a sister hotel, the Edgewater Gulf Hotel, in Biloxi, Mississippi, which closed in 1970. It was also designed by the same Chicago architectural firm.

The Chicago complex was composed of several buildings and recreation grounds. The Main Building, designed in the shape of a "forked cross," had 400 rooms and opened on June 3, 1916. Because of its success, in April 1923, construction began on a $3,000,000 19-story, 600 room tower addition to the south of the Main Building. The Tower Building, initially called the Annex, opened for occupancy on February 9, 1924, and was connected to the Main Building by a large hall.

The hotel featured a spectacular private beach and offered every imaginable amenity, including seaplane service to downtown Chicago. It also featured its own private radio station WEBH that was renowned nationwide for its live broadcasts of the big band music of Benny Goodman, Tommy Dorsey, Glenn Miller, Artie Shaw, Xavier Cugat, and many other popular music acts that appeared at the hotel. Locals flocked to the hotel to see them when they played outdoors on the hotel's famous Beach Walk, or in the hotel's elegant Marine Dining Room.

Over its lifetime, guests included: Babe Ruth, Lou Gehrig, Marilyn Monroe, Frank Sinatra, Judy Garland, Bette Davis, Charlie Chaplin, Tallulah Bankhead, Lena Horne, and Nat King Cole. It was also a favorite with the Washington elite, including United States Presidents Franklin D. Roosevelt and Dwight D. Eisenhower.

The 1951–54 extension of Lake Shore Drive from Foster Avenue to Hollywood Avenue cut the hotel off from having direct access to Lake Michigan,

1947 Press Photo of Phil Silvers and Frank Sinatra for a party on New Year's Eve. Courtesy: Pictorial Parade Archive

Sheet music from the 1962 Warner Brothers animated film, Gay Purr-ee. *Judy Garland, Robert Goulet, Red Buttons, and Hermione Gingold all performed voice-overs in the film.*
Courtesy: Authors Collection

leading to a reduction in business. So, a swimming pool was added in 1953; and, in order to compete with popular downtown hotels, the Edgewater Beach Hotel underwent a $900,000 renovation which included the installation of air conditioning in 1960.

In December 1967, after falling into disrepair, the Edgewater Beach Hotel closed its doors due to bankruptcy proceedings. Demolition of the hotel complex began in the fall of 1969 and was completed by 1971.

The Edgewater Beach Apartments, built in 1927 at 5555 N. Sheridan Road, and the last of the original structures left on the former hotel property, still stand. It was added to the National Register of Historic Places in 1994.

(Notes: John T. Connery was born in Bristol, Rhode Island, on January 10, 1861. He passed away in Chicago on June 5, 1937. In 1876, he took a job as a yard clerk for Ed Hedstrom and Company, coal merchants, and for more than 50 years worked in the coal industry. In June of 1904 John became President of the Miami Coal Company, which had its offices in Chicago.

James P. Connery, John's younger brother, was born in May of 1865. He died on June 30, 1929. Following the death of his oldest brother William M. in 1911, James became Secretary of the Miami Coal Company and continued on in that capacity for the remainder of his life, as well as being a major stockholder in the Edgewater Beach Hotel.

The rumor running rampant throughout Chicago was that the two Connery brothers were interested in purchasing the Chicago Cubs. When the deal fell apart they purchased the lot across from John's residence on Sheridan Avenue instead, where they built the Edgewater Beach Hotel. The elder brother was President of the Edgewater Beach Hotel from 1919 until his death.

Mary E. (Bidwill) Nelson, John's granddaughter, ran the Edgewater Beach Hotel with her husband John Lawrence Nelson until it was razed. Mary Bidwill Nelson died on Monday, August 8, 1994, at the age of 82. Mrs. Nelson's late father, Joseph Bidwill, served as clerk of the Circuit Court of Cook County.)

Even though there weren't a lot of items in the Edgewater Beach Hotel folder, what it did include was interesting. There was an article from *Variety*, a program, and a menu. Let's start with the article, which was published under "Unit Reviews," and dated April 12, 1967. Within eight months the Edgewater Beach Hotel would close. The review reads as follows:

"Minsky's Follies, Edgewater Beach Hotel, Chicago, April 6: *Minsky's Follies*, produced by Harold Minsky; choreographed and directed by Jerry Norman; featuring Lisa Duran, Debra Duke, Mikki Sharait, Barbara Curtis, Milt Douglas, Freddie Lewis, Danny Jacobs, David Walker, Larry Merritt, Ken Whitmer, Minsky Girls (7), Minsky Dancers (7); Opened April 6, 1967 at Edgewater Beach Hotel, Chicago; George Cook Orchestra (13); $3 - $4 cover.

The idea of a gaudy and bawdy burlesque show in the elegant setting of the Marine Room of the Edgewater Beach Hotel could be a sharp bit of booking. Or so it would seem from the SRO celeb turnout on opening night, one of the more gala nitery premiers in recent Windy City times. Whether the locals and conventioneers respond in kind to this sort of saucy and flashy nostalgia is a mite more iffy and will determine whether the four-week booking of the obviously expensive show is optimistic or not.

The show is handsomely mounted and briskly paced and the troupe in the main is first class. But as strong as the bill may be in total, it is sorely in need of a couple of sharper featured dancers and comics. Best of the former by far was Lisa Duran, a sinuous, supple, and sexy solo terper with a well-conceived turn. While a little less polished in her routine, Debra Duke has a great figure to show and was well received in her strip turn.

Comic Milt Douglas was appropriately brash in the traditional candy butcher oration, but missed or left out some of the time-tried bits of the ritual. Freddie Lewis, Danny Jacobs, and Barbara Curtis were okay in the old café drink-switching sketch, but didn't always maintain the gag pace of the veteran routine. The same applies to Douglas and Miss Curtis in a bickering couple skit – it drew occasional yocks, but couldn't sustain the laugh level. Monologist Ken Whitmer traveled some well-travelled comedic roads and was fine in his kidding on a variety of musical instruments.

Production singer David Walker was good in backing the strutting terp chorus and models and in several solos, and dancer Larry Merritt carried off his terp chores in fine style. The dance line was well-disciplined and the semi-nude models were uneven in their physical charm."

The program for the show reads: "Harold Minsky presents *Minsky's Follies*, Direct from Las Vegas! Edgewater Beach Hotel, Marine Room; World's most exciting girls!"

The show included a cast of 25, and that cast included: The Minsky Girls: Beth Avery, Pat Elliott, Linda Oliver, Darlene Larson, Jackie Peters, and Maureen Kelly. Some of the Minsky Dancers listed were: Arian Michele, Jean Kudia, Estelle Cole, Emily Byrne, Susan Ladd, and Marcia Gregg. And the show lists the following as features: Lisa Duran, Debra Duke, Barbara Curtis, Milt Douglas, Lyndon "Willie Dew" Cox, Danny Jacobs, David Walker, and Ken Whitmer. Al Alvarez and Bill Reddie were in charge of Orchestrations and Arrangements; and George Cook was the Musical Director. The show was Choreographed and Directed by Jerry Norman; the Company and Stage Manager was Don Kirk, and the Assistant to the Producer was Ava Minsky.

During the run of the show there were some cast changes which involved the Minsky Dancers and the Minsky Girls. The Minsky Girls now included: Betty Jo Alvies, Bettina Brenna, Bari Gibson, Maureen Kelly, Aria King, Darlene Larson, and Jackie Peters. The Minsky Dancers were: Juanita Boyle, Nikki Braniff, Marcia Gregg, Kitty McDonald, Arian Michele, Susan Sigrist, and Francine Storey.

Scenes in the show included: the opening candy butcher prologue "Sweetheart of 1937" by Milt Douglas; the "Pepsi Cola Café" skit performed by Freddie Lewis, Danny Jacobs, and Barbara Curtis; and "This is my Wife" with Milt Douglas and Barbara Curtis.

Barbara Curtis. Courtesy: Janelle Smith Collection

The biographical information on the back of the program was also interesting, and tells a bit about those involved in the show. It included Minsky, of course, but others in the cast and crew were covered, for example:

"Jerry Norman; choreographer and director of *Minsky's Burlesque Follies*, gave three years of his life to *West Side Story*, playing one of the Jets on Broadway, in the film, and on the European Tour. He now seems destined to give Minsky equal time, for he has been the choreographer of *Life Begins at Minsky's* and *The Wonderful World of Minsky*, both at the Silver Slipper in Las Vegas as well as *The Minsky Burlesque Follies*.

David Walker; whose appearances as a star of the Las Vegas Minsky shows indicates that he will have a long career as a singer in stage musicals, received his first Las Vegas job for Minsky and has appeared in several of his Silver Slipper shows there.

Miss (Lisa) Duran; a reformed adagio dancer, has been a headliner in clubs throughout America.

Debra Duke; is from the *Follies Bergere* in Las Vegas, has made movies in Rome and starred in a number of Minsky shows.

Milt Douglas; has been a favorite in vaudeville, nightclubs, and legitimate theatre. He replaced Jackie Gleason as the lead in the Broadway musical, *Follow the Girls*.

Danny Jacobs; is considered one of the world's greatest straight men and is a veteran of more than 50 years experience.

Barbara Curtis; is "one of the most talented talking women," who has played in theatres throughout the world.

Added attraction is Ken Whitmer, "Professor of Music," whose comedy and musical feats as a one-man band have been seen in Chicago at a number of theatres and nightclubs."

Lastly, I found the menu interesting – I planned to scan it for the book but sadly it was lost in the fire.

Also in this File was a folder for Elmwood Hotel and Casino, dated 1973.

The Elmwood Hotel and Casino complex, located in Windsor, Ontario, Canada, was owned by Al Siegel. The hotel was already open for business in the early 1930s, but underwent extensive reconstruction around 1944 - the Casino opened in 1952. The Elmwood Hotel, an art deco-style building with 103 rooms, was located on an 11-acre lot. Many top entertainers highlighted the nightly floor shows including: Tom Jones, Tony Bennett, Liberace, Ella Fitzgerald, Sammy Davis Jr., The Supremes, Smokey Robinson and the Miracles, Jimmy Durante, Sid Caesar, Milton Berle, and Wayne Newton.

Sadly, the Elmwood Hotel and Casino fell on hard times and owner Al Siegel could no longer afford the stars that the casino had supported throughout the years. Looking at the Agreement, you can tell payments for the *Minsky Burlesque Follies* were not handled the normal way. After filing for bankruptcy, Siegel closed the doors to the Elmwood Hotel and Casino in December 1974. Al Siegel was also a co-founder of the Windsor Raceway, a harness horse racing track. The Elmwood Hotel complex, in disrepair, was sold in 1983 and destined to become the Brentwood Recovery Home.

Included in the folder was an Agreement dated March 30, 1973; the show was to commence on Thursday, April 26, 1973 and run through and including Saturday, May 12, 1973. It was for two shows nightly, six nights per week, with Sundays off. Each performance was to last approximately one hour.

Minsky was to furnish and supply a cast of thirteen, along with all things necessary to present the show. The casino management was to supply rehearsal space, a follow spotlight and operator. They were also to furnish and pay for the orchestra, including rehearsal time and for all performances. The orchestra was to consist of seven musicians, including: piano, bass, drums, two trumpets, one trombone, and one saxophone.

Harold Minsky was to be paid $7500.00 per week; and $3750.00 for the additional three days. The dates he was to be paid were: April 28, 1973, May 5, 1973, and May 12, 1973. This section had a large section blacked-out and dates for payments retyped in.

Everything else is what would be in a typical Minsky contract regarding Workman's Compensation, taxes, and publicity. It was signed by Al Siegel for the Elmwood Hotel and Casino, and Harold Minsky.

The program included in the folder reads as follows:

"Fifteen of the most beautiful dancers and showgirls around have the stage at the Elmwood Casino starting Thursday, April 26, in *Minsky's Burlesque*, a musical revue produced by the famed Harold Minsky. The troupe has been called the greatest thing to happen to Las Vegas since faro was invented. Top Banana Tommy "Moe" Raft, according to one Las Vegas writer, is "Truly the greatest top banana in show business." Shows are at 9:45 and 11:45pm; Monday through Friday, $7.75 per person, $2.50 per person for the 2nd show."

There was also an article from *The Detroit News*, Sunday edition, April 29, 1973. It was titled "The Name is Minsky, Spell it b-u-r-l-e-s-q-u-e!," and written by entertainment columnist A.L. McClain. It reads:

"Scurvy Miller's baggy-pants hang somewhere on a rusty nail. Detroit's famous old burlesque comic hung them up some time ago. But seeing Scurvy pull out his oversized pants saying, "Wanna see my shoes," while strippers squirmed in the background, was a part of growing up for many males who are now middle-aged.

Scurvy Miller and Joan Arline working in a scene in 1955 at the Gayety Theatre in Detroit. Notice his nose. Courtesy: Joan Arline

The old Avenue Burlesque, scene of Scurvy's golden age of comedy, is now a lifeless place at Woodward and Congress. The National Burlesk Theatre, Detroit's surviving strip parlor, is hanging on by a G-string. There no longer is a prize "in each and every package" of candy. Burlesque, born in New York in 1908, now is a corpse waiting to be buried.

Harold Minsky, a happy cherub of a man with a famous name, would be an ideal choice to eulogize over the remains of burlesque. Only he thinks there is still life in the old girl.

His father, A.B. Minsky, introduced burlesque to this country on New York City's Lower East Side 65 years ago. And ever since the name Minsky has spelled burlesque – or burlesk – or burly-q.

Harold Minsky sees a new kind of burlesque rising from the empty and dirty stages of closed houses, although he knows that burlesque as it was once known will never return.

His show, *Minsky's Burlesque*, is playing the Elmwood Casino in Windsor through May 12. And the show is topless!

He has two other shows playing at the Playboy Plaza Hotel in Miami, Florida, and the Fremont Hotel in Las Vegas. "There's been a Minsky burlesque show playing somewhere in Las Vegas since 1950," he says proudly.

Minsky says that the only thing left to remind people of the old days in his show are the comics and strippers.

"Now we have choreographers, singers, and modern costumes. I remember that in the old days it used to take a girl four minutes just to take off her gloves. We've modernized it. One of our strippers, Denise Montego, doesn't just strip, she actually dances."

Minsky means burlesque. Harold has worked with the biggest names in the world of tease: Lili St. Cyr, Gypsy Rose Lee, Georgia Sothern, Margie Hart, Charmaine, Rose La Rose, Ann Corio, Tempest Storm, and Sequin.

The comics who worked for him include: Abbott and Costello, Phil Silvers, Red Buttons, Pinky Lee, and Robert Alda.

Autographed photo of Tempest Storm. Courtesy: C.F. Miller

"Some of them are still working," he said. "Only Ann Corio has stayed with the old-time burlesque, the same scenes and costumes. Rose La Rose died recently and left $700,000 in cash. Red Skelton was always hanging around the backstage, but he never worked for me. The last time Lili St. Cyr worked for me she was 50 and when she stripped, she looked swell."

Harold knew Scurvy Miller for many years, although the little comic, who always was dwarfed by the tall strippers, worked for a rival burlesque chain. "Scurvy was blue even by today's standards," Minsky said. "He would say anything."

Sequin posing alongside her sign at the Adams Theatre. Courtesy: Mary Jane Tamburello-Ellis

1964 Press Photo of Red Buttons, prepared to be used as a headshot to publicize the animated Warner Brothers film Gay-Purr-ee. *Buttons supplied his voice for a farm cat who goes to Paris. Judy Garland and Robert Goulet also performed voice-overs in the film. Courtesy: Authors Collection*

Rose La Rose. Courtesy: Burlesque Historical Society

*Lili St. Cyr.
Courtesy:
C.F. Miller*

Of the many strippers who worked for him, "I'd take none of them," he said. "But I would take Sophia Loren. Now there's a good-looking woman. She's a stunning woman, not a girl."

The Night They Raided Minsky's, a movie based on the Minsky family experience, was released several years ago. Harold Minsky said he thought it "was a cute film."

He added, "But I thought Tony Curtis would have been better in the part than Jason Robards. Elliott Gould, who played my uncle Billy, didn't look anything like him. He was too tall."

For a man whose lifetime work has involved shows with women taking off their clothes, he has some puritanical notions about nudity. "I don't think total nudity will ever be accepted. Partial nudity is more sexy than total nudity. There's no tease, no excitement in a completely nude woman staring at you," Harold Minsky says.

"F" is For...

"F" is for the Fremont Hotel and Casino in Las Vegas, Nevada. The Fremont is one of the resorts located in downtown Las Vegas that is currently part of the Fremont Street Experience. The property, at one time, had been owned by the pioneering Von Tobel family who had been in Las Vegas since the Land Auction of 1905.

The hotel was designed by architect Wayne McAllister and opened on May 18, 1956; it was the first high-rise hotel built on Fremont Street. It had 155 rooms, cost $6 million to open, and was owned by Ed Levinson and Lou Lurie. While Lurie owned the hotel, Levinson, who had started out at the Sands Hotel, was the President of the Fremont Hotel Corporation, which was the parent company of the resort. From the beginning, the Fremont became known for its food, and thought of itself as "a locals casino." Sadly, the roof of the hotel was a great spot for viewing the atomic bomb tests.

A mushroom cloud over Nevada. The Fremont Hotel is in right forefront of the photo. (Was this originally a newspaper photo?) Courtesy: Special Collection & Archives Research Center; Oregon State University

In 1959 Wayne Newton played his first Las Vegas Concert at the Fremont in its Carnival Lounge. In 1963, the hotel was expanded to include the 14-story Ogden Tower, a roof-top pool, and one of the city's first vertical parking garages.

In 1966, the Parvin-Dohrmann Company of Los Angeles, part owners of the Aladdin Hotel, bought the Fremont for $16 million. They added a 650-seat showroom called the Fiesta Room. Albert Parvin, head of the company, was connected to Ed Levinson and to the Teamsters, and his Foundation owned a share of the mortgage on the Flamingo.

In the late 1960s, Delbert Coleman and his Recrion Corporation obtained the Fremont Hotel, along with the Stardust on the Strip. By 1973, business pressures dictated that Coleman sell his casino interests, which included both hotels.

The hotels were encumbered by immense loans of $12 million dollars provided by the Teamsters Pension Funds.

In 1974, Recrion Corporation sold the Stardust and Fremont to Argent Corporation; the purchase was financed by a loan from the Teamsters Central States Pension Fund. Argent Corporation was owned by California real estate investor Allen Glick, who in 1976 expanded the Fremont at a cost of $4 million. He opened the first all female card room, and sponsored the "Battle of the Sexes" poker tournament. In the late 1970s, Glick got caught up in the Las Vegas gaming scandal and was ordered by the Nevada Gaming Commission to sell his properties.

The Golden Nugget and part of downtown Las Vegas in July 1968. Courtesy: Authors Collection

Downtown Las Vegas, late 1960s. Courtesy: Authors Collection

Enter Sam Boyd, and his son William, who would eventually buy the Fremont in 1983 to add to the Boyd Gaming group properties. Sam started out working as a dealer in the early 1940s. He worked his way up through the ranks of the Las Vegas casino industry, first to pit boss, then shift boss, and in 1952 invested $10,000 to become a part owner and partner in the Sahara Hotel and Casino. Sam Boyd left the Sahara to become General Manager and partner of The Mint Las Vegas; his gaming career took off from there. In 1973, Sam, and William, (a practicing attorney,) co-founded Boyd Gaming Corporation. In 1975, Bill joined his father full time in the gaming industry.

The Boyd's developed a reputation for running a squeaky-clean operation. As a result, the Nevada regulators turned to them for help following an investigation of skimming operations at both the Stardust and Fremont casinos in the early 1980s. The properties were notorious at the time for their extensive skimming operations. More information about the Fremont Hotel and Casino, the Boyd's, and the various owners and their "connections," can be found by doing research on the internet.

(Notes: The Edward Von Tobel Lumber Company opened for business in 1905 and remained in operation until 1976. It was founded by Edward Von Tobel Sr., and his partner and boyhood friend Jake Beckley, on South Main Street, south of the train depot. Jake Beckley, however, decided that perhaps what people needed more than Lumber and Hardware was clothes. So he and his brother Will bought a building on the south side of Fremont Street, on the corner of 1st Street, and they opened Beckley's Men's Wear. Shortly afterward, Jake amicably ended his partnership with Von Tobel. Active in community life, Von Tobel was elected to the city commission in 1911, and together with (among others), Jake Beckley, and Cyril S. Wengert, a prominent banker and utilities manager, was instrumental in the formation of civic and community service organizations in Las Vegas.)

The first item in the Fremont File was a "Letter Agreement" dated September 19, 1972, and it reads:

"This letter will serve as notice that Recrion will complete the unexpected term of their contract with Harold Minsky, to be played at the Fremont Hotel. The final two weeks of the existing contract shall be played at the Fremont Hotel rather than the Aladdin Hotel, and in addition to these two final weeks, Recrion hereby agrees to continue the show under the terms and conditions and for the same consideration set forth in the original contract of August 13, 1971 as amended by the Agreement dated November 1971 for a period of twenty-six (26) weeks, commencing December 27, 1972, with two sixteen (16) week options to be determined by March 6, 1973. All existing terms of the present contract shall remain in effect, except that the show MINSKY'S shall be produced at the Fremont Hotel main showroom and the Fremont Hotel shall be designated as the Operator in lieu of Prell Hotels, Inc. and Aladdin Hotel Corporation.

It is agreed and understood that in the event that there is a raise of minimum basic scales and working conditions thereof for principals, dancers and showgirls involved in Producer's production for Operator, the consideration agreed to be paid by Operator shall be increased in a like amount for the total number of employees designated in the agreement."

The Agreement was accepted and signed by: James J. Hill for the Fremont Hotel, Harold Minsky for Patava, Inc., and Art Engler from the Associated Booking Corporation, in Las Vegas.

Minsky's Burlesque Follies promotional photo from 1971, and the cast who performed at the Fremont Hotel. Courtesy: Janelle Smith Collection

The following item was part of the original Agreement from November 1971 between Prell Hotels, Inc., dbd as Aladdin Hotel, dba Aladdin Hotel Corporation, and Patava, Inc. The entire first page goes into all the legalese between this corporation doing business dealings as that corporation. This was not a normal Agreement due to all the different business names and explanations, but the bulk of the Agreement reads:

"Patava, Inc., performing under the stage name of MINSKY's, shall perform in accordance with said Agreement at the Aladdin Hotel on Las Vegas Boulevard South from the date of December 24, 1971, through and including June 1, 1972, constituting a period of twenty-three (23) consecutive weeks and shall continue to perform at the Aladdin Hotel for the balance of the term as set forth in the Agreement incorporated herein. Aladdin Hotel Corporation shall notify Patava, Inc. in writing no later than April 1, 1972 at the Aladdin Hotel that Aladdin Hotel Corporation desires Patava, Inc. to continue the performance at the Aladdin Hotel in accordance with the Agreements incorporated herein.

In the event that Aladdin Hotel Corporation does not notify Patava, Inc. in writing as set forth in the paragraph above, the Prell Hotels, Inc. shall present the performance of Patava, Inc., as set forth in the Agreements incorporated herein, at the Fremont Hotel in Downtown Las Vegas, Nevada, and Patava, Inc. shall perform at the Fremont Hotel in the same manner and to the same effect as is required of Patava, Inc. under the terms of the Agreement of August 13, 1971, and the RIDER attached thereto. In that event, Prell Hotels, Inc. shall pay all costs or expenses necessary or required to rearrange, modify or alter scenery or stage props in order to present the Patava, Inc. performance at the Fremont Hotel; and Patava, Inc. shall present to Prell Hotels, Inc. all statements of costs required in order to accommodate the performance of Patava, Inc. at the Fremont Hotel.

It is understood and agreed that costs and expenses shall not include any costs or expenses except those which may be necessary or required for stage props or scenery design and the alterations or modifications thereof.

The performance by Patava, Inc. at the Fremont Hotel shall continue for the balance of the term of the Agreement of August 13, 1971, unless otherwise extended.

Nothing herein contained shall relieve or release Prell Hotels, Inc. from any sums required to be paid or performance required to be done by Prell Hotels, Inc. under the terms of the Agreement of August 13, 1971, and the RIDER thereto, except for such payment or performance as may be done by Aladdin Hotel Corporation."

The Agreement was signed by: Sam Diamond, President of Aladdin Hotel Corporation, Moe Lewis, Entertainment Director of Prell Hotels, Inc., and Harold Minsky, President of Patava, Inc.

Even the person who typed up the Agreement for the Law Offices of Wiener, Goldwater, Galatz and Raggio, Ltd., located in the First National Bank Building in Las Vegas, could not keep track of the different corporations. Different names, titles, and corporations had "X's" typed through the positions listed above the Diamond and Lewis signatures.

The following came from a seven page October 1973 Agreement which was never officially signed or dated by anyone. It was also drawn up by of Law Offices of Wiener, Goldwater, and Galatz, Ltd., First National Bank Building, in Las Vegas, Nevada. Just some of the contract reads as follows:

"The Producer shall present, subject to Producer's supervision and control, a show consisting of a chorus and principals, a stage manager and one wardrobe mistress, together with a Director, Harold Minsky, in the main showroom on the premises at the Fremont Hotel, in Las Vegas, Nevada, for a period of fifty-two (52) consecutive weeks, commencing on the 6th day of February, 1974. The Producer shall provide sufficient personnel, to include the following: a chorus of fourteen (14) dancers and showgirls, eleven (11) principals, a stage manager and a wardrobe mistress. The Operator shall have the right to approve all performers that will appear in the production, which right of approval shall not be unreasonably withheld."

The Agreement continues on:

"For the basic consideration of $16,500.00 per week the Producer shall produce not more than thirteen (13) shows during any six (6) days of each week."

If the Operator requested additional shows during the week, or even additional shows on day seven, he would have to pay additional wages, including overtime, union benefits, and all federal and state taxes. The Operator also had the right to schedule the times for the shows, and the number of shows per day. Each show had to run for a minimum of seventy-five minutes. Harold Minsky was to be the Producer during the entire year, or run of the contract, and he was responsible for everything involving the show: personnel, costumes, production, choreography, direction, and musical arrangements.

The Operator was to furnish and pay for an orchestra of seven playing musicians for the shows and rehearsals. The rehearsals were to consist of approximately five hours for each two days prior to any opening of any new shows, or change of, or addition of any new principals.

The Operator would also provide stage lighting, as many persons as may be required by the appropriate union for stagehands, as well as an assistant wardrobe mistress, if needed. The additional personnel would also be provided for all rehearsals.

It was a basic Minsky Agreement with all the publicity and trademark stipulations, but I found the following paragraph an interesting read. It says the following:

"Except as hereinafter stated, it is hereby agreed that the duties and obligations required under this Agreement shall be suspended during the period of any strike or Act of God which prevents the presentation of any of the performances hereunder. In the event this Agreement shall be suspended by reason of a strike or lockout, and during the term of such strike or lockout, the Producer shall be obligated to pay its employees the minimum basic scale. The consideration to be paid by Operator to Producer during the term of such strike or lockout shall equal the applicable minimum basic scale for the Producer's employees and no more. It is further understood and agreed that in the event that there is a raise of minimum basic scales and working conditions thereof for principals, dancers, and showgirls involved in Producer's production for Operator, the consideration agreed to be paid by Operator shall be increased in a like amount for the total number of employees designated in the agreement."

The final "Letter Agreement" was dated January 2, 1975, and signed by: James J. Hill for the Fremont Hotel, Harold Minsky for Patava, Inc., and Art

Engler for the Associated Booking Corporation, located at 4055 South Spencer, in Las Vegas, Nevada. It reads:

"It is hereby mutually agreed that THE MINSKY SHOW which was to close at the Fremont Hotel, Las Vegas, Nevada on February 4, 1975, will instead close on January 9, 1975, and in consideration of this closing, it is agreed that the Producer, Harold Minsky, will be compensated in the amount of $6,177.00 per week for a period of three (3) weeks, plus pro rata eleven (11) additional shows, totaling $23,757.00.

This Agreement cancels the remainder of contract dated August 13, 1971 and RIDERS therein with no further obligation to either party."

There were also several articles and newspaper columns in this folder which I'm adding by dates. In all of these clippings musical arranger Ken Tiffany's name was misspelled as "Tiffiny." The first article from the *Las Vegas Sun* was dated November 20, 1972. There was also an advertisement included with the article; handwritten in a corner was: "SUN 11/6/72." The advertisement reads: "Audition Minsky Show for the Hotel Fremont; Showgirls 1:00pm November 8th Fiesta Room, see: Jerry Norman." The article reads:

"At Fremont Hotel Gals Audition For Burlesque; Las Vegas – Tell dancers and showgirls that Minsky is holding auditions for a new show, and then stand back to watch the bevy of beauties converge.

The crush of pulchritude occurred recently when famed showman Harold Minsky put out the word that he would be casting for the new *Minsky's*, set to premiere December 27 in the Fiesta Room of the Fremont Hotel.

There were tall ones, short ones, blondes, and brunettes. They came in all sizes, but all had one undeniable attribute – beauty.

Clad in attire destined to turn any healthy male's head, each damsel ascended the steps to the Fiesta Room stage. Watching the assembled hopefuls dance through various routines, Minsky selected the cream of the curvaceous covey for his new revue.

For some 40 years, Harold Minsky has been selecting the most gorgeous girls in the world to dress up the countless production shows he has produced in every corner of the globe.

To the delight of millions of burlesque aficionados, Minsky's spectaculars have showcased some of the most talented entertainers, lovely dancers and showgirls, lavish sets and dazzling costumes to be seen anywhere.

Beginning November 23, the Fiesta Room will be used exclusively for the elaborate preparations and rehearsals required for *Minsky's* Fremont opening night, December 27."

Harold Minsky and showgirl at rehearsal. Courtesy: Janelle Smith Collection

The next few paragraphs come from two separate columnists. The first, from Ralph Pearl, appeared in the *Las Vegas Sun* on January 1, 1973. It was a regular column called "Vegas Daze and Nights; People, Things & Stuff." It reads:

"It happened around the midnight hour last Wednesday night at the Fremont Hotel where the nation's number one girlie show provocateur, Harold Minsky, had just premiered his *Femme Frolic*. It was a sight that made not only his eyes sparkle but made the owners of the Fremont joyful because the showroom was packed for that midnight show while more than a hundred had already been turned away to come back another night.

Tommy "Moe" Raft and Berri Lee performing in a Minsky skit together in 1972. Raft greeting the photographer. Courtesy: Berri Lee

Yup, *Minsky's* is the greatest thing that ever happened to downtown Las Vegas since a speculator opened a faro game for a gang of railroad workers here in Las Vegas who were building the Union Pacific Railroad back in the 1930s. As for the revue itself, it has everything any Minsky burlesque show should have. Gorgeous gals, clad and unclad; exciting production numbers, and a little "Schlepper" (roustabout) by the name of Tommy "Moe" Raft, who is truly the greatest top banana in show business.

Put all together, *Minsky's* is a bawdy, saucy frolic that should stay at the Fremont until Christmas of '77 – at least."

The second, from Forrest Duke, appeared in the *Las Vegas Review-Journal* on January 7, 1973. It appeared in a regular column called "The Duke of Las Vegas," and this piece was called "Minsky moves in on Fremont Street." It reads:

"Girls, girls, girls opened to a capacity crowd in the Fiesta Room. The show is really burlesque at its finest. There are many scenes that are familiar but the show has a fresh contemporary feeling. When it comes to girls, Harold Minsky has done it again! He has picked 15 of the most beautiful dancers and showgirls to be found on any stage, and really, what more can you say about Tommy "Moe" Raft except that he IS top banana! Hopefully some of the audio problems can be worked out in three sequences Tommy appears in – a lot of his lines are lost to the audience because you can't hear them. His funniest bit by far is the classic of a bum trying to get arrested in the park. Suzette Summers has to be one of the loveliest, talented, exotic dancers in the business; she dazzles the audience with her interpretations to the music of "Black Magic Woman." The show was staged and choreographed by Jerry Norman, who pulled off an eye stopper with the 'space number' in black light with Don Crawford dancing on a spider web with a strong assist from the lead dancers and Minsky dancers. A salute goes out

Suzette Summers. Courtesy: Pat Elliott Minsky/ Burlesque Historical Society

to musical conductor Rudy Eagan and arranger Ken Tiffany for some great musical numbers as well."

The following *Variety* review was included in the folder and some of its words were used in promotional material created by the Associated Booking Corporation. The review was written by "Will" and dated January 16, 1973. In large letters the promotional material reads "Minsky's Means Money!" In medium letters, "All Minsky Burlesque and Minsky Follies Shows Produced by Harold Minsky, staged – choreographed by Jerry Norman. Exclusive Representation ABC – Associated Booking Corp." The review reads as follows:

"Fremont ($5.75 Dinner. $3.50 Midnight Minimum.) Las Vegas, January 15 – The coming of Minsky's to any Vegas establishment in the past has been the presage of good times. His special kind of burley revue has cured many an ailing hotel on the Strip. With the Fremont facing astronomical headliner fees and many of them leaving for better deals on the Strip, this downtown hotel turned at last to Doc Minsky for his guaranteed placebo for perking up the Fiesta Room.

Harold Minsky has evolved a format with choreographer-stager Jerry Norman, presenting a batch of typical nude dolls who can match any torso measurements extant and who can also zip around very well in the several production rounds.

This frontal attack on the senses is matched somewhat by the inclusion of blackouts with diminutive banana Tommy "Moe" Raft whipping up loads of yockables via his elastic puss, woebegone attitude, and top know how of verbal delivery.

Where at one time the fulcrum of a Minsky extravaganza was the batch of strippers, now a lone ecdysiast takes it off, but no further off than the showgirl nudes. Her name is Suzette Summers and she's one of the better peelers around, having a ripe body and tasty gestures in all disrobing gestures.

Raft's first sketch is a quickie with monolithic Janet Boyd, one-time stripper turned straight woman. Her looks, frame, and size contrast appreciably with the little guy. She does well in this bit, and in the "Courtroom" and "Trying To Get Arrested" blackouts. Jimmy Mathews adds to the howlarity with his rube schtick while Jerry Lucas takes on the straight in "Courtroom" and the cop in "Trying To Get Arrested," with aids from a couple of the line dolls.

Norman's choreos for the dancers and nudes are designed for fast action and razzle-dazzle steppery by all the femmes from opening "Harem Nights" through the cunning "Showgirl Strip;" as well as the far-out "Space Number" with Don Crawford and lead dancers Betty Francisco, Orie Tokay, and Dick Colacino. Warbling by Toni Shain, Barbara Swisher, and Joe La Vigna (Minsky Singers) is proficient for illustrating production numbers.

Josephine Spinedi's costumes executed by Eastwood, Wynn Strickland's set designs, and Don Dillingham's light effects are all instrumental for fine optic limnery. Ken Tiffany's musical arrangements are taken care of with brio by Rudy Eagan's septet.

Minsky's is in for an indefinite stay."

This same review ran in *Variety* with the date of January 22, 1973. There was a handwritten date of January 31, 1973 on the actual newspaper clipping. The only difference between the two included the following information:

"*Minsky's*, with Tommy "Moe" Raft, Suzette Summers, Janet Boyd, Jimmy Mathews, Jerry Lucas, Betty Francisco, Orie Tokay, Don Crawford, Dick Colacino, Minsky Dancers (5), Minsky Showgirls (8), Minsky Singers (3); choreographed and staged by Jerry Norman; costumes designed by Josephine Spinedi; set design, Wynn Strickland; lighting design, Don Dillingham; musical arrangements, Ken Tiffany; produced by Harold Minsky; Rudy Eagan Orchestra (7); $5.75 dinner, $3.50 midnight minimum."

The last item in this folder was a newspaper article from *The London Free Press*, dated April 13, 1974. It was titled "Minsky's Burlesque never raided, outlasting big name competition," and written by Bill Webster. It reads:

"Harold Minsky of burlesque fame explained, "Thank God we have never been raided." In the small office which forms a part of his home in Las Vegas, he outlined the early days of burlesque in America.

Sheet music from the Ziegfeld Follies of 1924. Albert Vargas designed several different art covers for a variety of songs from the Follies and they are highly collectible. Courtesy: Authors Collection

"My father, A.B. Minsky, was the one who had the trouble," he continued. "He had problems with churches and the police in New York. Earl Carroll's Vanities was also raided at that time."

"What about Ziegfeld with his Follies?" I asked.

"Ziegfeld was a different story," Mr. Minsky said. "He had influential backers, people like William Randolph Hearst with Marion Davies."

Rotund, good-natured and soft-spoken, Mr. Minsky smiled and sometimes laughed as he recalled his own early years and some of his father's problems. As a teenager he worked backstage at the Minsky Burlesque in New York. He can still remember some of the raids in which girls and comedians were hustled into police paddy wagons and taken to the nearest precinct station. His father would somehow manage to get bail money so he could get them back for the next show. The cases were always thrown out of court.

Lobby card from 1922 film Beauty's Worth, *with Marion Davies. The men seated on the box are Gordon and Johnny Dooley; vaudevillians, famous for their comedy dance routines. Courtesy: Authors Collection*

He is pleased with the way the film *The Night They Raided Minsky's* came off. "It's pure fiction as to events that happened, but I enjoyed it. It is a charming little picture which comes off quite well, and has done well at the box office too. Each member of the family had to agree to its being made and we each have a small piece of it."

Minsky's father started in show business with a nickelodeon, and was a contemporary of Sam Goldwyn, the Loew's, and the Selznick's. His grandfather was a construction contractor and had built a theatre in New York. When the man who was to lease the theatre backed out of the deal, Minsky's father leased the theatre with his own father as landlord.

"My father had a friend in burlesque and he thought it would be a good idea to start one of his own," Minsky said. "Burlesque had a different connotation in those days (1910 through the 1920s). The competition was keen too, there were so many burlesque theatres. There was no stripping in those days, it was the day of the belly dancer, especially after Little Egypt was such a hit at the St. Louis Fair. Comedy was the big thing then. Gradually the spotlight and attention swung over to women."

Minsky has operated his burlesque show (currently playing the Fremont Hotel) in Las Vegas continuously for the past 24 years. "I keep enough of the old burlesque comedy to provide some nostalgia for the older generation," he said. "At the same time, we find it appeals to the younger generation who come to burlesque to see just what it was their fathers found so interesting. Outside of these reminders of the past, we are contemporary, especially with our sets and production numbers."

Minsky owns the registered name "Minsky" or "Minsky's Burlesque." He does all the auditioning when filling roles in a new show, and during the weeks of rehearsal he is a busy man supervising every detail.

"A showgirl in our chorus earns $270 to $275 per week, doing 13 shows which run one hour and 15 minutes each. She works a five-day week," Minsky said. "Rehearsal weeks are tougher of course, but once the show is on, well, where else can you earn that money for those hours? The girls come mostly from the ranks of secretaries, dental assistants, and legal secretaries. Many of our present cast have been with us for a long time. Some are married with families and they all make their homes here. The disadvantage is the same as it is in all show business – there is no security."

Minsky went into the business under his father in 1933 and took over the business when his father semi-retired in 1937.

Harold Minsky enjoys his work still after 41 years. "You work up a new show and you get your bounce back," he says. His son Robert, known as Danny

Minsky, currently is managing the touring show which should be ready to open this month.

After a pleasant afternoon with this gentle man of burlesque, we saw his show that night at the Fremont. We noted the sequences of old burlesque comedy, not really all that funny, but genuine bits of old burlesque.

The production numbers are splendid achievements of stagecraft and lighting, especially one where in bursts of psychedelic lighting and exciting music, we see a spider snare with a pretty girl in a silver web so huge it fills the entire stage."

"F" is also for the Fairmont Hotel, in New Orleans, Louisiana, and the Fontainebleau Hotel, in Miami, Florida.

The history of the Fairmont Hotel began in 1893, as the Grunewald Hotel; a 200 room, six-story hotel named for owner Louis Grunewald, when it opened near the fabled French Quarter in New Orleans. Grunewald added a 400 room, 14-story annex in 1908, which became the hotel's main entrance. He also opened what may have been America's first nightclub. Originally called "The Cave," the supper club featured waterfalls, stalactites, and chorus girls dancing to Dixieland jazz. Revues, similar to the Ziegfeld Follies, were presented on a nightly basis.

In 1923, Theodore Grunewald, who had inherited the hotel when his father died in 1915, sold the hotel to a business group headed by Joseph, Felix, and Luca Vacarro. After renovations were made, the hotel was renamed the Roosevelt Hotel in honor of Theodore Roosevelt.

In 1934, the hotel was once again sold, this time to several New Orleans business leaders headed by Seymour Weiss, then President of the New Orleans Roosevelt Corporation, who went on to become principal owner and managing director of the Roosevelt Hotel from 1934 until its sale in 1965. It attracted people from across the country who wanted a taste of the rapidly growing culture of New Orleans. The Roosevelt Hotel offered many fine restaurants and dining, and was located near many other nearby attractions. "The Cave" was closed in favor of a much larger venue called the "Blue Room" which became a nationally prominent music venue.

During its reign as the Roosevelt, the hotel flourished under the leadership of Seymour Weiss. He was an elegant man who became friends with famed politician Huey Pierce Long Jr., who soon established his campaign headquarters in the hotel and moved in shortly after winning the governor's race.

Throughout the 1930s, Weiss brought many acts to the Roosevelt. These acts included: Don Bestor, radio and television star, perhaps best known for directing the orchestra during the early years of the old Jack Benny Program; Dorothy Blaine, mistress of song; Dolly Arden, who toured the globe as a professional acrobatic dancer; and Jane Moore and Billy Revel, internationally famous "Royal

Jesters of Dance." The talent he hired was national rather than local. The "Blue Room" would also have 'Opportunity Nights' every two weeks, and on the week in between they would hold auditions for the upcoming opportunity night. One winner was pianist Emile Parra, who soon signed on with the Bill Bardo Orchestra. The 1940s and 1950s were a rapidly growing time for music in New Orleans, and the "Blue Room" always offered nationally-renowned musical acts, as well as locally famous Jazz musicians.

In 1965, Weiss sold the Roosevelt, and it became known as the Fairmont New Orleans. The Fairmont continued the tradition of being a grand hotel; pampering its guests with gracious hospitality. Everything remained very much the same, and the nightclub continued to operate as a high-class venue for entertainment, hosting acts such as: Lena Horne, Joel Gray, Tony Bennett, Ray Charles, Tina Turner, and Bette Midler. The "Blue Room" also hosted WWL, a live radio station.

However, as the Fairmont Hotel began to experience numerous changes in management, those changes negatively impacted the nightclub's performance. In the mid-1970s, the club stopped making money on shows, so instead began to focus on a profit from the food service. This led to experimentation with acts that were brought in, leading to the booking of more local and lesser-known acts.

In 2005, the Fairmont New Orleans Hotel closed following serious damage caused by Katrina. The hurricane flooded the basement with over ten feet of water, destroying all of the mechanical equipment, while the rain caused most of the guest floors to be heavily damaged.

In early July of 2009, the hotel reopened under new ownership, as the Roosevelt New Orleans Hotel following a $145 million refurbishing. The "Blue Room" itself reopened on August 4, 2009, along with a large banquet that included a jazz big band fronted by Pete Fountain and Tim Laughlin.

What follows was the Fairmont New Orleans Hotel Agreement with Harold Minsky; it was signed by Klaus Kelterborn and dated August 30, 1976.

AGREEMENT

"This Agreement, made and entered into this 25th day of August, 1976, between, Fairmont Hotel, New Orleans, Louisiana, hereinafter referred to as the Operator and Shokow, Ltd., a Nevada Corporation, hereinafter referred to as the Producer.

I

Operator hereby engages the Producer to secure, provide and supply a package "Musical Revue" known as "Minsky's Burlesque" in the capacity of an Independent Contractor for and to the Operator, for presentation in the room now designated as the Blue Room in the Fairmont Hotel, New Orleans, Louisiana for a flat guarantee of three (3) weeks commencing Monday, January 24, 1977 through and including Saturday, February 12, 1977.

Each performance is to last approximately one (1) hour and be presented six (6) nights weekly with two (2) shows each night, Sundays off.

II

Producer agrees to furnish and supply, at his sole expense, a cast of no less than thirteen (13) persons.

Producer further agrees to supply all costumes, shoes, hose and accessories, scenery, backdrops, props, musical arrangements and special material and any and all things necessary for the presentation of the show.

III

Operator hereby agrees, at his sole expense, to furnish and supply the premises above (including all necessary times for rehearsals) and a fellow spotlight and operator for all rehearsals and performances.

Operator shall furnish and pay for the orchestra for necessary rehearsal times and all performances for this engagement and the orchestra shall consist of a minimum of ten (10) musicians, with the instrumentation to be advised.

IV

For and in consideration of the package "Musical Revue" as above described to be supplied and furnished by the Producer, the Operator hereby agrees to pay the Producer the sum of Ten Thousand ($10,000.00) Dollars per week to Shokow, Ltd., or its representative, on Saturday of each week.

V

Operator shall provide eight (8) gratis rooms for the cast for the run of the show, plus rehearsal period maximum of three (3) days before opening. In addition, Operator is to provide gratis rooms during rehearsal period for Producer, Choreographer and Manager.

VI

Producer warrants that he is providing at his expense, all Insurance required by law, such as Workman's Compensation Insurance, etc. relative to his employees. Operator warrants that he will carry the necessary third party liability insurance to hold the Producer harmless from third party claims in connection with the presentation of said "Musical Revue."

VII

Producer's capacity herein is that of an Independent Contractor exclusively and in no manner, shape or form, shall be construed or interpreted as that of being a partnership, joint venture or otherwise.

It is further agreed that the Producer, as Employer, is solely responsible for the payments of all salaries of all performers, including the required withholding and unemployment taxes, and Workmen's Compensation relative to any and all employees of the Producer.

VIII

Operator agrees to use the Registered Trademark (TM) insignia in all advertising including, but not limited to, table cards, lobby displays, billboards, newspapers, etc.

Producer agrees that it will use the Trademarks "Minsky's," "Minsky's Follies," "Minsky's Burlesque," and "Minsky's Burlesque Follies," in the New Orleans metropolitan area, during the term of this engagement and any renewal thereof, exclusively for shows produced by Producer for Operator. Producer reserves the right to inspect any pictures and written material for publicity and advertising to insure that said Trademarks are being properly used.

Operator and Producer acknowledge that no rights to said Trademarks have been or are transferred to the Operator by this Agreement.

Any billings by the Operator of "Minsky's," "Minsky's Follies," "Minsky's Burlesque," or "Minsky's Burlesque Follies," shall be headline billings.

In all advertising, signs or billings, wherein the names "Minsky's," "Minsky's Follies," "Minsky's Burlesque," or "Minsky's Burlesque Follies," are used, the words "Minsky" or "Minsky's" shall be in larger type than any of the other words used in any advertising or billings. Harold Minsky, shall whenever possible be identified as the Producer in all advertising and billing.

The words "Minsky" or "Minsky's" as it may be associated with "Follies," "Burlesque," or similar words, shall not be used by Producer in any other capacity in the New Orleans metropolitan area during the term of this Agreement.

In WITNESS WHEREOF, the parties hereto have set their hands the day and year first written above.

RIDER to accompany contract dated 25 August 1976 between the Fairmont Hotel by K. Kelterborn (Operator) and Minsky's Burlesque (Artist).

Artist agrees not to render services in any Night Club or Supper Club within the New Orleans area from the signing of the contract to the commencement of the engagement hereunder; and further agrees not to appear in any advertised personal appearance within a two-hundred (200) mile radius of the Fairmont Hotel sixty (60) days prior to the commencement of said engagement without written permission of the Operator. Artist agrees not to make any personal appearances in the New Orleans area (including benefits) during the period of this engagement hereunder.

Pursuant to Paragraph III; Operator agrees to furnish Artist with necessary rehearsals to be held on necessary times to be set at the Fairmont Hotel, with no cost or expense to the Artist.

It is understood and agreed to that during Artist's forthcoming engagement commencing on Monday January 24, 1977 for a three week period (Saturday February 12) at the Fairmont Hotel, the length of the Artist's performance shall not exceed fifty-five (55) minutes in length or be less than forty-five (45) minutes in length.

Artist agrees to perform two (2) shows nightly at approximately 9:30pm and 11:30pm except Sundays. If the second show goes overtime due to the length of the performing time by the Artist, (any time beyond 1am) the Artist shall be expected to pay overtime costs incurred by the musicians and any other staff of the Blue Room; and the Fairmont Hotel management is not liable for these extra costs. If the second show does not start as scheduled due to any fault of the hotel, the Artist shall not be held liable for overtime costs.

The check for the final week's services of the Artist will not be issued until Artist pays for all personal expenditures incurred during Artist's stay at the Fairmont Hotel. If these expenditures have not been paid for, the amount owed to the Fairmont Hotel will be deducted from the Artist's last week's check.

The weekly salary for the Artist includes transportation expenses as stated in the minimum AGVA wage agreement.

Operator agrees that the Artist shall receive 100 percent sole star billing in any and all publicity releases and paid advertisements including but not limited to programs, fliers, signs, lobby boards, and marquees.

Operator agrees to furnish Artist at no cost or expense to Artist an orchestra consisting of the following instrumentation: 3 trumpets, 1 trombone, 4 sax, 1 fender bass, piano, drums; leader, Dick Stabile.

Artist may postpone this contract for not more than one year, and the services rendered hereunder, without liability, on sixty (60) days notice to Operator, prior to commencement of the within engagement, in the event Artist's engagement hereunder would interfere with the preparation or rehearsal of, or performance in, any motion picture, legitimate stage production, or live pre-recorded, or filmed television series of eight (8) weeks or more, TV spectacular, or special in which Artist may appear or a Nevada engagement.

It is understood and agreed that Operator will provide gratis, 3 rooms beginning Friday January 21, 1977 and 8 twins beginning January 21, 1977 thru February 12, 1977, during the length of the engagement hereunder.

It is understood and agreed that the Artist shall have approval of any and all supporting acts in conjunction with said engagement hereunder.

Operator shall deduct 10 percent (ten percent) of Artist's salary and forward it to: 3 rooms January 21 thru January 23 only.

Accepted and Agreed: Klaus Kelterborn, Fairmont Hotel, August 30, 1976."

(Notes: The rooms section was crossed out; and Tony Papa, Vice President, Associated Booking Corporation, was named on the original contract.)

1976 Press Photo for the Minsky's Burlesque Follies appearance at the Fairmont Hotel Blue Room. Courtesy: Authors Collection

There were several newspaper clippings in this folder, including the January 21, 1977 Calendar Section from the *New Orleans States-Item*, which reads:

"Burlesque is back… Who says burlesque is dead? Not Harold Minsky. He's the man who put the strippers, the bump-and-grind girls, and the baggy-pants comedians on the stage of the old Gaiety Theatre on Broadway.

Today, the bump-and-grind and the specialty acts are gone but the long-legged girls, the splashy costumes, the spectacular sets, the comedians, and the blackouts remain, all entwined in a modern Las Vegas-type act.

Minsky's Follies opens Monday in the Blue Room of the Fairmont Hotel for a three-week run."

Maud O'Bryan, the Advertising Reporter for the same newspaper, on the same date, wrote:

"Burlesque at Blue Room Hotter than Vaudeville; *Minsky's Follies*, a blending of old-time burlesque, spectacular sets, exotic dancers in fanciful costumes, will open Monday in the Blue Room of the Fairmont Hotel.

Harold Minsky, son of Abe Minsky who kept the Minsky name on burlesque theatre marquees since 1908, will direct and produce the local extravaganza.

Burlesque "died" years ago, along with vaudeville, but Las Vegas kept it alive – with strippers, bump-and-grind girls, baggy-pants comedians, other comics playing three instruments at once, choruses that shake, shimmy, sparkle, rattle, and roll.

Some of this razzmatazz will be visible in the Blue Room Monday through Saturday evenings at two shows, starting January 24 for three weeks."

On January 23, 1977, *The Times-Picayune*, another New Orleans newspaper, published the following:

"Blue Room Burlesque, the Real Thing – Minsky; Harold Minsky, son of Abe Minsky who made burlesque famous since 1908, will present Minsky's Follies in the Blue Room of the Fairmont Hotel, January 24 for three weeks – except Sundays. Burlesque? Never on Sunday!

To some people the show might seem to glorify Bourbon Street, to others it's a take-off of Las Vegas, where *Minsky's Follies* played for 20 years after burlesque "died" in New York.

Anyhow, Harold Minsky, in true show biz tradition, promises, 'The most beautiful girls in the world, and the most outrageous costumes.'"

On January 25th, 1977, the *New Orleans States-Item* ran the following review, "Blue, Blue: They Whirl, They Twirl – By Allan Katz."

"Pretty girls in pasties and G-strings cavorting on the stage of the venerable old Blue Room? And, a male lead dancer clad in silver jock strap and boots?

Yes, it's all part of *Minsky's Follies '77*, a reasonably well-done fleshy extravaganza that last night opened a three-week stand in the flagship room of the Fairmont Hotel.

While unclad women aren't exactly a novelty in New Orleans entertainment, the Minsky show is closer to being a mini-Las Vegas revue than the honky-tonk striptease acts that dot Bourbon Street.

There are some reminders of old-time burlesque – a mild striptease by one of the dancers and a deluge of clever one-liners and sight gags by veteran comic Dick Richards. In particular, Richards and his straight lady, Angel Duke, do some pretty good variations on the old Abbott and Costello "Who's on First" routine that goes back many years in American comedy.

But, the real show is the dance routines. The lightly clad troupe of seven girls and Tom Vagadori give it all they've got, holding nothing in reserve. Well, hardly anything.

It's a fun show that swingers will enjoy. The dancers are not only attractive people but their numbers are well-choreographed, overcoming the Blue Room's postage stamp-sized stage. Richard's one-liners are raunchy and blue, just as burlesque is supposed to be.

There is an overly long, rather painfully unfunny comedy sketch toward the end of the sixty-minute act that could well be replaced by another dance number. Singer Scott Evans is okay and provides the dancers with a chance to catch their collective breath.

Overall, Minsky's is a winner."

The final item came from the January 26, 1977, morning edition of the New Orleans newspaper, *The Times-Picayune*. The article, "A Review: Minsky's Comes to Fairmont," was written by Joe Darby and reads as follows:

"*Minsky's Follies*, a combination of old-time burlesque and modern Las Vegas, although based on a theatrical tradition decades old, offers some fast-paced, refreshingly different entertainment.

The Follies, which opened at the Fairmont Hotel's Blue Room Monday and will run through February 12, has all the ingredients to be expected from such a show.

There are seven – count 'em, seven – pulchritudinous dancing girls – and one athletic dancing boy.

There is the fabulous Miss Suzette Summers, an exotic dancer who takes us back to Bourbon Street circa 1959. Better make that Bourbon Street circa 1965, after the stripperies were forced to clean up their acts.

There is the smooth-voiced singer, Scott Evans, who entertains with a few love ballads while the girls change their costumes – admittedly a male chauvinist viewpoint, but a viewpoint which is nice to have at a burlesque show.

There are straight man Jerry Lucas and the gorgeous talking woman Angel Duke, both foils to the comic, Dick Richards.

Richards, a pint-sized, pot-bellied, pug-faced veteran of burlesque, couldn't more look the part of a top banana if he had been chosen by a casting director wanting to film the history of burlesque.

Clad in a full-length black coat, topped by a derby and carrying a cane, Richards holds the whole show together. As soon as the ringside patrons see him amble onstage with that mischievous look in his eyes, they know they'll be in for some mild insults.

Some of the jokes probably go back to the time of Teddy Roosevelt, but no one minds. With Richards' rapid-fire delivery and impish expressions, they're just as funny now as they were 70 years ago.

The risqué material doesn't have the titillation effect it once had, what with X-rated movies and 'adult' television shows, but it's still as much fun.

Dick Richards. Courtesy: Lorraine Lee

The dancing girls are as leggy and as smilingly provocative as they were in grandfather's day – although when all six chorines plus lead dancers Lori Palmer and Tom Vagadori were onstage at the same time, things seemed to be at close quarters on the Blue Room's small platform.

The troupe's hour-long show goes by all too quickly, probably because they dispense in such abundance what entertainment should be all about - plain, old fashioned fun."

"F" is also for the Fontainebleau Hotel in Miami, Florida...

The Fontainebleau Miami Beach (also known as Fontainebleau Hotel) is one of the most historically and architecturally significant hotels in Miami Beach, Florida. Opened in 1954 and designed by Morris Lapidus, it was arguably the most luxurious hotel in Miami Beach at the time, and is thought to be the most significant building of his career. The hotel was built by hotelier Ben Novack

The Fontainebleau Hotel in 1955, a year after its grand opening: Courtesy: Library of Congress; Gottscho-Schleisner Collection

on the Harvey Firestone estate. Novack owned and operated the hotel until its bankruptcy in 1977.

In 1978, Stephen Muss bought the Fontainebleau Hotel for $27 million, rescuing it from bankruptcy. He injected an additional $100 million into the hotel for improvements and hired the Hilton Company to manage it. In 2005, the Muss Organization sold the Fontainebleau to Turnberry Associates. The hotel closed a large part of its property in 2006 for expansion and updates, although one building did remain open to hotel guests. The hotel and its new condominium buildings reopened in November 2008. On December 22, 2008, the Fontainebleau Hotel was added to the National Register of Historic Places.

The File itself contained very little; a newspaper ad, a table card, and the following Agreement signed by Harold Minsky and Ben Novack Sr. It reads as follows:

AGREEMENT

"This Agreement made and entered into this 22nd day of January, 1973 between Ben Novack, Fontainebleau Hotel, Miami Beach, Florida per Ben Novack hereinafter referred to as the Operator and Patava, Inc., a Nevada Corporation, hereinafter referred to as the Producer.

I

Operator hereby engages the Producer to secure, provide, and supply a package "Musical Revue" known as "Minsky's Burlesque" in the capacity of an Independent Contractor for and to the Operator, for the presentation in the Boom Boom Room of the Fontainebleau Hotel, Miami Beach, Florida for a term of:

Four (4) consecutive weeks commencing Friday, February 9, 1973 through and including Thursday, March 8, 1973.

Six (6) nights weekly; Mondays off:

Two (2) shows nightly, three (3) shows each Saturday, plus one (1) additional show to be determined by Operator each week; for a total of fourteen (14) shows weekly.

Operator has an option of extending this engagement for an indefinite period of time. Option to be exercised on or before Friday, February 23, 1973; if option is exercised then the engagement shall be subject to four (4) weeks' notice of termination.

II

Producer agrees to furnish and supply at his sole expense a cast of twelve (12) people.

Producer further agrees to supply all costumes, shoes, hose and accessories, scenery, backdrops, props, musical arrangements and special material, and any and all necessary things for the presentation of the show.

III

Operator hereby agrees, at his sole expense, to furnish and supply the premises above (including all necessary times for rehearsal) and a follow spotlight and operator for rehearsals and performances.

Operator shall furnish and pay for the orchestra for necessary rehearsal time and all performances for this engagement, and the orchestra shall consist of no less than five (5) musicians, instrumentation as follows:

Organ
Drums
Trumpet
Trombone
Saxophone

IV

For and in consideration of the package "Musical Revue" as above described to be supplied and furnished by the Producer, and Operator hereby agrees to pay the Producer Five Thousand Dollars ($5000.00) weekly.

<u>Payments shall be made by the OPERATOR to the PRODUCER as follows:</u> to Patava, Inc., and presented to the Company Manager each week. In addition, Operator shall provide seven (7) gratis rooms and two (2) gratis meals daily to all cast members and manager - meals to be provided in coffee shop only.

Producer warrants that he is providing at his expense all insurance required by law, such as Workman's Compensation Insurance, etc., relative to his employees. Producer to provide evidence of said insurance prior to initial date of performance. Operator warrants that he will carry the necessary third party liability insurance to hold the Producer harmless from third party claims in connection with the presentation of said "Musical Revue."

V

Producer's capacity is that of an independent contractor exclusively and in no manner, shape or form, shall be construed or interpreted as that of being a partnership, joint venture or otherwise.

It is further agreed that the Producer, an employer, is solely responsible for the payments of all salaries of all performers including the required with-holding and unemployment taxes, also AGVA welfare payments relative to any and all employees of the Producer.

VI

Producer agrees that it will use the trademarks "Minsky's," "Minsky's Follies," "Minsky's Burlesque," and "Minsky's Burlesque Follies," in the counties of Dade and Broward in the state of Florida respectively, during the term of this engagement, and any renewal thereof, exclusively for shows produced by Producer for Operator.

Producer reserves the right to inspect any pictures and written material for publicity and advertising to insure that said trademarks are being properly used.

Operator and Producer acknowledge that no rights to said trademarks have been or are transferred to the Operator by this Agreement.

Any billings by the Operator of "Minsky's" "Minsky's Follies," "Minsky's Burlesque," or "Minsky's Burlesque Follies," shall be headline billings.

In all advertisements, signs or billings, wherein the name "Minsky's" "Minsky's Follies," "Minsky's Burlesque," or "Minsky's Burlesque Follies," are used, the words "Minsky's" or "Minsky" shall be in larger type than any of the other words used in any advertising or billings. Harold Minsky shall whenever possible be identified as the Producer in all advertisings and billings.

The words "Minsky's" or "Minsky" as it may be associated with "Follies," "Burlesque," or similar words shall not be used by Producer in any other capacity in the counties of Dade and Broward in the state of Florida, respectively during the term of this Agreement.

VII

It is agreed and understood that the above parties to this Agreement shall comply with all union regulations of any unions or guilds that might have jurisdiction over any employees, of either party to this Agreement.

IN WITNESS WHEREOF, the parties hereto have set their hands this day and year as first written above."

Sunny Dare performing as belly dancer Nejma. Courtesy: Sunny Dare

(Notes: Should you do research on the Fontainebleau Hotel, you may be taken aback by the Novack family drama and what you discover. I will always find the hotel of interest because while taking nursing classes by day, Sunny Dare performed there at night as the belly dancer Nejma.)

"G" is For...

The next section is all about Granny's Dinner Playhouse, a 700-seat dinner theatre located in Dallas, Texas. Though small, the playhouse introduced their patrons to good acts, as well as showcasing many famous performers and celebrated

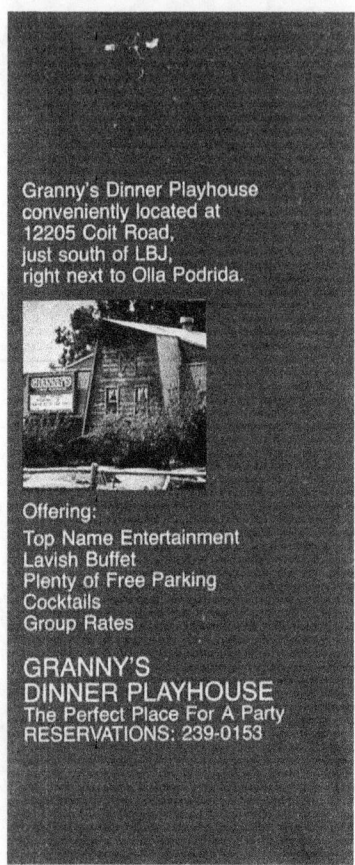

Granny's Dinner Playhouse flyer. Courtesy: Dallas History & Archives Division/Dallas Public Library; Adrianne Pierce

musicians into the 1980s. I actually found very little information regarding "Granny's." However, Minsky's shows played at the venue twice, in 1975 and 1977. Contracts for both shows were very similar. I have only included the contract from 1975.

AGREEMENT

"This Agreement, made and entered into this 4th day of February, 1975 between Granny's Dinner Playhouse, hereinafter referred to as the Operator and Shokow, Ltd., a Nevada Corporation, hereinafter referred to as Producer.

I

Operator hereby engages the Producer to secure, provide and supply a package "Musical Revue" known as "Minsky's Burlesque" in the Capacity of an Independent Contractor for and to the Operator, for presentation in Granny's Dinner Playhouse, 12205 Coit Road, Dallas, Texas for a period of eight (8) consecutive six (6) day weeks commencing Tuesday, April 8, 1975 through and including Sunday, June 1, 1975.

Each performance to last approximately two (2) hours, plus an intermission and shall be presented six (6) nights weekly, Tuesday through Sunday, Mondays off, and eight (8) shows weekly, not to exceed two (2) shows in any one night. Operator may hold performances on Mondays, if another day during the performing week is substituted as a day off and at least one week notice is given performers.

II

Producer agrees to furnish and supply, at his sole expense, a cast of no less than fifteen (15) persons.

Producer further agrees to supply all costumes, shoes, hose and accessories, scenery, backdrops, props, musical arrangements and special material and any and all things necessary for the presentation of the show.

III

Operator hereby agrees, at his sole expense, to furnish and supply the premises above (including all necessary times for rehearsals) and a follow spotlight and operator for all rehearsals and performances.

Operator shall furnish and pay for the orchestra for necessary rehearsal time and all performances for this engagement and the orchestra shall consist of five (5) musicians, with the exact instrumentation to be advised.

IV

For and in consideration of the package "Musical Revue" as above described to be supplied and furnished by the Producer, the Operator hereby agrees to pay the Producer the sum of Eight Thousand Two Hundred Fifty Dollars ($8,250.00) per week as follows: one (1) weeks salary is the amount of Eight Thousand Two Hundred Fifty Dollars ($8,250.00) made payable to Associated Booking Corporation, 919 North Michigan Avenue, Chicago, Illinois 60611. Said payment shall represent the last weeks payment for this engagement. Weekly payments shall be made each Saturday to Shokow, Ltd., by cashier's check or cash.

V

Operator shall provide and pay for transportation from Dallas International Airport to lodging site for this engagement, and upon conclusion of said engagement, shall provide transportation to Dallas International Airport for all members of the cast, including luggage, props, instruments, etc. In addition, Operator shall provide transportation from lodging site of the cast to the Theatre and return for each performance.

VI

Producer warrants that he is providing at his expense, all insurance required by law, such as Workmen's Compensation Insurance, etc., relative to his employees. Operator warrants that he will carry the necessary third party liability insurance to hold the Producer harmless from third party claims in connection with the presentation of said "Musical Revue."

VII

Producer's capacity herein is that of an Independent Contractor exclusively and in no manner, shape or form, shall be construed or interpreted as that of being a partnership, joint venture or otherwise.

It is further agreed that the Producer, as employer, is solely responsible for the payments of all salaries of all performers, including the required with-holding and unemployment taxes, and Workmen's Compensation relative to any and all employees of the Producer.

VIII

Operator agrees to use the registered Trademark ™ insignia, in all advertising including, but not limited to table cards, lobby displays, billboards, newspapers, etc.

Producer agrees that it will use the Trademarks "Minsky's," "Minsky Follies," "Minsky's Burlesque," and "Minsky's Burlesque Follies," in the metropolitan area of Dallas during the term of this engagement and any renewal thereof, exclusively for shows produced by Producer for Operator. Producer reserves the right to inspect any pictures and written material for publicity and advertising to insure that said Trademarks are being used properly.

Operator and Producer acknowledge that no rights to said Trademarks have been or are transferred to the Operator by this Agreement.

Any billings by the Operator of "Minsky's," "Minsky Follies," "Minsky's Burlesque," and "Minsky's Burlesque Follies," shall be headline billing.

In all advertising, signs or billings, wherein the names "Minsky's," "Minsky Follies," "Minsky's Burlesque," and "Minsky's Burlesque Follies," are used, the words "Minsky" or "Minsky's" shall be in larger type than any of the other words used in any advertising or billings. Harold Minsky shall, whenever possible, be identified as the Producer in all advertising and billing.

The words "Minsky" or "Minsky's," as it may be associated with "Follies," "Burlesque," or similar words, shall not be used by Producer in any other capacity in the metropolitan area of Dallas during the term of this Agreement.

IN WITNESS WHEREOF, the parties hereto have set their hands the day and year first written above."

The contract was signed by Perry Cloud, for Granny's Dinner Playhouse, and Chuck Eddy, Vice President, Associated Booking Corporation. There was an additional RIDER attached which did have Harold Minsky's initials. It reads:

"Thunder Chicken Club, Comstock Park, Michigan for three (3) weeks and three (3) days commencing Thursday, March 13th, 1975 through and including Saturday, April 5th, 1975 with the following days off: Monday, March 17th; Friday, March 28th; and Monday, March 31st – all in the year 1975.

Granny's Club, Dallas, Texas for eight (8) consecutive weeks commencing Tuesday, April 8th, 1975 ---- eight (8) shows per week with Mondays' off."

A copy of the program, for *Minsky's Burlesque '75*, listed the following cast: Comics, Herbie Barris and Jimmy Mathews; Exotic Dancers, Cassandra Lee and Sugar Kane; Straight Man, Eddie Innes; Talking Woman, Bobbye Mack; Singer, Darcy Schanz; Lead Dancers, Hector Nunez and Gail Martin; Dancers, Rise Clemmer and Candi LaSpina; Showgirls, Betty Jo Karsen, Eileen Woods, Awassa Greaves, and Ellen Burch. The crew included the following: Staged and Choreographed by Betty Francisco; Costumes by Eastwood; Production Manager, Jerry Lucas; Musical Arrangements by Ken Tiffany; Musical Conductor, Jerry Samuels; and Lighting by Tuna Howell. Cassandra Lee performed her "Dance of Fire" in Act I, and Sugar Kane's routine was listed as "The Las Vegas Sexsation" in Act II.

The back of the program included the following: "Our next show, Jo Anne Worley, starring in *Lovers and Other Strangers*; Opens June 3 – You Can Make Your Reservations Tonight."

The following article appeared in "The Arts" section of the *Dallas Times Herald* on Sunday, May 11, 1975. It was written by Bob Porter, and reads as follows:

"Minsky: Finding new life in Burlesque; "I always liked Phil Silvers and Red Buttons – my dad took him out of the Catskill Mountains to put him in our shows. Abbott and Costello started in burlesque. Pinky Lee came out of vaudeville. Rags Ragland and Jack Albertson also worked in burlesque – although Albertson was a straight man.

Phil Silvers. Courtesy: John Springer Collection

So was Bob Alda (Robert Alda, whose big movie roll was playing the life of composer George Gershwin, and who is also the father of Alan Alda). I remember his son, Alan, coming backstage when he was a boy. Milton Berle never played burlesque but he knows all of the burlesque routines. Mickey Rooney is doing burlesque things in his dinner theatre dates. So is Martha Raye."

1962 Press Photo; the many faces of Red Buttons. Courtesy: Authors Collection

Press Photo of Roberta Alda from 1944. Courtesy: Authors Collection

That was Harold Minsky, reminiscing about burlesque. It is a natural enough act. Minsky's dad Abe founded the famed *Minsky's Burlesque* at the Gotham Theatre in New York, which he joined himself in 1933 as a youngster. He has carried the family banner over the years for this rather unique form of Americana in the theatre, which now seems to be witnessing something of a rebirth of interest.

Minsky is a man of wry humor who can view this particular theatrical format in perspective. "I think the current popularity of burlesque (as represented in *Minsky's Burlesque '75*, now playing at Granny's Dinner Playhouse) comes from a combination of interests – nostalgia for those who haven't seen a burlesque show in years and years, and a generation born in the 1940s that has never seen a burlesque show. And, of course," he adds with a twinkle, "a girl show goes all of the time."

Shapely showgirls, and strippers, are a burlesque staple, along with baggy-pants comics dealing mainly in broad, blue comedy. While most of our veteran comics cut their professional teeth on various burlesque stages, so have there been famous strippers over the years. "I guess the one with the most class was Lili St. Cyr. Ann Corio in her heyday was very good. Georgia Sothern was very pretty. But I never considered Gypsy Rose Lee a stripper. She was a performer. There was more comedy than stripping in her routines," said Minsky.

Lili St. Cyr. Courtesy: C.F. Miller

Burlesque, by definition, is a comic reworking, something which "makes a travesty of that which it represents." As the strippers moved more to the forefront, back when the audiences were principally male, the accent, and image, turned toward showing bare flesh. Now when you can see about as much flesh, or more, on a public beach as in a burlesque theatre, the accent has, in a sense, moved back to comedy. The audiences also now contain as many females as males.

"We have kept the old comedy skits and routines intact in our own approach to burlesque these days, and the strips, and combined all that with contemporary music and choreography," said Minsky. "The costumes are also more elaborate than in the old days. They may not be on the par with the big French shows in Vegas, but I think they compare favorably with what you find in Vegas generally.

Some of the old jokes are so old they are now new. Yet, the music is timely," said Minsky, seeking an explanation to the current popularity for burlesque styled shows on the dinner theatre and summer stock theatre circuits. (Such as Casa Manana in Fort Worth which is returning *This Is Burlesque* this season, one of last season's box office hits.)

While a number of male comedy stars emerged from burlesque to stardom at large, few females have gone on to other things. Of course there is Valerie Perrine, the former Vegas showgirl who got an Oscar nomination for the movie *Lenny*, and is about the hottest thing on screen at the moment.

Ann Corio. Courtesy: C.F. Miller

UPI Press Photo from June 14, 1958; At work in her sewing room, Gypsy Rose Lee fits an old costume, which she is making over, onto a dressing dummy. Throughout her long show business career, Gypsy always worked on her own costumes. Courtesy: Authors Collection

"A couple of former Las Vegas showgirls are on *Hot L Baltimore*, the television show," said Minsky. "But not more than one in 10,000 girls is ever anything but a showgirl." And what is the stage life expectancy for a showgirl? "It varies but probably on the average of about 15 years. Some girls can be 37 or 38 and look like they are 23 or 24; other girls at the age of 25 look like they are 42 – especially when they have burnt themselves out. That is always a tragedy."

And what about the fabled stage-door Johnny of old, waiting in tails and limos to shower showgirls with diamonds? Minsky grinned. "Now I guess, it is the Bar Johnny, waiting for the girls to get through with the show, sitting at the bar." An offer for a free drink has replaced diamond bracelets it would seem, among other contemporary innovations."

In 1977 Minsky entered into a similar contract with Perry Cloud, and returned to Granny's Dinner Playhouse in mid-June with *Minsky's Burlesque '77*. From Dallas, the cast and crew went on to Chicago, Illinois, and performed at the Blue Max nightclub at the Hyatt Regency O'Hare, into late August.

The 1977 program from Granny's tells us the following performers were in the cast: Comics, Dick Richards and Jimmy Mathews; Straight Man and Woman, Jerry Lucas and Mary Scott; Exotic Dancers, Francine Farrar and Cassandra Lee; Singer, Scott Evans; Lead Dancers, Ron Santos and Brigid Itnyre; Dancers, Pamela Meneley and Jeanette Telders; Nude Dancers, Dona Reynolds, Pam Schmidt, Peri Rocan, and Clarita Diaz. The show was Produced and Directed by Harold Minsky; Staged and Choreographed by Betty Francisco; Production Manager was Jerry Lucas; Musical Arrangements by Joe Fernandez and Ken Tiffany; Stage Manager and Light Designer was John Schubert; and Costumes were by Eastwood.

On June 22, 1977, the *Dallas Times Herald* ran the following short article:

"Granny's burlesque show gets a little bit 'too' hot; evidently things were a little too hot at Granny's Dinner Playhouse.

The dinner theatre was visited this week by a representative from the Dallas Marshal's office, informing the theatre that one of the stripper's featured in the

Brigid Itnyre and Cassandra Lee at Granny's Dinner Playhouse. The show went on to play the Blue Max nightclub at the Hyatt Regency in Chicago. Courtesy: Brigid Itnyre

current show, *Minsky's Burlesque '77*, could no longer do her specialty number, a fire dance. The theatre was instructed to stop dancer, Cassandra Lee, from doing her fire dance because it was in violation of the Dallas Fire Code.

Perry Cloud, owner of Granny's, said that the news was no surprise as he has talked with a number of theatre and nightclub owners around the country recently who have been paid visits by local fire authorities.

"It probably has something to do with the recent fire in Kentucky," said Cloud. "Stopping Cassandra from doing her dance doesn't bother me, but it will probably bother her – it's her act."

Cloud said that Cassandra will still be featured nightly in the revue, doing her dance in her usual Indian outfit – only without the fire."

I'm also including a review from the 1977 show; it was not the only review in the File. Reviews were written for both the 1975 and 1977 show and published in *The Dallas Morning News*. However, the man writing those reviews wrote in such fragmented sentences that when typing them over for this book everything showed up "in red;" so, I gave up. The review I am including is titled "Minsky's Revue, Dallas June '77," and it was written by Roy Honeycutt. I don't know the publication it ran in. It reads:

"*Minsky's Burlesque '77* opened here at Granny's Dinner Playhouse June 14 and will run through July 3. Like all good reviewers I went to the show expecting to find something that I wouldn't like, that I could pan. It just didn't work out that way as there wasn't a second in the whole show that I didn't like. From beginning to end it is tops. Assembled by Harold Minsky, with Jerry Lucas in charge, the show is a very lavish and perfectly staged extravaganza. Certainly not to be ignored is the talent which is first rate. Jimmy Mathews and Dick Richards are the two comics that provide most of the laughs in some of the funniest and most outrageous skits I've ever seen. Jerry Lucas also has his moments in these slap-stick situations. Mary Scott is a comedienne and straight person to the comics and I would suggest that the show business world get ready for her because she is going to be a star. She is absolutely tremendous doing some very complicated material. Cassandra Lee (who is a Liza Minnelli look-alike) and Francine Farrar are the most charming exotic dancers ever to grace a stage. Francine does a very sexy Gypsy routine. Cassandra did a real hot number featuring fire handling, until our local officials decided it was too dangerous. Now she does it without the fire. Maybe they would okay sparklers! Scott Evans does very well as the handsome singer with shirts cut down to his beltline and has a really good voice. Scott did his best number during the finale, "Higher and Higher." Ron Santos is the lead dancer with Brigid Itnyre. They do best in the opener, "A Touch of Class." Brigid is a real charmer who reminds me of Barbara Eden. Any normal man would crawl over broken glass and bottle caps for Brigid. Pamela

Meneley and Jeanette Telders are two lovely ladies that are also real fine dancers and are in most of the numbers. Dona Reynolds, Pam Schmidt, Peri Rocan, and Clarita Diaz are the featured nude dancers and I just don't have the space to describe them. It would take a year to put all of the adjectives in. Let's just say that they are heavenly and leave it at that. Bring out more of that broken glass and bottle tops! From the cast to the costumes to the material you just really can't find any faults with the show. It is as solid as any show to ever perform in Dallas.

The buffet type food is not great, but it is good and the service is excellent. Granny's is a well planned and smoothly operated playhouse which is a compliment to Perry Cloud and his Public Relations man, Bob Lawler. There is a Tuesday night special for $7.95.

Granny's has two late shows scheduled for Friday's and Saturday's. Matinees are scheduled for Sundays. With the prices of movies going up to the level of a day's pay, it is even more of a bargain to get out and see a real happening. Be sure and take your glasses. You don't want to miss a thing."

(Notes: Perry Cloud died in April of 2017.)

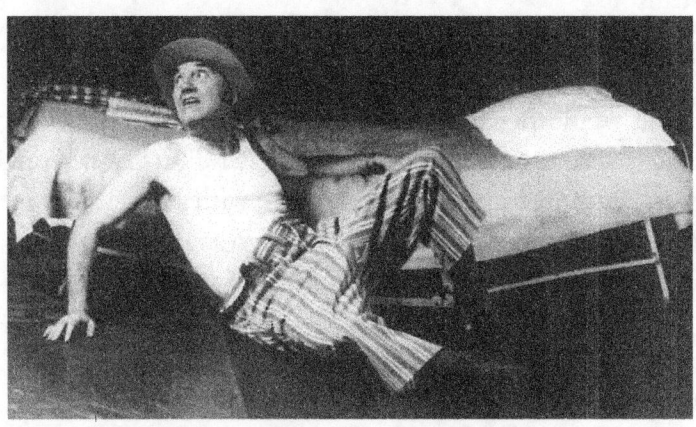

Jimmy Mathews. Courtesy: Pat Elliott

Jimmy Mathews took me to a Las Vegas gathering in 2001 where I met a few of the dancers who worked for Harold Minsky in some of the last shows he produced. In late 2016 I asked Brigid Itnyre (stage name) what she remembered about the Minsky shows she worked in and this is what she wrote:

"Oh my, I still think that we got to make one of the coolest entrances ever at Granny's Dinner Playhouse. We were in rhinestone gowns, with big slits up one leg, and boas; and we got to ride down out of the ceiling with our singer, who looked a bit like Tom Jones.

The Blue Max was so far out of the heart of Chicago – I MUCH preferred being at the Playboy Club because it was in the heart of the city!

Cassandra Lee was my roommate in Dallas and she did an Indian maiden strip that was very clever and classy. I honestly don't know if Cassandra Lee was her real name or not. I remember she was SO careful about her skin and hair

Jeanette Telders, Mary Scott, club manager, Brigid Itnyre, and Cassandra Lee in front at the Blue Max. Courtesy: Brigid Itnyre

care. I think it may have been the first time I became aware of ladies looking for THE very best of products; whether it was food, makeup, hair products, etc."

Regarding my question about retiring, Brigid responded, "Oh my, no...!!! I bring in actors and we perform for the patients at one of the medical schools here. It all started with a combination class between the medical school and the theatre department at UNLV back in 2005. I was also helping teach dance with a tango partner up until last summer. I just couldn't keep up with the late night rehearsals and classes, and then early mornings at my other job. I ended up getting sick and discovered the hard way that it was time to get off the "hamster wheel," that was so easy to deal with as a youngster!" (Brigid has since retired.)

It was also in late 2016 when I last talked to Lorraine Lee; I currently stay in touch with her by mail. Lorraine, in 2016, was a proud 95 years young; now, at 100 years of age, she still lives in her own home with her dogs, but no longer drives a car. She often worked for Minsky with her late husband Dick Richards, and I mentioned that conversation to Brigid. I asked what she remembered about Lorraine Lee and Dick Richards. Brigid wrote, "Lorraine...wow! She is a STRONG woman! I can still see the two of them. She and Dick were so great about taking those of us who loved sightseeing to various sites around New England when we played the Chateau de Ville Dinner Theatres."

Lorraine Lee. Courtesy: Lorraine Lee

"H" is For...

"H" is for a variety of things! The Blue Max nightclub at the Hyatt Regency O'Hare was briefly mentioned in the "G" File, so we're going to start there.

The first article was an interview Harold Minsky gave to the *Chicago Tribune* which appeared in the July 3, 1977 newspaper to promote the performances at the Blue Max at the Hyatt Regency. The article was written by Larry Kart, who's listed as the Night Life Critic. It reads as follows:

"Old-time burlesque survives and takes off with new zip; the trouble with burlesque, an authority on the subject once said, is that either it has been too dirty or it hasn't been dirty enough. Sex, more or less disguised, has always been the name of the game, even though a remarkable roster of comedians got their start in the field.

But, now, when every American city has its string of X-rated movie houses and massage parlors, burlesque's brand of commercialized cupidity is not an easy thing to sell. One man who still does is Harold Minsky, the only member of the famous Minsky clan who continues to put feminine flesh on display. His *Minsky's Follies* will be at the Blue Max of the Hyatt Regency O'Hare Friday through August 20.

Photo from the Minsky program of the dancers appearing in the show. Courtesy: Nancy Schuneman

The Minsky brothers – Abe (Harold's father), Billy, Herbert, and Morton – got into the business in 1908 when their father put them in control of his National Winter Garden Theatre on Manhattan's Lower East Side. On the ground floor was a hall that had been built for Boris Thomasevsky, the Yiddish tragedian. On the top floor was the theatre that eventually became the burlesque capital of New York after a mixture of movies and vaudeville had failed to fill the seats.

Two things made Minsky's a success – the decision to switch from overblown, Lillian Russell types to younger, slimmer girls; and an emphasis on what

Lillian Russell was an extremely popular performer during the late 19th and 20th centuries. She was well known for her musical comedy roles with the Weber and Fields Burlesque Company. I have a lot of sheet music with her pictured on the cover, along with her autobiography. Courtesy: Authors Collection

The Mutual Burlesquer, *a magazine cover from 1929. Courtesy: Dusty Sage*

Harold Minsky refers to as "a more modern approach." Others, particularly *Variety* publisher Simon "Sime" Silverman, would call it dirty.

"Yes," Minsky recalls, "he wasn't our friend at all. Old man Silverman believed that all show business should be like the days of the Keith vaudeville circuit. At the time, our burlesque was the strongest, bluest type of entertainment around, even though compared to what you see now it was like a church show. But that's what the generation coming up wanted. The proof is that the "wheels" went broke while we stayed in business.

Wheels? That's burlesque parlance for circuits, the string of theatre's road shows would play. There were two of them, the Mutual and the Columbia; and in their heyday, they used to run 40 weeks a year. But what Minsky's used to do was called stock. We'd stay in the same theatre and build a new show every week."

Harold Minsky entered the family business in 1931 at the age of 18 and took over from his father in 1937. Those Great Depression years were hard on other forms of stage entertainment, but they brought good fortune to Minsky's.

"That's when we did the best," Minsky says. "We gave 'em a show that up to 1 o'clock in the afternoon you could

A very early photo of the Rialto Theatre in Chicago. Courtesy: cinematreasures.org (It's a wonderful web site.)

get into for a quarter. A fellow used to look for a job from 8 in the morning until noon. Then he was tired and wanted a place to sit down. So he took his quarter, spent three or four hours in a burlesque theatre, and went home to tell his wife that he's been looking for a job all day. People were at a low ebb, and we gave them laughs and girls at a price they could afford.

From 1936 to 1939 there must have been 14 burlesque shows in Greater New York alone, but that ended for us in 1939 when Mayor Fiorello La Guardia took away our license. Then I operated the Adams Theatre in Newark and the Rialto in Chicago.

Remember the Rialto? It was right opposite Goldblatt's on State Street. The only reason I closed both theatres is that my leases expired, and in each case, I couldn't find another location downtown, where the action is. You can't put a burlesque house in a suburban shopping center; there's no drop-in trade."

When it comes to female burlesque performers, Minsky, who has seen them all, has definite opinions. "Lili St. Cyr was the best. Her idea of a strip was completely unique; they all copied her. She'd choose a number from *Carmen* and do a little story line with her strip. Or we'd have a tub and she's take a bath – getting undressed, getting into the tub, and so forth. And it was all in

Lili St. Cyr. Courtesy: C.F. Miller

excellent taste. She was a beautiful woman and the classiest strip in the business.

Gypsy Rose Lee? I wouldn't classify her as a stripper. She was a comedienne who joked with the audience while she took off her clothes. And she never took off very much. Don't get me wrong, she was a clever performer; but for a man who wanted to see a girl strip and get an illusion, Lili was tops. Ann Corio was very good in her day, too. And there were other types – Georgia Sothern, for example. She was a big star who did a cooch dance or a shake."

Fond as Minsky is of the burlesque queens; his heart really belongs to the comedians. He played a key role in the careers of Phil Silvers, Red Buttons, and Pinky Lee, taking them out of vaudeville and putting them in burlesque where they learned valuable lessons in comedy.

"You'll notice," Minsky says, "that each of them appeals to kids. It's because they're visual, not just stand-up comics. Unfortunately, now that burlesque is almost gone, there's no training ground. I see those fellows on the Carson show; they do two shots, and all of a sudden they're getting $5,000 a week. And some of them don't even know how to walk onto a stage.

Gypsy Rose Lee in Star and Garter, *which played at the Music Box Theatre for 609 performances from June 24, 1942 to December 4, 1943. Courtesy: C.F. Miller*

Press Photo of Ann Corio from 1961. Courtesy: Authors Collection

*1956 Press Photo of Phil Silvers.
Courtesy: Authors Collection*

*1962 Press Photo of Red Buttons, who could perform in both comedic and dramatic roles.
Courtesy: Authors Collection*

One guy I really admire though is Harvey Korman from *The Carol Burnett Show*. He really knows how to do a sketch right. And a lot of the comedy they do on TV is just old burlesque routines switched around. I should know."

The show Minsky is bringing to the Blue Max retains a lot of the old-time comedy, but the costumes and the choreography will be a bit fancier than they were at the Winter Garden or the Rialto. And, of course, there will be a stripper, or, as Minsky puts it, "an exotic dancer."

"Our audiences range from people in their early 30s on up. And the women love it. In the old days, you know, it wasn't considered nice for a woman to go to a burlesque theatre. They had to practically sneak in. But now our audiences are 50 percent women.

As for the men, we have two groups – people who remember the old Rialto or a theatre in New York, or in their hometown. To them it's nostalgic. The younger fellows, though, have only heard about burlesque. From their point of view it's like the late, late show. If you've never seen the picture, then it's new to you," Minsky said.

Harold Minsky would know."

Also included in this folder were two table cards from the Blue Max which promoted the show, as well as a handwritten list of all of the same performers and production crew who worked for Minsky in his 1977 revue at Granny's Dinner

Playhouse. The exception was the musical conductor; there was no name listed for that role, just several question marks.

Also in this folder was a quick paragraph written by Robert J. Herguth, of the *Chicago Sun-Times*, for his column "Public Eye." It reads:

"There may be no doctor in the house when *Minsky's Follies* prances nightly at the Blue Max. But there's always a registered nurse. Strawberry-blond Brigid Itnyre, 24, the troupe's lead dancer, earned her R.N. degree at Wesley Hospital School of Nursing. "My mother was a nurse. You can't dance all your life, so it's good to have something to fall back on," says Brigid, who also attended Academy of the Sacred Heart at 6250 N. Sheridan."

After Harold's death, his widow Pat produced a show that also played at the Blue Max nightclub at the Hyatt Regency O'Hare. The only thing in the folder regarding that show was the following newspaper article written by Laura Schmalbach, which appeared in Chicago's *Daily Herald* on Friday July 14, 1978.

"Follies mix old with new: When chorus girl Pat Minsky married her husband Harold in 1967, she had been hoofing her way through his *Minsky's Follies* burlesque show for four years.

"I saw it as an easy, glamorous way to make good money. It was a lot better than getting $60 a week for a nine-to-five job in a New Jersey publishing house," she recalled. "The nudity never bothered me, and the costumes were gorgeous. I loved it."

True to show business tradition, the boss took an interest in the young woman he'd hired, and despite the couple's 24-year age difference, they were married. "I always said I was the smartest girl on the line," said Pat with a smile.

Pat dropped out of the show shortly after the wedding, and spent the next ten years traveling with her husband, the son of founder Abe Minsky, and the rest of the venerable burlesque troupe. She watched as the emphasis switched from striptease to more complicated dancing, and listened to Harold's stories about "the good

Front cover from a Latin Quarter program. Courtesy: C.F. Miller

old days," when burlesque was thriving at clubs like the Copacabana and the Latin Quarter.

Now she's back, but behind the spotlight, not in it. Named associate producer after her husband's death last year, Pat is now responsible for overseeing musical arrangements and auditions and "making sure that the show is done in good taste ... that the old traditions are still there."

She was watching closely last week as dress rehearsal for the show at the Hyatt Regency O'Hare's Blue Max got under way. The opening number was "The Most Beautiful Girls in the World," and a chorus line of seven young lovelies paraded in elaborate floor-length pink costumes. In short order, the fancy clothes fell to the floor as the old bump 'n grind took over, complete with garter belts, silk stockings, and next-to-invisible G-strings.

Is the show true to the tradition of *Minsky's Follies*? Perhaps not, but as Pat points out, the "old traditions" are rapidly giving way to a new format that began even before she took over the reins from her husband.

"It's really tough to find good strippers now, and you can't get any tassel-twirlers anymore," said Pat with a grin. "It's all go-go dancing, and it's just not the same. A lot of college girls go into these topless-bottomless places for the money," she added. "In the days of Lili St. Cyr, everyone was trying to become a star; each one tried to top the other. That's gone now."

Pat Elliott Minsky.
Courtesy: Janelle Smith Collection

So the current show, while featuring the traditional "baggy-pants comics" and a variety act or two, has only one striptease routine. The songs, with the exception of "Most Beautiful Girls...," are current standards, and there's just as much emphasis on dancing skills as on good looks.

There are still plenty of elaborate costumes, all made in Las Vegas, but the "risqué" nature of burlesque has lost some of its punch.

"When stripping went into the legitimate theatre, through shows like *Pal Joey*, it became more accepted," said Pat, "and it took away some of the fun of seeing something naughty. We were playing the Playboy Club a few years ago, and one critic said the show was disappointing; that there wasn't enough nudity."

It's not quite the same, to be sure, as those Great Depression days when out-of-work men would sneak into the burlesque houses for a quarter, explaining their absences later with the excuse that they were looking for jobs.

Still, Pat doesn't bemoan all the changes from her husband and father-in-law's heyday. She still remembers the nights at the Silver Slipper when she would work three shows a night for eight days in a row – the times when, "You had to go out there and smile no matter what you felt."

Not only are the hours easier these days, but the audiences are becoming more diversified. According to Pat, attendance at the *Minsky's Follies* shows both on the road and in Las Vegas, the troupe's home base, is evenly divided between men and women. The age level is mid-30s; too young to remember the old routines with Tempest Storm, Gypsy Rose Lee, and comics like Red Buttons and Phil Silvers.

But, with or without the original flavor of *Minsky's Follies*, the show goes on. And Pat Minsky is happy to be right where she is, studying from the sidelines and trying to blend the old with the new.

"You know, the first couple of years I missed it," she said. "But I quickly realized that burlesque isn't something you can do all your life."

And this, she adds, is next best."

"H" also stands for the Hacienda Hotel and Casino in Las Vegas. Included in the Minsky Files were two newspaper articles written long after Harold's death, regarding a burlesque tribute produced by Maynard Sloate and performed at the Hacienda in 1986. I am only including one of the articles. The second, "Hacienda

Postcard of the Hacienda Hotel and Casino in Las Vegas, Nevada. Courtesy: Authors Collection

Burlesque Show enough to scare Minsky's Ghost," appeared in the *Las Vegas Review-Journal* on October 17, 1986. To me, it read like a personal attack on Minsky. I'm sure a copy can be located if you truly want to read it.

(Notes: Maynard Sloate, a member of the BHS, passed away on November 4, 2019.)

Frankie Ray Perilli and Maynard Sloate at the 1998 BHS gathering held in Venice, California.
Courtesy: Authors Collection

The article I am including was from the *Las Vegas Sun* and dated September 23, 1986. It appeared in the Ralph Pearl column "Las Vegas is my Beat." It reads:

"Harold Minsky lives again in Hacienda Hotel's Tribute"

"Back in 1941, as a New York City newsman, I was sent out by my City Editor to write a piece about Harold Minsky, then the King of Burlesque, who had just been dethroned by New York City Mayor Fiorello La Guardia. The Mayor believed that *Minsky Burlesque* and other burlesque shows of a smaller nature didn't belong in his town because they were "too raw," so he closed them down.

Nine years later in Chicago, *Minsky Burlesque* was all the rage in the Windy City with Top Banana Irving Benson one of its stars. I didn't see Minsky again until 1957, when his *Minsky Burlesque* started a long run in the Dunes Hotel with Irv Benson. And for the next twenty years, *Minsky Burlesque* would play a Las Vegas showroom a couple months a year. But it all came to a tragic end when in the Christmas week of 1977 Harold Minsky died.

Now, nearly ten years later, producer Maynard Sloate of the Sahara was bringing back a tribute to the great Harold Minsky, who had been a dear friend to the Hacienda Hotel. And sharing the headlining spot was none other than Irving Benson, the great Top Banana for the past fifty years, along with an exotic, sensuous dancer by the name of Bambi Jr., who brought back memories of other exotic, sensuous ladies who had played Las Vegas in the 1950s and 1960s, such as Lili St. Cyr, Tempest Storm, Gypsy Rose Lee, and Sally Rand.

Benson had worked for fifty years with almost every top name star, been Johnny Carson's favorite guest on *The Tonight Show*, and played in many of the

Bambi Jr. Courtesy: Bambi Jr.

Bambi Sr. (aka Bambi Brooks, Bambi Jones, etc.) appearing at Talk of the Town in Tucson, Arizona in 1952. Bambi Sr. was a close chum of Jennie Lee's and has been a member of the BHS for decades. Courtesy: Bambi Sr.

Strip and downtown hotels during the past thirty years. But his latest effort, this tribute to Harold Minsky, has to be his most pleasing one. There is no greater Top Banana in show business than Benson.

And if Harold Minsky was watching the show from "Upstairs" that night, he must have been pleased, even though Fiorello, sitting next to him, probably scowled all through the show. *Minsky Burlesque* is back where it belongs, here in Las Vegas. And judging by the response of the opening night sell-out crowd, it'll have a long run."

(Notes: We rarely read anything about Harold's family. His father Abe, who died in 1949, was married to Molly Wachtler Minsky, who died on May 14, 1964, at age 69; and he had a sister Sylvia Minsky Elkman, who had a son named Alan.

After her husband's death in 1949, Molly was an adviser to Harold, on his various productions. Formerly, she was Secretary and Treasurer of the Burley Amusement Corporation, the operator of the New Gotham Theatre on East 25th Street, in New York City.

For 35 years Mrs. Minsky was also the President of the Daughters of Israel Day Nursery at 220 East Fifth Street; she was also an organizer of the Charlanna

Philanthropic League. Molly was survived by her two children; a brother, three sisters, and multiple grandchildren.)

Also in the "H" File was a program from the New York Hilton, dated December 13, 1967. Part of the program reads:
"Meyer Davis Productions and Cass Harrison, Executive Producer, presents *Life Begins at Minsky's*. The 47th Annual Christmas Party for the Salesmen's Association of the American Chemical Industry, staged and produced by Harold Minsky."

Barbara Curtis.
Courtesy: Janelle Smith Collection

It listed officers and directors from many of the major chemical and oil companies in the country. The menu included: Supreme of Fresh Fruit Au Kirsch, decorated with berries in season and served in silver crowns. Roast Prime Ribs of Beef Au Jus, string beans and mushrooms sauté, and rissole potatoes. The meal concluded with, a Christmas Log, black cherry sauce, petit fours, and large coffees.

Cast members for the show included: Jeannie Linero, Orie Sasaki, Don Crawford, Mike Martin, Dick Bernie, Barbara Curtis, Danny Jacobs, Marilyn Mayblum, Jimmy Lewis, Milt Douglas, Marcia Gregg, Arian Michelle, Jack Rosen, Penny Damone, and Lisa Duran. The scenes included: "He-Haw," "Life-Saver," "Max and Cherie, a Happy Marriage," "School Days," and "Minsky Lunacy."

Also included was an obituary for Charles Hogan from the *Chicago Sun-Times* dated Tuesday, November 24, 1970. It was titled "Rites Wednesday for Charles Hogan, Bob Hope Agent," and reads as follows:
"Requiem Mass for Charles E. Hogan, 68, personal appearance agent for comedian Bob Hope for more than forty years, will be offered at 10am Wednesday at St. Luke Church, 528 Lathrop in River Forest. Burial will be at St. Mary Cemetery in Evergreen Park.
Mr. Hogan, of 1020 Monroe in River Forest, died of a heart attack Sunday night at West Suburban Hospital in Oak Park. He had been released from the

hospital earlier Sunday after convalescing from a previous heart attack for six weeks, but he suffered a second heart attack upon returning home and died at the hospital.

Mr. Hogan was the first agent to give Hope a break in show business. He booked him into the Stratford Theatre on the South Side for a one week engagement that stretched to six months. Mr. Hogan remained with Hope until his death.

Minsky's Burlesque and the Oriental Theatre also were counted among Mr. Hogan's clients over the years. He owned and operated a theatrical booking agency at 203 N. Wabash.

Mr. Hogan is survived by the widow, Patricia; a daughter, Patty Anne, and two sisters, Dorothy Fennerty and Betty Scherer.

Hope has announced that he will attend the funeral. Visitation will be on Tuesday at Drechsler-Brown Funeral Home, 203 Marion in Oak Park."

A second clipping in the folder was from the same newspaper, and also dated Tuesday, November 24, 1970. It was from "Kup's Column" and reads as follows:

"There are days when a reporter doesn't feel like meeting his deadline. This is one of those days brought on by the death of a longtime friend, Charles Hogan, the popular theatrical agent. Mr. Hogan had spent the last six weeks at West Suburban Hospital, convalescing from a heart attack. His daily calls, after the doctor permitted him to use the telephone, helped brighten our day. There always was a cheerful ring to his conversation, especially as the date approached for his release from the hospital. He was especially ecstatic on Saturday. The doctor reported his last electrocardiogram indicated he had fully recovered and could return home. He did return home on Sunday, but he suffered another attack and was rushed back to the hospital, where he succumbed.

Mr. Hogan's career had been intertwined with that of his No. 1 client, Bob Hope. They were more than business associates. Bob and Charlie were inseparable friends over a 40-year period. Their relationship started in 1929, when Hope, a struggling young comedian, would parade in front of the Woods Theatre Building on Randolph, as did dozens of young performers of that era, seeking employment from the agents who occupied the building. Mr. Hogan was the first to give Hope a break. He signed him for a one week engagement at the old Stratford Theatre on the South Side. The one week stretched into six months, after which Hope was on his way to the highest rung in show business.

No matter how high or far Hope traveled, Mr. Hogan usually was at his side. Bob had other agents, including one for TV and one for movies, but Mr. Hogan, who handled all his personal appearances, was closest to him. Throughout their long association, they never bothered with a written contract. The bond between them was sufficient.

Sheet music from the 1948 film, The Paleface, starring Jane Russell and Bob Hope. Courtesy: Authors Collection

Hope was in town over the weekend, and his first words to this reporter were, "Hey isn't the news about Charlie great? He's going home." Now we had to phone him and his wife Dolores at their Palm Springs (California) home to break the news. Both were distraught. Their first thoughts were for Mr. Hogan's widow, Patty, whom they would phone later and invite to their desert home. Hope will fly here to join the mourners at Mr. Hogan's funeral Wednesday morning.

We once asked Hope why he continues to work as hard as he does, making so many appearances at state fairs, colleges and auditoriums, between his TV and movie commitments. "Certainly you don't need the money." Hope responded, "I don't, but Charlie needs the 10 percent." It was a facetious reply but one that indicated the 'Gemütlichkeit' feeling between the two.

Mr. Hogan, with his mop of white hair and cherubic face, stood only 5 feet 3. But he was a giant of a man."

"I" is For...

"I" is for the International Theatre-Restaurant, owned and operated by Jack Silverman. A little background information is followed by the contents of the File.

Jack Silverman's International Theatre-Restaurant, a nightclub located downstairs on Broadway at 52nd Street, was a vastly expanded version of Jack Silverman's Old Romanian Restaurant, which for years flourished at 169 Allen Street. Originally, it was a 75-seat restaurant featuring a 75 cent dinner and a wandering accordion player, but it expanded into a 500-seat business featuring some of the great names of the Jewish stage, including Boris Thomashefsky, Ludwig Satz, and Sadie Banks, whose name eventually became synonymous with the Old Romanian. She came to work for a weekend and remained twenty-five years. It was written in a 1946 *Billboard* magazine that Sadie Banks was as permanent at the Old Romanian as the bar. Sadie ended her career working only occasional club dates, and weekends in the Catskills.

Record album cover from "Sadie Banks Sings."
Courtesy: Dusty Sage

In Marta Becket's 2014 autobiography *To Dance On Sands*, she wrote, "The Old Romanian had a line of girls, and a big woman who sang bawdy songs in Yiddish, cracked jokes, and announced the acts. Her name was Sadie Banks. She was known as the Sophie Tucker of the East Side."

It was at the Old Romanian that Paul Muni courted his wife, Bella; and Sholom Secunda sketched out many a musical comedy on its table cloths, including a new tune called "Bei Mir Bistu Shein." The song was part of a Yiddish operetta called *I Would If I Could*, written in 1932 by Abraham Bloom, with music by Secunda and lyrics by Jacob Jacobs. At the height of his fame, Rudy Vallee took his entire floor show from the Hollywood Restaurant on Broadway to perform at the club in honor of Thomashefsky. Comedian Milton Berle also once emceed the Old Romanian floor show, and regaled the audiences for hours while carrying around a plate of soup.

In 1956 the city declared that there would be a housing project established on the site, so the Old Romanian moved to Broadway, became the New Romanian, and was eventually renamed the International Theatre-Restaurant. It operated on a big name policy, and

A very young Milton Berle.
Courtesy: Authors Collection

among the entertainers who performed at the nightclub were: Sophie Tucker, the Ritz Brothers, Julius La Rosa, Ted Lewis, Joey Adams, Lennie Kent, Jean Carroll, Eileen Barton, Sid Gould, and Myron Cohen.

Sophie Tucker.
Courtesy: Burlesque Historical Society

The Ritz Brothers. Courtesy: C.F. Miller

Silverman, a native of Rumania, came to this country as a boy. He was in banking and quilt manufacturing before beginning a forty-year career in the restaurant business. A proud member of "The Friars Club," Jack retired in 1965 as the operator of the International Theatre-Restaurant. He died on June 15, 1974 in White Plains, New York. Jack Silverman was 86 years old.

What this folder contained about the show that played at the International included a variety of short columns and newspaper clippings. Nothing was very long; most were from the run in 1964, but Minsky also put a show on at the club in 1962.

The first clipping, the only one from 1962, was from the *Las Vegas Sun*, and dated October 29, 1962. It was written by Ralph Pearl and reads:

"For almost twenty years veteran comic Irv Benson tried breaking into the show business picture in his native New York. He'd have gladly settled for a walk-on part in a Broadway show or café. But his luck was bad. Being in burlesque, Irv had to go out of town and work the second rate clubs in such towns as Buffalo, Scranton, and Walla Walla. After all, he and his wife had a terrible habit; they liked to eat regularly.

Irving Benson. Courtesy: Pat Elliott Minsky/ Burlesque Historical Society

Three years ago he got his big break. Harold Minsky brought Irv out to work in his *Scandals* at the Dunes, later at the New Frontier. His fame as a top banana spread. However, it hadn't spread to New York. Irv still couldn't break into the Manhattan café or Broadway theatre scene. Then it happened!

Two weeks ago, the *Minsky Follies* opened on Broadway at Jack Silverman's Club. Irv Benson was the top banana in that girlie fracas. Now he's the darling of the town. All the top columnists, Winchell, Sullivan, Sobol, and Wilson write about him almost every day.

It now begins to look like little Irv has cracked through after twenty futile years. Evidently fame knows no calendar. The sweet taste of success is now lingering in Benson's long time starved palate. And it couldn't happen to a nicer gent."

Jack Thompson wrote the following article "Minsky Follies True to Form," which appeared in the *New York Journal-American* on September 25, 1964. It reads as follows:

"The autumn officially welcomed at Jack Silverman's International Theatre-Restaurant last night a sparkling new show *Minsky's Follies of '65* produced by the old master, Harold Minsky, himself.

The mixture is much as before with gorgeous showgirls, several of whom are alumnae of the Latin Quarter and Copacabana, and low comedians. The large audience gave the show a most cordial welcome.

Most unusual of the acts is a juggle-acrobat-dancer, Georgie Carl, who is reminiscent of the late, great Jimmy Savo with his innocent leer, as he performs his delightful, if overlong, act.

Those old Minsky standbys, Milt Douglas and Priscilla, are in the current show as their usual bickering married couple. Their act is considerably changed for the better, and it was always good. She remains remarkable for her ability to deliver startling double entendre lines while acting a perfect lady. Douglas is her equal as her husband.

Besides being a featured showgirl, the wide-eyed and spectacularly constructed Venus Christy, and you can bet she was christened that, plays straight for the other comedians and is really something worth watching.

At this rather late date Mr. Minsky has added a belly dancer to one of his shows. Her name is Rahmina and she is only moderately skillful in her art. The stripping is in the hands of Barbara Carroll, who is some sort of successor to the great Hinda Wausau, of a previous generation.

Minsky has again used his famous courtroom scene utilizing the talented Irv Benson, Jack Mann, Bob London, Larry Allen, Venus Christy, and another doll worth noting, Eva Nolan. It is pure, unadulterated old fashioned burlesque and utter chaos from start to finish and for the most part, extremely funny.

It's a long time since the International has had so diverting a show and it should be around for months to come."

(Notes: Jimmy Savo was born in New York City as James Vincent Sava on July 31, 1895. He was a comedian, juggler, singer, and mime artist, who performed in vaudeville, nightclubs, burlesque, films and television, as well as on Broadway. Charlie Chaplin once stated that Savo was "the best pantomime in the world."

In 1938, Savo originated the role of "Dromio" in the successful film *The Boys from Syracuse*. In 1942, Isidore "Izzy" Herk and the Shubert Brothers co-produced a Broadway show called *Wine, Women and Song*, starring Jimmy Savo and Margie Hart. The show, which opened on September 28, 1942, was advertised as a combination of vaudeville, burlesque, and Broadway revue; it ran for seven weeks. The revue, which included a striptease, shocked some of the audiences and was closed by court order on December 3, 1942. Two of his most remembered songs were *River Stay 'Way from my Door* and *You Get No Bread with One Meat Ball*.

Jimmy Savo died from a heart attack in Terni, Italy on September 5, 1960. He wrote two books: *Little World, Hello!* which was published in 1947; and a book published after his death in 1963, *I Bow to the Stones; Memories of a New York Childhood*. I'm tickled to say I found a copy of his 1963 autobiography to add to my collection.)

Jimmy Savo. Courtesy: Authors Collection

Margie Hart. Courtesy: Janelle Smith Collection

In Earl Wilson's column "It Happened Last Night," which appeared in the *New York Post* on September 25, 1964, Wilson wrote:

"I looked in on *Minsky's Follies of '65*, the new show at the International, and MAN, what beauties (Bellyrina Rahmina, Venus Christy, Eva Nolan, Marian Silva, and Barbara Carroll)! And busting me up with this, "I made a lot of money in a parking lot parking cars. My first night I made $360… How? I sold two cars," was comedian Irv Benson."

On September 25, 1964, the *New York World-Telegram and Sun* carried the following article by Leonard Harris, titled "Minsky's Back – in the Flesh." It reads:

"That most hallowed of institutions, Minsky's, returned last night – in the flesh – to Jack Silverman's International.

The current edition is *Minsky's Follies of '65* and it represents some smart quarterbacking on the part of veteran impresario Silverman. The play worked, so he used it again.

Two years ago, the Minsky revue brought a successful season to the huge International. It should do the same this year.

The girls are there – all there. Their sequins catch the raucous spotlights; their anatomies are something to marvel at. The comedians are raw, corny, and funny. And there's even a belly dancer, a belated nod in the direction of the 1960s.

But it's the old stuff that is wanted. And it is delivered with great gusto by comics Irving Benson and Jack Mann, Milt Douglas and Priscilla, and an acrobatic, dancing, juggling imp named Georgie Carl.

As a comedian, Benson is from the old school, and one of its star pupils. All eyes, leers and double takes, he is a master at the burlesque art.

As for the girls, it is hard to pick from the score of prime specimens that glide by, but several stand out. One is Marian Silva, who must be seen to be disbelieved; another is Venus Christy, who is the best rounded "straight man" in town; a third is a milky skinned dancer, Eva Nolan, whose magnificent eyes are so arresting you don't even notice what she's not wearing."

The last couple of mentions, of the show or performers, comes from "On the Town" columns written by Charles McHarry, that appeared in the *New York Daily News*. On September 30, 1964 he wrote:

"Burlesque comedians Irving Benson and Jack Mann are back at the International with a handsome new edition of *Minsky's Follies*. Go prepared to laugh your head off."

And on October 12, 1964 McHarry wrote:

"Barbara Carroll, featured in *Minsky's Follies* at the International will soon graduate to TV commercials. Agent Mickey Alpert has taken her under his wing."

(Notes: George Carl was born on May 7, 1916 in Ohio and started his comedy career during his teenage years performing acrobatics and pantomime with a

George Carl. Courtesy: Pat Elliott Minsky/ Burlesque Historical Society

Press Photo from December 1944 of Jerry Lewis and his father Danny, in Jerry's dressing room. Danny was a straight man in burlesque. Courtesy: Authors Collection

variety of circuses. He eventually attained international fame as a clown, vaudevillian, and slapstick comic; his work often mirrored that of Charlie Chaplin, and Laurel and Hardy.

With only a microphone and a microphone stand, Carl would seemingly become tangled up in the cord, get his thumb stuck in the microphone stand, and, through a flurry of silent bits, wind up accomplishing absolutely nothing at all in the time he spent onstage – and audiences loved him.

In 1995 George Carl made his screen debut at the age of 79, portraying an eccentric music-hall comedian in the film *Funny Bones*. The film also starred Jerry Lewis, whose father, Danny, was a straight man in burlesque.

Georgie Carl died from cancer at his home in Las Vegas on January 1, 2000.)

"L" is For...

"L" is for the Latin Casino Theatre Restaurant in Cherry Hill, New Jersey.

The Latin Club, which first opened in 1948, was originally located in Philadelphia; the struggling club, which could seat 600 people, was purchased in 1951 by Daniel "Dallas" Gerson and David Dushoff. The new club owners booked stars such as: Frank Sinatra, Sophie Tucker, Joe E. Lewis, and the Mills Brothers. However, frustrated by Pennsylvania's restrictive liquor laws, limited parking space, and conflicts with city officials, the men relocated to nearby Cherry Hill, New Jersey in 1960 where they built a plush 1,500-seat, Vegas-style dinner theatre. They formally named their new venture the Latin Casino Theatre Restaurant, even though casino gambling was not included. It was considered one of the largest, fanciest, and hippest nightclub experiences of that time featuring dinner, drinks, and a showcase of top entertainment. It was billed as the

Photo of the Mills Brothers from a piece of 1932 sheet music. The song was "How'm I Doin?" They were billed as "Four Boys and a Guitar." Courtesy: Authors Collection

Vintage photo shows part of the stage and dining area from inside the Latin Casino in Cherry Hill, New Jersey. Courtesy: thedailyjournal.com

"Showplace of the Stars," and Gerson was a gracious host who had a knack for putting people at ease.

Many of the top entertainers who performed at, or frequented, the club included: Harry Belafonte, Jimmy Durante, Sammy Davis Jr., Frank Sinatra, Dean Martin, Liza Minnelli, Don Rickles, Johnny Mathis, the Temptations, B.B. King, Tom Jones, Jerry Lewis, Milton Berle, Lena Horne, Louis Armstrong, Danny Thomas, Totie Fields, and Joey Bishop.

Yet, Gerson and the Latin Casino ran into trouble during the mid-1970s with the New Jersey Alcoholic Beverage Control Division and the Internal Revenue Service. Officials from the state liquor board received complaints when a lineup of chorus girls went topless in the *Folies de Paris Revue*. The girls were told to cover up, and the show went on.

The IRS ended the long battle with the club by filing a judgment in default against New Latin Casino Incorporated for $2.5 million. Gerson's solution to his tax problem was to dissolve the company named in the judgment and create a new firm, the Latin Casino Corporation. The new company bought a new liquor license and went on without missing a beat. However, the IRS eventually seized the casino's liquor supply and the new liquor license. In

NBC Press Photo of Jimmy Durante. Courtesy: Authors Collection

1978, the Latin Casino was forced to close. Everything was auctioned off from the napkins to the silverware, including a 1967 Rolls-Royce limousine that once transported Frank Sinatra.

Five months later, at the height of the disco craze, the Latin Casino reopened as an exotic disco club, called the Emerald City. The club exhibited a neon light show over the dance floor that cost in excess of one million dollars. After a couple years Emerald City shifted from disco to rock, hosting major and up-and-coming acts of the time including Prince on his debut tour. It finally closed for good in December 1982, and was torn down in the mid-1980s after a fire demolished the club. The headquarters of Subaru of America was then built on the site, opening in 1986.

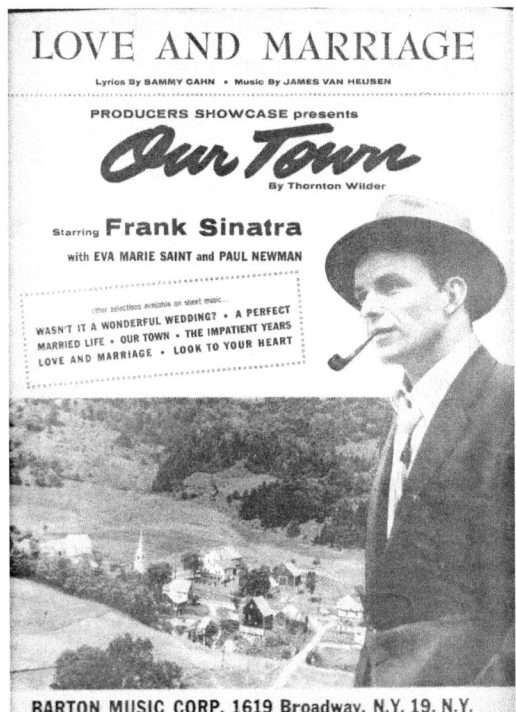

Sheet music from the 1955 production of Our Town, *starring Frank Sinatra. Courtesy: Authors Collection*

There were several celebrity incidents that drew media attention at the Latin Casino. Brenda Lee broke her neck onstage during a June 12, 1962, performance. On September 29, 1975, Jackie Wilson suffered a massive heart attack and collapsed onstage while singing his hit song "Lonely Teardrops" during a Dick Clark show. Wilson lived in a nursing home until his death in early 1984. Tom Jones was also jumped outside the back door following one of his performances by two fanatical women. He was not hurt but the ladies were banned from the club and from attending any future Tom Jones performances.

(Notes: Born in Poland in 1908, Daniel "Dallas" Gerson booked the acts and kept the Latin Casino going for thirty years until it closed in 1978. Gerson, 83, a resident of Lower Merion, Pennsylvania died on April 16, 1991 in a one-car accident in Springfield Township, Delaware County. According to the authorities, he apparently suffered a heart attack while driving and was killed when a rib punctured his heart.

Gerson had a passion for expensive cars, like Rolls-Royces and Bentleys. Not only was he content to drive them, but he could change into overalls and become a grease monkey overnight. How appropriate he died driving a car he probably loved.

David Dushoff often used practical jokes, buffoonery, and brashness to woo top entertainers into performing at the Latin Casino. Dushoff, at age 61, died on December 20, 1972 in Philadelphia, Pennsylvania.

In-part the following obituary ran in the *Reading Eagle,* on December 22, 1972. I didn't include his surviving family members or when the services were held.

"Philadelphia, PA (AP) - Latin Casino owner David Dushoff, who sometimes disguised himself as a taxi driver or chauffeur to meet show business celebrities and lure them to his nightclub, is dead at age 61. Death came late Wednesday at Hahnemann Hospital where he had been admitted December 4 after suffering a heart attack.

The flashy, $3 million theatre-restaurant, located in suburban Cherry Hill, New Jersey, was a struggling nitery in downtown Philadelphia when Dushoff, operator of two tile firms, bought it with a partner in 1951.

Dushoff, vowing to resuscitate the club by bringing in big names, flattered them with buffoonery and practical jokes as well as the disguises.

"Celebrities are like grownup children," he once remarked in an interview. "They have to be made a fuss about. When you're with a celebrity, always let him have the floor." After business grew, Dushoff moved the casino to New Jersey to beat the Pennsylvania blue laws and to provide more parking spaces.

Not all of his hobnobbing with entertainers went smoothly, however. Diana Ross and the Supremes walked out of an engagement at the club in 1969 after one of her dogs died from eating cyanide tablets, placed near dressing rooms to ward off insects; and comedian Joey Bishop quit his appearance at the club in 1970 after a heckling incident.")

Joey Bishop.
Courtesy: Burlesque Historical Society

The *Minsky's Burlesque Follies* played the Latin Casino in 1967. Included are three articles that were written about the show. "Burlesque Appeals to Crowd at Latin," written by Jerry Gaghan, appeared in the *Philadelphia Daily News* on February 21, 1967. It reads:

"Gals and gags, bared bosoms and buffoonery are in happy mixture at the Latin Casino, where *Minsky's Burlesque Follies* is making its area nitery debut. Headwaiter Al Turner swings right into the spirit of the things with the greeting, "Get your Nestlé's chocolate bar before you go down the aisle." Unlike the exclusively male attendance at the burlesque houses, there are plenty of women in the café audience. The crowd also has a different attitude and they are laughing before the desert is served. Not only laughing but impatient, the diners started spurious applause to get the show started when the opener ran a few minutes late. The strip is still very much in vogue in burlesque, but the Minsky entourage serves nudity in supermarket shipments. The eight stately showgirls flash plenty of epidermis, their main article of attire being the headdress. For the most part, the pasties and the G-string enhance the femme forms.

Debra Duke. Courtesy: Pat Elliott Minsky/Burlesque Historical Society

At the press table was Sid Brown, a brother of columnist Leon Brown, and now a resident of San Francisco. Pasties would be considered a fraud in the city by the bay, where "topless means just that." But after eight months in the nudist Athens of the west, Sid felt that pasties made the showgirls more attractive and the production more artistic. Another nearby font of information was New York public relations man Eddie Jaffe, a burlesque advance agent for three decades and the press representative for Rowland Barber's definitive book, *The Night They Raided Minsky's*. In addition to the prancing showgirls, there is a dancing chorus only slightly more encumbered for the ensemble stepping. The striptueses – Debra Duke and Lisa Duran – accentuate their peeling with some bona fide terping, and petite Mikki Sharait is the featured ballerina.

Since people come for the comedians, this boisterous business is entrusted to such burley veterans as Freddie Lewis, Dick Richards, and Milt Douglas, with blonde Barbara Curtis serving as straight woman for all three. The boys come from the old school and so do most of their jokes. They resort to puns and double entendre and if the laughs don't come fast enough, throw in comic vulgarity for shock hilarity. Lewis does a delayed take as the phone fails to ring. Finally he answers, "Who is this? Phil Wasserman? Are you positive?" Richards comes on in antic getup, swinging a cane, "I know what you're all thinking… just another Italian singer." Miss Curtis in a domestic bit asks husband Douglas, "Honey, would you cheat on me?" He replies, "Who else?" David Walker sings for the ensembles that add revue atmosphere, and La Vaughn and Maximilian break up the burleycue with an okay hoofing segment."

(Notes: Yes, the words "striptueses" and "terping" were used in this article – they are not typos.)

The next article, dated February 22, 1967, comes from the Camden, New Jersey *Courier-Post*. It was written by Charles Petzold, a staff member of the newspaper, and titled "Modern Burlesque Is Not the Same." It reads as follows:

"Burlesque has changed since the good old days. There are plenty of almost bare-bosomed babes in *Minsky's Burlesque Follies* at the Latin Casino, but the Cherry Hill revue fails to capture the nostalgia of true burly.

Where for example, are the baggy-pants comedians of the days gone by? They're not evident in the Minsky version.

Where are the 25-cent packages that used to have balding men digging deep into their pockets for two-bits worth of unknown pleasures? Also missing. Even the G-strings are gone.

A very young Barbara Curtis. Courtesy: Burlesque Historical Society

Milt Douglas. Courtesy: Burlesque Historical Society

Lest the Legions of Decency be outraged by that last remark, we should set the record level. The girls never get as far as the G-string. They wear bikini pants over full-length net tights. Debra Duke reaches near-nudity, but the lights dim before the final coverings are removed.

For those who like the flesh, however, Minsky's immodest maidens more than fill the bill in perhaps the scantiest costumes (or lack of costumes) in Latin Casino history.

And to the show's credit, the girls all are a-peeling (to steal a line). There is not a vintage or overweight stripper in the wine basket.

On the debit side, the dialogue is difficult, sometimes impossible to hear (particularly when waiters lean on the back of your chair and comment loudly). Improvements are definitely needed in the sound system.

At one point, diners began pounding on their tables and shouting "louder." Barbara Curtis, one of the show's bright lights, raised her voice. Others seemed not to care.

Despite some obvious drawbacks in a show which almost certainly will be improved, diners are filling the tables in the theatre-restaurant for both shows, a rarity early in the week.

One act which draws favorable reaction (and a few laughs) features Mikki Sharait wearing only pasties and bikini pants and Larry Merritt in a similar costume, sans pasties. The laughs appear to be for the nearly nude male, although he is a fine dancer.

Dancers La Vaughn and Maximilian also draw cheers. They deserve it.

Blonde Lisa Duran headlines the strippers (there are only two). Debra Duke is the other peeler. Unfortunately, they seem to rush through their routines. Here's one man's vote for allowing them more time.

Minsky's revue continues twice nightly through Sunday."

(Notes: I can see Barbara Curtis reacting to an audience shouting "louder." She attended the BHS gathering in Las Vegas at the Gold Coast Hotel and Casino in 2000, where we set up a small stage and presented an impromptu show. Barbara performed, and when the audience got a bit loud with their chatter, she stopped what she was doing onstage, and sort of "bellowed" for quiet. I thought it was great. I thoroughly enjoyed my brief encounter with the late, great Miss Barbara Curtis.)

The final article was from the Philadelphia *Evening Bulletin*, dated February 22, 1967. It was from the "Man About Town" column written by Frank Brookhouser. It reads:

Straight man Danny Jacobs, comic Dick Richards, and talking woman Barbara Curtis. Courtesy: Pat Elliott Minsky/ Burlesque Historical Society

"Nothing is missing – not even the candy butcher. In the person of Milt Douglas, one of the comics, he delivers his hard-sell spiel from the stage at the onset to set up the proper atmosphere for the proceedings after the girls have briefly simulated an out-of-step chorus line of 1937 vintage.

What follows in the new show at the Latin Casino, the barest and most abundant in feminine flesh it has ever presented, is exactly what the billing says, *Minsky's Burlesque Follies*.

It is a modern version of old-fashioned burlesque. The mannequins are prettier – and if I remember correctly – slimmer than the old style. The dancers are better dancers. The band is on the balcony stand rather than in a pit, and it plays better. The strips are … well, more refined, with the bumps and grinds held to a minimum. And there is no popcorn with prizes.

But basically, this is the way it was and, while the girls in this neatly-staged revue from Las Vegas clad principally in only pasties and G-strings – and headdress – are romping about in the old familiar manner, old-timers in the audience can have a fling with nostalgia.

The opening show customers, comprising a hefty percentage of women, seemed to love the activities, even if they had never made the trek to the Troc or the long defunct Bijou.

And truth to tell, with what takes place today in the legitimate theatre, on the movie screen and in book pages, nothing seems as bawdy as it once did. In a fashion, the show is like a fun trip to another era, a more innocent time in our lives.

Both of the strip stars, Lisa Duran and Debra Duke, not only have the dazzling figures but dancing skills to go with the fundamentals of their act. And Mikki Sharait, the featured dancer, is a cute and agile performer.

Aside from the lively routines furnished by the chorus of six girls and Larry Merritt and what might be called the occasional and random but effective movements of the eight mannequins, there is an exciting tap specialty by the team of La Vaughn and Maximilian.

The handsome young singer for the production number is David Walker and the ribald comedy is provided by Douglas, Danny Jacobs, and Dick Richards (three burlesque veterans), with blonde Barbara Curtis playing the straight woman in the style straight out of 1937.

The comedy is the same vintage. The gags are as broad as the Delaware. The double-entendre lurks behind the most innocent lead-in line. Rowdy is the word to cover it.

Wife: "My ancestors can be traced." Husband: "If the wind's in the right direction… Talking about funerals, are you going to my brother's wedding tomorrow?"

So, if the dancing is much, much better and the girls much slimmer and prettier in this modern version of old burlesque, the comedy hasn't changed an iota. And it has gone through a certain test of time."

(Notes: The late night shows, starting at 11:30pm cost $3 per person. All other shows cost $6 per person and included food and liquor.)

"L" is also for the Lookout House in Covington, Kentucky. The Lookout House, a thriving nightclub, was located in Fort Wright for several decades; just south of Covington.

Previously, there was a one-story brick building on the site, known as Rush's Tavern, which was torn down in 1886 for the construction of the new facility. The tavern was famous for excellent food and accommodations. The new three-story brick structure included a large cupola on top of the building, a slaughterhouse, and an underground passageway that was used as a natural cooling system for storing freshly cut meat.

In 1912, after the original owner died, William Hill bought the business for $25,000. Hill had a reputation as being a successful saloon owner, and under his management, Lookout House as it was now called, flourished as a nightclub. However, the business later struggled during the era of Prohibition. So, Hill sold Lookout House to Jimmy

An early photo of the Lookout House. Courtesy: nkyviews.com

A photo of the Jimmy Brinks era of the Lookout House. Courtesy: nkyviews.com

Brink in 1933. Brink remodeled the property extensively, brought in gambling, as well as big name entertainment; the club also almost immediately interested the Cleveland Syndicate. Throughout the 1930s, into the 1950s, it was a very popular nightclub; many openly talked about its mafia ties. Brink was charged numerous times but never convicted. In 1941 Brink decided to negotiate a deal with the Cleveland Syndicate, and sold Lookout House for $125,000, retaining 10 percent of the profits and remaining as the local manager.

In 1948 Brink, as manager, was again charged with permitting gambling on the Lookout House premises. Several witnesses appeared in court and testified against him. It was also during this time that investigators uncovered a connection between Brink and the Chicago-based Capone crime organization.

In 1952, Brink died in a suspicious private plane crash at an airport in Atlanta, Georgia. The Kenton County Circuit Court ruled, "There was a possibility Brink caused the crash through negligence by turning over the controls of the plane to Charles Drahmann." At the time both men had been facing prosecution on gambling charges, and there were signs that organized crime was involved in the restaurant.

An inside view of the Lookout House – "Show Place of the Nation." Courtesy: nkyviews.com

Local authorities eventually clamped down on the club, business declined, and by the early 1960s, it was closed. In 1963, the club was bought and renovated by the Schilling brothers (Dick and Bob) and brought back to prominence. The restaurant had white tablecloths, an upscale menu, and a very formal atmosphere. Sadly, Lookout House burned down on August 14, 1973.

The Shillings sold the property prior to the fire; however, they also owned the Beverly Hills Supper Club which, too, was destroyed in a fire, killing many people.

Chris Mayhew wrote the following obituary for Richard "Dick" J. Schilling Sr., which appeared in *The Cincinnati Enquirer* on May 15, 2002. Schilling Sr., retired in 1987 and moved to Florida. In-part the obituary reads:

"Richard J. Schilling Sr., former owner of the Beverly Hills Supper Club in Southgate, died Tuesday at his Florida home, weeks shy of the 25th anniversary of the devastating fire at the nightclub once billed as "The Nation's Showplace." The Fort Lauderdale resident was 79.

On May 28, 1977, fire erupted at the club, killing 165 people, many of whom had come to see singer John Davidson. Nothing has been built on the hilltop site since.

The state fire marshal's office investigation revealed that there were not enough fire exits to safely evacuate patrons when the building was at full capacity. Investigations also revealed problems with electrical wiring. Lawsuits stemming from the fire set precedents in class-action law.

One statement from then-Kentucky Governor Julian Carroll in a 1977 special task-force report called the Beverly Hills building "an electrician's nightmare." No one was ever indicted for any crimes related to the fire following a grand-jury investigation. Civil suits against the owners were settled out of court in 1980. The nightspot had originally been built in 1937 and operated as a casino until the early 1960s.

Mr. Schilling, a former resident of Villa Hills, and his three sons, Richard J. Jr., Ronald, and Raymond, owned and managed the 4-R Corporation and the club, which was deeded to the Schillings in December 1969. The Schillings upgraded and reopened the club in 1971 and attracted top-flight entertainers.

An exterior view of the Lookout House, as the fire raged in 1973. Courtesy: nkyviews.com

In a 1997 interview with *The Cincinnati Enquirer,* Mr. Schilling rejected any suggestion he shared responsibility for the tragedy. "To blame?" he said. "No sir. That was unfair. That was a low shot."

As for accusations that cost-cutting during construction and improperly installed wiring contributed to the disaster, Mr. Schilling said, "That's not so. It never was so." After the fire, Mr. Schilling maintained a low profile and participated in some of his sons' ventures, building or remodeling homes in Villa Hills and Fort Lauderdale.

"Since the Beverly Hills burned, there has never been another showplace east of the Mississippi with that kind of top-name entertainment," said Joan Vandergriff, a waitress from the club's opening until the fire in 1977."

(Notes: The Lookout House Supper Club and the Beverly Hills Supper Club are only connected by ownership, and the strange fact that they both burned down – but maybe that's not so strange. Back in those days buildings didn't have sprinkler systems, and were not built up to the fire codes that we have in today's society. The main focus of this section is Lookout House; to learn more about the Beverly Hills Supper Club fire do some research, there is plenty of information on the internet. Normally the club site is off limits, but it is open once a year for the anniversary memorial service. From I-471 South, take Exit 2 at Alexandria Pike; turn left, and Beverly Hills Drive is up a bit on the right. There is a historical marker on site.)

So, let's start with the Agreement between Lookout House and Harold Minsky. It reads:

"This Agreement made and entered into the 4th day of October, 1971 between, Business Management, Inc., d/b/a Lookout House, Covington, Kentucky per Alan Kirkpatrick, hereinafter referred to as the Operator, and Patava, Inc., a Nevada Corporation, hereinafter referred to as the Producer.

I

Operator hereby engages the Producer to secure, provide and supply a package "Musical Revue" known as "Minsky's Burlesque" in the capacity of an Independent Contractor for and to the Operator, for presentation in the Lookout House, Covington, Kentucky, for a term of:

Ten (10) out of Eleven (11) weeks commencing Monday, November 22, 1971 through and including Saturday, February 5, 1972 with the week of Monday, December 20 thru Saturday, December 25, 1971 off.

Six (6) nights weekly: Sundays off. Two (2) shows nightly: Three (3) shows each Saturday plus One (1) additional show to be determined by Operator each week; total of Fourteen (14) shows weekly.

Operator has the privilege of closing the show any time after January 8, 1972 by giving four (4) weeks advance notice of such closing in writing. If Operator gives such advance four (4) weeks' notice of closing, the Operator shall pay Three Thousand Five Hundred Dollars ($3,500.00) per week for any unplayed weeks of the original ten (10) out of eleven (11) week period.

II

Producer agrees to furnish and supply at his sole expense, a cast of fifteen (15) people.

Producer further agrees to supply all costumes, shoes, hose and accessories, scenery, backdrops, props, musical arrangements and special material, and any and all necessary things for the presentation of the show.

III

Operator hereby agrees, at his sole expense, to furnish and supply the premises above (including all necessary times for rehearsal) and a follow spotlight and operator for rehearsals and performances.

Operator shall furnish and pay for the orchestra for necessary rehearsal time and all performances for this engagement; and the orchestra shall consist of no less than six (6) musicians, instrumentation as follows: organ, drums, trumpet, trombone, saxophone, and electric bass.

IV

For and in consideration of the package "Musical Revue" as above described to be supplied and furnished by the Producer, the Operator hereby agrees to pay the Producer as follows:

Eight Thousand Five Hundred Dollars ($8,500.00) weekly for each of the ten (10) working weeks, total contract price for the entire engagement shall be Eighty-Five Thousand Dollars ($85,000.00).

<u>Payments shall be made by the OPERATOR to the PRODUCER as follows</u>: Eight Thousand Five Hundred Dollars ($8,500.00) to Associated Booking Corporation, 919 N. Michigan Avenue, Chicago, Illinois 60611, upon completion of this Agreement; said monies to be held in escrow and shall represent the final week payment for this engagement, and commencing Saturday, November 27, 1971 and each Saturday thereafter the sum of Eight Thousand Five Hundred Dollars ($8,500.00) to Patava, Inc. and presented to the Company Manager each week.

V

Producer warrants that he is providing at his expense all insurance required by law, such as Workmen's Compensation Insurance, etc., relative to his employees. Producer to provide evidence of said insurance prior to initial date of performance. Operator warrants that he will carry the necessary third party liability insurance to hold the Producer harmless from third party claims in connection with the presentation of said "Musical Revue."

VI

Producer's capacity is that of an Independent Contractor exclusively and in no manner, shape or form, shall be construed or interpreted as that of being a partnership, joint venture or otherwise.

It is further agreed that the Producer, as employer, is solely responsible for the payments of all salaries of all performers including the required withholding and unemployment taxes, also AGVA welfare payments relative to any and all employees of the Producer.

VII

Operator shall have the right of approval of all performers in the cast of the show; said approval shall not be unreasonably withheld.

It shall be the Operator's responsibility to attend, at his own expense, the casting call and auditions in Las Vegas and to audition any other performers in the show at the location where they shall be appearing prior to the casting of the show.

VIII

It is agreed and understood that the above parties to this Agreement shall comply with all union regulations of any unions or guilds that might have jurisdiction over any employees, of either party to this Agreement.

IN WITNESS WHEREOF, the parties hereto have set their hands this day and year as first written above."

The Agreement was signed by Alan Kirkpatrick, per James L. Downey, for the Lookout House; and Chuck Eddy for the Associated Booking Corporation, per Harold Minsky.

From a handwritten note in the File we discovered just some of the names penciled in for the cast, and their salaries. As one reads the articles and reviews for the shows, it's not really clear who was actually in the cast. Two of the names on the list included comic Dick Richards, $500.00, and dancer Suzanne Vegas, $250.00; however, neither appears to be in the cast for the show. Just some of the others on the list included dancers: Janet Schoolcraft, Patty Smith, Marilyn O'Brien, Patti Gregory, Barbara Sheehan, and

Janet Schoolcraft and Lorraine Lee at the 1999 BHS reunion held at the Imperial Palace in Las Vegas. Courtesy: Authors Collection

Nancy French; as well as Aldo Calderazzo, who appeared as the fighter in scenes. The dancers were paid $225 per week; Calderazzo, $200.

The first article was from *The Cincinnati Enquirer* and dated November 21, 1971. It was written by Tom McElfresh and titled "Burlesque's Back." It reads:

"Two 'remember when's' turn into 'back again' Monday night when *Minsky's Burlesque Follies* opens a six-to-ten week stand in a refurbished relic of palmier days – the red-velvet-rococo Casino Room at the Lookout House.

Production burlesque – meaning with a line of chorines, statuesque show girls, a tenor to sing the production numbers, a ballet (well, that's what they called it), and a certain air of tarnished innocence – but barely survived the war years of World War II at the Gayety. The last years it limped along, alternating solo strippers and comics of dubious ability.

Big-time production nightclub shows – meaning two or three specialty acts, with a chorus line and a headline attraction – ended abruptly with George Ratterman's election as sheriff of Campbell County.

Now – in slightly updated and mutated forms – both are returning. The "Follies" opening here is a new show, but resembles in style and content the shows Harold Minsky has produced for several years at various Las Vegas oases and at the Playboy hotels in Miami, Lake Geneva, and New York.

Looney Lewis, who is Minsky's favorite comic, will share the "Follies" spotlight with Diane Lewis, the star ecdysiast. (That's H. L. Mencken's $11 euphemism for a stripper.)

The Casino Room's mirrored walls and ceiling, the stretches of white plaster scrollwork, the flickering candles and shimmering sconces – restored just as they were in plush pre-war days – should provide just the proper ambience for these rackety resurrections."

The next article, also written by Tom McElfresh, was from November 24, 1971. It was also from *The Cincinnati Enquirer* and titled "An Enjoyable, Spicy 'Minsky's Burlesque' At Lookout House." It was a review of the show and reads:

"Need you ask? Certainly, it has all the subtlety of the Roller Derby. Certainly, it's spicy and very long on exposure. As my date for the evening – my lady wife – said, "What else but pearls would you wear with basic skin?"

Minsky's Burlesque '72 – which unveils itself (pun, weakish though it is, intended) twice nightly save Sundays on the stage, under the mirrored ceiling of the Lookout House Casino Room – offers no apologies. Nor need it do so. It is what it is.

Nor need I offer any for having enjoyed the show thoroughly. Mindless? Pointless? Sure. Save for the saving grace of laughter and a kind of innocent titillation. The things that were the stock in trade of burlesque in the classic 'What the hay?' days. And still are; and are, point enough.

Looney Lewis, in a home-grown fright wig, heads the bill as comedy star. Maybe there are some young burlesque top bananas somewhere. If there are, I never saw one. Age is just part of the polish, it seems. He romps through a boxing match with two straight men and a talking woman – a sketch that might be brand new or 200 years old. I can't vouch. I've never seen it before, but that doesn't prove anything. The bits are as timeless in effect and in appeal as the startling proportions of the four tall, mainly undraped (topless), showgirls. Walkers, they're called in the trade.

Lewis also leads the company through a reading of one of the most classic burlesque sketches, "Crazy House." It's been spiced up a bit with a kidding reference to a couple of local politicians, but the basic routine might have been played before Nero or Caligula. In Latin, of course – but the results would have been the same. Tried, true, and amusing.

Diane Lewis – who knows whether they're related? I didn't ask. I was too busy looking. Anyway, Diane Lewis does the solo strip number. Her way with a fringe defies any anatomical training I have ever had and any muscular dexterity I ever saw on *Wide World of Sports*. No, she doesn't do it like a lady – the way Gypsy Rose Lee did. But she does disrobe with a certain flirtatious and flippant air that sets her apart and above from the run-of-the-mill tassel stripper.

Eddie Cantor and Louise Hovick (aka Gypsy Rose Lee) in the 1937 20th Century-Fox film, Ali Baba Goes to Town. Courtesy: Burlesque Historical Society

There are four chorus dancers in various pink, brown, and mirrored versions of minimal attire who dance with assurance and attractive abandon.

And there's a dance team. The girl's stage name is Troika. She displays a nice blend of fire and grace. Her male partner – who is sometimes nearly as sparsely dressed as she – gives the ladies in the house an alternative view, and dances with athletic vigor.

There is one switch. If you remember the film, *The Night They Raided Minsky's*, you'll recall silver-haired Denholm Elliott intoning some inane tenor tune as he introduced the lazy lovelies "upon the illuminated runway." In the Lookout show, the production singer is a toothsome girl of handsome proportions. Name,

Carla Manning. Funny – I didn't miss either Elliott of the illuminated runway a bit. Oh yes – she sings quite nicely.

Ted Raymore is leading the six-man band which backs the show. The entire production – about seventy minutes long – depends on light, vivacity, and elaborate costumes for production glamour. No sets.

No. Definitely. Minsky is not in the art business. Was anybody in burlesque ever? But – as burlesque, it's a beaut of a show."

The final article in this folder had no date and no newspaper was listed. Titled, "And So Is The Covington-Newport Area," the article was written by John Alexander. It reads:

"Whoever it was that said burlesque was dead or that Covington and Newport would never again be open had better look again… twice.

Because the theatre of the belly laugh is alive and well, thank you, and it is thriving at the Lookout House, which is thriving along with a couple other spots in the Northern Kentucky area.

And it isn't second–rate burlesque in a second-rate spot.

It's a show specially produced by Harold Minsky, it stars one of the top burlesque comics of all-time – Looney Lewis – and features top-name stripper Diane Lewis, leading straight man Pat Burns, a second banana who was familiar to Barn Dinner Theatre audiences here by the name of Bernie Cedar, and dancers as flashy as any you'll find in Miami, Las Vegas, or New York.

And it's all in keeping with the new atmosphere prevailing in Northern Kentucky. The Lookout House, which now has all rooms open and is featuring the floor show in the old Casino Room, is as posh as it was in its brighter moments a decade ago – plush carpets, doormen, tapestry on the walls, and chandeliers.

Manager Alan Kirkpatrick (he formerly managed the Cincinnati Playboy Club) says the emphasis now is on bringing top-flight entertainment into the area, which is within a day's drive of about half the nation's population. The gamble is that there are enough people willing to pay a cover charge to justify the entertainment – and some of the names to come include: Sarah Vaughn, Frankie Laine, Rosemary Clooney, Billy Eckstein, Lou Rawls, and John Gary.

But the immediate show is Minsky's Burlesque, and while the room will be closed Christmas week, it opens again December 27, and will continue to feature the show at least through January.

No Generation Gap – Burlesque, for those who can't remember, isn't nearly what La Guardia made it out to be when he forced its closing in New York.

W.C. Fields, Red Skelton, Will Rogers, Danny Thomas, Abbott and Costello, Fanny Brice, Sophie Tucker, Rowan and Martin, Al Jolson, and Eddie Cantor are just a few of the much-honored American artists, who began in burlesque, or took the basic talent and specialized and perfected it; and were loved for it by millions.

W.C. Fields.
Courtesy: Burlesque Historical Society

1984 Press Photo of Lou Costello and Bud Abbott promoting films coming to the Seattle Center. Everyone still loves Abbott and Costello. Courtesy: Authors Collection

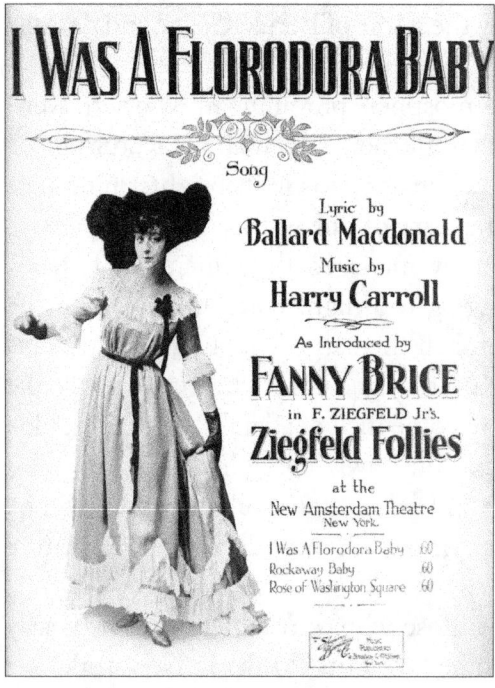

Sheet music from 1920, "I Was a Florodora Baby," sung by Fanny Brice in the Ziegfeld Follies at the New Amsterdam Theatre in New York City. Courtesy: Authors Collection

1922 "Silver Swanee" sheet music, lyrics by Eddie Cantor. Back in the day popular performers like Eddie Cantor, Al Jolson, and even Bert Williams, a Bahamian black man, performed in "black face." During the turn-of-the-century it was a fairly common form of entertainment and certainly not recognized as being unacceptable. I'm including this as a way to inform, and not meaning to offend; it's a part of history. Courtesy: Authors Collection

Minsky has kept it modern and with the times – but not too far ahead, for if it became that it would cease to be burlesque.

This particular production, the same cast and basic routine as that used to open the Playboy Plaza in Miami Beach, combines some of the best talent available with modern dance numbers.

Anybody who remembers burlesque from the days of the wheel will remember Looney Lewis. If they don't, and see his sketches as the boxing champion, and in "Crazy House," will remember once they've seen them. And they can learn what was so funny about original burlesque.

If you can laugh at yourself, you can laugh at burlesque. It deals with basic things and simple situations and by being so forthright and direct brings a belly laugh as opposed to a polite giggle.

There's no generation gap, either. The young set and their elders seem to enjoy it about equally. As Lewis says, "No matter what age, we're all human beings and we laugh and weep at about the same things."

As proof, consider his cast mate. Pat Burns, the straight man, is middle-aged. He brings as many guffaws from the young as the old. Bernie Cedar, the second banana, is in his 20s – and brings as many laughs from the over 60s as from the younger crowd.

Cedar, by the way, was featured in the Barn Dinner Theatre's *Girl In My Soup*, production a couple of summers ago. He got into the field of comedy, then into burlesque, and his sense of the ridiculous and comic as well as of timing may well give him considerable futures if he chooses to follow it.

Sophisticated – Be aware the show is sophisticated. Some of the chorus line hoofers are topless – and some are not – and the costuming is done in such good taste that it takes a while to notice that some are topless.

But assuming you appreciate sophisticated nightclub entertainment, you'll find this production as delightful as burlesque ever was, even though the thumping bass beat is now a thumping rock beat throughout every number. It is a fast moving, action packed production.

And as is true always in burlesque, it's full of surprises. Light and sound man John Adams Jr., makes his stage debut in this show, with stone-face skill in the "Crazy House" scene.

People from the audience are apt to do the same, as burlesque comics are notorious for locating prominent guests and inviting them for surprise walk-ons.

It's a welcome change from the usual formula of dance bands, singers, and whatever – a true floor show with flashy (and classy) costumes, tricky lighting, intricate dance steps and top talent."

The next folder in the "L" File was labeled "Bert Lahr." The first newspaper article was from the UPI and dated November 30, 1969. It reads:

"Bert Lahr in Hospital; New York (UPI) – Bert Lahr, whose career as a comic star spans nearly 60 years, was reportedly seriously ill at Columbia-Presbyterian Medical Center.

A spokesman for Lahr, 72, said he was "feeling a little better" but would give no further information.

It was learned that Lahr was admitted to the hospital last Wednesday for treatment of a bad cold which developed during the filming here of *The Night They Raided Minsky's*, in which he has a leading role. An informed source said the cold developed into pneumonia and Lahr's condition became complicated by a back ailment.

Lahr ran away from his home at 15 to go into vaudeville and was starring in burlesque as a comic two years later. His first Broadway hit was *Hold Everything* with Victor Moore in 1928. He became a movie immortal in 1939 with his portrayal of the cowardly lion in *The Wizard of Oz*.

1964 Press Photo of Larry Blyden and Bert Lahr performing in a skit on an unknown television show.
Courtesy: Authors Collection

Lahr's versatility was demonstrated in 1965 in Samuel Beckett's existentialist play, *Waiting for Godot*, and in the 1966 Ypsilanti, Michigan Greek Theatre production of Aristophanes' *The Birds*."

Sadly Bert Lahr never recuperated from his illness and the following article honors his memory. From December 4, 1967:

"Veteran Comic Bert Lahr Dies in Hospital at 72; New York (AP) – Bert Lahr, who charmed millions as the Cowardly Lion in *The Wizard of Oz* and in other stage and screen roles, and found new fame and fortune by eating potato chips on television, died today.

The 72-year-old Lahr was working on the movie *The Night They Raided Minsky's* when he had to be hospitalized November 21 because of a back ailment. Later he developed pneumonia, but had been reported improving.

His death at the Columbia Presbyterian Medical Center was blamed on a massive internal hemorrhage.

Although he had played every type of comedy on the stage and screen and in television, Lahr recently confided that he had never been recognized by passers-by on the street until he did a series of television commercials for a potato chip company.

He amused new millions of all ages as the old gentleman – or old lady – who couldn't "eat just one."

One of the great comic actors, Lahr's career spanned some 50 years and ranged from the classic Cowardly Lion in *The Wizard of Oz*, to Estragon in the difficult *Waiting for Godot*.

Which did he like best?

"Strangely enough," he said once, "it was *Waiting for Godot*. It was controversial. Those that hated it, spit at it. Yet it had its cult, and it created a different type of audience for me. It was like – it was like playing Carnegie Hall. It changed my whole career. Before that I was a buffoon; this gave me a chance to play Shaw and Moliere."

Sheet music from the 1939 film The Wizard of Oz.
Courtesy: Authors Collection

But it is as a clown that Lahr will be remembered by millions who saw him – and who will see him – as the Cowardly Lion.

Lahr was born in New York City on August 13, 1895, not far from the expensive Fifth Avenue apartment that came with success. As a teen-ager, he joined a children's vaudeville act called, "Nine Crazy Kids."

"It was horrible, but I got the bug, you know. Vaudeville and burlesque," Lahr said, "provided the birthplace of the true funnyman. I mean the real comics – the clowns," he said in 1953. "The real comic is one who can come out and say 'Hello' and make the audience laugh at him. Bobby Clark and Ed Wynn can do it. You can't name any more. The trouble with most present-day comedians is that they're all alike. They stand up and tell jokes. That's all they do, and they're only as funny as the jokes that are written for them."

Press Photo from 1953 of Bobby Clark and Bert Lahr for the CBS television program Omnibus. Courtesy: Authors Collection

NBC Press Department Photo of Ed Wynn. Courtesy: Authors Collection

Brooks Atkinson, former drama critic of *The New York Times*, once said of Lahr:

"Mr. Lahr is the sort of expansive clown who can fill a theatre with wonderful nonsense without crouching behind a microphone or assaulting the audience with a murderous drumfire of wisecracks. He radiates a kind of genial though lunatic good nature."

Time magazine said: "He can lose his head splendidly when all about him are stodgily keeping theirs."

Lahr made his debut on the legitimate stage in 1927 in *Harry Delmar's Revels* and went on to star in many hit musical comedies, including *Flying High* in 1930, *Du Barry Was a Lady* in 1939, and *Life Begins at 8:40* in 1934. His first movie was *Faint Heart* in 1931.

In 1963, Lahr's performance as Bottom in *A Midsummer Night's Dream* was judged the best Shakespearean performance of the year by the American Shakespeare Theatre and Academy.

The next year he was back as a romping, roaring clown in *Foxy*, a musical loosely based on Ben Johnson's Elizabethan classic *Volpone*. "Lahr," a critic wrote, "is at the peak of his career – a running, roaring fool with startled eyes and a 'Happy Hooligan' countenance."

Foxy was set in 1897 during the Klondike gold rush and the Canadian government invited the production to try out for seven weeks in the Yukon town of Dawson City during the "Gold Rush Festival" in 1962. Lahr's dislike for flying forced re-arrangement of rehearsal schedules, and a month-long trip from New York by train, steamship, and bus."

The following article, from December 5, 1967, was the last in the Bert Lahr folder and reads as follows:

"Favorite of 3 Generations, Brief Illness Ends Life of Comedian Bert Lahr; New York (UPI) – Bert Lahr, 72-year-old king of comics, died yesterday after a short illness that had interrupted filming of his 27th movie in a career that spanned nearly 60 years on stage and screen.

Death came to the actor of baleful visage at 4:30am at Columbia Presbyterian Medical Center as the result of massive intestinal hemorrhaging. He entered the hospital November 22 for treatment of a back ailment which was later complicated by pneumonia. Lahr was reported recovering last week but his condition deteriorated over the weekend.

A funeral service was scheduled for tomorrow afternoon at the Frank E. Campbell funeral chapel.

The fatal illness forced Lahr to drop out of the filming of *The Night They Raided Minsky's*, a movie about the heyday of burlesque during which Lahr rose to fame. Producer Norman Lear said Lahr's performance with Britt Ekland and Jason Robards was "too exquisite" to cut out of the unfinished film altogether.

Lahr's career had come full circle, ending on location in the old Gaiety Theatre on lower Second Avenue where he often appeared in his vaudeville and burlesque days, In addition to films, he has appeared in 17 Broadway productions and several national tours.

Lahr's most memorable performance was the role of the cowardly lion in *The Wizard of Oz*, a 1939 film hit which is a popular television rerun. Today's younger generation is more familiar with Lahr as the compulsive gourmand in a current television commercial for potato chips.

Bert Lahr taking a break from filming The Night They Raided Minsky's. *The 1968 film was released after Lahr's death in December 1967. Courtesy: New York Daily News Archives*

Autographed photo of Ray Bolger in a scene from the 1939 film The Wizard of Oz. *I wonder why Bolger didn't use a photo that included Bert Lahr? Courtesy: Authors Collection*

Born Irving Lahrheim to an immigrant German family in New York's Yorkville section, Lahr dropped out of school at 15 and joined a child vaudeville troupe. He toured the nation, learning the techniques of older comedians so well that he was hired by the Columbia Burlesque Circuit at age 18 for $35 a week.

Lahr boosted his earnings to $165 a week in seven years by perfecting a "Dutch" dumb cop character with a hilarious German accent. The comic's bulbous nose, Basset Hound eyes, and a voice that could wheeze, howl, bray, or bleat typed him as an unforgettable stage personality.

His first Broadway appearance was in the 1927 musical revue, *Delmar's Revels*, a near-flop which escalated Lahr to fame in the role of prize fighter Gink Schiner in *Hold Everything*, with Victor Moore the next season. A star was born and Lahr was able to command $4,500 a week when he repeated his Dutch cop act at the Palace Theatre.

Lahr's dignified lunacy and clean humor – in the great tradition of burlesque – brought comic brilliance to a series of shows including: *Hot-Cha, Flying High, Life Begins at 40, George White's Scandals, The Show is On*, with Bea Lillie, *Du Barry Was a Lady*, with Ethel Merman, as well as *The Seven Lively Arts, Two on the Aisle*, and *Hotel Paradise. Foxy*, a 1964 production, was his last stage show."

Sheet music from The Show Is On, *1936. Courtesy: Authors Collection*

Sheet music from Du Barry Was a Lady, *1939. Courtesy: Authors Collection*

The final folder in the "L" File was simply titled "Letters." Now we all know Harold Minsky probably received thousands of letters over the course of his years in burlesque. I can only assume these were special.

The first letter was addressed to: Mr. and Mrs. Harold Minsky – (Harold was married to Dardy Orlando, Lili St. Cyr's sister, at that time) – Dunes Hotel, Las Vegas, Nevada. It was written on "Person to Person" stationery, which included the names Edward R. Murrow, John A. Aaron, and Jesse Zousmer. It reads:

Person to Person – CBS
501 Madison Avenue
New York
June 25, 1959
Dear Mr. and Mrs. Minsky:

This week, Jesse Zousmer and I will be ending our six-year association with PERSON TO PERSON to try our hand at some new program ideas for television.

As you can see from the enclosed, we have attempted – perhaps inadequately – to express publicly our thanks to you and the other guests who "helped make this program possible."

But we do want you to know that without your patience, kindness and wonderful cooperation, we could not have carried through all these years.

We are grateful.
All good wishes,
John A. Aaron

(Notes: As the 1950s began, Edward R. Murrow was just beginning his television career by appearing in editorial "tailpieces" on the *CBS Evening News* and in the coverage of special events. This came despite Murrow's own misgivings about the new medium and its emphasis on pictures rather than ideas. Jesse Zousmer and John Aaron proposed, researched, and wrote the news portion as well as Murrow's word-for-the-day; Murrow wrote the "tailpiece" analysis for each broadcast. The three men also worked together on *Person to Person*.

Person to Person was a popular television program in the United States that originally ran from 1953 to 1961. Edward R. Murrow hosted the original series from its inception in 1953 until 1959, interviewing celebrities in their homes from a comfortable chair in his New York studio. His opening was always: "Good evening, I'm Ed Murrow,

Edward R. Murrow. Courtesy: Austin Film Society

and the name of the program is *Person to Person*. It's all live – there's no film." Although Murrow is best remembered as a reporter, he was a pioneer of the celebrity interview.

The program was well planned but not strictly scripted. As many as six cameras and all lighting necessary were installed to cover the guest's moves throughout their home, as well as a microwave link to transmit the signals back to the network. The guests wore wireless microphones so they could move around the home or its grounds. The interviews were done live. The two 15-minute interviews in each program were typically with very different types of people, such as a movie star and a scientist. Guests often used their appearance to promote their latest project or book.)

The next letter in the folder was from Patrick J. O'Conner and dated November 8, 1960. It was on Mr. O'Connor's own letterhead with an address of 845 Northwestern Bank Building, Minneapolis 2, Minnesota. I admit I don't understand the "2" between Minneapolis and Minnesota.

Mr. Harold Minsky
5712 Kelly Lane
Las Vegas, Nevada
Dear Harold:
I am finally getting around to thanking you for undertaking the responsibility for producing the show at the Johnson Rally. Despite all the complications it went off very well and Senator Johnson was very impressed.

I certainly enjoyed the time I spent with you and Major and am looking forward to seeing both of you when I return to Las Vegas. I am going to try to get out there for a few days prior to the first of the year.
Yours very truly,
Patrick J. O'Connor

The following letter was written on the letterhead of Lyndon B. Johnson, United States Senate, Office of the Democratic Leader, Washington D.C., and dated November 19, 1960. It reads:

Dear Harold:
Pat O'Connor wrote you the other day in my behalf and I was delighted. While I know, with you, I don't need to say it, I want to say it anyway ---- so, thank you again, my friend, for many things, not the least being all you did to make that Las Vegas rally an outstanding one.

Lady Bird and I leave this evening for the NATO Conference. She joins in sending you warmest regards and best wishes.
Sincerely,
Lyndon B. Johnson

(Notes: Do I need to explain who Lyndon B. Johnson was?

Patrick J. O'Connor Sr., 85, a Washington lawyer and lobbyist who became a formidable fundraiser and power broker within the Democratic Party, died on May 9, 2005 at his home in Minneapolis. He was born in Eden Valley, Minnesota, and was treasurer of the Democratic National Committee in the late 1960s and early 1970s, and raised hundreds of thousands of dollars for the party. He cultivated key friendships, including fellow Minnesotan Hubert H. Humphrey. Their relationship dated to the mid-1940s, when O'Connor campaigned for Humphrey during a Minneapolis mayoral race.

O'Connor was heavily involved in the campaigns of nearly every Democratic presidential candidate since Adlai E. Stevenson, including the bids of John F. Kennedy, Lyndon B. Johnson, Jimmy Carter, Walter F. Mondale, Michael S. Dukakis, Bill Clinton, and Al Gore. Patrick O'Connor Sr. was also a former director of the John F. Kennedy Center for the Performing Arts and the Washington Symphony Orchestra.)

The next letter, which had two addresses at the top of the document, was dated August 28, 1964. Handwritten in ink, at the top of the page was "Sept 14."
Danava, Inc.
c/o General Artists Corporation
640 Fifth Avenue
New York, New York

General Artists Corporation
640 Fifth Avenue
New York, New York
Gentlemen:
It is hereby agreed that the agreement of January 17, 1964, duly executed by and between us, in connection with the production of a motion picture based on Minsky shows, is hereby cancelled and revoked in all respects.

In consideration for said cancellation, we agree to pay you the sum of $1,500.00 payable as follows:

$500.00 with-in forty-eight (48) hours after the delivery of a copy of this agreement duly signed by each of you;

$500.00 ninety (90) days after date of delivery of the copy of the agreement as aforesaid;

$500.00 one hundred and eighty (180) days after date of the delivery of a copy of the agreement as aforesaid;

You will please indicate your agreement to the above by signing two copies of this agreement and returning same to this office.
Yours very truly,
Sandy Howard
Arthur Steloff

Read and Agreed
Danava Inc.
Harold Minsky
General Artists Corporation
B. Howe

The next letter in the folder was dated April 21, 1967.
Mr. Eddie Jaffe
156 West 48th Street
New York, New York
Dear Eddie:
Following are a list of dates booked on the Minsky Show. All of these places must be serviced with advertising and publicity. This should be done starting now. I would greatly appreciate your getting this material out to them immediately.

June 12-25; The Latin Casino, Cherry Hill, New Jersey, Attn: Mr. Jerry Katz.

August 22-27; Colonie Summer Theatre, Latham, New York, Attn: Mr. Eddie Rich, 133 E. 34th Street, New York City.

August 28 – September 3; Cape Cod Melody Tent, Hyannis, Massachusetts, Attn: Mr. Ed Holtzman, 251 Central Park West, New York City.

September 8-17; Mardi Gras Club, Baltimore, Maryland, Attn: Mr. Vince Bonolis, 68-10 Harford Road, Baltimore, Maryland.

August 15-20: The Music Circus, Lambertville, New Jersey, Attn: Mr. Jerry Krone, 1545 Broadway, New York City.

Best Regards.
Sincerely,
Norman Weiss
Cc: Mr. Harold Minsky, L.V.

(Notes: Eddie Jaffe was known as "The Press Agent of Broadway," and died in the Bronx on Tuesday, March 25, 2003 – he was 89 years old.

Robert Sylvester, a longtime entertainment columnist for the *New York Daily News*, devoted a chapter to Ed Jaffe in his 1970 book titled *Notes of a Guilty Bystander*. Describing him as "A small wiry man with a shock of wiry hair," Sylvester wrote, "underneath the hair is an imagination that knows no bounds, great energy,

Ed Jaffe. Courtesy: Dusty Sage

and a basic nature so kindly that, thinking over everybody who is left from this act, I cannot name a single person who puts the knock on him."

Edward Jaffe was born in Duluth, Minnesota, on October 22, 1913, the son of Isadore and Ann Jaffe. His father was a tailor from Lithuania who borrowed the money for a passage to America from a woman acquaintance who assumed he would then send for her and marry her. When he did not, she came over herself, tracked him down and got a rabbi to perform the ceremony.

At age 16, Eddie left for New York and got a job in the advertising department of the *New York Telegram*, working afternoons and evenings, and going to high school in the mornings. He also covered the area school sports teams.

He soon drifted into publicity work, starting with vaudeville and burlesque acts that, he figured, had little to lose in hiring him. When Walter Winchell published Eddie's column item calling stripper Margie Hart, "The poor man's Garbo," her pay skyrocketed from $250 to $2,500 a week. Jaffe's career took off as well.

Margie Hart. Courtesy: Janelle Smith Collection

Jaffe also did publicity for scores of films, mostly clunkers, but some good ones, too, like *King Kong*, *Sunset Boulevard*, and *The Red Shoes*. As a stunt, he once bought an electric chair to promote a 1959 Mickey Rooney prison movie, *The Last Mile*, but it was never delivered. No one would help him track it down, either. His advice to posterity, "Don't pay for an electric chair until it arrives."

After a stint in Hollywood promoting films, he returned to

New York and moved into a three-room walk-up apartment on the top floor of 156 West 48th Street. It became a perpetual party zone and refuge for aspiring starlets and actors, including Marlon Brando, who was just attaining stardom in *A Streetcar Named Desire*.

Throughout the years he continued to promote television, movies, shows, and revues, all with mixed results. Eddie Jaffe also promoted boxing and helped set up some of the earliest pay-per-view closed circuit television fights.)

One of my favorite letters was from Norman Lear, of 6725 Sunset Boulevard, Suite 307, Hollywood, California – Telephone 462-6686. It was dated May 25, 1967 and reads:

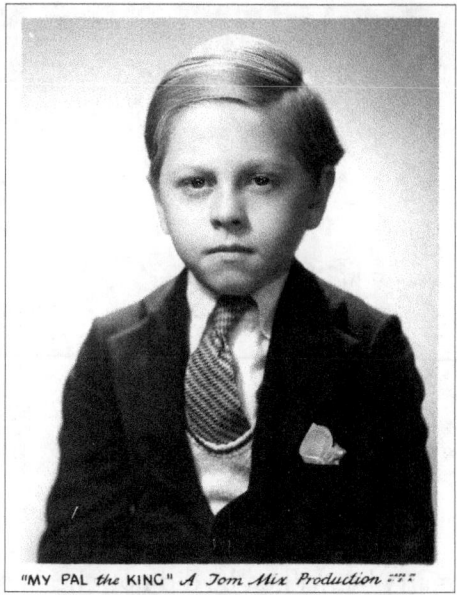

Lobby Card from the 1932 film My Pal the King, *starring a young Mickey Rooney. Courtesy: Authors Collection*

Mr. Harold Minsky
THE SILVER SLIPPER
Las Vegas, Nevada

Dear Harold,
Just a quick note to thank you for being such a charming, generous host and for providing such a wonderful evening. Besides thanking the host part of you, I'd like to express particular appreciation for you as a producer. That's a hell of a show you deliver.
Hope to see you again soon.
Best regards,
Norman Lear

(Notes: You really should know who Norman Lear is!)

The next letter was on Harold Minsky stationery, which included his home address of 5712 Kelly Lane, Las Vegas, Nevada 89109. It also included Patava, Inc. – the name of the Minsky Corporation - and his home phone number of: (702) 736-3013. It was a very simple letter.
October 2, 1969
Mr. Sid Fields,

Please accept this as your two weeks' notice to close after the last show on October 16, 1969.
Harold Minsky
Accepted: Sid Fields

(Notes: Sid Fields, was born Sidney H. Feldman on February 5, 1898 in Milwaukee, Wisconsin. He started performing in local theatres as a boy; by his teens, he was working carnivals and tent shows in the Midwest, and later he partnered with Jack Greenman to become part of a comedy team. The burlesque and vaudeville duo eventually made it to New York City and was cast by Harold Minsky in his Follies, but the team split up when Fields went to Hollywood to work on a feature film.

Fields kept busy working in radio, television, and occasionally in movies with Eddie Cantor, Ben Blue, Rudy Vallee, Fred Allen, Milton Berle, and so many others. During the 1930s, Fields appeared in some small comedic film roles, and served as the assistant director on one of Cantor's funniest films, *Ali Baba Goes to Town*. He also began an eight year association with Abbott and Costello, not only working on their radio shows, but also appearing in several of their films - the first being a small role in the film *The Naughty Nineties*. Though Fields had roles in several of their films, it was in *Mexican Hayride* where his scene as an overly talkative reporter interviewing the hapless Costello that was considered by many to be a highlight of the movie. From 1951, he supported Abbott and Costello in NBC-TV's *The Colgate Comedy Hour*, and in 1952, he was cast in the television series *The Abbott and Costello Show*. The show ran for two seasons and played in syndication for decades.

It was his two seasons on *The Abbott and Costello Show*, playing the duo's hot-tempered, greedy landlord, that he achieved immortality. With his bald-head and beady eyes, coupled with his expressive voice, Fields was the perfect nemesis for the baby-faced Lou Costello. Even though he was the perpetrator, Fields was also just as likely to get a pie in the face. Whether he was doing a slow burn, or seething in anger over some mishap caused by Costello, Fields was often

Sheet music from the 1937 film Ali Baba Goes to Town, *starring Eddie Cantor. Notice who else is in the cast – Louise Hovick – better known as Gypsy Rose Lee. Courtesy: Authors Collection*

1949 Press Photo of Danny Kaye and Sid Fields during a round of golf in Surrey, England. Courtesy: Authors Collection

one of the funniest characters on the show.

Those filmed shows became his legacy; even though Fields continued to work on network television for another dozen years, including regular appearances on top-rated programs like *The Jackie Gleason Show*, where he often did sketches with Gleason, also a veteran of burlesque. He also worked with Red Buttons, and appeared on *The Ed Sullivan Show*. Fields came to Las Vegas in the 1960s, initially to work as part of Pat Moreno's *Artists and Models Revue*, but he decided to make a permanent move, and stay in Vegas. After his move Fields continued to play small roles in television shows; he found short-term work in a Minsky Revue, and he also worked as a writer for Jackie Gleason.

Sid Fields officially retired in 1975, after spending 64 years in the entertainment field. He died of lung cancer on September 28, 1975 at the age of 77, but his work lived on after him in the hearts and minds of fans everywhere. His wife Marie, who was seriously ill in the hospital at the same time as Sid, passed away shortly thereafter. Sid Fields is buried at Woodlawn Cemetery in Las Vegas, Nevada.)

The next letter was written by Harold Minsky, accepted by Art Engler of the Associated Booking Corporation, and dated October 25, 1968. It was sent from Las Vegas, Nevada and reads:

Associated Booking Corporation
9477 Brighton Way
Beverly Hills, California
Gentlemen:

Upon entering into an Agreement in writing with the Aladdin Hotel, Inc., for the production and presentation of a show at the Aladdin Hotel in Las Vegas, Nevada, by Patava, Inc., Patava, Inc. agrees that ten percent (10%) of the gross sums received for the production and presentation of said show by Patava, Inc. at the Aladdin Hotel, shall be paid each week to Associated Booking Corporation, on the condition that two and one-half percent (2½%) of the ten percent (10%) to be paid by Associated Booking Corporation, to Charles E. Hogan, 203 N. Wabash Avenue, Chicago, Illinois.

The sum of ten percent (10%) agreed to be paid herein shall be paid directly by Patava, Inc., to Associated Booking Corporation, as the sums required to be paid to Patava, Inc., by the Aladdin Hotel are paid to Patava, Inc., and shall not be deducted from any agreement between Patava, Inc., and Aladdin Hotel, Inc.

Patava, Inc., further agrees that if it enters into an Agreement for the production and presentation of any shows in which Edward Torres is associated or is general manager, the agreements set forth herein for the payment to Associated Booking Corporation, shall remain in full force and effect.

It was signed by both Harold Minsky and Art Engler.

The following letter, dated August 13, 1969, came from *The Dramatic Publishing Company*. The letterhead states it was incorporated in 1887, and that Charles H. Sergel was the Founder. At that time it was located at 86 East Randolph Street, in Chicago, Illinois; the company still exists but has moved to 311 Washington Street in Woodstock, Illinois. The letter was addressed to Mr. Harold Minsky, Kelly Lane, Las Vegas, Nevada.

Dear Mr. Minsky,

What we're planning is a dictionary of the language of show business.

We specifically do not want definitions on hardware, things like cleats, lash lines, teaser, tormentors, etc. This sort of thing is easy, obvious, has been done a thousand times, and it's dull.

What we're after are definitions of words and phrases like:
Bench act
Chautauqua
Rag show
Tag show
Tab show
Hokum
Next week East Lynn
Corn
Give 'em the skull (?), etc. etc.

We want anything that you can think of or remember, and don't worry about duplications, that's our problem.

The attitude to take on these is to explain them in the terms you would use if a niece of yours came into town from Ohio and, let's assume, she's married to a nice engineer. Then, suppose you are all sitting over cocktails discussing show business. Then this young lady asks you what this or that phrase means. Define the term the way you would to her. Make it a story, give an example, and if you have an anecdote, better yet. We want the dictionary to be readable, useful, and fun.

It's perfectly alright to send the material on at your convenience. Send it along in dribs and drabs if you want to. If you remember a few words or phrases a few weeks after the first shipment has gone off to us, fine. Send 'em. We would also like to have a picture and biographical data for your listing as one of the contributing editors.

The deal is that 10% on the book will be split up in equal shares among all contributing editors on the first 2,500 copies. On the next 2,500 copies 12½% will be shared equally, and after we have sold 5,000 copies 15% will be divided equally.

I don't think it is a big deal but it should be a fun thing to do, and useful, and I am delighted that you seem to be inclined to help. For you have a knowledge and a fund of experience that no one else on earth has and it should be gotten down.

Sincerely yours,
The Dramatic Publishing Company
Sherman L. Sergel

The next letter came from Liliane Pavard, an agent in Paris, France; it was dated March 17, 1970, and addressed and written to Harold Minsky on Pavard's personalized stationery.

Mr. Harold Minsky
5712 Kelly Lane
Las Vegas, Nev. 89109
U.S.A.

Dear Sir,

I take the liberty to inform you that I am handling Miss Christiane Couty's contracts, (LULU LAMOUR) her artist's name. She says that she wrote you and sent me your reply dated February 25, 1969, in which you are asking for some details about her performance.

LULU has appeared for three years at the "Crazy Horse Saloon" in Paris, and after in the best Cabarets and Casinos of Europe. She is presently in a show at Freeport, Bahamas; the lounge of the Lucayan Hotel, where you may see her if you wish, until April 20th, her closing date. She would be extremely happy to follow up to the United States and particularly in Las Vegas.

Her present act is very sexy and danced and I believe that it can be presented in all establishments.

I should be very happy to hear from you. Hoping to receive a positive reply, I remain...

Yours sincerely,
Liliane Pavard

The next is a two-part letter; an original, and a copy, which was sent on to a group of other gentlemen. The original was on Associated Booking Corporation stationery, and dated April 7, 1971 – as was the copy. The original reads:

Mr. Harold Minsky
5712 Kelly Lane
Las Vegas, Nevada 89109
Dear Harold,

Thought you might be interested in this interoffice note I sent to the fellows who I hope will be of some help to us.

Kindest regards,
Sincerely,
Chuck Eddy
Vice President
Associated Booking Corporation

The copy reads:
From: Chuck Eddy
To: Oscar Cohen, Joe Sully, Frank Musiello, Fred Williamson, Dave Bendett, Art Engler, Tony Papa, John Hitt, Bob Phillips, Frank Rio, + Billy McDonald
Dear Fellows:

I am enclosing pictures of the MINSKY SHOW. Would like to emphasize that MINSKY is wide open and does not have a show playing at this time. It is imperative that we come up with something for MINSKY.

I have a deal starting in September for eight weeks in Detroit but we need something as soon as possible. We can probably deliver 13 to 15 people for around $7500 a week for from 4 to 8 weeks depending on the transportation costs involved, as the show would originate from Las Vegas.

I also want to emphasize again that every place that we have booked MINSKY he has done business and as a matter of fact has done better than 95% of the name people in show business because MINSKY is a name.

We owe it to this man to do everything we can to get him booked as he has paid us tens of thousands of dollars of commissions in the past 3 years and there is no reason why we can't make a lot of money with MINSKY in the future.

If any of you get any kind of nibbles, please let me hear from you.

Sincerely,
Chuck Eddy

The following was a draft of a letter written by Harold Minsky to "Dick," who may have had connections to the Union Plaza Hotel in Las Vegas. It reads:

Dear Dick,

Photo of the Pioneer Club with the Union Plaza Hotel and Casino in the background; late 1960s or early 1970s. Courtesy: Authors Collection

Pursuant to our last meeting when we discussed the possibility of a MINSKY SHOW for the opening of the Union Plaza Hotel on or about July 2, 1971, I would like to fill you in briefly on the past history of THE MINSKY SHOW that goes back sixty years playing every major city all over the United States and foreign countries. After all these years, a motion picture, *The Night They Raided Minsky's* was produced by United Artists and is currently showing all over the world. Up to the present time, the picture has grossed in excess of $3,000,000, and is still being exhibited.

Dick, I don't know if you are aware, but for the past twenty years THE MINSKY SHOW successfully played most of the major showrooms in the various hotels on the Strip. One of the most spectacular and successful engagements was for a period of over five consecutive years at the Dunes Hotel. It was during the run at the Dunes Hotel where a policy was initiated during certain times of the year that name stars such as Frankie Laine, Jayne Mansfield, Tony Bennett, Johnnie Ray, etc., were added to the show. Obviously, this was a double marquee value. For the most part, THE MINSKY SHOW played very successfully without benefit of the above names. It is my sincere opinion that for the Union Plaza Hotel the same basic format could be followed with names

1957 photo of Tony Bennett from the sheet music "In the Middle of an Island." Courtesy: Authors Collection

added at various times during the year such as Phil Silvers, Mickey Rooney, Dan Dailey, Red Buttons, etc.

I am sure you are aware that one of the main reasons that THE MINSKY SHOW has sustained all these years in the State of Nevada is due primarily to the great asset the show has been for casino operations.

After careful study, I feel that the type of show best suited for your operation would be a show consisting of a total of 25 people, MOSTLY GIRLS, plus one wardrobe woman, new costumes, scenery, music, sets, etc.; in other words, a complete package. Please understand that this show would be specifically tailored for your operation at the Union Plaza. On a basis of a 16 week guaranteed period, the show could be delivered for the price of $15,000 per week. This price does not include the addition of any name stars you may wish to add from time to time.

Sincerely,
H.M.
P.S. Dick, THE MINSKY SHOW played every place in the country except downtown Las Vegas. This would definitely be a first!!

The next letter was from the Associated Booking Corporation, and dated October 18, 1971. It was sent to Harold at his home on Kelly Lane.

Dear Harold,
I am enclosing date RIDERS covering the engagement arranged and secured by this office for the Minsky Show at the Aladdin Hotel commencing December 24, 1971 for a period of fifty-one (51) consecutive weeks.

Please sign all copies of the RIDER, retain one copy for your files, and return the four remaining copies to me for distribution.

Kindest regards,
Art Engler
Vice President
Associated Booking Corporation

The next letter came from Kavanagh Entertainments Limited, 170 Piccadilly, London. It was written by Peter Prichard and addressed to Harold in Las Vegas; it was dated March 27, 1972.

Dear Harold,
Further to our recent conversations, this is to confirm that I have a good chance of lining up your Revue for a tour in Europe. However, it is imperative for you to fly over to London as soon as possible to meet with the various Managements.

At the same time I think we should make a trip to Scandinavia as well as France and Germany. After which, if you have time, we should cover some of the Managements on the Mediterranean Resorts.

Please let me know when you will be arriving.

Kindest personal regards.

Yours sincerely,

Peter Prichard

Photo of Peter Prichard from 1964; it was used in his obituary which ran in The Telegraph. *Courtesy: Rex Features*

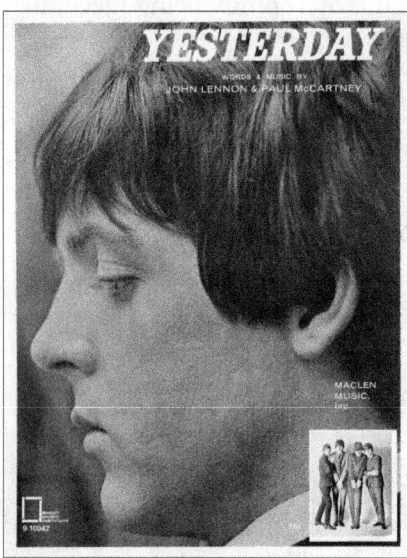

Sheet music from the 1965 song "Yesterday." Words and music by John Lennon and Paul McCartney of The Beatles. Courtesy: Authors Collection

(Notes: Peter Prichard, born in West London on November 30, 1932, and died on August 30, 2014, was thought to be the longest-serving show business agent in Great Britain. He was known as "the last of the old-time agents." In a career spanning more than sixty years, Prichard represented dozens of variety entertainers and comedy actors.

In February 1964, Peter Prichard was responsible for securing the Beatles live American television debut on *The Ed Sullivan Show*, where they were seen by an estimated 73 million viewers. As well as the Beatles, he introduced American audiences to the Rolling Stones, The Singing Nun, and a hugely popular Italian puppet mouse called Topo Gigio. Prichard also helped promote British concert appearances by: Frank Sinatra, Danny Kaye, Bob Hope, the Beatles, and Bill Haley and the Comets. He was also on hand whenever stars such as John Wayne, Gene Barry, Bing Crosby, and Ginger Rogers visited London.

Prichard earned a reputation as being tough, hard-working, fair, and scrupulously honest. A stickler for procedure, he never required his artists to sign a contract, always preferring a simple handshake. "That way, if they're not happy with what I'm doing for them, they can leave whenever they want," he once explained.

Away from show business, he served as a special constable with the Metropolitan

Police in London for many years, earning three commendations for courage and devotion to duty. Peter Prichard also worked in Fort Myers, Florida, as a patrolling volunteer deputy in the Lee County Sheriff's Department, a position which earned him a letter of thanks from President Obama. He was appointed Officer of the Most Excellent Order of the British Empire (OBE) in 1992.)

On March 28, 1972, Chuck Eddy wrote the following letter to Paul Raymond, at the Whitehall Theatre in Whitehall, London, England.

Dear Mr. Raymond,

In my conversation with your secretary today, I was extremely disappointed over the fact that Mrs. Raymond caught the Minsky show in the Playmate Lounge of the Playboy Plaza Hotel, Miami. This is not at all what we had in mind for a showing in England. I would like to emphasize that had I known Mrs. Raymond was going to be in the United States, I definitely would have had her go into Las Vegas to see the Minsky show that is currently on a one year contract at the Aladdin Hotel and, negotiations are now underway to extend the engagement for a total of two years.

I must strongly point out that the show in Miami is a very small, low-budget show playing in a lounge and in no way represents the lavish productions that Mr. Minsky presents in theatres and in Las Vegas. As a matter of fact, in order to straighten out this misconception, I would like to invite you personally, at our own expense, to come to Las Vegas at your earliest convenience to see the show there.

I am sure you are familiar with Lee Guber who operates the Music Fair Theatres in the East. As you know, Mr. Guber presents the very finest in entertainment, name stars, book shows, etc. Mr. Guber has committed himself to presenting the Minsky show in four of his theatres this late or early fall. This is certainly indicative of the faith that one of the best producers and talent buyers in America has in the production values of the Minsky show.

We strongly feel that the Minsky name has tremendous box office value in England, particularly in view of the fact that the motion picture, *The Night They Raided Minsky's* enjoyed considerable success in England and starred one of your famous British actors, Norman Wisdom. Again, I urge you not to close your mind to presenting the Minsky show based on a report of the show in Miami as this show is in no way indicative of the Minsky productions. However, in spite of the small cast and limited facilities, the show has completed a one year engagement and I am happy to say that I have just completed a contract to extend the show for an additional six months at the Playboy Plaza. This certainly indicates they are doing a great job.

May I please hear from you on the above at your earliest convenience?

Kindest regards.

Sincerely yours,
Chuck Eddy
Vice President
Associated Booking Corporation

P.S. Harold Minsky and I will be in London for one week commencing Sunday, April 16, 1972. I will call you on Monday, April 17, and per chance, we can get together to discuss further possibilities. C.E.

The next three letters and documents revolve around the Fremont Hotel; all were on hotel stationery. They read:

March 8, 1973
Mr. Oscar Cohen
Associated Booking Corporation
445 Park Avenue
New York, New York 10022

Dear Oscar,

This letter will serve as notice that the Fremont Hotel has exercised its option to extend the Minsky Show for a period of thirty-two (32) consecutive weeks, commencing June 27, 1973, through February 4, 1974.

Sincerely,
James J. Hill
President and General Manager
Moe Lewis
Director of Entertainment
Cc: Art Engler
Associated Booking Corporation

The next document was dated September 19, 1972; and there was an identical letter in the folder except it was dated October 10, 1973:

Associated Booking Corporation
4055 South Spencer
Las Vegas, Nevada

Gentlemen:

Upon entering into an Agreement in writing with Recrion Corporation, Las Vegas, Nevada for the production and presentation of a show at the Fremont Hotel, Las Vegas, Nevada by Patava, Inc., Patava, Inc. agrees that ten percent (10%) of the gross sums received for the production and presentation of said show by Patava, Inc. at the Fremont Hotel shall be paid each week to Associated Booking Corporation.

Patava, Inc., agrees that if it enters into any extensions of future agreements for the production and presentation of any shows at the Fremont Hotel, Las Vegas, Nevada, the agreements set forth herein for the payment to Associated Booking Corporation shall remain in full force and effect.

Patava, Inc.
Harold Minsky

The final letter was dated October 31, 1973, and reads:
Mr. Harold Minsky
President
Patava, Inc.
1001 Russell Road
Las Vegas, Nevada

Dear Harold,
This will confirm our agreement wherein the Fremont Hotel will extend the Minsky Show for a period of fifty-two (52) consecutive weeks beginning February 6, 1974, through and including February 4, 1975, under the same terms and conditions and for the same consideration as referred to in my letter of March 8, 1973.

This letter is subject to any necessary changes in the show, such changes, if made, to be mutually agreed upon by both parties.

Sincerely,
Moe Lewis
Director of Entertainment
ACCEPTED AND AGREED:
Patava, Inc.
Harold Minsky

One final letter from the Fremont Hotel came from James J. Hill, the President and General Manager. It was on the executive office stationery and dated December 11, 1974.

Mr. Harold Minsky
President
Patava, Inc.
1001 Russell Road
Las Vegas, Nevada

Dear Mr. Minsky,

This letter will serve as four weeks' notice to you that the Fremont Hotel is closing its showroom effective Thursday, January 9, 1975. Your contract will be terminated as of the last performance the evening of Wednesday, January 8, 1975. This closure is due to remodeling which has commenced.

At the receipt of this notice, we request that you immediately advise all persons in your employment connected with the Fremont Minsky show with respect to the closure so as to avoid any obligations which you may incur as a result of failure to notify.

Very truly yours,
Fremont Hotel, Inc.
James J. Hill
President and General Manager
Additional Copy to:
Harold Minsky
5712 Kelly Lane
Las Vegas, Nevada
Hand Delivered

(Notes: Why these letters were in this folder and not in the Fremont File is anyone's guess. For more Fremont information see the "F" section.)

The following four letters all dealt with donations of costumes to King City Joint Union High School in California.

February 4, 1974
Mr. Harold Minsky
Hotel Fremont
Las Vegas, Nevada
Dear Mr. Minsky,

So many fine things have been said about you, and deservedly. You have contributed so much to making people happy as well as your personal involvement in eradicating social injustices which have plagued mankind throughout his history.

Mr. Minsky, each year I do a "mini" musical revue for the less fortunate students of our high school. I do this on my own time and no budget to work with. We are a small high school in a valley primarily agricultural. Many migrants come in to pick vegetables and work the fields with their children. I try to bring a bit of enjoyment and beauty to their lives in presenting them in a little musical production. These are the good, hard working children one rarely hears of.

I pray that God bless you and when you clean out your storage rooms and you have any old remnants, flowers, faded jewelry, shoes, feathers, or garments which have outlived their usefulness, I could use just anything you might throw away. I would also be happy to defray any expense even if it means driving to Las Vegas. I did the same thing in Appalachia in West Virginia for the children of the miners there. Mr. Walters who was with the Latin Quarter sent me a number of items and I did a program that those wonderful youngsters are still talking about. They so look forward to it. They are not the "elite" or the intelligentsia of the school, and in some cases they are sometimes forgotten. Migrant children by the 1000s live in poverty, go hungry, suffer from malnutrition, but in addition live an incredibly uprooted life; such as few other American children live, and few children in other countries ever experience. The beautiful part is that they are humble, possess a basic sense of values, and strive to be successful the best they know how. We eat what they harvest, and it's such a harvest of shame for many.

Thank you, Mr. Minsky, and I wish you good health and happiness in your continued success.

Front cover from a 1949 Latin Quarter program. Courtesy: C.F. Miller

Most respectfully,
Frederick Santon
Chairman, English and Drama
P.S. Certainly whatever you might send would be tax deductible.

(Notes: There was a handwritten comment on the letter that simply states: "Answered February 15.")

The second letter from Frederick Stanton reads:
February 20, 1974
Dear Patricia Minsky,
We can never begin to thank you for the warm and generous letter expressing a desire to help our youngsters put on a show to bring some color and meaning to their otherwise colorless and meaningless existence. As I have said, they are truly nice boys and girls and they strive very hard to succeed in school, but so many

of their lives are so disrupted by planting and harvesting whenever it is done. In the Follies they have that "one" opportunity to be noticed and even applauded for their inherent talents. In the land of harvest a plenty, is also the harvest of shame.

Mrs. Minsky, just anything you may have I could use. As I said, I do this on my own time and no budget from the school. The Salvation Army, Goodwill, and St. Vincent de Paul are my haunts when I'm not teaching. I can get basic items here for little or nothing, but they are devoid of anything "stagey" – old feathers, jewelry, remnants, laces, hats, etc., costumes – but I don't ask for those. We can always add to, take away from, and piece together things of this nature to create a set of costumes. It's hard, and they don't always come out looking like "costumes," but they are interesting and we do it all ourselves. Old fur pieces, sequins, and things of this nature help a great deal. I could use just anything that has outlived its usefulness. Please, too, Mrs. Minsky, I would gladly pay the handling and the shipping charges.

Like you say, Mrs. Minsky, it is nice to know about people who care. I would like to believe that there are many who do, but somehow fail to get around to doing it. It does take time and money. It's so little to give and the inner reward is so profound and great when you look into the faces of happy and grateful students. It's an experience they never forget. It's nice to be a part of that experience. It's humane to share.

Mrs. Minsky, let me wish you and Mr. Minsky good health and happiness in your continued success. It's such a famous name. So you can see how grateful I am.

Sincerely,
Frederick Santon
English Department

The next letter reads:
King City High School
King City, California 93930
March 4, 1974
Dear Mrs. Minsky,
Words fail to express the happiness and gratitude on the part of all of us upon receiving your more than thoughtful packages to help us present a musical program that is worthy of the fine young students who have been working so very hard to put together things that would add color to their program. One of my girls, and a very sweet girl she is, said upon looking at the beautiful headpiece, "She must be a very wonderful person indeed wanting to help us. We must do something very nice for her, Mr. Santon." When we were sorting the items and

deciding how to use them one or two of the girls had tears in their eyes they were so happy.

Yes, whatever you send us is tax deductible. We are an educational-nonprofitable institution. I would be more than happy to sign the form you send. You should enjoy some tax relief because everyone knows the cost of costuming and the labor that goes into it. How wonderful you are they all said.

We will have pictures made of our program and I will send you a set hoping that you can recognize the items in them. Altogether I have 25 students in the show and it warms my heart to know that they are experiencing the most memorable moments of their young lives that they'll always look back on and say – "Some people did care!" It makes a better world of tomorrow for them and for us.

God love you and yours, and may I wish you happiness and good health in all the years to come.

Sincerely,
Fred Santon

And lastly in this series of letters was the following handwritten note, with no date. It reads:

Dear Mrs. Minsky,

Your love and consideration for less fortunate boys and girls have made a rewarding difference in their lives. We were able to have a nice good show with some colors in it – your accessories and other items made <u>all</u> the difference.

Thanksgiving is a time to be thankful for our blessings and I'll forever be grateful.

Fred Santon

The following letter was written on stationery from the Hong Kong Convention Center, and dated January 16, 1976. The bottom reads: "The Oriental Rooms, Palace, Noon Gun Lounge & Café, Hong Kong."

Mr. Tony Papa
Vice President
Associated Booking Corporation
9595 Wilshire Blvd.
Beverly Hills
California 90212
U.S.A.

Dear Mr. Papa,
Re: <u>Palace Night Club</u>

I am writing to confirm that the contract we have with Madame Bluebell will be expiring on August 31st, and it is advisable that you make a trip to Hong Kong so that we may be able to discuss the possibility of getting the Minsky Revue for a period commencing on September 1st.

Enclosed herewith please find copies of the Palace plan for your kind reference.

Yours sincerely,
David Lian
Entertainment Manager

The next letter was from April 2, 1976. It's a letter Oscar Cohen wrote to Michael Lapin at the Stardust Hotel in Las Vegas.

Mr. Michael Lapin
Executive Offices
Stardust Hotel
Las Vegas, Nevada

Dear Mike:

Per our telephone conversation, I would appreciate your considering booking the "Minsky Burlesque Show" into the Fremont Hotel. I am sure you are aware of the great success that the MINSKY Show has had throughout the county and in Las Vegas, in prior years. At this writing, we have approximately four MINSKY road companies touring throughout the country, and are doing exceptional business.

I assure you, it would be a pleasure for me to come into Las Vegas and sit down with you, your entertainment people, my associate Art Engler, Harold Minsky, and plan a new review with gorgeous girls, sensational comedy, and great production.

Hoping to have the pleasure of meeting you in the very near future, I am...
Sincerely,
Oscar Cohen
BCC: Mr. Harold Minsky
    Mr. Art Engler

On August 2, 1976, Marcus Glaser, of the Charles Hogan Agency, located at 203 North Wabash Avenue, in Chicago, Illinois, wrote the following to Harold Minsky at his home in Las Vegas.

Dear Harold,

First of all, how is my bum "Chaz" doing for you? Got a letter from him last week advising me you had extended his contract for two more weeks, and that he wanted more money. So I wrote him back and told him he should kiss your ass for holding him over and keeping him working. So he went along with me.

However just got a note from him that the show closes August 28th and he tells me that is one week short of the contract. So if there is any place you can put the character, would appreciate hearing from you.

Best wishes and kindest regards,
Sincerely,
Marcus Glaser

The next two letters were from Irving Siders, both written on his letterhead which reads: Irving Siders * Artists Management * 250 East 63rd Street * New York, N.Y. 10021 * 212 PL 1-2680. The first was dated December 31, 1976, and not sent to Minsky. It reads:

Mr. Tony Gillard
Entertainment Director
Ramada Inn
Industrial Hwy
Essington, Pa 19029

Dear Tony,

As per our phone conversation and your wire of confirmation, Harold Minsky of THE MINSKY FOLLIES has confirmed the following terms and conditions:

MINSKY FOLLIES with cast of ten (10) people opening Tuesday February 15th, 1977 for a minimum of six weeks with indefinite options thereafter subject to two week's notice by either party. The first option is to be exercised on or before third week of the initial six week engagement. Your wire indicated four weeks; however in our phone conversation of today, December 31st, 1976, you okayed six weeks. I have so advised Harold Minsky.

The terms are $5500.00 per week with a deposit in the amount of $5500.00 made payable to Harold Minsky, upon signing of contract. The show will be paid at the end of each week and the $5500.00 deposit will be used to pay the show for their last week's engagement.

THE MINSKY FOLLIES will perform nine shows per week. One show Tuesday-Wednesday-Thursday and two shows Friday-Saturday-Sunday. Time of shows will be determined by management of the Ramada Inn.

RAMADA INN will supply the following at no cost to the show:

Eight (8) rooms – no food;

Band consisting of organ, electric guitar, drums, and trumpet, (band will be available for rehearsal);

Follow spotlight and operator.

Under separate cover I have sent you publicity, and Harold Minsky is sending you whatever else he has. When I get back from my vacation next week, I will send you the contracts. Also, will arrange for my showing up at the Ramada to help set up the stage, lights, dressing rooms, etc.

Thanks again for your help and hope that this is the start of big things for the future.

Sincerely,
Irving Siders

The second letter from Irving was dated March 15, 1977.
Mr. Harold Minsky
5712 Kelley Lane
Las Vegas, Nevada

Dear Harold,

Wanted to write you sooner but have been rather busy getting ready to tour *California Suite* this summer.

I asked CBS regarding the special that they are talking about MINSKY BURLESQUE. The man that is in charge is Bernie Sofronski, CBS New York, and he promised to get back to me when he had more information. In the meantime I would suggest that you check into this. I believe that they are thinking of doing a History of Burlesque. In fact I represent a couple of writers that just did something for CBS and when I mentioned Burlesque they were both interested.

Have been on top of Mario Ciroli (Chateau de Ville) and am trying like hell to get him to take the show some time either early in the spring or summer. I'll keep on him and who knows, I may get a deal.

Incidentally, I am delighted about the Regency-Hyatt deal. Somehow since Chuck has been out, everything at ABC has gone down the drain. In fact, Oscar Cohen's attitude is so bad that I almost don't want to talk to him. Recently I had to talk to him about an act that they represent and he worked me over for nothing saying that I kissed myself in through Chuck on your show at Chateau and Granny's. Somehow Mr. Cohen has no knowledge of what goes on in his company as he never did anything with Chateau or Granny's until I got the deals, and if he did some thinking he actually got the free ride, not me. As far as I'm concerned until Chuck gets back I would rather deal with you and Irvin Arthur and merely forget ABC. Even the time that I got some dates with Lee Guber, Oscar until that time had nothing to do with the booking and since then hasn't had more than one act, Shirley Bassey with Music Fairs. I can work with Irv Arthur and I hope that between the two of us we can do you some good.

Always feel free to call or write as I like doing business with you.

Kindest regards,
Irving Siders

The following letter was perhaps the most difficult item I have had to copy over for this book – it describes Harold Minsky's death. It was dated December 31, 1977, and signed by Patricia Minsky.

Dear Dr. Katz,

I received your letter today having just returned from New York early Friday morning. Thank you for your sincere condolences. I think very highly of you professionally as well as personally, and wish to thank you for taking the time out of your busy schedule to telephone and to write.

I wanted to call you before we left Los Angeles. I had a few more questions to ask but decided that I really didn't want to know any more. I sensed it was only a matter of time and decided my questions were better off unanswered. Needless to say, I lost not only a fine husband but a best friend and despite the differences in our ages, our marriage worked quite well for almost eleven years.

The likeable personality you spoke of in your letter however was only a broken fragment of the man I had loved and married. Somehow the treatments and perhaps the disease itself destroyed much of the quality of his life. Being a man who greatly valued quality over quantity, I feel that he subconsciously started to give in when he left the hospital; holding out just long enough to make it home where he knew he was the happiest. From then on, he seemed to be going downhill at a very fast pace. He soon was unable to tolerate the feedings due to a feeling of extreme bloating and nauseousness. I cut down the total cc's per day from 3,720 to 3,000, being careful not to go below the 2,800 minimum requirements. That seemed to work out much better along with regulating the liquids to drip at a very slow pace. The next morning, Thursday, I woke to find a lot of bleeding around the bandage but noticed that the blood had dried and was not seeping. I immediately called Dr. Star and he explained that per his conversation with you a certain amount of bleeding could be expected. On Friday, I took Harold to Dr. Star's office. He cleaned out the wound and checked his vital signs. Everything seemed to be normal.

The evening before he passed away was the worst for either of us due to his almost continuous coughing and expectorating throughout the night. Saturday morning he was extremely weakened and in need of physical support even to walk. I found it somehow amusing that as sick as he was feeling that day he insisted on getting up early and going into the living room in order to watch the football games all the while desperately fighting the sleep he so badly needed. The coughing subsided later on that afternoon and he seemed calm and lethargic.

Harold Minsky, 1967. Courtesy: Pat Elliott Minsky/Burlesque Historical Society

He went to bed at 11pm, (Christmas Eve), at which time I started the last feeding for the evening. About forty minutes later, I was just about to jump into the shower, when he called to me saying he was frightened and wanted a Valium to calm himself down. I wasn't alarmed at the time as he expressed the same feelings the night before. I proceeded to shut off his feeding tube and put the crushed Valium along with some water into the syringe to attach directly to his tube, when it began to happen. He remained conscious for a short while. I sat on the bed next to him and assured him that everything was going to be alright.

Before I began to fully comprehend what was taking place, fifteen minutes had gone by and I realized that he hadn't blinked or responded in any manner to what I was saying. I was terribly frightened to leave him as all this time he was still breathing quite heavily through the mouth. I finally came to my senses and left the room long enough to call Dr. Star and explain what was happening. He arrived shortly after with his wife. He assured me that Harold was totally unconscious and in no pain. We both knew what had to be done. Nothing! But I thank God that I did not have to make that decision alone although I knew it was best to have it happen that way. Dr. Star stayed alone in the room with him until his heart finally stopped beating almost an hour after he first lost consciousness. But it was a peaceful death and at home and we were together. We had a memorial service the next day in Las Vegas then flew to New York with my sister and Ava on Tuesday for another service and burial.

So that is how it happened. My uneducated guess is that he probably hemorrhaged and lapsed into a coma.

Again, thank you for your kindness. I don't know when I will be in Los Angeles again. I have a few things to attend to here pertaining to business, etc. I may enroll in the University and submerge myself in class if there is still enough time to register for Spring semester. I thank God for giving me resilience and adaptability; two great assets that have assisted me in my life.

Take care and may the New Year bring you and yours much happiness and good health to you always.

Sincerely,
Patricia Minsky

(Notes: It was extremely difficult to read Pat's letter to Dr. Katz, and initially I thought of closing the book with it. But I decided to leave it in with the letters where it belongs. Knowing of Pat's struggle, dealing with ovarian cancer at the end of her life, also made reading this letter tremendously hard for me. Without her help, even while dealing with her own aggressive illness, the BHS would not have received the Minsky Files. Patricia (Trish) Minsky Shapiro is buried at Palm Memorial Park in Las Vegas. Harold Minsky is buried at the Montefiore Cemetery, Springfield Gardens, in Queens County, New York. Both are listed on the "Find A Grave" website; should you visit, please leave flowers and a note.)

More letters were written and received after Harold's death. The next letter comes from the University of Nevada, Las Vegas. It was written on January 31, 1978, and addressed to Mrs. Harold Minsky of 5712 Kelly Lane, Las Vegas.

Dear Mrs. Minsky,

It was so pleasant speaking with you this morning and remembering your visit to the library a few years ago to donate the book that Mr. Minsky had helped with. I remember at that time we had talked about historical material and the tape done by the Texan.

You mentioned that Mr. Minsky hadn't preserved much of his past but I wanted you to know that we at the University Library are interested in preserving what might have been saved such as letters, contracts, notes, scores, clippings, programs – anything that helps tell the story of the Minsky's in show business.

Since you are on campus taking courses, I'd appreciate your stopping into the library so I could show you some of the types of things we are doing in attempting to preserve the history of the area and it's individuals.

Sincerely,
Hal Erickson
Harold H. J. Erickson
Director of Libraries

This leads into the following letter from Southern Methodist University, written on February 23, 1978. It was addressed to Patricia Minsky at 1005 Russell Road, in Las Vegas.

Dear Ms. Minsky,

Thank you for your kind letter of February 21. We shall be happy to send you a copy of the tape your husband and I made in 1975.

Because of a writing project of my own, we have devoted most of the past two years to transcribing the film interviews taped for the SMU Oral History Project. That is about to come to an end, and your husband's interview will be the first up, once the film interviews are completed. We should have a bound copy of the transcription to you by the end of this year.

I was so sorry to hear of your husband's death. I enjoyed so much the afternoon we spent together. As a historian I am delighted to learn that his papers are being placed in a University archive.

If I can be of further service to you, please do let me know.

With warm regards,
Ronald L. Davis
Professor of History

The next three items were copies of notes written by Pat Minsky on Shokow, Ltd. stationery. The stationery included the following information; 1005 Russell Road, Las Vegas, Nevada 89119, and the telephone number: (702) 736–3013. They were all from August 1978, and in the order that they were written:

August 24, 1978

Dear Mr. Dearing,

I wish to express my appreciation for the article that appeared in the *Valley Times,* and the *Las Vegas Today* tabloids.

It was nice meeting you and talking to you about burlesque. Please thank Andrea for the flattering pictures.

Sincerely,
Patricia Minsky

August 27, 1978

Dear Professor Stevens,

I wish to express my appreciation for the excellent revue you wrote concerning the show at the Maxim Hotel and for the recent article you submitted to the *Las Vegas Magazine.*

I know that both of these articles required considerable thought and time on your part and are not without due recognition, on my part, for the time and effort you generously gave in their consummation.

Sincerely,
Patricia Minsky

And the last note simply reads:

August 28, 1978

Dear Mr. Delaney,

I wish to express my appreciation for the excellent article you wrote on the show at the Maxim Hotel and for your continuous mention of the show in your column.

Sincerely,
Patricia Minsky

"M" is For...

"M" is a very full File, containing articles about the Minsky show at the Maxim Hotel in Las Vegas, the show in Mineola, New York, music used in a variety of shows, information regarding the Minsky Trademark, and so much more.

We will start with an article from the *Evening Times*, out of Trenton, New Jersey, dated August 16, 1967. The article, by staff writer Annette Barshay, was titled "Minsky's at Music Circus Leaves Little to be Desired." It actually reads better than the title makes the show sound.

"LAMBERTVILLE – A good burlesque show, say the experts, should have two important ingredients: elegance and gaudiness.

Minsky's Burlesque Follies, opening at the Lambertville Music Circus last night, has both, though it is more stream-lined and less gross than the burlesque was in the days of Gypsy Rose Lee.

Twelve statuesque girls danced their way through the show dressed in gorgeous and often minuscule costumes. Six of them are highly skilled dancers.

True to form the stars have names in the old styles: Monique Monet, "The Girl With the Magic Hips;" Yolanda Moreno, "The Venezuelan Bombshell;" and Lisa Duran, "The Exciting Blonde Beauty."

Miss Duran, especially, who is a first-rate dancer, left the audience breathless.

The girls' numbers are interspersed with the traditional gags and jokes. The old-style comedians in baggy-pants, floppy jackets and tiny hats, got a lot of laughs with their crude jokes.

More sophisticated comic talent was shown by Milt Douglas, especially in a small bitter-sweet skit on married life.

The circular stage at the Music Circus, which can be a nuisance to

Yolanda Moreno. Courtesy: C.F. Miller

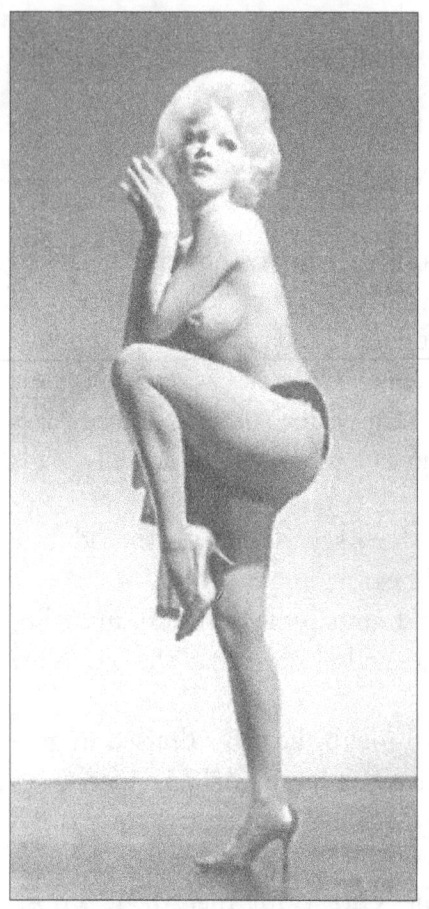

Lisa Duran. Courtesy: Pat Elliott Minsky/Burlesque Historical Society

actors in regular theatrical productions, was ideal for this show.

The troupe was always moving, leaving no segment of the audience with a poor view.

The costumes by Madame Golda of Las Vegas were extravagant. The stage was swirling with vividly colored satin and feathers, mink tails, and glittering sequins.

Direction and choreography is by Jerry Norman, and Mike Durso is the musical director.

Singer Frankie Vale provided vocal accompaniment to some of the dances, but suffered from a poor amplifying system.

This highly professional show was produced and staged by Harold Minsky, who has put on burlesque shows for the past 30 years. It will be at the Music Circus through Sunday."

Next, the Melody Tent review from the *Cape Cod Standard-Times,* dated August 29, 1967. It reads:

"Girl Watchers Recoup at 'Burlesque Follies;' This practically sunless summer has cheated beachcombing males by the thousands of their usual view of female epidermis, but the arrival of Harold Minsky's *Burlesque Follies* for a week's run at the Melody Tent in Hyannis changed all that last night.

For most of the audience it was actually a tent revival night as the two-act, 15-scene show eventually hit all the high spots of old-time burlesque.

The girls were there in generous portions of un-drapery, of course, but keeping them company were skits, lowdown jokes, baggy-pants comedians, and general tomfoolery that whipped up gales of hilarity.

Withal, last night's performance was a spirited job with colorful costuming, at the start of the numbers anyway, and some excellent production numbers, all backed in expert fashion by Mike Durso's Band. The result was a snappy package that should bring in the customers in droves to wind up the Melody Tent's season with a stuffed cash register.

A "School Days" skit with comedians Dick Bernie and Danny Jacobs as recalcitrant "pupils" of school marm Barbara Curtis, probably hit the highest

Barbara Curtis.
Courtesy: Janelle Smith Collection

Comics Bob Ferguson and Jack Rosen, 1957.
Courtesy: Joni Taylor

decibels on the laugh meter, although Milt Douglas, as a snappish hubby who always managed to verbally subdue his waspish spouse with the last word, gained a lot of cheers from frustrated males in the audience. Jack Rosen's skit work was well received also.

The show offered three specialty stars who shook up the audience with their various methods of shedding habiliments. In fact, so much came off, a stagehand hovered nearby with a basket to scoop up the finery as it came floating his way. Monique Monet offered "Girl with the Magic Hips;" Yolanda Moreno, billed as the "Venezuelan Bombshell," offered a pyrotechnic dance; and lithe Lisa Duran climaxed Act Two with a dance that reached the G-string and pasties level.

The show ran overlong and at times the pace was ponderous, probably because the Follies plays in theatres and nightclubs, rather than tent locations usually. The final skit titled "On Location," which depicted a drama rehearsal, misfired, became tedious and was overlong. It could be dropped to allow the performance to break before 11pm. The show peaked with Lisa Duran's spectacle anyway. J.F.S."

(Notes: In 1950, the Cape Cod Music Circus (currently the Cape Cod Melody Tent) became only the third musical tent to open in the United States. Over the years it attracted major stars of the Broadway stage and silver screen to its stages. The ensuing years has witnessed a variety of structural and performance changes from that once experimental summer theatre of the past; and sound and lighting

Postcard of the old Music Circus in Lambertville, New Jersey. Courtesy: Authors Collection

Vintage photo of the Cape Cod Melody Tent. Courtesy: Pat Elliott Minsky/ Burlesque Historical Society

equipment has been upgraded to state of the art systems designed specifically for theatres-in-the-round. Seating capacity has also been significantly expanded.

For nearly seventy years, the Cape Cod Melody Tent, has been presenting world-class entertainment in the scenic Massachusetts coastal community of Hyannis. It is one of only two continuously-operated tent theatres-in-the-round in the United States; and both are owned and operated by the South Shore Playhouse Associates, a not-for-profit organization dedicated to encouraging and supporting the arts, along with cultural and educational organizations in the area. The resident theatre company that was once established decades ago may be gone, but it has been replaced by touring performers of world-class caliber.)

The next "M" in the File is for Mineola, New York. The first article was from the December 7-13, 1966, issue of the *Las Vegas Reviewer*. There was no author byline. It reads:

"Minsky Producing New York Show, Sked January 17 Opener; Las Vegas show producer Harold Minsky has announced that he is now putting together a burlesque revue for the Mineola Theatre in Long Island, New York. Show will open January 17 and is set for an initial run of five weeks.

Minsky, who has produced and directed shows at the Silver Slipper for the past year, said the New York show will be similar in format to his Las Vegas burlesque revues.

He said the owners of the Mineola Theatre, a 1250-seat establishment, have reported the largest advance ticket sales in the theatres history.

New show will feature performers well-known to Las Vegans. Among them are dancer Mikki Sharait, who starred in *Cleopatra's Nymphs of the Nile*, at the Flamingo and later in two Minsky shows at the Slipper; singer Dave Walker, former Dunes and Silver Slipper production singer; and comic Dick Richards, a Silver Slipper performer for many years, dating back to the Hank Henry days.

Minsky is currently auditioning showgirls in New York. Show will consist of approximately 28 performers; 14 of them showgirls."

The following article appeared in *Newsday* on January 18, 1967. Written by Bob Greene, it reads:

Mikki Sharait. Courtesy: Pat Elliott Minsky/Burlesque Historical Society

Hank Henry. Courtesy: Burlesque Historical Society

"DA Studies Some New Briefs; Mineola - A bevy of beauties prancing across the stage with only miniscule pasties to ward off chest colds is legal in Nassau County but they can't be escorted by gentlemen who don't wear reasonably long trousers.

Such was District Attorney Cahn's considered decision yesterday. The ruling came after he and a cadre of serious-minded Nassau County police officers spent a six-hour afternoon at the Mineola Theatre, judicially viewing the dress rehearsal of *Minsky's Burlesque Follies* – all in the line of duty, of course. The show, which opened last night, was imported from Las Vegas, where most of the young ladies cut dry-cleaning costs by performing in the nude.

Cahn gave his legal opinion after viewing two scenes in which male dancer Larry Merritt, attired in high boots and a sort of bikini, swirled around the stage with pretty Mikki Sharait. Miss Sharait was costumed in two pasties and a G-string. Cahn stated his verdict succinctly. "That's too much," the district attorney ruled. "He's got to have pants on."

Cahn's only other objection came when flame-haired stripper Kelly Barton divested herself of several garments and danced a sort of shimmy, accompanied part of the time by a tuxedo-clad dummy. "The strip can stay," Cahn said, "but the dummy and the shimmy have to go." As an afterthought he added, "Her pasties better be a little bit bigger. I can hardly see them."

Otherwise it was all systems a go-go as far as Cahn and his sleuths were concerned as strippers stripped, (grinds, but no bumps) and chorus girls strutted Ziegfeld-style. "One has to take a very liberal view in these matters, because the courts have," Cahn explained. "My own personal views don't count." But he warned that he feels there is a difference between topless showgirls and topless waitresses. "The theatre is one thing," he said. "But I will prosecute any topless waitress operation."

Cahn, who was accompanied by, Nassau Chief of Detectives Edward F. Curran, Assistant District Attorney George Levine, and three members of the Nassau Police Vice Squad, sat next to Dr. Frank Calderone, the theatre owner, during the rehearsal. It was Calderone who ordered the changes Cahn

Dr. Frank A. Calderone checking out a set for an upcoming show at the Mineola Theatre. Photo from the mid-1960s. Courtesy: Calderone Theatre Collection/Hofstra University

desired. Later, Calderone said, "I quite agree with the few alterations suggested by Mr. Cahn. He was very fair, and I don't want anything that degrades my theatre."

Cahn said that he had asked to view the dress rehearsal after he had received a number of complaints from the public based on advance advertising for the show. Associate producer Norman Rothstein said the strip numbers, executed with maximum speed and minimum tease, were added to the show because the girls have nothing to strip in Las Vegas. "We've tailored the show to the community," he said.

When the rehearsal ended and Cahn left, producer Harold Minsky refused to comment or to let the performers talk to reporters. And as the last visitor left, Rothstein could be heard telling Miss Barton, "Kelly, honey, take out the man and put on bigger pasties. I love you, but I didn't write the rules."

Just to be sure that everything went off (or stayed on) as agreed to in the afternoon, Curran sat through the opening performance last night, where a mostly middle-aged, mostly male audience watched the show. "We were there to enforce the law," Curran said. "The show was run the way we agreed it should and there was no objection." Curran went on to say, "I'm no critic," when asked how he liked the show."

An advertisement from a November 18, 1966 edition of *Newsday* states the show was to run at the Mineola Theatre from January 17 through February 20.

The next article, by Robert McDonald and Frank McLoughlin, appeared in the January 18, 1967 edition of the *New York Daily News*. It was titled "Burlesque Catches DA's Eye, But He Proves Broad-Minded." It reads:

"'Cut it out!' replaced 'Take it off!' as the cry from the boys in the front row yesterday at the dress rehearsal of *Minsky's Burlesque Follies*, which opened last night at the Mineola Theatre.

"The boys," were Nassau District Attorney William Cahn and Chief of Detectives Edward Curran, along with more reporters than were ever assigned to a school board meeting on a frosty night.

They were there – the lawmen anyway – intent on "cleaning up" the show prior to its opening rather than issuing summonses later. Cahn said he had to attend personally because the assistant he had planned to send was suddenly assigned out of town. Cahn didn't say who did the assigning.

Asked why a burly show had to be censored in this day of topless waitresses, Cahn replied, "This isn't Fun City. We have to apply the standards of a residential community."

During the five-hour sneak preview, Cahn ordered only three changes in the performance. One involved a dance routine between Mikki Sharait and her male co-star, Larry Merritt, in which Mikki wears a G-string and pasties while Larry wears a G-string. Cahn ordered Larry to put his pants on.

True to the burly tradition to keep 'em waiting, the other changes come at the end of the story, since they come at the end of the show.

Cahn said he wasn't passing judgment on the show as a citizen, but as a law-enforcement officer.

"We only suggested changes that would bring the performance within the law, not changes that we would have liked to see," he said.

Both of the remaining changes involved the next-to-final act, a strip entitled "Dream Lover" by Miss Kelly Barton, in which her dream lover is a wooden dummy which pops out of a magic lantern.

Kelly Barton. Courtesy: Pat Elliott Minsky/Burlesque Historical Society

After some enticement by Kelly, a little life comes into the dummy's wooden bones and he gets a little frisky – too frisky for Cahn.

The DA also ordered Kelly to wear bigger pasties. "Why is it," he mused aloud, "that the biggest girls always wear the smallest pasties?"

Dr. Frank A. Calderone, owner of the theatre, promised that the changes would be made without affecting the quality of the show. Harold Minsky, the producer and son of the famous Abe, refused comment."

Apparently Minsky produced another show that played at the Mineola Theatre later in the year. In this same folder were two articles dated in late November 1967. The first, dated November 19, 1967, was from the *Long Island Daily Press*. Titled "Minsky's New Revue For Mineola," had no author byline. It reads:

"Harold Minsky, King of the Runway, is bringing his all-new revue, *Life Begins at Minsky's*, to the Mineola Theatre for three weeks, starting Tuesday and running through December 10.

Two extra performances have been added each Saturday at 2pm and 11pm. The Saturday 9pm show has been moved to 8pm.

Direct from the Silver Slipper in Las Vegas, *Life Begins at Minsky's*, features beautiful girls (for which Minsky is famous) and the baggy-pants comedians that

1966 view of the refurbished lobby and box office of the Mineola Theatre. Courtesy: Calderone Theatre Collection/ Hofstra University

are an integral part of the American burlesque scene.

The show is moving East in conjunction with the movie, *The Night They Raided Minsky's,* now being filmed in Manhattan's old burlesque and vaudeville houses.

The Minsky name is as famous in American burlesque as the *Follies Bergere* is in Paris. Harold Minsky's father, Abe, first produced shows in the Wintergarden Theatre in 1908. At one time there were over 15 theatres in New York filled with Minsky shows.

Harold Minsky is the man who wouldn't let burlesque die. When burlesque was driven out of New York, he took over the Minsky concept of beautiful girls onstage in lavish costumes and settings to Las Vegas and began another legend.

Harold is the sole remaining showman of the family, and the fifth Minsky to produce burlesque shows. His formula of beautiful girls in tasteful settings and slap-stick comedy has stood up against the toughest competition in the world."

The next article, written by Robert Sandler, appeared in the November 24, 1967 edition of the *Garden City Newsday*. Titled "DA's Visit Helps Cover Up This Case," it reads:

"Mineola – District Attorney Cahn isn't a theatre critic by trade, but the influence of his review of the present attraction at the Mineola Theatre is the sort of thing a professional aisle-sitter might well envy. Cahn, by his mere presence in the theatre, brought about what could be called a major script change – pasties.

Of course, the plot of the show in question, *Life Begins at Minsky's,* is fairly rudimentary. The trouble was, so was the costuming of several of "Life's" stars, at least until the intermission at Wednesday night's performance, which Cahn, Assistant District Attorney Richard Dellin, six detectives and other members of the district attorney's staff attended. The visit was unannounced, but the visitors did not go unnoticed.

Before the intermission, a Miss Lisa Duran worked her way from a silver Western costume down to a G-string and boots. Her performance was followed by that of Miss Jeannie Linero, who performed what was described as an oriental dance that left her in even worse condition; no boots. But when the curtain went up on the second half of the evening's entertainment, the young ladies who took off their clothes had put on pasties. And as Cahn's group left the theatre, manager Bob Walz told a member of the Cahn critics' circle that pasties would, from then on, be part of the standard operating equipment."

(Notes: Dr. Frank A. Calderone, born in 1901 and died in February of 1987, was an expert in preventive medicine and a leading figure in the World Health Organization. He also operated many theatres created by his father, Salvatore Calderone (1876 – 1929), until around 1980. In addition to those located in Nassau County, the company also owned and operated theatres in neighboring Suffolk County.

Photo from 1961, Dr. Frank A. Calderone standing next to a sign outside the Mineola Theatre that reads, "This Performance Sold Out." Courtesy: Calderone Theatre Collection/Hofstra University

Salvatore Calderone, who initially came to America in 1893 to work in the newspaper industry, went on to become an early American movie theatre magnate. He was the founder of the "Calderone Theatre Circuit," a chain of theatres located on Long Island, and became known as the "Master Showman of Nassau County." In the 1920s many of Calderone's advertisements read "Vaudeville Always," and noted that African-American performers were featured regularly at his Rivoli Theatre in Hempstead.

By 1927, the Calderone chain operated seven theatres in Nassau County, including two in Hempstead, and one each in Lynbrook, Valley Stream, Glen Cove, Westbury, and Mineola. From late 1928 through early 1929, Calderone entered into negotiations to sell his five large Nassau County theatres to Fox Theatres. The negotiated price was said to have been $3 million.

Sadly, Salvatore Calderone suffered a heart attack in the early morning hours of February 10, 1929 at his home in Hempstead, Long Island. At the time of his death local newspapers remarked, "His life is an example of what can be accomplished by those who come to America from other places. It shows that opportunities are always here for those who are ready to seize them."

Calderone's death put an end to the plan to sell his theatre chain to Fox Theatres. During Salvatore's life, the company built and managed most of its own theatres. The Calderone chain remained in operation by the family for many years after his death; however, after his death, the company began leasing out the theatres to other management chains.

Exterior view of the Mineola Theatre from 1972. Marquee reads, "Geo C. Scott in New Centurions." Courtesy: Calderone Theatre Collection/Hofstra University

Frank Calderone left the management of the company to others and did not return to have an active role in its management again until 1954. If interested, there are various articles online regarding the Calderone's and the Mineola Theatre. *The New York Times* obituary for Dr. Frank A. Calderone was published on February 24, 1987.

The Mineola Theatre, circa 1926 – 1927, was located at 120 Mineola Boulevard, Mineola; in Nassau County, New York. This theatre was under the management of Salvatore Calderone until just shortly before his death when it was turned back over to its owners who sold it in 1930. At some point after 1930 it returned to the Calderone chain and remained a part of it until around 1980-1982, when it was sold. It has since been demolished and replaced by an office building.)

Ann Corio acknowledges fans during the run of This Was Burlesque. Courtesy: Authors Collection

One other article in this folder, which also appeared in the November 19, 1967 edition of the *Long Island Daily Press*, relates to a burlesque show unrelated to the Minsky name. An author is not noted, but it is titled "Ann Corio to Make a Return Strip to LI." The article reads:

"Old-fashioned burlesque with beautiful girls and baggy-pants comedians, moves into Westbury Tuesday at 8:30pm, when shapely burlesque "queen of queens," Ann Corio brings the new edition of her touring show, *This Was Burlesque* into the Music Fair for a two-week stay through Sunday, December 3.

This Was Burlesque has been a howling success off-Broadway, on Broadway, and on tour ever since the curtain rose at the Hudson Theatre some five seasons ago. The brand new edition that Miss Corio is bringing into Westbury is loaded with funnier comics, leggier gals and a host of other surprises made to order for the tired businessman, the ladies, and young adults as well.

Harry Conley with a couple cuties from the cast of This Was Burlesque.
Courtesy: C.F. Miller

Co-starring in the show is one of the all-time original comic favorites of burlesque, television, and stage, Pinky Lee. Pinky, a long-time resident of California, is returning to the phase of show business which gave him and many of today's top bananas their start.

Miss Corio's *This Was Burlesque* is satirical. There's the offbeat little comely comedienne in the chorus who is always out of step, chews gum, and keeps it light. And, of course don't expect to see a "Twiggy" in the show. Miss Corio partakes in a parade of different costumes with her amusing comments between the acts; "discussions" of the styles and manners of burlesque during its hey-day.

This Was Burlesque has all the ingredients for a night of fun. There's Gloria LeRoy, Kelsey Collins, tassle twirler Taffey O'Neil, Harry Conley, comics Claude Mathis and Jimmy Mathews, a chorus of exotic cuties, and the exotic dancers. The show even has a take-off on a wrestling match featuring 'Cautious Klay.'"

(Notes: Taffey O'Neil, who is a member of the BHS, says she was never involved in the Ann Corio show, nor was she ever a tassle twirler!

Ann Corio, born in Hartford, Connecticut on November 29, 1909, was one of twelve children of Italian immigrant parents. While still in her teens, good looks and a shapely physique landed her roles as a showgirl that eventually led to Corio becoming a hugely popular striptease artist. Her rise to stardom as a featured performer on the burlesque circuit began in 1925, working in theatres such as the famous Minsky's Burlesque in New York City and Boston's Old Howard Theatre.

After Mayor Fiorello La Guardia closed down the New York City burlesque houses in 1939, Corio made her way to Los Angeles. Between 1941 and 1944 she appeared in several Hollywood "B" motion pictures. Ann Corio had a long successful career as a performer, and dancing onstage in burlesque.

In 1962 she put together the nostalgic off-Broadway show *This Was Burlesque*, which she directed and also performed in. In 1968, she wrote a book with the same title. During the 1970s she took *This Was Burlesque* out on the summer stock circuit for several seasons. In 1981, the show played Broadway at the old Latin Quarter, which was then known as the Princess Theatre, and tried to compete with *Sugar Babies* which was running just a few blocks up the street. In 1985, she mounted the show in downtown Los Angeles, at the Variety Arts Theatre, where it did not have a good run. A year or so later, the show played a dinner theatre in Florida, where it closed for good.

A resident of Cliffside Park, New Jersey, Ann Corio died at Englewood Hospital and Medical Center in Englewood, New Jersey on March 1, 1999.)

With the mention of Ann Corio in Minsky's Files, it allows me the opportunity to also include an article on Corio, provided by BHS member and burlesque legend, Ann Pett. Ann, and her husband Bob, were close friends of

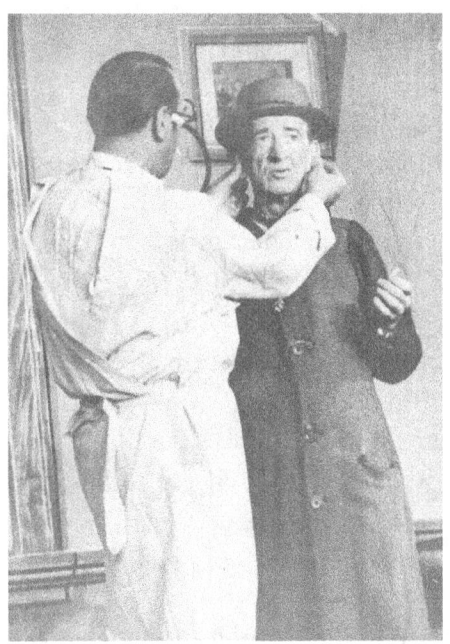

Steve Mills, in hat, in a scene from This Was Burlesque. *Courtesy: C.F. Miller*

PEPPER POWELL

Pepper Powell. Courtesy: C.F. Miller

Corio and her husband Michael P. Iannucci. Ann also sent a program from the Musicarnival in Cleveland when *This Was Burlesque* was touring in 1969. That edition of the show included the following cast: Ann Corio, Steve Mills, Harry Conley, Tami Roche, Claude Mathis, Harry Ryan, Count Gregory, Tom Dillon, Pepper Powell, and Beautiful Marlene. The show was staged and choreographed by Richard Barstow; with costumes by Rex Huntington.

The Ann Corio article appeared in the Albany *Times-Union* on August 9, 1973. It was titled "Burlesque's Ann Corio Today," and written by Mildred Mikkanen. (Mikkanen, before beginning her newspaper career, served as a chief yeoman in the USN WAVES during World War II. She died in 2010.) It reads:

"Burlesque queen Ann Corio doesn't pretend to give off the heavy aura of sex anymore. She doesn't particularly want to.

When she's gussied up in heavy white makeup, piles of red curls and exotic frills and ruffles for her nostalgic role in *This Was Burlesque,* she's more promoter than competitor of the busty young things who peel off their clothes to traditional strip tunes like "A Pretty Girl is Like a Melody."

She looks a bit drawn, and she works hard to move the show along. But catch her backstage and she looks great – tanned, lean, and athletic. And she projects energy, animation, and all the acumen and naturalness of the capable businesswoman she has become.

"Come in," she calls in answer to the knock on the door of her trailer dressing room behind the blue Melody Fair tent in North Tonawanda.

It's the same warm, husky voice that said "I am Tondeleyo," 30 years ago when she played the native girl in *White Cargo,* the shocker of her day.

But this is no Tondeleyo, clothed only in brown powder for a seconds-only glimpse before the first act curtain falls.

This is a frankly fifty-ish attractive woman with her hair rolled up in pink curlers, her tanned, freckled face devoid of makeup, and her 5-foot-7, 124-pound body sleek in a beige knit pantsuit.

"Sit down!" She motions the glass she carries to the divan in the sparsely furnished living room. "Let me get you something to drink – Wink, ginger ale, 7-Up; or how about spring water? That's what I'm drinking. It's pure! Not that I'm a health nut, but I eat nutritious things like skim milk, cheese, salads, and vegetables, so I can wear sample size 8. I eat no starches or sweets – oh, maybe a Neapolitan once in awhile; and when I can't stand it any longer, a big plateful of spaghetti."

She fetches a glass of Wink from the trailer refrigerator and sits down, warning that time is short, and that "It takes me an hour and 15 minutes to get ready for the show. I hate makeup and I spend the first 15 minutes just staring at myself in the mirror."

She also hates being called a stripteaser, always has. "I never did a bump or grind or a strip," she says. "I took off less and made more money at it than any other burlesque dancer. It was just a little peek-a-boo, and had more illusion and mystique than if I really did a strip. It doesn't take any talent to go nude the way they do in plays like *Hair*.

When I did *White Cargo*, I had pounds of brown powder on my body. That scene was beautiful and artistic and accepted although a buzz went through the audience.

I was only in burlesque three or four years, but that's where I made my name and everyone associates me with it. Actually I wasn't much of a dancer. I wanted to be in show business, but not in the chorus. So I devised my own routines and still do."

UPI Press Photo from June 14, 1958; Gypsy Rose Lee listens to a recording from her new album, "That's Me All Over," on her 1900 Victrola. Gypsy told the press she planned to tour in summer stock that season in the musical Happy Hunting. *Courtesy: Authors Collection*

She started out in her native Hartford, Connecticut, by winning a dance contest when she was 15. By 1934, Anna Maria Corio was known as the queen of burlesque, a title she later shared with her friend, the late Gypsy Rose Lee.

By 1940 Miss Corio had saved enough money so she could take a cut in pay to act in plays like *White Cargo* and *The Barker* on the summer circuit. She did several movies, among them *Swamp Woman, Jungle Siren*, and *The Sultan's Daughter*, which capitalized on her beautiful body image.

"Later I took plays like *Once More with Feeling, Rain*, and *Cat on a Hot Tin Roof*, on the road," she explains. "My role in 'Cat' depressed me and I got out of it."

But that was after it played in the theatre Michael Iannucci ran in Pittsburgh, Pennsylvania. A year later, in 1958, they were married. He is producer and general manager of *This Was Burlesque*, which is also the title of the book Miss Corio wrote in 1968 on the history of burlesque.

Press Photo from This Was Burlesque, *with Ann Corio and Jerry Lester. Courtesy: Authors Collection*

"It was Michael's idea that we do this burlesque type show and it was a good idea," she says. "We opened in 1962 in New York on a $15,000 budget and since have grossed $15 million. It played four years in New York and we've toured for nearly eight years."

The show is a nostalgic satire based on Miss Corio's recollections. It has scantily clad dancing girls, broad jokes by old-time comedians like Jerry Lester and Harry Conley, and three striptease artists who shed their clothes right down to one strategically placed pasty. Miss Corio acts as mistress of ceremonies, comedienne, and even dances and does an act of her own.

"Burlesque is very pure compared to what goes on in the theatre today," says Miss Corio, who is happy with the Supreme Court ruling allowing each community to make its own decision on what constitutes pornography and obscenity. "You cannot generalize on people's morals. Each community knows its own moral standards."

She's also a moralist when it comes to the shows she and her husband present in the summer theatre they own and operate in West Springfield, Massachusetts. They live in Suffield, Connecticut, where she

Male cast members from This Was Burlesque. *Courtesy: C.F. Miller*

relaxes by, "Cooking and baking like crazy, even making my own pasta like a good Italian should."

Stan Stanley, Jennifer Fox, and Harry Conley appearing together in This Was Burlesque. *Courtesy: Jennifer Fox*

"Michael's the boss in our family, the king of our house," she said. "I don't believe in women's lib, but I said to him, 'Michael, this is one point where I put my foot down – no vulgar plays in our theatre, no shows to which you can't bring kids.'"

Michael may be the business boss of *This Was Burlesque*, but according to Melody Fair officials, "Miss Corio is the whole shot when it comes to the production. She mothers the girls in the show, drills them in their acts, and feels very responsible for them. She runs a real tight ship."

She's also a hard-headed business woman. She and her husband own two clothing factories in Italy, and a boutique and a high fashion dress salon on the Piazza di Spagna in Rome. Their designer, Martieri of Rome, makes the clothes Miss Corio wears on and off stage. Her 19 luxurious show costumes are ankle length and long sleeved with deep necklines and slit skirts to show off her pretty neck and long legs.

Miss Corio scoffs at the idea that she's a sex symbol, or ever was. "I'm flattered if men appreciate and applaud me, but actually it's the women who applaud the most. And remember, I'm not exactly in my teens, and I am getting paid for this," Corio says."

The next folder in the "M" File was information regarding the Minsky Trademark. On May 16, 1973, *Variety* published a quarter-page sized legal notice dated May 8, 1973. It was similar to an advertisement, yet stated the following:

To Whom It May Concern:

Please be advised that the United States Patent Office has issued the following registered trademarks to the Harold Minsky Family Trust:

Name	Registration No.
Minsky's	956.287
Minsky's Burlesque	956.288
Minsky's Follies	956.289
Minsky's Burlesque Follies	956.990

These registrations were issued on March 27, 1973 for the production and staging of musical reviews, including burlesque shows, in class 107 (INT. CL. 41).

No use of these trade names or trademarks in the theatrical, stage or burlesque world made be made by any person, firm or organization except the Harold Minsky Family Trust, or its licensees. Any questions concerning these trademarks or trade names should be addressed to the undersigned as attorney for the Harold Minsky Family Trust.

Very truly yours,

Wiener, Goldwater & Galatz, Ltd.

J. Charles Thompson

What brought this about? There were three other items in this folder: a letter, a horribly faded Xerox of the front cover of a program, and a newspaper clipping attached to a copy of a newspaper advertisement.

The letter was on the stationery of Robert S. Fishko and John A. Prescott, 1681 Broadway, New York, N.Y. 10019, 541-9590. It was dated August 20, 1971, and addressed to Irving Siders, at 250 East 63rd Street, New York, N.Y. 10021. It reads:

Dear Mr. Siders:

Enclosed is a check payable to Patava, Inc. in the amount of Fifteen Hundred ($1,500.00) Dollars.

It is our mutual agreement that this payment is the full and complete compensation for the use by us and by the Colonie Coliseum Summer Theatre, Latham, New York, of the name Minsky in connection with a burlesque production starring Mamie Van Doren to be presented at the theatre August 24 through August 29.

It is our understanding that you represent Mr. Harold Minsky and are accepting this payment on his behalf, and you warrant and represent that you have the right to grant to us and the Colonie Coliseum Summer Theatre the right to use the name Minsky in connection with this production.

You agree that this payment covers all uses of the name Minsky in connection with this production, including but not limited to programs, advertising, signs and posters, and that Mr. Minsky will have no further claim against us or the Colonie Coliseum Summer Theatre.

Sincerely,

John A. Prescott

Accepted And Agreed To:

Irving Siders, for Harold Minsky

In the far upper left hand corner of this letter, in small print, and written in pencil, was: "Did not have permission to use the name Minsky."

The program in the folder reads: "Program Minsky's Follies, Colonial Inn, Hallandale, Florida." This also had the comment written in the corner: "Using the name without permission."

The last item was a copy of an advertisement attached to Harold Minsky's letterhead. The ad was from *Minsky's Burlesque of 1972*, performed at the Colonial Inn, at 6300 Gulf Boulevard, in St. Petersburg Beach, Florida. It reads: "By popular demand Frankie Mann returns to impersonate Flip Wilson, Buddy Hackett, Jackie Mason, Jerry Lewis, Herb Alpert, Harry James, and more." The show also featured: Denise Montego – Sophisticated Savage, Princess Laila – Belly Dancer, Art Daniels, and Clarence "Gatemouth" Jackson. The advertisement claimed it was "the best show in town," and goes on to give the hours, price, and a phone number. Outside of Denise Montego, it didn't sound like a Harold Minsky show to me at all.

The short newspaper article stapled to the page had a date of 1971 penciled on it, and it reads:

"Minsky, Inn Settle Suit; A suit by burlesque impresario Harold Minsky alleging that the Colonial Inn of St. Petersburg Beach fraudulently used his name has been settled out of court for an undisclosed amount.

"Settlement papers are being prepared for the approval of the United States District Court in Miami," said Joseph Pardo, Miami attorney for the Colonial Inn.

Minsky sued for more than $10,000 in damages when he learned last May that the resort was advertising its entertainment as "Minsky Burlesque."

"That was true," Pardo said, but the reason was that the show was run by G. Minsky Follies, Inc., a Miami corporation named for one of its stockholders. "The billing was discontinued at the request of Minsky," Pardo said, and was a move that expedited settlement out of court.

"The Colonial Inn found no benefit from the use of the name Minsky anyway," he said."

The next folder in the "M" File was labeled, "Music Fair, w/Martha Raye 1972; Painters Mill, Maryland, Shady Grove, Maryland, and Valley Forge, Pennsylvania." I was happy to find this material; I've always liked Martha Raye. The folder starts with a newspaper advertisement that reads:

"Harold Minsky needs girl-type girls to go on a four-month tour with Martha Raye. Auditions Tuesday, Performing Arts Studio, Commercial Center Arcade; showgirls and dancers, 1pm, girl singers, 3pm, Jerry Norman will choreograph."

There was only one actual newspaper article in the folder; the rest of the paperwork included contracts, financials, cast lists, and programs. So I am going to start with the article. It was dated October 11, 1972, and from *The Washington*

Post. The article, written by Megan Rosenfeld, was titled "Could This Be (Blush) Burlesque?" It reads as follows:

"LAS VEGAS – Everyone thinks he knows what a producer of burlesque looks like. He always wears a white tie and tails and a top hat, diamond cuff links and studs, and has two dolled-up cuties affixed to his arms at all times. He talks out of the side of his mouth and winks a lot.

But such is the tenor of our times that this character is with us no more – if indeed he ever was, outside of moving pictures. Just as burlesque shows have become almost family entertainment compared to what goes on in the movies these days – now that burlesque is neither bur-leekew nor burlesque but a show – producers are as sedate as bankers and perhaps more so.

Harold Minsky is a showgirl expert, one of a vanishing breed. His shows don't play in theatres anymore, (his father, the original Minsky, once owned seven of 17 burlesque theatres in New York City). They play in Las Vegas casinos, Playboy Clubs, or places orientated toward family entertainment like Shady Grove, where his newest revue opened last night.

Minsky has lived in Las Vegas for 15 years, where he seems to fit in just fine. He speaks, like almost all Las Vegas businessmen, with a slightly softened New York accent; "girl" comes out somewhere between "goil" and "gurl." For a man who's spent his entire adult life (he started the box office-stage manager-house manager route right after graduating from Columbus Grammar School) dealing with the flashiest part of show biz, he's very sedate. Aside from his diamond pinky ring, Minsky looks like a man who could be in the furniture business as easily as the burlesque business.

"In the old days we spent about $1,000 a show and we did a new show every week. Now we spend more like $100,000, but we only do two or three a year. A showgirl makes $265 a week for about five hours work a day, and they don't have to mingle with the customers or anything. The girls today treat it much more like a job – they come in, do their show, and go home. Actually, the old movie image of the gold digging showgirl wasn't very accurate – of course there were always the ones who were looking for live ones.

Yeah, I remember one of their favorite lines was to go up to a guy in the casino and say, 'Today is my birthday and I feel lucky.' So, he'd give her a hundred bucks; she'd play $25 and make $75 for herself.

Although, there was one I remember just like in the movies. She'd wear a polka dot dress and matching parasol and carry a little poodle – the whole bit. She married a very important guy who was Howard Hughes' right hand man. And there was this guy, dressed very conservative in a pin-striped suit and all, trailing around after her, carrying her bag. It was something to see."

Minsky says he never has any trouble getting showgirls. "Well, it's a pretty good job. You don't have to really do anything. You have to be pretty and have a good figure. And you have to have good breasts – they don't have to be big, but, you know, attractive, because they're bare breasted in the show. We never show total nudity though – I think something should be left to the imagination. And they have to be able to move a little. Our dancers are different; they have to have experience in jazz dancing or tap.

Yeah, I thought once the women's lib people attacked Hugh Hefner I'd be the next to go. But here's how I feel – my wife agrees with me, and she's very much a women's lib person, she subscribes to *Ms. Magazine* and everything – I feel that if a girl thinks there's anything immoral or wrong in my shows, she doesn't have to take the job. I don't hit anyone over the head to work for me."

Minsky's latest all-girl revue stars comedienne Martha Raye; although other female stars like Zsa Zsa Gabor, ("Boy! Was she terrible!"), and Jayne Mansfield, ("She was a very nice girl. Not too smart, but nice!"), have headlined the show, this is the first time a woman is taking the lead comic part. Originally, all the comics were men – the women were called "talking women" and were used primarily as set-ups and foils. Many of the old judge, doctor, and policeman sketches are being revived with Martha Raye as the judge, doctor, or what have you."

Autographed photo of Martha Raye from early 1970s. Courtesy: Authors Collection

The folder also contained a copy of the original Agreement between Minsky and Music Fair Enterprises, along with a copy of the Standard RIDER, which was dated and signed on July 24, 1972. It reads like many of the previous Agreements in this book, but I want to point out some of the specifics:

The show would be presented at: the Painters Mill Music Fair at Owings Mill, Maryland (Baltimore, Maryland suburb) on Tuesday, October 3, 1972 through Sunday, October 8, 1972; the Shady Grove Music Fair at Rockville, Maryland (Washington D.C. suburb) on Tuesday, October 10, 1972 through Sunday, October 15, 1972; and the Valley Forge Music Fair, Devon, Pennsylvania on Tuesday, October 17, 1972 through Sunday, October 22, 1972. At each location the show was to run for eight (8) shows weekly, and six (6) nights weekly with Mondays off.

The cast would consist of 19 performers, which included Martha Raye; as well as a musical conductor and stage manager. The cast also included: 12 dancers and showgirls, 2 striptease dancers, 1 singer, 1 comic, 1 straight man, and 1 straight woman. Minsky was also to supply all costumes, shoes, scenery, backdrops, props, music, and everything else that was standard in an Agreement for a show.

The following was very specific:

"Operator (Music Fair) shall furnish and pay for the orchestra consisting of ten (10) musicians for all rehearsals and performances. Rehearsals with the orchestra shall be four (4) hours the day prior to the opening and four (4) hours the day of the opening. Exact rehearsal time to be advised and exact instrumentation of orchestra to be advised. Rehearsal time is applicable to the Painters Mill engagement only; Shady Grove and Valley Forge rehearsal on opening day only, for four (4) hours."

Music Fair would provide all necessary personnel for the in-and-out of the theatres, plus hanging of the scenery, and operating the lights. They would also supply one (1) of each of the following: sound man, electrician, carpenter, prop man, and stagehand. Some things were scratched off and I believe the sound man was "not applicable."

I thought the following was also interesting:

"For and in consideration of the package "Musical Revue" as above described to be supplied and furnished by the Producer (Minsky), the Operator (Music Fair), hereby agrees to pay the Producer as follows:

Guarantee on Nineteen Thousand Dollars ($19,000.00) per week plus Fifty percent (50%) of gross receipts in excess of Fifty Nine Thousand Dollars ($59,000.00) per week plus Fifty Five percent (55%) of gross receipts in excess of Seventy Thousand Dollars ($70,000.00) per week. All monies will be payable to Patava, Inc., and delivered to Company Manager upon completion of each week."

Everything else was standard in a Minsky Agreement, but the last thing I found of interest was the billing arrangement.

"The exact billing of this show shall be as follows, in all advertising and publicity:

HAROLD MINSKY PRESENTS (50%)
MARTHA RAYE IN MINSKY BURLESQUE, 1972 (100%)"

The RIDER was a "Standard RIDER for Special Attractions." It covered the definition of Gross Receipts, and what happens if there is a strike, boycott,

"Act of God," or anything else the Producer may not be able to control. It also discusses programs and the sale of merchandise, and lastly "Area Restrictions." Area Restrictions were often covered in a Minsky Standard Agreement, not in a RIDER.

Another piece of paperwork in this folder was the AGVA Standard Form of Artists Engagement Contract signed between Martha Raye and Harold Minsky on July 6, 1972. It included the following RIDER:

Attached RIDER is hereby made a part and parcel of AGVA Contract #33775 dated July 6, 1972 between Patava, Inc., hereinafter called the "OPERATOR" and Martha Raye hereinafter called "ARTIST."

Engagements to be as follows:
Painters Mill, Owings Mill, MD – October 3, 1972, 1 week
Shady Grove, Gaithersburg, MD – October 10, 1972, 1 week
Valley Forge, Devon, PA – October 17, 1972, 1 week

Artist is to receive Seven Thousand ($7,000.00) dollars weekly, plus One Hundred ($100.00) dollars weekly, automobile allowance.

Ten (10%) percent commission is to be deducted weekly by Operator and sent to Coast Artists, Inc.

Martha Raye agrees to do sketches.
Billing to be as follows:
Harold Minsky (50%)
Presents
Martha Raye (100%)
In
Minsky's Follies (100%)
Or
Minsky's Burlesque (100%)
Accepted and Agreed to:
Martha Raye
Harold Minsky

Coast Artists, Inc. managed Martha Raye. They were located at 9454 Wilshire Boulevard, in Beverly Hills, California.

1976 Press Photo from when Martha Raye guest starred in "McMillan," a television series on NBC. Courtesy: Authors Collection

The full cast of the show included:
Comics – Dick Richards, Eddie Innes; Straight man – Ralph Clifford; Exotic dancers – Diane Lewis, Denise Montego; Talking woman – Paulette Powers; Production singer – Sharon Vanderbloom;

Lead dancers – Jerry Scott, Suzanne Vegas; and Adagio team – Jean and Marina. Dancers for the show were: Patti Smith, Marilyn O'Brien, Nancy Freidman, Judy Wallace, and Sandy Williams. The showgirls were: Janet Schoolcraft, Diane McGregor, Betty Jo Kaesen, Patti Gregory, and Lillian Langtree. Minsky was the producer and director; Jerry Norman staged and choreographed the show. The rest of the company included: Josephine Spinedi – costume design; costumes executed by Eastwood of Las Vegas; Frank W. Stevens – scenery; Ken Tiffany – musical arrangement; Marty Heim – musical conductor; and Jerry Lucas – company manager.

Painters Mill Music Fair, year unknown. Courtesy: baltimoresun.com

Notes in the folder included the following information. During the first week, at Painters Mill, the cast and crew would stay at the Townhouse Motel, in Pikeville, Maryland. The second week, at Shady Grove, they would stay at the Linden Hill Motel in Bethesda, Maryland. Lastly, the

Interior of Painters Mill Music Fair, year unknown. I believe all of the Music Fair buildings, inside and out, were similar in design. Courtesy: baltimoresun.com

third week, at Valley Forge Music Fair, the cast and crew would stay at the Tally Ho Motel, which was on the grounds of the theatre.

Also in the paperwork was a list of the various scenes, the order, and who would be doing what. Martha Raye appeared in two scenes, including: "A Day in Court," with Ralph Clifford, Eddie Innes, and Paulette Powers; and "Sloppy Joes," again with Clifford, Innes, and Powers. Raye also performed the closing act before intermission, accompanied by Marty Heim. There were three other scenes in the show: "St. James Infirmary," "Gaston," and "Double Trouble." Dick Richards appeared in "Gaston" and "Double Trouble." Denise Montego performed "Voo Doo Woman," and Diane Lewis performed "Bewitched and Beautiful."

Lastly, besides programs, there were two receipts for payment from the Music Fair. One dated October 8, 1972, which shows the week's gross receipts from the Painters Mill Music Fair to be $25,667.19, and the payment to Patava, Inc. was $19,000. The second was from the October 22, 1972 week's performance at the Valley Forge Music Fair. Gross receipts were $30,555.27, and again the payment to Patava, Inc. was $19,000. This receipt was signed by Jerry Lucas and Rick Gross.

(Notes: For those who need an introduction to Martha Raye, the following appeared as part of her obituary, which was published in *The New York Times* on October 20, 1994. It was titled "Martha Raye, 78, Singer and Comic Actress, Dies;" and written by Lawrence Van Gelder, then the senior editor of the Arts and Leisure weekly section at the newspaper.

"Miss Raye sang, she danced, she acted on Broadway, in Hollywood and on television, but the knockabout comic won perhaps her greatest renown as an indefatigable trouper who traveled thousands of miles through three wars to lift the morale of America's fighting forces.

"They ask so little and give so much," she said during the Vietnam War. "The least we can do back home here is give them the love, the respect and the dignity that they, our flag and our country deserve."

Her real name was Margie Yvonne Reed. She was born on August 27, 1916, into a show-business family in the charity ward of a hospital in Butte, Montana. Her father and mother, Pete Reed and the former Peggy Hooper, were Irish immigrants whose song-and-dance routine, under the name Reed and Hooper took them to carnivals and vaudeville houses around the United States.

"I didn't work until I was 3," Miss Raye was to say years later. "But after that, I never stopped."

Her mother taught her to read and write while the family, which also included her sister and brother, crisscrossed the country. From time to time, she attended schools in Montana, Chicago, and New York.

"Our home was in an old, broken down Pierce Arrow automobile which my father drove," Miss Raye remembered. "We put the scenery in the back seat and that was where we slept at night. We cooked on Sterno, and we went from town to town, looking for bookings."

She played burlesque houses, nightclubs and saloons, where she said she worked for tips only. "On a good night, I made a dollar," she said, "on a bad one, 25 cents."

At 15, she was singing, dancing, and clowning in a children's act. She picked the name Martha Raye from a phone book and piled up the credits. She was a member of the Benny Davis Revue and the Ben Blue Company, a trouper on the Loew's vaudeville circuit, a member of the Will Morrissey act, and a feature performer in *Earl Carroll's Sketchbook* and *Calling All Stars*.

Eventually she made her way to Hollywood. And on one of the Sunday nights when stars gathered and entertained one another at the Trocadero nightclub, she got a couple of her friends to play straight men to her comedy. Their names were Jimmy Durante and Joe E. Lewis. The producer Norman Taurog saw her perform, and the next day she was working with Bing Crosby on the 1936 film *Rhythm on the Range*. She did a slapstick drunk scene singing a song called "Mr. Paganini," and became a star overnight.

Press Photo from September 24, 1970; Jimmy Durante, 78, goes through his routine during one of his two shows a night at the Desert Inn Hotel in Las Vegas. Durante collapsed while working at the Frontier Hotel three months earlier. He died in 1980.
Courtesy: Authors Collection

Miss Raye appeared in films like *Waikiki Wedding*, *College Holiday*, *Give Me a Sailor*, *Hellzapoppin*, and *Keep 'em Flying*. In 1940, she starred on Broadway opposite Al Jolson in the revue *Hold Onto Your Hats*. She appeared on his radio show, and the programs of Eddie Cantor and Bob Hope.

During World War II, she began entertaining troops, and the 1944 film *Four Jill's in a Jeep* was based on a U.S.O. tour of bases in England and Africa she made in the company of Kay Francis, Carole Landis, and Mitzi Mayfair.

In 1969, the Academy of Motion Picture Arts and Sciences gave Miss Raye the Jean Hersholt Humanitar-

Milton Berle and Martha Raye, in uniform, backstage at The Hollywood Palace in 1966. Courtesy: Walt Disney Television

ian Award for her wartime efforts, and she was given the Presidential Medal of Freedom in 1993.

She was not happy about her Hollywood career, except for *Monsieur Verdoux*, Charlie Chaplin's controversial 1947 black comedy about a Parisian Bluebeard who marries and kills for money. "I must have made 35 or 40 movies and most of them were mindless," Miss Raye said. "But in those days actors didn't fight the system, back then we thought we were lucky to be under contract."

Her performance in *Monsieur Verdoux*, in which she portrayed Annabella Bonheur, a raucous, indestructible wife of the killer, was praised as brilliant by Bosley Crowther of *The New York Times*. "Do you know," she recalled in 1972, "that when Chaplin called to offer me the part, I hung up on him; I thought it was a joke."

Press Photo from 1947 of Charlie Chaplin in the film Monsieur Verdoux. *Courtesy:* Los Angeles Times

She blamed her decline in Hollywood on executives who focused on her shapely legs and ability to fill out a sweater. "They tried to make a glamour girl out of me," the brown-haired, blue-eyed actress complained. "Let's face it, I'm not a glamour girl. I'm a clown."

Despite her setbacks in Hollywood, she was far from finished. Milton Berle gave her a start in television, and by 1954, she was the medium's reigning female comedian. Ahead of her was more success in nightclubs, cabaret, and theatre.

Offstage, life was darker. "As an entertainer, she's a genius," one of her colleagues once said. "Socially, she's completely unsure of herself."

She married again and again. Among her husbands were the makeup artist Buddy Westmore, composer David Rose, businessman Neal Lang, dancers Nick Condos and Edward Begley, and policeman Robert O'Shea. Her last marriage was in 1991, to Mark Harris, her manager. She had a daughter, Melody, by Mr. Condos. In her later years, many people knew Miss Raye as the star of Polident commercials."

And now more about Music Fair Enterprises:

On April 12, 1955, radio broadcaster Frank Ford and nightclub owner Lee Guber went ahead with their wives' idea to create musical performances in a tent, which they called Music Fair Enterprises, Inc. Together with Shelly Gross, a television news anchor, the men raised the $100,000 they needed to get started by asking 100 friends to each contribute $1,000. Once the funds were raised,

Valley Forge Music Fair. Courtesy: Radnor Historical Society

they leased the Devon, Pennsylvania site, at the intersection of Route 202 and Route 83, which they named the Valley Forge Music Fair.

Construction was under way by early May 1955 for a bowl-shaped amphitheater at the west end of the area. It had a round, revolving stage in the center surrounded by terraced seating for more than 1,600 people over which a striped waterproof tent was erected. The tent, which was supported by 18 poles located throughout, meant some seats had obstructed views. Buildings and parking to compliment the theatre were also constructed.

The first season opened on June 23, 1955 with *Guys and Dolls*, starring Pat Harrington and Marilyn Ross. There were nine other summer stock musical shows that season, along with four shows for children. The entire first season of the Valley Forge Music Fair saw a profit of $52,000.

The success of their facility in Devon led to efforts to replicate the model, with the creation of other music fairs in suburban locations on the East Coast. An abandoned lime pit in Westbury, New York became the site of their second facility. The Westbury Music Fair, established in 1956, also originally housed in

Vintage photo of the Westbury Music Fair. Courtesy: newsday.com

Exterior of the Westbury Music Fair in Westbury, New York. It is still in operation. Courtesy: newsday.com

a tent, could accommodate 1,850 people and was developed for an investment of $150,000. In 1966, a concrete theatre-in-the-round building was constructed on the site, which cost a million dollars and could seat an audience of 3,000. It is still in operation.

In 1957, the men bought the Camden County Music Fair, also a tent complex, by the Cooper River in Cherry Hill, New Jersey; and in 1959, the group created the Storrowton Music Fair in West Springfield, Massachusetts. In later years they would open the Painters Mills Music Fair, in the Baltimore area, as well as the Shady Grove Music Fair in the Washington, D.C. area.

Initially, the idea was to use the music fairs on a rotating basis for performances by the road companies of Broadway musical shows. However, during the 1960s, musical tastes were changing and the chain began booking: rock, pop, jazz, soul, country, family, and comedy performers.

A vast amount of performers played the theatres. There were also "one-night" concert series that included the *Giants of Jazz* concert with Dave Brubeck, Stan Getz, and Dizzy Gillespie; and the *Golden Boys of Bandstand* concert with Frankie Avalon, Fabian, and Bobby Rydell.

Frank Ford left the group in the 1960s; and Lee Guber died suddenly in 1988. In 1992, beginning with the 38th season, Shelly Gross turned over the presidency of the Music Fair Group, Inc. to his son Rick Gross, who had been working at the Valley Forge Music Fair since his high school days. He felt Rick knew the contemporary music scene better and would make regular trips to view entertainers in all segments of the market and decide which of these the local audiences would prefer.

Even though, by 1996, the land where the Valley Forge Music Fair stood had a higher value as a supermarket, a full season was booked. The final performance at the Valley Forge Music Fair was the annual *Kenny Rogers Christmas Show* on December 19, 1996. After announcing the closing of the theatre, Gross recalled being conflicted, and having mixed emotions. It was reported he said, "It was like watching your mother-in-law drive off a cliff in your brand-new Mercedes." In May 1997 the Valley Forge Music Fair was demolished. The site of the theatre was to be replaced by a giant supermarket, which closed after only 16 months in business. It is now the site of the Valley Fair Complex.

Sheldon Harvey "Shelly" Gross was born on May 20, 1921, and died on June 19, 2009. Lee Guber was born on November 20, 1920, and died on March 27, 1988. Guber and Gross, old school-mates, built their business to become one of the biggest purveyors of live entertainment. The pair ran a concert division that arranged performances nationwide, including traveling productions of Broadway theatre hits.

Edward Felbin was a radio broadcaster widely known as Frank Ford. Felbin was born on September 30, 1916, and died on March 3, 2009. He hosted a late-night talk show on WPEN, becoming one of the first radio shows to use equipment that would allow the host to interact with callers on the air, unlike previous shows that had the host repeat the caller's comments. Guests on Ford's programs during his career included: Lenny Bruce, Abbie Hoffman, Sugar Ray Robinson, and Eleanor Roosevelt.)

The next folders in the "M" File were simply labeled "Music;" there were a couple music folders. One contained copies of the original scores from the movie *The Night They Raided Minsky's*. Material from the second folder is what follows. It may be difficult to record so the information is understood. There were a lot of handwritten notes throughout, some of which were hard to read. Those notes were also added by more than a few people – the handwriting is different on numerous pages.

I will start with the typed out list that was simply titled "Music." In the upper right hand corner, written in pencil, were the words, "Wardrobe Room Copy." There were notes all over the seven page document. The information below, that's in all CAPS, is what was typed on the document; the notes, which were written in pencil or pen, are in small letters and in parentheses. There were several additional pages of information that lists the running order and cues from several shows, as well as where the shows were performed. The years mentioned, according to the notes, mean the music was used in shows that were produced during those years. If UNLV is included in the notes, I assume the actual music was given to the school in the Minsky collection. The music was not in the Files given to the BHS. So let's begin. It reads:

MUSIC

A:
ALL OF YOU (VOCAL AND DANCE ORCHESTRATION)
    (3 Arrangements; Edwards 12/7/1961; 1958 and 1961; UNLV)
ACE IN THE HOLE (Hollywood; UNLV)
A MAN AROUND THE PAD (Thunderbird; 1st show; 1968)
AIN'T NECESSARILY SO (Harold Minsky, arranger; copy; 8/58; UNLV)
AFRO DANCE (Maxim; 1978)
ANDROID (Space number; Aladdin)
ARABESQUE (Thunderbird; 1st show; 2nd show; 1968) (2 Arrangements)
AFTER TODAY (Thunderbird; 2nd show; 1968)
ASK YOURSELF WHY (Aladdin; 1970)
ALL IS FAIR IN LOVE (1975)

B:
BEE BOOM (Slipper; 2nd show; Finale I – II; 1968)
BLUES OPENING - 1 AND 2 (SLIPPER) (California; 1966; Slipper;
    1st show; 1968)
BLUES FOR OPENING #4
BANGKOK COCK FIGHT (Dunes; Harold Minsky, arranger; 1958;
    UNLV)
BEGIN THE BEGUINE (crossed out in pencil; UNLV)
BAUBLES, BANGLES & BEADS (Dunes – Kismet; 1958; UNLV)
BRAZIL (and Reprise)
BUSY AS A BEE (copy cat; UNLV)
BIG MAMA CASS OVERTURE (Aladdin; 1969) (2 Arrangements,
    Overture, and extra parts)
BEAUTIFUL GIRLS (Dunes; Harold Minsky, arranger; 1958; UNLV)
BAREFOOT CONTESSA (Dunes; 1958; Bill Reddie – composer and
    arranger; UNLV)
BECAUSE OF YOU (Dunes; Registered 1957; UNLV)
BELLE OF THE BALL (Dunes; 1958; UNLV)
BEAUTIFUL BABY (Thunderbird; 2nd show; 1968)
BLUES FOR SCORPIO (Aladdin; 1970) (3 Arrangements)
BARNEY DOES IT ALL (Thunderbird; 2nd show; strip; 1968)

(The) BEAT GOES ON (Thunderbird; 2nd show; 1968)
BLACK MAGIC WOMAN
BLACK AND TAN FANTASY (Aladdin; 1973)
BLUES TO STRIP BY

C:
CINDY PART 2 (Home Cindy)
CARMEN (ARAGONESA, GYPSY SONG, HABANERA & TOREADOR SONG) (Dunes; 1958; UNLV)
CHERIE TANGO (Dunes; Harold Minsky, arranger; Registered 1956; UNLV)
CAKE WALK (Dunes; Pinky Lee; 1958; UNLV)
CUBAN EPISODE (Dunes; Bill Reddie, arranger; 1958; UNLV)
CALYPSO (Dunes; 1958; UNLV)
C'EST SI BON (Dunes; 1958; UNLV)
CA C'EST PAREE (UNLV)
CHAMPS ELYSEES (Dunes; Harold Minsky, arranger; Registered 1956; UNLV)
CARAVAN (Slipper; 2nd show; 1968)
CLEO'S ASP
CHICO (Thunderbird; 1967)
CHEERS (THUNDERBIRD SHOW) (Finale; 1967)
CHEERS OVERTURE (Thunderbird; 1st show; 1968)
COMIN' HOME BABY (Aladdin; 1970)
CHANNEL ISLAND (Aladdin; 1970) (2 Arrangements)
CENTRAL PARK NORTH (Aladdin; Finale; 1970)
CHANNEL ONE (Aladdin; Bill Reddie; 1969) (2 Arrangements)
CELEBRATION (Aladdin and Fremont)
CHEAPER TO KEEP HER
CHELSEA BRIDGE (Aladdin)
CINNAMON & CLOVE (THUNDERBIRD SHOW) (1967; 1st show; 1968) (2 Arrangements)
CITY OF BRASS (2 Arrangements)
CITY OF VEILS (PIANO ONLY; UNLV)
CORAZONE (1975)
CLOVE IN F MINOR

D:
DAN MAGREW (Slipper; 1ST show; 1968)
DAN MAGREW FINALE
DIE FLEDERMAUS WALTZ (Dunes; 1958; UNLV)
DRIVE MY CAR (2 Arrangements)

DON'T CHA' HEAR ME (Aladdin; 1970) (2 Arrangements)
DYNOMITE (1977)
DID YOU EVER STOP
E:
ESO BESO (Bosa Nova)
EBB TIDE (Dunes; 8/58; UNLV)
EBB TIDE REPRISE (Dunes; 1958; UNLV)
EASY TO LOVE (copy cat; UNLV)
ENTERTAINER (2 Arrangements)
EL CUMBANCHERO (STOCK MUSIC) (crossed out in pencil)
EVIL WAYS (Thunderbird; 1967; 1st show; 1968)
EVERYONE'S GONE TO THE MOON (Aladdin)
EASE ON DOWN THE ROAD (1977)
EXTRA PARTS
F:
FANTAIL
FROM THIS MOMENT ON (copy cat; UNLV)
FRENZY (TEMPEST STORM) (1958; UNLV)
FATE (Dunes; copy cat; UNLV)
FRENCH NO. (Dunes; Bill Reddie – arranger; 1958; UNLV)
FUNNY FEELING
FEELING GOOD (VOCAL)
FEELING
FACE
FOR ME (Aladdin; 1970) (4 Arrangements)
FABULOUS PLACES (Thunderbird; 2nd show; 1968) (3 Arrangements)
FANFARE (4/58)
FLIGHT MUSIC
G:
(The) GIRL I'M NEAR
GI GI (DARLING) (UNLV)
G MINOR PRELUDE (UNLV)
GIMBELS BASEMENT BLUES (Dunes; Bill Reddie – music and lyrics; 1958; UNLV)
GET MY KICKS
GOODBYE YESTERDAY (Aladdin; 1969) (2 Arrangements)
GROOVIN' HARD (Aladdin; 1973)
GET DANCIN' (1977)
H:
HYMM TO THE SUN (Harold Minsky, arranger; UNLV)

HOORAY TO HOLLYWOOD (UNLV)
HAJJI BABA (Thunderbird; 2nd show; 1968) (3 Arrangements)
HOLLER (circled in pencil)
HIGHER AND HIGHER (1977) (2 Arrangements)
HIGHER

I:
IN CROWD
I MET A GIRL (Dunes; 1957; UNLV) (2 Arrangements)
I FEEL PRETTY (Dunes; 1958; UNLV)
I MUST KNOW
IF I EVER LEAVE YOU (STOCK MUSIC) (crossed out in pencil; UNLV)
IT'S TODAY
I'LL TAKE ROMANCE (crossed out in pencil; UNLV)
I BELIEVE IN YOU (Thunderbird; 2nd show; 1968) (3 Arrangements)
IN THE MOOD (1977)
I FEEL THE EARTH MOVE (Aladdin; 1973) (2 Arrangements)
I'M A WOMAN (1975) (3 Arrangements)
I'VE GOT THE MUSIC IN ME (1975)
I LOVE MAKING LOVE TO YOU (2 Arrangements)
I BELIEVE IN MUSIC (1975)
I HONESTLY LOVE YOU (1975)

J:
JUST ONE OF THOSE THINGS (crossed out in pencil)
JET (Dunes; 1958)
JAMES BOND

K:
KILLER JOE (Aladdin; 1970) (3 Arrangements)
KEEP ON SINGING
KUNG FU FIGHTING (1976) (2 Arrangements)

L:
LOVE (Slipper; 2nd show; 1968)
LOVE FOR SALE (Bosa Nova)
LOVE IS A GAMBLE
LA BELLE HELENE (CAN CAN) (Dunes; Registered 1956; UNLV)
LES GIRLS (copy; 4/58)
LES GIRLS REPRISE
LOVER (Dunes; 1958; UNLV)
LOVER REPRISE (Dunes; 1958)
LIVE IT UP
LA BAMBA (New York)

LA BAMBA REPRISE
LESGINKA (UNLV)
LEGS, LEGS, LEGS
LOOK AROUND (Aladdin; 1969) (3 Arrangements)
LITTLE BIT OF SOUL (Aladdin; 1969)
LADDER BLUES (Opener; Bill Reddie)
LOVE STORY (Maxim; 1978)
LADY MARMALADE (1975) (3 Arrangements)
(Bad, Bad) LEROY BROWN (1975) (2 Arrangements)
LOVE FOR RENT (Aladdin)
LIVE AND LET DIE (1975) (4 Arrangements)
LOVE'S THEME

M:

MAS QUE NADA
MAID IN FRANCE (ONE OF THOSE SONGS)
MINSKY FINALE (ASSORTED) (Finale, Reprise; Bill Reddie – composer and arranger; 11/57; UNLV)
MINSKY A GO-GO (Slipper; 1st show; 1968)
MINSKY SHAKE (Dunes; Fanfare, Opening and Reprise; Bill Reddie – composer and arranger; 1957; UNLV)
MLLE DE PARIS
MISIRLOU
MOUNTAIN HIGH – VALLEY LOW (UNLV)
(The) MOST BEAUTIFUL GIRL IN THE WORLD (STOCK MUSIC) (UNLV)
MACARTHUR PARK (Thunderbird; 2nd show; 1968) (3 Arrangements)
MONITOR THEME (Thunderbird; 2nd show; 1968)
MINSKY PART 2 (Bill Reddie; to "Hub Caps and Tail Lights;" 1957)
(The) MAN I LOVE (STOCK MUSIC) (crossed out in pencil; UNLV)
MARION'S DITTY
MAMBO HABANERO (STOCK) (UNLV)

N:

NIGHT IN TUNISIA (crossed out in pencil; UNLV)
(The) NIGHT (Dunes; Harold Minsky, arranger; 1958; UNLV)
(The) NIGHT HAS A THOUSAND EYES (UNLV)
NOTHING CAN STOP ME NOW (2 Arrangements)
NO OTHER LOVE (3 Arrangements)
NEVER ON SUNDAY (STOCK MUSIC) (crossed out in pencil; UNLV)
NIGHT OF NIGHTS (Dunes; UNLV)
NIGHT OWL (1975) (2 Arrangements)

O:
ONE STEP ABOVE
ONE HELL OF A WOMAN (1977) (2 Arrangements)
ONCE YOU GET IT (1975)
OPENING & OPENING CREDITS (SLIPPER) (1966; 1st show; 1968)
OBA (Bosa Nova)
ORIENTAL NO. WITH ORIENTAL REPRISE, OPENING, AND PROLOGUE (Dunes; 1958; UNLV) (2 Arrangements)
OPENER 78 (Maxim; 1978)
OPENER PART 2
OPENER LAST PART
OPENING – MUSIC AND LYRICS (Dunes; Bill Reddie; 1958; UNLV)

P:
POSSIBILITIES
POWDER MY BACK (Slipper; 1st show; 1968) (2 Arrangements)
PARIS JAZZ DANCE (Opening)
PANT SIZE 50 (Maxim; 1978)
PARTY'S OVER (8/58; UNLV)
POMP AND CIRCUMSTANCE (STOCK MUSIC) (crossed out in pencil; UNLV)
PARIS OUI OUI (Dunes; Harold Minsky, arranger; Registered 1956; UNLV)
PADAM PADAM (Dunes; Harold Minsky, arranger; Registered 1956; UNLV)
PARIS HOLIDAY (Harold Minsky, arranger; UNLV)
PLASTERED IN PARIS (Harold Minsky, arranger; UNLV)
(The) PAPER MAN (Aladdin; 1970) (3 Arrangements)
PARTY'S OVER (Dunes; 1958)
PERSIAN MARKET

Q:
QUIET VILLAGE - INTRO
QUIET VILLAGE (2/58)

R:
ROLLIN' ROCK (UNLV)
RHAPSODY IN BLUE (crossed out in pencil; UNLV)
REAL LIVE GIRL (Slipper; 2nd show; 1968)
RISING SUN
RICKY-TICK (1972) (2 Arrangements)
REAL GOOD PEOPLE (1975) (2 Arrangements)
ROLLER DERBY (2 Arrangements)

S:

SATIN DOLL (Slipper; 1st show; 1968)
SHE LOVES ME (Slipper; 2nd show; 1968) (3 Arrangements)
SOMETHING BIG
STREET SCENE (Dunes; 1958; UNLV)
STREET SCENE OPENER (Dunes; Harold Minsky, arranger; 1958; UNLV)
(The) STRIP SONG (Dunes; Bill Reddie; 1957-58; AND 1962; With Tag; UNLV) (2 Arrangements)
START OF SOMETHING (UNLV)
SPLANKY (Thunderbird; 1967; 1st show; 1968)
SPELLBOUND (Dunes; 1958; UNLV)
SHANGRI LA (STOCK MUSIC) (crossed out in pencil; UNLV)
S'WONDERFUL (La Vaughn and Maximilian)

(Notes: La Vaughn and Maximilian were a tap dancing team from Boston.)

SHOUTIN' AGAIN
SO MUCH LOVING (1967)
SOME OF THESE DAYS (1958)
ST. PETERSBURG RACE (Aladdin; 1970) (3 Arrangements)
SHAFT (Aladdin)
(NEW) SHAFT (1977) (3 Arrangements)
SCARF DANCE (Maxim; 1978)
SHOW ME A MAN (1975) (3 Arrangements)
STEAM HEAT (1977) (2 Arrangements)
SOMETHING'S GOTTA GIVE (1975)
SONG OF INDIA (UNLV)
T:
TAKE 10 TERRIFIC GIRLS (BUT ONLY 9 COSTUMES) (Thunderbird; 1968) (Notes: From the 1968 film *The Night They Raided Minsky's*, sung by Dexter Maitland. The film featured original songs by Charles Strouse and Lee Adams. Check out "The Muppets" version of this song on YouTube.)
TOI, TOI, BIGUINE WITH YOU (DUET AND VOCAL SOLO) (Dunes; Harold Minsky, arranger; Registered 1956; UNLV)
TROPICALE (FROM JAMAICA) (2 Arrangements)
TROPICALE REPRISE
TAKE FIVE
THIS MUST BE THE PLACE (Dunes; Bill Reddie, music and lyrics; 1958; UNLV)
THAT REMINDS ME

TWISTED IMAGE (UNLV)
THIN MAN
THANK HEAVEN FOR LITTLE GIRLS (Dunes; 1958; UNLV)
THIS DREAM (THUNDERBIRD SHOW) (3 Arrangements)
   (Irv Gordon)

(Notes: Irving Gordon was a songwriter who was born on February 14, 1915, and died on December 1, 1996. Abbott and Costello often performed a baseball comedy routine, "Who's on First?," which they perfected during their years in burlesque. Gordon has been credited with writing "Who's on First?" although others have also claimed authorship; most notably longtime Abbott and Costello gag writer John Grant.)

TRACKS (Aladdin; 1969) (4 Arrangements)
TRAVELING ON (Thunderbird; 1st show; 2nd show; 1968) (2 Arrangements)
TEMPTATION (STOCK MUSIC) (crossed out in pencil; UNLV)
TANGA BOO GONK (Aladdin; 1973)
TIP TAP (UNLV)
U:
USHKA DARA (Aladdin; 1973)
V:
VEGAS NO. (WALK OUT) (Dunes; Bill Reddie; 1958; UNLV)
VEGAS NO. 1ST OVERTURE (Dunes; Bill Reddie; 1958; UNLV)
VEGAS NO. 2ND OVERTURE (Dunes; Bill Reddie; 1958; UNLV)
VOO DOO (Dunes; Harold Minsky, arranger; UNLV)
VALLEY OF THE DOLLS (Aladdin; 1969) (2 Arrangements)
VOCALS - MISCELLANEOUS
W:
WHY NOT (Slipper) (2 Arrangements)
WHAT THE WORLD
WHERE'S THE MENS ROOM (Dunes; Bill Reddie, music and lyrics; 1958; UNLV)
WHAT'D I SAY (Slipper; 2nd show; 1968)
WONDERFUL DAY LIKE TODAY
WINE, WOMEN & SONG (Dunes; Bill Reddie, music and lyrics; 1958; UNLV)
WALTZ AT MAXIMS (Dunes; Harold Minsky, arranger; 1958; from Gigi; UNLV)
WOMEN – WOMEN (Harold Minsky, arranger; Registered 1957-1958; UNLV)

WAR DANCE (Harold Minsky, arranger; UNLV)
WOMEN (Bosa Nova) (2 Arrangements)
WALKING HAPPY (Slipper; 1st show; 1968) (2 Arrangements)
WILD HONEY (2 Arrangements)
WACK-WACK (THUNDERBIRD SHOW) (1967; 1st show; 1968) (2 Arrangements)
WHERE IT'S AT (Aladdin; 1969) (2 Arrangements)
(The) WAY WE WERE
WINNING THE WEST (Aladdin; 1973)
WE'VE LOVED BEFORE (Aladdin; 1973) (2 Arrangements)
WITCHY WOMAN (1977) (2 Arrangements)
WAITING FOR THE ROBERT E. LEE

Y:
YES I CAN (Slipper) (2 Arrangements)
YOU MUST HAVE BEEN A BEAUTIFUL BABY
YOU CAN LEAVE YOUR HAT ON
YOU'RE NO GOOD (1975)
YOU AND ME AGAINST THE WORLD (1977)

Z:
ZING WENT THE STRINGS (Dunes; crossed out in pencil; 1958; UNLV)

OTHER FILES:
BOWS (BOW MUSIC 1 & 2)
FANFARES
ODD NUMBERS
REPRISES (SANDS OF TIME)
STRAYS
TAGS (STRANGER IN PARADISE TAG) (RACHMANINOFF TAG)
SHEET MUSIC
MUSIC NOT FILED
THUNDERBIRD SHOW

OPENING:
I BELIEVE IN YOU
BARNEY (STRIP NO.) BOY AND GIRL
TRAVEL ON

EAST INDIAN NO.
ARABESQUE
FABULOUS PLACES
HAJI BABA
MACARTHER PARK

FINALE:

MONITOR THEME
AFTER TODAY
BEAT GOES ON
<u>ALADDIN (FIRST SHOW '69):</u>
BIG MAMA CASS
WHERE IT'S AT
LITTLE BIT OF SOUL
CHANNEL 1
VALLEY OF THE DOLLS
GOODBYE YESTERDAY
TRACKS (THE OTHER SIDE OF)
LOOK AROUND
FIGHT SCENE MUSIC

Handwritten at the bottom was a listing of orchestration books: "Holliday for Strings," "From This Moment On," "Lisbon Antigua," "One O'Clock Jump," and "Oye Negra" (Latin). Music from *The Night They Raided Minsky's* was also written in pencil at the end of the list. I believe all of this music was given to UNLV with the Minsky collection.

(Notes: Considering how often Bill Reddie was mentioned in the list of music, it was not easy locating information on him.

William Henry "Bill" Reddie, was born in 1925 and became the founder of "Channel 1 Records." Reddie, was a longtime Las Vegas composer, musician, and musical director at the Dunes Hotel who would ultimately succeed Antonio Morelli as the Sand's music director. Morelli was credited with bringing classical music to Las Vegas, as well as being the music director for several Broadway musicals. Morelli was perhaps most well known for serving as orchestra leader for the famous Sands Hotel Copa Room in its Rat Pack heyday from 1954 through 1971. Antonio Morelli was born on July 22, 1904, and died on June 17, 1974.

As I continued the search it kept taking me to Buddy Rich. Bill Reddie penned perhaps Buddy Rich's most popular big band arrangement of a medley derived from Leonard Bernstein's *West Side Story*. The medley, a complex big band arrange-

Antonio Morelli. Courtesy: Las Vegas Review-Journal

ment, highlights Rich's ability to blend the rhythm of his drumming into his band's playing of the music. Rich originally received the medley arrangement in the mid-1960s and found it quite challenging. Bill Reddie received a 1968 Grammy Award nomination for his arrangement for the Buddy Rich Orchestra. Buddy Rich continued touring and performing until the end of his life. He was born on September 30, 1917, and died on April 2, 1987.

Cover of Fabulous Las Vegas Magazine *from August 5, 1950. Courtesy: C.F. Miller*

I also found a listing for a novelty album featuring Jayne Mansfield, which was produced in 1962 by 20th Century-Fox. It is a recording of her show *The House of Love* at the Dunes Hotel called "Jayne Mansfield Busts Up Las Vegas." Other artists on the album are Arthur Blake, Mickey Hargitay, and the Bill Reddie Orchestra; Bill Reddie conducting. Jayne Mansfield was born on April 19, 1933, and died on June 29, 1967.

The following was from a popular old Las Vegas magazine, *Fabulous Las Vegas.* Jack Cortez founded the magazine in December of 1946 and published it until his death in 1967. His wife Etta took over and ran the magazine until 1972. It's from an article Jack Cortez wrote in December 1964. You may want to read the entire article, "Bill Reddie – The Musician's Musician," which appears on lvstriphistory.com.

"Bill (a member of ASCAP) has composed and arranged music for choreographers and recording companies, and his star clientele includes such luminaries as: Betty Grable, Jayne Mansfield, Tony Bennett, Connie Francis, Eleanor Powell, Frankie Laine, Patti Page, *The Ed Sullivan Show, The Danny Thomas Show,* Debra Paget, Phil Harris, Hal Roach, Steve Allen, etc. These are but a fraction of the numerous credits that bear the Reddie signature.

Not only has Bill originated several large symphonic works, he created the entire original score for "Le Lido de Paris" at the Dunes Hotel, where he and his orchestra execute the inspiring musical background."

Cortez asked Reddie several questions; I'm only including three. Cortez: "In planning a musical score for a new Las Vegas show, which do you consider more important to the establishment of the correct mood, original music or recognizable old standards?"

In response, Reddie said: "Both. However, it depends on the type of show it is and what it is trying to convey to the audience. My own preferences lean toward original music for two reasons. First, I do not believe in the kind of negative thinking that proclaims an audience will not accept something new. Secondly, I feel that all of this adherence to nostalgia (no reflection on Christmas songs) has been overdone to the point of nausea. However, I have found that if the original music is good, the audience will accept it. Also consider that if original scores were detrimental to success, we would not have such things as Broadway musicals. Some of our best music has originated in this medium."

Cortez: "So much of your writing has been for choreographers and dancers. How important is music to the choreographer?"

Reddie: "Everything or nothing, depending on the individual. I would suggest a different wording of your question, however. It would be better to ask, 'To what degree of importance is the choreographer to the music?' Here, we reach the crux of the matter. The simple fact is that a good choreographer knows how to use good music to the best advantage. Good music serves as an inspiration to the choreographer. Conversely, an insensitive choreographer can literally destroy a good piece of music by insisting that it conform to conditions that are alien to a good performance."

Lastly, Cortez asks: "Why is it that there are so many good writers of music, yet only a relative few who gain national prominence?"

Reddie: "In many cases the successful writer possesses a unique style that appeals to a lot of people. Don't rule out the lucky breaks that come along. I would venture to say that one reason the condition exists is because the successful writer understands his clients and they, him. When planning the music for his clients, the writer leaves nothing to chance, no stone unturned. The result makes everyone happy and a healthy reputation is established.")

The final "M" folder was labeled, "Maxim, Las Vegas." In 1978, after Harold's death, Pat Minsky was the Associate Producer of a show at the Maxim. The information that follows is about Pat, and that Maxim show. Everything in this folder came from newspapers.

The first item was from a Joe Delaney column that ran in the *Las Vegas Sun* on July 28, 1978, and reads:

"Warm Maxim Showroom Offers Hot Minsky Show: *Minsky's Burlesque Follies* opened Tuesday at the Maxim Hotel with top banana Irv Benson; multi-faceted Jerry Lucas as straight man plus and excelling in every department; one of the best ecdysiasts in Cassandra Lee and a second femme banana peeler, Cimmaron, who is really quite different; a lead lady dancer, and two lads and five lassies who move extremely well.

The ingredients here are all first quality and the mix is vintage Minsky; the room is a warm, intimate 180-seater and the price, by LV standards, is right… With vacations and occasional cast changes, the show could run indefinitely.

Benson's timing, delivery, and reactions are impeccable examples of comedy playing; we have never enjoyed him better than here with Lucas as his foil… Our town should never be without a Minsky show; Tuesday night was an enjoyable 75 minutes of what was and what should be, always."

The next article may also be from July 28, 1978. Neither this, nor the Delaney piece, were from the original newspapers; they were copies. The following was written by A. Wilbur Stevens and titled "Maxim's Minsky Best Burlesque." It reads:

"The ladies are taking off and delightfully not running at the Maxim with the opening of *Minsky's Burlesque Follies*. As produced and directed by the ebullient Jerry Lucas, with the lovely Patricia Minsky as Associate Producer, this show certainly carries on the Minsky tradition for burlesque at its daring best. The costumes by Golda Eastwood are appropriately spectacular and lavish.

Meticulous and original choreography and staging by Betty Francisco highlight some of the changes which have emerged in burlesque in recent years. The company is highly trained, and the variety of effects which are realized in a lounge setting are amazing and, of course, more than titillating. Sex marches on.

Still, the "old" burlesque bawdiness is still here with a wallop in the person of Irving Benson, one of the last of the classic comics, whose bullet-like timing genius for the pregnant pause and never emptied bag of blue tricks had the opening night audiences falling under the tables. Benson is abetted in his hilarity by Jerry Lucas as straight man. Benson works in a kind of ancient jump suit, or

Irving Benson. Courtesy: Pat Elliott Minsky/Burlesque Historical Society

maybe it's an old-fashioned janitor's costume. As he says, "I'm just put together sloppy." In between his regular lines he heckles the audience. Some of his jokes go back to King Tut, but the audience loves it. Example:

Girl: "I'm game."

Benson: "You're a little out of season."

Casting for burlesque, especially with a comparatively small company, is a knotty problem. The company must sustain, tease, and interest. The present ensemble often gives the illusion of being greater in numbers than they are. The combinations are fairly traditional, but the versatility is exceptional. The nude dancers are Laurel Mock, Teri Gambino, Zoe Marshall, and Denise Esola (a real comer). The two boys are Kurt Sproul and Ron Ruge, well-known in strip dance circles. The lead dancer is impressive Michelle Demaria who is featured, among other numbers, in a superb adagio, the music from "Love Story," possibly the most exacting number of the show.

So you want to hear about the strips? Well, there's an exotic, most recently out of an acrobatic stint at the Royal Inn, named, simply, Cimmaron. (She told me she once used the name Cinnamon.) She does a "Little Red Riding Hood" which you won't find in all the story books, and culminates her proceedings with more acrobatics. And there is the stunning show-stopper, Cassandra Lee, who has been wowing them up to this engagement at the Jolly Trolley. Her work (for such it is) is artfully quiet at first and then breaks out into a silvery Dionysian riot. Using a red velvet suit and a fan, she moves through innumerable strip variations of Herbie Mann's "Cajun Moon."

Thus the company of eleven, working on the small stage of the Allegro Room of the Maxim, revives memories of the numerically larger Minsky shows of the past. The quality and excitement are still here."

(Notes: The Maxim Hotel and Casino originally opened on July 1, 1977; located at 160 E. Flamingo Road, it had 800 rooms. It was known for its lowered-floor casino and glittery lights that gave it the look of a disco club. Though smaller than typical Las Vegas resorts, the Maxim had a popular following because of its attention to personal service. It thrived during the 1980s, but went into decline as larger resorts opened on the nearby Strip. The hotel has since changed hands many times. Rapper Tupac Shakur, a passenger in a car, was shot in front of the Maxim in 1996; he later died from his injuries.)

The following article, published in *The Valley Times* on August 24, 1978, was also included in this folder. I really like the Abraham Lincoln quote that was printed on the newspaper's banner. "Stand with anybody that stands right. Stand with him while he is right, and part with him when he is wrong." The newspaper was published in North Las Vegas and cost 15 cents per copy. The article, "By Minsky's Widow – Burlesque Tradition Carried on in Vegas," was written by David Dearing, a staff writer. It reads:

"The acting credits for a recent University of Nevada, Las Vegas theatre production of the Greek tragedy, *The Bacchae*, included a junior theatre art major from Las Vegas by the name of Patricia Minsky.

It is doubtful that anyone would associate the Minsky name with a Greek drama and few people probably made the connection with the legendary burlesque king by the name of Minsky.

But in addition to her fulltime studies at the university, Patricia Minsky is carrying on the tradition of her late husband, Harold Minsky, and his father who gave burlesque a noble, if notorious, place in the history of American entertainment.

The lovely and charming Mrs. Minsky has "hung up her G-string" now for serious acting on a local basis, but still keeps the Minsky name synonymous with burlesque.

She is associate producer of Minsky's Burlesque shows in Las Vegas and Chicago along with her husband's partner for 10 years, Jerry Lucas, who is still onstage in the Vegas production as a straight man for classic burlesque comedian Irv Benson, who stars in the show.

Pat says she got into show business by accident. "I was working nine-to-five for a publisher in New York," she recalls, having left Newark for the Big Apple with an interest in a modeling career. "A girlfriend influenced me to audition for a part in *George White's Scandals*, but I didn't get a part."

Undeterred by her unsuccessful, albeit brief, brush with show business; she auditioned for Minsky's then playing at a dinner theatre in Yonkers.

She got a part as a showgirl and started taking dancing lessons. Pat stayed with the show for four years until a better proposition came along. "I married the boss," she says fondly.

She first came to Las Vegas in 1965 when still in the revue which Harold opened at the Silver Slipper. The show ran for two years and then moved to Chicago, and she and "the boss" were married shortly thereafter. Although her marriage ended her brief career on the stage, she remained close to the show.

"I always traveled with my husband," she says. "Producers' wives were always in the background but then again they really aren't. I was always there for meetings and had an influence on costumes, staging, and things like that."

The Minsky's reside in Las Vegas, where Harold had made his mark on the entertainment scene. He first came to Las Vegas in 1950 with a show at the Desert Inn. In 1957, he opened the first Las Vegas revue spectacular of its kind at the Dunes Hotel where he was affiliated until 1961.

Sheet music from 1924 with Charlie Chaplin pictured on the cover. Courtesy: Authors Collection

His brilliant career came to an untimely end with his death on Christmas Day, 1977, the same day the entertainment world lost another legend, Charlie Chaplin.

"It took a while to get over," says Pat, who decided to carry on with the Minsky tradition. "Now I try to keep up the standards he established for the show."

What kind of man was Harold Minsky? "He was very easy going," says Pat. "He looked more like a lawyer or businessman than a show producer. He was very well liked and always a gentleman; a decent man."

The burlesque Minsky loved and nurtured has declined but has yet to go the way of its companion art, vaudeville. "It's holding its own," says Pat, of the entertainment genre that dates back to ancient times.

Press Photo dated November 25, 1994 with an "NBC Photo" label on the back reading, "Abbott and Costello meet Jerry Seinfeld." Courtesy: Authors Collection

Sheet music from 1920, "Rose of Washington Square," sung by Fanny Brice in the Ziegfeld Midnight Frolic playing atop the New Amsterdam Theatre in New York City. Brice worked for both Ziegfeld and the Minsky's. Courtesy: Authors Collection

Burlesque flourished in this country in New York in the 1930s and 1940s until then Mayor La Guardia closed the popular burlesque palaces. The Minsky's weren't stopped by La Guardia, however, and cleaned up the shows to keep them going. Harold moved the shows from the theatres into supper clubs where they continued to thrive.

In its heyday, burlesque was the show business breaking in point for such great comedy stars as Fanny Brice, Abbott and Costello, and Phil Silvers, to name only a few. But would be comedy stars have other venues in the television age.

"Burlesque doesn't have the same effect today," says Pat Minsky. "Burlesque went into the movies and, in a sense, into legitimate theatre. No comics are breaking into it now. It was once the only way they had to get started. Now they all look for a shot on Johnny Carson, and they can make it overnight."

Press Photo of "Baby" Rose Marie and Phil Silvers rehearsing for the Broadway show Top Banana *in 1951. Silvers won a Tony award for his performance. Courtesy: Authors Collection*

Minsky's Burlesque in the Allegro Lounge of the Maxim Hotel and Casino is one of two national burlesque shows now in Las Vegas. The other is the *Wild World of Burlesque* at the Holiday Casino on the Strip.

The Minsky show has brought burlesque up-to-date with modern music and disco dance segments. The show has a cast of 11 – three lead dancers, (two male, one female), two strippers, a comic, and a straight man.

Vivacious exotic dancer Cassandra Lee is featured in the show which also showcases the talents of exotic dancer and comic straight lady, Cimmaron. Lead dancers are Michelle Demaria, and up-and-coming young male dancers Kurt Sproul and Ron Ruge. Rounding out the cast are beauties Laurel Mock, Teri Gambino, Denise Esola, and Zoe Marshall, all excellent dancers.

Pat says the show is doing "quite well" in the Allegro Lounge which seats about 180 people. She helps Jerry Lucas cast the show and comes in two or three times a week to make sure things are going well. The show, with performances twice on weeknights and three times on Fridays and Saturdays, uses topless dancers, she says, rather than showgirls. Betty Francisco choreographed the show.

"The primary thing we look for in casting is the dancing," Pat says. "Looks are incorporated and busts are of course, important. But the girls we use are slender because there is so much dancing." Jerry, she says with a laugh, checks out the girls' figures when casting a show.

Rehearsals are held for about two and a half weeks before a new show opens and then the show takes care of itself. Pat and Jerry will travel to check out a new show on the road before it opens to make sure it's okay, but booking agents and stage managers take care of the rest.

That leaves Pat time for her studies and to get involved in university and local theatre productions. "It's something I love," she says, adding that she's partial to Shakespearean plays. She predicts that along with the rapid growth of Las Vegas, theatre here will thrive.

It is there that lovely and talented Pat Minsky will probably make her own mark on the Las Vegas entertainment scene while continuing to carry out the Minsky tradition. "I hope so. I like living in Las Vegas. It's where the shows are. It's the place to be," she says."

The same exact article was printed in the August 29, 1978 issue of *The Las Vegas Today*, a weekly newspaper published in North Las Vegas. Looking through the advertising I noticed the Royal Dixie Jazz Band, who performed at the BHS Reunion held at the Gold Coast Hotel and Casino in 2000, was performing in Las Vegas at that time. Siegfried and Roy were performing at the Stardust. Their show cost $15 per person, plus tax, and included four cocktails. If you went to the early show, the dinner cost $2.50.

At Wonder World Discount Liquors on Maryland Parkway, a six-pack of Pepsi Cola cost $1.19; a case of Pabst Blue Ribbon cost $4.99; a case of Coors or Schlitz cost $5.79; a fifth of Hennessy Cognac cost $10.79; and all brands of cigarettes cost $4.49 per carton. Ice was free.

At the Circus Circus Hotel and Casino, you could buy a complete dinner for $3.95; at the Hacienda Hotel and Casino the brunch buffet cost $1.99, the 'all you can eat' dinner buffet cost $2.99; and round the clock drinks at the Island Bar cost 50 cents. The Mint Hotel had the cheapest lunch buffet at $1.75, and the Dunes had the most costly at $5.85. The Holiday International had the cheapest dinner buffet at $2.65; the most costly was $4.95 at the Maxim.

There was another article in this folder that was simply titled "The Minsky's" and it was written by A. Wilbur Stevens. I know it's from 1978 due to the content of the story; however, it was ripped out of the magazine it was published in. It reads:

"What is burlesque? Some feel, as the late Harold Minsky felt, that it was the one viable American tradition in the popular arts. "They want to see as much of the girl as possible," he said in an extensive interview he recorded in August of 1975 with Professor Ronald L. Davis of Southern Methodist University. I've heard the tape several times and have gotten some glimpse into the background of the famous Minsky tradition. I've also, through the kind auspices of Minsky's widow, Pat, watched the development of the *Minsky Burlesque Follies*, from its genesis through to its current showing at the Maxim Hotel. Of course the Follies at the Maxim is not "old" Minsky fare. It's a lounge show for a room holding 180 people with a bar which consumes too much space, but from which you get the best view of things.

But from way back to now at the Maxim is quite a history. Harold Minsky's father, Abe, started burlesque in 1908 in New York, There was that old theatre on Houston Street with shows which had their sources in the nickelodeon tradition. Eventually, Minsky's moved uptown and Harold, with (Abe's) brother Billy (they were later to part business-wise), filled such theatres as the Apollo and then the Gaiety on 46th Street. There Harold really went into the gamut of work which included box office, front-of-house chores, and finally backstage supervision.

The Minsky "business" never came into the Minsky household. A solid tradition of family living was maintained. There were European sojourns, private schools, summer camps – all the proper things of a proper New York family growing up in the 30s.

Here are some reflections on Minsky's part, going through the years in New York and then, in the 1950s in Las Vegas, where he settled and from where he ran his business.

The first great stripper was Charlotte Maine. She later went to Ziegfeld.

The best stripper was Lili St. Cyr. A fine production number done on and around a chaise lounge.

Margie Hart was a "strong worker." (The chief adjective used in burlesque parlance is "strong." This denotes and connotes a burlesque performance with the greatest turn-on effect.) Hart took off more than most.

Ann Corio used lots of fans, but not to Minsky's taste.

Sally Rand – not too talented.

Lili St. Cyr. Courtesy: C.F. Miller

Margie Hart.
Courtesy: Janelle Smith Collection

Rags Ragland. Courtesy: Mimi Reed

Comics; the list is endless: Phil Silvers, Red Buttons, Joe King, Rags Ragland, and Bud Abbott. Milton Berle is as knowledgeable in burlesque as any man, but was never in burlesque. He started in Vaudeville.

Soon, Minsky had theatres throughout the country. His decision to leave New York was based on the censorship rules under Mayor La Guardia and Paul Moss. By the time the Minsky formula reached Las Vegas, the old-time "bump-and-grind" routines had become more sophisticated. More women came to see burlesque. The comics became as important as the girls. The art was more refined and relaxed. Girls were chosen on the basis of dancing ability.

Minsky believed that burlesque would endure. He felt that you "have to keep your standards up." The older generation still likes it, and he can recall that burlesque was the mainstay of many men looking for work in the depression years. Still, more new people are needed in the business. Most importantly, it's hard to get good new strippers.

I watched, over a period of days, rehearsals for the current Maxim show. The main impression I received was the usual confusion which exists between the performers and production staff who know what they are doing, and the seemingly endless procession of local hotel and "four waller" entrepreneurs who feed various suggestions into the proceedings.

The girls, incidentally, work in straight dance clothes right up to opening night. Even for the dress rehearsal their breasts are covered. Then the show goes on.

Jerry Lucas and Pat Minsky (Harold's widow) have a hit which contains both the old and the new. The "old," of course, is Irv Benson, one of the last of the classic burlesque comics. He works in a kind of ancient jump suit, and regales his audience with marvelous insults. His material traces back to the French Revolution, but he has some modern flourishes which you won't soon forget. There's a sketch which he and Jerry Lucas (the straight man) has concerning an automobile and two girls that is dirtier than Aristophanes.

The dance numbers are superb, particularly the work of Michelle Demaria, who with Kurt Sproul and Ron Ruge, does a compelling adagio. The choreography of Betty Francisco is tops, even though in one number she has now added some blue actions which take away from the whimsy of the piece.

Cassandra Lee is, as usual, indefatigable in her "Cajun Moon" strip, and Cimarron is especially artful in her acrobatic perambulations.

The music throughout has a lot of disco emphasis which keeps to current vogue and inclination, but the Minsky tradition is being upheld. What its future will be is problematical, but in the Allegro Room at the Maxim the girls are coming on. Hopefully, *Minsky's Burlesque Follies* will be a turn-on for lots of people: the prurient, the resigned, and the hot.

Of course, the key to the Minsky operation lies in Patricia Minsky. She has at the helm Jerry Lucas, an amazingly efficient man, a rock of support who has been with the Minsky name 18 years. Jerry is an ex-cop; good background for the business. He is steady and charming. In all the rehearsals of the current show I never saw him give way nor be less than a producer.

Pat still feels her husband's death and a responsibility towards the show business tradition he set, but she is adamantly independent. She is not always at home in the expedient and fey milieu of Las Vegas, even though she came up through the showgirl burlesque ranks of New York and the long-run Silver Slipper days of Minsky in this town.

As a student at UNLV she is involved in acting (she was fine in a recent production of *The Bacchae*), drawing, and writing. She will work with the Minsky name and the frankly limited perquisites of the Minsky aims for some time, but sooner or later it seems to me, she will find more comfort in other directions. She does not disagree with this assessment."

There was one last article in this folder. It was not complete; there was no title and no author mentioned. It was a single page; could it have possibly be penned by Pat Minsky herself? It reads:

"Pat Minsky's brought this current edition to Las Vegas partly for sentimental reasons. "It just didn't seem right not to see the Minsky name somewhere on a Las Vegas marquee," she said. "Minsky's Follies was the forerunner of all the present, lavishly staged 'Follies' type shows. My husband pioneered the all-girl

Photo of some Minsky showgirls from 1953. Courtesy: Burlesque Historical Society

chorus line in Las Vegas back in the 1950s," she added.

Minsky noted that *Minsky's '78* features a modern motif with contemporary music, comedy, and dance numbers. Yet the key to the Minsky success has been and is the emphasis on pretty girls, funny skits, attractive strippers, and exciting dance routines.

The burlesque tradition goes back to the 5th Century B.C. and the Greek playwright, Aristophanes, according to Pat Minsky. Many Greek plays possessed ribald comedy routines and pretty girls. "Lysistrata is pure Burlesque," Minsky noted. The actual term "burlesque" comes from the word "Burla," which is Italian for "broad comedy." 19th Century burlesque-type shows were imported to the United States from England, where they were very popular. In America such well-known personalities of their day as Lydia Thompson and Adah Isaacs Menken brought much notoriety to the dance hall and burlesque stage with their innovative acts. Nonetheless, it took the master burlesque showman of his time, Michael Leavitt, to create a workable combination of gags, variety acts, and a grand finale patterned after the minstrel show which has been handed down to us in the form of classic vaudeville and burlesque.

It was the Minsky's who brought burlesque into the 20th Century. Louis, an immigrant originally from Minsk, Russia, who came to be called "Minsky" by his friends, gave his sons the National Winter Garden Theatre

Lydia Thompson.
Courtesy: Burlesque Historical Society

Republic Burlesque Theatre. Courtesy: Sandra Ellis

in New York City which became the original mecca for burlesque. The brothers, staging their own shows, brought burlesque into the big-time and opened multiple theatres. The Republic Theatre on 42nd Street, and Abe Minsky's Gotham Theatre were two of the most prestigious and sought-after burlesque and vaudeville showplaces. The Minsky's had shown the wide popular appeal of burlesque, and show business would never be the same.

Abe's son, Harold, was in charge of closing the Gotham Theatre during the winter season. One year, however, the enterprising 20 year old showman decided to keep the Gotham open during the traditionally "dead" winter. It was a rousing success; so much so that his father gave him the Gaiety Theatre, also in New York, to run full-time.

Harold Minsky then proceeded to "discover" such talents as Abbott and Costello, Phil Silvers, Red Buttons, Pinky Lee, and Rags Ragland. Early in 1948,

Red Buttons. Courtesy: C.F. Miller

March 1956 Press Photo of Pinky Lee. Courtesy: Authors Collection

Rags Ragland.
Courtesy: Burlesque Historical Society

Harold Minsky moved to Miami Beach where he produced the first show titled *Minsky Follies*. It was a happy blend of old-time burlesque, beautiful girls in gorgeous costumes and spectacular settings, plus the finest acts in show business. Then, in 1950, after having played almost all the large cities in America, *Minsky's Follies* moved to the show capital of the world, Las Vegas, where it enjoyed a tremendously successful two decades, playing virtually every major hotel in the city.

Thus the current rendition of Minsky's has a long and illustrious history behind it. It's nice to know that the venerable show business name of Minsky can still generate excitement and pleasure wherever it goes."

(Notes: Some cast members who often worked in skits in the last years of the Minsky shows included: Herbie Barris, Eddie Innes, Dick Richards, Irving Benson, Bobbye Mack, Jimmy Mathews, Pat Merl, Penny Powers, Rochelle Lea, and Jeanette Telders.)

N is For...

The first item in this File contained a very faded resume for choreographer Jerry Norman. I have typed it as it was written, and it reads:

JERRY NORMAN

Studied with Michael Panieff, Ernest Belcher, Eugene Loring, and Antonio Triana on the West Coast; and Igor Shvetsov, and Matt Maddox, as well as the American Theatre Wing, in New York.

Appeared in the Broadway shows ------ *West Side Story, Destry Rides Again, Bye Bye Birdie, Hello Dolly,* as well as *Ballet U.S.A.* In Las Vegas, *Bottoms Up Revues, Anything Goes, High Button Shoes, Ziegfeld Follies,* and several shows at the Dunes Hotel, Sahara Hotel, and Riviera Hotel.

Started his creative career in the area of staging and choreography in 1964.

Staged and Choreographed: *Minsky Shows* ------ five editions at the Silver Slipper, Las Vegas; Mineola Theatre, New York; Hilton Hotel, New York; Latin Casino, New Jersey; Edgewater Beach Hotel, Chicago; Lambertville Music Theatre; Two shows Thunderbird Hotel, Las Vegas; Three editions at the Aladdin Hotel, Las Vegas; Three shows at the Condado Hotel, San Juan, Puerto Rico; as well as the Playboy Hotels in Miami and Lake Geneva.

Watusi Stampede, Thunderbird Hotel and Bonanza Hotel, Las Vegas; *Mamie Van Doren Show*, Bonanza Hotel; *Milton Berle Show*, Caesar's Palace Hotel, Las Vegas; *Sock It To Me*, Review, El Casino, Freeport, Bahamas; and *Tickle Your Fancy*, Carillon Hotel, Miami Beach, El Casino, Freeport, Bahamas, and Stardust Hotel, Las Vegas.

Bottoms Up Revues ------ 1962-1972. Two editions at the Thunderbird Hotel, Las Vegas; Three editions Caesar's Palace, Las Vegas; Two editions at the International Hotel, Las Vegas; and Two editions at the Flamingo Hotel, Las Vegas.

Korean Kittens – Oriental Revue; Hacienda Hotel, Las Vegas.

Feminine Touch Revue, and *Fancy That Revue*; both at Harrah's Hotel, Reno, Nevada.

"N" also stands for the New Frontier Hotel in Las Vegas, where *Minsky's Follies '62* was to perform. The main article in this folder was a UPI newspaper article from the *Los Angeles Evening Herald Express*. The title of the article was "Vegas Hotel, Minsky Irate." It was dated December 11, 1961, and reads:

"Bandleader Louis (Satchmo) Armstrong today was named defendant in an $11.5 million damage suit by the New Frontier Hotel and show producer Harold Minsky.

The district court civil action stated that Armstrong signed a contract to perform at the New Frontier for 12 weeks at $15,000 per week – then refused to go through with the engagement.

The suit quoted Armstrong's manager, Joseph Glazier, as stating that Armstrong would not perform anywhere a Minsky- produced show had recently been billed because Minsky's shows were "indecent, immoral, and obscene," and that his future shows can be expected to have the "same unsavory character."

Minsky said he was "shocked" at the remarks about his background and that he has already spent $250,000 on staging the coming show – now being advertised as *Minsky's Follies of 1962 – The Show That Made America Blush*.

It is slated to open December 22 and Armstrong was to have opened in February after its closing.

The suit seeks $1.5 million for the anticipated loss of revenue to the hotel because of the contract repudiation; $4 million general damages, and $1 million punitive damages for allegations that the New Frontier was not providing anything but clean, wholesome entertainment. In addition Minsky seeks $4 million general damages and $1 million punitive damages for what he termed damage to his reputation.

Minsky, who has been retained to produce a show for next year's "Space Age Exposition" at Seattle, said stars such as Frankie Laine, Tony Bennett, Phil Silvers, and Red Buttons have appeared in his productions and Armstrong's allegations were uncalled for.

Named in the civil action filed by attorney Calvin Magleby on behalf of the hotel and Minsky was Armstrong, the Associated Booking Corp of New York; Arthur Engle, local associated representative, and Glazier."

The last folder in the "N" File stands for Newark, New Jersey – the Adams Theatre. There were a couple older articles in this file from the 1950s. They were both from *Focus Magazine* in 1953; no author is noted, and read:

"They have no Place to be Lousy; George Burns said it best, "The tragedy of kids breaking into show biz today is that they have no place to be lousy."

Looking for a place to "be lousy," tiny (5'2") Jacqueline Munsie, 18, recently left her native Bronx and crossed the Hudson River, bound for Newark and Minsky's Burlesque. She hoped to land a job in the chorus.

Choreographer Chuck Gregory auditioned her, but no job was offered to Jackie. Instead, she was invited to try again when she has picked up a little show-lore.

As she left, Jackie Munsie asked herself, "Where can you go to get experience?" - a question worn smooth by time.

Also from *Focus Magazine*:

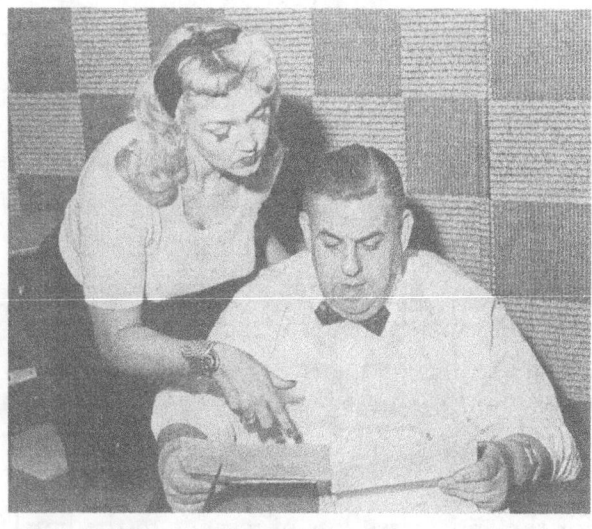

*Jennie Lee and Dave Cohn looking over a contract.
Courtesy: Burlesque Historical Society*

"Dave Cohn has America's most envied job. As burlesque's top agent, he sells sex. It takes a big man to hold down the job as the country's biggest burlesque agent – and Dave Cohn is just that – figuratively and literally. At a time when exotic dancers are helping burlesque make its comeback, Dave turns the wheels of progress as he helps his danseuses bump-and-grind their way to big money along the high voltage circuit.

His office, tucked away in the bustling Broadway district in New York City, is the meeting place, conference room, and stop-over for nearly every strip star who passes through the city. It was Dave who brought the western tornado, Tempest Storm, east for her first appearance here. "My first stop," says Tempest, "was to

Autographed photo of Tempest Storm. Courtesy: C.F. Miller

Gay Dawn; at least three women performed using that name in burlesque. Courtesy: C.F. Miller

see Dave. He's been booking me for a long time, and while I've spoken to him a dozen times on the phone, I've never met him." Tempest was captivated by his charm, as are his other clients – top names in the burly biz like Gay Dawn, Jessica Rogers, and others.

"My biggest asset," says Dave "is the telephone. I can't see all of my girls all of the time, but each one knows that I'm as close to her as the phone."

Jessica Rogers. Courtesy: C.F. Miller

Asked, "Do these beautiful dolls ever have any complaints or gripes?" Cohn's response was, "Not often, but sometimes; it's a matter of getting the right bookings – or more money, or conflict of engagements, or star billing – or doing too many shows. We always manage to get things straightened out." He must be able to work them out for he has at least one girl working at *every* burlesque theatre in

Victor McLaglen and Louise Hovick (Gypsy Rose Lee) posing for a scene from the 1938 20th Century-Fox film, Battle of Broadway. *Courtesy: Authors Collection*

Margie Hart. *Courtesy: Janelle Smith Collection*

the country *all the time*. For more than two score years he's been arranging itineraries and routes for the girls whom he pampers as though they were his own daughters. No backstage is ever closed to him and his phone rings continually – calls from New Orleans, Los Angeles, Chicago, or Miami clamoring for his damsels of the disrobe set.

Whenever possible, Dave attends the opening night show of every client

1943 Press Photo of Rags Ragland in 1943 film Du Barry Was a Lady. Ragland died in 1946. Phil Silvers was often his partner when performing in burlesque. *Courtesy: Authors Collection*

who plays near the New York area. He likes to watch his clients in action. Club and theatre managers claim he drops in to see how much of a house his artistes draw as well – so he can demand more money for them. If the crowd is good – no one has any objection in the long run – or the long green.

"Biggest headache," admits Dave, "is trying to get as many girls as possible to play Minsky's Adams Theatre. This theatre is to burlesque what the old Palace used to be to vaudeville – when you played there you've arrived."

Some of his big name clients draw as high as $2,500 per week – over $100,000 a year – which is a nice strip of money in any language. Dave recalls the old days, when the circuits were called "wheels" and the top stars got $100 a week. Exceptions in the much higher brackets: Gypsy Rose Lee, Ann Corio, and Margie Hart. Dave is also buddy-buddy with the top comics – the pie-in-the-face comedians who got their start in burlesque. Such men as: Red Buttons, Phil Silvers, Jackie Gleason, and the late Rags Ragland.

Dave pointed to his files; "I've got hundreds of clients – and I've seen every one of their acts. I'm father confessor, father, friend-in-need, and a shoulder to cry on for all their troubles – but I love 'em all."

Dave not only passes on all contracts, but he okays publicity, checks dances, and is critic to all the acts. Does he like his work? Cohn says, "Let me answer it this way, would you change jobs with me?"

Ahem, come to think of it, we would. Would you?"

Also included in this folder was a "partial article" that came from a small format publication. Was the entire article about Minsky? There is no way to tell, but I have included what I can from pages 18 and 19. I wish I had the entire article; I believe what follows was from the 1950s. It reads:

"Harold Minsky made up his mind to follow in his father's footsteps right after graduating from prep school. Right now his home base is the Adams-Minsky Theatre in Newark, New Jersey, since the runways across the river in New York have been dim for many years… at least legally.

The business of staging flesh shows brings Harold to the theatre seven days a week. He puts the shows together himself, and is always on the lookout for new talent… which, by the way, is becoming harder and harder to find. TV and Broadway take most of the better looking girls, even though they can make a lot more money for a lot less work with Minsky. He blames it on the bad reputation that Burlesque has gotten over the past twenty years. Why, he doesn't know, because his shows, at least, are clean… except for what thoughts his customers might have while watching…

Harold, who never goes backstage, must sincerely believe that there's nothing wrong with a girl stripping for a living because his wife is tall, statuesque Dardy Orlando, a headliner until three years ago. She's Lili St. Cyr's sister, and looks

Dardy Orlando. Courtesy: Burlesque Historical Society

Lili St. Cyr's photo was used on El Rancho postcards when she appeared at the Hotel. Courtesy: C.F. Miller

very much like her. Harold must have a point because backstage, between shows, the girls were busy killing time reading or just gabbing."

The final article from this folder was from the January 31, 1954, *New York Harold Tribune*; no author is listed. It was titled "Family-Style Burlesque is Smash Hit in Newark."

"Newark, New Jersey, January 30 – "Family-Style" burlesque has come to Newark. This may seem like a contradiction in terms, since burlesque has never been considered the ideal art form for women and children, but it is true. At the Adams-Minsky Theatre, where this cultural revival is flourishing, there are even special ladies-day matinees Wednesday afternoons, with coffee, tea, and cake for the patrons; and a fully dressed performer as hostess.

What is "family-style" burlesque? It seemed only proper to ask Harold Minsky, the local impresario for a definition.

"I mean a type of show that wouldn't offend anybody, man or woman," said Minsky, an amiable, stoutish fellow of thirty-eight. "It's definitely not a 'stag' show. Why, 50 percent of our Saturday night crowds are women. That's why we tried a ladies day matinee. And it went over so big that we decided to have one every week. Some people got the wrong idea about burlesque. Our comics aren't smutty; risqué, yes, smutty, no. We try to give a show that's a happy medium

Contract has been signed for Sequin to perform at Harold Minsky's Adams Theatre in Newark, New Jersey. Courtesy: Mary Jane Tamburello-Ellis

between old-time vaudeville and burlesque."

At the 2000-seat Adams, which Minsky says is the largest burlesque theatre in the country, four shows are staged daily, with an extra midnight show on Saturdays. Four striptease artists, three production numbers, a vaudeville act, three "scenes" with comedians, and a finale comprise the usual program. These shows alternating with second-run movies, last about an hour and a half, and operate on a continuous schedule, starting at 11am.

"We keep our comics in stock, too," Minsky said. "They'll stay maybe ten or twelve weeks, then go to the Rialto, a theatre I run in Chicago." Resident comedians at the moment are Irving Benson (thin) and Joe DeRita (fat), who are assisted by straight man Stanley Montfort and Waunita Bates, described by Minsky as a "talking woman."

He explained, "Most burlesque theatres take a girl from the chorus instead of using a girl in the scenes who can speak lines. You ought to see one of our dress rehearsals."

Dress rehearsals for burlesque? "Oh, our costumes aren't the usual burlesque stuff," Minsky said. "We rent our wardrobe from the Latin Quarter in New York, or have Mme. Bertha make them up for us. And the eighteen girls in our chorus, they're young dancers, not old hags."

He was right about the girls in the chorus. They are young and attractive, and their ensemble routines look rehearsed instead of dreamed. Nevertheless the show as a whole resembles

Photo of the front of the Latin Quarter in New York City. Courtesy: C.F. Miller

the old grind and isn't much different from non-family-style burlesque. An assortment of handsomely endowed women undress and undulate to music. One of them is abetted by a brilliantly plumaged parrot that flies off with strategically tailored garments.

It is all in the best tradition. Strippers and showgirls glitter with sequins and rhinestones. The comedians display the timing and ease that comes with familiarity. "Floogle Street," "This Must Be the Place," and other generic expressions are still used. The blackout is as effective as ever. And the sight gag of a man in underpants still gets an automatic laugh.

Minsky is assisted by Chuck Gregory, choreographer-director, in staging the shows. Rehearsals are held in the basement of the theatre between performances. A show that will open Friday begins rehearsing Tuesday. Dress rehearsals are held onstage after the final Wednesday and Thursday performances.

Minsky started in burlesque when he was eighteen, at the old Gaiety in Manhattan, where his father, A.B. Minsky, installed him as a cashier. A.B. and his brothers had built burlesque into a major theatrical attraction in New York until they were forced by the law to close in 1937. Harold Minsky assumed various jobs at the Gaiety and supplemented his practical experience with courses at Columbia University in lighting and direction.

Minsky's phone rang during the interview. "Hello Minsky-Adams," he said. "You're where? On 48th and Fifth? Just a moment." He told his secretary, Ruthie O'Grady, "Here's another one who wants to know how to get here from Manhattan." Ruthie took the phone and asked the caller if she could help him.

"She's become a transportation expert since we opened over a month ago," Minsky said. "People call from New York, the Bronx, Brooklyn, Westchester, even Connecticut, to ask directions. Guess they like our family-style burlesque."

Down in the basement, meanwhile, the next show was being rehearsed, with Gregory mapping the choreography while Harold Rausch, who conducts the orchestra, played the piano accompaniment. A visit to the rehearsal reaffirmed the family-style idea. Several of the showgirls were sitting around crocheting.

One of them, Stephanie Winters, a Newark girl who is being groomed as a strip soloist, seemed to be the expert. The others came to her for instructions and advice. Stephanie, who's tall, blonde and attractive, had crocheted a larger object than the others.

What was she crocheting? "Panties for my strip act," she replied.

"O" is For...

"O" is for "Other." There were two folders in this File; one contained mostly photos, the other contained a variety of odds and ends – blurbs, advertisements, paragraphs about Minsky, or people who worked for him. I am including them in order of their dates. Sadly, one item dated 1952 was a copy and can't be read in its entirety. It was an open letter about *Minsky's Follies* written by Frank Sennes.

The following paragraph came from the Louis Sobol column "New York Cavalcade" that appeared in the October 8, 1964 edition of the *New York Journal American*. It reads:

"Harold Minsky is off to London to snare the Windmill Theatre Burlesque Troupe for Broadway. (We itemed yesterday, that after these many years, when it boasted it had never closed, even during the Nazi bombing raids, the Windmill Theatre was finally giving up the ghost.)"

To be expected, Minsky's name appeared in several columns in 1967. I enjoyed reading the Jack O'Brian column, "O'BSERVATIONS," in the *New York World Journal Tribune* from March 12, 1967. It included nuggets about the Peggy Cass story of her blind date with Clark Gable; how Arthur Treacher reacted when Forrest Tucker attempted to give him a peck on the cheek during a Lamb's Club event, and how the columnist thinks Danny Kaye is simply marvelous. Just a quick note, Tucker once worked as a straight man in burlesque. This particular column also mentioned Bozo Snyder and Billy "Beef Trust" Watson, who were prominent burlesque comedic legends.

Tommy "Bozo" Snyder with stage makeup on. Courtesy: Lee Stuart

Billy "Beef Trust" Watson. Courtesy: Authors Collection

The paragraph mentioning Harold Minsky reads:

"The art of one Don Rickles eludes us: and we think some of the stars who retell on TV Rickles' blatant insolences to them in public places are managing to bury such humorless insults right in his back. The Rickles performing style is insult for the sake of lippy insolence; only Jack E. Leonard seems able to remain the proper mini-distance short of arrogant stupidity while needling. The sustained success of Minsky's Burlesque (burlesque remains still alive but barely kicking except under Harold Minsky's auspices) is because the last of a long 'Minskian' line knows a pretty girl when he sees one, plus the value of smart costumes – and good low comedians. Burlesque, too, can remain saucy, and daring; even explore the more cheerful vulgarities without exploding into filth. Please remember Mayor La Guardia only banned the rough-and-rowdy lowest art form when it grew so nastily bold as to advertise obscene words, phrases, and "in" smut right on theatre marquees."

Another section from a newspaper was cut out and tacked on to the same page as the O'Brian column. There was no date, or any other reference noted. It was titled "E.B. White Calls TV a Counterpart to Essay," and reads:

"The Carnegie Commission on Educational Television was in touch with more than organizations during its study. One correspondent was E.B. White, the author, and the following is taken from his letter:

"I think television should be the visual counterpart of the literary essay, should arouse our dreams, satisfy our hunger for beauty, take us on journeys, enable us to participate in events, present great drama and music, explore the sea and the sky and the woods and the hills. It should be our Lyceum, our Chautauqua, our Minsky's, and our Camelot. It should restate and clarify the social dilemma and the political pickle. Once in a while it does, and you get a quick glimpse of its potential."

The next came from "Kup's Column" in the *Chicago Sun-Times*, dated June 18, 1967.

"The Headliners: Patricia Elliott, one of the featured girls in the Minsky Revue at the Edgewater Beach Hotel, will marry the boss, Harold Minsky, in Las Vegas next week... Tony Curtis has signed to play the lead opposite Britt Eklund in *The Night They Raided Minsky's*, Harold Minsky's story, which former Chicagoan Billy Friedkin will direct."

Earl Wilson also mentioned the Minsky-Elliott union in his column, "It Happened Last Night." He wrote, "Harold Minsky said at Gallagher's he'll marry showgirl Patricia Elliott in Las Vegas next week."

Ralph Pearl wrote the following which appeared in his column in the *Las Vegas Sun* newspaper on June 16, 1967:

"Girlie impresario Harold Minsky married Pat Elliott, who used to dance in one of his Silver Slipper shows, Saturday at the Dunes."

The following clipping may have run in the same newspaper:

"Minsky Wed to Las Vegas Showgirl; Producer Harold Minsky, 52, has been married in Las Vegas to a 28-year-old one-time showgirl in one of his productions. He is presently connected with the Silver Slipper.

The bride is Patricia Elliott, of Las Vegas. The marriage was performed recently at the Dunes Hotel where Minsky once produced girlie shows."

One additional newspaper clipping was a Forrest Duke column called "The Duke of Las Vegas." There was no date, nor did it designate what newspaper it was from – his column once ran in 21 newspapers nationwide - but it did mention Harold Minsky. It reads:

"Phil Silvers, winner of the Tony Award for his performance on Broadway this season in *A Funny Thing Happened on the Way to the Forum*, was on *The Tonight Show* last week with Joey Bishop. Tony Sandler and Ralph Young, the Flamingo Hotel pactees, were also on the show, and they credited Silvers with their success, because he guided important agents to them when they were a lounge act at Lake Tahoe. Silvers told a story about the time he was speaking before a gathering which included Darryl Zanuck, his movie boss. Phil went into a long spiel about this wonderful man who gave him his big break and taught him everything he knows about the biz. Zanuck was smiling bashfully, and arranging his tie for when he stood up for his bow; Phil then said, "And that man is here tonight, sitting in the back – Harold Minsky!" Zanuck most certainly felt like crawling into a hole, and the pleasantly embarrassed Minsky was so surprised he almost fell out of his chair."

Press Photo from November 9, 1958 of Ed Sullivan showing Phil Silvers the award to be presented to him in the Friars Club Tribute on The Ed Sullivan Show on CBS television the following Sunday night.
Courtesy: Authors Collection

The final write-up comes from another Jack O'Brian column; sadly there was no date attached. I assume it comes from 1967 due to a comment in the column that says, "We're told by GM insiders '68 Caddies will have tail-fins again; customers want 'em." There were only a couple of lines regarding Minsky and they read:

"Harold Minsky's due to make such old tenants as T.S. Eliot and Leslie Howard among others roll over in their classical graves: Harold's dealing for a summertime Minsky burley show in the hallowed Henry Miller's Theatre."

Also included in this folder was a Xerox of a photo that appeared on a sports page in the *Las Vegas Review-Journal*, dated October 26, 1971. It was from a horse race at the Washington D.C. International Laurel Race Course. Coming in fourth was a horse named Minsky.

The last items included were advertisements that ran in *Variety* and *The Hollywood Reporter* regarding auditions being held for the new Minsky's Revue. The ads ran in publications on February 6-7, 1974. The choreographer was Anita Mann; and auditions were to be held on February 8, at the Stanley Holden Dance Center, located at 10521 West Pico Boulevard in Los Angeles. They were looking for boy dancers, girl dancers, showgirls, and female singers. The revue would be playing in New York and Miami Beach, and promised "steady work."

Another item I found in the "O" File surprised me, although I have been dealing with burlesque material long enough I shouldn't be surprised by anything anymore. The item was an article about the death of actor Dan Dailey, who died on October 16, 1978. It was stapled to a photo of the actor, and reads:

"Famed 'Song and Dance Man' Dan Dailey Dies; Hollywood (UPI) – Dan Dailey, the song and dance man who performed in dozens of Hollywood and Broadway musicals, died in his sleep at his home early Monday at the age of 62.

Al Melnick, his personal manager, said Dailey had suffered for several months from severe anemia. He said Dailey had been "virtually an invalid" since August 1977

Press Photo of Dan Dailey and Betty Grable from 1950 film, My Blue Heaven.
Courtesy: Silver Screen Collection

when he fell onstage during a performance of *The Odd Couple* at a dinner theatre in North Carolina and fractured his hip.

While the fall forced him to abandon plans to perform in a new Broadway show, *Spotlight*, Melnick said Dailey had hoped to continue his career by playing the part of the man in the wheelchair in *The Man Who Came to Dinner*.

His condition deteriorated in recent weeks, however. Dailey, who lived with a nurse in an apartment in Hollywood, was last seen by a doctor Sunday night and refused his advice to go to a hospital. He was found dead Monday morning. Funeral arrangements were pending.

Dailey, who received an Academy Award nomination for *Mother Wore Tights*, gained fame in a series of musicals; co-starring in several with Betty Grable.

In 1969-1971 he starred in the television series, *The Governor and J.J.*, and appeared on Broadway last year despite undergoing surgery for a fractured hip.

The New York-born actor always considered dancing a "lucrative hobby," even though his first film role with MGM in 1940 was that of a "heavy."

He grew up in a theatrical community and began taking dancing lessons when he was 14. Soon he and a schoolmate were working for $2.50 each hoofing in a minstrel show.

Dailey danced in the chorus line at Roxy's and on a cruise ship bound for the West Indies before he was introduced to burlesque king Harold Minsky, who put the dancer in a clown outfit with flappy shoes to entertain the audience before the women came onstage."

"P" is For...

The "P" File had several individual folders that actually started with the word "Playboy," but let's begin with the Palladium, Hollywood folder. The *Minsky's Follies* performed at the Hollywood Palladium from July 23 through August 30, 1975. The show was presented by "Playboy Productions." Monday through Thursday the dinner and show cost $13.50; on the weekends, Friday and Saturday, patrons paid $15.00. The Wednesday matinee cost $6.00 and the late shows at 11pm, on Friday and Saturday, cost $7.50. Burk-Hudson Public Relations at the Ambassador Hotel in Los Angeles put together the following fact sheet regarding the dinner theatre show. It reads:

"The Show: The show combines the classic elements of burlesque including baggy-pants comedians, the candy butcher, blackouts, and exotic dancers with a Vegas type show including long stemmed showgirls, exciting choreography, upbeat music, and excellent singing. The Nicholas Brothers, who are dancers extraordinaire, are the special guest stars.

<u>The Producer:</u> Harold Minsky is often called "the genial king of burlesque." His family has produced burlesque shows since 1908. Harold Minsky himself started his theatrical career in 1933. Since that time the Minsky name has appeared on theatrical marquees continuously, making it one of the best known names in show business. He is considered an authority on the subject of burlesque and was a contributing editor to the classic dictionary, *The Language of Show Biz*.

The Minsky's Follies Show is a Playboy presentation. A Minsky show broke all records at the Chicago Playboy Club, playing for 17 months.

<u>First Time In Los Angeles:</u> Although Minsky shows have played in virtually every major city in the United States, including long runs in Chicago, New York, Las Vegas, and Miami, this is the first time Los Angelinos will have the opportunity to see a Minsky show.

<u>Run:</u> The show is booked for six weeks – July 23 through August 30 at the Hollywood Palladium.

<u>Show Times / Prices:</u> Please see flyer for details. There are six dinner shows per week plus two late shows and a matinee. There is dancing before and after each show. The price is very reasonable for the package.

Red Buttons and Robert Alda who worked together in the 1930s Catskill summer resorts, are reunited on September 14, 1980 in HBO's Standing Room Only: Burlesque USA.
Courtesy: Authors Collection

<u>The Cast:</u> An outstanding cast of comics, exotics, dancers, showgirls, singer, and musicians has been assembled. For a fact sheet on any individual performer or more information, please contact Burk/Hudson at 387-7011, Extension 220.

<u>Background:</u> A Minsky show is first and foremost entertainment. The message is fun and enjoyment, and Mr. Minsky insists on good taste as a crucial element.

Webster's defines burlesque as "A type of theatrical entertainment characterized by broad humor and slapstick." Comedy is crucial to burlesque, and much contemporary humor stems from classic burlesque scenes. For example, "Hear Come de Judge" comes from a standard burlesque scene. Many famous comedians had their start in burlesque including: Abbott and

Vaudevillians Rose Louise Hovick and Baby June Hovick posing in 1922. Rose Louise was 8 and Baby June was 6. Courtesy: Burlesque Historical Society

Costello, Phil Silvers, Red Buttons, Pinky Lee, Jan Murray, Bob Alda, and Rags Ragland.

In addition to comedy, American burlesque includes beautiful girls – showgirls, dancers, and exotics. Spangles, feathers, and glitter are used in abundance to enhance the beauty of the performers. The exotic dancers are an important part of the show, combining a lot of tease with the strip and never going totally nude. The Minsky's show boasts two outstanding exotic dancers – Diane Lewis and Cassandra Lee. Probably the best known exotic dancer of past years was Gypsy Rose Lee, whose life story was the basis for the movie, *Gypsy*.

Burlesque is a classic American theatre tradition."

The cast of the show, according to the program, included: Comics, Looney Lewis and Charlie Vespia; Comic-Straight Man, Silky Silvers; Special Guest Stars, the Nicholas Brothers; Talking Woman, Margo Rogers; Boxer, H.R. (Rory) Calhoun (performed in "The Fighter" scene); Exotic Dancers, Diane Lewis and Cassandra Lee; Singer, Karen Philipp; Lead Dancers, Hector Nunez and Linda Lightfoot; Dancers, Elena Briones and Marisa Briones; Showgirls, Ginger Hill, Eileen Woods, Carye St. Clair, and Debbie

1940 opening of the Hollywood Palladium in Los Angeles. Courtesy: Los Angeles Times

Sheet music for the song "Everything's Coming Up Roses," from the 1959 film Gypsy. *Courtesy: Authors Collection*

Garner. Harold Minsky produced and directed the show; which was staged and choreographed by Betty Francisco. Jerry Lucas was the production manager; Gene Esposito the musical conductor; and the stage manager was Ava Minsky-Evans.

(Notes: Fayard (1914 – 2006) and Harold (1921 – 2000) Nicholas were considered by many to be the greatest tap dancers of their day. The brothers grew up in Philadelphia, the sons of educated African-American musicians who performed in their own band at the old Standard Theatre; their mother played piano and their father played the drums. The children grew up at the theatre which showcased most of the great African-American vaudeville acts and many of the early twentieth century jazz musicians. But the brothers loved the dancers the most and were fascinated by the combination of tap dancing and acrobatics.

During the years that the Nicholas family performed at the Standard Theatre, it was owned by John T. Gibson, an African-American, who envisioned affordable entertainment for everyone. The Standard's most successful years were from 1915 to 1930; however, in 1931, Gibson sold the Standard Theatre due to his losses from the Great Depression. The theatre was eventually turned into a movie theatre, and was officially closed in 1954. It was demolished in 1957; however, in 1992, the Pennsylvania Historical and Museum Commission placed a historical marker at the original location of the building, on the 11th block of South Street, to commemorate Gibson and the theatre.)

The following item appeared in *Tempo: A Guide to the Art of Living*. Mark Davidson wrote the article, no date was provided, and it was simply titled "Burlesque." It reads:

"In the thirties, he was America's foremost promoter of the striptease. In the fifties, he became a pioneer of topless. Now, in the era of topless, he has introduced Los Angeles to the old grind of old-time burlesque. And he insists he's still ahead of his time!

Silver-haired Harold Minsky, whose name has been synonymous with burlesque for most of the 20th century, is presenting a nostalgic production of his *Minsky Follies* – complete with baggy-pants comics reciting vintage jokes – at the Hollywood Palladium through August 30.

He concedes that topless is as far as the Minsky girls are allowed to go. That's where he draws the G-string. And no amount of chanting from the patrons of baldheaded row will persuade him to signal the girls to take it all off.

"I've never produced a totally nude show," he boasts. "I never will. I never will have to!"

Minsky thinks totally nude entertainment is tasteless and tedious. He believes the public is ready for a revival of the ribaldry that was burlesque.

"My show has played opposite the nude shows in many parts of the country in recent years," says Minsky, "and the crowds, men and women alike, always flock to us. That's because the striptease is sexier than total nudity, and also because the burlesque show consists of a lot of other entertainment besides."

The two-hour *Minsky Follies* actually consists of only two strips. In addition, there are four comedy sketches and six lavish production numbers, including the opening and finale.

Except for the show's contemporary rock music, everything is pretty much the same as when Minsky used to present such strippers as Gypsy Rose Lee and (the sister of the stripper who was his first wife) Lili St. Cyr. He also used to present such top bananas as Pinky Lee, Red Buttons, and Phil Silvers.

In the current production of the Minsky Follies, however, the star is burlesque tradition itself. It's a tradition with an interesting heritage.

Long before anyone ever heard of the striptease, the burlesque show was introduced to the United States by a troupe of English chorus girls who were billed as the British Blondes. The year was 1868.

By the turn of the century, the featured dancers in American burlesque were performing a provocative shimmy called the cooch. The cooch became a national craze as a result of the tireless efforts of a dancer called Little Egypt, who starred at the Chicago World's Fair of 1893.

How did the coy cooch evolve into the seductive strip? That's a mystery concealed by the gossamer of history.

"I really don't know," Minsky says, puffing reflectively on his pipe. "I've heard all kinds of stories. I was once told the strip was born one day when a cooch dancer accidentally dropped her bra."

On the other hand, millions of people who recently watched the telecast of *The Night They Raided Minsky's* were given a different impression. According to that movie, the strip began as an ad lib gesture of defiance – bringing down the house and the wrath of New York City plainclothesmen – perpetrated one spring night in 1925 by a willful 20-year-old cooch cutie known as Mademoiselle Fifi. Minsky, however, says the film was highly fictionalized.

Fifi was a dancer in the New York burlesque theatre that had been opened by Minsky's father, Abe, way back in 1908. While still in high school, Harold Minsky avidly assisted his father with backstage chores, only to become the new dean of burlesque with his father's retirement in 1936.

In the ensuing decades, Minsky took the shows on tours from Canada to Cuba, moving the Follies headquarters to Las Vegas.

Inasmuch as *The Night They Raided Minsky's* was before his time, he likes to remind people that he became a *cause célèbre* in his own right.

His introduction of topless dancing into Las Vegas about a dozen years ago resulted in the Nevada legislature's consideration of a bill designed specifically to put back the Minsky pasties. The statutory proposal, which the press referred to as the Bare Bosom Bill, was roundly defeated.

Today, he takes great pride in the continuing survival of his show, noting that his success in such diverse locales as Las Vegas and Grand Rapids proves that he continues to be in step with public taste.

But, if gentlemen prefer burlesque, why is it almost extinct? Why does even one of his own Las Vegas promoters refer to burlesque as "the whooping crane of show business?"

"Most burlesque shows closed down in recent years, because most of the burlesque theatres were situated in inner cities where the area had deteriorated. The general public has moved to the suburbs, and it doesn't want to go back to those shabby neighborhoods at night.

Another cause of the ruin of the runway," says Minsky, "is that the pioneer burlesque producers died off without leaving a second generation (like Harold Minsky) to carry on."

Harold Minsky has a grown son, Danny, but he's turned his back on the bright lights to become a computer programmer. This would seem to indicate that even the days of nostalgic burlesque are numbered – except that Minsky has a daughter who has sworn complete loyalty to the cause.

She's an attractive young woman named Ava. Like her father before her, she's become a behind-the-scenes apprentice to her father. Ava recently was married, but her husband, a Los Angeles clinical psychologist, has no objection to her becoming the heiress-apparent to the Minsky dynasty. "I guess I'm another example of women's liberation," Ava says.

"P" is also for "Payroll." Included in this folder were payroll figures involving shows and performers for just some of the early Minsky burlesque shows. One name in particular that caught my eye was that of talking woman and dancer, Wilma Horner; many of my Horner ancestors came from Pennsylvania. The following is just a little information I found on Wilma Horner.

From the *Pittsburgh Post-Gazette*, February 25, 1936:

"Wilma Horner Returns to Stage in *Jolly Girls*. Wilma Horner, Avalon Dancer, making her first appearance in burlesque in over a year and Charles "Red" Marshall, droll comedian, are the headliners of *Jolly Girls*, the current Independent Burlesque Association's show at the Variety. Miss Horner, whose career as a dancer was threatened when she sustained a broken back while playing an eastern theatre last year, was given a warm reception on her first appearance. Marshall, one of the best comics on the Independent Circuit had the opening day audience guffawing with his antics and wisecracks. "The War Debt" and the "Smith's Baby," two really funny bits, were Marshall's best."

From the *Pittsburgh Post-Gazette*, May 27, 1937:
"The Mack Davis's, she's Wilma Horner, the ex-burlesque queen are spending a month here with her family in Ben Avon." (Allegheny County)

Lastly, from "The Final Curtin" section in the October 3, 1942 *Billboard* magazine:
"Wilma Horner (Willie), 32, vaudeville and musical comedy performer and wife of Mack Davis Gershen, musical leader, died suddenly September 15 at her apartment in New York. She broke into show business as a chorine with tabloid units on the Joe Spiegelberg and Gus Sun circuits, later graduating to burlesque, where she soon became a principal. Later she appeared as the principal with various Harry Howard units in major vaudeville houses, her husband serving as musical leader with the same units. She did straights to Willie Howard in the latter's *Crazy With the Heat* Company, which opened in Boston Christmas week of 1940 and which later played New York. Horner is survived by her husband and several sisters and brothers."

(Notes: Wilhelmina Horner Gershen, born in 1910, is buried in New Stanton, Pennsylvania. Mack Davis Gershen died on October 25, 1976; he is buried in Queens, New York.)

Mack Davis and his Paradise Orchestra. The photo is from the 1924 sheet music, "When You and I Were Seventeen." Courtesy: Authors Collection

The following were the payrolls, cast lists, dates, and theatres included in the File. The file tab states this payroll paperwork was from "approximately 1938." Everything on the first list had names listed by first initial, and then the last name. I put together the pieces as best as I could; it does appear that the comics and straight men were all listed first.

For the Week of January 13: Brooklyn - $995.00: Bobby Morris and Charlie Harris,

$175.00; Jack Diamond, $140.00; Russell Trent, $85.00; Joey Faye, T. Chapman, J. Francis Jr., L. Murray, $85.00; L. Dixon, $75.00; M. Bartel, $120.00; V. McNeely, $110.00; A. Donaldson, $40.00; Castle and Company, $125.00; and Stage Manager, M. Kaye, $40.00.

Boston - $740.00: S. Weston, $75.00; Jimmy Dugan, $175.00; Harry Clexx, $175.00; Wally Sharples, $65.00; Herbie Barris, $65.00; Torchy Blair, $40.00; Jean Rose, $45.00; J. McCauley, $125.00; G. Clark, M. Voe; Marie Gundle, $35.00; Diane Johnson, $40.00; I. O'Donnell, $75.00; Dagmar, $70.00; and Stage Manager, E. Akin, $40.00.

Newark - $975.00: Billy Fields, $90.00; Bert Carr, $75.00; Jack Rosen, $80.00; Mervin Harmon, $85.00; Jim Walters, $70.00; H. Nickels, $50.00; B. White, $40.00; W. Clair, $50.00; G. Motormack, $65.00; Viola Spaeth, $45.00; S. Martin, $45.00; J. Amore, $45.00; Dot and Dash, $90.00; Zampini and Company, $100.00; and Stage Manager, J. Keller, $45.00.

Philadelphia - $1005.00: Joe Freed, $170.00; Happy Hyatt, $60.00; Johnny Cook, $70.00; Harry "Shuffles" LeVan, $50.00; Murray Green, $45.00; Charley Cane, $60.00; B. Harrison, $40.00; A. Bradley; Joan Barlow, $100.00; M. Lopez, $60.00; E. Lang, $65.00; K. Irwin, $75.00; C. De Vine, $75.00; J. White, $50.00; Rose Heatherly, $50.00; and Stage Manager, E. Ryan, $35.00.

Pittsburgh - $805.00: Harry "Stinky" Fields, $70.00; "Shorty" McAllister, $70.00; Benny "Wop" Moore, $75.00; Mac Dennison, $40.00; Lou Denny, $60.00; Joe Lyons, $55.00; Howard Montgomery, $45.00; P. Kerney, $40.00; D. Leland, $60.00; E. Whitney, $65.00; three names/companies, worthy of $195.00 in salary, were not legible due to a tear that was taped over; and Stage Manager, P. Cohen, $30.00.

Baltimore - $965.00: Steve Mills, $110.00; Herbie Faye, $125.00; Murray "Looney" Lewis, $50.00; S. Stone, $50.00; J. Elliott, $45.00; J. Devaux, $125.00; G. Kinnear, $60.00; Wilma Horner, $70.00; S. Slane, $75.00; Jean Carroll, $55.00; F. Moore, $60.00; S. Darling, $150.00; Barbara Janis, $100.00; F. Naomi, $45.00; Zulieka, $75.00; and Stage Manager, J. Kane, $40.00.

Republic - $1165.00: Jack Greenman, $100.00; Harry "Stinky" Fields, $95.00; Joseph K. Watson (went on to become a script writer in Hollywood,) and Willie Cohen, $200.00; Billy Arlington, $100.00; J. Steele, $55.00; L. Royce, $110.00; Joan Bell, $50.00; Margie Hart, $125.00; Rose La Rose, $50.00; L. Phelps, $50.00; Mae Dix, $50.00; E. Mae, M. Byron, $60.00; Carmen, $70.00; and Stage Manager, W. Miller, $50.00. Handwritten notes next to this list of names were: Allison, $60.00; Carmen, $60.00; and White, $75.00. I assume they were additions to the cast, or perhaps a salary change in the case of Carmen.

Brooklyn - $750.00; *Scan-Dolls* – the salary list for the week of September 22nd was as follows: Tom Bundy, $75.00; Edna Dee, $75.00; Charlie "Uncle Ezra"

Goldie, $50.00; Al Golden Jr., $55.00; Jewel Sothern and Lew Devine, $125.00; Harold and Reeves, $90.00; Lois Wray, $50.00; Dot Ahearn, $65.00; Frank X. Silk, $130.00; and Samuel Friedman, $35.00. The Captain of the line received an extra $5.00; and the chorus girls received $25.00 each.

Theatre – either Brooklyn or the Republic - $570.00; *Wine Woman and Song* – the salary list for week of October 6th was as follows: Buddy and Betty Abbott, $155.00; Murray "Looney" Lewis, $55.00; Sam Gould, $50.00; Gene Schuller, $85.00; Cynthia Mitchell, $50.00; Ruth Coburn, $50.00; Charles Robinson, $40.00; Rose Heatherly, $50.00; and Russell Carew, $35.00. The Captain of the line received an extra $5.00; and the chorus girls received $25.00 each.

Brooklyn - $1045.00; *Hi Hat Revue* – the salary list for week of October 13th was as follows: Billy Arlington, $100.00; Scotty Friedell, $50.00; Ann Winn, $60.00; Brownie Sick and Toots Brawner, $140.00; Marie Allely, $40.00; Eddie Lloyd, $60.00; Charley Cane, $60.00; Jean Rose, $50.00; Dolores Shaw, $50.00; Nazarro Hallo, $60.00; and Hughie Mack, $35.00. The Captain of the line received an extra $5.00; and the chorus girls received $25.00 each.

The following was added to the above list at a later time; the type was much darker, for some there were no first names, and the last name was handwritten in: Ceil Von Dell, $55.00; Maxie Furman, $75.00; Alma Maiben, $40.00; Simmons, $60.00; France, $65.00; and Reynolds, $45.00.

Republic - $783.50; *Pacemakers* – the salary list for the week of October 13th was as follows: Harry Bentley, $55.00; Max Coleman, $75.00; Jim Walters and Viola Spaeth, $90.00; Carlos and Gale, $100.00; Billie Hughes, $60.00; Sally O'Day, $60.00; Al Hillier, $73.50; Wen Miller, $60.00; Diane Johnson, $55.00; Connie Dale, $40.00; Ray and Really, $80.00; and Max Kroll, $35.00. The Captain of the line received an extra $5.00; and the chorus girls received $25.00 each.

Republic - $695.00; *Say It With Girls* – the salary list for the week of October 13th was as follows: Lew Black, $50.00; Harry White, $50.00; Charles Dane, $50.00; Dudley Douglas, $45.00; Frank C. Smith, $60.00; Herbie Faye and Barbara Janis, $125.00; Barbara Bow, $45.00; Hilda Allison, $50.00; Marie Gundle, $40.00; Condo and Allen, $85.00; Rose La Rose, $60.00; and Frank Engle, $35.00. The Captain of the line received an extra $5.00; and the chorus girls received $25.00 each.

The next folder is for "Publicity," but there wasn't much in it. It included multiple copies of a couple advertisements and a cast list.

The following was a list of the cast, crew, and scenes from *Minsky's Burlesque Follies '75*. Of course the show was Produced and Directed by Harold Minsky. The rest of the company included: Staged and Choreographed by Betty Francisco;

Production Manager, Jerry Lucas; Costume Designer, Anne Guertin; Musical Conductor, Jan Gallatin; Musical Arrangements by Ken Tiffany; Costumes Executed by Eastwood; and the Line Captain was Pat Merl. The cast included: Production Singer, Sandy MacTavish; Straight Man, Jerry Lucas; Talking Woman, Bobbye Mack; Covered Dancers, Annette Jops and Jewlie Elliott; Lead Dancers, Kurt Sproul and Linda Lightfoot; Comics, Dick Richards and Jimmy Mathews; Showgirls, Nancy Schuneman, Ginger Hill, Pat Merl, and Donna Reynolds; and Exotic Dancers, Saki Tumi and Donna Reynolds.

The scenes in the show included: "Handful of Nickels," "Kung Fu," "The School Room," "The Gun Ain't Loaded," and "Elk's Convention."

The first of several Playboy Files was a combined folder for St. Louis, Missouri, and Valparaiso, Indiana. It contained the Agreement, which was four pages long, along with a single page RIDER for the show, and a newspaper article.

The Agreement, dated December 17, 1974, seemed to be a standard contract between Minsky and the Playboy Clubs International. The show was to be presented in the Penthouse, at the Playboy Club located at 3914 Lindell Boulevard, in St. Louis, Missouri from April 25, 1975 through May 10, 1975. (The club closed in 1975.) Each performance was to last approximately one hour, presented six nights weekly, two shows nightly, and three shows each on Friday and Saturday; everyone had Sundays off. The third show on Friday night could be changed to any night, Monday through Thursday, as long as one week's advance notice was given of said change; those became known as a "floating show." The cast would consist of no less than twelve people; and maximum rehearsals were to be two, four-hour sessions. Minsky was to receive $6,650.00 per week, and to be paid on Saturday of each week.

Dancers from Minsky Burlesque Follies '75; the lead dancers were Linda Lightfoot and Kurt Sproul. Courtesy: Nancy Schuneman

The Agreement was signed by Harold Minsky, Irvin Arthur, Director of Entertainment for Playboy Clubs International, as well as Chuck Eddy of Associated Booking Corporation.

The RIDER gave the following performance dates as well:

Valparaiso, Indiana; May 13, 1975 through May 25, 1975 – this contract includes room and meals, and is for six days per week, fourteen shows per week.

Playboy Towers Hotel, Chicago, Illinois; Starting June 2, 1975 for a period of eight weeks – this contract includes room and meals, and is for six days weekly, fourteen shows per week.

The following article was written by Bob Goddard, and appeared in the Family Section of the *St. Louis Globe-Democrat* newspaper on Friday, May 2, 1975. It was titled "'Dean of Burlesque' Brings Show to Town," and reads as follows:

"The story is probably apocryphal, but it has been said that the first words Harold Minsky uttered as an infant when he caught sight of a pretty girl were, "Take it off!"

Minsky neither confirms nor denies voicing the immortal line, but it's fairly certain that he has heard that clarion call of burlesque more times than any man alive. It's ironic, too, in a way, because the proverbial "baldheaded row" at Minsky burlesque theatres never got all-out results from their exuberant shouts.

"No Minsky show has ever gone in for total nudity," Minsky said when he came to town for the opening of a brand-new show, *Minsky's Follies*, which will be at the St. Louis Playboy Club through May 10. "Bare breasts, yes, but it's much more provocative to leave something to the imagination. Matter of fact, yesteryear Minsky shows left almost everything to the imagination. In less permissive days, the showgirls and the striptueses wore flesh-covered tights, neckline to toe."

As today's "Dean of Burlesque," Harold Minsky admits that the lively art is long past its glory days, "but it will always survive and is doing especially well today, when nostalgia is the thing. Young folks who have never seen burlesque come to our shows to see what it's all about, and the older generation flocks back for an affectionate encore look at the baggy-pants comics, the straight men, the showgirls, and the exotics.

"Burlesque is light entertainment, and when done in good taste, as we do it, certainly nobody can be offended. That's what we're here for, to entertain. If you want a message, see Western Union," he said.

If anybody is qualified to speak with ringing authority about Burlesque, it's Minsky. Once dubbed the "Ziegfeld Follies for the Forgotten Man," the Minsky's burlesque chain was started by Harold's father, Abe Minsky, in 1908, when he opened his first theatre in New York City. He was later joined in the business by his three brothers, Billy, Herbert, and Morton. They flourished mightily and at one time operated 14 burlesque houses, mostly in the East.

Yesteryear New York Mayor Fiorello La Guardia, bound and determined to keep New York "pure," closed the last Minsky's New York theatre in 1937 when he saw to it that their license wasn't renewed. In spite of such reversals, Harold Minsky, who joined his dad and uncles in the business when he was fresh out of high school, has never been anything but a burlesque man in the 43 years since.

After the New York operation bowed out, he produced shows for a while in New Orleans, then moved to Las Vegas in 1950 and is still there, putting on burlesque shows regularly at the glitter spots and venturing afield every now and then to present his shows in Canada, South America, and throughout the United States. The current show at the St. Louis Playboy Club goes next to Chicago for a six-month run at the Playboy there.

"My dad wanted me to go on to college when I finished high school," Harold recalled, "but I was crazy about burlesque and talked him into letting me go to work for him. Incidentally, I was one of the most popular boys in high school. My father owned a burlesque show!"

Harold's longtime romance with burlesque included two of its practitioners; his first wife was a stripteaser, and the sister of famed exotic Lili St. Cyr. And his second and present wife, Pat, ("We're very happily married"), is a former burlesque showgirl.

The aforementioned Lili St. Cyr, by the way, was paid as much as $500 a week by the Minsky's, and Harold lists her as one of the most popular strippers of all time, along with Gypsy Rose Lee, Rose La Rose, Georgia Sothern, Ann Corio, and former Missourian Margie Hart.

Margie Hart.
Courtesy: Janelle Smith Collection

"They all worked for Minsky, and so did a lot of comics who made big names for themselves later on. My dad featured Abbott and Costello, Bert Lahr, Clark and McCullough, and Fanny Brice; and I myself started Phil Silvers, Red Buttons, and Pinky Lee in the business."

It was a grand era, and everybody came to Minsky's, not just the man in the street. The mink coat and top hat set came to be entertained, and stage-door Johnnies crowded the back entranceway to get a look at the girls. One of them, I remember, was an Egyptian prince or something, and he eventually married one of the showgirls, with the stipulation

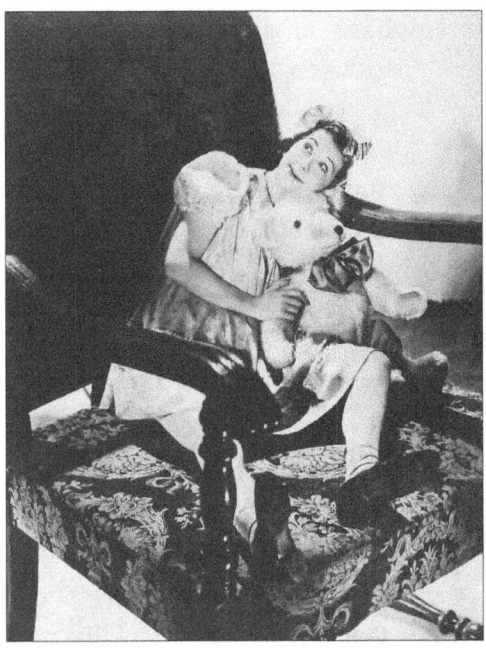

NBC Press Photo of Fanny Brice as Baby Snooks. *Courtesy: Authors Collection*

*Bert Lahr.
Courtesy: Burlesque Historical Society*

1965 Press Photo of Phil Silvers singing from Show Boat *sheet music. Courtesy: Silver Screen Collection*

One of four photos from 1962 Press Photo of Red Buttons. At that time he was the only actor to win both an Oscar and an Emmy. Courtesy: Authors Collection

that she would have to give him a male heir or the marriage was off. She did give him a male heir, and last I heard they were living happily ever after."

It wasn't really surprising that the so-called "quality folks" loved Minsky shows, as Minsky shows were always class productions.

"When you say the word burlesque," Minsky said, "the first word that comes to mind for most people is stripteaser. The exotics are, of course, an integral part of it, but the true essence of burlesque is its emphasis on satire. Pretty girls, sure. Double entendre humor, yes. But the keynote is fun. It's a happy kind of entertainment."

SAKI TUMI

Saki Tumi. Courtesy: C.F. Miller

The "happy entertainment" these nights in *Minsky's Follies* at the Playboy is no slapdash affair. The Minsky touch is ever present – in the beautifully-choreographed routines, the rousing music, the lookable showgirls, a beautiful Hawaiian stripper, Saki Tumi, (how about that?); baggy-pants comic Claude Mathis, and straight man Dexter Maitland, having a ball with the classic burlesque comedy routines, and a pretty young singer, Lynn Marie, making her professional stage debut here.

Straight man Maitland, by the way, played the straight man in the movie, *The Night They Raided Minsky's*, of which Harold Minsky served as a sort of unofficial adviser to producer Norman Lear.

Minsky, an affable, hale and hearty sort, figures he'll be keeping the Minsky tradition of quality burlesque alive for a long time to come, but if he ever gets around to thinking about an epitaph, he'll settle for the hit song from *Gypsy* - "Let Me Entertain You" - the musical about burlesque."

The next folder was labeled "Playboy - New York." It contained the Agreement, and a cast list of thirteen performers with weekly salaries to be paid to each, which was dated February 26, 1971. The cast list was handwritten on Patava, Inc. stationery, some of which was illegible. One name I could read, and know, is comic Dick Richards, who was paid $400.00. A few other names I could read were: Janet Schoolcraft, showgirl, $225.00; Joan Symes, showgirl, $225.00; Katherine Price, showgirl, $225.00; Sally Arena, dancer, $225.00; Harriet Lyn, singer and talking woman, $250.00; Jan Marts, lead dancer, $325.00; Richard Hamilton, lead dancer, $275.00; Coral Cooney, dancer, $225.00; Maurice Wayne

Oberlander, straight man and company manager, $325.00; and Jerry Spinner, dancer, $225.00. The strip, whose stage name was not listed, was paid $400.00.

Finding a typed list in the wrong folder, later, verifies the names, and wages paid. Of course some names were spelled differently between the two lists, so I hope I have them right!

The Agreement, a typical Minsky contract, was dated January 28, 1971 and signed by Arlyne Rothberg for Playboy Clubs International, and Chuck Eddy, Vice President of Associated Booking Corporation. The show was to be presented at the Playboy Club, 5 East 59th Street, New York City, in the room designated as the Penthouse. The show was to commence on February 26, 1971 and run anywhere from two to four weeks. Each performance was to last approximately one hour, and be presented three times nightly, and six nights weekly with Sundays off. The cast would consist of no less than thirteen performers.

The Playboy Club was to provide and pay for a spinet organ for all rehearsals and performances. They were also to provide and pay for four musicians, who were to include as follows: organist, drums, trumpet, and sax. The club was to pay $6500.00 per week; $650.00 to Associated Booking Corporation, and the remaining $5850.00 to Patava, Inc.

There was also a section towards the end of the contract, typical of all Minsky Agreements, which reads: "It is agreed and understood that the above parties of this agreement shall comply with all union regulations of any unions or guilds that might have jurisdiction over any employees of either party to the agreement." Handwritten under that section are the words, "We don't recognize AGVA." This was the first time I have seen that added to any of these contracts.

The next folder was the "Playboy Club - Lake Geneva, Wisconsin." It included Agreements for three separate years: September 3 through September 9, 1969; April 17 through June 21, 1970; and September 10 through November 21, 1971. The first two contracts were signed by Arlyne Rothberg, for Playboy Clubs International, and Chuck Eddy for Associated Booking Corporation. The 1971 Agreement was also signed by Chuck Eddy, but Arnold Morton signed as the Vice President for Playboy Clubs International. Shows for all three years were to include a cast of fifteen performers, and to be performed in what was designated as the Penthouse at the Lake Geneva Playboy Club.

The 1969 Agreement states the club was to pay $7500.00 weekly; $750.00 to Associated Booking Corporation and $6750.00 payable to Patava, Inc. The contract also stipulated that the Playboy Club would pay for "two prop boys for backstage and a follow spotlight and operator for all rehearsals and performances." The club would also pay for no less than eight musicians.

The 1970 contract paid $850.00 to Associated Booking Corporation and $7650.00 to Patava, Inc. for a total of $8500.00 per week. The 1970 contract stipulated the Playboy Club would pay for eight musicians, and they would also provide a follow spotlight and operator.

Lastly the initial 1971 contract paid $550.00 to Associated Booking Corporation and $5700.00 to Patava, Inc. for a weekly payment of $6250.00. The contract stipulates that the club would pay for six musicians, to include the following: organ, drums, trumpet, trombone, saxophone, and electric bass. It also stated: "All cast members are to receive gratis rooms and board; meals shall be gratis at the Sidewalk Café, Playmate Bar, or Playboy employee's cafeteria. If the cast members use any other restaurants at the Playboy Club Hotel, they shall receive a fifty percent (50%) discount on food and beverages." The contract also went on to give different weekly payments should the club extend their option for additional weeks of performances; the contract *was* extended for four additional weeks, for a total of fourteen, and the rate of pay was adjusted to $6000.00 per week. This is known due to the dates on Diane Marlo's contract.

The AGVA Contract, #33775, between Patava, Inc. and exotic dancer Diane Marlo, was dated and signed on October, 20, 1971. Marlo was to perform at the Playboy Club Hotel in Lake Geneva, Wisconsin for four weeks and three days; six shows weekly and two shows per day beginning on November 19th, 1971. She was to receive $350.00 per week, plus room and meals. Her agent was Roland Muse.

There were multiple lists of cast members' names in the folder; sadly, none revealed those performing in the 1969 show.

Barbara Curtis.
Courtesy: Janelle Smith Collection

Typed, on Minsky's personal stationery, was the following:

"Minsky's Burlesque '70 – Resume:

Barbara Curtis, Straight Woman; Patrick J. Burns, Straight Man; Pat Burns and Barbara Curtis who handle the "straight man" chores, are veteran performers in Vaudeville and the legitimate stage. They've been in Burlesque over six years.

Looney Lewis, Comic; Looney Lewis, is considered to be the Top Banana in Burlesque today. Looney has been in several Broadway shows and television specials in recent years.

Suzette Summers. Courtesy: Pat Elliott Minsky/Burlesque Historical Society

Jimmy Mathews. Courtesy: Jimmy Mathews

Richard J. Colacino, Lead Dancer; Ann C. Gubbins, Lead Dancer; Both Ann and Dick have been with the Follies Bergere and the Lido Club in Paris and are veteran Minsky Performers.

Candy Graham, Singer; Vocalist Candy Graham has been with the country's top groups and has been playing the Playboy Circuit.

Ferd Hernandez, Fighter; Spanish speaking Ferd Hernandez is a real fighter, and holds a decision over Sugar Ray Robinson to prove it.

Suzette Summers, Strip Woman; Suzette Summers is a protégé of Harold Minsky and recently closed at the Aladdin Hotel, Las Vegas, Nevada, and the Condado Beach Hotel, San Juan, Puerto Rico in order to open at the Sherman Hotel, in Chicago, Illinois.

Showgirls: Marcela Biddle, Sandra M. Carter, Mary A. Ellison, and Janet Schoolcraft.

Dancers: Laura Del Mar, Mary A. Kirby, Kathleen Ann Ruth, and Josephine Spinedi.

Staged and Choreographed by Jerry Norman; Produced by Harold Minsky."

There were two additional names on a similar list of names; Patricia Walsh and James Kimberlin.

Also, on a similar list, dated September 10, 1971, names and some salaries were penciled in. Salaries behind typed-in names included: Barbara Curtis Anger, $300.00; Richard J. Colacino, $325.00; Ann C. Gubbins, $300.00; Sandra M. Carter, $200.00; Laura Del Mar, $200.00; Mary A. Kirby, $200.00; Kathleen Ann Ruth, $225.00; and Josephine Spinedi, $250.00. Handwritten names and salaries included: Ferd Hernandez, $250.00; Satan's Angel, $400.00; Looney Lewis, $400.00; Candy Graham, $300.00; Diane Marlo, $350.00; Herbie Barris, $300.00; Ralph Clifford, Stage Manager/Company Manager, $250.00; and Jimmy Mathews, comic, $300.00.

There was one final list of names in this folder, which was under the heading of Patava, Inc.

There was no date, and there were no line dancers or showgirls names listed. The list reads: Looney Lewis, Comic; Willie Dew, Comic; Pat Burns, Straight Man; Barbara Curtis, Straight Woman; Lee Ballard, Production Singer; Satan's Angel, Strip; Alawn Don Jay, Strip; Ann Gubbins, Feature Dancer; Dick Colacino, Feature Dancer; Ferd Hernandez, Prize Fighter; Jerry Lucas, Stage Manager; Dick Albers, Trampoline Act; Miss Loni, Juggler; and "22 people in the cast."

The last item in this folder was a newspaper article; handwritten on it was: "Chicago Daily News, April 25, 1970." It was titled "Oh, Minsky! Oh, Womensky!" and written by Sam Lesner. It reads as follows:

"Harold Minsky, the genteel, soft-spoken, middle-aged and graying son of the founder of Minsky's Burlesque (1908), is presenting his *Minsky's Burlesque Follies of 1970* at the Playboy Club-Hotel at Lake Geneva without those silly breast patches (pasties) that hide virtually nothing.

Hardly anyone seemed to notice the absence of the frivolous cover-ups as Minsky's bare-bosomed strutters pranced among the frisky dancers in choreographer Jerry Norman's wildly gymnastic production numbers.

But that's the idea, Minsky explains – to keep a relentlessly aggressive tempo in the dance numbers, even if the burlesque comedy skits generally bog down.

Minsky has a patent on his burlesque formula, and he may be quite correct in his assumption that what looks old and tired to us oldsters now is being discovered by a younger generation for its campy freshness.

"This business is going to get bigger, not smaller," Minsky said after the opening night show of this current nine-week engagement.

"The kids today can look at burlesque without the initial shock and embarrassment that bugged us. But they've only seen strippers and go-go dancers, and not old-time burlesque. And with topless waitresses serving lunch and drinks today, pasties surely are archaic. The kids today are much more broad-minded," Minsky adds with a straight face, even though he laughs at the "Look, Ma, no pasties!" quip his revue inspires.

"In Puerto Rico, you still wear pasties. It's the rule. But in Cincinnati we did two shows recently for charity, at $25 a ticket, without pasties, and we even played Hyannis Port one week in the summer of 1968 with tremendous success – and no pasties."

Minsky says he hopes to take an expanded company out on the road this fall to play "all the Shubert houses, but no more playing in those decrepit, filthy burlesque houses." In Las Vegas, the parent company of Minsky's Follies is a continuous entertainment magnet.

Minsky says he retains a strong affection for Chicago (his burlesque occupied the Rialto Theatre on State Street for four years, until it was torn down in 1954).

His Playboy version of his famed Follies features lead dancers Ann Gubbins and Dick Colacino; singer Candy Graham, who sings loud and with a cutting edge; and burlesque comic Looney Lewis, who lets himself get vigorously slapped about with 16-ounce boxing gloves by authentic middleweight boxer Ferd Hernandez while they exchange insults in Shakespearean verse.

Autographed photo of Satan's Angel. Courtesy: C.F. Miller

Also, there is straight man Pat Burns, straight lady Barbara Curtis, Miss Loni, a juggler, and, best of all, stripper Satan's Angel, whose "Light My Fire" number, has twirling flaming tassels attached to where pasties used to be.

While its bargain-basement burlesque in quality, if you let yourself go, the show definitely has a number of buckle-busting yocks."

(Notes: Richard Colacino appeared in Off-Broadway Revivals of *Oklahoma* in 1958, and *The Boys from Syracuse* in 1963. He is also listed in the credits as a dancer in the 1969 Broadway show *Sweet Charity*, as well as listed as a waiter/dancer in the film version.

Boxer Ferd Hernandez won a national Golden Gloves title in 1960 and turned professional a year later. He fought as a middleweight from 1961-68, recording 33 wins in a 46-fight career. At one time, Hernandez even held the Nevada middleweight title. On July 12, 1965, in Las Vegas, Hernandez, at the peak of his career, scored a 10-round decision over former world welterweight and middleweight champ Sugar Ray Robinson, who was on the downside of his storied career. In 1966, Hernandez got his shot at a world middleweight title, fighting Jose Gonzalez to a draw. Two years later, a detached retina forced his retirement from fighting. Hernandez became a Nevada boxing referee in 1970, and continued in that capacity for 15 years. He also became a popular local Las Vegas bartender. He died in Omaha, Nebraska on July 17, 1996. Ferd Hernandez was 57 years old.

In his 2004 memoir, *Someday You're Not Coming Down*, Dick Albers, (Dick Albershardt) chronicles his career as an internationally known comedy trampoline artist. During his years at the University of Indiana, Dick won the North – South Championships in Sarasota, Florida in both 1954 as well as 1955. He also captured the 1955 NCAA Trampoline Championship and the Big 10 Trampoline Championship titles in both 1952 and 1956. Albers turned his trampoline skills and comedic talent into a livelihood and with family in tow Dick found himself performing with the Globetrotters, in Las Vegas, on television, in Minsky's burlesque shows, at the London Palladium, Madison Square Garden, and on tour with Bob Hope's USO show entertaining military troops throughout the war zones of Southeast Asia. According to his authors' page, Dick Albers performed throughout 49 states and 30 countries around the world; he considered every show date a new and exciting chapter in his life.

Miss Loni. Courtesy: Pat Elliott Minsky/Burlesque Historical Society

Miss Loni, was born Apolonia Van Voorden in 1926, and died in 2012; she grew up in Holland in a family of performing artists. When Loni was 10, her father began encouraging her to practice juggling, dancing on a wire, and spinning objects with her feet. Soon, Loni was foot juggling in the family circus. The wire act was dropped to emphasize her foot juggling, and her father gave her the stage name of Miss Loni. Her family toured Europe with her father's small circus, which included a variety of acts such as clowns, magicians, jugglers, trained bears, and acrobatics.

A representative from Ringling Bros. and Barnum & Bailey Circus discovered Loni in Europe and recruited her to join the circus in America. Miss Loni first came to America in her early 20s. She was giving her first performance with the circus at Madison Square Garden when film director, Cecil B. DeMille, asked to be introduced to her.

In the 1950s, the Ringling Bros. and Barnum & Bailey Circus toured major cities using multiple railroad trains. As a performer, essentially living on a train for two years, Miss Loni recalled how the "oddity" people from the sideshows had to stay in separate railcars. With all of the performance tents, a cookhouse tent, dressing-room tents, sideshows, and other appendages, the circus was a small town.

After a couple of years with the circus, she moved with her husband to Chicago and began performing in nightclubs, mostly in the Midwest, New York, Hollywood, and Las Vegas. They were big productions; Miss Loni would open for Liberace, or one of the big bands of the era. "It was certainly a more sophisticated life," she said. "But looking back, the circus was very nostalgic." After about 10 years on the nightclub scene, she decided to return to the circus.

Miss Loni appeared in two films, *The Greatest Show on Earth*, from 1952, starring Charlton Heston; and *Jumbo*, a 1962 film about a circus elephant that featured Doris Day, Jimmy Durante, and Martha Raye. While filming *Jumbo*, Miss Loni heard that two members of the Flying Wallendas, a family high-wire act, fell to their deaths during a performance in Detroit. At the time, Miss Loni had the same manager, and she was friends with the family.

Until the age of 60, Miss Loni performed with a variety of circuses. The items she juggled and spun with her feet included: a large ball, a cross-shaped object, lit lanterns, and an oversized playing card. During her career, she also performed with Bob Hope, went on tour with the Harlem Globetrotters, and appeared on a number of television shows, including *The Ed Sullivan Show*. Miss Loni died in 2012.

Mona Vaughn, the first member of the BHS, at a small gathering in Venice Beach, California in 1997, which included Sunny Lee and the author. Courtesy: Authors Collection

"You can take someone out of the circus," Miss Loni once said, "but you're never going to take the circus out of someone." Mona Vaughn would have agreed. See her chapter in *BURLESQUE: Legendary Stars of the Stage, 2nd Edition*.)

The next folder in the "P" File is for "Playboy – Miami; 1971 - 1974." There was a lot in this folder and I have sorted it out by year. There were three separate Agreements for 1971 alone. The shows ran consecutively starting on May 14, 1971, and ending November 13, 1971. The shows were performed at "The Lounge" in the Playboy Plaza Hotel, in Miami, Florida. Minsky would supply all costumes, shoes, hose and accessories, scenery, backdrops, props, musical arrangements, and special material, as well as any and all necessary things for the presentation of the show. These are typical stipulations in Minsky contracts.

The first 10-week long contract was signed by Arlyne Rothberg, for Playboy Clubs International; the other two were signed by Arnold Morton. All were signed by Chuck Eddy, and the second was personally signed by Harold Minsky.

All state that each performance was to last approximately one hour, and was to be presented six nights per week, three shows nightly, if needed, and everyone would have Sundays off. They also all state the club would provide a follow spotlight and operator for all rehearsals and performances. Minsky requested five musicians and instrumentation in all three Agreements for: organ, drums, trumpet, trombone, and saxophone.

In the first contract, for ten weeks, Minsky was to receive $5500.00 per week; of which a weekly payment of $550.00 was to be paid to the Associated Booking Corporation. The second contract, for six weeks, Minsky was to receive a weekly payment of $5167.50, and $375.00 of that was paid to the Associated Booking Corporation per week. This contract also stipulated that all cast members were to receive gratis rooms and board at the Playboy Plaza Hotel, Miami Beach, Florida; the gratis meals were to be in the coffee shop only. The final contract, for nine weeks, the cast received the same gratis room and board as in the second contract. Minsky was to be paid $5082.30 per week, and the Associated Booking Corporation received $375.00 per week. Of course from the money Minsky received he paid all the salaries, insurance, and costs for producing the show.

The next item will only be quoted in-part. It comes from a May 20, 1971 article by Paul M. Bruun in the *Miami Beach Reporter*. Initially I thought it was meant to be a review of *Minsky's Burlesque '71*, but reading the very long article I came to a different conclusion. The article was titled "'Chest' Gets Some Gripes off HIS." Because of its length and content, it made me think the man who wrote the piece was also the man who published the newspaper – he didn't seem to care what the article was about or the word count. The following were the only paragraphs in the entire article which mentioned the show, or the performers.

"To get down to the bare facts of Minsky's Playboy Revue by Harold Minsky, there is a solo stripper, Diane Marlo. And she knows what stripping, in exciting fashion, is all about. And she has the wherewithal from which to take her attire.

The star of Minsky's is Looney Lewis. He does a boxing scene that Chris Dundee must understudy. Ditto Cassius Clay. Shakespeare even gets into this act. Jerry Lucas is his opponent but I like Jerry's second better, and Maurie Wayne. The girls are Barbara Curtis and Deborah Duke. This is burlesque comedy at its very best. I am still laughing.

NASA should take pointers from "Everybody Gets To Go To The Moon." This song is by the Minsky star singer Bonnie Graham, and she sings this one in red sequin pants and poncho.

There is "The Crazy House." Looney Lewis is the star patient. I do not know whether Looney is his christened name but it sure fits him better than any name conceivable. Bonnie Graham has songs throughout. There is one male dancer, Bob Romaniak. Now fellows, here is a guy to be jealous of, the only real young man in the cast and all that feminine pulchritude everywhere around him.

The costumes are superior, the lighting can be improved, the routines are exciting and fast, the music is under the baton of Stan Musick with the orchestra under the direction of Charles Austin.

I have a suggestion which just might be workable. I am going back to burlesque of yesteryear, before most young punks of today were born. How about an old-time candy butcher to enliven things before each show starts, with salable items for his huckstering? It might add to the general theme and to the fun of an evening.

With some sharpening by management, this Minsky Revue, with occasional changes, should be able to play the Playboy Plaza forever. These girls I just might find reason to appraise another time, if Josephine will let me go alone again, and if it isn't opening night when and where everybody knows me.

Yes, I guess I am just a dirty old man, a devotee of old-time burlesque. And I know you are jealous of me, so stop complaining."

Also in this folder, with no date, was a listing that simply reads "Cast of Minsky Show Playboy Plaza Hotel." Was this the beginnings of a working cast list? It reads:

Comedian, Sammy Smith; Straight Man, Maurie Wayne; Talking Woman, Bobbye Mack; Exotic Dancer, Saki Tumi; Singer, Wyoma Winters; Lead Dancers, Michel Stany and Bonnie Fletcher; Showgirls, Francis Satcher, Michele Jourquin, Sunni Nelson, and Sara McKay; and Dancers, Nancy French.

Sammy Smith.
Courtesy: Burlesque Historical Society

On February 29, 1972, Chuck Eddy sent the following letter:
Mr. Arnold Morton
Playboy Clubs International, Inc.
919 N. Michigan Avenue
Chicago, Illinois 60611

Dear Arnold:

Your signature and Harold Minsky's together below will serve as a Letter of Agreement to the following:

It is agreed and understood that the contract between the Playboy Plaza Hotel, Miami, and Patava, Inc., a Nevada Corporation, dated July 30, 1971 and as revised October 18, 1971 for the current engagement of Minsky's Burlesque show in the Playmate Lounge shall terminate Saturday, April 8, 1972.

It is further understood and agreed that the producer, Mr. Harold Minsky, shall provide a completely new show to include a change in costumes, girl vocalist, exotic dancer, new burlesque skits and, in short, a complete new show utilizing some or all of the chorus members. Said new show shall commence, Monday, April 10, 1972 for twenty-six (26) consecutive weeks through and including Saturday, October 7, 1972. All terms and conditions of the original contract dated July 30, 1971 and as revised October 18, 1971 shall remain the same including the contract price of Forty Eight Hundred Fifty Dollars ($4,850.00) weekly.

It is further agreed and understood that the Playboy Plaza Hotel has the right to close the show upon four (4) weeks advance written notice. However, such notice cannot be given before Monday, June 12, 1972. In the event that Playboy Plaza Hotel elects to give four (4) weeks advance notice of closing, it is agreed that the Playboy Plaza Hotel shall pay Patava, Inc., the sum of Two Hundred Dollars ($200.00) per week for any unplayed weeks of the twenty-six (26) week period commencing April 10, 1972.

It is further agreed that the Playboy Plaza Hotel will provide gratis accommodations for the choreographer, producer, manager, and costumer during the rehearsal period for the new show for the ten (10) day period commencing April 3, 1972 for the purpose of staging, blocking, and rehearsing the new show.

Kindest regards.
Sincerely yours,
Chuck Eddy
Vice President
Associated Booking Corporation
It was Agreed, Accepted, and Signed by Arnold Morton and Harold Minsky.

A simple attached letter, dated May 5, 1972, reads:
Dear Harold,
Please attach the enclosed Agreement to your copy of the contract for your engagement in Miami.
Kindest personal regards.
Sincerely,
Chuck Eddy

On June 29th, 1972, on Harold Minsky stationery, Harold sent the following note:

"To the cast of Minsky Show, Playboy Plaza Hotel, Miami Beach, Florida…

Michel Zaplatilek
Roberta Fletcher
Nancy French
Toni Alley
Michele Jourquin
Sunni Nelson
Patricia Merl
Sara McKay
Barbara McAneney
Wyoma Winters
Saki Tumi

Please be advised your present contract shall run indefinitely; Subject to two weeks' notice.

Respectfully,
Harold Minsky
President
Patava, Inc.
Las Vegas, Nevada

There was one more letter in this folder regarding shows for 1972. It was written by Chuck Eddy, and dated September 20, 1972. It was sent to, and signed by Irvin Arthur. It read as follows:

Irvin Arthur
Playboy Clubs International, Inc.
8560 Sunset Boulevard
Los Angeles, California 90069

Dear Irvin,

Your signature and HAROLD MINSKY'S signature below will serve as a Letter of Agreement whereby you are extending the current engagement of shall be extended the MINSKY BURLESQUE SHOW now playing in the Playmate Lounge of the Playboy Plaza Hotel, Miami Beach, Florida, through and including Sunday, February 11, 1973.

All terms and conditions of the current contract including the modifications will remain the same.

It is further agreed and understood that Playboy Clubs International, Inc., has an option to extend his engagement beyond February 11, 1973, said option shall be exercised on or before Monday, January 29, 1973.

If option is exercised, then the engagement shall be on an indefinite basis subject to four weeks notice of termination by either party.
Kindest regards.
Sincerely,
Chuck Eddy
Vice President
Associated Booking Corporation

The next letter was written on Associated Booking Corporation stationery and dated March 29, 1973. In pencil, in the upper right hand corner someone wrote the following: "4/27/73," "Indefinite," and "No Copy." The letter was attached to an updated Agreement dated March 23, 1973. The letter was signed by Chuck Eddy, Irvin Arthur, and Harold Minsky. The updated Agreement was signed by Eddy, Minsky, and Arnold Morton, Vice President of Playboy Clubs International. The letter reads:

Mr. Irvin Arthur
Entertainment Director
Playboy International
919 N. Michigan Avenue
Chicago, Illinois 60611

Dear Irvin;
Your signature below will serve as a confirmation that the MINSKY SHOW'S opening date in Miami, Florida shall be Friday, April 27, 1973 in the Playmate Lounge. All other terms including the length of the engagement shall remain the same as the contract signed by Arnold Morton dated March 23, 1973.

It is further agreed and understood that the opening date for the MINSKY SHOW in the Penthouse of the Playboy in Chicago, Illinois shall definitely be Monday, May 21, 1973 also as per the contract signed by Arnold Morton dated March 23, 1973.
Sincerely,
Chuck Eddy
Vice President
Associated Booking Corporation

The updated Agreement states it was "for presentation in the room now designated as the Playmate Lounge, in the Playboy Plaza Hotel, Miami Beach, Florida for an indefinite period of time, subject to four (4) weeks' notice of termination by either party, with a minimum guarantee of 26 weeks. The guarantee period of 26 consecutive weeks shall commence on Friday, April 20, 1973 through and including Thursday, October 18, 1973; each performance to last approximately one (1) hour and presented six (6) nights per week; Sundays off; two (2) shows nightly, three (3) shows on Fridays and Saturdays."

Minsky was to provide a cast of twelve people, as well as all things necessary for the presentation of the show. The club was to provide the spotlight and operator, as well as an orchestra of five. All cast members were to receive gratis rooms and board at the Playboy Plaza Hotel in Miami Beach; the meals were to be provided only in the coffee shop. Minsky was to receive a payment of $5,000.00 on Friday of each week. From that payment Minsky paid the salaries of all performers, including all taxes and Workman's Compensation Insurance.

There was one final Agreement in this folder which stated it was made and entered into on October 5, 1973, between Playboy Clubs International, Inc., and Shokow, Ltd. (Minsky)

It was similar as far as the four weeks' notice of termination, and it being a twenty-six consecutive week contract, which was to commence on Tuesday, April 23, 1974, and run through, including Monday, October 21, 1974. The numbers of shows and the size of the cast and orchestra were all the same. The noticeable difference was Minsky was now to furnish the five members of the orchestra with, "one (1) set of costumes."

Playboy Clubs International was to pay Minsky: "The sum of Five Thousand, Six Hundred and Fifty Dollars ($5,650.00) per week for the first thirteen (13) weeks of the engagement, and Five Thousand Dollars ($5,000.00) per week thereafter."

The Agreement went on to say: "All cast members are to receive gratis rooms and the maximum number of rooms to be provided gratis by the hotel shall be seven (7) and shall be at the Playboy Plaza Hotel, Miami Beach, Florida. The Operator (Playboy) shall also provide gratis rooms for the Producer, (Minsky), Choreographer, Costumer, and Manager during the rehearsal period and for any necessary changes or notifications of the show during this engagement. All cast members shall also receive gratis meals at the Playboy Hotel, Miami Beach, Florida and the gratis meals are in the coffee shop only."

It was a typical Minsky contract regarding salaries paid out, insurances, and advertising; similar to those written up in this book. It was witnessed and signed by Harold Minsky, Irvin Arthur, and Chuck Eddy.

The final two items in this folder were newspaper articles. The first was from *The Miami News*, and dated May 20, 1974. It was written by Entertainment Editor Alex Ben Block, and titled "Times have changed; So has Minsky Burlesque." It reads:

"Less than four years ago Hugh Hefner's bunnies had arrived at the Plaza Hotel with hopes high and spirits inflated. Only four months after opening they installed Minsky's Burlesque in the Playmate Bar downstairs for the first of its annual runs.

It was to be a classic Playboy hotel, served by a classic burlesque show complete with flesh and feathers and baggy-pants comics. The music, of course, was the same honky-tonk show stuff that had served burlesque since the days measurements became more important than talent.

In the past month both these "classics" have quietly been phased out, possibly forever, replaced by new forms, new people and new styles. Playboy is gone from Miami Beach, and Minsky's has gone rock 'n roll.

It was a night of mixed feelings as I watched the new Minsky's on the last night of the Playboy's ownership of the Plaza. Even as you read this the Playboy name has been torn off, painted over wherever it showed on Miami Beach. The costumes and props displaying the sophisticated rabbit, official corporate seal of the sprawling Chicago based Playboy, Inc. empire, have been shipped back to world headquarters on Michigan Avenue.

Of 40 cotton tailed bunnies, 20 will stay on to become "Hyatt Honeys," another kind of glorified waitress in an abbreviated costume.

The last day was spent de-bunnyizing (if there is such a word). Professional sign crews removed the big symbols while others dashed about with cans of paint brushing out rabbit ears. Even the pictures of playmates from the magazines that have lined the wall behind the bar had to go, quickly hustled off the walls one jump ahead of the souvenir hunters.

The new owner is a fiftyish Connecticut real estate executive, Harold Cononer, whose dream has come true with the purchase of his first Miami Beach hotel, but who has had the sense to turn the day to day operation over to professional managers from the Hyatt chain.

Would Minsky's Burlesque be any different on Playboy's closing night, I wondered as I waited for the curtain to rise?

From the opening number I knew the answer was yes, the 1974 Minsky's is different; it's better.

Last year's revue was much like the classic described earlier, featuring some aging, sagging Miami girls on a strung out chorus; and some clowns whose gags were all straight out of Joey Adams comics handbook. It was depressing instead of erotic.

My, oh my, times have changed. The new Minsky's, populated by a bevy of beautiful long legged California girls, set to the pulsating beats of contemporary music, is an exciting lively compact mini-revue. It isn't as bizarre as some of the leather and feather revues we've seen in the past couple seasons, nor as raunchy as Redd Foxx, but it is fast, colorful and contemporary.

Choreographer Anita Mann, who originally cast and staged the show in Las Vegas with Harold and Danny Minsky, is regularly employed to stage production numbers for CBS Television in Los Angeles; and it is her fast pacing and tight numbers that make this show glistening entertainment.

The 90-minute or so show opens with a hot version of "Show Me A Woman That's Got A Good Man," done in sync to two female dancers in sequins and a male dancer wearing little more than a leather jock strap. The offstage voice is loud, powerful, sometimes piercing. We learn shortly it is Kae Cronin, a Helen Reddy lookalike.

In her several numbers, the thin blonde with her hair cut pixie short is loud, in tune and often relentlessly provocative. She doesn't convey much emotion, but she is obviously pumping the music from her heart.

The girl who really gives her heart is Suzette Summers, whose slow strip to beating, grinding rock is sensuous, enticing and erotic. As an artist swishes a brush across his canvas to convey beauty, Suzette sweeps across the stage with a gypsy thump and Marat Sade bump.

The comics are short round Charlie Vespia, who also throws in a surprisingly interesting baritone opera number; blonde Kurt Nagel, who fills his space without much reason; and baggy-pants slapstick star Herbie Barris, whose jokes are as shaggy as his pants are baggy.

The kids in the chorus are all appealing and attractive. The lead dancer is pretty blonde Kathy Bergeron. The lead male dancer, who carries much of the shows dance number from the primary pivot position in the chorus, is Hector Nunez. He moves with freedom and abandon, giving Minsky's a touch of Burt Reynolds appeal.

There is nothing very "dirty" about the new Minsky's. Not because it isn't risqué, because it is; but because times have put what we find titillating into a new perspective. When you can see nude sunbathers on the beach, and streakers in the street, there must be more than peep show mystery to propel a burlesque show.

Packed, paced, and packaged like television, with the added charm of beautiful nudity, Minsky's has something more. Beyond its substitution of rock for the usual win, place, and show music, Minsky's has a sophisticated charm last year's show lacked. Ready or not, the future is here."

The second article, dated July 24, 1974, was written by John Huddy, the *Miami Herald* Entertainment Editor. The title of the piece was, "Finally, a Minsky's With Real Style." It reads:

"Here's a happy, unexpected surprise: The "Minsky's Burlesque" showgirl revue, which opened quietly last week and was nearly lost in the shuffle when Playboy sold the hotel to the Hyatt chain, turns out to be the best little package on the Beach. Considering that we've never met a Minsky's show we didn't hate, the crack professionalism of the current revue is all the more startling, but there it is anyway.

The girls are young and pretty and glide like swans. There's not an ounce of silicone detectable in the show, which makes the production rarer still, and in virtually every department – choreography, costuming, pacing, arranging and band – the same excellence prevails. "Minsky's" does not look like a bare-to-the-bone compact revue, but one costing three times the estimated $7,500 budget. Give much of the credit to the producers – and especially the vibrant, energetic personnel.

Kathy Bergeron is a lovely lead dancer with unfathomable energy, and Suzette Summers is not a stripper at all but an elegant dancer (a startling innovation itself). Singer Kae Cronin, looking like Eddie Cantor's daughter with those huge, saucer eyes, is offbeat and funny with a crazy, squeaky voice, and the dancers, Claudine Ferrara, Pat Moreland, and Hector Nunez, add high spirits to an already lively revue.

Even the showgirls, so clumsy and silly in other Minsky revues, turn out to be sleek, agile, and more like high-velocity dancers than models on parade.

Press Photo of Minsky's Burlesque Follies *appearing at the Playboy Club in Chicago, May 1973. Courtesy: Authors Collection*

(There's a $3.50 beverage minimum per person in the downstairs lounge of the newly renamed Hyatt House.)

Sideshow at the Bar; the well-known maitre de of an even better-known, and still active, Miami Beach nightclub, goes to the bar and asks for a glass of water. The bartender, no pal, tells the man in the tuxedo to go to the toilet if he wants a glass of water. Wham-Bop-Pow, a furious brawl erupts at the bar – smack in the middle of the show that's just started on stage. The show does go on, the combatants are separated after five minutes of punching – and now the room has a new bartender and head waiter. And in the lounge of the Hyatt House, a newly arrived restaurant manager is aghast to discover a loud mouthed busboy clattering and cursing his way through the audience just before the "Minsky's" revue. "Fire that man!," the manager says – before discovering the busboy is actually Charlie Vespia, the comic-singer who opens the revue with the noisy stroll."

The final "P" folder in the File is simply titled "Playboy – Chicago." The material in the folder ran from 1973 through 1976. The first mention of the show was in "Kup's Column" in the *Chicago Sun-Times,* dated May 23, 1973. It was only a couple of lines that read: "If you dig nostalgia, *Minsky's Burlesque Follies* at the Playboy Club is your dish. We especially enjoyed old burlesque comedian Dick Richards and a new addition to the show, Chicago singer Kandi Moore. But the Minsky gals are hard-pressed to compete with the club's bunnies."

The first full length article was from *Now! – Chicago Today,* and dated Friday, May 25, 1973. Titled "Chicagoland Night Life," no writer is listed. It reads:

"*Minsky's Burlesque Follies* in the Penthouse of the Chicago Playboy Club is part traditional burlesque and part Vegas spectacle. In the first category are the risqué comedian, the straight man who heckles him, and the frequent strip routines. The Follies part with the Vegas aura applies to the showgirls – shapelier and prettier than the hard-as-nails stripper of the old Rialto.

Comedian Dick Richards pulls all the old punches and some new ad libs, leers through his double entendres, and is consistently amusing. Vocalist Kandi Moore is as lovely to look at as the undressed beauties, and featured dancer Denise Montego is worth watching even when she's not indulging in the tantalizing gestures of "take-it-off."

The show has much dancing, choreographed by Jerry Norman, who shows ingenuity in devising movements around the central theme of bumps-and-grinds. There is nice work by male soloist Kyle Banner who dances vigorously almost as undressed as his two girl partners.

The costuming is affluent, and the extravagant decorations are placed where they don't interfere with natural endowments. The well-endowed Minsky show will be at the Playboy Club until July 28."

The following item was not a standard AGVA contract, so it was copied as written. It was signed by Harold Minsky, Producer and President of Shokow Ltd., and Monroe "Monkey" Kirkland, on July 3, 1974. It was titled "Artist Engagement Agreement" and reads:

"Agreement made this 2nd day of July 1974, between Shokow Ltd., hereinafter called the 'Producer,' and Monroe Kirkland hereinafter called the 'Artist'.

1. The Producer (employer) hereby employs and engages the Artist and the Artist hereby accepts said employment and engagement. Under the direction, supervision and control of the Producer as a Comic at the Playboy Towers Hotel at 919 North Michigan Avenue in Chicago, Illinois for a period of four consecutive weeks, six days weekly, fourteen shows per week, commencing on July 8, 1974, for which the Producer agrees to pay the Artist, and the Artist agrees to accept, as full salary, the sum of $300.00 weekly, payable immediately preceding the first performance on the concluding night of each week's engagement hereunder, plus transportation between Houston, Texas and Chicago, Illinois, and return.

A very young Monroe James Kirkland, aka as "Monkey." Courtesy: Lady Midnight

2. Artist hereby gives and grants to Producer the option of extending the engagement indefinitely, see section 9, immediately following the conclusion of the original engagement hereunder, upon the same terms and conditions as contained herein for the original period hereof. The weekly payment during each option period shall be $300.00. On engagements for one week or less, Producer will give written notice on the day following the opening; on engagement of 2 or 3 weeks, the Producer will give at least one week's written notice and on engagements for 4 weeks or more weeks, the Producer will give at least 2 week's written notice.

In the event the employment and engagement of the Artist shall be continued by mutual consent beyond the expiration date of this contract (original term and option periods, if any) for a period of one week or more, the Artist shall be deemed to be engaged on a continuous employment basis, subject to one week's written notice of termination by either party to the other. All other provisions of the original contract shall continue in full force and effect throughout such continued employment and engagement.

3. The Artist hereby accepts such employment upon the terms set forth herein and under the terms prescribed. The Artist shall render his act in the variety field exclusively to the Producer throughout the term hereof unless otherwise provided herein or otherwise consented to by the Producer in writing. This shall also preclude any appearance on TV or motion pictures.

4. The provisions hereof are subject to Federal and State Law, and if any part hereof is in conflict therewith, such part shall be deemed inapplicable and, to the extent thereof, shall be deemed severed from this agreement. The remainder shall remain in full force and effect.

5. The Artist shall not be required to perform or appear, nor shall the Producer request the Artist to perform or appear in television, radio, films, or recordings without proper prior negotiations, unless strictly for the promotion of the show, without compensation paid to the Producer.

6. All grievances that may arise out of this contract, must be presented to Producer in writing within 30 days.

7. The Producer hereby accepts responsibility for all required contributions for Federal Insurance Contribution Act, State Disability Insurance Funds, State and Federal Unemployment Insurance and Workmen's Compensation Insurance, as required by State and Federal Law.

8. The Artist shall not be required to mix with nor solicit drinks from customers.

9. SPECIAL PROVISIONS AND/OR RIDERS: (Must be initialed by all parties to this contract.) The week of September 2nd will be a five day week and will be paid on a pro rata basis. This contract includes room and meals; 10 percent commission to be paid to Jess Mack Agency."

The actual Agreement for the show between Minsky's and the Playboy Clubs International in Chicago was basically a normal contract for a period of fifteen consecutive weeks beginning on Monday, July 8, 1974, and running through Saturday, October 19, 1974. There was to be a cast of thirteen people.

There was a stipulation in the contract that reads, "It is agreed and understood that 'Minsky's Burlesque' will be off on Labor Day, Monday, September 2, 1974, and the contract price shall be reduced by $535.00."

Minsky would receive $5,500.00 per week for the first fifteen weeks; if the Playboy Club kept the show on they would pay $5,000.00 per week plus room and board for all cast members. In addition they would pay for any additional transportation charges that might be applicable. If the show were to play at any other Playboy Club, other than Chicago, and where room and board was not provided, the contract price would be increased by $1,300.00 per week. It also stated that if the Playboy Clubs International wanted to play the show in any city other than Chicago, they must be consecutive weeks and within two days after closing in Chicago.

The contract stated that the Playboy Club would pay for fifteen round trip coach air fares from Las Vegas, Nevada to Chicago, Illinois; plus a maximum of eight gratis rooms for the cast, plus gratis meals for all members of the cast to be provided in the Delicatessen or the Living Room. In addition, they were to provide gratis rooms during the rehearsal period for Minsky, as well as the Choreographer, Costumer, and Manager.

This contract was signed by Chuck Eddy, and Irvin Arthur, Director of Entertainment for Playboy Clubs International.

There were a few articles in the folder regarding this show. The first was dated Friday July 12, 1974, and ran in the publication *Now! Chicago Today*. It was titled "Burlesque That's Worth Seeing," which ran in the column "Night Life." It was written by Lois Berger, and reads:

"They shake, they shimmer, and they sparkle plenty. Harold Minsky would be proud.

His burlesque babies are alive and well and baring their bods in the Playboy Penthouse. It's not quite the way it was in the old Rialto. These girls can actually dance, and there's hardly a bump or grind. The musical numbers are all choreographed and rock-orientated. The nearly naked neophytes nubilely swing to "Bad, Bad, Leroy Brown" and "Queen of the Roller Derby," as though they were starlets lifted from the nearest discotheque.

No more specialty acts with a fan or a bubbling bathtub. Dancer Cassandra Lee whips out a flaming torch and gets all fired up. Then, there are the ever-corny comedians who try those moldy-but-goodie blackouts, which somehow work, just because they are so old and everyone has forgotten the punch lines.

Old-timers Bob Mitchell and Monkey Kirkland are still in baggy-pants, bopping each other on the head, but it's their bits that bring a sparkle of nostalgia to the show, and somehow you know this is the way it was…"

The "Nightspots" column of the July 19, 1974 publication *In Chicagoland*, no author was mentioned, was titled "Minsky's Burlesque Headlines Playboy Club." It reads:

"*Minsky's Burlesque Follies of 1974* opened a 15-week engagement in the Penthouse showroom of the Chicago Playboy Club July 8 through October 20. The Follies came to Playboy direct from Las Vegas.

The famous shows by burlesque king Harold Minsky have become an institution. The magic ingredients of burlesque are still there: comedy routines, blackouts, and the ever-gorgeous platoon of long-stemmed showgirls whose presence lights up the stage. The costuming, choreography, staging, and music are executed with high professional polish, while ad-lib comedy keeps the show on a delightfully informal plane.

The featured artists include comics Bob Mitchell and "Monkey" Kirkland, straight man Kurt Nagle, exotic dancer Cassandra Lee, vocalist Kay Lowry, lead female dancer Suzy Williams, and lead male dancer Harry Laird.

Show times will be 8:30pm and 11:30pm Sunday through Thursday; and 8:30pm, 11:15pm and 1:15am Friday and Saturday."

The following full length article appeared in the *Chicago Tribune* magazine on November 7, 1976. The piece was titled, and sub-titled, "Burlesque Comedy: The grand old art just ain't what it used to be. But don't count it out just yet, not while old-timers like Dick Richards are still able to snuggle up to a buxom blond and fire off one-liners with the speed of a Gatling gun." It was written by Jack Hurst, and the very first paragraph makes me think of Blaze Fury when she said, "You saw more at the beach than you ever saw on a burlesque stage."

Dick Richards and lovelies performing in a comedy bit during a Minsky show. Courtesy: Lorraine Lee

(Notes: Dick Richards died on April 15, 1993. He was one of the last legendary burlesque comics to perform in the Chicago area; he was 78 years old. A resident of Fort Lauderdale, Florida, he died in the Manor Oaks Nursing Home. Richards performed in many of Harold Minsky's burlesque houses, as well as the Edgewater Beach Hotel and the Blue Max. His wife, Mary, an exotic dancer performing under the name of Lorraine Lee, also worked with him as a comic partner and straight woman. She was his only survivor; Hurst got Dick's age wrong in his article.)

The article reads as follows:

"The first and second squads of chorus girls had come out and taken off most of their clothes, the tall girl singer had belted out another verse of "What a Life!" while dancing with the chorus boy, and they all had cantered coyly off behind shimmering, tinsel strands of curtain.

Then Dick Richards, an almost pitifully overbearing gnome in white sneakers, a black derby, and a moth-eaten, floor-length, black overcoat, wandered grumpily into the spotlight from stage left. His eyes, looking (rightly) as if they had seen the insides of a lot of places worse than this, roved the Chicago Playboy Club's stage side diners and drinkers. He began to bluster, "Straighten up bud, ya look like yer sittin' in a pay toilet," he upbraided one well-dressed young blade. The blade, thus noticed, laughed happily.

"Well, lookit this little blond here. You fool around, baby? You do? Hmmm. Considerin' the face on that character yer with, nobody could blame ya." The balding man beside the blond grinned foolishly. Noting his sweat glistening head, Richards observed that it was difficult to tell whether the gentleman was sitting right side up or upside down. "You and that other fellow over there ought to get your heads together," he added, pointing out another hairline that had passed its zenith. "You'd make a perfect ass."

These Don Rickles-isms notwithstanding, Richards, 56, longtime resident of Staten Island, New York, and sometimes invader of Chicago, is not just another loudmouthed comic. His is a special business. One of the rarer relics in the entertainment field today, he is a member of a tiny fraternity of perhaps a half-dozen men who still work, whenever they can, at a once-shady business now generally considered dead. Fortunately for these few, it is not quite, and so Richards was back in Chicago again in the summer of this Bicentennial year for an eighteen-week Playboy Club engagement by *Minsky's Burlesque '76*. That's right: Minsky's Burlesque. Dick Richards is a burlesque comedian.

Gypsy Rose Lee writing backstage in her dressing room. Courtesy: C.F. Miller

Autographed Sally Rand Table Card from the Latin Quarter. Courtesy: C.F. Miller

You may not remember burlesque comedy, burlesque's memory having become synonymous now with exhibitionistic ladies of dubious renown, such as Gypsy Rose Lee and Sally Rand. Yet burlesque was also – in fact, first – the province of funny men; some of the most famous included Jack Benny, Red Skelton, Redd Foxx, and Milton Berle.

These men went on to finer things of course. Dick Richards didn't. He stayed where he was, watching the death of a tawdry American phenomenon that had given those more famous men their training. His 3½ hard decades in it weren't without their rewards. Burlesque gave him a living. It allowed him to travel. It introduced him to two of his three wives. It has even given him a certain loyalty to a tradition that tries to linger on.

After Richards had his fill of insulting the audience that night at the Playboy Club a few weeks ago, and after he rapidly told what seemed to be every Polish, Jewish, Irish, Italian, and black joke in the world, ("You got to include everybody," he would say later, "or it ain't fair."), a straight man came out, and he and Richards did some "routines." Most were unprintably bawdy, many silly and so old that they deserve to be called chestnuts. But that was what they were supposed to be, humor with a past, and they came in a flood, some of them funny enough to produce steady rounds of plainly amused, if not riotous laughter.

Richards: You take two nuts and hang 'em on your chest, what are they?

Straight man: I dunno.

Richards: Chestnuts. You take two nuts and hang 'em on your wall, what are they?

Straight man: I dunno.

Richards: Walnuts. You take two nuts and put 'em under the bed, what are they?

Straight man: I dunno.

Richards: Pee-cans.

They even did a couple of "scenes," as he calls them, although they certainly weren't as elaborate as they were when Richards first saw them done in the old days with casts of a half-dozen or more characters. But there was one in which Richards and the straight man advised each other on how to approach women, and another in which Richards and a buxom blond discussed, but never got around to getting into a bed at center stage.

At various intervals between these events, the tall girl singer, the two squads of chorus girls, and the chorus boy reappeared, followed eventually by one Miss Gina Bon Bon, an admirably chested, long-legged, and preoccupied creature who took off a lot of nice clothes to the lonely rhythm of one drum. When she had gotten virtually all of them off, the tall girl singer, the dancing girls, the dancing boy, Miss Bon Bon, and Dick Richards, all reappeared in the lights to accept a generous final applause. Then the lights dimmed and the first of two shows that night was, to use an overworked but in this case perhaps acceptable phrase, history.

A short while later, while relaxing in his plant and curio-filled room in the Playboy Towers, Dick Richards sighed as he talked about how the times and the people have changed since the autumn of 1939, when he entered this dying business.

"The other night," he mused, shaking his head a little wonderingly, "one of the Bunnies asked me, 'Why do they laugh when you say pecans?'"

His real name is Richard Gluck. It would probably be a perfectly good name to use today, he says, but he was advised by somebody who supposedly knew more than he did when he was starting out that it was unacceptable. So, because his first name was Richard, he became Dick Richards – thereby gaining, as he points out, a name like half the other people in comedy. "Everybody is Dick Richards," he says.

At one time, his father taught engineering at Cornell University, but when Richard was small the father had begun losing his eyesight and the family moved to Staten Island to join some other relatives in a shoe business. When World War II came along, Richards recalls, his father made a lot of money – and then lost most of it in real estate.

The youngest of three children, and the only son, Richards mostly just slept on Staten Island during his youth, he recalls; his waking hours he spent in Manhattan, often working and studying. Having taken piano lessons since the age of 8, he went two years to Juilliard and New York University before formal education ended abruptly for him when he signed on as a band member on a cruise to South America. When he returned, he thought he knew enough to make a living.

"I went up into the Borscht Belt, the old hotel circuit up in the Catskills, and I found out a comic could make more than a piano player," he recalls. "So I became a comic. I came down to the Eltinge Theatre on 42nd Street in New York, auditioned for a job, and got it. After a few days, the theatre manager said to me, 'Why don't you stutter anymore, like you did at the audition?' I said, 'I don't stutter. I was just nervous.' He told me he wanted me to put the stutter back in the act. So I stuttered for a while when he was watching until he forgot about it. At the time, I only figured I'd be in it for a couple of years. Burlesque was still a stepping stone to legitimate theatres and the movies and everything then. I thought I'd just hang around for a couple of years and look at the girls."

Burlesque is no stepping stone for comics anymore. There are hardly enough jobs in it to keep even the few regulars like Richards in year-round work. The scattered neon signs that still advertise burlesque usually spell it "burlesk," and

1932 exterior view of the Eltinge Theatre on 42nd Street in New York City. Courtesy: New York Daily News Archive

Rialto Theatre (Chicago) marquee promoting both stage and screen. Courtesy: cinemastreasures.org

about all they mean by it is that there are women inside the place who will get naked. There are certainly no baggy-pants comedians who tell off-color stories.

Somewhere between the Peace of Panmunjom and the Fall of Saigon, sex went public, outflanking and routing burlesque theatres where the subject had been winked at and joked about – burlesqued – since Reconstruction.

Within a few years after the founding of *Playboy Magazine* in 1953, Chicago's last great burlesque theatre, the Rialto, closed its doors and was torn down. The inner-city, working-class neighborhoods where burlesque houses had been located changed into places into which most people were afraid to venture at night. Finally, sex lost most of its humor and all of its mystery as Penthouse, Hustler, and other raunchy magazines started giving the world explicit, semi-respectable guides to the more popular locales of the female anatomy. "What can you do after you've done that?" shrugs Dick Richards.

Today's proliferation of total nudity in massage parlors, X-rated movie houses, and above-the-counter magazines dismays not only Richards but other longtime observers of the burlesque scene. These include Sally (Mrs. Harry) Greben of Chicago, erstwhile booker of burlesque circuits, and Harold Minsky of Las Vegas, onetime owner of Chicago's Rialto and now the producer of *Minsky's Burlesque '76*.

None of them is easily shocked, as you might expect. Burlesque had its towns like Baltimore or Calumet City where everything went, the wilder the better. But

Chicago wasn't one of these, they recall. Chicago had its police censors who came around to watch the first show every Friday and told the performers what jokes and wiggles had to be deleted.

Mrs. Greben recalls that strippers often had families and lived "normal lives when they weren't on the road," many putting themselves or their husbands through college on what they made exhibiting themselves. Between acts – four a day, five on Saturday – they often sewed or read, she says, adding that they always hung their robes just offstage when they were working because "God forbid that someone should see them undressed backstage."

Minsky recalls that the few troubles he had with the Chicago censors were usually caused by competition among strippers for applause. Emphasizing that he is no prude, Minsky simply disagrees with the strategy of today's new standards. "I just think," he says, "that you get more people turned on by teasing them than by coming out and showing them everything you've got."

At a point, long before Dick Richards auditioned at the Eltinge Theatre in New York, burlesque was purely the province of comics, comediennes, straight men, and dancing girls. Its performances once consisted entirely of burlesques of serious shows, plays, and songs, rendered for the masses.

There are several versions of how the stripping revolution began. Sally Greben says that according to her late boss, Chicago-based burlesque booking agent Milton Schuster, it all started in Boston when, in the middle of a routine, the elastic in the panties of a certain burlesque actress broke and the garment fell around her ankles. The reaction of the audience was so profoundly positive that when she came off the stage, the theatre owner ordered her to leave the embarrassing accident in the act.

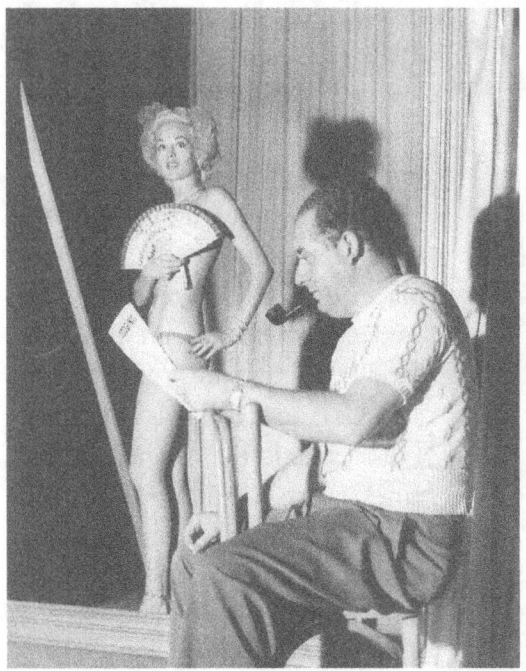

Harold Minsky and dancer rehearsing at the theatre. Courtesy: Janelle Smith Collection

The Minsky family, possessors of probably the best-known entrepreneurial name in burlesque, entered the field virtually by accident in 1908. Abraham Minsky and his brothers, through the help of their father Louis, acquired the National Theatre, a building of several stories with a sixth floor on which no business had been able to survive. A friend suggested they put in a burlesque show, and neither Abe nor his son, Harold, who entered the business in 1933, appear to have ever been ashamed of what they did.

"We were entertaining the working guy," the son says now. "Rich people had their Ziegfeld Follies, and the working guy had burlesque, where he could go to see a show for 50 or 75 cents."

At the height of his family's involvement in burlesque, he, his father, and a couple of his uncles owned 17 different theatres, Minsky says. Most were on the East Coast.

Both Harold Minsky and Dick Richards say the greed of the theatre own-

From the 1932 back cover of the Show Boat *souvenir program – a Florenz Ziegfeld production, direct from the Casino Theatre in New York City. Courtesy: Authors Collection*

ers was a principal cause of burlesque's decline and fall. Seeking more and more profits, the owners began to pare down shows, reducing the number of comics, chorus girls, and musicians while paying strippers higher and higher salaries. "They kept taking the feed away from the horse," Minsky puts it, "until one day the horse died."

Richards recalls watching the horse die in New York while playing the last shows in Minsky's Gaiety Theatre. The operators of several burlesque houses on 42nd Street had become so competitive that they put up pictures of their strippers on the street, ignoring the growing resentment of the congregation of a nearby church. The church appealed to Mayor Fiorello La Guardia, who closed down the theatres. They reopened again as "Follies Theatres," but the church people demanded and got the right to send delegations to see the shows, and approve the type of entertainment.

"It was a hectic week," Richards recalls. "The comics all did scenes that had no sex in them, the chorus girls dressed up, and the strips (strippers) went easy. But the regular patrons booed, and the church people weren't satisfied either. The places all lost their licenses."

Around 1950, soon after Abraham Minsky died, Harold took over his father's business and moved to Las Vegas. At about that time he rented the Rialto in Chicago, already a well-established burlesque theatre, and he had "a few good years" until his lease expired in late 1953, he says. By then the inner city was changing, he recalls, and it didn't seem economically feasible to follow his erstwhile patrons to the suburbs.

Even after the old burlesque theatres closed around the country, however, Minsky refused to give burlesque up for dead – primarily, he says, because "the Minsky name was synonymous with burlesque comedy."

Putting together a chorus line, a couple of strippers, a couple of baggy-pants comics, and a band (but with all new music and much flashier finery than his shows had displayed in the old theatres), Minsky took burlesque into upper-middle-class respectability at the Desert Inn in Las Vegas. It proved successful enough there that he raised other troupes for limited use in dinner theatres in Boston, New Orleans, and Florida. For four years now, he has sold one a year to Chicago's Playboy Club.

But when Minsky is asked if he believes burlesque will live forever, he declines to predict it will. Because Minsky, who is now 60, one wonders what Dick Richards will do when Minsky retires his family's well-known name from marquees for good.

Even now, burlesque comedy doesn't provide Richards with a year-round living. Between stints, he and his wife go back to an apartment on Staten Island. There he keeps some income flowing by occasionally playing a little piano in nightclubs near his home.

The much-improved, if rarefied, air of burlesque's respectable new surroundings is enjoyable when Richards can get the comedy bookings. During his latest run at the Chicago Playboy Club, he and his wife lived at the Playboy Towers. From the stage he has gotten to kibitz with such visitors as Johnny Carson, Joey Bishop, and Telly Savalas. Such a life keeps him young, he says.

"I'm still playing games," he says. "I'm still playing house with my wife for instance. When we close somewhere and there's no booking somewhere else, a lot of times we'll take the car and go down to Mexico. We've done that four or five times. When we close here this time, if there's nothing else booked, I'm going down to the Ozarks and go fishing. I've never been there before."

He has gone to a lot of new places in his life, places he wanted to go. After trips to South America and the Mediterranean in his young manhood, travel became a passion with him. Partly to indulge that passion, he got into burlesque for a couple of years to see the girls and maybe get picked for a Broadway show. He saw the girls. He saw them, in fact, virtually drive comics out of a business that had been started with comics. Then, of course, they went ahead and drove themselves right out of business, too, their inflated salaries unable to be reconciled with deflating audiences.

Richards says he never particularly liked strippers as a group; usually they were vain, overpaid, and underworked, he thinks. As individuals, they obviously impressed him differently; the last two of this three wives were stripping when he met them.

Does he wish he had left burlesque before it died? Asked that, his machine-gun manner of speech subsides abruptly; his lips purse. "Do you think you'll be doing the same thing 30 years from now, that you're doing now?" he counters, after a moment of reflection.

"Nobody thinks that, when they're young. Oh, I think I'd have been much better off now if I'd gotten out of burlesque. I think I'd have been better off if I'd gone into nightclubs. But I don't regret it. I took the easy way. I hate competition – you know, knocking the other guy out, or feeling like he's going to knock you out. If I saw eight guys waiting when I went to try for a job, I left. If I was the only guy, fine.

My father was the same way. One time there were two jobs I could have had, and I asked him which one I should take. He said, 'Tell me about them.' I said, 'One is a nice job, you have fun, but it only pays $40 a week. The other one pays $60 a week, but it's a tough job.' He said, 'Take the one where you'll enjoy yourself.'

A few years ago I got in this motion picture called *Grasshopper*. I spoke to the director, a nice young fellow, and he told me, 'You're an actor, you play parts well. What you should do is stay around Hollywood, be around when they need somebody. Maybe you can get your foot in the door, and then somebody will push you. But you gotta spend time at it.'

But I didn't do that. A guy came along and said, 'Dick, we got a show going to Puerto Rico, we're going to be down there 30 weeks.' Well, to me, that was a sure thing, 30 weeks of work, and Puerto Rico sounded fascinating. Me, I went to Puerto Rico."

(Notes: Jack Hurst was a staff reporter for the Nashville *Tennessean* for ten years, the *Philadelphia Inquirer* for three years, and a syndicated columnist for the *Chicago Tribune*. Hurst is the author of: *Nathan Bedford Forrest: A Biography*, and, *Men of Fire: Grant, Forrest, and the Campaign That Decided the Civil War*.)

The next article came from the Will Leonard column titled "Who says Burlesque is dead?" It ran in the *Chicago Tribune* on July 12, 1974, and reads:

"Burlesque and Vaudeville both have been dead longer than the interurban and the boat cruise to Milwaukee, but they both pretend to rear their funny little heads every now and anon. Burlesque is a phenomenon of the same indestructible stamp. It knows it's been dead since the era of that wonderful old melody, "The Strip Polka." But it won't admit it.

And neither will Harold Minsky. Harold, who comes from a long line of burlesque producers, used to be the man who put on strippers, the bump-and-grind girls, the baggy-pants comedians, and the blackouts, in the old Rialto at State and Van Buren Streets.

Almost all that hoary stuff is present and accounted for in Harold's, *Minsky's Burlesque Follies of 1974*, at the Playboy Club. Only now the show comes from Las Vegas, where Harold has been producing this energetic nonsense for a decade or more.

The Playboy Club? It sounds sort of funny, in 1974. Hugh Hefner has been exposing young ladies in their complete birthday suits for many seasons in his magazine. The ladies in Harold Minsky's show never go quite that far, except for an occasional show of boldness north of the navel.

Actually, in this era of X-rated movies and all other kinds of permissiveness, the old burlesque of Dad's day is laughably out of date. But when a modern version is put on with the vigor and vivacity of the revue at the Playboy, it's still lively and laughable, if not libidinous.

The girls' legs are as long as those of any you remember from yesteryear. The costumes shimmer with gold glitter and sequins. And there actually are some pretty good singers and dancers in the company. There's another factor that separates this from the burlesque shows of the old days.

One long, tall gal sings: "I'm a W.O.M.A.N.," as if she needed to tell you that. One comic, either Bob Mitchell or Monkey Kirkland, (we forget which is which) plays three instruments at once – trumpet, cornet, and trombone. Not every night you get a chance to hear that.

The Minsky's Burlesque Follies are getting to be an annual summertime tradition at the Playboy clubs. Some items of Americana still are sturdy and dependable."

(Notes: *Chicago Tribune* columnist Will Leonard died in January 1977, at age 64. He was carried from the newsroom after a heart attack that would prove to be fatal. Leonard sometimes wrote under a pseudonym, Eugenie Wells, combining the names of two streets near his Old Town neighborhood home.)

To wrap up 1974 were two articles from the *Where, Playboy Towers* publication. The first was from the week of July 20, 1974; the second from September 17, 1974. What I thought was interesting about the July publication is that Angela Lansbury was performing as Mama Rose in a production of *Gypsy* at the Opera House in Chicago through July 27, 1974. Kaye Ballard was also appearing in a new musical, *Sheba*, at the First Chicago Center. Ballard began her career in show business as a talking woman in burlesque. The first article, an "After Dark" column regarding the Minsky show, reads as follows:

"Burlesque, let it be known, is *not* dead. Indeed, whoever said it was? Certainly, not anyone, who's paid a recent visit to the Penthouse showroom of the Playboy Club of Chicago; there, burlesque – in the form of the famous *Minsky's Burlesque Follies of 1974* – is very much alive and kicking, with a modern-day flair.

All the magic ingredients of burlesque are included: comedy routines, blackouts, and the ever-gorgeous platoon of long-stemmed showgirls whose presence lights up the stage. Costuming, choreography, staging, and music are all executed with high professional polish, while ad-lib comedy keeps the show on an informal plane.

In the dance department, exotic dancer Cassandra Lee gives an attention-riveting performance in her featured "Fire Dance" number. And lead female dancer Suzy Williams sets a lively pace for line dancers Barbara Sheehan, Christina Sheehan, Diana Valentien, Stacy Lynn, Vicki Parsons, and Rhonda Feakes. Harry Laird is the talented male member of the dancing ensemble.

Bob Mitchell and "Monkey" Kirkland as featured comics of the show, inject new life into the most standard of routines. They are aided and abetted by straight man Kurt Nagle. Statuesque Kay Lowry performs the vocals.

This current Minsky's extravaganza – lavishly decked-out in spangles, glitter, and feathers – is a multi-faceted entertainment gala that has come to the Playboy Club direct from Las Vegas. It will occupy the Penthouse stage through October 20. Show times are 8:30 and 11:30pm. Sunday through Thursday; 8:30 and 11:15pm and 1:15am Friday and Saturday. The phone number is 751-8000."

The second article reads:

"*Minsky's Burlesque Follies of 1974*, choreographed by Anita Mann, produced by Harold Minsky; featuring "Monkey" Kirkland, Bob Mitchell, Kurt Nagle, Kay Lowry, Cassandra Lee, Harry Laird, Suzy Williams, Barbara and Chris Sheehan, Rhonda LaMont, Stacy Lynn, Diana Valentien, and Vicki Parsons: cover $5-$6.50.

While *Minsky's Burlesque Follies of 1974* isn't the old days, it's as close as the Chicago nitery scene has come to packaging a first rate Las Vegas style follies in a good while. The production has proved popular in the Playboy Clubs Penthouse room, and one good reason, besides the razzle-dazzle, may be the show's occupying the entirety of the stage, giving everyone a sight line.

Femmes are all leggy and there is just enough exposure to make it into the spicy category. Anita Mann, the show choreographer, has plotted out a fast paced hour of cheesecake interlarded with several baggy-pants comedy routines that are fun.

Highlights are the comedy routines involving Kurt Nagle, Bob Mitchell, and toothless Monroe "Monkey" Kirkland. The latter stumbles his way through the English language, as well as the hilarious dirty, old judge routine.

Vocalist Kay Lowry sharply turned in dusky-voiced renditions of upbeat pops, such as "Bad, Bad Leroy Brown." Cassandra Lee did a show-stopping strip cum-live-fire, and lead dancers Harry Laird and lush Suzy Williams nicely commanded the eye. – Jac."

This brings us up to 1975. There were two Agreements for Minsky shows to run at the Chicago Playboy Club that year; the first was actually written on September 20, 1974. It was a contract for a period of twenty-five consecutive weeks which was to begin on Monday, June 2, 1975 and run through Saturday, November 22, 1975. The show was to be presented six weeks nightly, two shows nightly; three shows each on Friday and Saturday. The third show on Friday night could be changed to any other night, Monday through Thursday, by giving one week's advance notice of said change; it was known as a "floating show." The cast was to consist of no less than twelve people; the orchestra would consist of five musicians, and the club was to provide a follow spotlight and operator. The cast and crew were given Friday, July 4, 1975 and Monday, September 1, 1975 off, which reduced the weekly payment to Minsky of $5350.00 per week by $535.00 for each of those two weeks. Minsky paid his cast and crew, and provided all things necessary for the show. The Playboy Clubs International also provided fifteen round trip coach air fares from Las Vegas to Chicago; plus a maximum of nine gratis rooms for the cast, plus gratis meals for all members of the cast to be provided in the Delicatessen or the Living Room. They also provided gratis rooms during the rehearsal period for the Producer, Choreographer, Costumer, and Manager. Everything else was pretty standard for a Minsky Agreement. It was signed by Irvin Arthur and Chuck Eddy.

The next Agreement was written on March 3, 1975, and was for a period of forty consecutive weeks and two days, beginning on Friday, December 26, 1975 and running through Saturday, October 2, 1976. Many things are similar to the previous contract including the weekly amount of money paid to Minsky, the allowance of having National Holidays off, and the amount paid during those weeks. The club would also provide air fare, rooms, and meals – same as the previous contract.

The two major differences between this and other typical Minsky contracts are below:

"It is agreed and understood that this contract price shall include a Cost of Living clause to be determined as follows: If there is an increase or decrease in the United States Government Cost of Living Index, this contract price shall be increased fifty percent (50%) of the Cost of Living Index percentage. For example, if the Cost of Living Index increases by five percent (5%), this contract price shall increase by two and one-half percent (2½%). The base point for this Cost of Living clause shall be any increase or decrease from January 1, 1975 to January 1, 1976. The Cost of Living increase or decrease shall also be determined for any increase or decrease between January 1, 1976 and May 1, 1976."

"It is agreed and understood that the Producer (Minsky) shall change all principal members of the cast, including comic, straight man, featured exotic dancer, and featured singer on April 5, 1976. In addition, Producer shall change all principals as mentioned above plus change two (2) production numbers including costumes on June 28, 1976. Operator (Playboy Clubs International) shall pay for any additional round trip transportation for all principals that are changed on the two (2) above mentioned dates. In addition, Operator shall provide gratis rooms for the Producer, Choreographer, and Costumer during the time periods necessary for changing the principals and/or the production numbers."

This contract was signed by Harold Minsky, Irvin Arthur, and Chuck Eddy.

There were only a few short articles and comments in newspaper columns regarding the Minsky show in Chicago in 1975. Perhaps what publicity was printed simply was not saved.

In the "Café Topics" column of the *Chicago Daily News* on June 13, 1975, Sam Lesner wrote:

"Burlesque can be beautiful: *Minsky's Burlesque '75* has settled into the Chicago Playboy Club for a run through November 22, and Minsky, at last, has found a choreographer who knows the difference between modern dancing and gymnastics.

The revue's burlesque comedy skits are still from the Stone Age of Vaudeville, but Minsky's primarily is a dance show. As such, with exotic dancer Saki Tumi featured, Harold Minsky again is honoring the memory of dear old Papa Minsky, who invented this form of fast-paced nudity which is an art, compared with the crudity of *Bottom's Up '75*.

Minsky's sole lead male dancer Kurt Sproul, is versatile and masculine."

And there was this from the June 15, 1975 issue of *Tempo Magazine*:

"The Playboy Club: *Minsky's Burlesque '75* headlines the show at the Penthouse showroom of the Chicago Playboy Club. *Minsky's Burlesque '75* comes to the Playboy direct from Las Vegas. The magic ingredients of burlesque are there, complete with comedy routines, blackouts, and the ever-gorgeous platoon of beautiful long stemmed showgirls. The costuming, choreography, staging, and music are executed with high professional polish, while the ad lib comedy keeps the show on a delightfully informal plane. Show times are 8:45 and 11:30pm Sunday thru Thursday; 8:30 and 11:15pm and 1:15am Friday and Saturday."

The following appeared in the *Chicago Tribune* on Sunday, June 15, 1975. It was part of the "On the Town" column, written by Will Leonard, and titled "It's Your Basic, Bawdy Summer." In-part it reads:

"At the Playboy Club; When Harold Minsky's young ladies worked in the old Rialto at State and Van Buren Streets, bras (or at least pasties) were the proper thing. Times have changed and the lovelies are topless now, as they are on bathing beaches in many sectors of the semi-civilized world.

But, aside from that, very little has changed in this quasi-burlesque since Harold Minsky's grandfather was new in the business on New York's Lower East Side. The girls, not quite as tall and stately as the ones in Las Vegas (though, goodness knows, they try), parade and change costumes and parade again, all the while smiling prettily.

A few of them gyrate to the rhythms of "Steam Heat," which was hot stuff 20 years ago in *The Pajama Game*, but is old hat now. Eventually, when you're beginning to wonder whatever happened to the old baggy-pants clowns, a couple of baggy-pants clowns come on, running through the same jokes that were unprintable in the days of the Rialto and still, today, are unprintable.

There's one element missing. At last it arrives. It's a comely stripper, a Japanese maiden with the impossible name of Saki Tumi. She is the prettiest thing you see all evening, and she closes the show on the right note."

The following appeared in the Maggie Daly column, which ran in the *Chicago Tribune* on July 11, 1975.

Saki Tumi. Courtesy: C.F. Miller

"Saki Tumi, the Polynesian fire dancer in *Minsky's Burlesque '75* at the Playboy Club, is taking dramatic lessons and hoping for a starring role in the remake of an oriental musical film. Bob Hope saw Saki's performance in the show about a year ago, but she was too shy to meet Hope. A couple of weeks ago when Bob saw the show in Chicago at the club, Saki went to dinner with Hope and the cast."

And lastly the following paragraph from *This Week in Chicago*, for the week of July 12-18, 1975; the "Miss Twic Sees…" column reads:

"That *Minsky's Burlesque '75*, the entertainment gala that brings back the authentic Las Vegas spectacular with a modern-day flair, is performing in the Penthouse showroom of the Chicago Playboy Club, at 919 N. Michigan Avenue. The famous show by burlesque king Harold Minsky has become an institution. The magic ingredients of burlesque are still there – complete with comedy routines, blackouts, and the platoon of beautiful showgirls. The showgirls, with their multi-colored costumes of glitter and feathers, are all first-rate singers and dancers. Two of my favorite numbers are their versions of "In the Mood," and "Shaft." One of the highlights of the Minsky show is Saki Tumi, an exotic dancer, whose really different act includes dance routines with fire."

R is For...

There were two folders in this File. The first was for Bill Miller's Riverside Hotel in Reno, Nevada. It primarily consisted of advertisements for a Minsky's Follies production performed at the hotel in October 1961. The show starred: Bert Wheeler, Tommy Dillon, Pat "Amber" Halladay, the Amin Brothers (acrobats), Peggy Womack, Karen Wessler, Bill DeBell, Penny Potter, and Alan Conroy. There was also a very long, personal article on Wessler, the female vocalist in the show. Beyond the advertisements, there was really nothing about the show. The Wessler article did not pertain to the show.

The second folder was identified simply as "Rialto, 1953." It contained a single article with a handwritten note which said: "Time Magazine, Minsky at Rialto, 1953." No author was listed. It reads as follows:

The Riverside Hotel in Reno, Nevada. Courtesy: Reno Historical Society

"Strippers' Retreat; The bald-headed men and the college boys celebrating New Year's Eve in Chicago shouted, "Take it off!" for the last time at Minsky's Rialto Theatre. When the curtain came down, at 1:35am, Harold Minsky's lease had expired. Costs were up, box-office receipts were down, and the new year saw wreckers razing the old buildings to make room for shops that will sell the kind of clothes that women put on. The Follies, a small nearby theatre just outside 'The Loop,' was burlesque's last stand in an area where, a generation ago, there had been a dozen "burly" houses. (The strippers retreated to blowzy joints west and north.)

A young Bert Wheeler. Courtesy: Burlesque Historical Society

Pat "Amber" Halladay. Courtesy: Burlesque Historical Society

Olive Sharron, a platinum blonde who has stripped in 37 states since she graduated from Detroit's Chadsey High School ten years ago, was gloomy about the Rialto's fate. "This was the peak of success in our business," she said. "The Rialto in Chicago was like the Palace in New York for vaudeville people. Now it's club work for me."

Lili St. Cyr, the star of the final show, wasn't worried. She had a full schedule ahead of her, although none of her dates would be in Boston, Massachusetts. Bos-

Older photo of the Rialto Theatre in Chicago, with Minsky's World Famous Burlesque marquee. Courtesy: cinematreasures.org

ton had done it again. In mid-November the police, cracking down on "lewd, indecent, and immoral shows" had suspended the licenses of the city's two remaining burlesque houses – Waldron's Casino and the venerable, 108-year-old Howard Athenaeum in Scollay Square. First financial repercussions came from Joe and Nemo's adjacent hot-dog stand, which was reported to be losing $500 a day.

Second Offense: It wasn't the first time that the famous "Old Howard" had been disciplined by the censors. In 1933 one of Ann Corio's torrid performances

Rose La Rose. Courtesy: C.F. Miller

Irma the Body. Courtesy: Burlesque Historical Society

snapped the Watch and Ward Society into frozen attention, and the theatre was closed for 30 days. A few days earlier, Boston's former Mayor Curley had eyed Miss Corio's art and found it absorbing.

The performers chiefly involved in the new Boston strip-out were Rose La Rose, Marion Russell, and a girl called simply Irma the Body. Their downfall was the result of special leg-work by Police Detective Peter DiSessa, who had provided himself with a movie camera and taken pictures from the balcony of each theatre. His evidence was good (or bad) enough to convince the Censorship Board and the present Mayor John B. Hynes. Less convinced was the Reverend Dr. Harry W. Kimball, pastor emeritus of a church in suburban Needham. In an article published in the *Boston Herald*, the 84-year-old clergyman said, "Filth in burlesque is governed by the mind of man." He was following the aesthetic lead of the late Oliver Wendell Holmes, who graduated from Harvard and the "Old Howard" to the Supreme Court and Washington's F Street burly shows.

Ironically, the weathered "Old Howard" building started off as a church in 1843, but show business took over a year later when the cult's religious leader slipped up on his prediction that the world would come to an end as of April 23, 1844. Perhaps by the way of compensation, the venerable Alvin Theatre in Minneapolis, Minnesota, which retired after 50 years in the burlesque business, has

The old Alvin Theatre in Minneapolis after it had become the Minneapolis Evangelical Auditorium. Courtesy: Minneapolis Tribune Archives

become the Minneapolis Evangelical Auditorium.

But despite the fact that Boston is, at least for the time being, through with burlesque, and Chicago nearly so, the general state of the union is such that the medium's strippers and slapstick comics are still able to earn a living wage.

Con and Pro: The future of burlesque, however, doesn't look so good to Milton Schuster, a 70-year-old booking agent for fourteen Eastern and Midwestern theatres. No one has a better right than Schuster to reminisce about the talent that emerged from burlesque the hard way – Eddie Cantor, Abbott and Costello, Fannie Brice, Buster Keaton, Mae West, Bobby Clark,

Press Photo of Eddie Cantor. Courtesy: Authors Collection

1947 Press Photo of Bud Abbott and Lou Costello wearing caps and holding baseball bats preparing to perform the "Who's On First" routine on NBC Radio. Courtesy: NBC Radio Collection

Fannie Brice was singing "Sadie Salome" in a Yiddish dialect when Florenz Ziegfeld first heard her sing. He hired her on the spot – the year was reportedly 1911. Courtesy: New York Daily News Archive

Sheet music from the 1923 song, "I Never Broke Nobody's Heart When I Said Goodbye," introduced by Mae West. Courtesy: Authors Collection

and W.C. Fields. But in Schuster's opinion, those days are gone forever. "The movies hurt us, and then the nightclubs and radio began taking the talent from our houses. Burlesque decided it had to change from comedy, vaudeville, and music. It was in 1928, when Hinda Wassau did the first striptease in Chicago's Haymarket Theatre. From then on the strippers became the most important part of the burlesque show. There's so little new talent and so little new material. There's no training of young comics and writers are too expensive for most old-timers. Some comics are using the same material I used when I quit the stage in 1919, and some of the jokes were in use when I broke in with Al Jolson back in 1900."

More sanguine was Orville Baldy, former manager of the disappearing Rialto and personal representative of the successful Miss St. Cyr. "Burlesque will last. It's the one form of entertainment you can't put on television," he insisted.

S is For...

There were a lot of folders in this File, so let's begin with the Silver Slipper folder from 1965 into 1968. The first item I suspect held memories for Harold, and Pat Elliott, the woman who would become his second wife. It was an AGVA contract; NO. 68183, signed between H.M. Enterprises and Patricia Elliott, on October 8, 1965. Pat was signed as a "Model" and was paid $200.00 per week. She was originally signed for four weeks, but agreed to the inserted clause to be signed indefinitely, for four week periods at a time. Pat was to appear in three shows daily, twenty-one shows per week. The contract was signed by Harold Minsky and Patricia Elliott.

"Model" Pat Elliott Minsky. Courtesy: Janelle Smith Collection

The only article from 1965 appeared in the *Las Vegas Sun* and was dated October 20, 1965. There is no author byline, but it was titled "Minsky's Follies: Historic Silver Slipper Opens Tonight on Strip." The article reads:

"The Silver Slipper, historic landmark of the Strip, will reopen tonight. Featured in the show room will be the first edition of *Minsky's Follies*, produced and directed by Harold Minsky, internationally known for his specialized productions.

Minsky said a policy of continuous entertainment will go into effect with "Follies" show times at 10pm, 12:30 and 2:45am. A musical group, "The Raves," will perform in the interims until 5am.

Minsky also announced that every Thursday at 4am a Watusi contest for the public will be held, with cash prizes for the winners.

The Silver Slipper is headed by Sam Diamond,

Silver Slipper postcard from Las Vegas. Note the marquee mentioning Minsky's Burlesque. Courtesy: Authors Collection

Photo from 1957, from inside the old Frontier Village, of the Silver Slipper. Courtesy: Authors Collection

Minsky's program from the Silver Slipper show. No year is mentioned within its pages. Courtesy: C.F. Miller

President; a twenty-year resident of Las Vegas with affiliations with the Flamingo Hotel, Pioneer Club, and Club Bingo. Diamond's associates include Shelby Williams, Executive Vice President, a retired Houston businessman, and a local resident; Jack Shapiro, Vice President, a leading diamond broker from Detroit; Thomas Bellsnyder Jr., owner and President of Jefferson Foundry in Birmingham, Alabama; Dr. Louis L. Friedman, owner of the Friedman Diagnostic Clinic in Birmingham, Alabama, medical textbook author, lecturer and real estate investment broker; and Ben Moss, Amusement Park Operator and owner of Uncle Ben's Kiddyland in the San Fernando Valley. Moss was also part owner of the old Eldorado Club in downtown Las Vegas from 1947 through 1949.

The Silver Slipper edition of *Minsky's Follies* carries on a tradition of the form of entertainment made famous by the Minsky family and in subsequent productions in Las Vegas, notably at the Desert Inn and the Dunes.

Featured in the "Follies" will be Irving Benson and Jack Mann, Dick Richards, Dave Walker, Clegg Hoyt, and spotlighted nudes Miken O'Day, Mikki Sharait, and Evelyn Clark. Minsky "Mannequins" are Debra Duke, Willa Jean Baty, Janet Schoolcraft, Virginia Lukacs, Patricia Elliott, Jane Hughes, Phyllis Metcalf, and Diane Wellington.

The show is staged and choreographed by Jerry Norman, with costumes designed by Winn Morton. Musical director is Alfred Alvarez. Special scores are composed by Raoul Romero."

Charlie Robinson. Courtesy: Lorraine Lee

Backstage at the El Rancho in Las Vegas, from left to right, Irving Benson, Jessica James, Eddie Lynch, and Jack Mann. Benson and Mann often worked as a team. Courtesy: Pat Elliott Minsky/Burlesque Historical Society

Also in this folder were some of the contracts for the 1966 Silver Slipper show starting in February. The following were signed and dated in February of 1966 by Harold Minsky and the performers involved, which included:

Charlie Robinson, comedian; three shows daily, six days a week for eight weeks was to be paid $350.00. If Robinson worked seven days per week, he would receive a weekly salary of $400.00. Minsky would also pay one way transportation to Las Vegas from Detroit.

Irving Benson, comic; three shows daily, seven days a week for eight weeks was to be paid $450.00 weekly.

Jack Mann, straight man; three shows daily, seven days a week for eight weeks was to be paid $450.00 weekly.

Benson and Mann often worked together in burlesque as partners, comic and straight man, and all contracts state, "Artist to work as directed by Harold Minsky."

Camille Traxler, dancer; three shows daily, seven days a week for eight weeks was to be paid $200.00 weekly. There was also an "Indefinitely" clause written into her contract; Traxler did not actually sign her contract, but Harold Minsky did.

The following two contracts were similar to those above, but for only two weeks, and they were written out and signed in May of 1966. Both had the "Indefinitely" clause written into their contracts, and were signed by Harold Minsky and the performers.

Venus Christy, talking woman; three shows daily, seven days a week for two weeks was to be paid $300.00 weekly.

Gloria Linero, exotic dancer; three shows daily, seven days a week for eight weeks was to be paid $300.00 weekly.

Outside of finding the show listed in the tiniest of print in a couple publications of the *Las Vegas Reviewer*, all I found regarding the February 1966 Minsky show at the Silver Slipper was a photo and caption from the Saturday, January 29, 1966 edition of the *Las Vegas Sun*. Also included in the folder were a couple pages torn from the September 1966 issue of *Sir!* magazine. As you can imagine there were more photographs than words, and nowhere did it mention the Silver Slipper.

The *Las Vegas Sun* ran the following about the show on October 12, 1966. In his "Vegas Daze and Nites" column, Ralph Pearl wrote:

"We talked with the quiet man of burlesque, Harold Minsky, on our TV show Sunday afternoon, about the many trials and tribulations a guy like himself runs into while guiding the destinies of his nightly girlie shows at the Silver Slipper. You'd never associate the gent with the pipe and shy manner as a girlie show operator. He looks more like the neighborhood pharmacist or insurance man. Yet, from the time he was a mere stripling of 15, he was closely associated in the business of learning about girlie extravaganzas through his famous uncle Billy and papa, Abe, who opened their first theatre in 1908.

"When I brought my girlie show, *The Minsky Follies*, into the Desert Inn in 1950, it was the first show of its kind ever to play there," said Harold Minsky. "Then, several years later, we went into the Dunes and stayed a couple of years and convinced a few Strip hotel owners they had to follow suit. Hence the long running, spectacular girlie shows at the Stardust, Tropicana, Dunes, and Desert Inn."

Recently the remarkable Minsky legend was put between covers, *The Night They Raided Minsky's*, and became a best seller. The late New York Mayor Fiorello La Guardia didn't realize it would become a legend back in 1940 when he outlawed Minsky Burlesque from all New York theatres. It's now being made into a movie."

Also included in this folder was a copy of an unsigned Agreement between H.M. Enterprises (Harold Minsky) and Shelam, Inc. (the Silver Slipper). This contract was a little different than some in the other Files. The show would consist of a minimum of eighteen employees, including Director Harold Minsky, for a period of fifty-two consecutive weeks. The show would be performed seven days a week; three shows nightly, with a minimum performance time of sixty minutes, commencing on January 3, 1967 and ending on January 1, 1968. Minsky was not allowed to change any personnel without the approval of the Silver Slipper, and he was required to be present, or on the premises of the Silver Slipper, a part of each day during seventy-five (75%) percent of the term of this agreement or any renewal of such agreement. During the term of the contract, the format and content of the shows were expected to change from time to time, but each new show was to remain for at least sixteen weeks – as long as it met the quality of previous shows. If the Silver Slipper did not approve of the new show, Minsky would have to create an entirely different show within four weeks. Every Monday the Silver Slipper agreed to pay Minsky $8,000 from which Minsky paid all of the costs of the show. Minsky was to pay Federal Withholding Tax, Federal Social Security Assessments, as well as Insurances – and the management of the Silver Slipper stipulated in the contract that they wanted to see proof that he made those payments. The hotel also included a clause stating that they would give notice on July 1, 1967 if they intended to extend this Agreement for an additional fifty-two weeks on the same terms and conditions; they would also supply a five piece orchestra. The contract also spells out that the Silver Slipper expected Minsky be in good standing with AGVA, and during such time pay the necessary fees for any performer requiring help through AGVA welfare programs or welfare benefits. The final paragraph was particularly interesting; it reads:

"In the event of the death of Harold Minsky during the term of this contract or any renewal thereof, the Operator (Silver Slipper) shall have the option to terminate this contract upon the giving of four (4) weeks written notice thereof. Whether or not the Operator shall exercise such option, the Operator shall nevertheless have an exclusive right to continue to use the names "Minsky," "Minsky's Follies," and "Minsky's Burlesque" as part of the title of any show put on in the Operator's premises after the termination of this Agreement, or any renewal thereof, or after the exercise of the option contained in this paragraph. However, as consideration for such use, the Operator agrees to pay to Ava Minsky, the daughter of Harold Minsky, a minor born on July 12, 1953, the sum of Five Hundred ($500.00) Dollars per week for so long as said names are used. During such use the said names shall vest exclusively in the Operator and no one else may use said names or be given the right to use said names."

Tommy "Moe" Raft. Courtesy: Pat Elliott Minsky/Burlesque Historical Society

This Agreement was never signed, but the show did go on! On April 6, 1967, H.M. Enterprises signed comic Tommy "Moe" Raft to a contract for eight consecutive weeks, seven days a week, and 3 shows per day. He would be performing at the Silver Slipper; the closing date was to be May 29, 1967, and it was a "No Options" contract. Raft was to receive $500.00 per week.

There were also a couple short paragraphs written about the show in the folder. From the *Las Vegas Sun*, on September 23, 1967, Ralph Pearl wrote:

"Show Must Go On Department; It happened an hour before show time of the *Minsky Follies* at the Silver Slipper Wednesday night. Leggy, beautiful Jill Harris, who figures prominently in three sketches with Irv Benson, Marty May, and Jack Mann, was suddenly taken ill and couldn't go on. Producer Harold Minsky rushed his bride, Pat, into the skits and the night was saved as Mrs. Minsky played it expertly to the antics of the trio of hilarious top bananas."

Silver Slipper newspaper advertisement from October 20, 1967 picturing Lisa Duran.
Courtesy: Janelle Smith Collection

The following paragraph was at the end of an article titled "Sammy Davis at Sands Tonight." It was written by S. P. Melnick in the column "Las Vegas Beat." There was no date but I am guessing it was from mid- to-late 1967.

"The Silver Slipper has Minsky's Burlesque to draw the crowds and draw it does. The comedy skits are knockouts and the girls are something to write home about."

The next folder in the File is identified as "Shubert Theatre, Cincinnati, Ohio, 2 Nights – 4/70." There were two individual contracts typed out and signed on Patava, Inc. stationery. You can tell the contracts were not for a regular show. The performance was to be held at the Shubert Theatre for two nights only, on April 10 and 11, 1970. The contracts in the file were for Willie Dew and Sandy McQueen; both were to be paid $200.00 – Willie was to receive transportation as well. The paperwork also had rehearsal times and dates listed. The contracts were signed by Harold Minsky, and the performers involved. The show was a salute to the Gayety Theatre for the benefit of WCET, a Public Broadcasting Service member television station in Cincinnati, Ohio.

Lew Weber and Joe Fields, the first comedy team.
Courtesy: Burlesque Historical Society

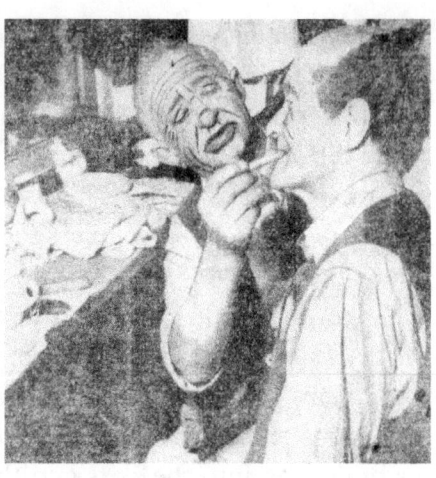

Vintage photo of Billy "Beef Trust" Watson and Billy "Grogan" Spencer. These men were partners on the burlesque stages for over forty years.
Courtesy: Burlesque Historical Society

Gypsy Rose Lee. Courtesy: Burlesque Historical Society

Rose La Rose in a Pepsi Cola promotion.
Courtesy: Burlesque Historical Society

(Notes: WCET was the first licensed public television station in the United States, and it is located in Cincinnati, Ohio. The Federal Communications Commission assigned Channel 48 to WCET in 1951. A corporate charter and construction permit were granted in 1953. WCET began broadcasting on July 26, 1954. The first day of programming began with *Tel-A-Story*, a half hour reading program by the Cincinnati Public Library. On March 11, 1955, the FCC granted WCET the first non-commercial educational broadcast license in the country. Originally, WCET was funded through local school levies. However, a failed levy in 1966 forced the station to seek other sources of funding. In 1968, WCET held its inaugural *Action Auction*, raising $31,000 in two days.)

A very faded copy of a flyer was enclosed in this folder regarding the "Salute to the Gayety for the benefit of WCET." It provided prices and reads:

"Since 1909 Cincinnatians have patronized that unique American art form – Burlesque at the Gayety. Generations of gentlemen and ladies, both young and old, with healthy curiosities and a broad sense of humor have enjoyed the erotica, humor, and pathos of Gayety Burlesque.

The stars of yesteryear and today, who have graced the stage of the Gayety, read like the who's who of show business: Weber and Fields, Sliding Billy Watson's Beef Trust, Sophie Tucker, Red Skelton, Gypsy Rose Lee, Pinky Lee, Robert Alda, Joey Faye, and of course, the perennial favorite Rose La Rose.

Alas! The Mistress of Vine Street is doomed to fall under the wreckers' ball in the next few weeks and with it will pass an era unique in local entertainment.

So, Join Us. Help us make this event long to be remembered.

On Friday and Saturday Night, April 10 and 11, friends of WCET are going to throw a farewell party for the Gayety. Contributions for this "Goodbye to the Mistress of Vine Street" will go toward the purchase of new equipment for WCET.

Enjoy the Gilt and Glamor of the Gawdy, Bawdy Burlesque at this once in a lifetime theatre party. See Burlesque once again on the grand scale that only Harold Minsky – the last remaining brother of the famous Minsky's can bring you. A musical revue with verve and vitality! It's beautiful Burlesque at its best! Direct from Las Vegas.

Minsky's Burlesque '70 – Two performances at the Shubert 8:30pm April 10, April 11, Friday and Saturday. This black tie event is in the form of a progressive farewell party. First the show at the Shubert featuring

1955 photo of the Shubert Theatre. Courtesy: Cincinnati Enquirer

Minsky's Las Vegas revue. Then the theatre party goes to the Gayety to toast the gay days of Burlesque on the Gayety stage and for a last look at an era never to be seen again. You will want to see and be seen at the Shubert's farewell party for the Gayety and for the benefit of WCET – America's 1st Educational T.V. Station."

On one end of this flyer was: ticket information, prices, a seat reservation section, and information where to send your check or money order. The section that tells you where to send your reservation reads: "To insure your seat selections we must have your response prior to March 31. Please enclose a self-addressed stamped envelope with ticket order. Orders will be filled according to postmark."

The ticket information and pricing read as follows:

"Top Banana – Orchestra Seat; Party onstage at The Gayety, (Tax Deductible $18.00) Ticket price - $25.00.

Second Banana – Mezzanine Seat or Lower Box Seat; Party onstage at The Gayety, (Tax Deductible $13.50) Ticket price - $20.00.

Exotic Dancer – Lower Balcony Seat; Party onstage at The Gayety, (Tax Deductible $10.00) Ticket price - $15.00.

Stripper – Upper Balcony Seat or Upper Box Seat; Party onstage at The Gayety, (Tax Deductible $6.00) Ticket price - $10.00."

Also enclosed was a program which included the list of acts and routines that were performed, a soliloquy, a history of the theatre, as well as a write-up about the show. Members of the cast, in the order of their appearance, included: Ann Gubbins, Dick Colacino, Lee Ballard, Willie Dew, Barbara Curtis, Pat Burns, Miss Loni, Looney Lewis, Ferd Hernandez, Jerry Lucas, Satan's Angel, Dick Albers, and Alawn Don Jay. There was no mention of Sandy McQueen.

Scenes performed included: "St. James Infirmary," "Fight," "Crazy House," "Peanut Brittle," and "Gone with the Wind."

The following was the write-up in the program about the show. It reads:

"The Show: While burlesque has drawn its last local breath, it could not be healthier than in the desert climate of Las Vegas, thanks mainly to one of the most famous names ever associated with the art. The name is Minsky, Harold Minsky.

The show you'll see tonight, *Minsky's Burlesque '70*, is another in the long line of rollicking revues staged by Minsky. It comes to Cincinnati directly from the Aladdin Hotel in Las Vegas and features some of the biggest names in the current era of burlesque.

Comedian Willie Dew is certainly one of the biggest names in the business, as is Looney Lewis, considered to be the Top Banana in burlesque today. Lewis has been in several Broadway shows and television specials in recent years.

Pat Burns and Barbara Curtis, who handle the "straight man" chores, are veteran performers in Vaudeville and the legitimate stage. They've been

Barbara Curtis. Courtesy: Janelle Smith Collection

in burlesque over six years. Ferd Hernandez is a real fighter, and holds a decision over Sugar Ray Robinson to prove it. Vocalist Lee Ballard has been with some of the country's top musical groups, recently playing the Playboy Club circuit.

Dancer Ann Gubbins and Dick Colacino both have been with the Follies Bergere and the Lido Club in Paris and are veteran Minsky performers.

Strippers, of course, are still a big part of burlesque, 1970 style. Alawn Don Jay is a beautiful newcomer to the art of ecdysis. Satan's Angel is the gorgeous temptress billed as the "most unusual act in Burlesque."

Trampolinist Dick Albers is a former national collegiate champion and two-time Big Ten champ while at Indiana University. Miss Loni's specialty act has been seen in circuses on several continents and two all-time great circus movies, *The Greatest Show on Earth*, and Billy Rose's *Jumbo*.

The production has a local flavor, too. Stage Manager, Jerry Lucas, (no relation to the ex-Royal hoopster), was a member of the Cincinnati police force before moving to Las Vegas. He's been with Minsky's for seven years.

Photo taken between 1939 and 1941 when the Minsky's were being harassed by Mayor La Guardia and Paul Moss. They renamed the Gotham Theatre "Tri-Boro Follies," but were still shut down. Courtesy: New York Daily News Archives

Harold Minsky has been producing burlesque shows since 1936. His father, Abe Minsky, put young Harold in charge of the Gotham Theatre in New York. Harold, his father, and uncles built the business to the point where, in 1937, Minsky shows were running in 15 New York theatres.

Then came World War II and the slackening of entertainment everywhere. After the

1955 photo of the Silver Slipper and the old Frontier Village sign. Courtesy: Authors Collection

war, Harold Minsky toured the country with his shows, settling in Las Vegas in 1950.

He's been a big part of the entertainment scene in the desert oasis ever since. His burlesque extravaganzas have been seen in the Desert Inn, the Dunes, the New Frontier, the Silver Slipper, and other famous Las Vegas nightclubs.

It seems only proper that the biggest name in burlesque today should help Cincinnatians ring out the end of an era here."

The history section of the program reads:

"The History: First a church; later the Gayety nee Empress burlesque house. Now, 122 years after its raising, comes its razing. It has heard the sermons of sin, the soliloquies of sadness, and the songs of sensuality. Soon, the music will be the crescendo of destruction. The "Mistress of Vine Street" will be a memory. Not always so. The decay of today is the last gasp of a once proud lady, whose genesis was religion. She first took form as the Vine Street Congregational Church. The interior walls, later to echo the humor of baggy-pants comedians, were resplendent with biblical art. Controversy has always been a part of her personality. In 1896, a young preacher named Herbert L. Bigelow upset the established Congregationalists by welcoming in several mavericks – inhabitants of the nearby flop houses. This move changed her face from somber to saucy. The church, now in the hands of liberals, prospered and grew. The congregation moved to other quarters and in 1909, hymns and sermons gave way to comics and Indian princesses. The Empress Burlesque Theatre was born.

The Empress Theatre in Cincinnati, Ohio. Courtesy: cinematreasures.org

Burlesque had been flourishing in this country for over 40 years. Its roots went back much further – to the great classic playwright of ancient Greece, Aristophanes. He was the first to employ satire and laugh at tragedy… and make his audience laugh in the process. That's what burlesque means. It comes from the Italian word "burlare"

Front and back covers of the sheet music from the 1934 film College Rhythm, *starring Joe "Wanna Buy a Duck" Penner. Courtesy: Authors Collection*

Bert Lahr in 1930, appearing in Flying High *at the Apollo Theatre. Courtesy: Authors Collection*

which means "to laugh at, to make fun of." In its embryonic stages, burlesque made its appearance on the London stage in 1600 and on this continent in 1727, nearly 50 years before this country was born. It's had a colorful history ever since. The bawdy flavor of burlesque was first seen in 1861, when a girl of impressive dimensions, dressed in tights, rode a horse on stage. Scandalous! By the late 1800s, girls had replaced end men and comedy teams such as Weber and Fields, and became headliners. In 1904, "Little Egypt" introduced the belly dancer to this country. Shortly, every burlesque show in the country had a belly dancer or "cooch" dancer as they were known. Enter the "Golden Age of Burlesque"… and, in 1909, the Empress Theatre at the 814-818 Vine Street sire. The next quarter century saw burlesque and the Empress Theatre at their height. Gracing the Vine Street stage were such names as: Sophie Tucker, Bert Lahr, Leon Errol, Gypsy Rose Lee, Al Jolson, Bozo Snyder, Joe Penner, and Bobby Clark. Although the Ziegfeld Follies and Earl Carroll's Vanities robbed Burlesque of some of its luster in the East during the teens, it flourished here. The Empress was busy. As the thirties arrived, the emphasis of burlesque shifted. The striptease became the prime attraction, although the comic still played a vital role.

In 1937, the Empress took on the "Gayety" name, one which had already been made famous by burlesque theatres in other cities. The local Gayety numbered among its attractions many legitimate stars who would later achieve fame in other show business arenas. Red Skelton, Pinky Lee, Abbott and Costello, Robert Alda, Joey Faye, Rags Ragland, and others brought chuckles and belly laughs to Gayety patrons. During this time and into the 1940s and 1950s the Gayety's glamour was enhanced by Ann Corio, Pepper Powell, Tempest Storm, Lili St. Cyr, Sherry Britton, Rita Atlanta, and Rose La Rose – gorgeous creatures who excited fathers and sons alike. These artists of the striptease will no longer exhibit their charms on Vine Street. Silent will be the comics, the singers, and the bands. Gone is the very special niche of entertainment known as burlesque. Gone is the Gayety – all its magnificent days and nights. But the melody lingers on."

The program included photographs or caricatures of the following women: Loo Ling, Princess Do May, Rita Atlanta, Irma the Body, Ann Perri, Tinker

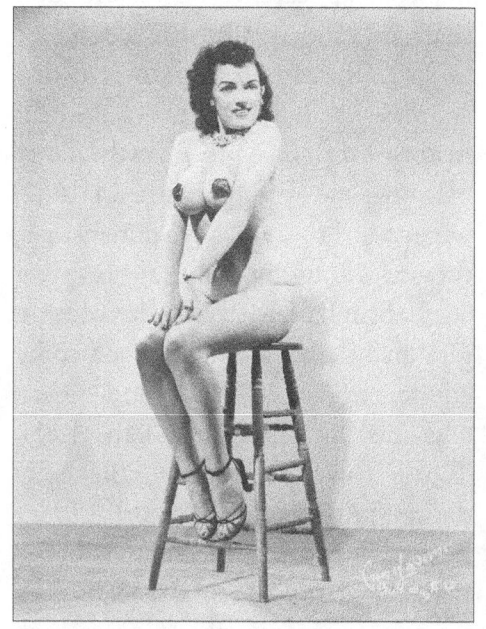

Ann Perri. "The Parisian Jane Russell" and "Empire Theatre, Newark 2, NJ" were stamped on the back of this photo. Courtesy: C.F. Miller

Autographed photo of Patti Waggin. Courtesy: Joni Taylor

Bell, Blaze Starr, Rose La Rose, Patti Waggin, Pepper Powell, Sunny Dare, and June Harlow.

The following article provided a bit more history about the Gayety Theatre. It was written by George Palmer and appeared in *The Cincinnati Enquirer* magazine on April 5, 1970; it was titled "Going... Going... Gone are the Days."

"And the walls continue to come tumbling down.

A native Cincinnatian who left his home town as recently as 30 years ago would wonder what has happened to downtown – if he returned for a visit.

Next, among other buildings to go, is the Gayety Theatre, at Vine Street and Gano Alley, between Eight and Ninth Streets.

Another parking facility is scheduled for the land area now occupied by the Gayety.

This theatre which has been playing burlesque since 1909 – first as the Empress, then the Gayety – was built as a Presbyterian church.

That was in 1846. In 1946, a Cincinnati newspaperman wrote that, "Elderly citizens remember the building as the favorite meeting place in their youth, when their young social consciences glowed with hopes of a better world here and now. It was the Vine Street Congregational Church then. That was back in the 1890s, and the early years of the current century."

Today, in these latter days of a former church, you may see pictures of semi-nude women on the entrance panels – women who wiggle a lot for a little money.

And you can see the old codgers who apparently depend on a little thrill to make the big life for them. They buy tickets.

Once the Gayety building, when it was a church, had walls gilded with the sayings of Jesus – His Golden Rule was painted there, for example.

Sunny Dare.
Courtesy: Sunny Dare

The Gayety Theatre, previously named Empress, in Cincinnati.
Courtesy: Leroy Griffith

And it was not old codgers in attendance but rather lodgers – who lived in the flop houses along Gano Alley.

A new preacher, young and vigorous, had come to the church. He was Reverend Herbert S. Bigelow. He walked down the alley and invited the lodgers to come to worship.

He offered them the front pews – and they came. The old parishioners were scandalized. Those had been their pews a far back as they could remember.

But Mr. Bigelow told them the original Congregational Church had been organized to help underprivileged people who were Negro slaves; that their forefathers had broken with the original Presbyterian Church over the issue of slavery – considered a sin against the dignity of man by them.

The old-timers left the church, and Mr. Bigelow found himself with, "flaming young liberals" who had gathered about him. "It was a new congregation," according to the writer who recalled the Gayety history back in 1946.

Apparently the young liberals didn't flame too long, or their fire was apathetic, because in 1909, the Vine Street church became a theatre.

The Congregational Church, which fell before the onslaught of exposed flesh, became the Peoples' Church, with services in the Grand Opera House, the Odd Fellows Temple, and the Railway Brotherhood building.

Some of the highlights of the Gayety down the years, without strict regard to the exact chronology include:

January 1948; It was New Years Eve the night before Louis Winkelman, who had been treasurer of the Gayety for some eleven years, dropped dead of a heart attack. Comics, girls, stagehands, all concerned found it difficult to present a New Years Eve show – but the show went on.

December 1933; The Theatre was called the Empress in those days. On Christmas Day, some ten chorus girls set up their own Christmas tree in the basement dressing rooms. They used colored footlights to decorate it, and exchanged gifts and greetings.

October 24, 1932; Police blamed labor troubles for an attempted bombing at the Empress, and an actual bombing at the home of theatre manager, Meyer Lantz. A janitor found the bombs at the theatre before they exploded, but the one at the Lantz home blew out several windows and a wall.

November 1940; No police report was filed by the manager of the theatre. The manager was Morris Zaidins. The newspaper report at the time stated that, "Men, frequenters of the places near (the Gayety) had threatened (Zaidins) with harm for attempting to protect his girl employees from suggestions that they lead a life of vice."

Editorial, November 1951; "The closing of the Gayety, last of Cincinnati's burlesque theatres, may be only incidental to the dark days which have fallen upon so many of the nation's live theatres under the dual impact of radio and television on one hand, and unduly high operating costs on the other.

The prime attraction increasingly became the feminine 'striptease' dancers, but throughout its history the burlesque house was a traditional training ground for comedians and vaudeville actors of all description.

It's to be hoped that the darkening of the local theatre is only temporary, and that it will come back again as it has previously."

That comment of almost 50 years ago would apply today – you most certainly can't train comedians, actors, and present 'striptease' dancers in a parking facility.

The Gayety reopened, blossomed briefly, until:

March 1952; "Cincinnati's only burlesque theatre – the Gayety – is to be reopened under new management March 28." – News Item.

December 1969; "The Gayety Burlesque Theatre is being 'bumped' as progress 'grinds on.' The site will become a parking lot."

But the Gayety is going down to demolition with some element of glory.

That old Presbyterian church and Congregational church and Empress and Gayety burlesque theatre will have a farewell party.

For the slaves of more than a century ago who found the building a refuge, for the lodgers on Gano Alley who came to worship; and for the comedians and strippers who learned a career there. They'll be the ghosts present when Cincinnati citizens of 1970 salute the Gayety Theatre next Friday and Saturday.

Harold Minsky, the famous burlesque name in New York, will bring his show, *Minsky's Burlesque '70,* into the Shubert Theatre for those two nights. It's a black tie affair.

And all the car owners who find parking more fun than burlesque can join the farewell ceremonies on the stage of the crumbling old Gayety Theatre.

There will be refreshments there – after the performance at the Shubert. And it will be fitting to toast the Mistress of Vine Street."

The next article in the folder had no date, but you know it was from around the same time period. It was titled "Gayety Reminiscence: One from the Boy in the Balcony," and written by Tom McElfresh. It reads:

"The smell got worse over the years, and the paint peeled more. A lot of seats were broken, and the band got smaller and smaller until, with the unions protesting, management switched to records. Then came films alternating with live entertainers. And now – the Gayety's going. Too bad; too many institutions of learning are closing.

It would be too much, I suppose, to ask some foundation to help preserve burlesque, as foundations preserve opera, and ballet, and the other museum arts: valid and valued rescues. Living memories…

Press Photo of Bert Lahr used in publications in both 1945 and 1947. Courtesy: Authors Collection

Ann Corio in her dressing room at the Old Howard in Boston. Courtesy: Boston Public Library

As it is, I can't recall the Gayety's palmy days – the great Bert Lahr and Ann Corio days. I never saw a chorus line kicking out of time – only single strippers alternating with blackout comedy routines. I never saw a name comic in front of that ugly red and yellow house curtain, or much of a production number behind it. I remember the middle years, lame at best, dying at worst. But fun; and yet dying with a bit of style and a smile. Long before the go-go grotesqueries got to it and made it lewd instead of provocative; before television deadened the comedy with poor playing.

Remember the great comedy bits – "This Must Be The Place," "Meet You Round The Corner," "Crazy House," and the classic of them all, "Here Comes Da Judge." I heard half a dozen different comics play that classic on the Gayety stage ... with no more than eight or ten words in the entire script changed. And, big house or small – the laughs came in the same places, as predictably as nightfall.

The girls: I made a farewell trip the other night, and found them a little younger, a little less exotic, and a lot less haughty and removed than the statuesque lovelies I recall.

I'll never forget the first headliner I saw at the Gayety. (Of course, I was underage and lied to get in. Of course, I sat in the second row. Of course, I bought the Nestle Bar and the genuine imported pack of French post cards; guaranteed to make my shirt roll up and down my back like a window blind. Of course, they were pictures of the Eiffel Tower, the Bridges on the Seine, and the Place de la Concorde.)

Her name was Minx Bradley. She wore black velvet, even black velvet pasties. She was a head taller than I am and was billed as "Manhattan Towers Herself!"

Evelyn West and her Treasure Chest. Courtesy: C.F. Miller

She probably danced poorly, and wasn't nearly as pretty as I thought, but she won me over.

I remember Evelyn West and her Treasure Chest. Enterprising girl; in the early 1940s she had her bosom insured for one month for $1,000,000 by Lloyd's. I'm sure that fine old London firm knew they were being taken, and loved it. She promoted herself with that same policy for years, never bothering to renew.

And the classic stripper of that time – better than Gypsy Rose Lee and Ann Corio – the one and only Rose La Rose. I remember her as sultry – Creole perhaps – and a fair tap dancer. In those days Rose La Rose could sell out the Gayety on a Saturday night. I hitchhiked in from out of town to see her. She started in red velvet, sang abominably, and took 20 minutes to get down to a

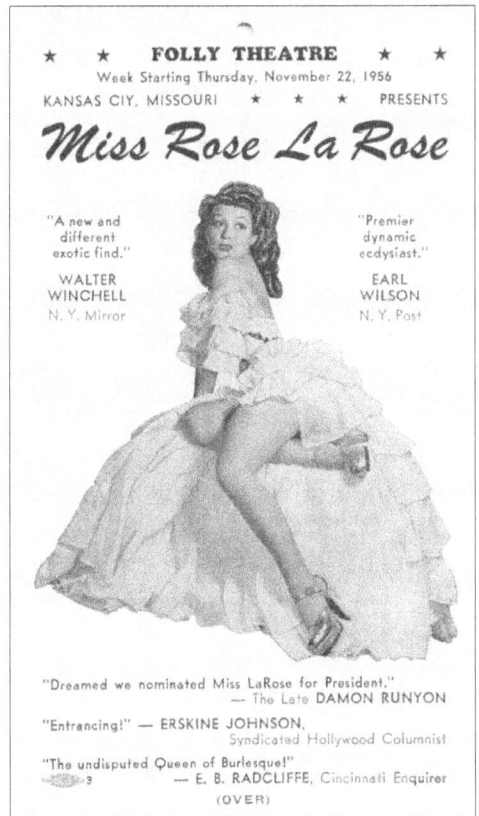

Front and Back of a Rose La Rose Folly Theatre Calendar from 1956-1957. Courtesy: C.F. Miller

white fox wrap, which she dropped "accidentally" in the curtain call at the midnight show.

There were lots of other memorable girls. One was too far over the hill to really tease. She made it funny and drew a good round of applause. Another had a sequined quarter note glued over her appendix scar. Another was too young; she looked pretty innocent to be up there. Pretty – she embarrassed us all, us apprentice dirty old men.

But, my favorite Gayety girls never appeared on the stage. At a cold December matinee, probably in 1954, I happened to glance back and saw three uniformed Salvation Army lassies lined-up, bright-eyed and wondering, in the back row. I knew why I was there; to learn anatomy. I've no idea what curriculum they were following."

Program from the 94th Season of the Old Howard, 1939-1940.
Courtesy: David Kruh

The final article in this folder was from *Time* magazine, dated April 27, 1970, and published in the Show Business Section. No author was listed and it reads:

"Grinding to a Halt; If vaudeville was king, burlesque was the nation's raffish, rococo old queen. Sixty years ago this week, Baltimore's New Monumental Theatre featured "Divorceland: A fantasy of song and jest, with sumptuous scenic environment and an ensemble of beauteous femininity prodigally clad in costly raiment." Throughout the 1920s and 1930s, pratfalls and epidermis at Minsky's warmed the Broadway night. From Boston's elegant Old Howard to the vulgar palaces of Midwestern river towns, innocently dirty old men of all ages whistled and stamped at the sultry writhings of Gypsy Rose Lee, Ann Corio, and Rose La Rose.

Fiftyish but still game, Rose was back at Cincinnati's Gayety Burlesk last week. But the beat at the Gayety was a dirge to the vanishing world of burlesque. In its rowdy, sixty-year history, the old grind house featured such titillating favorites as Tempest Storm, Trudine the Quiver Queen, and Moonbeam McSwine (complete with an armful of randy piglets). Like most such houses, it has been

Perhaps my all-time favorite photo of Tempest Storm, who died April 20, 2021. Courtesy: C.F. Miller

reduced in recent years to skin flicks, separated by the geriatric gyrations of faded strippers. Now the Gayety is being torn down to make way for a parking lot. To mourn the moment, the town fathers brought in Harold Minsky and his troupe from Las Vegas, and persuaded Rose La Rose to come out of retirement. The result was simultaneously salacious and a much too respectable salute to a bygone era.

Flit Guns; Cincinnati citizens turned the two-night extravaganza into a community project. The Minsky show was staged in the nearby Shubert Theatre, and post-performance parties were thrown at the Gayety. Some 100 lady volunteers scrubbed away part of the Gayety grime and even painted over the most unsavory washroom graffiti. Sixty years of libidinous musk was impossible to eradicate; however, before the opening-night party, Flit Guns filled with Nettie Rosenstein perfume were distributed among the ladies.

Nearly 4,000 black-tied gentlemen and bejeweled matrons turned out for the two performances. Catcalls and whistles echoed throughout the house as the curtain rose on a chorus line of topless dancers and intensified at the entrance of Alawn Don Jay, the "Sophisticated Blonde Beauty." Audiences paid $25,700 for the show. The highlight of the evening's entertainment was, Cece Ingram; a top-heavy lass billed as "Satan's Angel." Satan's little darling stripped down to a G-string

Autographed photo of Satan's Angel, who died in April 2019. Courtesy: C.F. Miller

and tassels, which she set aflame and proceeded to twirl in opposite directions. Cece sighs, saying, "It wrecks the breasts, but I've stayed in the business because, well, burlesque is my home."

Teasingly Yours; At intermission, traditional candy butchers did a thriving business in "surprise packages" containing little nasties and taffy at a dollar a throw. Later, at the Gayety, Rose held court in a silver gown, and signed men's shirt-tails with "Teasingly Yours, Rose La Rose" for $10. Bright young girls hawked pasties for $2 and tassels for $7.

John J. Strader, a wealthy Cincinnatian, lovingly cradled six boxes of G-strings and pasties as he said, "I've bought these to give to old friends, to the lovers of the better things in life." Added his wife, "We like to see a little of Americana left. If we don't preserve some of the things that make up our history, we'll end up with a country full of parking lots."

Alas, that seems to be the fate of all the Gayeties. Boston's Old Howard burned down nine years ago. "The Block" in Baltimore, once a glittering mecca of burlesque, is slated to be razed next year. Dirty movies and crass, ubiquitous nudity have virtually finished burlesque. A few bawdy old burlesque houses are left, but where they once were a cornucopia of good, smutty fun, now they are mainly a refuge for the pitiful and lonely. Where Lili St. Cyr and Pepper Powell once performed with lavish eroticism; Abba E. Bond and her Gaza Strip, and Terry and her Privates, now perform grim, grotesque imitations.

"What's worse," says Looney Lewis, "some of the top strippers these days are guys with silicone treatment around the hips and chest." Mourns Cece, of the flaming tassels; "It will never be the same again. I'll never be a Tempest Storm or a Lili St. Cyr. Burlesque is dead."

Vintage photo of the Landmark Hotel in Las Vegas. Courtesy: Authors Collection

The next folder was short, sweet, and somewhat confusing. Written on the tab was "Silverbird '77 – Mickey Rooney." However, inside was an unused contract for a show at the Landmark Hotel in Las Vegas. It was for a period of twelve consecutive weeks, from December 31, 1971 and ending on March 23, 1972. In the upper right hand corner, in pencil, was written: "Landmark (never used)." Was this a contract someone planned to copy over to use for a show at the Silverbird Hotel and Casino in 1977?

(Notes: The Landmark was a hotel and casino located in Paradise, Nevada – east of the Las Vas Strip and across from the Convention Center. Frank Carroll, a successful business contractor from Kansas City, purchased the property in 1960. He wanted to build a hotel-casino based on the style of the Hollywood Landmark Hotel, a lush establishment built in the mid-1950s in West Los Angeles that catered to celebrities. Carroll also envisioned Nevada's tallest building being constructed on the site; however, Carroll needed $10 million dollars to build the kind of tower he wanted, and he could not find a lender. To bide his time, he built a shopping center and a 120-unit apartment complex at the site and opened them just west of his uncompleted tower. In 1961, Carroll officially opened the Landmark Plaza, while Fremont Construction began to work on the adjacent thirty-one-story tall tower, with completion expected for early 1963. Because of a lack of financing, construction was stopped in 1962, with the tower nearly 80 percent completed.

For years, the partially built tower stood vacant while Carroll attempted to raise money. In 1966, the Teamsters provided a $5.5 million construction loan to finish the project, with ownership transferred to a group of investors that included Carroll and his wife; however, the Landmark's completion and opening was delayed several more times. The Landmark was completed in the spring of 1968; and the "tower" ended up resembling the "Seattle Space Needle." As construction was coming to a close, assault and battery charges were filed against Carroll. Because of the charges he withdrew his application for a gaming license and began searching for a buyer; the charges against Carroll were later dropped.

Through "Hughes Tool Company," Howard Hughes purchased the Landmark in 1969. It became the last of six casinos Hughes would own. He spent approximately $3 million to add his own touches to the resort, before opening it on July 1, 1969. The property was never a hit, and lost millions in its first year.

The Landmark continued to suffer financial problems after its opening and underwent several ownership changes, none of which resulted in success. Unable to compete with the new, larger megaresorts, the Landmark was closed on August 8, 1990. Three years later The Las Vegas Convention and Visitors Authority purchased the hotel and demolished it in 1995 to create a parking lot.

Also, the Silverbird began its existence as the Thunderbird Hotel, the fourth resort to open on the Las Vegas Strip. For more information see the "T" Files.)

After reading about the turbulent times of the Landmark and the Silverbird, maybe the timing just wasn't right for a Minsky show at either establishment.

But I know plans for a show at both hotels were being considered by the handwritten notes in the folder. Mickey Rooney was also being considered for the show; which one I don't know. The notes state the following:

Landmark: 7 days – 15 shows – 18 weeks; figured at 1971 scale. 28 people and wardrobe – line captains, swing girls, including extras and scenes = $11,850. Taxes, vacation, sick pay and insurance = $1,800. Miscellaneous, office accounting, petty cash and repairs = $350. H.M. = $2,500. Chorus – 14 people, Production Principals – 6 people, Principals – 8 people, and Wardrobe Woman – 1 person.

Silverbird: Figured at 26 weeks; 14 Chorus and 12 Principals = $17,500 to $18,500 depending on Principals. This figure includes all taxes involved with payroll and pertinent insurance. Approximately 60 costumes, figuring 3 Production Numbers = $27,000.00. Sets and Soft Materials = $15,000. Choreography = $4,000 to $5,000. Rehearsal 3 weeks X 20 people = $9,000. Music = $3,000. Lighting = $2,000.

There were additional handwritten notes in the folder; "chicken scratch," as my mom would have called them. It was apparent whoever wrote them was trying to come up with the numbers to sell a show. How much would they need in the budget to include: 7 musicians instead of 5; how much would a "straight" act cost – like a trampoline artist or dog act; and how much was needed for pre-production costs? It was very clear from the notes they wanted Mickey Rooney; his contact information was scribbled on a page, along with his current work schedule. There was also contact information for: dancer, Denise Darcel; music director, Mike Koroa; music writer and composer, Dick Winslow; writer and director, Dick Quinne; and comedy writer, Stan Davis. At the bottom of the page was: "Discussion – 4 weeks at $10,000; 6 weeks at $12,500; 6 weeks at $15,000; and 4 weeks at $17,500." The final figures had check-marks next to them. Lastly in this folder was a program for the show in which Mickey Rooney was currently performing, *Three Goats and a Blanket*, at the Windmill Dinner Theatre. No date, or year, was provided in the program.

Mickey Rooney appearing in the 1979 production of Sugar Babies. *Courtesy: Burlesque Historical Society*

The next folder in the File was labeled, "Scotsman Inn, West Paterson, New Jersey 1972." There were two pages of handwritten notes at the end of the Agreement paperwork, some of which was in an abbreviated format. There were two men's names listed representing Scotsman, Inc.; Arthur Knight and George Leitch. Knight was listed as President, and Leitch as Secretary/Treasurer. Harold Minsky and Chuck Eddy also signed the Agreement, which was dated March 20, 1972.

The contract was for four consecutive, six day weeks beginning on Thursday, June 1, 1972 and running through Wednesday, June 28, 1972. There were to be eight shows weekly, but no more than six nights per week, and no more than two shows on any one night. The OFF night was to be designated by the Scotsman at least one week in advance.

Minsky was to furnish and supply a cast of sixteen performers – eight chorus and eight principals. One of the handwritten notes reads: "If any member, or members, of the cast shall perform in such a manner as to be injurious to Operators License, Operator shall have the right to have that person or persons replaced at the Producers expense."

The Operator would also supply a follow spotlight and operator, and a light board operator for all rehearsals and performances. The Scotsman also provided a six piece orchestra for all rehearsals and performances, which included: piano, drums, trumpet, trombone, saxophone, and an electric bass.

The contract went on to read: "The Operator hereby agrees to pay the Producer as follows: Ten Thousand Dollars ($10,000) per week for four (4) consecutive weeks; total contract price for the entire engagement shall be Forty Thousand Dollars ($40,000). Payments shall be made by the Operator to the Producer as follows: Ten Thousand Dollars ($10,000) by certified check to Associated Booking Corporation, 919 N. Michigan Avenue, Chicago, Illinois 60611, no later than May 1, 1972; said monies to be held in escrow and shall represent the final week payment for this engagement, and commencing Wednesday, June 7, 1972 the sum of Ten Thousand Dollars ($10,000) to Patava, Inc., and presented to the company manager each week."

There was also a stipulation in the contract about extending the engagement for an additional four weeks at $8,500 per week, and if they extended the show beyond that the Scotsman would pay $7,500 per week on an indefinite basis. However, either party would have to provide a four week notice to terminate the show, should the show be extended beyond the eight weeks.

Above and beyond that it was a typical contract. Minsky agreed to pay the insurance, for all the costumes, sets, and performers in the show; the Scotsman agreed to Minsky's billing. The handwritten notes were scribbles on a piece of Scotsman stationery, some of which included: "Must tell before eighth week that the closing date is the 12th week." There was also: "50 miles covered by NJ clause;" "Must renew before end of second week;" and "Right of approval of performers; jeopardize liquor license, pasties, and obscene."

The Agreement and notes were all stapled, as well as paper- clipped together, and signed by George Leitch, Harold Minsky, and Chuck Eddy.

The Ralph Pearl column in the *Las Vegas Sun* on May 9, 1972 included: "Harold Minsky, back from London town, takes a quick breather and then starts auditions for girl and boy singers and dancers for his traveling company of "Minsky Burlesque," which will open in Paterson, New Jersey June 1, for eight weeks with options. The auditions will be held tomorrow at 1pm at the Richie Astone Studios on Paradise Road."

There were two more short articles, as well as a lengthy one in the folder. The short articles I believe appeared in *The Star-Ledger* and *The Jersey Journal*. The Journal piece reads:

"Minsky's Follies Returns to N.J.; New Jersey will get its first look at Minsky's Burlesque and Follies since 1957 when the all-new edition of the world-famous revue comes to The Scotsman on Route 46 in West Paterson beginning the night of June 1 and continuing until June 28.

Talent from Miami Beach and London will be brought in for the performances to augment the Las Vegas revue. Tickets are $6 and may be obtained only by advance reservation at The Scotsman."

The piece from *The Star-Ledger* reads:

"Burlesque laughter; Irving Benson, the "Top Banana" in *Minsky's Burlesque Follies '72*, playing nightly except Sundays, through June 28, at The Scotsman on Route 45, West Paterson, is having guests rolling off their chairs with laughter at each performance.

Benson, who has been associated with Minsky's Burlesque revues for some 27 years, heads up the comedy department in the fast-moving, action-packed Las Vegas spectacular which is complete with showgirls, singers, dancers, baggy-pants comics, and blackout skits produced by Harold Minsky, and staged by Jerry Norman.

Tickets which are priced at only $6 each may be purchased in advance at The Scotsman. Reservations for individual seats or complete tables may be made by calling The Scotsman. Special group rates for theatre parties and fund raising are also available on request.

Lenny Dian and his Orchestra, provides the music for the shows and dancing that follows the 9 and 10pm shows."

The last item was a rather lengthy newspaper article from the Thursday edition of *The Star-Ledger* dated June 1, 1972. The article appeared in the "Reporter at Large" column written by Mark Finston, and was titled "Comics, Acts,

Program from the Old Howard Athenaeum Theatre. Courtesy: David Kruh

Girls, Everything: Curtain Creaking up on a Minsky Burlesque." It reads as follows:

"You see, Harold Minsky is a word-purist. He's not at all happy about what has happened to the word "burlesque."

It's just not like the good old days when Minsky's father, Abraham, and Minsky's uncles, Billy and Herbert, had a grip on the burlesque market that General Motors would have envied in the auto market.

"Nowadays, every little nightclub with two or three strippers uses the word burlesque," sighs the 57-year-old Minsky. "This attracts people who think they're going to see a big show; comics, acts, girls, everything."

Minsky claims to be the last serious burlesque producer in the United States. (Someone like Ann Corio, who produced a show called, *This Was Burlesque*, he says, spoofs burlesque.)

One of his three shows will open tonight at a nightclub in West Paterson called "The Scotsman," which occupies the lower floor of a Teamsters Hall. The run is expected to be four weeks. Minsky's other two burlesque shows are long-running affairs in Las Vegas, where he now makes his home, and Miami Beach.

"I think there are three reasons for the decline of burlesque," said Minsky, a soft-spoken, affable man. At the time various members of his cast of 16 (including one male comic, one serious stripper and one comic stripper) were rehearsing onstage at "The Scotsman."

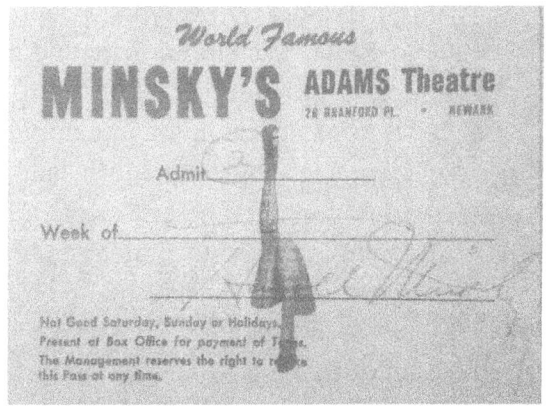

Minsky's Adams Theatre pass for two, signed by Harold Minsky. Courtesy: Dusty Sage

"One reason is there are no more burlesque theatres per se. I remember we had two in Newark: the Empire and the Adams. But burlesque theatres are in sections

1980 Press Photo promoting the Abbott and Costello 1952 film Lost in Alaska, *to appear at a local family movie theatre.*
Courtesy: Authors Collection

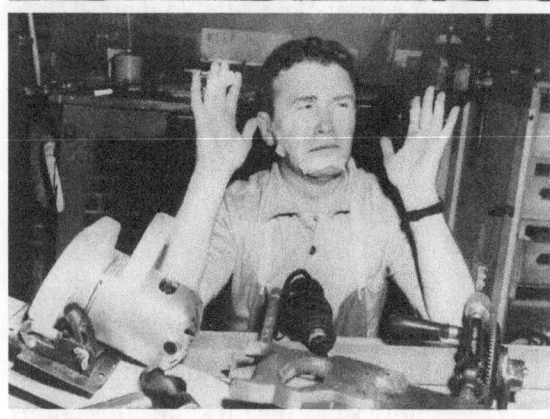

May 1953 Press Photo of Red Buttons. Who said, "Do it yourself?" Courtesy: Authors Collection

of cities that nobody wants to go to at night anymore."

Then there's the "anything goes" attitude in movies and onstage. Though burlesque is more than a strip show, a certain percentage of patrons were primarily interested in the stripper. These patrons can now get bigger and better kicks elsewhere.

"I'm against total nudity, not morally, but from a show business point of view," continued Minsky. "It's more effective if the girl is not completely naked. In this day and age, my show is really very tame."

His stripper, a five-foot, nine-inch woman named Zianne (36-24½-36), appears in a G-string. She performs completely topless in Las Vegas and Miami Beach; whether pasties will be added in West Paterson had not been decided as of yesterday's rehearsal.

"The third reason for the decline is the lack of burlesque comics coming up," said Minsky, who looked back fondly on the days when Abbott and Costello, Phil Silvers, and Red Buttons worked their way up from third comic, to second comic to top banana in burlesque.

"Nowadays, everybody wants to go on Carson and become a one-night success. The comics who appear in nightclubs – Henny Youngman, Mort Sahl, Dick Gregory – are stand-up comics; they get to a microphone and tell jokes. A burlesque comic has to do sketches. This takes a lot of training."

Most of the showgirls and dancers in the production have

no particular ambitions, no great drive to become the female equivalent of a top banana. (Dancers work harder than showgirls, and their costumes are not as skimpy.)

An exception is Kathy Price, 23, a tall, stunning brunette, who eventually hopes to become a top banana in the animal world; a veterinarian.

Miss Price has been a showgirl two years; she figures in four years she'll have enough money saved to take the necessary courses at UCLA.

Prior to being a showgirl, Miss Price worked for a teen-fan magazine and was a fashion model. "Both those businesses are more of a racket than this one," she said. "People were more brazen, more forward."

Well, she was asked, can anything be more brazen than people in the audience gawking at the shapely Miss Price – and gawk they certainly will. "It's only looking, not touching," answered Miss Price.

Stripper Zianne is 30, and has been in the business for 10 years. "I was born nude, so appearing nude doesn't bother me. I chose the name because my real name is Dianne. In the science of numerology, the letter 'Z' is a successful letter. I'm a student of the occult."

With an eight-year-old son by a previous marriage, Zianne is now married to Rod McCumber, a sometimes iron worker and welder.

"My fellow strippers hate those movies with all the nudity," she said. "How can a stripper compete with all that movie action? It hurts strippers in the pocketbook. I haven't been hurt because things are right astrologically."

If she had to do it all over again, Zianne wouldn't be a stripper. Instead she would choose from one of these four careers: psychologist, concert pianist, astrologer, or Buddhist nun. "And I'll only stay in stripping until the end of this year," she promised. "It's been a good life, but I'd still like to be a certified astrologer."

So Harold Minsky will lose another stripper, to add to his lost continent of old burlesque houses, and old top bananas.

There may be other losses, Minsky has two children; Ava, 19, a psychology major, and Danny, 24, a computer programmer.

"At one time Ava wanted to go into my business, but now she wants to work with disturbed children. I'm trying to get Danny to take over the business. Just a week ago I finally talked him into going to Florida to break in as company manager. He hasn't been interested, but maybe he'll take a liking to it, I hope…" he said sadly."

The next "S" folder in the File was for "Shoreham Hotel, Washington D.C." The Agreement was entered into and signed on October 30, 1974, and the show was to be presented in the Blue Room at the hotel starting on Thursday, November

7, 1974 and run through Wednesday, January 1, 1975. Additional information in the contract included:

Minsky was to furnish and supply a cast of no less than twelve people, along with all the costumes, props, scenery, musical arrangements, and special material. The Shoreham was to supply the spotlight and operator, along with the orchestra, which was to consist of six musicians; electric piano or organ, electric bass, rhythm guitar, drums, lead guitar, and trumpet. A side-note to all of this was either the guitar player or bass player had to be a strong contemporary vocalist.

Minsky was to receive the sum of Five Thousand Five Hundred Dollars ($5,500) per week, and be paid on Saturday of each week. The show was to receive a maximum of nine gratis rooms for the cast, plus meals for all members of the cast which were to be provided in the employee's cafeteria. Gratis rooms were also to be provided during the rehearsal period for the Producer, Choreographer, Costumer, and Manager. He was to pay his employee's, as well as provide all insurance required by law, such as Workmen's Compensation. Shoreham agreed to provide all the necessary billing and advertising, using the Minsky registered Trademark, as was typical to a Minsky contract.

The Agreement was signed by James Ballard, the Managing Director for the Shoreham Americana Hotel, and Frank Musiello, Vice President of Associated Booking Corporation.

Built in the 1930s, the Shoreham Hotel, in Washington D.C., has a "Ghost Suite." If you are curious check into Suite 870. In 1983 it became the Omni Shoreham Hotel. Courtesy: hauntedrooms.com

The following handwritten list was also in the folder. It tells us who was in the cast, and the costs for their transportation. It reads:

"Air transportation for the cast; Re: Shoreham Americana, Washington D.C. Make up separate P/R envelopes for transportation and have them sign.

Herbie Barris, $166.37; Charles Vespia, $166.37; Hector Nunez, $166.37; Gail Martin, $166.37; Darcy Schanz, $184.37; Stacy Lynn, $166.37; Cassandra Lee, $166.37; Eileen Woods, $166.37; Rita Brosh, $30.37; Rise Clemmer, $177.37; Betty Jo Kaesen, $207.74; and Maurice Wayne, $40.37. Total = $1,804.81."

I believe I have deciphered the handwriting correctly. Doing a quick search, I found Rise Clemmer was a cast member in one of the many productions (1983 perhaps) of *The Chorus Line* on Broadway.

The first article was from an unknown publication on November 18, 1974, and titled "Happenings," by Lou Byers.

"The Shoreham Americana Hotel is currently presenting *Minsky's Follies* in the Blue Room. The show, direct from the Fremont Hotel in Las Vegas, is a fast paced, lively one hour revue. The cast of 13 blend contemporary music, modern dancing, and nostalgic comedy into colorful entertainment. The emphasis is on glamour. There are four girls in the chorus, three specialty dancers and an exotic dancer – all 8 are young and attractive. Hector Nunez is the single male among them and a superb dancer. Comics, Charlie Vespia, pint-sized with a giant-sized voice, and baggy-pants-attired Herbie Barris offer situation humor and skits with the aid of straight man Maurice Wayne. Production singer Darcy Schanz has a varied repertoire of well balanced top tunes.

The accent is on youth, pace and sophisticated charm in the *Minsky's Follies*. The Blue Room offers dinner, dancing, and the show for $12.00 per person Monday thru Thursday, including free parking; and $15.00 Friday and Saturday. There's one show nightly at 9:00pm Monday thru Thursday, and two shows 9:00pm and 11:00pm Friday and Saturday."

Comic and singer Charlie Vespia. He passed away in 2012. Courtesy: findagrave.com/the Chronicler

For *Roll Call – The Newspaper of Capitol Hill*, Don Hearn wrote the following short article "The Good Life." It reads as follows:

"With burlesque beauties sharing election headlines during the month that was, the bare breast invasion of the Shoreham Americana Blue Room should come as no surprise.

For the uninformed – there are some I suppose – *Minsky's Follies* has set up shop in this somewhat staid show-bowl.

It's a grand change of pace. Frankly I had grown weary of those sweet little Florence Henderson types who seem to turn up here at the slightest whim of some agent.

Responsible for this busty, lusty, razzle-dazzle is ingenious showman Harold Minsky. He's a master at whipping the wraps off high class burlesque in high class saloons. He's proven it in such super spar as Las Vegas and Miami Beach.

The only reminders of the old days of bawdy burlesque are the baggy-pants comics. In this department the Follies has Herbie Barris and Charlie Vespia. Pros, my friends; their stuff is shaggy but who really cares. Laughs they get.

I guess it's a guy's show but Mr. Minsky hasn't forgotten the distaff set. A single, handsome male dancer flashes by garbed in little more than a sequin jock strap.

If you've hesitated going the Silver Slipper route, the Blue Room is a better bet. The price is right and the gals are gorgeous."

The following appeared in the *Washington Star-News* on November 12, 1974. It was an article titled "A Blue Blue Room," by Boris Weintraub. It reads:

"So it's come to this. The Shoreham Blue Room used to be the class place for a night on the town. Many are the tales of senior proms and New Year's Eves, of big dates and proposals on the dance floor.

No more, baby. Burlesque has come to the Blue Room, and the drapes and the rugs aren't the only things that are blue.

It is high class burlesque that the Minsky folks have brought in, if that isn't a contradiction in terms. It's called *Minsky's Follies*, and if there isn't anything that will warm the hearts of the women's movement – except, perhaps for the presence of one scantily clad male dancer – there's nothing that will offend too many people, either. Whether it will bring in enough to pay its way is another matter.

There IS nudity, almost. The women, who are mostly a pleasure to look at, always wear something, and though their breasts usually are uncovered, there's enough cloth in the general area to remind you of what clothes look like.

The highest marks go to the trio of comics, including a genuine, baggy-pants old pro named Herbie Barris who looks like Emmett Kelly without make-up. The jokes and skits were old when current TV comedians hadn't seen their first custard pie."

The next article in the folder came from the *Bethesda-Chevy Chase Tribune* and was dated November 29, 1974. It was written by Gardner Blake, and titled "Barely Burlesque in the Blue Room."

"She is the most exciting stripper you will ever see. I don't care whether you have a dislike for burlesque, or whether it turns you on, when you see this lady onstage, you can't help but admire her ability to move."

Kyle Brenner was describing Suzette Summers, the sultry and sensuous stellar attraction of *Minsky's Follies* in the Blue Room at the Shoreham Americana Hotel currently.

Brenner knows something about this sort of thing; he is the remarkably talented gent who held Maryland theatre patrons spellbound a couple of years ago, as the featured male dancer in Harold Minsky's revue at Shady Grove Music Fair.

"Suzette has a special kind of rapport with her audience," he enthused. "She puts you on the defensive. It's not a vicious or vulgar kind of thing, but it mesmerizes you. You see her as a mobile beauty as you watch her take her clothes off, and you sit there speechless because you're so hung up on the way she moves. Suzette is one of the truly gifted dancers in this business."

Most Washingtonians have finally recovered from the shock of finding a burlesque show booked into the traditionally circumspect Blue Room, (its past diversions have seldom been more raucous than Phyllis Diller or the Supremes). And from the standing-room-only audiences night after night, it would seem that they understand what Brenner was talking about.

With the possible exception of some unnecessarily smutty dialogue of the revue's comedians, *Minsky's Follies* appears to have found acceptance as a valid art form designed for a mixed patronage (there are as many women in attendance as men)... bare bottoms and breasts notwithstanding. Burlesque has become respectable. Well, almost.

Hector Nunez, who has replaced Kyle Brenner as the virile counterpart to all of that voluptuous female flesh, makes his presence felt adroitly in several production numbers that require exhausting athletic precision.

His performance is still more impressive when you understand that just a year ago he fell onstage and tore the cartilage in his right knee. He was told he might never walk again, much less dance.

The handsome Latin has had plenty of practice; his first job was in the chorus at the Lido de Paris, where he became principal dancer. He wound up ultimately at the Stardust in Las Vegas.

Last week at lunch at Agostino's on Connecticut Avenue, its amiable proprietor, Sandy Buttinelli, did the ordering for us... one of the numerous veal delicacies that are concocted in his "different Italian" kitchen. It was delicious, "But I have to watch my weight," Hector said. "It's the first thing women criticize about my performance."

His youthful enthusiasm for his work was contagious. "When I was dancing at the Lido," he recalled, "French laws required us to shave our bodies completely, and apply make-up from head to toe. That was pretty tedious; you can imagine what a relief it was to come to America where they don't mind a little hair here and there."

How does it feel to be dancing before mixed audiences with one small sequined triangle between you and the naked truth? "I was embarrassed at first, naturally, but it doesn't bother me anymore. You're too preoccupied with the choreography to worry about what you aren't wearing."

Georgia Sothern. Courtesy: C.F. Miller

Margie Hart during a World War II Bonds sale. Courtesy: Janelle Smith Collection

He and his wife Lydia, a beauteous showgirl in Las Vegas, have a healthy philosophy about dancing in the buff. "It's one of the reasons we get along so well," he said.

So do the girls in the Blue Room show. "But you wouldn't *believe* how modest they are," Hector chuckled. "Suzette, too; just barge into their dressing room without knocking, and they let out a scream. When they're standing offstage waiting for their entrances, they cover their breasts with their arms, or a make-up towel. And it's the same routine as soon as they leave the spotlights."

You could rest assured none of these would be taking headline-making dives into the Tidal Basin."

The last article in the Shoreham Hotel File was from *The Washington Post*, and dated November 11, 1974. It was from a column called "Donnelly's Revue" which was written by Tom Donnelly, and titled "Minsky's Follies: The Blue Room Takes on a Flesh Tone." It reads:

"Take it from the producer, *Minsky's Follies*, the new show in the Shoreham Americana's Blue Room, is especially designed to please "the older people and the younger people." Harold Minsky has put together a package that combines "a legit rock show – very contemporary music" with the kind of girls and gags any impresario named Minsky would just naturally order. "The girls don't chew gum or fall off the stage or do anything coarse but we still keep the mood. We give them the strip that's synonymous with Minsky." There are to be topless dancers in the Blue Room? "Yes indeed," Minsky said. That may be (and it is) a first for the Blue Room, but it's *de rigueur* for a Minsky show, as thousands of aging Georgia Sothern and Margie Hart fans can fondly attest.

Harold Minsky began his theatrical career in 1933 when "fresh out of prep school," he went to work in the box office of the Gotham Theatre, one of seven houses in the Minsky chain. His father, Abe Minsky, founder of the celebrated burlesque empire, wanted his boy to "learn everything there was to learn."

The senior Minsky had begun his own show business career in 1908 with a nickelodeon, along with the likes of Samuel Goldwyn and Marcus Loew. "I used to kid him that I could have been David O. Selznick if he had gone west with the others," Minsky said. "Selznick's old man was one of those nickelodeon pioneers. I really don't know if my father just couldn't see what a future the movies had or if he was just too much of a New Yorker to tear himself away."

In the heyday of the Minsky's (Abe had a partner, his brother Billy) they produced a series of shows with titles like: *Panties' Inferno, Ada Onion From Bermuda, Lotta Schmaltz From Greece, Iva Schnozzle From Red Hook*, and in response to the big Broadway musical, *At Home Abroad*, a small extravaganza titled, *A Broad At Home*.

In her autobiography Gypsy Rose Lee described the kind of Minsky "production number" that brought down the house: a tenor sang "The Bells of St. Mary's" while chorus girls dressed as angels with silver wings and glittering G-strings carefully removed their bras; "their eyes turned upward in saintly solemnity."

"The show at the Shoreham is a lot more sophisticated than that," Minsky says, and of course it's on a comparatively small scale; a cast of 13, including four chorus girls, three specialty dancers, plus "one exotic," one male dancer, two comics, a straight man, and a "production singer" named Darcy Schanz. She sings, among others, "I'm Woman," (A Peggy Lee number), and "Live and Let Die," (A James Bond number).

Minsky's headquarters are in Las Vegas; he's been putting on shows there since 1950. "The one at the Fremont Hotel is in its second year," he said, "with a chorus of 22 beautiful girls – 22."

When he was given the chance to produce shows on his own, Minsky hired Phil Silvers, Red Buttons, Pinky Lee, Rags Ragland, and Abbott and Costello. He said, "You notice how they all became successful in movies and TV shows that had big appeal for kids? Burlesque was a great training ground for that. I mean, in burlesque a comic really learned how to make great faces and pantomime big feelings, and just sort of project it out through the back wall."

The rivalry among those striptease queens was intense. Minsky said, "You had to watch them every minute. Always trying to outdo each other, and the only way they could outdo was by taking off a little more. Not Gypsy, though. She got by on con. She's a kid with the audience. Pat a bald guy on the head, or say,

Gypsy Rose Lee. Courtesy: C.F. Miller

'Hey young fellow, what are you doing out of school?' or go around with an apple for guys to take bites out of. She didn't really strip.

Gypsy's rivals took to doing more and more elaborate routines, pretending to be Cleopatra on a busy day and so forth. Some of those girls wanted to do 14 minutes," said Minsky. "I'd say, 'You gotta do it in eight minutes,' and they'd say, 'But that'll kill the whole story line!' Lili St. Cyr really started this trend with an ornate bathtub bit. She had very good taste and wore beautiful costumes. Women started going to burlesque to see her, whereas before it was just men. Now the audience is about 50-50."

Burlesque was outlawed in New York in 1941 because, said Minsky, "Paul Moss, the license commissioner, thought burlesque was a detriment to the city. Moss used to be with the Theatre Guild, you know. Cardinal Spellman was another one who didn't like it, and he was a man with an awful lot of power in those days. Mayor La Guardia had nothing against burlesque. He said to me right in his own office, 'There's nothing wrong with a naked girl.' But he went along with Moss. And you know something? When I see what you can see today on any stage or any screen or even on TV, I can't believe it! I just can't believe it!"

There are two classic sketches in *Minsky's Follies*. The one called "The Transformer," (the straight man tells his nurse that he's got a transformer that will cure all diseases – they go through the transformer into this dummy), and the one where three guys are standing on the corner and this girl comes by and drops her purse and a guy picks it up and gives it to her, and she does a bump-and-grind and says, "Thanks for that – you can meet me round the corner" and then another girl walks by…

Minsky went to consult with his baggy-pants comic, having first introduced me to one of the girls in his show, Rhonda LaMont. He said, "She used to be Rhonda Feaks."

The very blond, very slim Miss LaMont said, "He always kids me about changing my name from Feaks. But that's really no name for show business. Of course, my mother thinks 'LaMont' sounds phony."

I said, "Did you pick it through numerology?"

Miss LaMont said, "No, my mother thought it up." I said, "But I thought you said she thinks it sounds phony?" Miss LaMont says, "NOW she does. But when she thought it up she liked it."

Miss LaMont is the show's lead dancer. She said, "I'm the youngest, I'm 19." She's been dancing for five years and she does tap, ballet, Hawaiian, and jazz. "Jazz is my favorite."

I asked what her ultimate show biz ambition might be. "Where do I want to go? Everybody asks that. Show business has such a wide range I could go lots of places. I'd like to get into singing. You can only dance so long and then your body says, 'Uh-uh! No more!' I'd like to have my own company of dancers some day. If I'm in my 20s I'll dance. If not, I'll choreograph."

I said, "How about marriage?"

Miss LaMont said, "I could very easily give it all up to be a housewife. Later on, if I let the business start to age me too fast or start getting on my nerves, then I'll quit. I'd love to be married."

"Maybe you could do both?" I said.

"That would depend on my husband. I'd have to travel around. A lot of men don't dig that at all. Men in show business do, but most of the men I've met in the business I don't think I'd like to be married to. Touring is tough. I mean, roommates are really a hassle."

Miss LaMont said she does a variety of numbers in *Minsky's Follies*, including a topless bit and a "kind of bump-and-grind." Miss LaMont said she'd love to get a steady job as a member of a dance troupe on a TV show but how many weekly musical shows are there with choruses? "I'm very lucky to have this job," she said. "I consider myself very talented for 19, but when you realize there are a lot of dancers a lot more talented than I who are starving – well, it's depressing. That's what it is, depressing."

There was a folder included in this section that perhaps should have been in the "P" File. It had "Parodies" written on it, as well as "Sung and acted out by Burlesque Comics." There were a lot of them, but I only included about half; most have titles and many were not "politically correct." I included just one of those because it reminded me of Zorita.

Zorita's first professional photograph, taken at Robinson's Studio in Merced, California, on August 30th, 1936. Courtesy: Burlesque Historical Society

In one of her many letters she described her former husband's using some of the terminology used in the "Notre Dame" parody. You know, just by reading this material, they were used in the older Minsky shows. I typed them as they were written; now, because of the fire, I wish I had copied them all.

LEGS
Legs, Legs, First They Buy a Ticket
And You March Them Through the Door.
Legs, Legs, First You See a Little Bit
And Then You Want Some More.
Limbs Are So Attractive
They Can Make an Old Man Active.
Sure Cure for Your Blues
You're Bound to Loose With
Legs, Legs, Legs.

DARLINGS OF THE SHOW
When you see our versatility
We are sure you'll be back soon
'Cause watching us
Is the second best way
To spend a rainy afternoon… SWEET DADDY
Every gent
Will want to pay our rent
For our costumes leave no doubt
So if you are
More than three feet away
Take your opera glasses out
(And lift your eyes up)
Take your opera glasses out
(And get an eyeful)
Take your opera glasses out
(We don't wear falsies)
We're the darlings of the show.

ROSALIE
I made an awful blunder when I married Rosalie
I found out that she had tattooed her whole anatomy
But Rosalie went to the extreme
For stars of stage and movie screen

On our wedding night this was to be seen.
Chorus:
Rosalie – had Tyrone Power – on her chest was he
And Don Ameche – was there on her knee
Robert Taylor – right where he should be
On her back – Sonja Henie – just below – Andy Devine
And Rosalie had – Clark Gable – tattooed on her ankle
But she's mine – Rosaline mine.
2nd Chorus:
On her spine – was Edgar Bergen – the Ritz Boys – stood in line
And of course – Charles McCarthy – was right there
On – her – tummy and I'll – tell you folks after awhile
'Bout Barrymore's profile
And she covers with her panties
That schnozzle of Durante's
But she's mine – Rosalie mine.

OLD SPINNING WHEEL
There's a little white pot – in the bedroom
And we keep it in under the bed
We used to go out to the backhouse
But we're using the white pot instead
Some people have them fancy – and all decorated
Ours is only plain but oh so neat
And it fits all the family so cozy
'Cause it's better than the cold backhouse seat.

OVER THE RAINBOW (with added notes)
Some – where – over the rainbow
The pigeons fly
When – I – look up at the rainbow
Things hit me in the eye (they drop something in my eye)
Some – say – that's lucky – and means wealth
If that's on the square
So – with – all that luck
I should be a millionaire
Those pigeons fly up in the sky and say oh look there goes that guy
And things like that –
It really is – a dirty shame – they get all set – and how they can aim
At my new felt hat – but

Some day I'm going to get even
In a (our) plane I'll fly
If those damn pigeons can do that
Tell me – oh why can't I?

RIVERS STAY AWAY FROM MY DOOR
I was a lonely little fellow – but I got married one fine day
Bought myself a home – thought we'd live there all alone
But one day she took a boarder – and Charlie Rivers was his name
Since the day he came – things have not been the same.
Chorus:
I wish that he would go now – 'cause my wife says I'm too slow now
Rivers stay away from my door
He's just a wolf in sheep's clothing – he deserves all my loathing
Rivers stay away from my door
When we sit there together – he and my wife keep making eyes
He bought her some undies for Christmas – and he knew the proper size
They say put your troubles on the shelf – but I was a boarder once myself
Rivers stay away from my door.

YOU MUST HAVE BEEN A BEAUTIFUL BABY
Oh you must have been a beautiful baby –
    you must have been a marvelous child
But now you're twenty-one – and you've been having fun
I hear you drive the little boys wild –
    and I've been hearing rumors you're guilty –
Of doing things that nice girls wouldn't do –
You've been staying out all night – now you know that isn't right
So you've really got it coming and how
'Cause you're going to have a beautiful baby
For baby – look at you now.
2nd Chorus:
I must have been a beautiful baby – I must have been a marvelous child
They showed me to my ma – they showed me to my pa
And I nearly drove them wild – my father took a look and said what is it -
It looks like something I ought to drown
Then imagine my surprise – when I opened up my eyes
And I heard the doctor say "Don't frown –
For you really have a beautiful baby
But you're looking at him upside down."

WEEKEND OF A PRIVATE SECRETARY
She went to the mountains – to take a vacation
For $22.50 to spend a few days
She went to the mountains – to look for a he-man
Forget about business – do nothing but play
While searching for a local romance
She ran across a handsome guy
This guy's name was Max Shapiro
And Shapiro was her hero
He showed her the country and some of his etchings
Also a nightclub way up in the sky
One night he mentioned that the place was too loud
He said let's get away from the rest of the crowd
Now Max Shapiro was quite a fancy kid
And you could see it – for what nobody else did – Shapiro did
Now she's back in the office – punching the time clock
But you can see her mind's not on her work
It's up in the mountains – with handsome Shapiro
And now she is married to Goldstein the jerk – the clerk
Some girls can go to Europe and fool around and get in Dutch
The same thing happens in the mountains only it doesn't cost so much
Now when she has her baby and those things do happen
She may call it Louie Goldstein or Nero
But it will still look like Shapiro.

THANKS FOR THE MEMORY (Chord the verse)
They had us both up in the courtroom
To try and find out which one
Was guilty of a lady's downfall – and the father of her son
The girl accusing us then testified – and told her tale
And we began to wonder – how we'd look in jail
Chorus:
But thanks to her memory – she couldn't quite recall
Which one had caused it all – the night she learned the facts of life
From someone in the hall – how lovely that was
And thanks to her memory – she couldn't place the blame
Or give the fellow's name – but 'till we knew that she was dumb
We hung our heads in shame – how lucky we were
The judge looked at us with suspicion – but he couldn't give a decision
He was scared that the kid might be his'n

So at us he'd wink – as she tried to think
But thanks to her memory – because it was so short
The whole case came to naught – then 16 other worried guys
Stood right up in court – and thanked her – so much.

I MARRIED AN ANGEL
In the next house to me – there lives a family named Engle
They're rich as they can be – with a homely daughter you should see
And to my brother once her father said – with his check book in his hand
Sam, if you'll wed my homely daughter – I'll give you fifty grand
Chorus:
Have you heard – he married an Engle
But there is an angle there that he didn't see
The next day his wife had a baby – so he called her father up
And said, "What have you done to me?"
Sam said, "She's no angel" and her pa said, "I'm glad
That you confided in me – now I'll confide in you too
If you think my daughter is no good – just wait 'till you try to cash
That check that I gave to you."

BEACH AT BALI-BALI
It happened on the beach with Rudy Vallee –
He kissed her once and she said Rudy don't
It happened on the beach with Rudy Vallee –
He kissed her once again and said I won't
And then he took his girlie to the sea shore
Now his intentions were the worst you bet
And when he brushed the sand out of his trousers
He said I bet I get that damn thing yet
Then he told her that he loved her
Said he'd buy her anything
She said after what has happened
You had better buy me a wedding ring
It happened on the beach with Rudy Vallee
And he's mighty sore I'm telling you
For soon there'll be another little crooner
To sing Boo Boo * Boo Boo * Boo Boo * Boo Boo * Boo Boo.

SERENADE IN THE NIGHT
Sarah made in the night – Sarah wasn't too careful

Sarah's favorite joy was to be with a boy out on a big date
Sarah made in the night – now according to Winchell –
Sarah's going to be blessed with a blessed event
Which makes things complicated -
Although – they all know who the maw will be
No one – will know who the paw will be
Sarah made in the night – Sarah wasn't too careful
Now Sarah's lawyer who's wise – is suing six of those guys
Sarah made in the night.

BIST DU SHANE
My dear sister Shane – please let me explain
I think I'm being framed by your daughter Ann
I took her out once or twice – but why should I pay the price – when
There wasn't any vice I'm not the man
It could be Phil or Bill or even Sam or Lee
Somebody plowed the furrow but it wasn't me
What do you hear from the mob – one of those guys did the job
So kiss the kid and tell him he's not mine.

POCKETFULL OF DREAMS
I bet on a horse named Jake – as a race horse Jake's a fake
Now I've got a pocketful of dreams
He was sure to win that day – but he ran the other way
Now I've got a pocketful of dreams
I thought I had a sure thing – I figured I can't lose
When he caught up and passed the others – I lost my blues
That race was, how could he miss
If he didn't stop to take a _____ drink
Now I've got a pocketful of dreams.

I CAN'T GIVE YOU ANYTHING BUT LOVE BABY
All night long I walk the floor with my baby
Walk a million miles or more with my baby
All alone – no one home – to take my place
The poor kid moaned – then he groaned
I didn't scold him – but I told him
Gee I hate to see you aggravated baby
I hope your mother doesn't stay out late baby
And if you're hungry you'll have to wait baby
For, I can't give you anything but love.

MARGIE
I got a room in a Lenox Avenue Hotel –
    the manager said the bed bugs they won't bite –
He thought he knew – what he said was true
In the middle of the night – when I turned on the light
Chorus:
They were marching – them boys weren't creeping – they were marching
They had me weeping there was squads to my right and squads to my left
They just sneaked right up and took a bite and kept on marching
It was an inspiration just for one to see
They advanced without fear – and they bit me in the rear
And - kept on marching on me.

FRIVOLOUS SAL
They call her fan dancing Sal – a sexy sort of gal
Without any clothing – in nightclubs she's posing
She's my old gal – she flitters hither and there
But most of my sweetheart is bare
It's really uncanny – how she fans her fanny
She's my gal Sal.

ISLE OF CAPRI
'Twas on a pile of debris that I found her
Oh she was drunk as drunk as could be
And you could still smell the gin for miles around her
When we met on that pile of debris
I was tight but she was a little tighter
And as she laid there she was pretty to see
I was tired so I laid down beside her
When we met on that wonderful spree
You could hear her softly mutter
As she sadly shed a tear – this is my own private gutter
What the hell are you doing here?
And when the cops found us both in the morning
Oh we were friends it was easy to see
And when we kissed with the dawn in the morning
'Twas goodbye to that pile of debris.

SONNY BOY
(Shots offstage; run on with burlap bag & stuffed chicken)
I never saw one man make such a fuss over one dead rooster – mister rooster

You being so popular I'm naming you Sonny Boy
(Break into song)
Climb into my sack Sonny Boy – no need looking back Sonny Boy
The hot grease am waiting – no need hesitating
I'll eat you, feet and all Sonny Boy – then we'll stick together
Thru all kinds of weather – just you and me Sonny Boy
I'll get your mother – your sister and your brother
Like I got you Sonny Boy
You came from the hen house and I know you're worth
I'm going to eat you until my stomach will burst
The whole wide world it knows that you
Taste much better than beef stew
You've chased your last hen – Sonny Boy.

CHANGE PARTNERS
They all laughed when my girl came to the ball dressed up in slacks
But when she stooped they split – then somebody cracks
You better change panties or else go home
'Twas on the night that Orson Welles broadcast that play so vividly
I got so scared that my lady friend said to me
You better change panties or dance alone
She said go sit this one out someplace by yourself
Or I'll tell the waiter to tell you you're wanted by the Board of Health
If Orson Welles ever does that thing again
No matter when – I hope that I'm not living then
'Cause I know I'll have to change panties again.

NOTRE DAME
Shame – shame on old Notre Dame –
    the Jews and the Polacks have stolen your fame –
Why put Mellocovitch into the line – why not O'Hara or O'Brien
You give all the plays to the Wops and French
And keep all the Irish sitting on the bench
Everyone wonders what became – of the Irish of Notre Dame.

TREES
Of all the things that I could be – I thank the Lord I'm not a tree
A tree that stands out in the street
With little doggies at its feet
Is nothing more or less – a comfort station in the grass

A tree that lifts its arms to pray
Stay away little doggie stay away
And what is more I couldn't bear
A nest of pigeons in my hair
If it's to be – or not to be
I thank the Lord – I'm not a tree.

LORD YOU MADE THE NIGHT TOO LONG
Verse:
Trousers dragging – simply dragging down the street
And their dragging you could hardly see my feet
I'm not finding fault at all
They're so big and I'm so small
But Sam you promised to make ends meet.
Chorus:
You made the coat and vest – fit the best
You made the stitches good and strong
But Sam you made the pants too long
You made my coat lapel look so swell
Who am I to say you're wrong
But Sam you made the pants too long
Now I've got a belt and I've got suspenders
So what have I got to lose?
But what good is the belt and what good is the suspenders
When the pants are hanging over my shoes
I get the darn'dest breeze
Thru my B.V.D's –
My fly is where my tie belongs
Oh Sam you made the pants too long.

"S" also stands for "Show Costs." Most of what was in the folder revolved around orchestrations, set, and lighting costs. But there were a couple of items that dealt with payroll as well, so let's begin there. I like payroll items because normally they are lists of names; sadly, it was sometimes difficult to read the handwriting.

The first item was handwritten on stationery from the Edgewater Beach Hotel in Chicago, Illinois. It was dated May 9, 1967, and in large letters at the top of the page were the words "Breakdown on Payroll."

Dancers: A. Michaels, J. Boyle, Marcia Gregg, Kitty McDonald, Estelle Cole, Francine Storey; and line captain and swing girl, Susan Sigrist. The dancers were paid $175.00 per week; Sigrist was paid $243.75 per week.

Showgirls: Betty Jo Alvies, Beth King, Pat Elliott, Darlene Larson, Jackie Peters, Bari Gibson; and line captain and swing girl M. Kelly. The showgirls were paid $175.00 per week; Kelly was paid $200.00 per week.

Principals: Barbara Curtis, $300.00; Milt Douglas, $425.00; Debra Duke, $400.00; Lisa Duran, $550.00; Danny Jacobs, $275.00; Barbara Johnson (wardrobe) $150.00; Fred Lewis, $325.00; Larry Merritt, $325.00; Ken Whitmer, $630.00; Dave Welker, $350.00; and Don Kirk, $250.00.

The other payroll item in this folder was a copy of the unsigned letter/contract, dated November 5, 1973, written by Harold Minsky, and addressed to Anita Mann.

Miss Anita Mann
15130 Mulholland Drive
Los Angeles, California 90024

Dear Miss Mann:

We are pleased to learn that you have agreed to choreograph our show at the Playboy Plaza Hotel, Miami Beach, Florida which is scheduled to open on or about April 23, 1974. As per our previous conversations with your representative, Mr. Gershenson, our agreement for your services is as follows:

1. In consideration of the services to be rendered by you as the choreographer for this show, SHOKOW will pay you the sum of $4,000.00, payable as follows: $2,000.00 when rehearsal commences and $2,000.00 on the opening day of the show.

2. In addition to the foregoing, SHOKOW agrees to pay to you weekly, a royalty of $75.00 per week for each week that the show plays at the Playboy Plaza Hotel, Miami Beach, Florida, beyond the first 26 weeks.

3. You will be required to devote to SHOKOW the following time as a choreographer: two weeks of full rehearsal in Las Vegas which will be preceded by several one day trips to Las Vegas for various meetings, auditions, etc. When the show moves to Florida you will be present for three days of rehearsal immediately prior to opening night and remain for two days following the opening.

4. We will provide to you or reimburse your expenses for all transportation to Las Vegas and Florida together with your transportation while in Las Vegas and Florida.

5. SHOKOW will provide or reimburse you for your living expenses while you are in Florida and during your brief trips to Las Vegas prior to the two weeks of full rehearsal.

6. Although SHOKOW cannot guarantee the content of billings which are paid for by the Miami Playboy Plaza Hotel, we will request and put forth our best efforts to see that you receive billing as the choreographer in all paid advertising and printed promotional material.

If this agreement is acceptable to you please execute he enclosed copy and return the same to me.

Sincerely yours,
SHOKOW, Ltd.

(Notes: Information about Anita Mann can be found online; she remains very active and has a web site.)

Also, there was a statement from Dillingham and Associates, located at 1551 Rawhide, Las Vegas, Nevada 89119, to Harold Minsky, at 5712 Kelly Lane, Las Vegas, Nevada. It was dated January 15, 1973.

The bill was for: Lighting Directors Fee, $1500.00; 10 Color Wheels at $15.00 each, $150.00; 5 4" Kliegl Lekos at $65.00 each, $325.00; 2 6" Kliegl Lekos at $50.00 each, $100.00; and Rental of 2 modified Cramer Projectors (Value $350.00 each) at $10.00 per week for 26 weeks, $260.00. The bill totaled $2335.00, but below it were some additional handwritten notes. 1/29/73 - $1500.00; 2/8/73 - $835.00 and $235.00; 2/15/73 - $600.00 and $300.00; and lastly 2/23/73 - $300.00 and $300.00. Below that final date and numbers was a large zero, with a line drawn through it.

Another statement comes from Cinema Services/Las Vegas, Inc. The letterhead mentions lights and lighting equipment, as well as grip equipment. The address for the company was 3420 Polaris, Las Vegas, Nevada 89102. There were two statements; one was for items Minsky bought, the second for items he rented. All of the items were to be delivered on December 21, 1971 to the Aladdin Hotel and Casino; the items were paid for in cash.

The rental statement, 0406, was for the following items: 12 – 2 for 1 Adapters at $1.00 per week, $12.00; 2 – 50' 12/3 Stage Cable at $1.00 per week, $2.00; and 1 – 50 Gallon Fog Barrel at $10.00 per week, $10.00. The total bill was for $24.84; $24.00 for the items, and 3½ percent tax for 84 cents. The invoice date on the bill was January 5, 1972; it was marked paid on January 11, 1972 – as was the second invoice for the items sold to Minsky.

The sold to statement, 0405, was for the following items: 24 – Mini-Strobe Lights at $4.00 each, total $96.00; 48 – Lamps for Mini-Strobe at $1.00 each, total $48.00; 48 – 9-Volt Batteries for Above at 36 cents each, total $17.28; 4 – A F2 Carousels Complete 4 to 6 Zoom Lens at $230.00 each, total $920.00; 3 – Medium Flash Pots at $16.50 each, total $49.50; 1 – Large Flash Pot for $24.80;

1 – Pound Common Flash Powder for $20.00; 4 – E H R 400 Watt Quartz Lamps at $9.50 each, total $38.00; 1 – B C K Quartz Projector Lamp for $9.85; Repair and Service Kaleidoscope for $20.00; and 1 – 12" Glass Disc for Above for $6.20. The total bill was for $1,293.37; the items cost $1,249.63 and the tax of 3½ percent came to $43.74.

The next two proposals and contracts were for sets and scenery. The paperwork mentioned the various sets commissioned, the prices to be paid, and drawings. The drawings were not in Minsky's Files; if they still exist they may be at UNLV. Both contracts were between Patava, Inc., and the Las Vegas Display Company, 3049 Rigel Street, Building A, Space N1, Las Vegas, Nevada. The contracts were signed by Fredric K. Josephs, and initialed by Harold Minsky. Could it be that what once was Rigel Street in Las Vegas in the early 1970s may now be Rigel Avenue?

The first contract was dated November 15, 1971, and the scenery was to be delivered to the Aladdin Hotel no later than December 19, 1971. It was for a total of $13,075.00. $3,500.00 was due upon signing the contract, and the following was attached to the paperwork which reads as follows:

"EXHIBIT "A" – On November 29, 1971 an additional $1000.00. Upon delivery of completed sets an additional $2500.00. Commencing on the first Friday February 1972 an additional $1000.00 and each Friday thereafter an additional $1000.00 until March 10, 1972 where a balloon payment of $1075.00 will conclude the total amount of $13,075.00 will be paid in full."

In the margin, notes were made in ink regarding the various payments. On November 29, 1971, payment was made by check number 5430. Additional payments were made on December 21, 1971, February 4, and February 10, 1972, as well as $1000.00 paid on March 10, 1972. A handwritten note states, "Leaving $75.00 due."

The scenery delivered to the Aladdin Hotel included:

"Opening Set as per drawings No. 1, 2, & 3, Less Lacework, cost $3500.00; Finale Set as per drawings 4, 5, 6, 7, & 8, Less Glass Beads, cost $3725.00; Strip Number as per drawing No. 9, cost $850.00; Panel Cyc. as per drawings No. 10 & 11, cost $2250.00; Credits, Screens & Hole Sleeves as per drawings No. 14, cost $625.00; Spider-Space Number, as per drawings No. 15 & 16, cost $1350.00; Interest until March 10, 1072, $100.00; and Flying Mirrors as per drawings No. 12 & 13, cost $675.00."

The second contract was dated November 13, 1972, and the scenery was to be delivered to the Fremont Hotel no later than December 19, 1972. The total cost for the scenery was $3,834.00; $1,917.00 due upon the signing of the contract, the balance due upon the delivery of the completed scenery. Again payments were noted in the margin of the contract; payments of various amounts were made on November 14, 1972, as well as on December 6, and 29, 1972, and finally on January 5, 1973.

The scenery delivered to the Fremont Hotel included:

"Opening Set: Build and cover new flats, cut down existing scenery, cost $537.00; Lace Credit Screens: Remake into traveler curtain, and add panels, cost $140.00; Show-Girl Strip: Modify existing units, as per sketch, cost $416.00; Space Number: Build and mount caster wagon units, and rig webs to hang, cost $280.00; Finale: Build new finale flats and center unit as per sketch, cost $1,538.00; Panel Cyc.: Cut down existing units to working height, cost $675.00. Total labor and material for scenery, cost $3,584.00. Trucking (two ways) plus forklift rental, cost $250.00; Total, $3,834.00."

Finally, this folder was for "Orchestrators and Arrangers." There were several contracts, all dating from 1971 to 1974. Those named on the contracts included: Eddie Freeman, 1971; Irv Gordon, 1971; Bob Hammer, 1971; Dick Alber, 1972; and Ken Tiffany 1972 - 1974. Minsky signed several contracts with Ken Tiffany. Amounts paid range from: $405.20 to Eddie Freeman; $524.00 to Irv Gordon; $290.38 to Bob Hammer; $100.00 to Dick Alber; and $3,545.00 to Ken Tiffany.

Tiffany was asked to orchestrate the song "Ricky-Tick," and to reorchestrate the following: "Arabesque," "Mac Arthur Park," "For Me," "Bows," "I Feel the Earth Move," "I'm A Woman," "Show Me," "Cheaper to Keep Her," "Roller Derby," "Night Owl," "Leroy Brown," "Live and Let Die," "The Way We Were," and "Keep on Singing." Tiffany was also hired to transpose and rearrange music for five or seven piece bands, as well as to add reed and alto parts to a number of orchestrations. The other gentlemen were hired to do the same but Minsky worked with Tiffany more than the others.

Irv Gordon was asked to reorchestrate the following: "Don't cha Hear Me Callin," "Killer Joe," "Channel," "St. Petersburg," "Paper Man," "Central Park," and "Scorpio." It appears that Gordon and Eddie Freeman may have worked on some of this music together.

(Notes: Musician and arranger Kenneth (Ken) M. Tiffany Jr., was born in Hutchinson, Kansas on February 17, 1936, and remembered as always having a love of music. After learning a variety of instruments he decided the trombone was his favorite. He played professionally all over the country with many noted swing bands before settling in Las Vegas, Nevada, where he was the lead trombone player at the Sahara Hotel for many years. Tiffany also played in other Las Vegas hotel bands, participated in a 76 Trombones concert in Ham Hall on the campus of UNLV, and arranged music for many showroom headliners. Ken Tiffany passed away at the age of 63 on July 28, 1999, and is buried at Memory

Gardens Cemetery in Las Vegas. A collection of his scores, as well as some photos of Tiffany, are housed at UNLV.

There is extensive information regarding jazz pianist, composer, and arranger Howard Robert "Bob" Hammer online. He was born on March 3, 1930 in Indianapolis, Indiana.

Richard Royal "Dick" Alber was born May 31, 1938 in Lincoln, Nebraska, and died December 27, 2019 in Las Vegas, Nevada. He played lead trumpet for a time in the early 1960s when Warren Covington was fronting the Tommy Dorsey Orchestra. He then moved his family to Las Vegas where Richard, known as Dick Alber, continued a long and varied music career. He played in a multitude of house bands including those at the Dunes, the International, and the Stardust. The bands backed many well-known names as well as his personal favorites Steve Lawrence and Eydie Gorme. He also wrote and arranged original music as well as standards for use in local bands. Alber, and the Las Vegas Music Company, is also listed in a 1971 catalog of copyright entries with a song entitled, "Would You Believe Seven?" In 1974, according to a newspaper article in the Albuquerque Journal, Dick Alber was the lead trumpet player at the Flamingo Hotel. He performed with the Vincent Falcone Orchestra at the Rio Hotel in 1999; and Las Vegas newspaper articles in 1999, and again in 2001, mentioned Dick playing trumpet in a multi-piece band for the Buddy Greco show at the Flamingo-Hilton Hotel, and at the Blue Note Las Vegas. He retired in 2003.

There is also a lot of information about Irving Gordon online. He was born on February 14, 1915 in Brooklyn, New York and died on December 1, 1996 in Los Angeles, California. Gordon was credited with Abbott and Costello's baseball comedy routine, "Who's on First?" (See Notes in Music Section.) If this is true, it may also connect him to the first generation of Minsky's Burlesque; check him out.

Is Eddie Freeman, (named on the contract connected to Irv Gordon), the jazz musician born in London on November 10, 1909? Like so many professional musicians Freeman played many instruments in several different orchestras: the violin, guitar, tenor banjo, trumpet and piano to name a few. He moved to the Bronx in New York in the early-mid 1940s, which is where he may have met Irv Gordon. By the early 1950s Freeman and his family moved to Oceanside, California where he supported himself as a pianist in clubs, piano tuner, transcriber, and teacher. Eddie died on November 23, 1987 in Dallas, Texas.)

The final folder in the "S" File was titled "Songs/Skits." It's a bit confusing since it solely contained copies of the before-mentioned Parodies, two skits, and the cast list from *Minsky's Burlesque '75*.

I'll start with the cast list, which included: Comics, Dick Richards and Lou Ascol (Equal Billing); Straight Man and Woman, Eddie Innes and Ilona Adams; Exotic Dancers, Janet Boyd and "Robin;" Specialty Acts, Berri Lee; Singer, Joseph La Vigna; Lead Dancers, Donald Crawford and Rhonda LaMont; Dancers, Barbara Sheehan and Christina Sheehan; Showgirls, Robin Duran, Barbara Hunt, Dona Reynolds, and Robin Zito. The show was Produced and Directed by Harold Minsky; Staged and Choreographed by Betty Francisco; Musical Arrangements by Ken Tiffany; Costumes by Eastwood; and the Production Manager was Jerry Lucas.

Comic Lou Ascol.
Courtesy: David Hanson

The scenes for the show were to include the following performers. The first act: "The Flirt," with Dick Richards, Eddie Innes, and Ilona Adams; "School Room," with Lou Ascol, Ilona Adams, Janet Boyd, and Eddie Innes; and "Gaston," (The Lover) with Dick Richards, Eddie Innes, and Ilona Adams. The second act: "19th Hole," with Lou Ascol and Ilona Adams; and lastly "Cut Up and Bleeding," with Lou Ascol, Dick Richards, Eddie Innes, Ilona Adams, and Janet Boyd.

The next item was titled, "Introduction for Miss Martha Raye." In the top right hand corner, written in pencil, is: "Valley Forge Music Fair." The skit is typed to provide variations to the old courtroom scene called, "How Did I Know He Was After My Money." The original scene, included as a variation to this skit, is not included; however, it is in one of my other books. The rest of the scene is typed exactly as it was written, and reads as follows:

Straight man: (center stage) Ladies and Gentleman; I want you to meet a truly great star of the entertainment world. A lady in the absolute tradition of the theatre. Her name and talent forever imprinted on our minds and hearts and beloved by all. She was destined to be a star from that moment when she was born in a dressing room of the Gayety Theatre, St. Louis, Missouri, eighteen seventy five---------

Martha: (on and loud) Eighteen seventy five??

Straight man: (right on it) Martha Raye!

Martha: (after acknowledging audience) What's that eighteen seventy five?
Straight man: Oh, that's the street number of the theatre.
Martha: Well, for a moment you scared me. I thought maybe you were right. Okay, what do we do now?
Straight man: We do the Judge scene and you are the Judge. (assist Martha on with the judge's robe, which should be handily placed on bench or nearby chair)
Martha: This should be some kind of a first for burlesk, putting it on instead of taking it off. I'm glad it's this way, after what happened to me at that nudist camp. The first day I took my clothes off, they threw me out for indecent exposure. (takes position behind judge's stand)
Straight man: Heil to the Judge, etc.
Martha: What's the first case on the docket?
Straight man: First case your Honor is that of a man whose wife gave birth to a red headed baby, and he claims that he is <u>NOT</u> the father.
Martha: Bring in the father…
Straight man: What??
Martha: Bring in the baby… The husband… Bring in somebody.
Straight man: (offstage) Send in the husband. (man enters)
Martha: You are the husband?
Man: Yes your Honor.
Martha: And you claim that you are <u>NOT</u> the father of the baby??
Man: That's right.
Martha: Why???
Man: Because the baby has red hair…
Martha: Anyone in your family or your wife's family have red hair?
Man: No!!
Martha: Did your grandmother have red hair?
Man: No…
Martha: Did your grandfather have red hair?
Man: No… No one in my family had red hair!
Martha: Let me ask you a personal question… How often do you make love to your wife?
Man: Twice!!!
Martha: Twice????
Man: Yes, once in the winter and once in the summer.
Martha: (to straight man) This man makes love to his wife twice a year… His baby doesn't have red hair!!!
Straight man: What is it??
Martha: That's R U S T!! Case dismissed… What's the next case??

Straight man: The next case is a divorce action on the ground of incompatibility.
Girl: (enters and sits, right of judge's bench)
Martha: Listen you, stop using those big words, just say they couldn't get along.
Straight man: Well, that's incompatibility.
Martha: Then just say, they couldn't get along on account of incompatibility and we'll know what the hell you're talking about. (to girl) All right young lady how long have you been married?
Girl: Six years.
Martha: (to girl) Now why do you want a divorce? Just tell the Judge everything, don't leave out anything, and in your own words, I'll understand.
Girl: Well, my husband has a Suzuki… And I have a Kawasaki.
Martha: That's a beautiful way of expressing it. It sort of gives it an exotic secret of the Orient. Go ahead…
Girl: Well, lately, my husband just can't keep his hands off my Kawasaki.
Martha: Is that so? Well, maybe you should stop going to those drive-in sex movies.
Girl: He's always after me wanting to ride my Kawasaki.
Martha: All you have to do is refuse.
Girl: I do but somehow when I'm not looking, he sneaks up on it, and away he goes.
Martha: That guy must be damn fast or you're awfully slow. Doesn't he give you a hint, some warning, you know a kiss or something, take off the bra, nosh a little?
Girl: Once he gets his leg over it, that's it.
Martha: I see. You're a pushover for a leg.
Girl: If it wasn't for the man next door, I don't know what I'd do.
Martha: Now it's beginning to get real interesting. What about the man next door?
Girl: Well, he has a Yamaha.
Martha: He has a Yamaha? A Yamaha? Is that anything like a Suzuki?
Girl: About the same, but the Yamaha is six inches longer.
Martha: Cheese and crackers, what the hey, holy gesschawtz. (good spot here to belt the straight man with the bladder)
Straight man: Judge, Judge, control yourself.
Martha: I can't, my controller is busted. A Yamaha? Lady, that's a Yamaha, ha, ha, ha…
Girl: The first time he gave me a ride on it, I was tickled silly.
Martha: I read or heard somewhere, that extra six inches makes a more comfortable ride. Okay, divorce granted, and may you find many pleasant hours with your Suzuki, Kawasaki, and that Yamaha.
Girl: (exits)
Straight man: You know of course, she was talking about motorcycles.

Martha: Motorcycles?

Straight man: What did you think she was talking about?

Martha: The same damn thing that guy over there was thinking. (pointing to audience member) Next case…

Straight man: Your final case is of a man walking around town without any pants on… Practicing nudism, or in other words, he was picked up for indecent exposure.

Man: (during above dialogue, enters and stands at side of judges bench)

Martha: Young man what have you got to say for yourself? How old are you cutie? Well, let me put it another way, are you married?

Man: Yes, I've been married now for two years.

Martha: Any children?

Man: Yes, we have nineteen.

Martha: You have been married two years and have nineteen kids?

Man: Right.

Martha: Case dismissed.

Man: (exits)

Straight man: But Judge, you saw for yourself he wasn't wearing any pants.

1939 Press Photo of Joe E. Brown and Martha Raye. The scene is from the Paramount film, $1,000 a Touchdown. *Courtesy: Authors Collection*

Martha: Married two years and having nineteen kids, that guy never got a chance to put his pants on.
BLACKOUT

The last item was a skit written by Jess Mack for the Minsky Show starring Martha Raye. Prior to becoming an agent, Jess was himself a straight man in burlesque, and worked with many notable comics. This is an adaptation of the "Restaurant Scene," and was typed as it was written.

Cast:
Martha Raye
Comic
Straight man
Girl

Stage setting:
Bar on one side; table and two chairs on other side; and hall tree center stage.

Props:
Small table
Two chairs
Hall tree
Straw hat each show
Bar
Four quart bottles filled with water and whiskey (tea) color
Tall ten-ounce plain glass
Mixer
Cigar box with sawdust
Bar towels
One egg each show
Bottle of seltzer
Small red flag

Wardrobe:
Tall white chef's hat (Raye)
White apron (Raye)
White coat (Comic)

Raye: (to comic) Now, this is your first day on the job... Remember, I am the boss... You will be the chef and I will be the waitress. Anyone orders anything... I will call it out to you and you repeat it... Do you understand?

Comic: Okay... I'll be the chef... Here comes some business... (Straight man and girl enter)

Straight: Here we are dear... They say they serve excellent Chinese food here.

Raye: (to comic) Chinese food? (looks at him) How much would you charge to sour up a bottle of milk?
Comic: Pint or quart? I'm going into the kitchen… (exits)
Raye: Hello folks… Just be seated…
Straight: My hat… (hands her straw hat) Hang it up…
Raye: Okay… (business of breaking same on hall tree, upstage)
Straight: Waitress… I think you broke my hat.
Raye: You think? Take another look… Have a seat (he does)
Straight: (to girl) Dear… What do you want?
Girl: Oh sweetheart, you know what I want.
Raye: You'd better eat first…
Straight: Maybe you can suggest something?
Raye: Me, suggest something to eat in here? Not me… I eat around the corner. Come to think of it, how about some nice lambs tongue?
Straight: I'll have you know that I never eat anything that comes out of an animal's mouth!!
Raye: How about some eggs?? Maybe you'd like to have some "zoop"?
Straight: Some what?
Raye: Some zoop… (spells) Z… you double P… Zoop (in eye)
Straight: What kind of soup do you have?
Raye: We have chicken and pea soup…
Straight: Okay… I'll have a bowl of chicken soup.
Raye: (calls offstage) One bowl of chicken soup…
Comic: (offstage… repeat) One bowl of chicken soup.
Straight: I've changed my mind miss… Instead of chicken soup, I'll have pea.
Raye: (calls offstage) Hold the chicken and make it… Pea!!
Comic: (enters) Hey Martha, the garbage man is here.
Raye: Tell him we don't want any.
Comic: Better take two cans!
Raye: What for?
Comic: For the soup. (exits)
Straight: Cancel the soup; I think I'll have a ham sandwich.
Raye: With or without?
Straight: Without what?
Raye: Ham…
Straight: I want a ham sandwich… With ham…
Raye: Do you want bread with it?
Straight: Certainly… How can you make a ham sandwich without bread?
Raye: You could put it on a piece of matzo… Or on a bagel.
Straight: Forget the ham sandwich… Do you have any specials??

Raye: You lucky people… Today is Tuesday and every Tuesday we have a Blue Plate Special… Beans ala tot!
Straight: Never heard of it… What's beans ala tot?
Raye: First you eat the beans… Then ta tata tata ta tot…
Straight: No, I don't think I want that.
Raye: How about some macaroni and beans??
Straight: What's the macaroni for?
Raye: Gives it that ripe organ effect…
Straight: Never mind the beans… A little while ago you said something about eggs.
Raye: Yes, we have strictly fresh eggs.
Straight: I think I'll have two eggs.
Raye: (calls offstage) Two eggs…
Comic: (offstage) Two eggs…
Raye: How do you want them?
Straight: Fry one on one side… And… fry one on the other…
Raye: (calls offstage) Fry one on one side…
Comic: (offstage) Fry one on one side…
Raye: And fry one on the other…
Comic: (enters) What the hell is this? Fry one on one side and one on the other?
Raye: Don't you know how to do it? I'll show you… First you take one egg and fry it… Okay? That's fried… Put it on the side and forget it. Now you take the other egg and flip it…
Comic: Flip it??
Raye: Yes, you flip it… (business of hands and arm ala Italian)
Comic: It can't be done… Tell him to order zoop or get the hell out of here. (exits)
Raye: Sorry, we're all out of eggs… (to girl) How about something to drink?
Girl: A good idea… I'll have an eggnog.
Raye: (calls offstage) One eggnog…
Comic: (offstage) Fry one on one side… (enters)
Raye: You don't fry an eggnog. You've got to mix it. Come over here and I'll show you. (business of mixing drink with tall glass, mixer, sawdust, egg, a couple of bottles – gin and whiskey colored, and bottle of seltzer. When she gets to the seltzer bottle…) This is what they call go-zint-ta water.
Comic: Go-zint-ta?
Raye: Yes, this goes into that… (squirts seltzer into tall glass until it runs over, and then squirts comic in fly of pants)
Comic: (pants and leg business) Did you see a tall dog pass by??

Raye: No.
Comic: Must have been an inside job…
Raye: (continues with drink, uses bar rag, and wrings some into glass. Take small red flag and puts it into glass. Walks to table and sets it on table with hand in it)
Girl: You don't expect me to drink that do you?
Raye: Not if you have good sense.
Girl: You've got your fingers and everything in it!
Raye: Not everything.
Girl: I have never been so insulted… I'm leaving. (exits)
Straight: I'll pay you for the drink. How much do I owe you?
Raye: Thirty-five cents…
Straight: Thirty-five cents? That is cheap… How do you make any profit?
Raye: Well to tell you the truth… I am not really a waitress. The real waitress is upstairs with my cheating husband… And what my husband is doing to her upstairs, I'm doing to his business downstairs.
BLACKOUT

"T" is For…

There were four folders in the "T" File. The first two solely contained contracts for shows held in 1975. The first contract, dated June 24, 1975, was with Town & Country Dinner Theatre in East Rochester, New York. It reads in-part:

"For presentation at the Town & Country Dinner Theatre, 445 West Commercial Street, East Rochester, New York commencing Thursday, September 4, 1975 for two (2) weeks and four (4) days through and including Sunday, September 21, 1975.

Each performance to last approximately two (2) hours, including intermission and shall be presented six (6) nights weekly, Tuesday through Sunday, Mondays off; and eight (8) shows weekly, not to exceed two (2) shows in any one night.

Producer (Minsky) agrees to furnish and supply, at his sole expense, a cast of no less than fifteen (15) persons."

From there it seems to be a typical agreement stating the theatre would supply rehearsal space, and a follow spotlight and operator for all rehearsals and performances. They would also furnish and pay for all the advertising, as well as the orchestra, which would consist of five musicians: electric piano, electric bass, electric guitar, drums, and trumpet. Minsky would pay the performers salaries, withholding taxes, as well as Workmen's Compensation Insurance.

The theatre agreed to pay; $8,250 per week, plus one-eighth (1/8) of the weekly salary per each additional show, as well as one (1) week's salary in the amount of $8,250 made payable to the Associated Booking Corporation, 919 North Michigan Avenue, Chicago, Illinois 60611, upon the signing of the contract. Said payment shall represent the last week's salary for this engagement. The theatre made weekly payments on Saturday by cashier's check or cash.

Barry Tuttle signed the agreement, for the Town & Country Dinner Theatre, and Chuck Eddy, for the Associated Booking Corporation.

(Notes: The Town & Country Dinner Theatre in East Rochester, New York played host to some of the biggest names in entertainment during its very brief history.

The place was the brainchild of longtime Producer Barry C. Tuttle, and East Rochester Mayor Anthony Della Pietra, whose family owned a lumber company. Together they brought the dinner theatre concept, popular in big cities, to the area. Milton Berle opened the theatre with a two-week-run in late December 1974. Many big name performers played the club, which leaned toward entertaining an older audience. Tuttle and Pietra found the right demographic — at least at first — and often drew sellout crowds of 700 people or more. However, the camaraderie didn't last long. Soon, the owners were involved in lawsuits against each other, the Organized Task Force raided the place, and bills went unpaid. Each man wanted to buy the other out, and lawyers and courts got involved.

The Town & Country Dinner Theatre closed in 1977 due to bankruptcy. Tuttle reopened the place in late 1982 as the Barry Tuttle Dinner Theatre, but the venue closed again a few months later. The building, as of 2014, at 445 W. Commercial Street, had been converted into an office complex.)

There was an "experimental" Minsky show performed at the Thunderbird Dinner Theater in Michigan. Although there was no actual contract, the show was performed in March 1975. The following article was from *The Grand Rapids Press*, Arts Section, dated Sunday, February 9, 1975. "Burlesque Will Open Dinner Theatre," was written by David Nicolette, and reads:

"A dinner theatre opens in the Grand Rapids area in March. The Thunder Chicken, at 5707 Alpine Avenue NW, will bring in *Minsky's Burlesque Follies* in a dinner-show program for performances Thursday through Sunday, March 13, 14, 15, and 16.

Richard Bichler, General Manager of the Thunder Chicken, said he and Kenny Gordon, popular local entertainer, have worked out an arrangement for the special engagement of the touring burlesque company.

"We designed this place as a supper club," said Bichler, "but we haven't been able to work in that direction until three weeks ago, when our kitchen was completed."

Large and handsomely furnished, the Thunder Chicken appears ideally suited for a dinner theatre program, with two-level seating for about 525 diners, a stage, well-planned lighting, and a good sound system.

Since its opening nine months ago the night spot has been a popular gathering place for the younger crowd interested in hearing contemporary music by name groups.

Bichler was cautious in plans for future shows. "This first show is an experiment," he said. "We'll see how it is received."

He admitted that Gordon "talked me into this," but indicated that he didn't need too much convincing.

"We want to try it," he said. "But we plan to continue bringing in the entertainment the young people like. They're what made this place go and we've been very successful so far."

Advance reports of the Minsky show, with four companies on the road year-round, indicate its appeal spans all ages, and Bichler hopes he'll be pleasing his regular patrons, the college crowd and just beyond, as well as the older groups.

And just so there's no confusion, if Bichler decides to continue both the music programs and the dinner-show entertainment he plans to use the name Thunder Chicken Rock Theater in announcing music bookings, and Thunderbird Dinner Theater when shows are scheduled.

Plans now are to offer a buffet and the burlesque for $9.50 per person on Thursday, $10.50 on Friday, and $11.50 for the Saturday performance. Details for the Sunday show haven't been worked out.

Gordon said Minsky's Follies draws on old-time burlesque, with tastefully costumed dancing girls, the old-time longtime comic, and skits. "It's really a lively show and all done in good taste," he said.

The company booked for the Thunder Chicken – or Thunderbird – is in rehearsal in Las Vegas now, and is scheduled to play the Chicago Playboy Club for six months following the appearance here.

Neither Gordon nor Bichler would make a flat statement on the length of the engagement here, but it appeared that if the initial response warrants it, the show could be held over.

Gordon, who is associated with Conquest Productions, a local booking agency operated by partners Doug Banker and Dan Jakary, also revealed that he and Bobby Charles, his former partner, will get together again to form a new band which will be used in the Minsky production.

"Bobby's coming back – he's been on the road selling sound equipment – and we'll be in rehearsal as soon as we can to prepare for the dinner theatre opening," said Gordon. "Bobby and the band will play for the show, then we'll do some numbers for dancing between shows."

In working out details in the presentation of a stage show, Gordon and Bichler agreed little would have to be changed in the large room except for proper table arrangements for comfortable dining and viewing, and construction of a runway for the burlesque production.

"This place couldn't have been designed better for a dinner theatre," said Gordon. "I think this is going to be a really big entertainment breakthrough for Grand Rapids."

Gordon's enthusiasm is understandable. He's been working on the dinner theatre idea for almost two years – and was thinking about such a program long before that.

Bichler appears to be catching some of the enthusiasm, though he's a bit more cautious. "It's quite an investment," he said.

Part of the investment, though a small part, was the installation of additional telephones to handle dinner-show reservations starting Monday. The number is 784-3074."

The next article appeared in the same newspaper, but on March 16, 1975. "Minsky Recalls Old Burlesque" was also written by Nicolette. It reads:

"In the audience opening night of *Minsky's Burlesque Follies* at the Thunderbird Dinner Theater was a man with a name synonymous with this form of entertainment.

Harold Minsky is Producer-Director of the show and the son of the famed A.B. Minsky, whose New York 14th Street National Winter Garden Theatre flourished from 1908 through 1930 before moving uptown to the Broadway area. But World War II literally killed it.

"That's when burlesque in New York came to an end," said the soft-spoken Minsky as he waited for the latest of his shows to have its first performance. "The city wouldn't issue any more licenses. I guess there were some people who thought the soldiers coming into the city would be corrupted."

Minsky has been around burlesque all his life. "My father operated a nickelodeon theatre back when Lowe and Selznick and the others had them along the same strip," said Minsky. Those were the forerunners of the movies.

While others in the trade went into motion picture productions, much later, that is, a friend urged A.B. Minsky to open a burlesque show in the theatre his (Minsky's) father had built.

The place had its ups and downs with the police, but the crowds continued to attend and son Harold was educated in private schools and the family lived well.

Minsky said his father's business didn't appear to affect his gaining friendships with other boys in the private schools, though such entertainment was generally frowned upon. "That didn't give me any trouble," he said. "I had more trouble, if you want to call it that, because I was a Jew."

After schooling, father took his son into the business, first in the box office, then as stage manager and later as manager. As he took over the business he expanded and opened burlesque houses in Chicago (the famed Rialto) and in Newark.

As burlesque business eased off, those houses were closed and in 1950 Harold Minsky went to Las Vegas, adapted the productions to the more acceptable revue style booked into the hotel lounges there and Minsky's Burlesque has been a mainstay in the gambling-entertainment center in Nevada for the last 25 years.

He has one company there, another on the road in the East, the troupe that opened here and will travel on to Chicago for a six-month stay at the Playboy Club, and another forming in a month in Las Vegas to tour another section of the country.

The father of two grown children, Minsky isn't certain whether he will be the last of those with the famed name in the business.

His son Danny showed interest for a time, then switched to computer programming. Daughter, Ava, also showed interest, but that was before she married a psychiatrist. Minsky hasn't given up hope, however. Danny's wife is expecting a baby in June.

Perhaps the theatrical chain will miss one generation link and grandson will learn at grand-dad's knee."

The *Greater Grand Rapids Visitor*, Volume 37, Issue 5, March 2-thru-16, 1975, produced a cover with a photo of the *Minsky's Burlesque Follies*, and the following article:

"Minsky's is coming March 13-16 to Grand Rapids Thunderbird Dinner Theater. *Minsky's Burlesque Follies* has been called "the greatest thing that's happened to downtown Las Vegas since a speculator opened a faro game back in the 30s." Minsky's four touring companies have played to packed houses in virtually every major city in the U.S.

And now Minsky's is coming to Grand Rapids. On Thursday, March 13th, Minsky's show opens at the Thunderbird Dinner Theater, 5707 Alpine Avenue NW. (As of March 13th, Thunder Chicken becomes Thunderbird Dinner Theater and Thunder Chicken Rock Theater.)

Minsky's Burlesque Follies is variously described as "spectacular, sophisticated, hilarious, glittering, and surprisingly contemporary." Minsky's was summed up by *Chicago Today* dance critic Ann Barzel, as follows:

"Stripping is part of the show, but much more is going on in the department of humor, dancing, and singing. Unexpectedly, the show is inoffensive. You could even say it is in good taste."

According to Dick Bichler, Thunderbird General Manager, the show is slated to play March 13, 14, 15, and 16th. Advance sale of tickets and reservations for 'Buffet-'n-Burlesque' indicate that the *Minsky Follies* should be 'held over.' Our information reports that the Follies will continue through the first week in April. Performances will be presented Tuesday through Sundays – no performances on Mondays. The added 'held over' schedule will start on March 18th. Prices will remain the same for various evenings, as they appear in their advertisement on the opposite page. The Tuesday and Wednesday time schedule and prices will be the same as the Thursday, March 13th column in their advertisement.

Reservations are important, to you and to the show, so may we recommend that you call the Thunderbird Dinner Theater right away, for the current dates thru the 16th or for the newly released 'held over' schedule starting the 18th. The Box Office is open daily from Noon to Five, reservations accepted via the telephone – the number is 784-3074. All of the details concerning the 'Buffet-'n-Burlesque' Tickets and Reservations will be covered via the telephone.

The Thunderbird (Thunder Chicken) location is 5707 Alpine Avenue on Highway M-37, approximately two-and-a-half-miles north of 4-Mile Road. (4-Mile Road and M-37 are shown on the Visitor Map in the upper left corner for your information.)"

(Notes: The cost of the Sunday show was later listed as $10.50; and beer and wine only to be served on Sunday. The above mentioned Visitor Map was in the center of the publication. The other item in the folder was a newspaper ad; exactly the same advertisement that ran in the *Greater Grand Rapids Visitor* publication.)

The second folder contained a contract regarding a show to be held at the Thunderbird Dinner Theater in Comstock Park, Michigan. Each performance was to last approximately two hours, including an intermission; one show nightly, and two shows each Friday and Saturday. The show was to commence on Tuesday, November 25, 1975 for three consecutive weeks and five days, through and including Saturday, December 20, 1975.

The show was to have a cast of fourteen; the theatre would provide rehearsal space, a follow spotlight and operator, and an orchestra of five, with the exact instrumentation to be determined. In many regards, it was a typical agreement. Minsky was to pay the performers, withhold taxes, and cover Workmen's Compensation Insurance. The theatre would handle third party liability insurance, the advertising, and billing per Minsky's requirements.

The theatre was to pay the sum of $7,250.00 per week, plus one-sixth (1/6) of the weekly salary per each extra day, contract price for the entire engagement was $27,791.66. Payments were to be made as follows: $3,625.00 to the Associated Booking Corporation, in Chicago, on or before Saturday, November 1, 1975; and an additional $3,625.00 to Associated Booking Corporation on or before Saturday, November 15, 1975. The total deposit of $7,250.00 was to represent the last week's salary of this engagement.

The theatre was also to provide transportation from the Grand Rapids airport to the Presidents Motel and from the Presidents Motel to the Thunderbird Dinner Theater and return, prior to and following each performance and from the Presidents Motel to the Grand Rapids airport upon completion of the engagement.

Richard Bichler signed the agreement for the Thunderbird Dinner Theater, and Chuck Eddy, for the Associated Booking Corporation.

(Notes: The Thunderbird Dinner Theater, also known as the Thunder Chicken Rock Theater, was a popular venue for touring musical concerts and nightclub entertainment. Richard Bichler died on June 4, 2006.)

There was another Agreement in this folder; it was a RIDER written on Shokow, Ltd. stationery, and signed by the man Minsky refers to as the "Artist," Jerry Lucas. It reads:

"Thunderbird Dinner Theater, Grand Rapids, Michigan; This contact commences Tuesday, November 25th, 1975 for a period of three (3) weeks and five (5) days. The five (5) days to be paid on a Pro Rata Basis on a weekly salary of $450.00. Artist shall work six (6) days per week and eight (8) shows per week.

Royal Hawaiian Supper Club, Falls Church, Virginia; This contract commences December 22nd, 1975 for a period of two (2) weeks and five (5) days. The five (5) days to be paid on a Pro Rata Basis on a weekly salary of $450.00. Artist shall work six (6) days per week, eight (8) shows weekly. Off days shall be December 24th and 25th, 1975 -- January 1st and 5th, 1976. Contract concludes January 11, 1976."

The final folder in the "T" File is regarding the Thunderbird Hotel in Las Vegas. The Thunderbird Hotel was the fourth hotel to open on the Las Vegas Strip on September 2, 1948. It was built by developer Marion Hicks and owned

Two 1955 photos of the old Thunderbird Hotel in Las Vegas. Courtesy: Authors Collection

by the Lieutenant Governor of Nevada, Clifford A. Jones. The hotel was located across from and just south of the El Rancho Vegas. In 1955, articles surfaced in the *Las Vegas Sun* stating that Meyer Lansky and other underworld figures held hidden shares in the hotel.

The Thunderbird Hotel had a Native American theme featuring portraits, a Navajo-based restaurant, a bowling alley, a showroom that featured Minsky's Burlesque show in the late 1960s, and Joe's Oyster Bar – a favorite hang-out for the Las Vegas locals. The Thunderbird has the distinction of being the resort where singer Rosemary Clooney made her first appearance in Las Vegas in 1951, and where Judy Garland made her final Las Vegas appearance in 1965.

Photo of Rosemary Clooney from the 1950 sheet music "Me and My Teddy Bear." Courtesy: Authors Collection

Sheet music from the 1954 film A Star is Born. *Courtesy: Authors Collection*

A four-story addition to the hotel was completed in late 1963, and in 1964 the casino was purchased by Del Webb for $10 million. He ran the resort until 1972, when he sold it to Caesars World, owner of Caesars Palace, for $13.6 million. A 2,000 room resort was planned for the site, but Caesars was unable to find financing, and sold the property four years later to banker E. Parry Thomas at a loss of $5.7 million. Thomas later sold it to Major A. Riddle, of the Dunes Hotel, who renamed the hotel the Silverbird in 1976.

The Silverbird opened on January 1, 1977, and by 1980, the resort had 400 hotel rooms. In 1981, after Riddle died, Ed Torres bought the hotel from the Riddle estate. Torres renamed the property El Rancho, after the nearby El Rancho Vegas, which burnt down in 1960.

So, let's start with some short items from Las Vegas columnists Murray Hertz, Forrest Duke, Joe Delaney, and Ralph Pearl in the two local newspapers, the *Las Vegas Review-Journal* (Hertz and Duke) and the *Las Vegas Sun* (Delaney and Pearl). The items mentioned in these columns ranged in dates from November 17, 1967 through November 23, 1967.

On November 17, 1967, Hertz wrote:

"Harold Minsky's pulling out of the Silver Slipper to go over to the Thunderbird means the end of a long association – one that has endured since the Silver Slipper reopened a number of years ago. Minsky, as was itemed in this column many weeks ago, had been talking with T'Bird execs and finally decided to make the switch. He'll open a completely new show at the Thunderbird on January 3rd of 1968 with a cast of 36. I also understand that his new show will not be strictly burlesque as in the past. He wants to drop the burlesque and follies tag and go in for something a little more sophisticated. Will he drop nudes? I doubt it. Minsky without nudity would be like Davis without Reese (or vice-versa)."

On November 21, 1967, the Hertz column had the following:

"Thoughts while Shaving: Harold Minsky's move to the Thunderbird could be just what the doctor ordered for the trouble-plagued 'Bird. Minsky has always been a sure-fire draw, even since his Las Vegas beginning many years ago at the Dunes Hotel when he actually introduced bare bosoms to this resort city."

On November 23, 1967, Hertz wrote:

"Well, Class, today is T'Bird Day, so let's talk about that hapless hotel that has had more than its share of problems in the past few years. On the negative side, hotel manager George Benson resigned – a good man, Benson had been with the organization since the Del Webb regime took it over. Another long-timer, chef Tommy Collins also turned in his apron. Understand Bobby Rydell is out of the show, *That Certain Girl*, and is off to Venezuela. Ditto for Phil Foster who is also out of the show due to some sort of squabble over billing, but don't give up hope.

Benny Binion's Horseshoe Hotel and Casino.
Courtesy: Las Vegas Review-Journal

Here comes the plus. The 'Bird has an unusual junket coming in a week or so. This one is all the way from London and it's called, *The Northeastern Sportsmen's Club*, and don't forget Minsky. He'll soon help to put the place on the map again."

Also on November 23, 1967, Joe Delaney wrote in his column "On & Off The Record" the following short bit:

"Memo to Ev McCarlie: Bringing Harold Minsky into the T-Bird main room was an excellent move. Harold is hot and the forthcoming motion picture will make the Minsky name even warmer. There is only one Irv Benson and Harold has him. Good stroke!"

(Notes: Eugene Everett McCarlie Sr., born in 1912 and died in 1999, was a pioneer in the casino business. McCarlie moved to Las Vegas in the early 1950s and worked for the legendary Benny Binion at the Horseshoe.)

In a column from December 21, 1967, Delany simply wrote:
"Minsky will make a mint for the Del Webb Organization."
Ralph Pearl wrote in "Vegas Daze and Nights," from the same date, the following:
"Jerry Schafer and the T-Bird have parted company and all future entertainment problems will be handled by Harold Minsky, who comes in with a four-year pact for his exciting *Minsky Scandals*, starting the first week in January. Meanwhile, Minsky is off for New York to launch his travelling company on a four weeker at the Mineola (Long Island) Theatre. And while in Manhattan, Minsky will be talent hunting for his new edition at the T-Bird."

The next article appeared in the *Las Vegas Sun* on Thursday, November 23, 1967. No author was mentioned, and it was titled "Minsky Inks Pact at Thunderbird."

"Dana S. Bray, President of the Thunderbird Hotel, and Martin J. Kehoe, Executive Entertainment Director and Secretary-Treasurer, last night signed veteran showman Harold Minsky to a long-term exclusive production contract. The all-new Minsky spectacular will open January 3, 1968, in the Continental

Theatre of the Thunderbird. The show will consist of a cast of 36 people, featuring comedy and variety acts, and of course, the famed Minsky showgirls.

The show will be performed twice nightly during the week and three times a night on Fridays and Saturdays. As yet, a name has not been set for the new production, but the theme will be "the Modern Minsky."

Well-known dance director, Jerry Norman, has been signed to choreograph the show.

Of the show, Minsky is quoted as saying, "I think the Thunderbird Hotel facilities lend themselves perfectly to the presentation of a spectacular musical variety show. My new production will have something for everyone to enjoy. It will feature what you may call, 'family burlesque.'"

As one eastern newspaper put it, "The new Minsky format features the same old grind, but now Paw brings Maw!"

The Minsky name has been synonymous with the best in burlesque since 1908, when Harold Minsky's father, A.B. Minsky and his two brothers first entered the business. Harold himself has been producing burlesque musical variety shows since 1933.

Press Photo of Bert Lahr, starring in the production of Romanoff and Juliet *in March 1959, under the auspices of the New Orleans Opera Guild. Courtesy: Authors Collection*

He is responsible for furthering the careers of such well-known comedy figures as Phil Silvers, Red Buttons, Abbott and Costello, Pinky Lee, Bert Lahr, and many others.

In 1950, he brought the first package production show to the Desert Inn Hotel in Las Vegas. In 1957, he produced a main room production at the Dunes Hotel which ran for five years. Another Minsky production ran for a year and a half in the main room of the Frontier Hotel, and subsequent to that, a smaller Minsky production enjoyed two years of capacity business at the Silver Slipper.

The Minsky shows in Las Vegas were the forerunners to the French extravaganzas, and many of Minsky's earlier shows employed top-flight European variety acts that are still playing on the Las Vegas Strip.

Harold Minsky not only set the pace for the large package variety shows, but he also introduced nudity to Las Vegas, in that he was the first producer to present undraped showgirls on a Las Vegas stage.

Press Photo from the 1969 film The Night They Raided Minsky's, *with Forrest Tucker and Britt Ekland. Tucker actually was a straight man in legendary burlesque. Courtesy: Authors Collection*

Aside from his Las Vegas interest, Minsky has a show presently playing at the Edgewater Beach Hotel in Chicago, and will have another opening soon at the Mineola Theatre in Long Island, New York.

In the past years, a Minsky production has played every major city in the United States.

Shortly after the signing of his new contract with the Thunderbird Hotel, Minsky boarded a plane for New York City, where he will be consulting on a Norman Lear motion picture titled, *The Night They Raided Minsky's*. The motion picture deals with the early career of the Minsky family in burlesque, and stars Jason Robards, Bert Lahr, Britt Ekland, and Forrest Tucker, and is scheduled for release early next summer.

Upon his return, Minsky will begin casting his new production."

The following are more tid-bits from several columns published in Las Vegas newspapers during the month of December 1967. The columns were written by Forrest Duke, Joe Delaney, and Ralph Pearl. They mentioned specific burlesque performers, Harold Minsky, or the upcoming show at the Thunderbird Hotel.

Forrest Duke wrote:

"Jack Mann is to be congratulated for the splendid way in which he coordinated the recent backstage activity at the successful *Nite of Stars* benefit for St. Jude's Ranch For Children in Boulder City for Father Jack Adam. Not only does Mann, a show biz veteran, know everything there is to know about the fascinating profession – he knows just about every star, manager, and agent, all of whom respect his know-how. Mann is still doing his fine work onstage as straight man to the wonderfully hilarious Irving Benson at the Silver Slipper's Minsky Revue. If he ever decides to get on this side of the footlights, some hotel owner would be wise to appoint him as entertainment director. As a Las Vegan, one of Mann's strong assets is knowing what kind of shows brings players into the casinos!"

Male cast members from the 1950 Michael Todd production of Peep Show. *From left to right: Ben Hamilton, Dick Dana, Harry Conley, Jack Mann, "Bozo" Snyder, and "Red" Marshall. The show was written by Bobby Clark and ran for 278 performances at the Winter Garden Theatre. It was a good example of how Broadway looked to Burlesque for its comedians. Courtesy: Burlesque Historical Society*

(Notes: Jack Earl Mann was born in New York, New York on November 1, 1920, and died on April 5, 1993 in Ashland, Oregon. He appeared in many television shows between 1957 through 1961.)

Joe Delaney wrote:
"Harold Minsky's first effort under his new contract slated to open January 3rd… Prediction: Chalk up another hotel "save" for HM."

There were several bits from Ralph Pearl, who used to write his "Vegas Daze and Nights" column about all sorts of "People, Things and Stuff." The following appeared in separate columns:

"The first thing Del Webb did when he took back the T-Bird the other afternoon was to assure Harold Minsky that he and the other top execs at the Webb Stores are most happy about, the upcoming *Minsky Follies* are coming to the T-Bird January 3. Webb has appointed Jess Hinkle as the new T-Bird General Manager."

"Harold Minsky, is bringing in a large girlie revue first week in January to the Thunderbird, will audition singers at 2pm Saturday in the T-Bird showroom and showgirls and dancers at 3pm."

Autographed photo of Lili St. Cyr sitting in her dressing room. Courtesy: C.F. Miller

1956 Press Photo of Dagmar as Madame Du Barry. *Courtesy: Authors Collection*

"As itemed in this space 10 days ago, the new Minsky show might open at the T-Bird New Year's Eve, while the Barry Ashton show, *Wonderful World of Burlesque,* replaces HM at the Silver Slipper. Tommy "Moe" Raft, truly one of the greatest top bananas in the business, will headline the Ashton frolic which premieres January 1st. Silver Slipper boss Sam Diamond is looking for a singer in his Red Garter lounge. Call him at the Slipper any night. Ben Blue, after 15 weeks in the Frontier lounge, opens tomorrow with Lili St. Cyr and Dagmar in *Bravo Burlesque* at the San Carlos Theatre outside San Francisco."

And lastly:

"Joe E. Ross and Liz Renay will headline the new *Minsky Follies* at the T-Bird January 3rd."

The following appeared, probably in a Las Vegas newspaper, in April or May 1968. There was no official date or author noted on the article, which was titled "Says Harold Minsky Pretty Girls Dime a Dozen." It reads as follows:

"A man who looks more like an advertising executive or college professor than a show producer is presently guiding the fortunes of a big musical revue.

Harold Minsky, a member of the famed show business family, opened his *Thoroughly Modern Minsky* revue at Hotel Thunderbird four months ago and from the opening night it has proven to be a splendid success.

Minsky has an undeniable theory about the success of his show. "The formula is simple," Minsky said. "Certainly it's important to have attractive girls and good costuming, but the key is to present it in good taste."

Burlesque to Minsky is an art. "It's a delightful combination of vaudeville and legitimate theatre," Minsky said. "It's a matter of precision timing and pace. We want people to laugh and relax and have fun. It is our only purpose."

Minsky girls are really special. In the course of a year Harold looks at well over a thousand girls and all are the cream of one crop or another. But few are chosen.

"Pretty girls are a dime a dozen," Minsky says. "Pretty girls who have talent are perhaps the scarcest commodity you can imagine."

Meanwhile, Harold does magic in developing talent. He has hired girls who were secretaries, waitresses, and a host of other things before becoming Minsky girls. And the success of the show proves the success of his theory.

At present, Harold Minsky is working on the mechanics of producing a new edition of his Thunderbird show.

The new offering will incorporate the theme of the movie about to be released (*The Night They Raided Minsky's*) with updated burlesque humor.

The show will be a flashback to the early days of burlesque and vaudeville, and will bring the show goers from the old days to modern times in a fast-moving 90 minute spectacle of lavish costuming, brilliant choreography, traditional skits, and, oh yes, beautiful girls."

Pat Elliott Minsky and the World Famous Burlesque Thoroughly Modern Minsky marquee at the Thunderbird Hotel in Las Vegas. Courtesy: Pat Elliott Minsky/ Burlesque Historical Society

The following articles all came from *The Saharan* magazine, a product of the Sahara Hotel. The publication explains that the Thunderbird Hotel is a next-door neighbor to Hotel Sahara, making "the north end of the famed Strip the place to be for great restaurants and entertainment." The Sahara-Thunderbird corner of the Strip sounds like it was the place to be in the late 1960s. Because of their sister-like existence, *The Saharan* helped promote shows at the Thunderbird.

*The Sahara Hotel in Las Vegas, Nevada.
Courtesy: Authors Collection*

In the April 1968 publication there was an article titled "Sahara-Thunderbird offers complete Resort Complex," in which the author writes about the restaurants and entertainment provided at both hotels. Regarding the entertainment it reads:

"The Thunderbird, presently offering the highly popular *Thoroughly Modern Minsky* revue, has long been a showplace of stars and delightful musical comedies.

Consider stars like: Jack Benny, Judy Garland, Michael Callan, Walter Slezak, Bobby Rydell, Steve Allen, Robert Goulet, and others. All have appeared at Hotel Thunderbird along with top Broadway shows such as *Flower Drum Song*, and *South Pacific*.

Meanwhile, at the Sahara, top stars such as: Buddy Hackett, Johnny Carson, the Smothers Brothers, Donald O'Connor, Danny Kaye, and others head the Congo Room lineup and the swingingest lounge in town. The Sahara's Casbar Theatre, lists top artists such as: Don Rickles, Billy Eckstine, Count Basie, Norm Crosby, and The Treniers."

Also in this publication was a bit of information on "Top Banana" Irving Benson, and "Top Producer" Harold Minsky. They read as follows:

"Irving Benson, for years the "Top Banana" in the field of burlesque comedy, has never been better than he is as the star of *Thoroughly Modern Minsky* at Hotel Thunderbird.

Seen and known by millions of television viewers as the "heckler" that frequently appeared on Milton Berle shows as a pain in the neck named Sidney Spritzer.

To millions of others he is a hilarious standup comic who has turned in top performances on *The Johnny Carson Show* and *Hollywood Palace*.

*In 1973, Irving Benson in front of the marquee at the Thunderbird Hotel in Las Vegas, promoting the Minsky show.
Courtesy: Irving Benson*

Benson, a leading comic for more than 30 years, has also registered well in legitimate theatre, starring in productions *High Button Shoes* and *Anything Goes*.

In the Minsky revue, Benson is at his best as he romps through skits and fast burlesque sketches as well as a quick show opener in the role of that likeable trouble maker, Sidney Spritzer."

The words on Minsky were:

"A man that looks more like an advertising executive or a college professor these days is guiding the fortunes of the most lavish production revue in Las Vegas.

Harold Minsky, a veteran of thirty years in the business of entertaining people, is producing *Thoroughly Modern Minsky*, in the showroom of Hotel Thunderbird.

Great revues, always presented in good taste, are the hallmark of the Minsky family name and this theory has never been more evident than in the current Thunderbird show.

With a delightful blend of pretty girls, excellent choreography and traditional burlesque skits, "TMM" is fast moving and highly acceptable to virtually any entertainment taste.

Minsky is modest about his successes. "We simply try our best to give people a fun show, something to make them relax, and laugh," Minsky said. "If we have been successful, it's because of the hard work of the people in the show."

Perhaps this is the key to Minsky's success. His performers never fail to give a good performance. "I guess it's just plain respect for Harold and the Minsky name and manner," as one observer put it."

In June 1968 this was written in *The Saharan*:

"Girl watching – A serious business. A man who looks more like an advertising executive or college professor than a show producer is presently guiding the fortunes of the finest musical revue in Las Vegas.

Harold Minsky, a member of the famed show business family, opened his *Thoroughly Modern Minsky* revue at Hotel Thunderbird four months ago and from the opening night it has proven to be a splendid success.

Minsky has an undeniable theory about the success of his show. "The formula is simple," Minsky said. "It's a matter of precision timing and pace. We want people to laugh and relax and have fun… it is our only purpose."

Minsky girls are really special. In the course of a year Harold looks at well over a thousand girls and all are the cream of one crop or another. But few are chosen.

"Pretty girls are a dime a dozen," Minsky says. "Pretty girls who have talent are perhaps the scarcest commodity you can imagine."

Meanwhile, Harold does magic in developing talent. He has hired girls who were secretaries, waitresses, and a host of other things before becoming Minsky girls. And the success of the show proves the success of his theory.

At present, Harold Minsky is working on the mechanics of producing a new edition of his Thunderbird show.

The new offering will incorporate the theme of the movie about to be released, (*The Night They Raided Minsky's*) with updated burlesque humor.

The show will be a flashback to the early days of burlesque and vaudeville and will bring the showgoer from the old days to modern times in a fast-moving 90 minute spectacle of lavish costuming, brilliant choreography, traditional skits, and, oh yes, beautiful girls."

The final article from *The Saharan* was from July 1968. It reads as follows:

"Minsky unwraps edition "Undressed" up for summer. The summer edition of *Thoroughly Modern Minsky* at Hotel Thunderbird is set to bow Wednesday, according to show producer, Harold Minsky.

All new, the revue will include the talents of veteran burlesque comedian Irving Benson, the diminutive comic capable at rapid fire zingers or traditional zingers.

Benson, who appears frequently on television with Milton Berle, is the delightful heckler Sidney Spritzer who gives Berle the business from a ringside seat. Example: "I've spent half my life in comedy," said Berle. "How come we have to suffer through the other half," cracks Spritzer (Benson). And on and on it goes.

With this edition of "TMM," much of the delightful exchange is recreated and with the aid of another veteran comic, Sid Fields, the skits and sketches are better than ever.

Add to this, two starring exotics and the show should be a smash. One of the two, Lainie Miller, is the girl who did the stripper scene in the recent motion picture success, *The Graduate*. Lainie, a tiny 5'1" dancer, is easily one of the best in the business and this show might well be her last, since she has enrolled in UCLA for the fall term.

The second girl, another beauty, is Jodi Lawrence, an accomplished dancer and an entertainer equally adept as a stripper or as an integral part of one of the brighter skits.

For this edition, producer Harold Minsky has brought back the song styling's of Kay Houston. The dark haired beauty returns after nitery engagements in San Francisco, Los Angeles, and Seattle.

As in other Minsky shows, the revue will accent brilliant costuming, excellent choreography, and plenty of fun… all presented in traditional Minsky good taste.

And, oh yes, the show also will have plenty of pretty girls."

A million dollar fire demolished the older section of the Sahara Hotel on July 20, 1968. Some guests jumped from the second story windows, others were evacuated. There were no serious injuries. Courtesy: Authors Collection

(Notes: *The Saharan* was published monthly by the Hotel Sahara Publicity Department. The staff in 1968 included: Dave Bradley, Editor; Ron Erickson, Associate Editor; Earle Thompson, Herb McDonald, Jerry McLain, Howard P. James, John Romero, and Jess Hinkle, Editorial Advisors; Regina Riley, Helen Bruno, Leonard Norman, and Harry Mann, Editorial Staff. Photography was done by the Las Vegas News Bureau.)

U is For...

This File is all about the Minsky Collection which was donated to the University of Nevada, Las Vegas. After meeting at a burlesque reunion held in 2000, Patricia Minsky Shapiro, donated at least some of the same material to "The Golden Days of Burlesque Historical Society" in September of 2004. Sadly, all the donated materials were lost in an explosion and house fire on July 5, 2018. The written manuscript for this book was only saved by grabbing my laptop as I escaped the fire. I have since come to the conclusion that the BHS received some of the same materials, and some different, as UNLV. With that in mind, let's begin with the material in this folder, most of which were letters and lists.

The first item was a brief introduction of Pat Minsky – there is no date. It reads:

"Patricia Minsky, now associate producer of the Minsky shows, began her career in 1963 when she auditioned as a showgirl for her late husband. The show was at the Westchester Town House, in Yonkers, New York. She then appeared in his show at Jack Silverman's International Supper Club, Broadway and 52nd Street, and in 1965 moved to Las Vegas to appear in his show at the Silver Slipper.

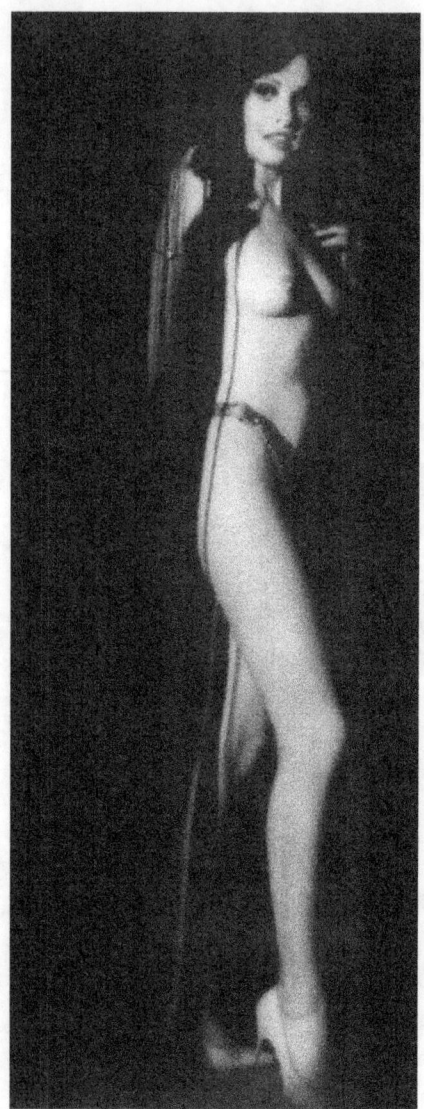

Pat Elliott Minsky. Courtesy: Janelle Smith Collection

In 1967 she married her boss after he flew to Chicago and proposed to her between shows at the Edgewater Beach Hotel where his show was then appearing. One might say that she hung up her G-string and retired from show business into married life and the rearing of the teenage step-daughter Ava. During the ten years of their marriage she traveled extensively with her late husband to openings of his many road shows, and assisted him in his many productions.

Three years ago she enrolled in the University of Nevada, Las Vegas, and is presently working on a degree in Theatre Arts, and has become an active member of their productions."

The following letter, written on UNLV stationery, was dated January 31, 1978 and addressed to Mrs. Harold Minsky, 5712 Kelly Lane, Las Vegas, Nevada 89119. It reads as follows:

Dear Mrs. Minsky:

It was so pleasant speaking with you this morning and remembering you visit to the library a few years ago to donate the book that Mr. Minsky had helped with. I remember at that time we had talked about historical material and the tape done by the Texan.

You mentioned that Mr. Minsky hadn't preserved much of his past but I wanted you to know that we at the University Library are interested in preserving what might have been saved such as letters, contracts, notes, scores, clippings, programs – anything that helps tell the story of the Minsky's in show business.

Since you are on campus taking courses, I'd appreciate your stopping into the library so I could show you some of the types of things we are doing in attempting to preserve the history of the area and its individuals.

Sincerely,
Harold H. J. Erickson
Director of Libraries.

(Notes: The *Las Vegas Sun* ran Harold "Hal" H. J. Erickson's obituary on Wednesday, November 15, 2000. It is interesting to note that Erickson came to Las Vegas in 1965 to work as a librarian for what was then Nevada Southern University, and which later became the University of Nevada, Las Vegas. In 1969, Erickson started the UNLV library endowment fund with $1,000 in donations he received in memory of Al Cahlan; a former editor of the *Las Vegas Review-Journal* who at the time of his death was a columnist for the Las Vegas Sun. By the year 2000, at the time of Hal's death, the fund's estimated worth was $2 million dollars. Erickson became director of library development in 1981 and retired in 1990. During his years at UNLV, the James R. Dickinson Library, under Erickson's guidance, grew to six times its original size. Much of that success resulted from his hard work and devotion to reach out to the community during the library's infancy. The development of the Special Collections Department is probably the accomplishment for which Erickson will be most remembered.)

The following letter written on Shokow, Ltd. stationery, showing the Russell Road address in Las Vegas, was dated February 21, 1978. It was written to Ronald L. Davis, Professor of History, at Southern Methodist University in Dallas, Texas. It reads:

Dear Professor Davis,

I am very much interested in obtaining a copy of the interview that you taped during your meeting with my husband in 1975. The interview was in reference to an Oral History Project on the performing arts in America that you were doing at the time.

Since my husband's death, Christmas Day of last year, I have been collecting various materials that pertain to his career in show business. I plan to donate a number of his personal letters, contracts, etc., to the University of Nevada of which I am a student in the Theatre Arts department.

Harold Minsky with cast and crew during rehearsal in the 1960s. Courtesy: UNLV

For that reason, and for my own personal keeping, a copy of the tape would be very much appreciated. I will be very glad to pay for any expenses that might occur.

Thank you for your time. Unfortunately, I did not get to meet you while you were in Las Vegas. However, I remember my husband telling me how much he enjoyed your interview with him.

Sincerely yours,
Patricia Minsky

(Notes: Ronald L. Davis has been a film buff since he was old enough to go to the movie theatre every Saturday afternoon in the late 1940s. Davis is a retired professor of American Cultural History at Southern Methodist University, and author. He also served as director of the Oral History Program at SMU. The oral histories span the years 1974-1991 and include more than 500 volumes of largely biographical interviews with actors, directors, producers, singers, composers, writers, cameramen, production technicians, stuntmen, vaudevillians, and burlesque performers. The goal of the Oral History Program was to gather primary source material for future writers, researchers, and cultural historians on all branches of the performing arts.

Davis has written multiple books on legendary Hollywood, including: *Hollywood Beauty: Linda Darnell and the American Dream*; *Van Johnson: MGM's Golden Boy*; *The Glamour Factory: Inside Hollywood's Big Studio System*; and *Just Making Movies: Company Directors on the Studio System*; all of which made extensive use of many of his oral history interviews.)

The following letter was also written on February 21, 1978, but on Harold Minsky stationery, which includes the address, 5712 Kelly Lane, Las Vegas, Nevada 89109, and the telephone number: (702) 736-3013. It reads:

Dear Ms. Howard,

I just want to let you know that your card of condolence was forwarded to me in Las Vegas. Thank you also for the newspaper clipping that you included.

Harold and I were married for almost 11 years and in spite of the 24 year difference in our ages, enjoyed a beautiful relationship. I was a showgirl-dancer when we met, and worked for him also. I always said that I was the smart one in the line, as I managed to marry the boss. I mean that sincerely as he was, as you know, a wonderful human being. We will all miss him.

If you will read the enclosed letter, you will find that I am donating, to the University of Las Vegas, various materials that pertain to his long career in show business. I feel that we need to preserve the history of burlesque, in particular, the Minsky contribution to the theatre. In this way, valuable information will remain on permanent record for years to come, when a bygone era is forgotten.

The problem is, Harold not being a hoarder of information, unfortunately did not save any materials pertaining to his shows in Newark, New York City, etc. In fact, I have little information on anything prior to his shows in Las Vegas

Eddie Lynch backstage, later on in his career.
Courtesy: Maureen Girard

(about 1957) when he opened at the Dunes. I was wondering if you might like to contribute to this broken link in the form of newspaper clippings, or pictures of yourself. Even a personal letter expressing your feelings about him as a boss would be appreciated. Anything that cannot be used I will gladly return. I would also be glad to pay for any mailing costs, etc.

Also, if you are still in contact with other entertainers who might do likewise, I would appreciate information on how I can get in touch with them.

Thank you for your time. Eddie Lynch, who is now stage manager at Caesars Palace, remembers you well.

Sincerely,
Patricia Minsky

The following letter was a simple note dated April 2, 1978. It included Pat's private and business phone numbers: (702) 736-6405 and (702) 736-3013. Even though no last name was mentioned, upon reading the closing line I know it's a note Pat wrote to Irving Benson – she mentioned his wife Lil. She writes:

Dear Irv,

As you can see by the attached letter, I plan to donate a number of items to the Special Department of Records at the University of Nevada, Las Vegas. Whatever things I may have that will tell the story of the Minsky name in show business.

I feel that we need to preserve the history of burlesque, particularly the Minsky contribution to the theatre. In this way, valuable information will remain on permanent record for years to come long after a bygone era is forgotten.

I would like to include with this collection a file on you and your relationship with Harold over the years. Any way that you could contribute to this collection would be greatly appreciated.

Stay well. Love to Lil.
Sincerely,
Patricia Minsky

Old friends, burlesque comics Joey Cowan and Irving Benson. Courtesy: Irving Benson

The following note was from Cliff Segerblom, on his stationery that says, "Art and Photography For Reproduction – Cliff Segerblom & Associates." The bottom of the page gave his address as: Post Office Box 36, Boulder City, Nevada 89005. The note was dated June 29, 1981. It reads as follows:

Mr. and Mrs. Philip Shapiro
1128 Pinehurst Drive
Las Vegas, Nevada 89109

Dear Mr. and Mrs. Shapiro:
I appreciate your making a book contribution in my name. Your Burlesque collection brought back many memories and will be very meaningful to the University in the years to come.

And good art books are hard to come by.
Cordially,
Cliff Segerblom

(Notes: Cliff Segerblom, born in 1915, spent more than fifty years dividing his creative energies between photography and painting. Originally from California, Cliff attended the University of Nevada on a football scholarship, but majored in art. In 1938, when visiting Boulder, he accepted a position with the Bureau of Reclamation and became the first official photographer of the Boulder Canyon Project – his initial project was to take photographs of the recently completed Hoover Dam. His work was featured in several magazines including *Life, Time, National Geographic*; and one Segerblom photograph of the Hoover Dam is in the Museum of Modern Art collection in New York. In 1939, while "on loan" to the Bureau of Indian Affairs, Segerblom documented the Havasupai Indians in their Grand Canyon home; and in 1941 he photographed the Third Locks Project on the Panama Canal. Perhaps the highlight of all his assignments came in 1969 when Cliff was invited by the Secretary of the Navy to record the splashdown of Apollo 12.

Cliff Segerblom also excelled in watercolor and acrylics, and his studies of Nevada's vanishing towns and terrain were often shown in exhibitions across the state. In 1984, he was a recipient of a Nevada Governor's Art Award; he died in 1990.

And for those wanting information on Pat's second husband, the *Las Vegas Sun* carried the following Associated Press obituary: "Philip Shapiro, Co-Founder of 'Al Phillips Cleaners,' Dies Following Brain Surgery, on Wednesday, August 11, 1999, at 5:07am." It reads:

"OAKLAND, California - Philip Shapiro, who, along with his brother Melvin, founded one of the most successful dry cleaning businesses in Nevada, died Wednesday in an Oakland, California hospital of complications following brain surgery to help control Parkinson's disease. He was 72 years old.

Originally from New York, Philip Shapiro found a home and made dry cleaning history when he and his brother moved to Las Vegas in 1964. They bought a dry cleaning plant in Commercial Center on Sahara Avenue. The original owner was a man named Al Phillips and the brothers decided to keep the name because of the clientele it already had and because they couldn't afford to change the sign. Today "Al Phillips the Cleaner" is nationally known as one of the innovators in the dry cleaning business.

Philip Shapiro was born in Brooklyn, New York on October 3, 1926. He went to high school there and later took special courses before going into the dry cleaning business.

In 1964, the Shapiro brothers moved to Las Vegas and opened the dry cleaning shop. Mel had a show business background and felt the stars playing Vegas would appreciate quick, quality service. They made the move and as they say, the rest was history. Philip kept active in the business even though the Parkinson's disease cut down on his daily routine.

Over the years, Philip Shapiro had received numerous awards recognizing the innovations he had brought to the dry cleaning industry. His idea of "drive thru" service was the first in the industry and set a trend for the entire nation.

Philip Shapiro leaves his wife Patricia, three grown children, Robert Shapiro, Lorrie Krasny, and Susan Christensen. There are seven grandchildren and one great grandchild. Philip was active in the Parkinson's Foundation, having served as president of the local chapter. He was a member of the Las Vegas Country Club and was involved in a variety of charitable organizations.

Funeral arrangements are still incomplete but services are expected to be held Sunday, August 15, 1999. The family said details would be announced."

Pat Minsky died from cancer on November 6, 2004; both Philip and Patricia "Trish" (Minsky) Shapiro are buried at Palm Memorial Park in Las Vegas, Nevada.)

There was also a short list in this folder from Design Concepts, 5365 South Polaris Avenue, Las Vegas, Nevada 89118; telephone number: (702) 736-8333. Design Concepts constructed sets for a variety of production shows in the area. The list contained the "Estimated Value of Scenery belonging to Patricia Minsky," and was signed, "Respectfully submitted by Hugh Van Gorder." The items listed included the following: 5 each Steel Frame Panels 3' wide X 10' high, covered on two sides with vinyl. 6 each Steel Frame Panels 4' wide X 10' high, covered on two sides; value $1,650. 1 Simulated Spider Web, steel construction of approximate 8' X 14' dimensions; value $800. Lastly, 1 Turntable 9' diameter X 1' high; value $350.

The last of the letters and Memorandum of Gifts in this file were all on University of Nevada, Las Vegas stationery, which lists the street address as 4505 Maryland Parkway, Las Vegas, Nevada 89154. Some also said: College of Arts and Letters, Department of Music (702) 739-3332; Special Collections Department; or simply, Library (702) 739-3286. The following letter, from July 10, 1981, was signed by Kenneth M. Hanlon, Chairperson. It reads:

July 10, 1981
Mr. and Mrs. Philip Shapiro
1128 Pinehurst Drive
Las Vegas, Nevada 89109

Dear Mr. and Mrs. Shapiro:
I was recently informed by Mr. Harold Erickson, the Director of the UNLV Dickinson Library, that you donated funds for five new volumes to be added to the music library in my honor. I would like to take this opportunity to thank you both for the honor and for helping us improve our music library resources. It is only through the generosity of interested members of the community such as yourselves that we will be able to build a library collection that will properly meet the needs of our students.
Sincerely,
Kenneth M. Hanlon
Chairperson

(Notes: Kenneth M. Hanlon, was born in Baltimore, Maryland in 1941, and began studying music at the age of ten as a percussionist. Switching to the trombone at the age of thirteen, he began playing in dance bands a year later. At the age of sixteen, Hanlon entered the Peabody Conservatory as a scholarship student. During his undergraduate years, Hanlon joined the Hank Levy Big Band as lead trombonist. He also studied music arrangement with Levy, whose credits include composer/arranger for the big bands of Stan Kenton, Sal Salvador, and Don Ellis. As a junior, Hanlon was invited to join the Peabody Preparatory School faculty as its youngest member.

Hanlon performed with the Baltimore Symphony Orchestra, played for traveling Broadway shows at the Morris Mechanic Theatre, and at the Club Venus where he backed up such acts as Gladys Knight and the Pips, the Temptations, Theresa Brewer, Sandler and Young, and many others.

In 1968, after moving to Las Vegas, Hanlon went on the road with the Si Zentner Band, and upon his return began working as a showroom musician in various "Strip" hotels, including: Caesars Palace, the Flamingo, the Tropicana, Sahara, Thunderbird, Bonanza, Stardust, Las Vegas Hilton, Landmark, and the Sands. While working in those showrooms, he recorded live albums as lead trombonist for Jack Jones and Buck Owens. Hanlon also worked as an arranger for numerous acts that included: Frank Sinatra, Edie Adams, Jerry Lewis, Lena Horne, Joanne Worley, Petula Clark, Paul Anka, Liz Torres, and Andy Williams. He also penned arrangements for *The Ed Sullivan Show*, and the *Siegfried and Roy Television Special*.

While continuing to perform on the "Strip," Hanlon joined the music faculty at UNLV in September 1970 and became the chair of the Music Department during his second week on campus. Hanlon, was instrumental in the establishment of the Nevada School for the Arts, the Nevada Dance Theater (now the Nevada Ballet Theatre), New World Brass Quintet, Sierra Winds, Las Vegas Opera Association, Las Vegas Chamber Players, Las Vegas Jazz Society and other arts organizations. In 1984, he received the Nevada Governor's Arts Award as an arts educator.

In the early 1990s, while working on a biography of jazz trombonist Carl Fontana, Hanlon realized just how many big band alumni were living in the Las Vegas area. In 1992, Hanlon organized a posthumous eightieth birthday celebration for Stan Kenton, which featured many Kenton alumni. A similar gathering was organized around Woody Herman alumni in the spring of 1994.

In the fall of 1994, Hanlon was asked to join the UNLV administration as Associate Provost of Academic Budget and Facilities. In July of 2000, Hanlon became the Director of the Arnold Shaw Popular Music Research Center.

He produced 15 albums for TNC Jazz, as well as was awarded a grant by the Nevada Humanities Committee to produce the 2002 KUNV radio series, *Jazz Las Vegas*, which provided programs on a variety of artists who lived or have lived in Las Vegas. He also reviewed jazz CDs and concerts for the Las Vegas Jazz Society.

In May 2017, Kenneth M. Hanlon retired from UNLV after a long and entertaining career; he died on November 27, 2018.)

There were three Memorandum of Gift letters from UNLV, all signed by Patricia Minsky Shapiro and Harold H. J. Erickson. The first, dated October 5, 1982, simply reads: "Minsky Collection. Primarily music deposited October 5, 1982." The second, dated June 15, 1983, reads: "Minsky Collection. Primarily music and contracts deposited for examination and evaluation June 19, 1980;

officially donated October 5, 1982." The third and final letter was dated June 15, 1983, and reads: "Minsky Photographic Collection. 500 prints and negatives deposited for examination and evaluation June 16, 1981; officially donated October 5, 1982."

The following letters were both written to Mrs. Patricia Minsky Shapiro by Harold H. J. Erickson, Director of Library Development at UNLV. The first was dated December 23, 1982; the second, June 16, 1983. They read as follows:

Dear Mrs. Shapiro:

The library has received your two donations of the Minsky Music Collection.

This collection is valuable research material not only for our music students but our drama students as well. Its relationship to Mr. Minsky's Las Vegas years is also important to our collection of historical material relating to show business in Las Vegas. As this history is written, the Minsky Collection will be one of the prime research collections used.

We thank you for donating it to the University Library.

Sincerely,
Harold H. J. Erickson
Director of Library Development

Dear Mrs. Shapiro:

Thank you for your letter of June 15, 1983, designating all of the various portions of the Minsky Music Collection as officially donated to the University with the last deposit which occurred on October 5, 1982.

With your official designation of the entire collection as University property, you have given us permission to make the collection available to the researcher. Any use of material in printed form will comply with university rules and regulations and will credit the Harold Minsky Collection.

On behalf of our students and faculty, I want to express our appreciation for your kindness in making this collection available for research.

Sincerely,
Harold H. J. Erickson
Director of Library Development

(Notes: The Burlesque Historical Society received minimal actual music or arrangements, and we received no photos of costumes. There were definite differences between the two collections, but there may have also been similarities. For those who want to do even more research, visit UNLV; or seek out the Harold Minsky Collection in their Special Collections Library online. There you will find lists of photographs, music, papers, contracts, and additional documentation. Pat gave me the items I've used for this book when she learned she was terminally ill and dying from cancer. She knew I would share the history; much of what I received from her is in this book. Sadly, the materials were lost; but I still have her emails.)

W is For...

There wasn't a lot in this File; the first folder had "World's Fair, Seattle '62" written on it. Included was an advertisement that states *Minsky's Follies of '62* opens on June 19, at the Orpheum Theatre. The stars of the show were Pinky Lee and Lili St. Cyr, "in her daring bubble bath."

(Notes: Seattle's 5th Orpheum Theatre was built in 1927, and opened on August 28, 1927, showcasing Orpheum Circuit vaudeville performers and silent films. It had a large neon rooftop sign and was equipped with a special Wurlitzer organ. It was closed for almost a year during the Depression, and was reopened by John Hamrick solely as a movie house under his Evergreen State Amusement Company. During the 1940s and into the 1950s, it was home to the Seattle Symphony Orchestra. In the early 1960s the stage was bricked off from the main house and it became a movie theatre once again. The Orpheum closed on May 9, 1967. On June 27, 1967 the contents of the theatre were auctioned off, including the Wurlitzer organ, and on August 6, 1967 demolition began. It took 10 weeks to raze the building; the Westin Seattle Hotel now occupies this site.)

April 1971 Press Photo from the Denver Post backstage at the University of Colorado Memorial Ballroom. Pinky Lee is rehearsing his lines in preparation for the annual Trivia Bowl. Photo by Steve Larson. Courtesy: Authors Collection

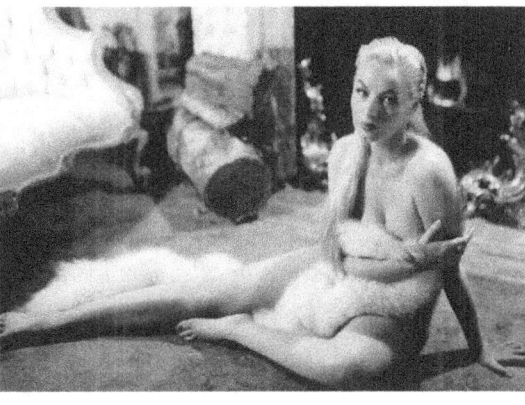

Lili St. Cyr. Courtesy: C.F. Miller

Photos of the Orpheum Theatre in Seattle, Washington. Two show the exterior of the building; there is also a photo of the stage. Courtesy: cinematreasures.org

There was also a partial Xerox of a *Variety* article dated April 25, 1962. It was saved solely for the headline which reads: "Seattle: Minsky & Stravinsky." The entire article, written by Joe Cohen, was not saved; however, the opening paragraphs read:

"Nudes in high, ditto prices. Seattle's $100,000,000 Century 21 Exposition has given this city a New Look which might be called look-the-other-way. Seattle is seeing things it never saw before in the Expo's Show Street and elsewhere. Despite the space age theme, Century 21 is down to earth.

The Fair's officially opening Saturday (21) revealed a new world that extends from Minsky to Stravinsky, from the primitive arts of the carnival to the exhibitions of the fine…"

(Notes: The rest of the article continued on page 51.)

The other item in the folder was also incomplete. It was typed and the first page was titled "Minsky's Follies of 1962."

"For five generations the name Minsky has been synonymous with show business, and girl shows. In the last ten years Minsky's show have moved from the burlesque theatres of

Broadway to the lush resorts of America. Featuring lavish productions and the most beautiful girls in the world.

With his knowledge of show business and twenty-five years of experience Harold Minsky is planning on bringing to Seattle for the World's Fair a spectacular revue. Featuring twenty-eight of the most beautiful girls to be found in the world. Minsky's talent for selecting showgirls is universal, his prime belief being youth. 'Everyone enjoys seeing a lovely young girl, properly displayed in beautiful costumes, with lighting that gives her the best advantage possible.' Mr. Minsky is devoting all of his time between now and his opening in Seattle, searching for the girls for this show, here and in Europe, and promises each one will be carefully selected, and presented as only he can.

Costumes for the show are already being planned. Max Berman and Sons, well known Hollywood costumers, will execute over one hundred elaborate creations, which will take months of preparation, in the designing and beading work. Berman's have costumed the Minsky showgirls, for all the productions presented in Las Vegas, and are well equipped to handle this elaborate show.

The numbers which have already been started are, "Minsky Goes to Paris," a colorful production depicting what happens to Paris when the "Minsky Girls" arrive. The wardrobe for this number will be 'haute couturier' fashion. With designs copied from the top fashion houses of the world. Also planned, is "Ebb Tide," an undersea ballet fantasy. Featuring a skin diver, who finds a watery world of feminine sea creatures. An ultra violet effect will produce dozens of colorful fish swimming among 'SEAGIRLS' dressed in iridescent fish scale gowns to create…"

The next folder, "Westchester Town House – 1964," had even less in it. There was solely a photo with the following caption: "Touring – Newark's Patricia Elliott performs in *Minsky Follies of 1964*, currently at the Westchester Town House Dinner Theatre." There was also a Xerox of an advertisement.

The following folder was interesting, it had two words written on it: "Wardrobe, Inventory." There were three copies – one was handwritten, and two were typed; it is typed as it was written. It was dated October 1968 and reads as follows:

Red and White Showgirls: 8 hats, 8 G-strings, 8 white skirts and cummerbunds, 8 collars, and 8 gauntlets.

Dancers: 6 skirts, 6 bikinis, and 6 bras. (bras all need replacing)

Pink: Blue and yellow eyelash dress; 9 nudes and 6 dancers.

White Petal: 7 bras and bikinis, 14 nude bikinis, and 5 bras. (dyed)

Powder My Back: 5 pink, 1 white, 1 black, and 12 Puffs. (2 on sticks)

Satin Doll: 8 coats and 7 mirrors.

Yellow Showgirls: 9 jeweled with trains, 6 G-strings, 6 harnesses, and 6 hats.

Dancers: 6 bras, 6 bikinis, and 6 hats.

Blue Feathers Showgirls: 6 hats, 6 G-strings, 5 harnesses, 7 tails, and 7 tops. (needs rewiring and ostrich)

Dancers: 6 hats, 6 bras and bikinis, 6 tails, 1 G-string hat (original), and Singer leotard and top.

Harem Showgirls: 9 hats, 9 sets of pants, G-strings and tops (need jewels) - 1 set original, 9 hoops (need Marabou), 9 pairs of armbands, 7 G-strings, and 3 body stockings.

Dancers: 6 hats, 6 bras and bikinis (gold), 6 pink ribbon tops and bikinis (1 original), and 6 pink hats. (1 original).

Spanish (red) Showgirls: 10 dresses, 10 hats, 10 G-strings and harnesses, 10 pairs of arm frills (black fur and pale blue), 10 hats, 10 blue tights, 10 coats, 10 plastic yellow ribbons, and 1 lead hat and costume, G-string, harness and top.

Purple Showgirls: 8 coats, 5 G-strings, and 6 hats.

Dancers: 6 bras, 6 hats, and 6 G-strings with fox tails. (need rewiring)

Opening Gold Showgirls: 10 coats, 10 hats, 10 pants, 10 harnesses, and 2 leads harnesses and bikinis. (1 singer, 2 boys)

Dancers: 10 bras and bikinis, 10 fringe dresses and hats.

Tropical Showgirls: 10 G-strings and trains, 8 hats (green), and 10 helmets.

Dancers: 10 purple skirts, 10 tops and G-strings, and 5 white skirts. (1 singer, 2 boys)

Brown and Pink Showgirls: 10 hats, 10 skirts and tops.

Dancers: 10 hats, 10 sets of tops and bikinis. (1 singer, 2 boys)

Black and White Showgirls: 10 wigs, 10 leotards, 9 hoop dresses, and 5 boys black pants and shirts. (1 singer)

Indian Showgirls and Dancers: 20 Sari's.

Showgirls: 8 coats, and 10 wigs with pearls.

Dancers: 10 bras, 10 pearl collars, 10 bikinis with jewels, 10 wigs with pearls, 5 boys gold pants, and 5 boys green coats. (1 singer)

Opening Showgirls: 10 pink bras, 10 bikinis, 10 skirts, 10 hats, 10 bustles, and 10 hats. (orange and yellow).

Dancers: 10 pink bras, 10 bikinis, 10 hats. 2 purple bras, 2 bikinis, 2 hats, 10 bustles, 5 boys suits, and 5 boys white pants and tops. (1 singer)

The last "W" folder in this File was listed as, "Windmill Dinner Theatre, Houston, Texas 1978; After Harold Died." The show was simply called *Minsky's Burlesque*. The cast and crew were billed as follows: Produced and Directed by, Jerry Lucas; Associate Producer, Patricia Minsky; Choreographed by Betty

Francisco; Costumes by Eastwood; Musical Arrangements, Joe Hernandez; Comics, Jimmy Mathews and Dick Richards; Acrobatic Act, Luciana Reberte and Alberto Colombo; Variety Act, Higa the Magician; Straight man, Stan Stanley; Singer, Manolo Meza; Lead Dancers, Jamie Lawrence and Lisette Doyle; Covered Dancers, Jeanette Telders and Donna Lambusta; and Nude Dancers, Debbie Garner, Nancy Schuneman, Dona Reynolds, and Terry Jory.

Dick Richards scenes included: "Handful of Nickels" and "Gaston;" and Jimmy Mathews scenes were "Lady Cop" and the "Flirtation Scene."

At this time, the Windmill staff included Perry Cloud as Chairman of the Board and Producer, President Robert (Bob) T. Mathis, Stage Manager Bill Austin, and General Manager Dee Garrett. There was nothing in the program that states the actual dates of the production.

Jeanette Telders and Jimmy Mathews performing together in a skit. Courtesy: Jeanette Telders

There was also a Xerox of the "Review" column written by William Albright in the folder. There was no newspaper header or date; the closest we get to knowing the date is in the final paragraph. The column reads:

"In its heyday – the 1920s, 1930s and into the 1940s – I guess the name Minsky's came to mean Burlesque like Ziegfeld meant Follies. And *Minsky's Burlesque '78*, the Windmill's latest show, wasted no time in getting down to business and showing us that burlesque – at least the way it ended up – is where the only women with clothes on are in the audience.

The striptease was under way as soon as the singing introductions to "The Most Beautiful Girls in the World" were over. It featured all the classic moves – taking off the gloves with the teeth, a finger at a time; plenty of hip swiveling, the works – by four of the show's five well-built G-stringed girls who went topless. Two more chorus girls wore bra-like tops throughout the press preview performance.

Minsky's Burlesque '78 had more than shapely, scantily clad dancing girls, though. There were lots of flashy costumes awash in feathers and sequins, several outrageously hilarious, old-fashioned bawdy comedy sketches, a pair of comedy acrobats, a magic act, and a singer; all of which added up to an entertaining and fast-moving show.

Dick Richards, a real throwback to the good-bad days of vaudeville and burleyque, was my favorite of the two "blue" comics. Dressed, in his first sketch, in a derby and long black coat like Arte Johnson's 'Tyrone,' and speaking in nasal New York-ese like an old-time ring announcer, he combined Don Rickles insult comedy and barrages of ethnic and sexual one-liners that maligned every nationality and sexual preference. He left no entendre undoubled or lewd gag gagged.

Jimmy Mathews, who with his bent-up hat, clown face and dumb-guy (in this case dumb-Texan) character reminded me of Red Skelton, was literally a baggy-pants comic, and often a funny one. But his brand of sketch comedy, which had perhaps even more leer and corn than Richards', went in more for rude noises and off-color body English.

Higa the Magician, did some card manipulation tricks (seemingly pulling them out of thin air) and the Chinese rings bit (mysteriously linking and unlinking apparently solid metal hoops). He ran a huge needle and thread through a balloon without popping it. His big finish was a disappearing act with a $100 bill – somebody in the audience's though, not his own.

Lisette Doyle and Jamie Lawrence were the lead dancers. She was good; his somewhat uninvolved and blank-faced work lacked snap. But he did have the muscle to partner her in the many athletic lifts and catches.

Minsky's Burlesque '78 – a Las Vegas show featuring a cast of 15, produced and directed by Jerry Lucas, is at the Windmill Dinner Theatre through July 2."

There was one more box of Harold Minsky Files that ran from A through Z. It mostly contained personal letters, from performers seeking to work for Harold Minsky, as well as plenty of 8 X 10 photographs. Needless to say, all of those items, along with the original material that this book was written from, was destroyed. A box of additional photos to be used in this book were also destroyed in the fire – all original material. I'm just happy the words were written for this book and that I had time to grab my laptop.

I have spent many years working with this material. I believe Harold Minsky was loyal to his show concept, his performers - whom he used in his shows over and over again, and especially to his family. He seems to have been a most honorable man; writes someone looking at this from the outside in. So, if this book has intrigued you at all, get on the computer or take a trip to Las Vegas, and view the Minsky treasure trove in person at UNLV. Enjoy your journey!

My favorite photo of Harold Minsky, which comes from an old Minsky show program. Courtesy: Janelle Smith Collection

www.ingramcontent.com/pod-product-compliance
Lightning Source LLC
Chambersburg PA
CBHW080719300426

44114CB00019B/2418